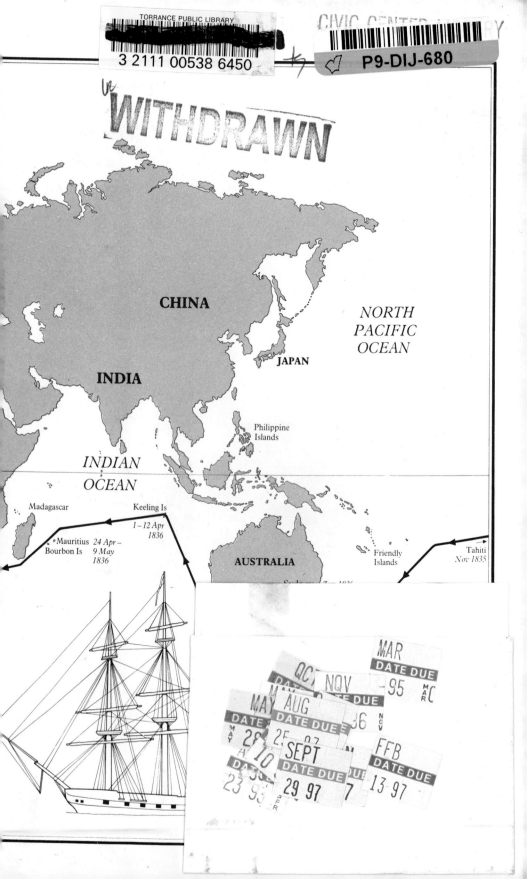

CHINA

INDIA

JAPAN

NORTH
PACIFIC
OCEAN

Philippine
Islands

INDIAN
OCEAN

Madagascar

Keeling Is

1–12 Apr
1836

Mauritius   24 Apr –
Bourbon Is   9 May
1836

AUSTRALIA

Friendly
Islands

Tahiti
Nov 1835

CHARLES DARWIN

A New Life

JOHN BOWLBY

W·W·NORTON & COMPANY

New York   London

Printed in the United States of America.

Manufacturing by the Maple-Vail Manufacturing Group.

ISBN 0-393-02940-9

W.W. Norton & Company, Inc., 500 Fifth Avenue, New York, N.Y. 10110
W.W. Norton & Company, Ltd., 10 Coptic Street, London WC1A 1PU

1 2 3 4 5 6 7 8 9 0

Contents

List of Maps

Preface

I first became interested in Charles Darwin as a personality, and as a scientist and invalid, thirty years ago when I read the new and complete version of his *Autobiography*, edited by his granddaughter, Nora Barlow. In it, amongst much else, he makes brief reference to the chronic ill-health from which he suffered over many years and the nature of which, I knew, had for long been a subject of controversy, the major issue being whether his symptoms were caused by an organic illness or were of emotional origin. At the time, I was working on the psychological ill-effects that are apt to follow a childhood bereavement and so, when I learned that Darwin's mother had died when he was eight years old, I began to wonder whether that might have played some part in the genesis of his troubles. A little later, when the medical controversy erupted again, I made a brief contribution raising the issue. Having many other commitments at the time, I was unable to pursue the idea further, though I hoped it might one day be possible.

During the autumn of 1983 my interest was sparked afresh when the British Psychological Society decided to hold a symposium on Darwin's contribution to psychology (in connection with the centenary of his death in 1882) and invited me to contribute. Although my brief paper was confined to a discussion of Darwin's study of the emotions in animals and man, and to the way in which his ideas foreshadowed those now being followed so productively by present-day researchers, the occasion proved a trigger. Much new information about Darwin was by then available.

First, an important new book on his ill-health had been published by a New York psychiatrist, Dr Ralph Colp, Jr.. In it he not only gives a comprehensive account of the symptoms from which Darwin suffered at different times of his life but also undertakes an exhaustive review of the manifold theories that have been advanced in the attempt to explain their nature and origin. His work, *To be an Invalid*, (1977), is thus an invaluable source book. Furthermore, his conclusions, which endorse much expert opinion previously published, that Darwin's symptoms are much more likely to have been of emotional than of organic origin, are now commonly accepted.

Nevertheless, once that is granted, further problems remain. If Darwin suffered from emotional troubles, what was their nature and why should he have come to develop them? In explanation, some students of the problem invoke constitutional factors. Others draw attention to family and professional situations that may have caused him stress. The possible role of his relationship with his father has been implicated by several; but few other influences deriving either from his earlier years or from current situations have received systematic attention, except from Colp.

When I first became interested in the possible role of Darwin's early bereavement, little was known about his mother, and nothing whatever about her invalid state and fatal illness: of that I was assured by Nora Barlow. That there is, apparently, nothing of consequence in the voluminous Darwin archives I believe to be no accident. In recent years, however, searches in the Wedgwood archives at the University of Keele have revealed information of the greatest interest. Much of that has been published in a history of the Wedgwood family by Barbara and Hensleigh Wedgwood entitled *The Wedgwood Circle* (1980).

Another extremely valuable source of information, in this case about Darwin's thoughts and feelings, which hitherto had not been easily accessible, is the series of volumes containing his complete correspond-ence, splendidly edited by Frederick Burkhardt and Sydney Smith and published by Cambridge University Press. The four volumes so far in print contain all the letters written by Darwin and all those addressed to him that come from the first half of his life, from his schooldays until 1850 when he turned forty-one. In addition, the volumes contain, in notes and appendices, a wealth of other useful information. Since in Darwin's time letter-writing was in its heyday, an extraordinarily rich picture of his life during those years is revealed. They were years of the greatest consequence both for his health and for his scientific work.

Thus much more is now known about the early years of Darwin's life than was formerly available. Furthermore, there have been significant advances in psychosomatic medicine and developmental psychiatry. These provide a greatly improved scientific framework within which to understand Darwin's medical symptoms and the origins of his emotional troubles.

Although initially I conceived this work within fairly narrow limits, as it progressed I found myself captivated by Darwin as a maturing personality and gifted scientist, and also by the large extended family in which he grew to manhood, by his devoted wife and their numerous children, by his circle of scientific friends and colleagues, in short by the whole drama of his eventful, troubled and extraordinarily productive life. As a result I found that what I was writing had become a biography, though a biography with a special slant and inevitable limitations. Thus it gives far more attention than is usual to the subject's formative years, to his emotional life, to the pattern of family relationships he was born into, to the ups and downs of his scientific life, to the medical problems that dogged him and to the anxieties and miseries that too often afflicted him. What is missing is a full description of the great variety of Darwin's scientific activities and, above all, any evaluation of the magnitude and range of his achievements. Since, however, without some account of these activities and achievements the picture presented would be sadly ill balanced, I have done what I can to sketch them in.

Only in the light of this history can the unusual way in which my biography starts be understood. In the Prologue I give an outline of Darwin's life, including a reference to the medical problems that have proved so puzzling; then, after describing the symptoms in greater detail and discussing some of the varied ideas that have been advanced to explain them, I state my own position, identifying those ideas advanced by others that I adopt and why I do so, and, in particular, outlining the developmental perspective in which I believe the symptoms can most fruitfully be considered. Since in that perspective the events of family life and the pattern of family relationships a person encounters during his childhood and adolescence, and the ways he reacts to them, are regarded as of key importance, those are the themes to which close attention is given in the biography that follows.

Finally, it should be added that any reader not interested in the puzzle of Darwin's ill-health is advised to skip the Prologue and start at Chapter 1.

Acknowledgements

Throughout the writing of this work I have been encouraged and guided by my wife, Ursula. Not only have we had innumerable discussions about the unfolding story and how best to understand it, but she has read every word of manuscript in a succession of drafts, leading to abundant suggestions for improvement. To her I am, as always, deeply grateful.

For eighteen months during 1984 and 1985 Christian Jackson acted as my research assistant in examining unpublished material in Cambridge University Library and the libraries of Christ's College, Cambridge, and the University of Keele, which holds on temporary deposit manuscripts belonging to the Wedgwood Museum. I am greatly indebted to him for having identified and brought to my attention much material of relevance to my purpose. In this task he was assisted by the staff responsible for the manuscripts. Special thanks are due to Christine Fyfe, archivist of the library at Keele, and to Philip Gautrey, until recently under-librarian at Cambridge, who put at my disposal his unrivalled knowledge of the Darwin literature.

In pursuing my interests I have been assisted throughout by Margaret Walker and the staff of the Tavistock Centre Library, who have been tireless in arranging for me to borrow books and other materials from the Document Supply Centre of the British Library. Without their help this biography could never have been written.

To Mary Sue Moore I am indebted for having guided me to literature on the hyperventilation syndrome, and especially to the work of Peter Nixon, Laura Freeman and Ashley Conway; and to Ashley Conway I am grateful for his having read through my drafts on the subject and suggested improvements. Ken Adam directed me to the model of psychological and psychosomatic disorder that I have sketched in the appendix.

I welcome this opportunity to thank once again Dorothy Southern, my secretary for forty years, who has typed a succession of drafts with her customary zeal and accuracy, and has helped me in many other ways. For editorial suggestions, and for preparation of the bibliography, the Who's Who and the index, I am indebted to Molly Townsend. Linden Stafford has acted as overall editor, in the course of which she has improved my English and identified a number of areas that called for clarification, expansion or addition.

For permission to use unpublished extracts from Charles Darwin's correspondence, my thanks are due to the Master and Fellows of Christ's College, Cambridge, and to the Syndics of Cambridge University. My thanks are due also to the University of Keele for making available to me unpublished Wedgwood family letters in their archives which are the property of the Wedgwood Museum. Permission to quote from these is by courtesy of the Trustees of the Wedgwood Museum, Barlaston, Stoke-on-Trent, Staffordshire, England.

For permission to quote from published works, I am greatly indebted to the Cambridge University Press respecting the many quotations I have taken from *The Correspondence of Charles Darwin*, Volumes I-IV (edited by F. Burkhardt and S. Smith), *The Beagle Record* (edited by R. D. Keynes) and *Charles Darwin's Beagle Diary* (edited by R. D. Keynes); and to Collins Publishers for quotations from *The Autobiography of Charles Darwin* edited by Nora Barlow.

Picture Acknowledgements

The author and the publishers would like to thank the following for their kind permission to reproduce the illustrations that appear in this book:

American Philosophical Society Library (p. 422 *top*); Blackie & Sons Ltd from *Darwin's Moon*, Amabel Williams-Ellis, 1966 (p. 315); The Bodleian Library, Oxford (pp. 43 *top*, 108, 136, 235, 361, 286 *bottom*); the Trustees of the British Museum (*frontispiece*, pp. 105 *bottom*, 209 *bottom left*, 269 *top right*); Cambridge Philosophical Library (p. 191); the Syndics of Cambridge University Library (pp. 183, 383 *top*); Cambridge University Press, from *Beagle Diary*, ed. R. D. Keynes, 1988, (p. 144 *top*), and from *Beagle Record*, ed. R. D. Keynes, 1979, (p. 175); Lt Col R. D. Crombie (p. 95 *bottom*); the Darwin Museum, Down House (pp. 42 *top and bottom*, 43 *bottom*, 59, 119, 144 *bottom*, 175, 227, 243 *top and bottom*, 251 *bottom*, 294, 295 *top and bottom left*, 302, 303, 309, 339, 381, 423, 438 *top right, bottom*, 439, 446); Edinburgh City Libraries (pp. 84–5); Mrs Sophie Gurney (p. 295 *bottom right*); The Hulton-Deutsch Collection (pp. 64, 95 *top*, 356, 405, 422 *bottom*, 453 *top and bottom*); Linnean Society of London (p. 257); the Mansell Collection (pp. 144–5, 209 *top*, 251 *top*, 314, 357, 399 *top*, 452 *bottom*); the Mary Evans Picture Library (pp. 375 *top left*, 399 *bottom left and right*); the Mitchell Library, Sydney (p. 156); The Museum of Comparative Zoology, Harvard University (p. 277); the National Maritime Museum, London (p. 128); the National Portrait Gallery, London (pp. 17, 27 *top left and right, bottom right*, 105 *top*, 209 *bottom right*, 375 *top right*, 391, 452 *top*); Penguin, from *Darwin and the Beagle*, Alan Moorehead, 1971, (pp. 144 *top*, 163, 221); the Royal Botanic Gardens, Kew (p. 322); President and Council of the Royal Society of London, (pp. 27 *bottom left*, 438 *top left*); Scottish National Portrait Gallery (pp. 269 *top left, bottom left and right*); Shropshire Libraries, Local Studies Department (p. 69); Miss Marjorie B. Sirl of Bega, New South Wales (p. 203); the Trustees of the Wedgwood Museum, Barlaston, Staffordshire (pp. 23 *top and bottom*, 22 *top and bottom*, 49 *top left and right*).

Brief chronology

1809, 12 February	Born Shrewsbury, the second son and fifth child of Dr Robert Darwin, a leading physician, and Susannah, eldest daughter of Josiah Wedgwood, the potter
1817, 15 July	Mother died
1817–25	Educated Shrewsbury School
1825–27	Edinburgh University, studying medicine
1828–31	Cambridge University, studying for the church
1831, December to 1836, October	Naturalist on board survey ship HMS *Beagle*, on voyage round the world
1836, October to 1838, December	Bachelor, living in London; working on *Journal of Researches* (1839) and geology of the voyage
1839, January	Married his cousin Emma Wedgwood; continued living in London
1839, December	Eldest son, William, born; first breakdown in health
1841, March	Eldest daughter, Annie, born
1842, September	Moved to Down House, near Orpington, Kent
1842–56	Eight more children born

1844	Drafted unpublished essay on evolution theory
1846	Completed studies arising out of *Beagle* voyage
1847	Began eight year study of barnacles
1848, Nov	Father died; second breakdown
1849, March	First tried hydropathy, at Malvern
1851, April	Eldest daughter, Annie, died
1855	Began drafting major work on evolution theory
1858, July	Joint paper, with Wallace, read at Linnean Society
1859, Nov	*Origin of Species* published
1863, March to 1864, April	Lyell disappoints: third breakdown
1865, Spring and Summer	Relapse
1861–67	Working on *Variation under Domestication* (1868)
1868–70	Working on *Descent of Man* (1871)
1871–72	Working on *Expression of Emotions* (1872)
1872–81	Published five books on plant physiology, and another on *Earthworms* (1881)
	Also wrote Autobiography and Memoir of his grandfather, Erasmus Darwin (1879)
1882, 19th April	Died at Down

Prologue

I

Charles Darwin, whose life spanned much of the nineteenth century, is the most influential biologist to have lived. Not only did he change the course of biological science but he changed for ever how philosophers and theologians conceive of man's place in nature. An outstanding scientist who excelled first as an observer and later as a theorist and experimenter, he was also a singularly attractive character beloved by family and colleagues alike. Yet for thirty years of his life he suffered from chronic ill-health which for periods of months at a time prevented him working. Among his varied array of symptoms were persistent gastric pains and retching, and palpitations and pain around the heart. The nature of his ill-health and, in particular, the question whether it was of organic or psychological origin are the subject of an extensive literature.

Despite sporadic claims still heard that Darwin suffered from an organic illness, perhaps an infection contracted in South America, the weight of medical opinion today very strongly favours a psychosomatic diagnosis. Against an organic diagnosis are the nature and course of his symptoms and the fact that during the final decade of his life he was in better health than he had been during the previous thirty years. In favour of a psychogenic diagnosis are not only the nature of his bodily symptoms but also the severe psychiatric problems from which he also suffered. Evidence shows that he was prone to panic attacks, in which he feared he would die, and also that on two occasions he was incapacitated for months on end by depression.

Once it is concluded that Darwin's ill-health was of psychological origin, the question arises how it may be explained. Here there are two principal schools of thought. One is that it was the expression of an inherited constitutional weakness, the other that he developed a vulnerable personality as the result of a childhood shadowed by an invalid and dying mother and an unpredictable and often intimidating father, and that his symptoms can be understood as responses to stressful events and situations, both family and professional, that he met with during later life. It is the latter view that I believe the evidence favours.

My purpose in this work, therefore, is to explore this way of explaining Darwin's long-lasting troubles, setting out such evidence as there is in its support and examining the difficulties. In doing so I am drawing on the now substantial body of work supporting the view that stressful life events, including bereavements, play a major role in causing emotional disturbance and disorder. The conceptual framework adopted for understanding mental health and ill-health is the one advanced in my volumes on attachment and loss.

For readers unfamiliar with Darwin's life the following preliminary sketch may be useful.

II

Charles Darwin was born on 12 February 1809, the fifth child and second son in a prosperous professional family. His father, Robert, not quite forty-three at the time, was a prominent physician in Shrewsbury whose practice extended over the border into North Wales. His mother, Susannah, elder daughter of Josiah Wedgwood the potter, was eighteen months older. Within a few years of his birth she developed a serious illness, from which she died in July 1817 when Charles was eight. Dr Robert did not remarry and Charles was cared for within the family, largely by two elder sisters, Caroline and Susan, respectively nine and six years older.

Charles was educated briefly at a small local school and then, between the ages of nine and sixteen, at Shrewsbury School, where he was a boarder. He was not good at his lessons and he especially disliked the classics. From early days he was a keen collector, at first of any and every item of natural history, but later was more selective. In addition, he read Shakespeare with enthusiasm, and enjoyed carrying out chemical experiments in a shed in the garden with his brother, Erasmus, four years his elder.

When Charles was sixteen his father sent him, together with his elder brother, to Edinburgh, where both were to study medicine. In going there they were following a strong family tradition, since their grandfather, the great Dr Erasmus Darwin, their father and also his elder brother had all studied medicine in Edinburgh. Although Charles found most of the lectures tedious, he made friends with a young lecturer in zoology, Robert Grant, with whom he collected specimens of marine life on the shore, and from whom he heard favourable comment about Lamarck's theory of evolution.

After two years in Edinburgh Charles decided he did not care for a medical career. This was deeply disappointing to his father, who expressed much concern lest his son become a good-for-nothing. The alternative decided upon was that Charles should go to Cambridge, study for the church and become a country parson. Despite some doubts whether he could subscribe to all the church's tenets, Charles thought this a reasonable prospect and was happy to fall in with his father's wishes.

During his three years at Cambridge, 1828 to 1831, Charles once again scamped the required courses and, as in Edinburgh, busied himself with extra-curricular activities. These included shooting game birds and hunting foxes, but much else besides. His long-held enthusiasm for collecting became focused on beetles so that he spent much time scouring the nearby fens for specimens. This brought him into contact with the Professor of Botany, the Reverend John Henslow, thirteen years his senior, who was fond of organising field trips for his students. Henslow was soon struck by Darwin's intelligence and gifts and they became friends. In this way during his final year Darwin joined the group of scientifically minded dons and students who met for evening discussions at Henslow's house. Stimulated by these meetings, Darwin did some serious reading. In consequence, although at the time there was no degree course in science, during his three years in Cambridge he absorbed much of the scientific thought and knowledge then available there.

At the end of his time and as his final examinations neared, Darwin concentrated on the set subjects for a degree, classics and mathematics, and managed to obtain a respectable place among those who did not seek honours.

By this time Darwin's hopes were set on travel and the pursuit of his scientific interests. To equip himself better, during August 1831 he joined the Professor of Geology, the Reverend Adam Sedgwick, whom he had met at Henslow's house, on a geological field trip to North Wales. As the first of September drew near Darwin's only thought was to be over at his Wedgwood cousins' house in Staffordshire, a day's ride from Shrewsbury, for the start of the partridge-shooting season. Stopping *en route* at his home, however, he found a letter from Henslow which was to change the course of his life.

The Admiralty was commissioning a small ship, HMS *Beagle*, to survey the east and west coasts of South America. The captain, Robert FitzRoy, was willing to give up part of his cabin to a young man willing to accompany him without pay as naturalist and companion. Henslow himself had been approached but felt constrained by family responsibilities and was now suggesting Darwin as a suitable alternative. Although Charles was eager to accept, his father was again deeply concerned lest it diverted his son from pursuing a proper profession and therefore pressed refusal. Fortunately, however, Charles's Wedgwood uncle, Josiah II, thought differently and persuaded Dr Robert to relent.

After meeting FitzRoy and being approved as a suitable companion on a long voyage, Darwin was duly appointed as naturalist. Time was short and preparations urgent. At the end of December the *Beagle* sailed from

Plymouth on what was intended to be a two-year voyage. In the event she was away for four and a half years. Having at length completed her survey of the coasts of South America as far as the Galapagos Islands, she returned west across the Pacific to Australia and on round the Cape of Good Hope to the Atlantic.

During his four years of voyaging Darwin spent much time ashore in South America while the ship moved up and down the coast surveying. He rode long distances across the Argentine pampas, and later, on the west coast, undertook ambitious expeditions in and across the Andes. Except for much seasickness and a severe fever in Valparaiso, which kept him in bed for six weeks, he was fit and extremely active throughout these years.

His duties as naturalist were to observe and to collect all items of possible interest, tasks for which he was well equipped. Carefully labelled with particulars of where found and expertly packed, large cases full of his specimens were from time to time dispatched to England addressed to Henslow in Cambridge. Included were rocks, fish and other marine life, insects, birds, mammals, plants and fossils. Almost all were strange to him and, although he was able to identify many specimens from the books on board, by far the most had to wait for examination by the appropriate specialists in England. In addition to the collecting, for which he had the help of a full-time assistant, he kept a detailed diary and field notebooks in which he recorded a huge variety of observations, geological, zoological, botanical and human; he also speculated on the significance of his more striking observations for the understanding of changes in the earth's crust, the geographical distribution of animals, and the relation of fossil species to living ones. From time to time all his doings and collecting were described in long letters to Henslow, with priority always given to geology. A regular correspondence with his sisters was also maintained, though, thanks to the ship's uncertain itinerary, their monthly letters from home were often much delayed in reaching him.

A few months before the *Beagle*'s eventual return in October 1836 Charles learned from his sisters that the semi-technical bulletins he had been sending to Henslow were creating a stir in scientific circles. In fact, news reached Shrewsbury that Charles Darwin looked destined for a distinguished career in science. Dr Robert was delighted and relieved that Charles had found a proper role. Thereafter he had no hesitation in supporting his son's work by providing him with adequate finance.

On arrival back in England Charles received a warm welcome from some of the leading scientists of the day. This enabled him, though not without using a good deal of persuasion, to arrange for the different parts of his collection to be examined by a range of suitable experts, mainly in London and Cambridge. He himself took responsibility for the geological specimens.

Exploiting the fruits of the *Beagle* voyage was to take Darwin the next nine years, during which, though often delayed by ill-health, he published three major works on geology and oversaw the publication of a large series of monographs detailing the findings of the other specialists in their various fields. He also wrote and published his *Journal of Researches of the Voyage of the Beagle*, which met a ready readership among a public already fascinated by a succession of travel books describing new discoveries in strange lands.

In addition to all these public activities, which were earning him a place among the foremost young scientists of the day, Darwin was busy in private trying to formulate a theory which might explain the processes whereby the natural world had come to present the picture it does. Before the end of 1838, hardly two years after the *Beagle*'s return, he had articulated the main features of his theory of evolution by means of variation and natural selection; and a few years later he had written up his reasoning and conclusions in a long memorandum which he put away for safe keeping.

Meanwhile he had decided to marry, and had proposed and been accepted by his cousin, Emma Wedgwood, whom he had known all his life. Married in January 1839, she gave birth to a rapidly increasing brood of children which gave Charles great pleasure but also much intense anxiety. For their first three years of marriage they lived in the Bloomsbury district of London, but then moved to a village a few miles south of Bromley on the southern outskirts of London. There they lived at Down House until Charles died in 1882, aged seventy-three.

Darwin was a workaholic who followed a rigorous routine day in and day out seven days a week, reluctant always to take a holiday. During those forty years at Down he produced a steady stream of monographs and books, as well as innumerable short and long papers for journals. Until 1846 he was employed completing publications arising from the *Beagle* voyage. Next he spent no less than eight years studying barnacles, by the end of which period he had published a series of monographs which were, and have remained, definitive. Not until 1854 did he decide it was time he wrote up his ideas on evolution, and another five years elapsed before his famous book, *On the Origin of Species*, was published. There followed twelve years of fierce controversy, 1860 to 1872, during which Thomas Huxley was enjoying his self-appointed role as Darwin's bulldog, while Darwin himself, when not incapacitated by ill-health, was busy completing a series of weighty volumes on topics relating to evolution, which included two volumes on the *Descent of Man*. Thereafter, during the final ten years of his life, he devoted himself to path-breaking experiments in what would later be called plant physiology, on which he also published extensively.

Although Darwin spent most of his life at Down, he was far from isolated. Being close to London he could travel easily to attend scientific meetings there and to see relatives, while relatives and scientific friends could visit Down for a few weeks, for weekends, or even for the day. Since postal services were amazingly fast and efficient, he was able to carry on a huge correspondence with scientific colleagues, both professional and amateur, not only in Britain but in every continent. In scientific circles his reputation grew steadily. In 1853 the Royal Society conferred on him one of its Royal Medals, in recognition of his barnacle study as well as of his contributions to geology; and eleven years later he received the society's highest award, the Copley Medal. Meanwhile he had become well known to the reading public, first for his *Beagle Journal* and later for his *Origin of Species*, the source of one of the most intense controversies of the nineteenth century. Deeply loved by family and friends, and widely revered, he at length received national recognition by being laid to rest in Westminster Abbey.

III

Charles Darwin suffered chronic ill-health from the age of thirty until he was sixty. During the last decade of his life, however, he was much better, and he lived to be seventy-three. In the Darwin archives there are plentiful papers giving detailed information about his condition, often monthly and for some periods even day by day.

The symptoms on which attention has tended to be concentrated and with which in later years Darwin himself was constantly preoccupied are the gastric ones, which afflicted him especially at night. They included flatulence, gastric pain and a symptom variously referred to as sickness and vomiting. Another symptom about which he worried from time to time and which preceded the gastric symptoms by nearly ten years was palpitations. In his *Autobiography* he gives few details. The palpitations he describes as having first afflicted him during the weeks before the *Beagle* sailed at the end of 1831, when he was only twenty-two.[1] The gastric symptoms he describes as 'violent shivering and vomiting attacks' brought on by the excitement of meeting people.[2] In his letters, however, much else of relevance to his health is described.

By far the most complete description of the symptoms is given in a long account Darwin wrote on 20 May 1865. Representative extracts from the first half, with his numerous insertions placed here in brackets, run as follows: 'For 25 years extreme spasmodic daily and nightly flatulence: occasional vomiting, on two occasions prolonged during months. Vomiting preceded by shivering (hysterical crying) dying sensations (or half-faint) . . . ringing in ears, treading on air and vision. (focus and black dots) . . . (nervousness when E. leaves me) – What I vomit intensely acid, slimy (sometimes bitter) consider teeth. Doctors (puzzled) say suppressed gout – No organic mischief, Jenner & Brinton . . .' A note added in Emma's

---

[1] Notes to the main text begin on p. 467.

writing runs: 'Does not throw up the food.' In the second half he refers to his pulse ('58 to 62'), his appetite ('good'), evacuation ('regular'), urine ('scanty'), eczema ('now without'). and lumbago. He notes also: 'always tired – conversation or excitement tires me much.'

Over the years Darwin's symptoms waxed and waned, but there were three periods, each lasting one or two years, during which they were especially bad. The first began in the last days of 1839 after his marriage and a day or two before the birth of his first child. The second was in 1848–9 during his father's terminal illness and after his death. The third was three years after the publication of the *Origin*, during 1863–4, with a relapse a year later: it began immediately after he was bitterly disappointed by a senior colleague whose support for his theories he deeply craved. In addition to the symptoms listed, he suffered on some other occasions from a skin eruption which affected his face, lips or hands and which he usually referred to as eczema.

During the course of his life Darwin consulted most of the leading physicians and surgeons of his day, but none of them ever found anything organically wrong. Although a number of physical illnesses that could not have been diagnosed last century have since been proposed – for example, chronic cholecystitis, hiatus hernia, arsenic poisoning – the only one to receive any serious attention in recent years is Chagas's disease. This is a form of trypanosomiasis, an infective condition common in South America which is transmitted through the bite of an infected bug. This diagnosis was first proposed by Professor Saul Adler, an Israeli parasitologist, in 1959.[3] Although examined in the greatest detail in 1965 by another parasitologist, Professor A. W. Woodruff,[4] of London, and rejected decisively by him in favour of a psychosomatic diagnosis, the idea was revived in 1984 by Dr Ralph Bernstein[5] and remains current in some quarters.

The arguments for and against a diagnosis of Chagas's disease are set out in the appendix. Among the many objections are, first, that at least one of Darwin's symptoms, palpitations, was present before the *Beagle* sailed for South America, and possibly his gastric troubles as well.[6] Secondly, there is abundant evidence that his cardiac symptoms were brought on not by exercise but by meeting people and by anxiety generally. In fact, despite the symptoms, Darwin's exercise tolerance seems to have been excellent until his final years. As his son Francis wrote, Darwin 'walked with a swinging gait' and 'moved about quickly and easily enough' when interested in his work.[7] Much evidence, moreover, points to an emotional origin for his gastric symptoms. In his summing up, Woodruff emphasises that, while none of the points taken individually could exclude Chagas's disease, when 'taken collectively they make a case of overwhelming strength against it'.

Woodruff's diagnosis of psychosomatic illness is shared by at least two other distinguished clinicians, both of whom emphasise that Darwin's improved health during the last decade of his life constitutes a telling argument against almost all organic diagnoses.

Thus Sir George Pickering, formerly Regius Professor of Medicine at Oxford, after making a careful analysis of both the symptomatology and the circumstances in which the symptoms started, argues strongly against any organic diagnosis.[8] The palpitations and several of the other symptoms he attributes to Da Costa's Syndrome, now known as hyperventilation syndrome, a diagnosis first advanced by Professor Douglas Hubble in 1943.[9] He notes Darwin's description of his condition prior to the *Beagle*'s departure: 'These two months at Plymouth were the most miserable which I ever spent, though I exerted myself in various ways. I was out of spirits at the thought of leaving all my family and friends for so long a time, and the weather seemed to me inexpressibly gloomy. I was also troubled with palpitations and pain about the heart, and like many a young ignorant man, especially one with a smattering of medical knowledge, was convinced I had heart disease. I did not consult any doctor, as I fully expected to hear the verdict that I was not fit for the voyage, and I was resolved to go at all hazards.'[10] 'This description is typical of Da Costa's syndrome' is Pickering's comment, and he points especially to the circumstances in which the symptoms originated. When such a patient is examined, his heart-rate is raised and he is usually overbreathing. Among the effects of overbreathing are faintness, tingling and a sense of weakness, from all of which Darwin suffered.

Yet a further point made by Pickering is the deeply adverse effect on the patient of authoritative medical advice that his heart is seriously affected. In September 1837, a year after the *Beagle*'s return, when Darwin was working very hard writing up his various findings, he starts a letter to his old Cambridge tutor, J. S. Henslow: 'I have not been very well of late with an uncomfortable palpitation of the heart, and my doctors urge me *strongly* to knock off all work and go and live in the country for a few weeks.'[11] These medical opinions went far to confirm his suspicions that he was indeed an invalid. This conclusion of his was strongly reinforced during subsequent years, not least by his father, whose medical opinions he treated as gospel.[12] For example, in July 1841, after the gastric symptoms had started, Darwin wrote to another mentor, Charles Lyell, 'My father scarcely seems to believe that I shall become strong for some years.'[13]

Another medical specialist, this time a former President of the Royal College of Surgeons, Sir Hedley Atkins, has also examined the records, giving special attention to the gastric symptoms.[14] His conclusion is compatible with Woodruff's and Pickering's: 'We are accordingly not only thrown back on a diagnosis of neurosis, but we can muster an unequalled array of evidence in a positive way in favour of it. It is interesting that nearly every medically qualified man who has written on this subject is inclined to the view, with a variable degree of conviction, that Darwin's symptoms were mainly, if not entirely, psychogenic. Those who oppose this view are almost exclusively not medically trained.'

IV

A re-examination of Darwin's somatic symptoms in the light of recent research leaves no reasonable doubt that Hubble and Pickering were right in attributing them to Da Costa's syndrome, or hyperventilation syndrome in today's terminology.[15] In this condition both physiological and psychological factors play their parts, and factors of each type provoke those of the other to create a vicious circle. In current nomenclature, when the diagnostic orientation is physiological the condition is named hyperventilation syndrome and, when it is psychological, anxiety disorder with panic attacks. One of the earliest descriptions of the condition was given by Freud, who in 1895 proposed the label 'anxiety neurosis'.[16] Other labels used in the past include 'effort syndrome' and 'Soldier's Heart'. There is still no satisfactory or widely agreed definition.

The immediate cause of the symptoms is an increase in the arousal level of the patient's autonomic nervous system, with an ensuing increase in his breathing without his engaging in energetic action. In ordinary circumstances such increased arousal and oxygen intake occur only in conditions when increased energy consumption is called for, such as those of physical danger when it prepares the organism for fight or flight. In the absence of the appropriate energy consumption, as occurs in sedentary town dwellers who are especially prone to the syndrome, the increased and unstable breathing leads to a number of physiological changes, among which a persistently lowered and fluctuating level of carbon dioxide in the blood is critical. It is these fluctuations that produce the symptoms of which the patient complains.[17]

A common condition is one in which, as a result of persistent overbreathing often so slight as to be imperceptible, the carbon dioxide in the blood comes to be maintained continuously at a level only just above that at which symptoms are produced. As a result, any situation, however commonplace, that increases arousal and lowers the level still further will produce symptoms. It is thus that situations that are seemingly trivial such as the animated conversation in which Darwin liked to engage, or even a heavy sigh, can bring them on. Evidence, reviewed later, suggests strongly that Darwin was often in this condition.

Given that state of affairs, much turns on how the symptoms are then construed. Trouble starts when the patient believes that they indicate some serious organic illness affecting, perhaps, his heart or stomach. If they are construed in this way, the patient becomes increasingly alarmed, the level of autonomic arousal increases still further, the symptoms become worse, and he suffers a full-blown panic attack. During it he is beset by frightening thoughts, for example of a heart attack, a stroke, loss of control, often of dying, thoughts which are all too clear and credible and which he finds difficult to exclude.[18] Fear of being left alone and a consequent demand for some trusted person to be constantly at hand commonly follow.

At this stage the medical advice a patient receives is crucial. Should the condition be diagnosed for what it is, and appropriate explanation and reassurance be given, the vicious circle is aborted. Should the doctor misdiagnose or prevaricate, however, the patient's worst fears persist and the circle becomes ever more vicious.

A major finding from careful and informed research is that in many cases, probably the great majority, the tendency to overbreathe is due to the person's being in a state of chronic anxiety caused by one or more severely adverse events that have occurred in his life and are continuing to affect him. Among the salient events that have been found to have initiated the condition, none is more frequent than those involving separation or loss, or the threat of such happenings: bereavement, marital breakdown, loss of job. Other situations are those in which a person becomes intensely angry with someone, for example an employer, but must on no account express it.

All these findings, which are discussed further in the appendix, are held to be of great relevance to the present study. Another finding, equally relevant, is that these patients have a pronounced tendency to avoid referring to the event or to their having been distressed by it. Furthermore, they do not need to be consciously aware of having been reminded of the event for it to affect their breathing. This means that, without skilled investigation, which should be carried out only as part of a therapeutic procedure, the disturbing event or continuing situation responsible for the condition is likely to remain hidden. Findings of these sorts go far to explain occasions when the onset of symptoms occurs for no obvious reason, as often happens – for example while reading a newspaper or watching TV.

V

Let us return now to the symptoms from which Darwin suffered and consider how current knowledge of the hyperventilation syndrome can help us understand them.

The evidence, which because embedded in the story of his life is best understood as the story unfolds, strongly suggests that at various times in his life and for weeks or months on end Darwin was persistently overbreathing and his physiological state precariously balanced so that almost any increase in arousal, however trivial, led to an onset of symptoms. Furthermore, there is no lack of evidence that emotional factors played a major part in accounting for these periods of chronic overbreathing as well as in precipitating an attack. Darwin himself was keenly aware that being anxious or upset brought on the symptoms. Examples are his misery at the prospect of leaving family and friends before the *Beagle*'s departure, anxiety about pressure of work following her return, and the humiliation he felt when a serious criticism was made of one of his geological papers. In later years his descriptions of the chronic symptoms often imply a conviction that they were of organic origin. Yet evidence to the contrary is abundant: Darwin had a strong tendency to respond to adversity with both acute and chronic anxiety and sometimes also with depression. Note, for example, the revealing phrase inserted into the detailed account of his somatic symptoms: 'hysterical crying'.

Another ailment from which Darwin suffered, but which is not part of the hyperventilation syndrome, was the skin eruption that affected his face, lips and hands. The circumstances in which these outbreaks occurred suggest strongly that, here again, emotional factors were at work. The first recorded outbreak occurred when he was aged twenty and felt deeply responsible for a shooting accident in which a companion had been hit (fortunately much less seriously than at first appeared). Another example was shortly after he had accepted the invitation to join the *Beagle*. Yet another occurred when he was 'burning with indignation' over the behaviour, towards a friend, of a colleague he had come to hate.

Skin eruptions of this sort occurring in conditions of stress are well recognised by dermatologists.[19] They are often associated with a disturbance in the body's ability to regulate temperature and, as in the case of hyperventilation, they are especially prone to occur in individuals who strive to suppress their feelings and who are given to low self-esteem and overwork.

These features, both physiological and psychological, are recorded as having been characteristic of Darwin. First, temperature regulation: 'Like most delicate people', his son Francis recalled, 'he suffered from heat as well as from chilliness; it was as if he could not hit the balance between too hot and too cold; often a mental cause would make him too hot, so that he would take off his coat if anything went wrong in the course of his work.'[20] Secondly, low self-esteem and overwork: work was constantly used by Darwin as a means of diverting his attention from his bodily discomforts and also, as he frequently insists, from thoughts about whatever was causing him anxiety or depression. Time and time again in his letters he refers to the anaesthetic effects of work. When not yet forty he writes to his wife: 'I was speculating yesterday how fortunate it was I had plenty of employment ... for being employed alone makes me forget myself.'[21] Ten years later, on 4 February 1861, after telling his close friend Joseph Hooker that he is 'never comfortable except at work', he adds: 'the word "holiday" is written in a dead language for me, and much do I grieve it'.[22] During his mid-fifties, in 1864 and 1865, he writes in similar vein to no fewer than three of his regular correspondents: to his cousin William Darwin Fox, that work 'is the only thing which makes life endurable to me'; to Joseph Hooker, 'I have my hopes of again some day resuming scientific work, which is my sole enjoyment in life'; and, most revealing of all, to Alfred Russel Wallace commiserating with him on a broken engagement: 'Do try what hard work will do to banish painful thoughts.'[23] Not only Darwin himself but members of his family were keenly aware of the role of work in his life. Thus in 1860, when he was fifty-one, his wife writes to a friend: 'Charles is too much given to anxiety, as you know, and his various experiments this summer have been a great blessing to him.'[24] Similar views are expressed by two of his sons in their reminiscences. Francis, who edited the three volumes of *Life and Letters*, reflecting on times when his father had taken a holiday after a period of overwork, writes: 'it seemed as though the absence of the customary strain allowed him to fall into a peculiar condition of miserable health.'[25] Leonard, the fourth son, recalled vividly that, when on one occasion one of his brothers had encouraged his father to take some rest away from home, his father had replied 'that the truth was that he was *never* quite comfortable except when utterly absorbed in his writing'. On this Leonard comments: 'He evidently dreaded idleness robbing him of his one anodyne, work.'[26]

Thus the evidence is unmistakable. Darwin's scientific work, from which biology and other sciences have benefited so hugely, served also as an indispensable refuge from the troubles that beset him. Small wonder he overworked. He was a workaholic who pursued his studies according to a daily routine, week in and week out until he could continue no longer.[27] Then, starting in 1849 and continuing for many years, he would resort to a hydropathic establishment and follow a regime of cold baths and douches. He also tried a multitude of other forms of treatment, both orthodox and unorthodox. The detailed description of his symptoms quoted earlier was written for a doctor whose sovereign remedy was ice-packs to the base of the spine. Viewed superficially, he has appeared to some as an all-too-typical Victorian hypochondriac.

Yet these troubled areas of his life stand in extraordinary contrast to the high spirits of his Cambridge years,[28] and the enterprise, vigour and unflagging industry of his five years in the *Beagle*. They stand in contrast, too, to the immense productivity of the thirty years during which his health was hardly ever good and sometimes very bad – more than a dozen substantial books and monographs and a prodigious number of papers. He was much loved by friends and colleagues, to whom he was generous of praise, sometimes to a fault; he was father to a large, affectionate and united family; and his wife, Emma, spared nothing in the devoted care she gave him. That is the other and no less vital part of the story.

VI

In the belief that Darwin's symptoms were responses to stress, psychiatrists and other medicals have advanced a plethora of ideas about what the stressors may have been and why he was vulnerable to them. These are reviewed in the appendix, with my evaluation of each. The hypotheses I favour and which inform the biography can be summarised. For Darwin's vulnerability, I see his relationships within his family as providing the keys: first, his relation with his mother and her early death, especially his elder sisters' insistence that no reference be made to her thereafter; secondly, his subsequent difficult, though far from bad, relation with his father during boyhood and adolescence. As regards the current situations that exacerbated his symptoms and account for the periods of increased disability, for Darwin's first two breakdowns I look to situations that either threatened or constituted a family loss and, for the third, to certain special aspects of how the *Origin* was received. Principal features of my thesis are that his mother's early death, and especially the way in which members of the family responded to it by sealing it in silence, made him intensely sensitive to any illness or possible death in the family, while his father's disparaging criticisms of him made him especially vulnerable to any criticism from emotionally significant senior colleagues.

Not unexpectedly, there is evidence to suggest that these two strands of psychological causation interacted from the start, one vulnerability factor influencing the development and effects of the other, and current situations of the two kinds sometimes coinciding and thereby augmenting each other's effects. In what follows, therefore, whenever any one link in these causal networks is under discussion the roles of the other links must constantly be borne in mind.

One other factor must not be forgotten, namely the profound influence on Darwin of the opinions of his medical advisers. As Pickering and many others have emphasised, to indicate or even to imply to a patient with Darwin's symptoms that he might be suffering from a bad heart or a diseased stomach is to increase the anxiety from which he already suffers. Furthermore, it not only focuses the patient's attention on some internal organ but diverts it from the situation that is making him anxious. This diversion of attention away from the source of the patient's troubles, and channelling it into a blind alley, enormously exacerbates his problems.

Although the evidence strongly suggests that for many years Darwin's condition was made worse by the medical opinions expressed and the advice he received, it must be remembered that in the middle of the last century medical knowledge was still elementary and diagnostic instruments primitive. In consequence any condition that did not give rise to unequivocal signs of its nature remained a mystery, and the medical advice offered turned on the fashions of the day and the whims and biases of the practitioners concerned. So long as it was so difficult to exclude organic conditions with any degree of certainty and psychosomatic conditions remained so little understood, in a case such as I believe Darwin's to have been there were only two choices: one was to adopt a safety-first approach to guard against some hidden organic disease, which led inevitably to a state of invalidism; the other was to dismiss the patient as a hypochondriac. Evidently the advice Darwin received swung from one such viewpoint to the other. No attempt to see his problems in a psychological perspective appears to have been made; if any attempt was made, it must have proved abortive.

If the diagnostic assessment of Darwin's troubles outlined above is well-founded, I believe that with our present knowledge he could have been given a great deal of help both for his psychosomatic symptoms and for his emotional troubles, even though he might well have continued to be oversensitive to situations of certain kinds.

The first therapeutic step in the programme would be to establish the diagnosis by means that would give the patient confidence that his fears of organic disease had been taken into account and had proved unfounded. That would require both a thorough medical history and a thorough medical examination. The next step would be a discussion of the nature and origin of the condition and the patient's introduction to the therapeutic measures recommended. These would include procedures aimed to help him avoid overbreathing, which would be the province of a physiotherapist, and also procedures aimed to help him psychologically, which would be the province of someone trained in psychoanalytic psychotherapy. Sketches of both types of procedure are given in the appendix.

I see no reason why Darwin would have been an especially difficult patient. As far as his psychosomatic symptoms are concerned, it would have been fairly easy to show him that they were due to overbreathing and that he tended to do it when he was anxious or excited – which he half knew already. As regards helping him gain an understanding of the nature and origin of his anxieties and other emotional troubles, the first and indispensable step for the psychotherapist would have been to recognise, and gradually to counteract, the powerful influence on his patient of the strongly entrenched Darwin tradition that the best way of dealing with painful thoughts is to dismiss them from your mind and, if possible, forget them altogether. That brings us back to the family in which Darwin grew up and the way in which it influenced his development.

In order to obtain a clear understanding of the current relationships existing between members of any family it is usually illuminating to examine how the pattern of family relationships has evolved. That leads to a study of earlier generations, the calamities and other events that may have affected their lives and the patterns of family interaction that resulted. In the case of the family in which Darwin grew up, I believe such study to be amply rewarding. For that reason alone it would be necessary to start with his grandfathers' generation. A second and equally weighty reason is that it was his grandfathers' generation that shaped so much else in Darwin's life: the social and economic circumstances in which it was lived, the political causes he favoured, the kind of scientific problem that fascinated him and, not least, the direction that his theorising took.

ONE

Two distinguished grandfathers:
Erasmus Darwin and Josiah Wedgwood

I

Both of Charles Darwin's grandfathers were men of great energy, ability and distinction who, during the second half of the eighteenth century, were famous throughout Britain. His father, Robert, was the youngest son by the first marriage of the famous physician, scientist and author, Dr Erasmus Darwin of Lichfield. His mother, Susannah, was the eldest and favourite daughter of Josiah Wedgwood, who, starting from almost nothing, had by skill, ingenuity and enterprise established one of the principal potteries of Britain. For many years these two outstandingly able men lived and worked in the same county, Staffordshire, just north of Birmingham. Exact contemporaries, they first got to know each other well about 1765 when they were in their mid-thirties and both raising young families.[1]

Although they came from very different social backgrounds, one having had the best of education and the other self-educated, they had a great deal in common. Not only were both exceptionally talented but both were given to original thinking and action. In politics both favoured liberal, and indeed radical, opinions. Both were excited by the scientific discoveries of the day and especially by the technical innovations and inventions that were at the heart of Britain's industrial revolution, then in its heyday. The two became firm friends and for many years looked forward to the time when the two families would be united in marriage. That, however, did not occur until 1796, a year after Susannah's father had died at the age of sixty-five. Robert's father lived another six years and died, aged seventy-one, seven years before his grandson, Charles, was born. Thus Charles never knew either of his grandfathers personally.

II

Erasmus Darwin, Charles's paternal grandfather, born in 1731, was the youngest of a family of seven. His father, a lawyer and naturalist, lived on a small estate he had inherited from his mother on the borders of Lincolnshire and Nottinghamshire. Among Erasmus's numerous brothers and brothers-in-law were another lawyer and two country parsons.

Erasmus was educated at school near Sheffield where he was well grounded in the classics; thence, between the ages of eighteen and twenty-two, he was at Cambridge where he not only studied medicine but became proficient in writing English verse. After two years of further studies in Edinburgh, the leading medical school of the day, he qualified. A year later he settled in practice in Lichfield, a small cathedral town in the heart of England. There he prospered, built up an extensive practice, and became the centre of a large circle of friends, some of them literary, others scientific. Soon he had married a young local girl, Mary Howard, who during the ten years spanning 1758 to 1767 bore him three sons and two daughters, both the daughters dying in infancy. The third son, Robert, who would in due course father the famous scientist, was born in 1766.

Much else was happening in Erasmus Darwin's life during that decade. Since his practice covered a large area around Lichfield, he travelled far and wide in his specially designed single-seat carriage and became familiar with many influential personages. Among these was Josiah Wedgwood, whose new and thriving pottery was at Burslem, some thirty miles north-west of Lichfield. First acquainted in the roles of doctor and patient, they soon discovered a mutual interest in technology and invention.

Erasmus Darwin himself was both scientist and inventor, finding the time to think and invent during the long journeys he undertook to see his patients; indeed the single-seat carriage in which he travelled was itself built to his own design. During the early 1760s he was not only experimenting with gases and formulating new laws, later recognised as fundamental, but scheming to put his discoveries to use. Steam-engines were still primitive and needed to be improved. Matthew Boulton (1728–1809), a metal manufacturer in Birmingham, was the recipient of Darwin's ideas for a steam carriage, about which Darwin wrote in his characteristically enthusiastic style: 'As I was riding Home yesterday, I concider'd the Scheme of the fiery Chariot, and the longer I contemplated this favourite idea, the [more] practicable it appear'd to me', and ending up, 'As I am quite mad of this Scheme, I begg you will not mention it or shew this paper, to . . . any Body.'

Another great interest of Darwin's at this time was the building of canals; and it was the project for a strategic canal for the Midlands that brought Darwin and Wedgwood closely together.

Dr Erasmus Darwin, Charles's paternal grandfather 1731–1802

ERASMUS DARWIN OF LICHFIELD AND DERBY

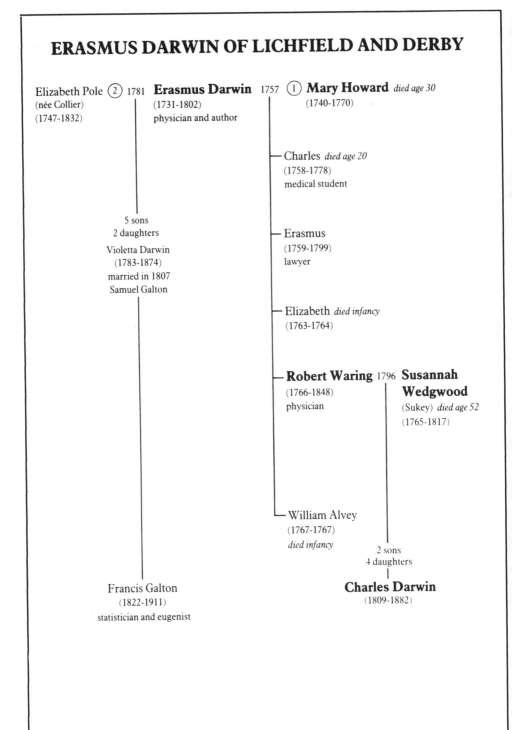

Elizabeth Pole ② 1781 **Erasmus Darwin** 1757 ① **Mary Howard** *died age 30*
(née Collier)   (1731-1802)   (1740-1770)
(1747-1832)   physician and author

Charles *died age 20*
(1758-1778)
medical student

5 sons
2 daughters

Violetta Darwin
(1783-1874)
married in 1807
Samuel Galton

Erasmus
(1759-1799)
lawyer

Elizabeth *died infancy*
(1763-1764)

Robert Waring 1796 **Susannah**
(1766-1848)   **Wedgwood**
physician   (Sukey) *died age 52*
                             (1765-1817)

William Alvey
(1767-1767)
died infancy

2 sons
4 daughters

Francis Galton   **Charles Darwin**
(1822-1911)   (1809-1882)
statistician and eugenist

JOSIAH WEDGWOOD OF BARLASTON AND ETRURIA

Josiah Wedgwood 1764 **Sarah Wedgwood** (Sally)
(1730-1795)   (1734-1815)
Master Potter

Robert Darwin 1796 **Susannah** ——
(1766-1848)   (1765-1817)
                    died age 52

2 sons
4 daughters

Jane Allen 1794 John ——
(1771-1836)   (1766-1844)

3 sons
3 daughters

Richard ——
(1767-1768)
died infancy

Elizabeth Allen 1792 **Josiah II** ——
(Bessy)   (1769-1843)
(1764-1846)

5 sons
4 daughters

Thomas (Tom) ——
(1771-1805)

Catherine (Kitty) ——
(1774-1823)

Sarah ——
(1778-1856)

III

Josiah Wedgwood, a few months older than Erasmus Darwin, was born into a clan of potters in a district known as the Potteries in north-west Staffordshire where the principal towns are Newcastle-under-Lyme and Stoke-on-Trent. He was the twelfth and last child of Thomas Wedgwood, who, like many others of the clan, owned a small pottery making rough earthenware goods in the village of Burslem. When Thomas died at the age of fifty-four, Josiah was nine years old, with only two years of schooling behind him; even so he had immediately to leave school to help in the pottery, which had passed to his elder brother, another Thomas. Two years later he was a victim in an epidemic of smallpox, became extremely ill and was left with an infected and crippled right knee. This limited his activity in the pottery but gave him time to practise modelling in clay.

Josiah's mother, Mary, was the daughter of a Unitarian minister in nearby Newcastle-under-Lyme, the Reverend Samuel Stringer. An intelligent and enterprising woman, she gave Josiah much encouragement and no doubt provided him also with further education.

At the age of fourteen Josiah entered into a formal five-year apprenticeship with his brother, thirteen years his senior. On its completion he hoped to be taken into partnership but this was refused. Nothing daunted, he entered into partnership with neighbours. This lasted a further five years, after which he became dissatisfied with the arrangement since he had set his heart on manufacturing ware of much higher quality than his partners were interested in. Fortunately there was another neighbour, a much older man, who, evidently valuing the initiative and skills Josiah brought with him, gave him the opportunity he sought.

It was during this partnership, which lasted four years, 1754–8, and which proved happy and productive, that Josiah started to blossom. In the evenings at the pottery be began the brilliant series of experiments in which he tried out, with results recorded in secret code, an array of different clays, mineral earths and metallic oxides in an effort to perfect new bodies, new glazes and new firing techniques. In addition, he broadened his education by reading books lent him by, and subsequently discussed with, a much older brother-in-law, another Unitarian minister in Newcastle-under-Lyme.

In 1758 Josiah, now twenty-eight and engaged to be married to one of his many Wedgwood cousins, decided to set up on his own and leased a small building from two uncles of his fiancée. By this time he had not only acquired all the traditional skills of a master-potter but had invented a new and far more refined type of earthenware, known as creamware, which proved extremely popular. With growing demand, he could appoint a reliable and well-qualified cousin to act as supervisor of his workforce. On the sales side an elder brother, already a merchant in London, could be appointed as agent. Within four years he was requiring much larger premises and in 1762 took a lease of one of the biggest in Burslem, comprising a substantial house with workshops and kilns at the rear.

Soon too he was in a position to marry. Sarah, or Sally, an intelligent and capable woman, came from a better-off branch of the family and was also better educated. At the time of their engagement some five years earlier, her father, hardly enthusiastic about his daughter's marrying a penniless young man, had stipulated that he would give his consent only if Josiah could match the dowry of £4000 that he intended to settle on her. By 1763, when Josiah was thirty-three and Sally twenty-nine, he was able to find this not inconsiderable sum, and they were duly married early the following year. Initially she was able to help him in his work, keeping records of his experiments and giving feminine advice on taste and design. Their first child, Susannah or Sukey, was born a year after marriage, to the delight of both. When she was forty-four Susannah would give birth to her fifth child and second son, Charles Darwin of the *Origin*.

Meanwhile Josiah was proving a singularly successful entrepreneur. Technically skilled himself, he was able not only to transmit those skills to his growing workforce but also to find and enlist the help of men who could make good his limitations. One such was Thomas Bentley, a man of his own age who owned an import–export warehouse in Liverpool and whom he had met almost by chance.

Liverpool, some fifty miles to the north-west of Burslem, had come to play a key role in Josiah's affairs. On the one hand, it was the port of entry for the high-quality clay which he required for his new wares and which was shipped from the West Country for overland transport to Burslem; on the other, it was the outlet for his growing export trade to North America and the West Indies. From time to time he visited the port, and on one such occasion in 1762 while he was riding there his injured knee received a blow that required three weeks of bed rest in Liverpool before he was fit to return. The surgeon who attended him, Matthew Turner, was a practical chemist and also moved in literary and artistic circles. It was through Turner and during this enforced stay in Liverpool that Wedgwood met Bentley as well as another gifted man, also due to play a significant role in his life, Joseph Priestley.

Thomas Bentley, who came of a property-owning family, had had a good education and he then served an apprenticeship to the cotton and woollen trades. After travelling on the continent, he had started a successful import–export agency in Liverpool where he had become an influential citizen. Like Wedgwood and Darwin and so many others in this story, he was a nonconformist in religion and a radical in politics. With a large house where he could entertain and broad interests, he had everything in education, knowledge of aesthetic taste and social connec-

Sarah Wedgwood, wife of Josiah I, Charles's maternal grandmother, 1734–1815, by Joshua Reynolds, 1782

Churchyard Works, Staffordshire, birthplace of Josiah Wedgwood I, 1730

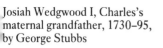

Josiah Wedgwood I, Charles's maternal grandfather, 1730–95, by George Stubbs

y House Works, Staffordshire,
'edgwood's first factory, 1759

tions that Wedgwood lacked. Despite these differences, however, they quickly found common ground, and Bentley invited Wedgwood to spend a week or two's convalescence in his house before he returned to Burslem. Wedgwood gladly accepted and before leaving, enterprising as ever, he had appointed Bentley's firm as his sole agents in Liverpool.

From the first, Wedgwood nurtured this new friendship, which quickly became yet one more source of education and advancement for him. Bentley could advise him on current literature to read and artists to employ, and could also guide him on the latest taste in aristocratic circles and how best to sell his wares there. By 1765 Wedgwood ware was becoming fashionable in the Midlands, and news of its merits had already reached London. After one of Queen Charlotte's household had acquired a tea-service, the Queen herself gave an order; and soon Josiah was given permission to style himself 'Potter to Her Majesty', and to describe his creamware as 'Queen's Ware'. By the following year Wedgwood had perfected another original ceramic, one also to become immensely popular, the unglazed black stoneware he named basalt. Meanwhile, Queen's Ware boomed. 'It is really amazing', he could write at this time, 'how rapidly its use has spread over the whole globe.'

Not surprisingly, Wedgwood's meteoric rise impressed Bentley, whose Liverpool business was no longer flourishing. By the end of 1767 Wedgwood, employing his characteristic combination of charm, enthusiasm and unrelenting pressure, had persuaded Bentley to join him as a partner. For the next thirteen years, until Bentley's untimely death, the firm, trading as Wedgwood & Bentley, went from strength to strength.

IV

From the time Wedgwood began importing clay and exporting finished ware through Liverpool, land transport had been a constant problem. With nothing but rough tracks, goods had to be carried both ways either by pack animals or by heavy wagons which were precarious as well as slow. In 1761 the first canal to be built in Britain was opened to bring coal ten miles from Cheshire to Manchester. Its success led to more ambitious schemes. One such was to build a canal from the Mersey near Liverpool through the Potteries to join the east-flowing river Trent south of Derby. In this way goods could be transported to and from the growing industrial Midlands from either the west coast or the east.

Needless to say, Wedgwood was enthusiastic about the plan. Nevertheless the building of such a canal, soon to be named the Grand Trunk, was a huge enterprise that for its success required wide-ranging public and political support as well as engineering and technical expertise and large amounts of capital. A number of influential public figures were needed to help promote it and among those to whom Wedgwood turned was his multi-talented physician, Erasmus Darwin. Darwin responded with the greatest enthusiasm. He urged well-heeled patients and friends to support the scheme and bombarded Wedgwood with ideas and advice. Letters and meetings between them burgeoned. Thus began the close friendship that was to have momentous consequences for science in the following century.

It is testimony to Wedgwood's enormous energy and his capacity to mobilise likeminded and able allies that the Mersey–Trent canal received parliamentary approval so quickly. Work began during the summer of 1766 under the direction of James Brindley (1717–72), the talented and experienced hydraulics engineer who, among other achievements, had already built the coal canal into Manchester. Wedgwood himself, officially styled treasurer but always the driving force, cut the first sod on ground owned by his family. 140 miles long, the canal had to rise up a stairway of locks to a height of nearly 400 feet before descending down another stairway to the Trent. At the summit a tunnel was necessary, a tunnel no less than a mile and a half long. It was ten years before the canal was completed. Freight rates could then be cut to a fraction of their former levels and those who had backed it made a handsome profit. That the canal happened to make a detour just in front of the splendid new factory Wedgwood was building outside Burslem was hardly fortuitous and did not escape criticism. On Darwin's suggestion the factory was named Etruria, reflecting his belief that Wedgwood had rediscovered a decorative technique previously known only to the Etruscans.

V

During the late 1760s Erasmus Darwin's genius for friendship bore remarkable fruit. For some years he had been gathering around himself a circle of scientists, inventors and technically minded manufacturers. With the arrival in Birmingham of a Scots physician, William Small (1734–75), these disparate individuals came together in a club which met monthly and would later call itself the Lunar Society, so named because it usually met at the time of the full moon which made it easier and safer to drive home at night. Like Darwin, Small was not only a physician; he was also a mathematician and astronomer who for seven years had taught at William and Mary College in Virginia and had had Thomas Jefferson as a most appreciative student. He had been introduced to Matthew Boulton, the Birmingham manufacturer, by the experimental scientist and statesman, Benjamin Franklin (1706–90), then acting as spokesman in Britain for the American colonists.

It was a group of diverse talents and interests. Manufacturing was represented by Wedgwood (ceramics), Boulton (metal working), John Wilkinson (iron founding), John Baskerville (printing), James Keir (alkalis and glass), John Whitehurst (instrument making) and James Brindley (civil engineering). Among the scientists and inventors were

Darwin in the fields of physics and mechanics, Small, in mathematics and astronomy, and some of the manufacturers, for example Keir in chemistry and Whitehurst in geology.

Links at a distance were made with many others, two of the most gifted of whom subsequently moved to Birmingham and became principal members. One was James Watt (1736–1819), a gloomy Scot whose radical improvements to the steam-engine revolutionised steam power. After he entered into partnership with Boulton in 1773, the Boulton & Watt engines they designed were to power British industry through the nineteenth century and into the twentieth. Another gifted scientist who moved to Birmingham and finally joined the society in 1780 was Joseph Priestley (1733–1804), who combined serving as a Unitarian minister with experimental chemistry, for which he would become famous. To leaven what might otherwise have been rather solemn proceedings, the high-spirited Erasmus introduced two younger men, Richard Edgeworth (1744–1817), a prolific inventor who, like Erasmus, was versatile in the extreme, and Thomas Day, a wealthy eccentric of literary interests and great eloquence who had no scientific pretensions whatever.

The glue that held them all together was friendship with the self-effacing Small; while the very diversity of their fields of work limited the likelihood of jealousy. As a result, even the most precious or controversial of new ideas could be expressed freely; and in allowing others to take credit for his ideas and inventions Darwin himself was among the most generous. At any one meeting there were seldom more than half a dozen present. Never a scientific society, the Lunar Club was little more than an inspired gossip-shop.

VI

As a forum for the interchange of ideas and experiences, the Lunar Society was a model for scientific stimulation and industrial innovation. Erasmus Darwin was not only its architect but also one of its principal beneficiaries. Already well versed in many of the topics discussed, he was thereby enabled to extend his knowledge still further. Here lay one source of the encyclopaedic scope of the literary works he was soon to start writing.

In 1770 his wife Mary died at the age of thirty, leaving him with three young sons, then aged twelve, eleven and four. Fortunately his elder unmarried sister, Susannah (1729–89), was free to take charge of his household. Still only thirty-nine, he remained a widower for the next eleven years. Mary's early death cast a shadow, the consequences of which, I believe, can be discerned in the lives of her sons and grandsons and are considered in the next chapter.

During his eleven years as a widower, Dr Erasmus was a regular attender at the Lunar Society, then at its most thriving, and he also began

Matthew Boulton, manufacturer, 1728–1809   James Watt, engineer, 1736–1819

Joseph Priestley, chemist, 1733–1804   Benjamin Franklin, American scientist
and statesman, 1706–90

Four members of the Lunar Society

the literary works for which he would become famous. One of the first was an ambitious medical text which, twenty years later, would be published under the title *Zoönomia*.

Erasmus Darwin was no mean scientist. In 1757 he had carried out ingenious and critical experiments on water vapour and other gases, reports of which were published in the *Philosophical Transactions of the Royal Society*, and soon afterwards, he was elected a Fellow of the Society. After Priestley's arrival, Darwin's interest in physics and chemistry was renewed. Having done further experiments, he informed Watt that water is not an element, as was then widely believed; and he was also one of the first to abandon the phlogiston theory of combustion. The canal, with its cuttings and long tunnel, in which fossil bones and shells were found, fired his interest in geology and stirred in him the ideas about evolution that would appear in *Zoönomia*. Another growing interest was botany. In 1777 he bought eight acres outside Lichfield on which bubbled a clear cold spring at the head of a little rocky valley. This he planted as his own botanic garden, which he would later celebrate in verse.

Early in 1781 Dr Erasmus married again. His bride, Elizabeth Pole (née Collier), was the thirty-four-year-old widow of a landowner near Derby with three school-aged children, a son of eleven, heir to the estate, and two daughters of ten and six. In accepting him she stipulated that he move to Derby. Although it was no doubt a wrench, entailing his abandoning much of his medical practice, his botanic garden and his Lunar Society and other friends, he did not hesitate. The new Mrs Darwin was vivacious, intelligent and generous, and their marriage proved a success.

There was a crowd of children in the new household. In addition to Elizabeth's three, there was the twenty-four-year-old illegitimate son of her first husband. Darwin brought another four, his two surviving sons and two illegitimate daughters aged nine and seven, the offspring of a mistress who had shared his house during his widowhood. These family events, and especially the sudden death from septicaemia of his gifted eldest son at the age of twenty, which had occurred in 1778, and was an extremely severe blow to him, had far-reaching repercussions. For that reason a full account is postponed to the next chapter.

For the first two years of their marriage the Erasmus Darwins lived in the big country house outside Derby where Elizabeth had lived with her first husband. This arrangement did not suit his medical practice, however, and late in 1783 they moved into a town house in Derby. Already during their time in the country Elizabeth had given birth to two further children; the younger of them, Violetta, would become the mother of the distinguished scientist Francis Galton. The next seven years, in Derby, saw Elizabeth give birth to five more children, four of whom survived. Altogether by 1790 when he was nearing sixty, Erasmus Darwin had fathered fourteen children, all but three of whom reached maturity.

Dr Erasmus seems to have had no difficulty in building up a new medical practice, partly because he was already well known in the vicinity and partly because there was some overlap with the practice he had left in Lichfield. There was, however, a considerable change in his way of life. Now aged fifty and too far from his old circle of friends, he became much more domesticated and, without the stimulation of the Lunar Society, gave up experimenting and reduced the time he spent inventing. Henceforth his priority would be literary works. Even so, he much regretted the Lunar meetings. As he told Boulton at the end of 1782 in his typical prose style: 'I am here cut off from the milk of science, which flows in such redundant streams from your learned lunations; which, I can assure you, is a very great regret to me. . . . Pray if you think of it, make my devoirs to the learned Insane of your Society.'

From his schooldays onward Dr Erasmus had excelled in literary composition, and while in Lichfield had moved within a literary circle presided over by Canon Seward in the cathedral close. As an accomplished versifier he had helped the canon's daughter, Anna, to achieve success as a poet, and to earn her title as the 'Swan of Lichfield'. It was not surprising, therefore, that in the relative isolation of Derby he should devote time to literary productions.

His first works to be published were botanical. Classification and nomenclature had been in chaos before Carl Linnaeus (1707–78) produced his seminal work, *Genera Plantarum*, which had first appeared in 1740 and had subsequently gone through many editions. The current edition was translated from the Latin by Darwin and published in four volumes during the years 1783 to 1787 under the titles *System of Vegetables* and *Families of Plants*. Since this great work had been begun in Lichfield, where he had founded an abortive botanical society, authorship was attributed to the society, though Darwin had received only meagre help from its few other members.

Steeped as he then was in botanical science, Dr Erasmus turned his literary talents to composing an encyclopaedic poem in which he presented the whole of botanic knowledge in sparkling and polished couplets. Under the overall title *The Botanic Garden*, the work appeared in two parts (in reverse order), Part II, *The Loves of the Plants*, in 1789 and Part I, *The Economy of Vegetation*, two years later, each backed by copious scientific notes. Cast in the idiom of the day, they took the literary world by storm and propelled their author to literary fame. Though today no longer honoured for his poetry, Erasmus Darwin is well recognised by historians as the inspiration of the Romantic poets.

His next publications were two massive volumes on animal life. Titled *Zoönomia*, they appeared in 1794 and 1796 and were another great success, with many translations and reprints. The work remains notable for the chapter describing evolution, a chapter that his grandson, Charles, would read when a medical student and would be more influenced by than he seems ever to have realised. The theme of evolution appears again as the subject of Erasmus Darwin's last work, a long poem published posthumously in 1803 under the title *The Temple of Nature*, which is judged by his biographer, Desmond King-Hele, to be his finest achievement. The ideas on evolution, presented in more detail in this work, resemble closely, and antedate by some years, those of the well-known French naturalist, Jean-Baptiste Lamarck (1744–1829).

Before his death in 1802 Dr Erasmus had published two further works. One was a slim volume setting out his ideas on education, strongly influenced by Jean-Jacques Rousseau, whom he had met briefly during the latter's visit to England in 1766. Girls should be properly educated, he believed, so that they would grow up 'sound in body and mind'. The book was written for his two illegitimate daughters, Susan and Mary Parker, born in 1772 and 1774. The mother of these two girls, a Miss Parker with whom Dr Erasmus lived openly during his widowhood, had the status of a servant in the household; what her relationship was with his elder sister, who was also resident in the house, is obscure. In any case, Dr Erasmus gave the girls a good education and encouraged them to set up a school in a house a few miles outside Derby.

In 1800 Erasmus Darwin published a substantial survey of vegetable life under the title *Phytologia*, in many respects a companion volume to *Zoönomia*. It contains a quantity of up-to-date botanical science, among much else describing photosynthesis more fully than anyone had done before. It also advocates a number of technical innovations, for example sewage farms, the biological control of insects, and the boring of artesian wells, the geological principles of which he had been the first to describe.

Although always respected as a great physician and in later years famous for his literary works, Erasmus Darwin's politics made him a highly controversial character. A confirmed radical, he strongly supported both the American and the French revolutions. An agnostic before Huxley had coined the term, he lived his seventy-two years fearing neither God nor man. In the fields of science and technology his ideas were original and daring, never more so than in biology. By introducing an evolutionary perspective into the family's thinking, he paved the way for his grandson's breakthrough to an extent that is still not adequately recognised.

VII

Charles Darwin has often been criticised for failing to give credit to his grandfather for the hoard of valuable ideas bequeathed to him and which he absorbed during his student years as part of the Darwin family culture. There were several good reasons for that failure, to which attention is given in later chapters. Here I am concerned only with the nature of the ideas.[2] Some are of a general kind and direct attention to areas and interests that merit study, such as the natural world and how it is to be conceived and understood; the nature of knowledge and the philosophy of scientific method; social problems, ethical judgements and political action. Many others concern salient areas of biology and geology which include, of course, the fertile ideas on evolution proposed by Charles's grandfather.

From the last decades of the eighteenth century onwards, interest in natural history, both in its own right and for what significance it might have for humanity, became a major topic among the educated and leisured classes. Botany in particular became fashionable. The Royal Botanic Gardens at Kew were founded in 1760, natural history societies multiplied, the record of Gilbert White's lifetime of observations in a Hampshire parish, published in 1789, became a best seller. While country parsons provided much of the basic data, theologians were busy formulating theories that would explain the findings in terms consistent with the Biblical record. One of the most influential of these was *Evidences of Christianity* (1794) by the Reverend William Paley (1743–1805). In it he drew attention to the host of ingenious devices for survival to be found in living organisms and, using the analogy of a watch being intelligible only by inferring the existence of a watchmaker, argued that design in nature required the inference of an omniscient Creator. Not only was the natural world therefore of the greatest intrinsic interest but its study also provided lessons of the greatest importance for mankind. By the 1790s Dr Erasmus had advanced an evolutionary alternative to that explanation, but his ideas were ignored in academic and theological circles. Only when his grandson, sixty-five years later, followed in his footsteps and buttressed the theory with an abundance of impressive and interlocking evidence, while simultaneously detailing a plausible mechanism of evolutionary change, would it be taken seriously.

The similarities of approach, of interests, of ideas and often even of language between Charles Darwin and his grandfather are often striking. Both tried to study nature as a whole and approached it with reverence, enthusiasm and piety. Both combed the scientific and travel literature of the day for relevant information. Both were alive to the significance of geological findings and the value of taxonomic studies. Both saw nature as an endlessly unfolding and changing spectacle in which design and adaptation are crucial. Both recognised the roles of sexuality in promoting variation and of superfecundity in necessitating some means of reducing numbers. Both saw that the selection procedures of the breeders of domestic animals provided clues to what might be happening in nature. As possible mechanisms for explaining evolutionary change both of them considered the inheritance of acquired characters as well as natural selection.

The grandfather favoured the former; the grandson emphasised the latter, but he always kept the inheritance of acquired characters as a reserve to be invoked if necessary.

In no way were all these similarities the product of chance. On the contrary, as King-Hele shows, there is plentiful evidence, from the marginal comments and underscorings, that Charles read his grandfather's works with the greatest care. Thus it was no accident that when in 1837 he began his *Notebooks on Transmutation* he used the heading 'Zoönomia', nor that his great work on evolution carried the title *The Origin of Species*, a clear echo of the title *The Origin of Society* adopted by Dr Erasmus for one of his works but later discarded by him.

The differences in their thinking, which are many, are due mainly to the extreme thoroughness with which Charles worked out his thesis and presented his evidence, much of which had been recorded at first hand by himself, in contrast to the inspired speculations of his grandfather. Yet, we may ask, had Dr Erasmus been able to devote almost his whole life to solving the problem, might his efforts have been crowned by success? In fact, that is unlikely. Before Charles's breakthrough would be possible, much further spadework in relevant scientific fields would be required. None would be more fundamental than the major reformulation of geological theory, the life-work of Charles Lyell (1797–1875), who, as a distinguished and older scientist, was destined to play a pivotal role in Charles Darwin's emotional life as well as in his scientific career.

In his scientific work the method adopted by Dr Erasmus was the one in favour today but not in his own time, namely formulating one or more possible hypotheses and gathering data for and against each, by means of experiment whenever feasible. Although Charles claimed at times that he adopted the exclusively empirical procedures of Francis Bacon, in fact he followed steadily in his grandfather's footsteps. As he remarks in later life,[3] every time he identified a problem, a possible hypothesis entered his mind, and all his work was to consist of weighing the evidence for or against one or another of them.

Finally, let us look briefly at the influence Dr Erasmus had on the political opinions and social values of later Darwin generations. Both Charles's father, Dr Robert, and Charles himself were concerned about all the same social problems that had been the lively concern of Dr Erasmus and his Lunar Society friends. Although never as outspoken as Dr Erasmus himself, Dr Robert, Charles and the other grandchildren were strong supporters of the Whigs, and later of their successors, the Liberal Party, and were committed to widening the franchise, abolishing slavery, eradicating poverty, and building a society that turned its back on racial and warlike policies. Firmly held views on all these issues are repeatedly expressed in Charles's letters home from the *Beagle* and in his later voluminous correspondence with his friends.

VIII

While tracing the fortunes of Dr Erasmus and the Darwin family from the mid-1760s onwards, we have almost lost sight of Josiah Wedgwood and his manifold interests.

For him the late 1760s were a period of great commercial success, but this entailed his shouldering many responsibilities and caused him much worry. His building programme was then in full swing. Not only were the canal and the new factory under construction but he was also building a substantial house for himself and his growing family at Etruria, a smaller one for a senior manager there and numerous dwellings for his work people. These soaring outlays meant that working capital was often short; while the organising of production at two factories a few miles apart, the one at Burslem continuing to produce for the popular market and the new one at Etruria concentrating on high-value decorative pieces, posed awkward management problems.

It was therefore doubly unfortunate that at this time Josiah's damaged knee was giving further trouble. Reluctantly, his medical advisers, headed by Dr Erasmus, decided it was necessary to amputate the leg above the knee, an operation which, without anaesthesia, was a gruelling procedure. Nevertheless in May 1768 it was successfully performed. Once healed, he was fitted with a wooden peg-leg which he used for the rest of his life.

Although the leg seems to have given no further trouble, Josiah was in low spirits at this time. Besides business worries and the loss of his leg there was much else on his mind. Only days after the operation, his second son, Richard, aged ten months, died of an acute gastric infection. A few months later Sally's father became ill and she went over to care for him, leaving Josiah to fend for himself. Moreover, a disaffected employee was spreading malicious rumours that the pottery was heading for bankruptcy. Josiah suffered from insomnia and headaches, and he also began worrying about blurred vision and complained of seeing dots in front of his eyes. The verdict of Dr Erasmus was that at one time or another everyone had that experience but that 'everybody *did not look at them*'. Evidently Josiah was depressed and a little hypochondriacal.

In 1769 the family moved from Burslem to Etruria, briefly occupying the smaller house until Etruria Hall was ready. Since their marriage five years earlier, Sally had given birth to four children: Sukey, now aged four, John aged three, Richard, the baby who died, and another son Josiah II, born that year. Two years later another son, Tom, was born – which made five children within seven years. It was hardly surprising perhaps that after Tom's birth Sally was in poor health and depressed. During the spring of 1772 Josiah took her to Bath for a few months, but to no avail. After their return to Etruria, Dr Erasmus stepped in and took her to stay in the Darwin household, still at Lichfield. Although this led to improvement, she relapsed after returning to Etruria. During the winter of 1772–3 she ran a high temperature and there were fears for her life. Josiah's elder sisters came to lend a hand and in due course Sally recovered. A year later her widowed father, Richard, joined the family and was a much-welcome resident until his death in 1780. During the five years following her recovery Sally bore three more babies, all girls. The youngest, Mary Ann, born in 1778, was mentally handicapped and died at the age of eight.

Even when no more than the bare facts of their lives are displayed, it becomes evident that the burdens on the wives of the successful men of those times were onerous to a degree. Small wonder that some succumbed to ill-health and depression. The anxieties arising when children are ill and the often devastating effects on parents when they die, whether in infancy or in later years, are too often given scant attention. They account, I believe, for a great many of the breakdowns of health and spirits that appear in the records.

In Josiah Wedgwood's public life, we find that, despite the many problems facing him, the pottery was thriving. When in 1767 he had recruited Bentley, his plan had been that Bentley would take charge of the Etruria factory and live in the smaller of the two new houses, Little Etruria Hall. Bentley, however, did not fancy a future confined to the Potteries. Instead, with Josiah's agreement, he went to London to take charge of the firm's new showrooms and act as chief salesman. This arrangement proved conspicuously successful, since Bentley enjoyed his role of introducing the fashionable, the wealthy and the aristocratic to the ceramic marvels being produced at Etruria. A dinner service of nearly a thousand pieces, each with a different pictorial design, made for Catherine the Great of Russia was the most prestigious of the many orders the firm was securing. Bentley, moreover, was at home in the artistic world. He engaged skilled painters to decorate plain ware delivered from the factories and, during the late 1770s would commission distinguished artists to design special pieces.

Meanwhile in the cellars of Etruria Hall, specially designed for the purpose, Josiah was busy experimenting, as always in the closest secrecy, with yet further new materials. Already by 1770 the pottery was producing ware of six different types, and a few years later Josiah had perfected yet one more which he called jasper, a ware that would take a range of delicate colours one of which was to be the famous Wedgwood blue.

During these years the Lunar Society was in its heyday and Josiah a zealous attender. He and Erasmus saw much of each other – at the regular monthly meetings, over matters medical, and also in connection with a horizontal windmill that Erasmus had designed for grinding colours at Etruria.

Another interest shared by the two men was education. Since there was no suitable school in the Potteries, the alternative for Josiah's children was education at home or boarding school. Initially Josiah opted for boarding school, partly, perhaps, to ease Sally's burdens. Whether so or not, from 1772, when Sukey was only seven and her brother John only six, these two went away as boarders to different schools. In due course the two younger boys followed. These arrangements proved unsatisfactory, however, and the children's health suffered. After three years as a boarder Sukey left. Finally, in 1779, Josiah decided to start a school of his own, the Etruscan

School, to be attended by five of his own children, ranging from Sukey, now fourteen, to Kitty, aged five, and a few from neighbouring families. Among these for a while was Erasmus Darwin's youngest son, Robert, now aged thirteen. It may have been at this time that the idea was born that Robert and Sukey might one day make a match.

England during the 1770s was rocked by the American Declaration of Independence and the subsequent war. Opinion in the Lunar Society was sharply divided. The majority, dissenters in religion and including Josiah and Erasmus, backed the Americans, to the disgust of the conservatives headed by Boulton and Watt. It is greatly to the credit of the members that the society held together and that meetings continued.

Another effect of the war was that it hit export trade, especially after the French joined in on the side of the Americans. Despite much-reduced exports for some years and economic depression at home during the early 1780s, when the firm of Boulton & Watt was in financial difficulties, the Wedgwood enterprise managed to weather the storm. It also managed to survive the premature death of Bentley in 1780. His loss was a severe blow to Josiah. None the less he succeeded in replacing him. A nephew, Tom Byerley, son of one of Josiah's sisters, had worked for the firm in earlier years but had proved restless and on two occasions had left to seek his fortunes elsewhere. Now, in his mid-thirties and given full responsibility for the London showrooms, he fulfilled his promise and became a mainstay of the firm. By the mid-1780s, when the war was over and distinguished artists, headed by the sculptor John Flaxman, were contributing designs, demand boomed.

The 1780s saw Josiah at the height of his career, both rich and becoming a public figure. To mark his 'arrival' he had arranged in 1780 for a portrait of the whole family to be painted by George Stubbs, who, not unexpectedly, insisted that the elder daughter Sukey be shown mounted on her pony. Two years later, Josiah commissioned Sir Joshua Reynolds to paint portraits of Sally and himself. Meanwhile, he had invented a new type of thermometer able to measure accurately at very high temperatures, indispensable for firing the highest-quality ceramics. This he described in a paper read to the Royal Society, of which he was elected a fellow soon afterwards. In mid-decade Josiah, with a few likeminded industrialists, met to found a General Council of Manufacturers to lobby the government in connection with trade treaties then being negotiated with Ireland and later with France. Elected the first president, Josiah found himself in conference with none other than the Prime Minister, William Pitt, first Earl of Chatham. In this role, however, he was out of his depth; and he came in for scathing criticism from fellow manufacturers and newspapers alike, an experience that much upset him.

Another source of worry during the late 1780s was that none of his three sons showed much enthusiasm for succeeding him in the pottery. The eldest, John, now turned twenty, had spent a year at Edinburgh

University and had then joined Byerley in the London showrooms. He was a silent and depressed young man, dissatisfied with life and clearly unfit for a managerial role. The second son, Josiah II, three years younger, was more promising. Having spent a year at Edinburgh, he now joined his father as a personal assistant. Although practical and reliable, he was something of a plodder. Moreover, with plenty of money in the family, he preferred the idea of becoming a country gentleman to following his father into industry. The third son, Tom, still in his teens, had the brains. After spending a year at Edinburgh as his brothers had done, he had been installed at Etruria to carry out chemical experiments under the guidance of his father and an able chemist, Alexander Chisholm, who had worked there for some years. One of Tom's special interests was pioneering an early form of photography. Tom, however, suffered from chronic ill-health and changeable moods. When, a few years later, old Josiah came to make his will, he would leave the Etruria estate, houses and factory to Josiah II, the other sons receiving more in the form of investments.

There were also of course, three daughters, each of whom would be well provided for in her father's will. In contrast to their brothers, all three were clever, strongminded and more interested in intellectual pursuits than most girls of their day. The two younger ones were still of school age, but Sukey (henceforward to be referred to by her proper name, Susannah) was in her early twenties and enjoying an active social life. She was a regular visitor to Derby, where Dr Erasmus and his family were now living, giving him piano lessons and also attending dances with her future husband Robert.

By 1790 the Lunar Society was crumbling. Dr Erasmus had moved too far from Birmingham to attend: William Small and other members had died. The *coup de grâce* came a year later when a mob burned Priestley's house, destroying his library and laboratory. The assault, on the second anniversary of the fall of the Bastille, was engendered by his public support of the French Revolution, which, like the American revolution, was welcomed by all the dissenters, to the fury of the more conservative members of society. Soon afterwards Priestley emigrated to America, where he later died.

As an offset to the bad news of these years, Josiah, back in his familiar role as expert and pioneering potter, scored the triumph of his life. An excavation near Rome during the seventeenth century had uncovered a sarcophagus, dated AD235, in which was found a vase of dark-coloured glass decorated with white cameo figures. Purchased in Italy by Sir William Hamilton and brought to England, it had been bought at auction by the Duke of Portland and became known as the Portland Vase. Josiah had already been entranced by it and had set his heart on making replicas. Although beaten at auction by the duke, he had obtained permission to borrow it and, after several attempts, had at last succeeded in his aim. In midsummer 1789 Josiah was able to send his old friend Erasmus Darwin the first perfect copy of the vase. Only a few months earlier Erasmus had himself sent Josiah an advance copy of *The Botanic Garden*, the long poem that was to earn him literary fame. The two had reached the pinnacle of their respective careers at the same time, and each was generous in his praise of the other.

By 1791 Josiah had turned sixty and was beginning to feel his age. The firm, now named Wedgwood, Sons & Byerley despite the marginal contributions of two of the sons, continued to prosper; but the early nineties were to be Josiah's last years. Before he died, in January 1795, however, he would see his two elder sons married and starting on their careers as fathers of large families.

In August 1792 Josiah II and his elder sister Susannah went to the Haverfordwest Assizes, in West Wales, and there met Elizabeth (Bessy) Allen, the eldest of nine daughters of John Allen, owner of a large local estate, Cresselly. Now aged twenty-three, Josiah II fell in love at first sight with this charming and sociable woman, five years his senior. After a pressing courtship, Bessy agreed to marry him, prompted perhaps by her desire to escape from a somewhat tyrannical father who had been left a widower two years earlier. The ceremony took place at Cresselly in December and was the start of what was to be a singularly happy married life. Their large brood of children, who would be contemporaries of the six cousins to be born to Robert Darwin and Susannah Wedgwood, were to play a large part in Charles Darwin's life. Indeed, their youngest child, Emma, was to become his wife.

The following year, Josiah II's elder brother, John, now aged twenty-seven, followed his brother's example by marrying another of the Allen daughters, Jane, aged twenty-two. Thus began the complex intertwining of three large families, the Darwins, the Wedgwoods and the Allens, that was to pervade the social life of the coming generations.

The future of Tom, the third of Josiah and Sally's surviving sons, was much less happy. In 1792 he suffered a breakdown, gave up his pioneering ventures in photography and became what in later days would be called a hippy. He was to join a literary circle and to become a close friend of Coleridge. Like the latter, unfortunately, he became an opium addict and was to meet an early death.

During the autumn of 1794 Josiah I was failing. Visits with Sally to Blackpool and Buxton failed to restore him. His jaw became infected and inflamed, and he died on the second day of the New Year, aided in his passing by a copious supply of laudanum prescribed by Dr Erasmus.

TWO

Parents to genius

I

When Charles Darwin's father, Robert, married Susannah Wedgwood in 1796, he was not quite thirty and had already built up a thriving medical practice in Shrewsbury. With the aid of a handsome dowry settled on Susannah by her father, he built a substantial house, known as The Mount, in ample grounds on a site overlooking the river Severn. There the six children of the marriage were born and there Dr Robert lived until his death fifty years later.

Robert had not had an easy life. Not only had his mother died when he was four years old but the elder of his two older brothers had died in tragic circumstances when Robert was twelve. Since I believe that these deaths account in large part for the emotional troubles from which Dr Robert suffered and that this had an adverse effect on his children, there is reason to give them attention.

Robert's mother, Mary Howard (1740–70), was barely seventeen when she married Dr Erasmus Darwin, nine years her senior, at the end of 1757. She is described by a contemporary as 'blooming and lovely', with a lively mind, and as 'a capable as well as a fascinating companion'.[1] She was one of the two surviving children of a Lichfield solicitor, Charles Howard, whose wife had died, aged forty, when Mary was only eight. During the ten years after her marriage, Mary gave birth to five children, two of whom died as infants. The eldest of the three survivors, all boys, was born eight months after the marriage and named Charles after his maternal grandfather, becoming the first Charles in the Darwin family. He was closely followed by another son, named Erasmus (after his father) and whom I shall call Erasmus II. Robert was born in May 1766, seven and a half years later. During the interval there had been a daughter born who had died, and a year after Robert's birth there was a fourth son, who had also died.

Even before Robert was born, his mother was in poor health, and during his early childhood she became progressively worse, dying shortly after his fourth birthday. Particulars of her illness are given in some detail in a letter dated 5 January 1792 from Dr Erasmus to his son, Robert, then aged twenty-six, who had evidently enquired about the danger of hereditary ill-health in the family.[2] Dr Erasmus describes how, during the four or six years before her death, Mary had suffered severe pain 'about the lower edge of the liver', a pain which led to 'violent convulsions . . . sometimes relieved by great doses of opium'. She 'took to drinking spirit and water to relieve the pain, and I found (when it was too late) that she had done this in great quantity, the liver became swelled and she gradually sunk'. The severe pains from which she suffered initially sound like colic, perhaps from gallstones or a renal stone. Later it was evidently alcoholism with liver damage. Her father died a year after Mary and, according to Dr Erasmus, also died of drink: 'he was a drunkard both in public and in private.'

Towards the end of his letter, in an effort to reassure his son, Dr Erasmus explains that, although alcoholism is in some degree hereditary and, he suspects, a cause of epilepsy and insanity, many children in these families escape such troubles. Finally, in the same letter to Robert, Dr Erasmus makes a revealing reference to how Robert himself had responded to his mother's symptoms: 'I well remember when your mother fainted away in these hysteric fits (which she often did) that she told me, you, who was not then 2 or 2½ years old [would] run into the kitchen to call the maid-servant to her assistance.'

After Mary's death in 1770 Dr Erasmus was able to persuade his elder and unmarried sister, Susannah, to keep house for him, as she had before his marriage, and to care for the three boys, now aged twelve, eleven and four. Robert was said to have become 'deeply attached' to his aunt and to have spoken of her in later years 'as the very pattern of an old lady, so nice looking, so gentle, kind and charitable, and passionately fond of flowers'.[3] Whether she continued to care for him after his father's mistress, Miss Parker, was installed in the household is not clear.

When Robert was twelve years old another tragedy befell the family. The eldest son, Charles, then a medical student in Edinburgh, cut his finger during a post-mortem on a child, developed septicaemia and died within days. He is described as 'a young man of extraordinary promise' who had already distinguished himself as a medical student by winning the gold medal of the Aesculapian Society for 'an experimental enquiry on pus and mucus. Notices of him appeared in various journals; and all the writers agree about his uncommon energies and abilities.' One of his professors recalled him 'with the warmest affection' forty-seven years later when his namesake, Charles Darwin of the *Origin*, was himself a young medical student in Edinburgh.[4]

Charles's sudden and untimely death in May 1778, shortly before his twentieth birthday, was a devastating blow to Dr Erasmus. All his hopes had been centred on this favourite son whose death he never ceased to

mourn. Unlike Charles, Erasmus II, the second son and now eighteen, did not promise well. Although highly intelligent, he was quiet and retiring and, judging by his unhappy future, almost certainly depressed. Moreover, he shared none of his father's scientific interests. Manifestly disappointed in this young man, Dr Erasmus focused all his hopes on his third son, Robert, who was promptly cast in the role of his father's successor, despite his having no particular interest in medicine. Thereafter Robert is said to have suffered from headaches and depression.[5]

Information about Robert's education is scanty. Soon after he had been earmarked for medicine, his father sent him to the Potteries to attend a course of lectures on chemistry with the elder of Josiah Wedgwood's sons, John; and the two boys also received personal instruction from the lecturer during the mornings. It was around this time, too, that Robert was attending the Etruscan School with other members of the Wedgwood family. Back in Lichfield Dr Erasmus engaged a French prisoner-of-war to teach Robert French; and this proved so successful that the tutor was engaged for a year to teach in the Etruscan School.[6]

In 1781 when Dr Erasmus remarried and moved to Derby, Robert was fifteen. A year or so later he went to Edinburgh to qualify in medicine, which he duly did, probably in 1786. A year after that, when he was twenty-one, his father set him up as a physician in Shrewsbury, about twenty-five miles west of the Potteries and on the Welsh borders. From the first, he seems to have prospered and soon had a large practice.

II

For all his admirable qualities which were widely acclaimed, Dr Erasmus was not always an easy man; and he could at times be impatient and intimidating. Since fathers' intimidation of sons seems to have been a Darwin tradition through several generations, and unquestionably played a major part in the emotional troubles from which Charles Darwin of the *Origin* suffered, it is revealing to trace its history. Much of what follows is culled from Charles's own writings, namely his 1879 memoir of his grandfather and his own *Autobiography*, both written during the last decade of his life.

Charles Darwin lists the adjectives most frequently applied to his grandfather in letters and elsewhere as: benevolent, sympathetic, generous and hospitable. He held the communication of happiness and the relief of misery to be the only standard of moral merit. 'But it is fair to state from my father's conversation', writes the grandson, that Dr Erasmus 'had acted towards him in his youth rather harshly and imperiously, and not always justly; and though in after years he [Dr Erasmus] felt the greatest interest in his son's success, and frequently wrote to him with affection, in my opinion the early impression on my father's mind was never quite obliterated.'[7] This account of the effect of father on son is remarkable for two reasons: first, other evidence suggests it is a true description; second, it is also as vivid a description of how Dr Robert treated his own son, Charles, as could well be imagined. The sequence is a classic example of a parent adopting towards his own child the very same treatment as the parent himself had experienced from his own parent when he was a child.

There is some evidence that during his childhood Dr Erasmus had also experienced a similar combination of paternal intimidation alternating with generosity and concern. In 1754, shortly after his own father's death, Dr Erasmus, then aged twenty-three, had described his father as having been 'very tender to his children, but still kept them at an awful kind of distance'.[8]

Because in his memoir of his grandfather Charles describes his grandfather's treatment of his father, and its effects, in words that fit so exactly his father's treatment of himself and the effects it had on him, we may wonder whether Charles's report of the older generation is to be trusted. Evidence from independent sources about Dr Erasmus, how-ever, suggest it can be. For example, there are various reports of his being domineering and riding roughshod over others, and also of his occasion-ally being sarcastic. Sarcasm always inflicts a deep wound, and none deeper or more enduring than when it comes from a parent to a child.

Two other family reminiscences of Dr Erasmus, reported in Charles's memoir, support the picture. Charles quotes his father as saying: 'he was

Dr Robert Darwin,
Charles's father,
1766–1848

View over the Severn
from The Mount

The Mount, Shrewsbury,
Charles's parental home

Susannah Darwin, née
Wedgwood, Charles's
mother, 1765–1817

sometimes violent in his anger, but his sympathy and benevolence soon made him try to soothe or soften matters.' Charles had also heard (probably from one of Dr Erasmus's second brood of children) that his grandfather was 'not always kind' to his second son, Erasmus II, 'being often vexed at his retiring nature and at his not more fully displaying his great talents'.[9]

Another feature of this giant figure which appears to have had a powerful influence on later generations of the Darwin family was his way of dealing with his feelings, especially painful ones. In his memoir Charles reports that Dr Erasmus had 'a strong dislike . . . to any display of emotion in a man. He therefore wished to conceal his own feelings', and that 'it was his maxim, that in order to feel cheerful you must appear to be so.'[10]

In keeping with this maxim was his way of dealing with feelings about his bereavements, described in a letter to his old friend Josiah Wedgwood after the death in 1780 of Wedgwood's partner, Thomas Bentley. In it he is certainly referring to the death two years earlier of his favourite son, Charles, and may also be referring to that of his first wife, Mary, in 1770. After expressing his very great concern at the news of Bentley's death, he continues: 'and a train of very melancholy ideas succeeds in my mind, unconnected indeed with your loss, but which still at times casts a shadow over me, which nothing but exertion in business or in acquiring knowledge can remove. This exertion I must recommend to you, as it for a time dispossesses the disagreeable ideas of our loss.'[11] Many years later we find the grandson recording that his father, Dr Robert, agrees with the opinion of Dr Erasmus that 'the only cure for madness is forgetfulness'.[12]

At the end of 1799 another unforeseen blow befell the family: Erasmus II committed suicide by drowning. He had just turned forty and had recently bought a small estate outside Derby. During a thunderstorm he walked into the river Derwent, which flowed at the bottom of his garden.

In the memoir of his grandfather Charles gives some account of his uncle's life and death, an account derived from his father.[13] He describes Erasmus II as having had very considerable abilities but as always being 'quiet and retiring'. He had 'his own particular tastes, viz. genealogy, the collecting of coins, and statistics'. As a boy he had made a census of the inhabitants of Lichfield, later confirmed to have been correct. Qualified as a solicitor, he practised in Lichfield but was already planning imminent retirement to his newly acquired property. He had never married. Prior to his suicide it appears that he had been depressed for at least two years. From having been 'an excellent man of business', he 'had become dilatory to an abnormal degree'. He neither paid his bills nor collected money owing to him. In a letter to his youngest son, Robert, Dr Erasmus had described Erasmus II's condition as a 'defect of voluntary power. Whence he procrastinated for ever!'[14]

Looked at in the psychiatric perspective adopted here, Erasmus II's depressive condition and suicide can be regarded as the long-term effects of his early bereavements, exacerbated by his father's lack of sympathy, impatience and frequent unfavourable comparisons with his brilliant elder brother. A telltale pointer in support of this view is a little episode that clearly impressed the family and is reported in Charles's Memoir. 'Among the property of Erasmus II my grandfather found a little cross made of platted grass . . . gathered from the tomb of Charles, who had died twenty years before.' This little cross was bequeathed by Dr Erasmus to Robert, and from Robert it passed to the younger Charles, who reports it as being still in his possession.[15]

A possible reconstruction of Erasmus II's problems is as follows. During his childhood his mother had been seriously ill for several years, before dying when he was aged eleven. Thereafter he had come to look to his brother Charles, one year older, for emotional support and companionship. Charles's tragic death when Erasmus II was nineteen came as a second and sudden blow to a youth still mourning his dead mother. From childhood onwards, I suspect, he was chronically depressed and during his late thirties some kind of adverse event or events in his personal or professional life proved too much for him.

The suicide of his son was a terrible blow to Dr Erasmus, who described it as 'the greatest shock he had felt since the death of his poor Charles'; and in a letter to Robert he refers to himself as being 'in great anguish of mind'. A little over two years later Dr Erasmus was himself dead. That left Robert, at the age of thirty-six, the only survivor.

III

By the time his father died Dr Robert had been married six years and already had two small daughters. His wife, Susannah, known earlier as Sukey, was now thirty-seven and would give birth to four more children, of whom Charles was next to last.

In the previous chapter some account was given of Sukey's life before her marriage. During the six years after her birth, her mother Sally Wedgwood, had had four sons, of whom one had died aged nearly a year. Sally had become severely depressed and was in poor health. Perhaps partly for these reasons Sukey had been sent off to boarding school at the age of seven in the company of two little cousins, her father's nieces. Josiah himself escorted the three little girls to their school, which was near Manchester.[16] Sukey did not thrive, however. In mid-June 1773, a year after she had gone there, Josiah, writing to his friend Thomas Bentley, described how Sukey 'after sitting and sewing at school for twelve months is so full of pouks and boils and humours' that he was taking her with her cousins to the seaside near Liverpool, where they were to spend five days. Despite this bad beginning, it appears that Sukey continued at boarding school until she was ten, when she was sent to London to live with Thomas Bentley and his wife while attending a local day school.

Eventually, when Sukey was fourteen, she was able to attend the Etruscan School held in her own home.

Sukey as a girl is described as being very like her father both in appearance and in temperament: quick-witted, extraverted and aggressive, in all these respects differing greatly from her rather pathetic younger brother John, who, having been sent away to boarding school at the age of six and continuing there for several years, had become lethargic, unassertive and anxious to please.

Sukey or Susannah (also known as Susan) was not married until 1796, and information about her twenties is scanty. She enjoyed music, played the spinet and took an interest in the comings and goings of fashionable society. A great favourite of old Dr Erasmus, she was often over at Derby, staying with him and his large family and giving him piano lessons. In 1792 she accompanied her younger brother Josiah II on his visit to Pembrokeshire where he met his future wife, Bessy Allen. A couple of years later, after another brother, John, had married Bessy's sister Jane, Susannah sometimes stayed with them in London.

Apparently Susannah suffered from ill-health and was constantly consulting doctors and trying new treatments, which included, among others, taking the waters at Bath. During the winter of 1794–5 when her father was dying, Susannah, who was helping her mother nurse him, is said to have been so deeply affected that she became ill herself.

Eventually, in April 1796, the long-planned marriage of Susannah to Robert Darwin took place. It was to last twenty-one years and to be ended by Susannah's death in July 1817, at the age of fifty-one, after a long and painful illness. Owing to the wall of silence erected by her daughters around her memory, information about her remains extremely scanty. From the scraps available we have the picture of an active, sociable woman, well liked by relatives and neighbours, and interested like her husband in natural history.

Fifty years after Susannah's death, a London journalist, Eliza Meteyard (who had already written a book about Josiah Wedgwood), drawing on some Wedgwood papers she had discovered and such other information as she could glean, wrote an account of the younger Wedgwoods and their friends during the period from 1795 to 1815. In it she gives a description of Susannah Darwin. Since nothing from other sources contradicts her account, it is given here in full.

After a reference to Susannah's 'gentle, sympathising nature', Meteyard continues:

She entered zealously into all her husband's pursuits; and as he took almost as much interest in botany and zoology as his father, Erasmus Darwin, their gardens and grounds became noted for the choicest shrubs and flowers. They petted and reared birds and animals; and the beauty, variety, and tameness of 'The Mount pigeons' were well known in the town and far beyond. But the wife of the leading physician of an important provincial city like Shrewsbury had, in those days more especially, a multitude of other duties, that only a woman of education and tact could effect. There was often to receive, sometimes entertain, high-class patients in her husband's absence; to give dinner and supper parties; to be on visiting terms with the gentry of a wide neighbourhood; to take an interest in the town and town-folks; and not omit what was one of the established customs of the place, two great yearly feasts to the chief medical practitioners of town and country. To this Mrs Darwin added much assistance to her husband in his large correspondence.[17]

The first four children of the marriage, three daughters followed by a son, were born within the first nine years. Apparently child-bearing was difficult and depressing for Susannah. During her second and third pregnancies, in 1800 and 1803, she was confined to bed for several months. During the second one she wrote to one of her brothers, 'Everyone seems young but me.'[18]

Although Susannah was mostly at home keeping house for her husband and children, there were times when she was able to visit members of her family, sometimes with a couple of the children, occasionally with her husband. Most of these visits were to her brother Josiah II and his wife Bessy, who for a few years were living in the south of England but who from about 1805 were within easy reach of Shrewsbury.

IV

Soon after Josiah I died, his two elder sons, John and Josiah II, decided to indulge their ambitions to become country gentlemen. Both moved from the Potteries to the south of England and left management of the business in the hands of Tom Byerley. John became a partner in a London bank and acquired an estate near Bath. Josiah II as owner of the business maintained links with the firm but moved to Surrey. Both these ventures miscarried disastrously, however, making the first decade of the new century one of severe financial strain for the pottery as well as for the Wedgwood family.

For some years the elder Wedgwood brothers lived extravagantly and far beyond their means. At one time Josiah II was travelling between Surrey and Staffordshire in a grand coach drawn by four grey horses as though he were royalty. Early in the decade the London bank into which John had put most of the money he had inherited got into financial difficulties and became a source of acute anxiety. For a time both the bank and John himself were on the verge of bankruptcy, putting the financial reputation of the whole Wedgwood family in jeopardy. John therefore had to sell his estate in the south and, with his wife and growing family, take up residence in Etruria Hall to earn his living in the business. In his new role as deputy works manager he was imaginative and enterprising in introducing new wares and new designs, both of which were sorely needed. Financially, however, he was as impractical and extravagant as ever.

By 1803 Josiah II realised he had to spend more time at the pottery and so acquired the long lease of a house and estate in the vicinity, Maer Hall. His idea was to remain in the south and to stay in Staffordshire for a few months each summer. It was soon clear, however, that, if the firm was to survive, far more attention was needed. In 1805, therefore, he sold his estates in the south and moved the family permanently to Staffordshire.

By this time the financial affairs both of the family and of the business were in a tangle. Large loans had been made to John by Josiah II and also by other members of the family, and some of them necessitated mortgaging the factory. 1810 was a crisis year. The faithful Tom Byerley, who had for many years kept the firm going, died; and demand for products collapsed as a result of a ban on all exports because of the Napoleonic war. Drastic action was required and after much heart-searching Josiah II took it. The London showrooms were closed and the extravagant John was asked to resign, which he did. The business survived, though it remained in low water for some years yet. To enable John to avoid bankruptcy, members of the family contributed to a trust fund, set up with John's elder sister Susannah Darwin and younger brother Josiah II as trustees.

Despite John's many failings, he still has one claim to fame. A keen horticulturist, he gathered together a group of likeminded enthusiasts and is recognised as the founder, in 1804, of the Royal Horticultural Society.

The third brother, the gifted but wayward Tom, had died prematurely at the age of thirty-four in 1805. Tom was only two years younger than Josiah II and the brothers had been close companions, despite their opposite temperaments; the loss was a severe blow to Josiah, who missed Tom's sparkling imagination and also the talented friends he introduced.

Josiah II was reliable and sensible but unenterprising. As head of the family ever since his father had decided to leave him the pottery in preference to his inadequate elder brother, he filled the position conscientiously and proved a stabilising influence. The role he liked best, however, was being squire of Maer Hall.

Maer Hall and the large family of Wedgwoods residing there were destined to play a crucial role in Charles Darwin's life. A large Elizabethan house set in an estate of a thousand acres, it had woods, a lake and plenty of sporting facilities. Being little more than twenty miles north-east of Shrewsbury, it was within a day's ride or drive of the Darwin family, who became regular visitors. Moreover, being only nine miles south-west of the Wedgwood factory, it enabled Josiah II to enjoy his taste for country living and also to ride over to his office for the day. In addition, it was possible for him to bring his widowed mother, Sally, now aged seventy and his two unmarried sisters, Kitty (thirty) and Sarah (twenty-seven), over from Etruria where they had continued to live after Josiah I's death and to install them at a house, Parkfields, on the estate. Sally lived there until her death in 1815 at the age of eighty-one. Kitty and Sarah

Josiah Wedgwood II, 1769–1843,
of Maer Hall, Staffordshire,
Charles's uncle and father-in-law

Bessy Wedgwood, née Allen, 1764–1846,
wife of Josiah II and
Charles's mother-in-law

Maer Hall, Staffordshire, the home of Josiah II and Bessy Wedgwood

stayed on for some years longer. At Maer Hall itself the sociable Bessy kept open house. Allens and Wedgwoods as well as Darwins came and went in a succession of short and long visits. For thirty years Maer was to be the happy hub of the three clans.

Josiah II proved in the end reasonably successful in presiding over the business and provided an equable and stable background for his wife's generous hospitality. Given to few words, he was the target of Sidney Smith's ironic remark that he was an excellent man, though it was a pity he hated his friends.[19] He and his brother-in-law, Robert Darwin, had known each other since boyhood and now saw a good deal of each other. Not only was Dr Robert medical adviser to all his Wedgwood in-laws but he became their financial adviser as well. When John's bank was in financial straits, he was brought in to engage John in some plain speaking about what his responsibilities were and how he should meet them. When Josiah II acquired Maer, Dr Robert advanced funds. When the firm's accounts were in disarray, Dr Robert audited the books.

Where money was concerned, Dr Robert seems never to have made a wrong move. He would evidently have been a far more successful businessman than any of the Wedgwood brothers, and he would undoubtedly have preferred such a career to following his father into medicine.

V

There is no lack of information about Dr Robert, much of it coming from Charles's own accounts. To the original draft of his *Autobiography* he added an extra section in which he records much that his father had told him as well as describing his own observations and experiences. In the memoir of his grandfather Charles repeats some of this but adds a few further facts. Another source of information is the recollections of Charles's wife, Emma, as recorded by their daughter, Henrietta Litch-field. There is also interesting material derived from Wedgwood sources in *The Wedgwood Circle*. The picture is consistent and vivid.

In many ways Robert Darwin was larger than life. Not only did he stand 6 feet 2 inches in height, but he had broad shoulders and for most of his life was grossly overweight. When he last weighed himself he was 24 stone (336 pounds). He was always extremely busy in his practice and did not care for exercise. A great talker, he tended to dominate a room. Since he was exceedingly sensitive and given to an occasional angry outburst, many people were afraid of him. Yet he was said to be much loved by his patients, rich and poor alike, and renowned for the sympathetic ear he gave their troubles. Charles, who idolised him, insists: 'His sympathy was not only with the distresses of others, but in a greater degree with pleasures of all around him. This led him to be always scheming to give pleasures to others, and, though hating extravagance, to perform many generous actions.'[20] Charles himself was to be one of the principal beneficiaries of that generosity.

When Robert's brilliant elder brother had died after the post-mortem tragedy in Edinburgh, Robert had had no desire to become a doctor and had done so only on his father's insistence. In later life he told his son that he had 'at first hated his profession so much that if he had been sure of the smallest pittance, or if his father had given him any choice, nothing should have induced him to follow it. To the end of his life, the thought of an operation almost sickened him.'[21]

In his medical practice, as in most of his opinions, Dr Robert modelled himself on his father. Like Dr Erasmus, Dr Robert had a light single-seat carriage, known as a sulky, in which he went long distances to see patients around Shrewsbury, sometimes travelling westwards into Wales. He was keenly alive to the emotional problems of his patients, especially ladies, for whom he became, according to Charles, 'a sort of Father Confessor. He told me that they always began by complaining in a vague manner about their health, and by practice he soon guessed what was really the matter.'[22] So successful was he in his guesses that he gained the reputation for reading people's thoughts. Although many of his patients were well off and no doubt paid handsome fees, the poor, especially those in the poverty-stricken area through which The Mount was approached, were treated free, as was commonly the custom in those days.

In keeping with Dr Robert's interest in psychological factors was his belief 'that the general talking about any disease tends to give it, as in cancer, showing effect of mind on individual parts of body'; this was an opinion later recorded by his son in one of his notebooks.[23] Though he had clearly inherited the family intelligence, Dr Robert's mind was not a scientific one. In fact, his paper on 'Ocular Spectra' published in the *Philosophical Transactions of the Royal Society*, which led to his election to fellowship at the age of twenty-two, had, according to Charles, been largely written by his father.[24] However, even if his gifts were purely intuitive, these, combined with a deep sympathy for suffering and considerable psychological insight, made him one of the best clinicians of his day.

Although usually in good spirits, Dr Robert was not always so. The picture that emerges from the Wedgwood account is of a man who as a rule responded to setbacks with over-activity but who on occasion lapsed into a brooding withdrawal. Apparently he was in one of these dark moods after his father's death in 1802. Otherwise he was constantly on the go. In his medical practice his concern to alleviate suffering may well have led him to be a compulsive caregiver.* He was undoubtedly a compulsive eater: his single-seat carriage was as stuffed with edibles as his father's had been full of papers on science and technology. When not working he

---

*Someone with a very strong disposition to give care to others and to expect none for oneself.

busied himself with his library, his investments, his superb collection of Wedgwood ware and, in later years, his greenhouse. He was probably not an easy man to be married to.

Suffering distressed him intensely and, like his father before him, he did all he could to avoid unhappy memories. This was the more difficult because not only had he an extraordinarily retentive memory but he had suffered some tragic experiences, starting in his early years with his mother's suffering and death. That, I suspect, had always coloured his outlook. The events he could not help recalling were not happy ones. When in old age he was asked by his son why he did not drive out of the town for a change of scene, 'he answered, "Every road out of Shrewsbury is associated in my mind with some painful event." ' The same was true of dates, for 'if he once heard a date he could not forget it; and thus the deaths of many friends were often recalled to his mind.'[25]

It is more than probable, I believe, that the deaths he was especially anxious to forget were those of members of his family: of his elder brother Charles in 1778, of his other brother (by suicide) in 1799, of his father three years later, and, consciously or unconsciously, of his mother when he was only four years old. Robert's concern during his early years for his mother's deteriorating health and attacks of severe pain, which led him to summon the servant to her aid, may well have set a pattern for his life: intense distress at suffering, combined with deep sympathy for the sufferer, and also, a habit learned from his father, his determined efforts to forget. These proclivities, so well attested to by Charles in the *Autobiography*, are major clues, I believe, to an understanding of the way in which the family responded to Susannah's early death.

THREE

A tragic loss;
a formidable presence

I

The family into which Charles Darwin was born on 12 February 1809 consisted of Dr Robert, nearing forty-three, his wife Susannah, turned forty-four, three daughters – Marianne, coming eleven, Caroline, eight and a half, and Susan, five and a half – and an elder son, Erasmus III, aged four. Fifteen months after Charles's birth another daughter, Catherine, arrived.

Except for the children growing bigger, life at The Mount seems to have continued much as before during Charles's earliest years. Letters in the Wedgwood archives, mainly those from Susannah and Dr Robert to Josiah II, give some picture. Apart from the weather, the main topics are family finances, health and visits from one family to the other. An example is a letter from Susannah to Josiah II in mid-June 1813 expressing the hope that he, Bessy and the girls would all come over soon: 'we are looking very gay, and are in the midst of our hay harvest *in the orchard* – the Dr and young ones join in.' The sisters-in-law, Bessy and Susannah, had become close friends.[1]

Among other letters the following two, also from Susannah to Josiah II, are not untypical. At the end of 1810 (when Charles was approaching his second birthday) she begins by referring to work she has been doing on the perennial task of sorting out the financial affairs of their brother John. She continues: 'My whole time has been taken up since our return home in nursing sick children and I have still four very poorly – most violent colds, and attended with considerable fever. [The baby, Catherine] is got quite well again, and regained her lost flesh – We are in daily fear too of the scarlet fever, it is become so prevalent.' They were avoiding seeing neighbours who had it, but 'our danger is more from the Dr who is so much at Sundorne, where four of the children and one of the Servants have it – He has slept there many times, and is just sent for again to-night.'[2]

Five years later, on 21 November 1815, the picture is much the same.

DARWINS OF THE MOUNT, SHREWSBURY

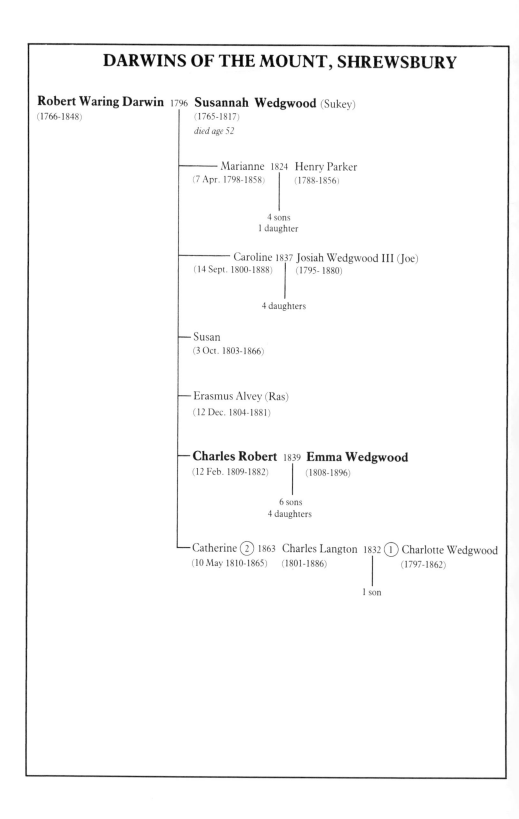

Robert Waring Darwin 1796 **Susannah Wedgwood** (Sukey)
(1766-1848)   (1765-1817)
                                         died age 52

———— Marianne 1824 Henry Parker
(7 Apr. 1798-1858)   (1788-1856)

                    4 sons
                    1 daughter

———— Caroline 1837 Josiah Wedgwood III (Joe)
(14 Sept. 1800-1888)   (1795- 1880)

                    4 daughters

— Susan
(3 Oct. 1803-1866)

— Erasmus Alvey (Ras)
(12 Dec. 1804-1881)

— **Charles Robert** 1839 **Emma Wedgwood**
(12 Feb. 1809-1882)   (1808-1896)

                    6 sons
                    4 daughters

— Catherine ② 1863 Charles Langton 1832 ① Charlotte Wedgwood
(10 May 1810-1865) (1801-1886)   (1797-1862)

                                       1 son

WEDGWOODS OF MAER HALL, STAFFORDSHIRE

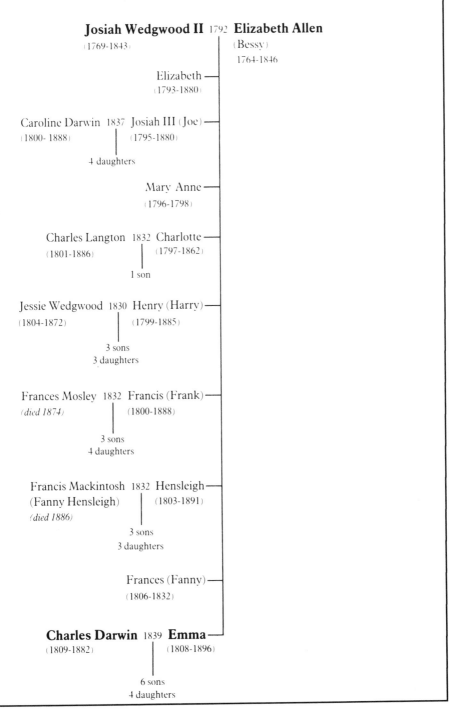

Josiah Wedgwood II 1792 **Elizabeth Allen**
(1769-1843) (Bessy)
1764-1846

Elizabeth
(1793-1880)

Caroline Darwin 1837 Josiah III (Joe)
(1800- 1888) (1795-1880)

4 daughters

Mary Anne
(1796-1798)

Charles Langton 1832 Charlotte
(1801-1886) (1797-1862)

1 son

Jessie Wedgwood 1830 Henry (Harry)
(1804-1872) (1799-1885)

3 sons
3 daughters

Frances Mosley 1832 Francis (Frank)
(died 1874) (1800-1888)

3 sons
4 daughters

Francis Mackintosh 1832 Hensleigh
(Fanny Hensleigh) (1803-1891)
(died 1886)

3 sons
3 daughters

Frances (Fanny)
(1806-1832)

Charles Darwin 1839 **Emma**
(1809-1882) (1808-1896)

6 sons
4 daughters

Difficulties over their brother John's financial affairs continue, with complaints about 'his great aversion about saying anything about money matters'. Susannah also refers to her two unmarried sisters, Kitty and Sarah, as being the residuary legatees in their mother's will. 'Our poor Invalids make but slow progress,' she continues, 'they are certainly better than they were at one time, but there is nothing to lead us to hope they are getting well – A week ago Erasmus [eleven] came home with mumps. . . . For fear of infection he is kept quite aloof from all the rest which makes a great addition to my trouble nursing so many, and I have not now help from the Dr as a nurse' (because every night he was sleeping at the house of a patient who was very ill). 'I am pretty well myself which is very fortunate just now.'[3]

By the New Year the family seem to have recovered, and late in January 1816 Susannah took the two elder girls Marianne (seventeen) and Caroline (fifteen) to join a large Wedgwood party for a fortnight's social life at Bath. Earlier in the month the girls had all been having lessons in singing, dancing and drawing in Shrewsbury.[4]

By mid-March, back at The Mount, news is much as before. Marianne is again unwell and Susannah busy mastering details of the Budget – 'The Dr says my old head is crammed so full of the Chancellor of the Exchequer, Property tax etc., that I must be much better qualified to write upon matters of finance than himself' – and she proceeds to make comments on the family accounts.[5]

From the letters, we see how during these years Susannah was devoting herself to the welfare of her family, and also how she had inherited some of her father's business abilities. The doctor, it seems, was so busy attending patients that his family got neglected.

Since the letters of early 1816 make no mention of Susannah's health, it would appear that the serious illness from which she was soon to suffer had not yet manifested itself. Indeed, the first reference in the archives appears to be from 7 March 1817, when Dr Robert ends a letter to Josiah II: 'your sister sends her love. I am sorry to add that she has been very indifferent of late.'[6] Four months later, in midsummer, she was dying. It seems that by then she had been ill for some months, perhaps a year, because she is referred to as having been an invalid. Since Dr Robert prescribed laudanum for her, the illness was evidently painful. A letter dated 14 July 1817 from one of Susannah's sisters in the Wedgwood archives describes her last days, when she was suffering from acute gastric symptoms. She had evidently had a chronic gastro-intestinal condition, possibly a gastric ulcer but more probably a carcinoma, and died from peritonitis following a perforation.

During the last fortnight of Susannah's illness the four younger children were kept from seeing her, and when the end came it was sudden. She was taken ill with severe abdominal pains, and her condition rapidly worsened. Her two younger sisters, Kitty and Sarah, were summoned from Parkfield and joined Marianne and Caroline to help nurse her. The situation they found was already grave, as Kitty reported to her brother at Maer: 'The Doctor has not the slightest hope and her suffering is terrible. The pain indeed is gone that was her first illness, but she has such severe vomitings and sickness that he says he does not think her suffering much lessened . . . this evening she is worse, and he is very wretched . . . Marianne and Caroline are always with her and keep up pretty well.' Within forty-eight hours she was dead – on Thursday, 15 July.[7]

That evening Sarah conveyed the news of her sister's last hours to her brother at Maer and described how Marianne and Caroline had 'nursed her with heroical fortitude, they have wept very much and expressed their sorrow fully since her death which gives me hope that they will be pretty well soon.'[8] The funeral was arranged for the following Monday.

Dr Robert's immediate reaction to the calamity was characteristic, as is described by Sarah in another letter to Josiah II telling him of arrangements for the funeral: 'but the Doctor would be glad to see you and John sooner if it is convenient for you. He is obliged to go tomorrow to Denbigh [a town in North Wales no less than fifty miles distant] to see a patient who is very dangerously ill; he will return on Saturday evening. He thinks the journey and being obliged to think of other things will do him good.'[9]

After Susannah's death the two elder daughters, Marianne and Caroline, took charge of the household, including responsibility for the younger children. They were aided, of course, by a staff of servants, which included Nancy, the nanny, who had probably been with the family for some years and who remained with them for many years longer.

Since we know that Caroline, nearly seventeen, took over the two youngest children, Charles (eight) and Catherine (seven), it is likely that Marianne acted as housekeeper. The third daughter, Susan, was not yet fourteen; the elder son, Erasmus III, aged twelve, was a boarder at Shrewsbury School. The family restructuring was probably made easier because their mother had been an invalid and Marianne and Caroline may already have been filling their respective roles.

While the household continued to function much as before, the family atmosphere became tense and gloomy. Susannah's death proved to be a blow to Dr Robert from which he never fully recovered. Throwing himself frantically into his practice, on his return home in the evenings he was often depressed and irritable. According to the Wedgwoods, 'The depression which occasionally had struck him in the past seemed never to lift now, and the atmosphere at The Mount was one of never-ending gloom. Robert's wit turned to sarcasm and bullying.'[10]

It was extremely fortunate for Dr Robert that his closest friend and brother-in-law, Josiah II, lived not far away. It was perhaps even more fortunate for the Darwin children, since their uncle and aunt, with their large and cheerful family, always made them welcome. There were eight children at Maer, four boys and four girls, a fifth girl having died early in childhood. The two sets of cousins were near contemporaries, with the Wedgwoods all a little older. When their aunt Susannah was alive, the two elder Wedgwood girls, Elizabeth and Charlotte, had enjoyed visiting Shrewsbury. After her death they felt very differently about doing so.

For example, three years after the tragedy, the eldest Wedgwood daughter, Elizabeth, now twenty-seven, gives an account of a Sunday afternoon at The Mount, where she and her sisters had gone for a singing class with the Darwin girls the previous evening. Writing from The Mount to one of her many Allen aunts (Bessy's younger sisters), Elizabeth describes the scene. Dr Robert was out, probably seeing patients. 'Sunday we dined at half-past-one, drest afterwards, and sat about 3 hours expecting the tide to come in about dark, and rather stiff and awful the evening was.'[11]

Many years later, one of Darwin's granddaughters, Nora Barlow, drawing on family records, describes Dr Robert and the atmosphere he created: 'His was a compelling presence, and all sense of liberty vanished when he entered a room, for no one could feel at ease to "go on about their own talk". A busy and successful doctor, he yet had time for a two-hour monologue each day before dinner. Visitors to the Mount were full of praise of the order, correctness and comfort, but a week was long enough; the doctor's talk was fatiguing.'[12]

II

It is time to look at this sequence of events from Charles's point of view. He has left two accounts of his childhood, the longer one written in 1838 when he was twenty-nine and engaged to be married, the other written some forty years later as the early part of his *Autobiography*.[13]

The most striking thing about these accounts is Charles's failure to recall anything of significance about his mother – despite being over eight years old at the time. In his earlier account, the 'Fragment', all he says is: 'When my mother died I was 8½ years old, and [Catherine] one year less, yet she remembers all particulars and events of each day whilst I scarcely recollect anything . . . except being sent for, the memory of going into her room, my father meeting me – crying afterwards. I recollect my mother's gown and scarcely anything of her appearance, except one or two walks with her. I have no distinct remembrance of any conversation, and those only of a very trivial nature. I remember her saying "if she did ask me to do something . . . it was solely for my good".'

In the later account his description is even briefer: 'My mother died in July 1817, when I was a little over eight years old, and it is odd that I can remember hardly anything about her except her death-bed, her black velvet gown, and her curiously constructed work-table.' He then gives his

half years. During the spring of 1817, shortly before his mother died, Charles started at a local day school. 'Before going to school,' he tells us, 'I was educated by my sister Caroline, but I doubt whether this plan answered. I have been told that I was much slower in learning than my younger sister Catherine, and I believe that I was in many ways a naughty boy. Caroline was extremely kind, clever and zealous; but she was too zealous in trying to improve me; for I clearly remember after this long interval of years, saying to myself when about to enter a room where she was "What will she blame me for now?" and I made myself dogged so as not to care what she might say.'[16] The well-intentioned effort of the teenaged Caroline to improve her younger brother, with its undesirable effects on him, which was soon to be reinforced by the equally moralistic Susan, provided over many further years a ground-base to family relationships.

The day school to which Charles went (with Catherine) at the age of eight was kept by the minister of the Unitarian chapel to which Susannah Darwin and the children used to go.[17] Many of Charles's recollections of the year that he spent at the school are self-critical. In the 'Fragment' he tells us that he was 'very timid', that he was afraid of the dogs he met on his way to school and that he could not get up courage to fight the other boys. Moreover, there are further self-critical references to showing-off, both in the *Autobiography* – 'I may here also confess that as a little boy I was much given to inventing deliberate falsehoods, and this was done for the sake of causing excitement'[18] – and in the 'Fragment': 'I was in those days a very great story-teller – for the pure pleasure of exciting attention and surprise. . . . I scarcely ever went out walking without saying I had seen a pheasant or some strange bird . . .; these lies, when not detected, I presume, excited my attention, as I recollect them vividly, not connected with shame, though some I do, but as something which by having produced a great effect on my mind, gave pleasure like a tragedy.' Since his year at day school coincided with his mother's death, the statement following is unexpected: 'I have no particular happy or unhappy recollections of this time or earlier periods of my life.'

Other memories of these years concern his early interests in natural history and collecting which he reports were well developed before he started at day school. 'I tried to make out the names of plants, and collected all sorts of things, shells, seals, franks, coins and minerals. The passion for collecting . . . was very strong in me.' Here again, however, he dwells on his peccadilloes. 'One little event during this year has fixed itself very firmly in my mind, and I hope that it has done so from my conscience having been afterwards sorely troubled by it; . . . I told another little boy . . . that I could produce variously coloured Polyanthuses and Primroses by watering them with coloured fluids, which was of course a monstrous fable.'[19] Curiously enough the other little boy grew up to become a well-known botanist. In old age he recalled Charles Darwin as a schoolfellow:

one day Darwin had brought a flower to school and had told 'that his mother had taught him how by looking at the inside of the blossom the name of the plant could be discovered'.[20] In addition to confirming Charles's tendency to recount 'monstrous fables', this little story indicates that Charles's interest in natural history is likely to have been encouraged by his mother, who, it will be recalled from the account in Chapter 2, shared her husband's enthusiasm for botany and zoology. Other memories of this time include 'collecting stones etc., gardening, and . . . often going with my father in his carriage, telling him of my lessons, and seeing game and other wild birds, which was a great delight to me.' He ends this passage in the 'Fragment' with the comment, 'I was born a naturalist.'

In view of Darwin's failure to recall much about his mother and nothing about her funeral, it may be relevant that the only other incident of his time at day school that he could recollect was the funeral of a dragoon soldier: 'it is surprising', he writes, 'how clearly I can still see the horse with the man's empty boots and carbine suspended to the saddle and the firing over the grave. This scene deeply stirred whatever poetic fancy there was in me.'[21] Since, however, it was a dramatic occasion, well calculated to impress itself on a small boy's memory, it may perhaps be of little consequence.

There is nevertheless a record of unusual behaviour by Charles during the period after his mother's death that seems unmistakably to be of relevance to understanding his disability. He reports it in his *Autobiography* in the following passage: 'I have heard my father and elder sisters say that I had, as a very young boy, a strong taste for long solitary walks; but what I thought about I know not. I often became quite absorbed, and once, whilst returning to school on the summit of the old fortifications round Shrewsbury, which had been converted into a public foot-path with no parapet on one side, I walked off and fell to the ground, but the height was only seven or eight feet.' Rather surprisingly, in the brief comment that follows he makes no reference to being hurt but gives an emotionally detached, scientific account of his mental processes: 'Nevertheless, the number of thoughts which passed through my mind during this very short, but sudden and wholly unexpected fall, was astonishing, and seem hardly compatible with what physiologists have, I believe, proved about each thought requiring quite an appreciable amount of time.'[22]

Charles's mental state during these long, solitary and absorbed walks is more than likely to have been that referred to technically as a fugue, a state akin to sleepwalking in which the individual is oblivious of what he is doing. This is a state that is known to occur sometimes in persons who have failed to recover from a bereavement.

III

The school to which Charles was returning on the occasion of his accident was the big Shrewsbury School which he first attended in the summer of 1818, aged nine, after his year at day school. The headmaster, the Reverend Samuel Butler (1774–1839), had been appointed at the early age of twenty-four and had so improved it that Shrewsbury had become one of the leading schools of England. Now in his mid-forties, he was near the height of his career. Despite the school's being hardly a mile from The Mount, Charles was a boarder. This, he tells us, enabled him to keep in touch with 'home affections and interests' by running there and back during longer intervals in school routine as well as to live 'the life of a true school-boy'.[23]

Although school athletics were limited, since neither cricket nor rowing had yet been introduced, Charles seems to have joined in zealously with what there were; and he had plenty of friends. He played the local version of fives, was apparently one of the best at high jumping and enjoyed fencing. One of his sons, George, recalled how, when he and his brothers were young, their father taught them to lunge and parry.[24]

During later years Darwin was always very disparaging about his seven years at Shrewsbury School. 'Nothing could have been worse for the development of my mind than Dr Butler's school, as it was strictly classical, nothing else being taught except a little ancient geography and history. The school as a means of education to me was simply a blank.' He felt incapable of learning languages and no good at verse-making. Even so, 'I was not idle, and with the exception of versification, generally worked conscientiously at my classics, not using cribs.' He sums up: 'I believe that I was considered by all my masters and by my Father as a very ordinary boy, rather below the common standard of intellect.'[25] Nevertheless the standard of the school was high, and records show that his school marks were about average.[26]

Throughout these years Charles's interest in natural history provided some compensation for the barren days at school. A family holiday spent with the Wedgwood cousins during the summer of 1819 at the seaside near Towyn, on the north coast of Wales, he recalled with especial pleasure. Moths and other flying insects not seen in Shropshire surprised him and almost led him to decide to collect all the dead insects he could find (since to kill them merely for his collection was frowned on by his sisters). He also found much pleasure in watching birds and kept notes on their habits, stimulated by reading Gilbert White's *Natural History of Selborne*.

The following year, in July, Charles, now eleven, and his elder brother Erasmus, known in the family as Eras or Ras and now fifteen, went for a riding tour into North Wales to see a famous waterfall, a distance of

Shrewsbury School

perhaps forty miles each way. In July 1821 they were far more ambitious. Together with the two younger Maer boys, Frank (twenty-one) and Hensleigh (eighteen), Ras and Charles rode to Bangor in north-west Wales to see Telford's suspension bridge being built across the Menai Straits to Anglesey. They covered 255 miles in the course of about ten days.[27] Later that summer Charles, with Caroline and Catherine, stayed for a time at Woodhouse, an estate a few miles from Shrewsbury and the home of William Mostyn Owen and his large family of children. The eldest daughter Sarah had become a bosom friend of Susan Darwin. For the next ten years Woodhouse was destined to play a part in Charles's social and sporting life second only to Maer.

It was at Woodhouse that Charles learned to shoot, taught by the master of the house, who was probably teaching his eldest son, another William, at the same time. 'In the latter part of my school life I became passionately fond of shooting', Charles tells us, 'and I do not believe that anyone could have shown more zeal for the most holy cause than I did for shooting birds . . . This taste long continued and I became a very good shot.'[28] Until his departure on the *Beagle* Charles was to spend many a happy day shooting at Woodhouse.

Although in his *Autobiography* Charles makes no mention of the extensive riding tour to Bangor, he does refer to a couple of briefer tours during the following summer, 1822. The first was with his sister Caroline, riding due south from Shrewsbury, and the second with Elizabeth (probably his cousin Elizabeth Wedgwood) south-west into Wales. The tour with Caroline, he noted in the 'Fragment', was the first occasion he could recollect of taking pleasure in scenery, which ever after was to give him vivid delight.

That same year Ras left school and went to Cambridge to read medicine. Becoming interested in chemistry, he converted a toolshed in the garden at The Mount into a chemical laboratory. There Charles assisted him in his experiments and also read some of his chemistry books. 'This was the best part of my education at school, for it showed me practically the meaning of experimental science,' he records; 'we often used to go on working till rather late at night.' News of their unprecedented activities reached school and Charles was nicknamed 'Gas'. Dr Butler disapproved strongly. Rebuking Charles publicly for the shocking waste of time, he used a term Charles did not understand and presumed it to be 'a fearful reproach'.[29]

Another way in which Ras influenced Charles in a direction of much benefit to his career was by lending him books and encouraging him to read. In fact by the time he left school Charles had already become a reader. 'I used to sit for hours reading the historical plays of Shakespeare, generally in an old window in the thick walls of the school. I read also other poetry, such as the recently published poems of Byron, Scott, and Thomson's *Seasons*.'[30] He also read popular books on science and technology. One of these, *Wonders of the World*, he mentions especially as having stimulated a wish in him to travel in remote countries, a wish to be amply fulfilled some ten years later. For the rest of his life Charles would be an omnivorous reader.

A number of letters from Ras, studying medicine in Cambridge, to his younger brother, still at school, have survived from the years 1822–5.[31] They contain enthusiastic accounts of laboratory equipment and minerals available in the Cambridge shops, requests for books on physiology and biology to be sent to him from The Mount, reports of his medical studies, and requests to be passed to their father for the payment of some of his bills. There are also proposals for refitting their private laboratory. Charles visited Ras at Cambridge on at least one occasion, June 1823, and certainly replied to his letters, though none has survived.

After three years at Cambridge, Ras was due to complete his medical qualifications by spending the academic year 1825–6 in Edinburgh. Charles was still only sixteen but doing so poorly at school that Dr Robert decided he should leave and go to Edinburgh to read medicine with Ras.

IV

By the summer of 1825, when Charles left Shrewsbury School for Edinburgh, his three elder sisters were grown up. Social life seems to have continued unabated after Susannah's death. Wedgwoods and Darwins were as close as ever with parties and joint summer holidays. For singing and dancing lessons at The Mount they were often joined by the elder Mostyn Owen girls.[32]

Marianne had become engaged to her father's partner, Dr Henry Parker (1788–1856), and was married in December 1824. She was amiable and sociable but perhaps a little dull. 'Marianne Parker', writes Bessy, 'is as happy as the day is long, with a very small income and a small house they give no dinners and she being of a very retired nature likes it all the better.'[33] During the next ten years Marianne produced four sons and a daughter. Once she had moved out of The Mount, Charles saw little of her and she played no part of consequence in his future life.

It was very different with Caroline and Susan. Both were tall, good looking and had a considerable presence. Caroline, although not regularly handsome, had 'brilliant eyes and colouring', and black hair growing low on her wide forehead. In the opinion of her cousin and exact contemporary, Frank Wedgwood, 'she looked like a Duchess'. Her 'dominant personality and sense of humour' reminded Josiah II of his elder sister Susannah, Caroline's mother. Vivacious and popular, with a passion for riding, Caroline is thought none the less to have had some of the formality and stiffness associated with the Darwin household.

In 1822 Caroline and Susan, following a common practice among well-off, liberal-minded families of the time, had started an infant school in the nearby poor district of Frankland, financed by the ever generous Dr Robert. After visiting there Bessy Wedgwood expressed admiration for Caroline's work in the school, noting especially 'her perseverance [and] her gentleness to the children', and adding: 'I thought all the time how happy the man who should call her his wife, and how much I should like my Joe to be that man.'[34] Bessy in fact had set her heart on Caroline's becoming the bride of her elder son, Josiah III, known always as Joe, who was five years Caroline's senior. Joe, however, was a very slow starter and something of a worthy dimwit. The romance which Bessy was so keen to encourage took a long time to mature – another dozen years in fact. Meanwhile Caroline remained at home keeping house and acting as hostess at what Charles called the 'fuss dinners' given by his father.

Whereas Caroline was rather serious and given to worrying, Susan was always in high spirits. In the words of Charles's granddaughter, Nora Barlow, 'Susan was her father's favourite. She too was tall and more beautiful than Caroline, with a beauty that endured, an immense flow of high spirits, and a power of enjoying the little details of life. . . . She could infect her father with her own rollicking enjoyment.' Although she was a famous flirt, especially at the numerous Wedgwood parties, the family were aware that she 'had a settled resolution against marrying'.[35] In the event, she never did; instead she lived at home and after Caroline's marriage would keep house for her father until his death in 1848. As she grew older she got a reputation in Charles's family for her fussiness and for always discovering 'disagreeables'.

There is abundant evidence that after his mother's death these two elder sisters were powerful influences in Charles's life. Devoted to him and constantly concerned for his mental and moral welfare, they were none the less a little overwhelming in their efforts to improve him. It may be that this dedication was due to their mother, during her last illness, having charged them with the responsibility for caring for their younger brother and sister. Although ten years later Charles described Caroline as having been 'a mother to me during all the early part of my life', he also addressed her in one of his letters (when he was a rising young scientist of twenty-nine), 'you being my Governess' – a role which seems, in fact, to have been nearer the truth.[36] Something similar applies to Susan. In the many letters he would write home from the *Beagle* he usually refers to her as his 'Granny', whose duty it was to correct his errors.

Since in the explanation of Charles's subsequent ill-health much emphasis is placed on the wall of silence that Caroline and Susan imposed against any reference to their dead mother, it is of interest to consider why they should have done so. One obvious possibility is that it was intended to protect their father. We know that before losing his wife Dr Robert had already suffered more than one sudden bereavement and that he could be haunted by unhappy memories. The Wedgwood records, moreover, describe how he became inconsolable after Susannah's death. It could well be that the course of her illness reminded him all too forcefully of the time when he was four years old and his mother was dying. Furthermore, there was also the strong Darwin family tradition of trying to avoid unhappiness by burying memories and diverting attention to other things – a tactic notable in Dr Robert and one that his daughters would inevitably have learnt from him.

Before we consider the central issue of Charles's relationship with his father it is useful to look briefly at his relations with his brother Ras and his younger sister Catherine.

Charles was always on the most cordial terms with Ras, who, of a gentle and unassertive disposition, was completely unlike the intensely ambitious Charles. Accounts of their chemistry experiments together suggest harmonious co-operation and, as we shall see in Chapter 5, during the year they were together at Edinburgh Ras was concerned always to be of help to his younger brother. After that they saw less of each other, largely because their interests diverged. Ras was not the least interested in natural history or in hunting foxes and shooting birds – which became

Charles's passions at university. Instead he preferred literary circles and a quiet London life. Nevertheless, when Charles was away on the *Beagle* Ras would act as his agent. He would make all arrangements for the purchase and dispatch of books and equipment to far-distant lands and would also plan for the reception of Charles's specimens in England. After the *Beagle*'s return they would live close by each other for some years in London, and after Charles moved out he would usually stay with Ras whenever he was in London. Moreover, for many years Ras would accompany Charles and his family on summer holidays.

Ras was often depressed. In the *Autobiography* Charles describes how 'his health from his boyhood had been weak, and as a consequence he failed in energy. His spirits were not high, sometimes low, more especially during early and middle manhood. He read much even whilst a boy.'[37] Bessy Wedgwood's description of him at the age of eleven when he was holidaying at Maer was to prove prophetic, if unduly negative: 'he is an inoffensive lad'.[38]

Finally, we come to Catherine, the youngest of the six children and only fifteen months younger than Charles, whose playmate she was when they were small. Quick and intelligent, she learned to read more quickly than he did, but she seems always to have been an anxious and unhappy person. The uproarious parties with the Mostyn Owen family at Woodhouse, into which her elder sisters entered with enthusiasm, she could not enjoy; after one such occasion she assessed her enjoyment as only 'about half as much as Susan's'. Charles she came to treat censoriously, adopting, it is clear, her elder sisters' attitude towards him.

In later years she came to have a great admiration and affection for Charles, but this was not reciprocated. On her fairly frequent visits to him and his family at Down she was apt to behave in a rather high-handed way which, in the words of her nephew Francis, 'used to make us children boil with indignation'.[39] Charles forgave her, however, as, very characteristically, 'he wished to avoid a quarrel'.

For most of her life Catherine seems to have lived with her father and Susan at The Mount. Eventually, at the age of fifty-two, she would marry the widower of one of her Wedgwood cousins, the Reverend Charles Langton. After her early death only three years later family letters refer to her 'high capacities', 'noble qualities' but 'abortive life'. 'I remember her father used to joke about Cath's "great soul",' writes Fanny Allen, Bessy's youngest sister; 'what he spoke in jest she had in earnest, but somehow it failed to work out her capabilities either for her own happiness or that of others.' Charles Darwin's daughter, Henrietta, recalling her aunt's visits to Down when she was a child, comes to her aunt's defence, however: 'She was a very kind and stimulating companion, taking an interest in my reading and what I was doing.'[40] Furthermore, on these visits she made herself useful to her brother by copying out some of his notes, for example lists of books, in a beautifully legible hand.[41]

Shrewsbury from the Severn

V

Immensely influential on his life though Charles's elder sisters were, they were not more so than his father. Inevitably Charles stood in awe of this formidable man. Recognising that it did not pay to cross him, he seems early to have developed effective ways of placating him. One of these ways, which became ingrained in his character, was to accept all his father's pronouncements as ultimate truths that were never to be questioned. 'His reverence for him was boundless and most touching' is how Charles's son Francis describes his father's attitude. 'He would have wished to judge everything else in the world dispassionately, but anything his father had said was received with implicit faith.'[42]

If Charles Darwin's idolisation of his father seems extreme, the circumstances of his developing it have to be remembered. First and foremost his father had many admirable qualities. He could be very kind and was always generous; he was highly intelligent and well read, so that his views were to be respected. Furthermore, in Charles's own words, his father 'was of an extremely sensitive nature, so that whatever annoyed or pained him did so to an extreme degree. He was also somewhat easily roused to anger.'[43] Most important of all, his father was the only parent he had. There was no loving mother to whom he could retreat should relations with his father become strained, while his elder sisters seem most unlikely to have been sympathetic to a younger brother who had been foolish enough to have roused their father's wrath. On such occasions probably all suffered. As Nora Barlow puts it: 'Subjection to the benevolent tyrant was implicit in the family atmosphere, combined with a real reverence for his opinions and deep mutual affection.'[44]

Throughout the years of Charles's boyhood Dr Robert seems always to have shown his special combination of great kindness and generosity coupled with an overbearing manner and an occasional outburst of sharp criticism. An example of the former is an episode in June 1819 in which an adolescent son of John and Jane Wedgwood had developed symptoms and had been sent over to Shrewsbury to consult Dr Robert. The outcome is described by Bessy Wedgwood: 'Dr. Darwin . . . talked to him with so much kindness that he comforted him very much. The Dr. said he thought his illness arose from anxiety. He told the Dr. that he was in debt £20 which lay very heavy upon him; the Dr. said that he would venture to promise him that it should be discharged without distressing his father and mother even with the knowledge of it.'[45]

Later that summer there had been a combined Darwin and Wedgwood family holiday on the Welsh coast, for which Dr Robert had paid. Unfortunately one of the Wedgwood girls had fallen ill *en route* at Shrewsbury and been left behind with Dr Robert. Bessy knew all too well how she would be feeling in that situation and was anxious lest she might risk her health by returning to Maer precipitately: 'but as I believe she would be left tête a tête with the Doctor she certainly will come away as soon as she can.'[46]

Dread of being left alone with Dr Robert was shared by all the Wedgwoods and Allens. Years later Bessy's youngest sister, Fanny, was to write: 'Sad, sad Shrewsbury! which used to look so bright and sunny; though I did dread the Dr. a good deal, and yet I saw his kindness.'[47]

Even though a submissive and placatory attitude towards his father became second nature to Charles, there were still times when he became the target of a biting outburst. On one celebrated occasion, probably when Charles was at Cambridge, his father exploded: 'You care for nothing but shooting, dogs, and rat-catching, and you will be a disgrace to yourself and all your family.' In relating this episode in his *Autobiography*, Charles describes the 'deep mortification' these words caused him, but proceeds at once to exonerate his father: 'But my father who was the kindest man I ever knew, and whose memory I love with all my heart, must have been angry and somewhat unjust when he used those words.'[48]

After Charles's death his daughter Henrietta would recall his saying 'with the most tender respect, "I think my father was a little unjust to me when I was young, but afterwards I am thankful to think I became a prime favourite with him." She [had] a vivid recollection of the expression of happy reverie that accompanied these words, as if he was reviewing the whole relation, and the remembrance left a deep sense of peace and gratitude.'[49]

Another source of information about Charles's childhood and his relations with his father comes from Emma, Charles's wife. When their son Francis was drafting his 'Recollections' of his father, he had a special talk with his mother about what she knew of Charles's childhood and her memories of her father-in-law. As the youngest member of the Maer family, she had known her uncle, Dr Robert, from childhood, long before her marriage. In his manuscript Francis records his mother's opinions, though they do not appear in the published version. The picture she paints is not a happy one, as Francis reports:

She thinks decidedly that Dr. D. did not like [my father] or understand him or sympathise with him as a boy. He was a fidgety man and the noise and untidiness of a boy were unpleasant to him . . . . Everything in the household had to run in the master's [way] so that the inmates had not the sense of being free to do just what they liked. Conversation could not be split with two or three or tête a têtes but was all more or less directed at Dr. D. – My mother quotes the way in which he would say 'What's Emma saying?' when she said something to one of the other girls – The consequence was they never felt at ease, and she used to be extremely glad when the Dr went off on a long journey, and sorry to see him come back again. My mother thinks that the affection which Dr. D. felt for my father sprang up chiefly after the return from the voyage.'[50]

There is indeed ample evidence that Emma was right about that, and also for Charles's belief that his father came to have the deepest admiration for his scientific achievements and that this was a source of great comfort to him. Nevertheless this was only half the story. Lurking always in the back of Charles's mind, ever ready to emerge, was a deep uncertainty. Was he the disgrace to his family his father had so angrily predicted, or had he perhaps made good? On this vital issue Charles oscillated. Again and again he knew he had made good – there was abundant evidence of it. Yet from time to time he was less sure; and occasionally his doubts became certainties.

Throughout his scientific career, unbelievably fruitful and distinguish-ed though it would be, Charles's ever-present fear of criticism, both from himself and from others, and never satisfied craving for reassurance, seep through. In order to defend himself against these nagging fears, he devised a formula. 'Whenever I have found out that I have blundered,' he tell us in his *Autobiography*, 'or that my work has been imperfect, and when I have been contemptuously criticised, . . . it has been my greatest comfort to say hundreds of times to myself "I have worked as hard as I could, and no man can do more than this".'[51] Unflagging industry and a horror of idleness were to dominate his life.

FOUR

A vulnerable personality

I

In the previous chapter we noted certain prominent features of Charles Darwin's personality that were already present during his earliest years and considered some of the influences exerted on him by members of his family. In this one I dwell on those features that I believe made him especially vulnerable to adverse events and show how most of them were the price, paid in psychological suffering, exacted by characteristics that friends and colleagues often prized.

As an adolescent of sixteen Charles was a popular member of his family's social circle. At Maer he was especially welcomed by his uncle, Josiah II, who was reminded of his long-dead and still-missed younger brother Tom. Like Tom, Charles was tall and slender, athletic and passionately devoted to shooting and fishing; other similarities were collecting and experimenting. Another household in which Charles was always welcome was that of the Mostyn Owens at Woodhouse. The head of the family was an old friend and admirer of Dr Robert and a decade later he recalled with pleasure the times when he was teaching the teenaged Charles to shoot.[1]

It is apparent from his boyhood onwards that Charles was regarded by older men as a particularly agreeable companion, a personal characteristic that was to be manifested during his university years as well as during the decade after the *Beagle*'s return. Always enthusiastic and quick to learn, he would have been especially attentive to the older man's personal interests and respectful of his opinions, unlike some brash young men. Welcome though such attitudes may be in youth, they can become excessive in later years. Then, not only is the status of others given undue respect and their opinions given undue weight but, far more important than that, the person's own worth and own opinions may be commensurately under-valued. This was undoubtedly true of Charles Darwin and was derived, equally certainly, from his childhood relations with his father and with his elder sisters.

No less than four of Darwin's children remark on their father's exaggerated respect for authority and the opinions of others, and/or on his tendency to disparage his own contributions. In his 'Memoir' of 4 January 1883 William, the eldest son, writes: 'A very strong characteristic was his deep respect for authority of all kinds and for the laws of nature. He could not endure the feeling of breaking any law [even] of the most trivial kind. . . . This feeling partly explains his great respect for a title. . . . No man could feel more intensely the vastness or the inviolability of the laws of nature, and especially the helplessness of mankind except so far as the laws were obeyed. He had almost a terror of any infringement, however slight of the laws of health.'[2]

In his 'Recollections' another son, Francis, writes: 'He sometimes expressed surprise that so few people thanked him for his books which he gave away liberally; and the letters he did receive gave him much pleasure, because he habitually formed so humble an estimate of the value of all his works, that he was genuinely surprised at the interest which they excited.' Some pages later Francis comments: 'To some, I think, he caused actual pain by his modesty; I have seen the late Francis Balfour quite discomposed by having knowledge ascribed to himself on a point about which my father claimed to be utterly ignorant.'[3]

His daughter Henrietta, who in his later years used to read his drafts and make suggestions for revision, recalled that 'He was always so ready to be convinced that any suggested alteration was an improvement . . . and he used almost to excuse himself if he did not agree.' Lastly there is the testimony of the fourth son, Leonard, who in his brief memoir of his father describes how 'the modesty of his nature . . . led him to concentrate his attention on possible defects in his own character and to ignore probable merits'.[4]

A characteristic and dramatic example of the combination of surprise and pleasure at praise for his work, referred to by Francis, is found in a letter written near the end of his life to his closest friend, Joseph Hooker, to whom he had sent a copy of the *Life of Erasmus Darwin*: 'Your praise of the life of Dr. D. has pleased me exceedingly, for I despised my work, and thought myself a perfect fool to have undertaken such a job.'[5] Here we find an unmistakable echo, more than sixty years later, of the 'self-contempt' he had felt as a young boy over being 'vain'.

Time and again throughout his life his desire for attention and fame is coupled with the deep sense of shame he feels for harbouring such motives. As a young boy, he tells us, on the one hand he was intent on being admired for his boldness and perseverance at tree-climbing and his pleasure in exciting attention and surprise by telling tall stories, but also, on the other, he felt shame and contempt for himself when he recognised he was vain. In his 'Recollections' Francis describes the 'contempt' his father had felt 'for the love of honour and glory' and notes that in his letters he 'often blames himself for the pleasure he took in the success of his books'.[6]

It is sometimes suggested that Darwin's contempt for his desire for fame was in some way a reflection of the culture of his times. I see no grounds for this. Not only is there no trace of such sentiments in the letters of his distinguished contemporaries, but Darwin's self-contempt stems from his nursery years. Most small children show off on occasion. Those who do it most are those who feel in danger of being overlooked; and in this connection it should be noted that Charles was only fifteen months old when his sister Catherine was born. An older child is very often jealous of a new baby and the shorter the age-gap the greater the jealousy. That leads me to believe that Charles as a young child was markedly jealous of Catherine and that his showing off was a natural expression of it. This was evidently treated by his elders with a heavy moralising hand, so that the contempt expressed by them for his desire for attention turned early into a nagging self-contempt which was always with him.

Whose the heavy moralising hand was we shall never know. It is most likely to have been his mother's. Not only is a child's mother usually the main influence in such matters during the early years but nothing we know about Susannah is incompatible with this idea. Also influential would have been the strongly moralising attitudes of Charles's elder sisters; but, here again, by far the most likely person to have produced such attitudes in them would have been their mother, whose values they are likely to have absorbed. Wherever the truth may lie, what is certain is that Charles grew up with an overbearing conscience which never left him.

It was especially at night that Darwin's overactive conscience burdened him. Francis notes that 'at night . . . anything which had vexed him or troubled him in the day would haunt him, and I think it was then that he suffered if he had not answered some troublesome person's letter.'[7] On occasion his nocturnal worries led him to unexpected steps to rectify matters. The vicar of Downe, with whom Darwin was on most cordial terms, notes an episode when after the discussion of 'some disputed point of no great importance' at a meeting of the parish council, he had been 'surprised by a visit from Mr Darwin at night. He came to say that, thinking over the debate, though what he had said was quite accurate, he thought I might have drawn an erroneous conclusion, and he would not sleep till he had explained it.'[8]

Darwin's eldest son, William, recalled a similar episode. One evening in 1866 discussion turned to a heated controversy then current about the merits of the privately financed prosecution of the Governor of Jamaica for the death of a slave, which had resulted from maltreatment. Characteristically, Darwin felt very strongly about it and remarked that he had subscribed to the costs of the prosecution. Hearing this, William, then aged twenty-seven, facetiously remarked that the money had probably been squandered on a dinner. At this, William proceeds, 'My father turned on me almost with fury, and told me, if those were my feelings, I had better go back to Southampton' (where he was living). 'Next morning at 7 o'clock, or so, he came into my bedroom and sat on my bed, and said that he had not been able to sleep from the thought that he had been so angry with me, and after a few more kind words he left me.'[9]

Throughout his life Darwin was acutely anxious lest he became angry and deeply troubled when, very occasionally, he did. Nothing roused his ire so readily as cruelty, of which he had a deep loathing. When, later in life, he was giving evidence before the Royal Commission on Vivisection (to which he gave heavily qualified approval) he surprised himself by coming out with very strong words about cruelty: 'It deserves detestation and abhorrence.' About this episode Francis comments: 'When he felt strongly about any similar question, he could hardly trust himself to speak, as he then easily became angry, a thing which he disliked excessively. He was conscious that his anger had a tendency to multiply itself in the utterance.'[10]

Darwin's horror of cruelty and fear of his own anger, which are clearly connected, started, like so much else in his character, very early in life. In the *Autobiography* he recounts that , 'whilst at the day-school, or before that time, I acted cruelly, for I beat a puppy I believe, simply from enjoying the sense of power; but the beating could not have been severe, for the puppy did not howl, of which I feel sure as the spot was near to the house. This act lay heavily on my conscience, as is shown by my remembering the exact spot where the crime was committed.' The fact that, as a general rule, he was humane as a boy he attributes 'entirely to the instruction and example of my sisters'.[11]

While there is so much to admire in the absence of pretension and in the strong moral principles that were an integral part of Darwin's character and that, with much else, endeared him to relatives, friends and colleagues, these qualities were unfortunately developed prematurely and to excessive degree. That made him prone to self-reproach and depression; and it also proved a major handicap when he met with opposition. In the 'Fragment', it will be remembered, Darwin describes how, when he first started day school, he was very timid and afraid to stand up for himself. This continued throughout his life. Hostile criticism devastated him and, had it not been for friends and admirers, he would have been crushed.

There were occasions when even his closest friends were exasperated by Darwin's inability to protest. Such an episode is recounted in the biography of Joseph Hooker.[12] Darwin had sent Hooker a manuscript for comment, as he often did, but through mischance this script had been put into the drawer used for the Hooker children's drawing paper. By the time the error was discovered nearly a quarter of the script had vanished. The quick-tempered Hooker would have blown up had it happened to him.

Not so Darwin. In a letter to Huxley, Hooker describes his feelings: 'I feel brutified, if not brutalised, for poor Darwin is so bad that he could hardly steam up to finish what he did. How I wish he could stamp and fume at me – instead of taking it so good-humouredly as he will.' It was probably this same aspect of Darwin that led Leslie Stephen to remark after meeting him that there was 'something almost pathetic in his simplicity and friendliness'.[13]

II

In the Prologue we saw that a person prone to develop the hyperventilation syndrome is likely to have suffered one or more severely adverse events, often including a childhood loss, and likely to be reluctant or unable to refer to them but to develop symptoms when something reminds him of one, even though he may be unaware of having been so reminded. Furthermore, a sufferer is often a person who is apt to find himself in situations in which he has strong cause for anger but must on no account show it. In view of Darwin's early loss of his mother and the strong pressures brought to bear on him by his father and elder sisters, it is hardly surprising that he should have grown up to be just such a person.

So far the discussion of Darwin's ill-health and the vulnerability of his personality has focused on his physical (somatic) symptoms because they are the ones that have aroused so much controversy. It must also be borne in mind, however, that in addition to those symptoms he suffered from periods of chronic anxiety and episodes of fairly severe depression. Psychiatric conditions in which, over a period of years, a changing mixture of symptoms of these kinds occur are not uncommon and have posed knotty problems for those eager to fit every patient into a tidy psychiatric classification. An alternative is to take the view that symptoms belonging to this array are to be looked at as commonly springing from a set of closely related causes giving rise to minor variations in the expression of a common psychopathology. Though the issue is far from settled, there is today substantial evidence supporting the second of these viewpoints.[14]

No finding has been more regularly reported than the observation that patients who suffer from one or another of this array of symptoms – those of the hyperventilation syndrome, panic attacks, depression – are significantly more likely to have lost their mother in childhood or to have had a chronically difficult relationship with her than are comparable individuals who are healthy. Since in this study so much emphasis is being put on the death of Darwin's mother when he was eight, further discussion of the evidence for its importance, and especially how it comes to have adverse consequences for the motherless child, is called for. The antecedents of a depressive breakdown are the ones best documented.

Evidence that those who have lost their mother, either through death or desertion, during childhood and adolescence are more prone to become depressed than are those who have not is no longer controversial (see appendix). Even so, it must be recognised that it is only a minority of those who suffer an early loss who become vulnerable – which means that there is now an active search to identify variations in experience that may account for why some do and others do not. Among variables found by a London research group to be associated with an unfavourable outcome is the child's having received inadequate substitute care after the mother's loss.

A closely related variable to which attention is drawn by those engaged in psychotherapy (though only recently the subject of systematic research) is the extent to which a bereaved child is helped to mourn his lost mother. Mourning entails opportunities to ask questions about what happened and why, to express his longing for his mother's return and his anger and grief when told she never will. Only very slowly does a child come to accept these hard truths, and only after being given many opportunities to go over the ground does he do so. To enable a child to progress favourably through the painful and bewildering months of mourning requires a clear understanding of how a mourner (of any age) thinks and feels and sympathy for the intense distress that he will express only when he feels sure of an understanding response. Without understanding and sympathy there is a danger that the child's thoughts and feelings will become locked away, as though in a secret cupboard, and there will live on to haunt him. Then, whenever some adverse event or threat of it penetrates to that secret cupboard, with or without his realising it, he becomes anxious and distressed and prone to develop symptoms, the reasons for which neither he nor his family may understand. (It is a calamity that for so long wishful thinking on the part of grown-ups and a failure to perceive that a bereaved child is sad and perplexed and needs help and comfort have led to the myth that children cannot and do not grieve, that they soon forget. Unfortunately, children's ready capacity to lock away thoughts and feelings that the adults in their world are unwilling to recognise or accept still tends to support this myth.)

It was, of course, recognition of states of mind of this sort that led Freud to postulate the existence of a dynamic unconscious. Although the existence of active mental systems segregated from the person's principal system of consciousness was formerly controversial, recent experimental research by cognitive psychologists throws much light on the issue and also suggests ways in which two systems, one of which may be active only episodically and without the person's being aware of it, may become segregated from each other, one being in effective control most of the time, the other only occasionally.[15]

III

Returning now to the experience of Charles Darwin, it is all too clear that after his mother's death he received little or no help in mourning her. Instead, an iron curtain descended. That, I believe, caused all his thoughts and feelings about her to go unexpressed and instead to be banished from consciousness, but nevertheless to live on to haunt him. In support of that view are some striking examples in the records of his childhood and later life that show how actively he maintained the repression of all thought and feeling about her.

One such episode occurred in 1842 when he was aged thirty-three. A cousin, who had become a close friend when they were undergraduates together at Cambridge, had lost his wife after a longish illness. Darwin wrote him a consoling letter in which we find an astonishing sentence: 'Your affecting account of the loss of your poor wife was forwarded to me yesterday . . .; I truly sympathise with you though never in my life having lost one near relation, I daresay I cannot imagine how severe grief such as yours must be.'[16]

Another episode, no less striking, is recounted in the memoirs of one of Darwin's granddaughters.[17] In the Darwin family a word-game had become popular in which a word could be stolen from another player and a new word then constructed by adding a letter, thereby changing its meaning. The story goes that on one occasion Darwin saw someone add an M to OTHER so as to construct the new word MOTHER. After looking at it for a long time he objected, 'MOE–THER; there's no such word MOE–THER.'

Both these episodes occurred in later life. Records of the years shortly after his mother died, already referred to in the previous chapter, also contain evidence that I believe supports the view here advanced. In his *Autobiography*, where Darwin emphasises how odd it is that all he can recall about his mother's death-bed were her black velvet gown and her curious worktable, there is nothing whatever about her as his mother, about how she may have treated him or how he had felt about her. Emotion is completely missing. In the 'Fragment' there is slightly more, though still very little. The only interchange between them that he records seems to refer to a minor issue of discipline – her saying that 'if she did ask me to do something . . . it was solely for my good'. Once again emotion is missing.

Another item recorded in his *Autobiography* (and described earlier) that I believe is related to his failure to mourn his mother is his strong taste for long, solitary walks during which he was so absorbed in thought that on one occasion he walked off the footpath along the old Shrewsbury fortifications and fell seven or eight feet, without his having any recollection of what he might have been thinking about.

If my ideas about Darwin's state of mind after his mother's death are on the right lines, these long, solitary walks, which are so uncharacteristic of young boys in general, can be regarded as occasions when a mental system preoccupied with his missing mother, and still hoping to find her, was temporarily in control despite being outside ordinary consciousness. A number of examples of adults bereaved as children who are found in a dazed condition, in circumstances indicating a search for their lost mother, are on record.[18] A dramatic example is given in the appendix.

There is a good deal of evidence that an individual who has been prevented, for whatever reason but usually by his family, from expressing feelings of anxiety, sadness or anger during childhood and from recognising the situations that have given rise to them is likely to have considerable problems with certain feelings in later life. These include difficulties in expressing such feelings, difficulties in identifying the situations that have given rise to them and that may still be doing so, and even difficulty in identifying what the emotion is that has been stirred within him. Thus it can happen, for example, that a person who has suffered a serious loss or some severe setback in his working life and has subsequently become depressed is unable to recognise that his state of depression is a response to the loss or the setback. Once the connection between response and situation is grasped the depression becomes intelligible; so long as the connection goes unseen it is deemed a symptom. The same is true of the physiological expressions of anxiety or of anger, for example a thumping heart or sweating hands. Once the person concerned understands what they are and how they arose, he ceases to regard them as symptoms and sees them instead as the ordinary human responses to danger or frustration. The same goes for his medical advisers.

Thus, when Darwin's emotional development and periods of ill-health are considered in this perspective, I believe it becomes possible to understand why he grew up to be especially sensitive to certain types of stressful situation and apt then to develop various combinations of psychosomatic symptoms and chronic anxiety, together with episodes of depression. Even so, until he reached the age of thirty, during his years at university and aboard the *Beagle* his problems hardly surfaced except the once when he was anxious and depressed before the voyage began. On the contrary, throughout these years he was almost always in high spirits and vigorous good health.

FIVE

Science and natural history
at Edinburgh
1825–1827

I

In late October 1825 Charles arrived in Edinburgh together with Ras. Both of them were to study medicine – Charles, who was not yet seventeen, as a beginner, Ras for some more advanced courses. They found comfortable rooms very close to the university, signed the matriculation book and explored the city. First impressions both of the city and of its inhabitants were most favourable, as they promptly reported to their father.

As it turned out Charles was to spend two academic sessions there, each an unbroken six or seven months starting in early November and ending in early June, leaving a very long summer vacation. Ras stayed for only four months of the first session, after which he returned to Shrewsbury, where he began doctoring the poor living near The Mount. Charles had the impression that even if Ras qualified in medicine he never really intended to practice, and he never did so.

When Charles himself began his medical training he took a keen interest and worked hard. During the summer before starting at Edinburgh he had begun attending some of the poor people in Shrewsbury, chiefly women and children. He had written as full accounts of his cases as he could and had then read them to his father, who had advised on the next steps. 'At one time', he tells us, 'I had at least a dozen patients, and I felt a keen interest in the work.' His interest evidently continued for most of his first session at university. He signed on for five courses of lectures, registered for borrowing at the library and attended regularly the clinical wards in the hospital. Some of the lectures he found appallingly dull: 'Dr Duncan's Lectures on Materia Medica at 8 o'clock on a winter's morning are something fearful to remember,' he recalls in his *Autobiography*. Moreover, the lecturer on anatomy he disliked extremely, and the subject matter so disgusted him that he never learned to dissect. This he later came to regard as having been 'one of the greatest evils' of his life. Even so, there were other lecturers about whom he was enthusiastic. Writing to his sister Caroline in early January 1826, he speaks highly of Dr Hope's lectures on chemistry: 'I like both him and his lectures *very* much'; the clinical lectures on sick people in the hospitals he also liked '*very* much'.[1]

Lectures, however, were never to Darwin's taste: he found reading to be much more profitable. During his schooldays he had become a great reader, and he continued to read extensively at Edinburgh and for the rest of his life. During 1825–6, it is recorded, he and Ras borrowed more books than any other students.[2] The comparison is hardly surprising, since those borrowed by Charles himself during his first seven month session make a most formidable list; they show well the wide range of his interests around his seventeenth birthday: *The Study of Medicine*, in four volumes; *Diseases of the Abdominal Viscera*; *A Course of Lectures on Natural Philosophy* (i.e. science) *and the Mechanical Arts*, in two volumes; *The Philosophy of Zoology* (structure, functions and classification of animals); *The Animal Kingdom* (a translation of Linnaeus's system of classification with more recent additions); two volumes of *Entomology*; *Illustrations of the Linnean Genera of Insects*, in two volumes; *Introduction to the Study of Conchology* (i.e. shells); Newton's *Opticks*; and Boswell's two-volume *Life of Samuel Johnson*.

The shift in his reading from medical subjects at the beginning to works on zoology and science later on is of some relevance, since his interest in medicine was already waning during this first session. There were two quite distinct reasons for this. One was that, when attending the operating theatre in the hospitals, he had witnessed two very bad operations (conducted, of course, without an anaesthetic), one of them on a child. He had found the scene unbearable, had rushed away and never attended again. 'The two cases fairly haunted me for many a long year,' he recalled later. The other reason was that he 'became convinced from various small circumstances that [his] father would leave [him] property enough to subsist on with some comfort.' The context suggests that in reaching this conclusion he may have been influenced by Ras. In any case his belief in his father's intentions was sufficiently firm to check 'any strenuous effort' he might have had to learn medicine,[3] and thenceforward his interest became purely scientific.

Among his many other activities during this first session he made friends with the curator of the university museum, William MacGillivray (1796–1852), an ornithologist and field naturalist from the Hebrides, learned to stuff birds, and studied French. Although in his *Autobiography* he insists that he was 'incapable of mastering any language',[4] this was not true so far as reading was concerned. He was later able to read scientific books in French fairly easily and also to struggle through those in German, though not without many a groan.

Throughout Charles's first session at Edinburgh his sisters wrote to him regularly. Altogether thirteen of their letters and three of his have survived. Apart from a single letter he addressed to his father shortly after his arrival, all communications between him and his father were conducted by means of messages conveyed in his correspondence with his sisters. This mode of communication continued later when he was in Cambridge and also when he was aboard the *Beagle*. The absence of letters is no accident. In a rare and brief exception, a letter written to Charles fourteen months after the *Beagle* had sailed, his father ends: 'You know I never write anything besides answering questions about medicine and therefore as you are not a patient I must conclude.'[5]

The surviving letters from his sisters are long, affectionate, gossipy and informative. In them they give detailed accounts of their active social lives which comprised visits, long and short, to Maer and Woodhouse and return visits to Shrewsbury by their Wedgwood cousins and the two elder Mostyn Owen girls, Sarah and Fanny, both of whom were lively and very popular. Other topics include books they have been reading and visits to the theatre. There is much concern about the dogs belonging to Charles and Ras which had been left at Shrewsbury and were proving miserable or troublesome; one of them later died, to everyone's sorrow. However, the most striking thing about their letters, even those of the fifteen-year-old Catherine, is their strong and unremitting efforts to improve their brother.

No sooner had Charles written his first letter home, addressed to his father and describing their first activities and impressions, than Catherine dispatched one in return: 'Papa sends his best thanks for the very nice letter he received from you this morning. I shall hope soon to hear from you again, my dear Bobby,* and remember that every little particular will be interesting – I must just mention that Edin*burgh* is spelt with an *h* at the end; and *altogether* has only ONE *l*, not *all*together, as you spelt it in your letter to Papa; do not be very cross at this, dear Charley.'[6]

Charles's relationship to Susan is well illustrated in their correspondence. During the winter of 1825–6 Susan, now aged twenty-two, starts one of her letters, 'My dear Charley, I am very glad to hear you are such a good boy about your French', and in another she refers approvingly to Charles's promise to write to her 'in such a good hand'.[7] At the end of January 1826 Charles, replying, starts by thanking the whole family for writing to him so often and then describes some parties he and Erasmus have been to. He continues 'I have been most shockingly idle, actually reading two novels at once. A good scolding would do me a great deal of good, and I hope you will send one of your most severe ones.'[8]

A couple of months later a scolding arrived. Dissatisfied with some of the lectures, losing interest in medicine and perhaps also a little homesick, Charles had written to say he was thinking of cutting the last week of the

---

*Charles's second name was Robert. Catherine sometimes addressed him as Bobby, though more often as Charley or Charles.

session and returning home early. His father disapproved, and so did Susan: 'I have a message from Papa to give you, which I'm afraid you won't like; he thinks your plan of picking and chusing [*sic*] what lectures you like to attend, not at all a good one; and as you cannot have enough information to know what may be of use to you, it is quite necessary for you to bear with a good deal of stupid and dry work: but if you do not discontinue your present indulgent way, your course of study will be utterly useless. Papa was sorry to hear that you thought of coming home before the course of Lectures were finished, but hopes you will not do so.'[9] In the event he stayed until the session ended, reaching home at the end of May.

Caroline strikes a more affectionate note. Shortly before Susan dispatched her scolding, Caroline, now twenty-six, had written a long, newsy letter, mainly about the social events surrounding the Assizes recently held in Shrewsbury. She continues more intimately: 'dear Charles I hope you read the Bible and not only because you think it wrong not to read it, but with the wish of learning what is necessary to feel and do to go to heaven after you die . . . it made me feel quite melancholy the other day looking at your old garden, and the flowers, just coming up which you used to be so happy watching – I think the time when you and Catherine were little children and I was always with you and thinking about you was the happiest part of my life and I dare say always will be.'[10] To this Charles replied a week or two later, thanking her for her 'very nice and kind letter. It makes me feel how very ungrateful I have been to you for all the kindness and trouble you took for me when I was a child. Indeed I often cannot help wondering at my own blind Ungratefulness. I have tried to follow your advice about the Bible, what part of the Bible do you like best? I like the Gospels . . . Do write to me again soon, for you do not know how I like receiving such letters as yours.' He adds that, though he is longing to return home, he is glad he stayed, since he has been to some very good lectures on electricity.[11]

In two further letters, written in April 1826, Catherine describes how they are making Erasmus very useful 'by taking him about among the Poor; he has acquired a very high reputation for doctoring them and has got a great many patients'; while Caroline, after thanking Charles for his very kind affectionate letter, mentions that Charles will shortly be receiving a letter of introduction to an Edinburgh family, the Horners, who were to play a significant part in his life in later years.

Edinburgh from the base of
Nelson's monument, 1827

BELOW LEFT Edinburgh University

BELOW RIGHT The harbour of Leith

II

Returned home at the beginning of June 1826, Charles soon set off on 'a long walking tour with two friends with knapsacks on our backs in North Wales. We walked thirty miles most days, including one day the ascent of Snowdon.'[12] By the 20 August he was at Maer for the start of the shooting season and subsequently at Woodhouse for more shooting. In late October he went on a riding tour with Caroline, once again into North Wales, accompanied by a servant, also mounted and carrying their clothes in saddlebags. Thus did the long five months' vacation pass with only a limited amount of time at The Mount. That was no accident, since, we are told, Charles wished to spend as little time as possible there.[13] This was presumably to avoid his father's uncertain moods and overbearing presence and perhaps also too big a dose of his sisters' improving pressures.

In describing this and his later long summer vacations while at university, Darwin in his *Autobiography* remarks that they were 'wholly given up to amusements', adding, 'though I always had some book in my hand which I read with interest.' That is probably an understatement. There is reason to think he read a great deal, and it is not improbable that it was during the summer of 1826 that he read his grandfather's *Zoönomia*, since we know he had already done so before starting his second session at Edinburgh on 6 November 1826.[14]

Darwin's activities during this second session were to prove very different from those of the first. Ras was now in London continuing his medical education, eventually qualifying as a Bachelor of Medicine of Cambridge in 1828.[15] That was an advantage, since Ras had acted as a restricting influence: Caroline had complained that he had refused to make use of the various introductions to people in Edinburgh that she had arranged for him.[16] The upshot was that during the session Charles made a number of scientific friends from among his contemporaries and the younger graduates, and took only two lecture courses, one in 'the practice of physic and medicine' and the other in natural history.[17]

The latter course covered a wide area – zoology, geology, meteorology, hydrography and some botany. Rather surprisingly, since it was a course of which others thought highly, he found it 'incredibly dull': 'the sole effect [the lectures] produced on me was the determination never as long as I lived to read a book on Geology, or in any way to study the science.'[18] By contrast, others who took this course, given by Professor Robert Jameson, spoke of the professor's 'enthusiastic zeal [and] wonderful acquaintance with the scientific literature'. Darwin's adverse judgement was evidently of a piece with his aversion to lectures in general. It is also possible that some of it was at too advanced a level for him.

On 28 November 1826, three weeks after starting the new session,

Darwin was elected a member of the Plinian Natural History Society, a student body which met weekly during the academic session. A week later he was elected one of the five members of its council, a fact which suggests he was already well known for his knowledge of and enthusiasm for the subject. Of the nineteen meetings he attended all but one and took part in the discussion at four. Topics were wide-ranging, covering among much else the natural history of the cuckoo, the chemistry of the Cheltenham waters, oceanic and atmospheric currents, the anatomy of expression, and instinct.

Darwin's membership of the Plinian Society led to many scientific friendships during this second session, and also to the first of the almost endless sequence of discoveries he would make. One of these friends was Dr Robert Grant (1793–1874), a physician and zoologist sixteen years his senior who at that time was lecturing on invertebrate anatomy. They explored the coast of the Firth of Forth together, searching for specimens of marine life which they could later dissect and examine under the microscope. Other specimens Darwin obtained from the local fishermen, whom he sometimes accompanied when they dredged for oysters. At that time the identity of some of these specimens was often still unknown, so there was always a chance of finding something new. On 27 March 1827, towards the end of the academic session, Darwin reported two of his findings to the Plinian Society. The first was that what were then believed to be the ova of *Flustra*, one of the *Bryozoa* or sea-mats, possess organs of locomotion, and the second that some small black globular bodies hitherto believed to be the young of a seaweed were really the ova of a leech (*Pontobdella*). In a paper on this species, later published in the *Edinburgh Journal of Science*, Grant describes these ova (subsequently found in fact to be cocoons), and states that 'the merit of having first ascertained them to belong to that animal is due to my zealous young friend Mr Charles Darwin of Shrewsbury, who kindly presented me with specimens of the ova exhibiting the animal in different stages of maturity.'[19] As it happens, another Scots biologist had already made the same discovery but had not published it.

After describing these discoveries to the Plinian Society, Darwin wrote a report of them in the notebook he was keeping of his observations, naming also the various authorities whose works he had consulted. The motility of the so-called ova of *Flustra* (later identified as the larvae of another species), he writes, 'does not appear to have been hitherto observed either by Lamarck, Cuvier, Lamouroux, or any other author.'[20] The reference to Lamarck is of some interest since it shows that Darwin was familiar with Lamarck's work on invertebrate taxonomy. He had, it appears,[21] copied out a classification chart from Lamarck's *Système des animaux sans vertèbres* (1801), a volume containing, as a prefatorial chapter, a lecture that includes the first statement of Lamarck's theory of evolution. This theory, which became widely disseminated during the early part of the century though usually dismissed as either heretical or absurd, advances the view that species have changed and become improved during the course of geological time, and also that these changes have been caused by the presence within each organism of 'an innate tendency towards perfection'. Whether Darwin read that chapter we do not know: his serious reading of Lamarck was to be many years later, in 1839.

Darwin's notebook of observations and other documents from this period demonstrate how seriously he took his field studies. They show also that, by the time he left Edinburgh, having just turned eighteen, he had already 'acquired the methods of collecting and identification of specimens and the faculty of careful observation and interpretation' that were to be the hallmarks of his work during the famous voyage of a few years later.[22]

There is little doubt that most of Darwin's increasing skills were due to his friendship with Robert Grant.[23] Grant was a very capable zoologist who had spent a winter ten years earlier in Paris studying under the great Georges Cuvier (1769–1832) and was familiar with the work of all the other French biologists, including that of Lamarck. Evolution had for long been an interest of his; indeed he had referred to Erasmus Darwin's *Zoönomia* in the thesis he had written for his degree. It is hardly surprising therefore that when Charles Darwin, a bright young student with a famous name, crossed his path he welcomed him on his field trips. Nor is it surprising that on one of them he should have spoken enthusiastically of Lamarck's ideas on evolution. Darwin describes the occasion in his *Autobiography*: 'I knew [Grant] well; he was dry and formal in manner but with much enthusiasm beneath this outer crust. He one day, when we were talking together burst forth in high admiration of Lamarck and his views on evolution. I listened in silent astonishment, and as far as I can judge without any effect on my mind. I had previously read the *Zoönomia* of my grandfather in which similar views are maintained.'[24] Although Darwin insists that these ideas had no effect on him, he does concede that 'hearing rather early in life such views maintained and praised may have favoured my upholding them under a different form in my *Origin of Species*. At this time,' he adds, 'I admired greatly the *Zoönomia*.' Clearly, the notion that over the course of time one species can evolve to give rise to one or several new species was already thoroughly familiar to him, even though, as he well knew, it was deeply abhorred by established opinion.

It was during the course of his friendship with Grant that Darwin learned for the first time about rivalry and jealousy in the scientific world, as many years later he was to tell his daughter Henrietta, who recorded it among the notes she made about her father after his death.[25] On making his discovery about the so-called 'ova' of *Flustra*, Henrietta reports, 'he rushed instantly to Professor Grant who was working on the subject [and was due to give his paper on it a few days later] to tell him, thinking he would be delighted with so curious a fact. But was confounded on being told that it was very unfair of him to work at Professor Grant's subject and in fact he would take it ill if my Father published it. This made a deep impression on my Father,' Henrietta continues, 'and he has always expressed the strongest contempt for all such little feelings – unworthy of searchers after truth.' Darwin would continue to feel contempt for all yearnings after priority – a vanity of vanities, he would think – but he would later find it very hard to stifle his own intense desire to be accorded priority for the revolutionary new theories about the origin of species that he was to take so long to hatch.

The story of Robert Grant's future is of interest both for the light it throws on the scientific politics of the day and for the part played by a rising young zoologist, Richard Owen (1804–92), who, as ambitious as he was hard-working and able, would in later years be Darwin's most bitterly hostile critic.

The same year that Grant was talking to the young Darwin about Lamarck, 1827, saw him appointed to the chair of zoology at the newly founded University College in London. His scientific reputation, especially his work in comparative anatomy, was high and outweighed any misgivings there might have been about his avowed adherence to Lamarck's ideas and to the radical left-wing politics that went with it, both of which he shared with several other Scots who had been studying in Paris. Welcomed to London as the future Cuvier of Britain, he was soon elected to the councils of the principal scientific societies, Linnean, Geological and Zoological, and in 1836 became a fellow of the Royal Society. In London he became well known as the leading advocate of Lamarck's views, about which he published extensively. Then he disappeared from the scene, although he continued to hold the chair. To Darwin on his return from the *Beagle* voyage the eclipse of his brilliant friend was to be inexplicable.[26]

The explanation was the malevolent rivalry of Richard Owen.[27] Both men were pioneers in the new field of comparative anatomy and, for dissection purposes, both required the corpses of any dead animals available at the Zoological Society. As fellow members of the society's council during the early 1830s both had access to them. Owen, however, seems to have resented the competition and in 1835 determined to oust Grant; after intensive lobbying, no doubt exploiting the deep anxiety then prevalent about all ideas originating in revolutionary France, he succeeded. Grant lost both his place on the council and his access to material for dissection. His morale shattered, he did no further work of consequence. It was because Owen's destruction of Grant took place while Darwin was away from England that Darwin remained in ignorance of the cause of his friend's eclipse.

Returning now to Darwin's second academic session in Edinburgh, we find that in addition to his activities at the Plinian he was also a member and regular attender at the Royal Medical Society, 'but as the subjects were exclusively medical I did not care much about them.' Moreover, he adds, 'much rubbish was talked there'.[28] On other occasions he was Grant's guest at the Wernerian Society, the principal natural history society of Edinburgh, where he heard the American ornithologist John James Audubon (1785–1851) discoursing on the habits of North American birds. Another time he was a guest at the Royal Society of Edinburgh, whose president, a little incongruously, was Sir Walter Scott. On that occasion he was the guest of Leonard Horner, to whom his sister Caroline had earlier arranged an introduction.*

Darwin left Edinburgh at the end of April 1827 but before returning home undertook a tour of cities in central Scotland, Dundee, St Andrews, Stirling and Glasgow, and also visited Belfast and Dublin. No sooner had he arrived back at Shrewsbury than he paid a visit to Paris in the company of his uncle, Josiah II, and his sister Caroline. It was to be the only visit he ever paid to the Continent.

Now that he had given up medicine, Darwin's future was uncertain; and it was not until eight months later, in January 1828, that he resumed an academic life. Nevertheless Darwin's two sessions as a medical student in Edinburgh were far from wasted. He had been educated in the rudiments of anatomy and physiology, trained in the methods of field biology, and inducted into the world of science. On the debit side he had taken to snuff, which later became a near-addiction.

No doubt correspondence with his sisters had continued as before, but no letters have survived. This is unfortunate, especially as we have no detailed records of how Dr Robert reacted when he heard, through Charles's sisters, that he did not wish to become a physician. Plainly he was disappointed and angry. All Charles says about it in his *Autobiography* is that 'he was very properly vehement against my turning an idle sporting man, which then seemed my probable destination.'[29] The solution Dr Robert proposed was that Charles should become a clergyman, a proposal that Charles asked for time to consider.

III

Although the life of a country parson attracted him, with visions no doubt of Gilbert White and having plenty of time to work at natural history, he nevertheless had scruples about declaring his belief in all the dogmas of the Church of England. 'Accordingly I read with care *Pearson on the Creed* and a few other books on divinity; and as I did not then in the least doubt

---

*Leonard Horner (1785–1864) was an industrialist in the linen trade, a Whig concerned with education and social problems, and also a geologist and fellow of the Royal Society as well as being the father of a large family. A few years later one of his daughters was to marry Charles Lyell (1797–1875), the leading geologist of his generation, who was to become one of Darwin's most influential mentors and friends.

the strict and literal truth of every word in the Bible, soon persuaded myself that our Creed must be fully accepted.'[30] Since to become ordained required that he go to an English university, it was agreed he should go to Cambridge. That meant a return to the classics, which he had been spared at Edinburgh. To his dismay he found that what little he had learnt at school had completely disappeared, and so had to be recovered with the aid of a tutor in Shrewsbury. His knowledge being still insufficient for him to start in the autumn of 1827, he eventually went up to Cambridge in the New Year.

There was thus a long interregnum between Edinburgh and Cambridge. Whenever possible during those months he was at Maer or at Woodhouse, welcomed alike by his uncle and aunt, Josiah II and Bessy Wedgwood, and by the Mostyn Owens. Both houses held great attraction for him. Both were occupied by cheerful families of contemporaries, and life in both was relaxed and free. Both were situated in pleasant countryside affording ample opportunity for walking and riding. Come the shooting season, both provided ample opportunity for sport. At Maer there were the added attractions of good conversation and music, and the opportunity to get to know his uncle, and at Woodhouse there were the feminine charms of Sarah and Fanny, the eldest of the many daughters of the house.

The pages in Darwin's *Autobiography* describing these visits, which were continued during his vacations from Cambridge for the next three and a half years, show these times to have been among the happiest in his life. 'In the summer the whole [Wedgwood] family used often to sit on the steps of the old portico, with the flower-garden in front and with the steep wooded bank, opposite the house, reflected in the lake, with here and there a fish rising or a water-bird paddling about. Nothing has left a more vivid picture on my mind than these evenings at Maer.' He then tells how attached he was to his uncle and how greatly he revered him. 'He was the very type of an upright man with the clearest judgement. I do not believe that any power on earth could have made him swerve an inch from what he considered the right course.' Josiah seems to have reciprocated these sentiments. Although he was notoriously taciturn and could appear forbidding, Charles refers to the occasions when his uncle unbent: 'he sometimes talked openly to me'.[31]

During the late 1820s Josiah II, as the owner of the Wedgwood factory, still had major responsibilities for its management and its chronic financial problems. Consequently he often had to go over to Etruria for the day, riding each way. His eldest son, Josiah III, was competent and reliable but uninterested and not up to taking charge. Frank, the third son, was far more capable and also far more interested. In November 1827, therefore, Josiah II reorganised the business, taking these two sons into partnership and giving each a quarter of the shares while he retained half. Thenceforward Frank took increasing responsibility and in due course became head of the firm, restoring its finances and the reputation of its wares.[32]

During the latter half of 1827, when Charles was spending so much time at Maer, a distinguished Whig politician and historian was in residence there. This was Sir James Mackintosh (1765–1832), who had married, as his second wife, Kitty Allen (1765–1830), Bessy's next younger sister. Depressed by his failure to be appointed to the new coalition cabinet, he had retired to the country to work on his ambitious *History of England*, the first volumes of which were to appear three years later. Enjoying an admiring audience of young people, he often held court in the evenings. Charles was sometimes present and was vastly impressed by Mackintosh's erudition and powers of conversation: 'I listened with much interest to everything which he said, for I was as ignorant as a pig about his subjects of history, politicks and moral philosophy,' he recalled. Afterwards he heard 'with a glow of pride' that Mackintosh had remarked, 'There is something in that young man that interests me.' Reflecting on that many years later, Darwin comments: 'To hear of praise from an eminent person . . . is, I think, good for a young man, as it helps to keep him in the right course'; though very characteristically he also deplores that it is 'apt or certain to excite vanity'.[33]

It was during the years when Charles was at university that his passion for shooting was at its height. 'My zeal was so great that I used to place my shooting boots open by my bed-side when I went to bed, so as not to lose half-a-minute in putting them on in the morning; and on one occasion I reached a distant part of the Maer estate on the 20th of August for black-game shooting, before I could see: I then toiled on with the gamekeeper the whole day through thick heath and young Scotch firs.' Not only was he extremely fit and enthusiastic during these years, but he was also manifestly competitive: 'I kept an exact record of every bird which I shot throughout the whole season.'[34] This led to his being the target for a practical joke.

At Woodhouse Charles used to shoot with the eldest of the Mostyn Owen sons, William, a couple of years or so Charles's senior. William had noticed Charles's habit of keeping his score by tying a knot in a piece of string he kept for the purpose, and one day, with the help of a cousin, played a trick on him. Charles recounts the story in his *Autobiography*: 'every time after I had fired and thought that I had killed a bird, one of the two acted as though loading his gun and cried out "You must not count that bird, for I fired at the same time," and the gamekeeper perceiving the joke backed them up. After some hours they told me the joke, but it was no joke for me for I had shot a large number of birds, but did not know how many, and could not add them to my list.' The truth is Charles took his shooting very seriously. Years later he reflected that perhaps he had been a little ashamed of his zeal, 'for I tried to persuade myself that shooting was almost an intellectual employment; it required so much skill to judge where to find most game and to hunt the dogs well.'[35]

Among the other attractions of Woodhouse were the two eldest daughters of the house, Sarah, now about twenty-four, and Fanny, about nineteen and Charles's contemporary.[36] Both were exceedingly popular. In her letter to Charles in Edinburgh in January the previous year, Catherine had written, 'I never saw such merry agreeable girls as Fanny and Sarah are; talking so easily and naturally and so full of fun and nonsense. They are very much admired and get plenty of partners at the Balls.' A few months later Catherine reported: 'Fanny Owen has quite the preference to Sarah among all the gentlemen, as she must have everywhere; there is something so very engaging and delightful about her.' Charles found them irresistible and from the autumn of 1827, if not before, enjoyed flirting with both. A lively and light-hearted correspondence ensued. Evidently the letters they wrote to him during the next four years – 'so full of fun and nonsense' – meant much to him, since he kept them and they still survive, though his, not surprisingly, have perished. Both girls married into local landed families, Sarah in the autumn of 1831 shortly before the *Beagle* sailed, Fanny eighteen months later. The letters each wrote him telling of their engagements show that, with each, beneath the inconsequential banter there was much genuine mutual affection.[37]

SIX

Sport, beetles and
philosophy at Cambridge
1828–1831

I

Darwin's career at Cambridge is complicated by his starting very late in the academic year 1827–8 and then having to spend three complete years there to meet the conditions for a degree. Since in his *Autobiography* he refers to these complete years (1828–9, 1829–30 and 1830–1) as his first, second and third, I shall refer to the period from January to June 1828 as 'year zero'.

As it turned out year zero was a period of great consequence for Darwin, since during this time he made friends with his second cousin, William Darwin Fox (1805–80), who, being a few years older, had preceded him to Christ's College but had not yet taken his degree. The friendship ripened fast; and Fox became the earliest and most intimate of all Darwin's many friends. After Fox completed his degree in January 1829 he left Cambridge and thereafter the two men saw relatively little of each other. An advantage from our point of view is that throughout their lives they corresponded regularly and over 150 letters from Darwin, most of them long, intimate and informative, have survived. Unfortunately there are none of Fox's; as a personality, therefore, we see him dimly and only through Darwin's eyes.

Fox, who like over half Darwin's Cambridge friends and acquaintances was destined for the church, was a keen and capable naturalist. Very early in their friendship he introduced his cousin to entomology, which at once became one of Darwin's ruling passions. Fox also introduced him to the Professor of Botany, the Reverend John Stevens Henslow (1796–1861), who also was to become a close friend, and was destined to play a most beneficent and key role in Darwin's life.

Darwin's purpose at Cambridge was to take a degree and, after further study, to be ordained as a clergyman in the Church of England. In doing so he was simply falling in with his father's plan for him, which was the line of least resistance. His doubts about the church persisted, but no immediate decision regarding ordination was required and in any case

Christ's College, Cambridge

William Darwin Fox, 1805–80,
aged 43 in 1848.
Charles's second cousin and
life-long intimate friend, who
initiated him into the joys of
beetle collecting

three years at Cambridge would be agreeable. Fortunately, only an ordinary degree was necessary. The examination, which he took in January 1831, the middle of his final year, covered classics, mathematics and philosophy. A year before sitting it he had to take the preliminary examination (or Little-Go). Before each of these hurdles he put in a few weeks of hard work and passed without difficulty: his place in the finals was a good one, tenth on the list of 178 who passed.[1] Apart from these brief spells of degree work and attending a few compulsory lectures, he spent his time in other ways, some of which were to be of the greatest value to his future.

Just under six feet tall, and slim, in physique he was more Darwin than Wedgwood.[2] In his features, however, he clearly took after the Wedgwood side of the family and, from such pictures of her as are available, seems to have resembled his mother. Always fond of the outdoors and full of energy, he spent much of his time during the spring and summer collecting beetles. In the autumn it was shooting; and during the winter fox-hunting. In addition, he enjoyed long walks and long rides with friends. Throughout these years he was extremely sociable and mixed in at least three distinct sets. One was the fox-hunting fraternity, which included 'some dissipated low-minded young men. We used often to dine together in the evening', he writes in his *Autobiography*, 'and we sometimes drank too much, with jolly singing and playing at cards afterwards.' Recalling these occasions in later years he thinks, very characteristically, that he 'ought to feel ashamed of days and evenings thus spent' but has to admit that 'as some of my friends were very pleasant and we were all in the highest spirits, I cannot help looking back to these times with much pleasure.'[3]

A second set of friends comprised men of intelligence, varied interests and aesthetic tastes with whom he walked and rode and who stimulated his interest in pictures and music. He came especially to enjoy choral services in King's College Chapel and engravings in the Fitzwilliam Museum.

A third set were the entomologists and other scientists, with several of whom he kept in touch for many years and some of whom would become famous. Although in later years Darwin was always apt to stress that he had wasted his time in Edinburgh and Cambridge, he did no such thing. Deeply immersed in natural history and what would later become ecology and exposed to the finest scientific minds of the day, Darwin was being prepared for the career in science upon which, did he but know it, he was soon to embark.

II

The academic year at Cambridge consisted then as now of three terms, with two short vacations at Christmas and Easter and a much longer one in the summer. Darwin's mode of travel between Shrewsbury and Cambridge was by coach via London. Since for much of this time Ras had rooms in London, Charles often broke his journey and spent a few days in town, meeting scientific colleagues and going to the opera. In December 1829, when he was working for his Little-Go and took only a brief Christmas break, he passed the whole three weeks in London. In all but his final year he stayed in Cambridge during the Easter vacation. Throughout the long summer vacations his aim was to spend as little time as possible at The Mount.

The summer vacations began in early June and extended until October, giving four clear months. During the first of them he determined to study mathematics, which he found horribly difficult. Accordingly, for eight weeks during July and August he went with a tutor and a couple of friends to Barmouth, on the west coast of Wales, to work during the mornings and to walk, beetle-hunt and fly-fish for trout during the afternoons. Unfortunately the tutor, a young don, proved 'a very dull man' and Darwin's progress was excessively slow. 'The work was repugnant to me. chiefly from my not being able to see any meaning in the early steps in algebra.'[4] The scenery and walks were to his liking, however, and the beetle collecting exhilarating, as he reports in long letters to Fox.

During September and the early days of October he spent as much time as possible shooting at Maer and Woodhouse, and he also managed a first visit to Fox's home, Osmaston Hall, in Derbyshire. Some of his feelings about Shrewsbury emerge in a thank-you letter he wrote to Fox after his return: 'I stayed two days at Maer . . . and on Monday returned to sweet home. Home is doubtless very sweet, but like all good things one is apt to cloy on it; accordingly I have resolved to go to Woodhouse for a week. This is to me a paradise, about which . . . I am always thinking; the black-eyed Houris . . . are real substantial flesh and blood. Formerly I used to have two places, Maer and Woodhouse, about which, like a wheel on a pivot I used to revolve. Now I am luckier in having a third . . . Osmaston.' Throughout his Cambridge years 'la belle Fanny' was especially in his mind, and their correspondence continued. In the winter of 1829–30, when Charles spent his Christmas vacation in London, Fanny was deeply disappointed he was not at The Mount when she was a guest there.[5]

Unfortunately none of his sisters' letters have survived, so we remain ignorant of the atmosphere at home. In his long letters to Fox, Charles makes few references to the family, though we learn that in the autumn of 1829 Dr Robert was seriously ill with erysipelas: 'My sisters appear to have been terribly alarmed, as I suppose on Wednesday he was in imminent danger.' Charles was in mind to return to see him but was discouraged by the doctors, who insisted he be kept quiet. On a more cheerful note, he tells Fox how pleased his father had been when he had presented him with two live death's-head moths. His father's comment had been that 'if he himself had thought for a week he could not [have] picked out a present so acceptable'.[6] From childhood days a shared interest in natural history had been their only area of common ground.

III

At the beginning of the last century collecting articles of natural history had become a fashion. No country house was complete without its cabinets of stuffed birds, butterflies, beetles, fossils and other specimens. Many a countryman augmented meagre earnings by selling items he had collected to the local big house, and professional collectors were starting to market items from Europe and elsewhere. Good prices could be obtained for rare, curious and beautiful articles. It was hardly surprising, therefore, that undergraduates of the time were sharing the craze. Recalling the years when Darwin was at Cambridge, a local vicar, Leonard Jenyns (1800–93), whom Darwin came to know well, reported: 'Never before . . . was natural history so in favour in the University; nor has it ever since held the place it then occupied.'[7] Entomologists, Jenyns continues, were especially numerous.

Numerous indeed they were. Introduced to the brotherhood by Fox, Darwin with his long-established passion for collecting was soon to become the most enthusiastic and successful of them all. He invented two new methods of acquiring specimens, he tells us in the *Autobiography*: 'I employed a labourer to scrape during the winter, moss off old trees and place [it] in a large bag, and likewise to collect the rubbish at the bottom of the barges in which reeds are brought from the fens, and thus I got some very rare species.' Much to Darwin's rage one of the men he employed proved to be a double-agent and was giving a rival first pick: Darwin promptly sacked him.[8]

Soon after leaving Cambridge for Shrewsbury at the end of the summer term of 1828, Darwin is bewailing to Fox that he is 'dying by inches, from not having anybody to talk to about insects'. He had captured a few and was trying to identify them. A sister had been enlisted to make drawings which he was enclosing. Three weeks later he wrote again on the same topic. Among the books he had consulted was Lamarck's comprehensive work on invertebrates, which he had acquired in Edinburgh. 'On Wednesday', he reports, 'I set out on my Ento-Mathematical expedition to Barmouth; by the blessings of Providence I hope *the science* will not drive out of my poor noddle the Mathematics.'[9] In later years one of his companions at Barmouth, J. M. Herbert (1808–82), recalled that on their afternoon expeditions 'Darwin entomologised most industriously, picking up creatures as he went along. . . . And very soon he armed me with a bottle of alcohol, in which I had to drop any beetle which struck me as not of a common kind.' Another companion, T. Butler (1806–86), recalled that Darwin's enthusiasm had inoculated him with a taste for botany which had stuck with him all his life.[10]

The beetles that Darwin collected at Barmouth proved to be exceptionally good ones, including a few previously unknown. Having left the party at the end of August to start the shooting season at Maer, he writes back to Herbert asking him to collect some additional specimens and telling him, 'I have taken some of the rarest of the British Insects, and their being found near Barmouth is quite unknown to the Entomological world: I think I shall write and inform some of the crack Entomologists.' Write to them he did, and before returning to Cambridge in early November he spent time with one of them, the Reverend F. W. Hope (1797–1862), who after seeing his collection announced that for a long time 'he had not seen such a rich case collected in one year', as Darwin reported in a letter to Fox, adding: 'My head is quite full of Entomology.'[11]

Darwin's contact with Hope continued. During five days in London the following February, he spent two with Hope, whose collection he found 'most magnificent'. Moreover, Hope gave him 'about 160 new species' and also, it seems, introduced him to another leading entomologist, J. F. Stephens (1792–1852), who was busy producing his *Illustrations of British Entomology*, a work being issued in a series of parts which had started in 1827 and would continue for another eight years. Darwin showed his specimens to Stephens and a few months later, in July 1829, had the immense satisfaction of seeing his name in the current number of the series. 'No poet ever felt more delight at seeing his first poem published than I did at seeing in Stephens' *Illustrations of British Insects* the magic words "captured by C. Darwin, Esq."' is how he recalls the event in his *Autobiography*. In the completed work, no fewer than thirty-five species are listed as taken by Darwin.[12]

Hope's appetite having been stimulated by his young friend's exploits in Wales the previous summer, the two arranged a joint expedition for the following one. They set out together in mid-June but Darwin fell sick and, to his deep mortification, had to retreat to Shrewsbury. In gloomy mood he reports to Fox in a letter of 3 July 1829: 'I started from this place about a fortnight ago to take an Entomological trip with Mr Hope through all North Wales: and Barmouth was our first destination. The two first days I went on pretty well, taking several good insects, but for the rest of that week, my lips became suddenly so bad, and I myself not very well, that I was unable to leave the room, and on the Monday I retreated with grief and sorrow back to Shrewsbury.' Mr Hope had done wonders, he continues, securing several rare species: 'I am determined I will go over the same ground that he does before Autumn, and if working hard will procure insects I will bring home a glorious stock.'[13]

The trouble Darwin had with his lips had started some months earlier. The first we hear about it is in a letter to Fox written from Shrewsbury at the end of the previous January: 'My life is very quiet and uniform, and what makes it more so, my lips have lately taken to be bad.'[14] Although he gives no further information about the symptoms, he does describe the circumstances in which they had begun. Two things were on his mind. One was the Little-Go examination that he was due to take the next term and for which he was working, and the other an unfortunate shooting accident at Woodhouse. 'About the Little-Go I am in doubt and tribulation,' he reports to Fox. He was wrestling with Adam Smith, probably his *Wealth of Nations*, and Locke's *Essay Concerning Human Understanding*, and was far from confident about the exam. Apparently he had cause to be, since on his return to Cambridge his tutor advised him to postpone taking it for a year, which he did.

The shooting accident had occurred quite recently and had been a great shock. He had gone over to Woodhouse for a week and on the first day with his very first shot had hit one of the younger Owen boys. It 'cut his eye so badly . . . that he has been in bed for a week – I think I never in my life was so much frightened.'[15] The damage had been done by a copper-cap, which may well have flown off at an angle and presumably hit the boy's eyelid. No doubt everyone feared for the boy's sight and Darwin felt deeply responsible.

Though in his letter to Fox Darwin does not attribute his symptoms to these two tribulations, the fact that first one and then the other are described in the same paragraph and immediately following the reference to his lips shows how closely associated they were in his mind.

It seems likely that his lips were giving trouble off and on throughout the first half of 1829, for there is a further reference to their 'not being quite so well' in a letter written in gloomy mood to his cousin a couple of months later (1 April 1829). Fox, having taken his degree, had left Cambridge for good and Darwin was missing him. Moreover, Fox had not written. Chiding him for not writing and bewailing his absence, Darwin continues: 'I find Cambridge rather stupid, and as I know hardly anyone that walks, and this joined with my lips not being quite so well, has reduced me to a sort of Hybernation.' An old Shrewsbury contemporary, now at St John's, C. T. Whitley (1808–95), was proving some sort of substitute, however, and they had just begun a series of regular walks together.[16]

Just what it was about the entomological trip to Wales with Hope that led to Darwin's lips becoming so bad is not clear. One possibility is an episode of conflict between them that caused ill-feeling. The reason for raising this possibility is that during these years Darwin was intensely competitive and it seems that Hope was too. At their initial meeting, when Hope had presented him with a large number of specimens, Darwin had been impressed by Hope's generosity. Later he revised his opinion. In August 1830, a year after the abortive trip, he was on another visit to

Wales with Hope, though this time in a larger party. In giving Fox an account of his doings he says he has become 'quite disgusted with Hope's egotism and stupidity' and how much he wished Fox was in the party instead.[17]

Since Darwin was almost always ashamed of being vain and of enjoying fame, the uninhibited competitiveness he reveals in the letters written to Fox from Cambridge comes as a surprise. In mid-May 1829, at a time when beetle-hunting was at its height, he tells Fox of the brilliant success of a mutual acquaintance and continues: 'My success also has been very good amongst the water-beetles. I think I beat Jenyns in Colymbetes.' Two months later, when proudly telling his cousin, 'You will see my name in Stephens's last number', he adds: 'I am glad of it if only to spite Mr Jenyns.' The following spring his campaign against the poor vicar continued unabated. In March that year (1830) he was in an elated mood, having just heard he had passed his Little-Go. Reporting the joyful news to Fox, he insists his cousin join him for a few days in Cambridge: 'what fun we will have together, what beetles we will catch, it will do my heart good to go once more together to some of our old haunts . . . Heaven protect the beetles and Mr Jenyns, for we wont leave him a pair in the whole country.'[18]

The Reverend Leonard Jenyns was the vicar of a nearby fenside parish and an expert naturalist. How it came about that Darwin became so competitive with him is not clear, though one possibility is that it had originated with Fox. Darwin himself, however, had formed an unfavourable impression of Jenyns. From time to time they met to swap specimens and Darwin judged him to be rather mean. Eighteen months later, however, his opinion radically changed. 'What a good naturalist he is,' he tells Fox. 'I have seen a good deal of him lately, and the more I see the more I like him.' In his *Autobiography* Darwin confesses his initial error: 'At first I disliked him from his somewhat grim and sarcastic expression . . . ; but I was completely mistaken and found him very kind-hearted, pleasant and with a good stock of humour.'[19] They were to maintain contact with each other and, after the *Beagle*'s return, it was Jenyns who would undertake the examination of the fish.

On the issue of meanness, there is an interesting sequel. Many years later when Darwin and Jenyns met and were recalling old times, Jenyns reminded Darwin of an occasion when they had been exchanging specimens and Darwin had insisted on retaining a specimen that Jenyns had especially wanted. 'Oh yes,' Darwin replied, 'I remember it well: and I was selfish enough to keep the specimen when you were collecting materials for a Fauna of Cambridge.'[20]

IV

Among the many friends that Darwin made at Cambridge, two stand out as the most intimate and influential, his cousin and contemporary Fox, and Henslow, Professor of Botany and thirteen years his senior. Before coming up to Cambridge Charles had heard about Henslow from Ras, who had commended him as a man who knew every branch of science. Darwin therefore made a point of attending his lectures, which were so extremely clear and well illustrated that he signed on for them for all three years he was up.[21] Furthermore, Henslow kept open house once every week during term-time and all undergraduates interested in science were welcome; several senior members of the university were also regular attenders. After being introduced by Fox, Darwin never missed an evening. Since Henslow's knowledge was considerable in a wide range of sciences, discussion covered topics in botany, entomology, chemistry, mineralogy (of which Henslow was formerly professor), and geology. In addition, 'Henslow used to take his pupils, including several of the older members of the University, field excursions, on foot, or in coaches to distant places, or in a barge down the river, and lectured on the rarer plants or animals which were observed.'[22] The day ended in high spirits over dinner in a local inn.

On these excursions Darwin was in his element and, although not an official student of botany, in due course attracted Henslow's attention. The friendship ripened slowly. Henslow's name first appears in Darwin's correspondence towards the end of his second year, when in April 1830, he mentions to Fox, 'I have been seeing a good deal lately of Prof. Henslow, I took a long walk with him the other day: I like him most exceedingly, he is so very good natured and agreeable.' A month later he reports that 'the more I see of him the more I like him. I have some thoughts of reading divinity with him the summer after next.'[23]

During his Cambridge years Darwin's ideas about his future were probably in a state of flux, though the balance seems usually to have favoured ordination. Most of his friends, including Fox, were moving in that direction; and there was no obvious alternative. Nevertheless he still had his doubts about the Thirty-nine Articles, which formulate the beliefs of the Church of England and to which adherence is necessary, and he felt at times they would be an insuperable obstacle, as Herbert, his companion at Barmouth in the summer of 1828, later recalled.[24] Henslow's influence was strongly towards orthodoxy. 'He was deeply religious, and so orthodox, that he told me one day, he should be grieved if a single word of the Thirty-nine Articles should be altered.'[25] Thus for Darwin a possible plan for the future was to prepare for the ordination examination by studying divinity with Henslow.

It was during Darwin's third and final year at Cambridge that the friendship between the two men was cemented. Darwin went up early in October in order to read for his degree examination to be taken in January. Most of his friends had gone down, and he complains to Fox on 8 October that 'there is not an individual up whom I know'. Working for his degree, he had no time for anything else. 'I have not stuck an insect this term,' he reports a month later, 'but really I have not spirits or time to do anything. Reading makes me quite desperate, the plague of getting up all my subjects is next thing to intolerable.' The one bright spot was Henslow: 'Henslow is my tutor and a most *admirable* one he makes, the hour with him is the pleasantest in the whole day. I think he is quite the most perfect man I ever met with – I have been to some very pleasant parties there this term – his good nature is unbounded.'[26]

Darwin never had reason to revise his profound admiration for his tutor or to qualify his deep sense of gratitude to him. His feelings are well expressed in the *Autobiography* and, at greater length, in a letter written to Jenyns after Henslow's death.[27] Henslow, indeed, had great qualities. In addition to being very knowledgeable he was a brilliant lecturer who took immense trouble to help his students, whom he encouraged in every possible way. Darwin was struck especially by the absence of jealousy and selfishness in Henslow's character. 'He was free from every tinge of vanity or other petty feeling; and I never saw a man who thought so little about himself or his own concerns,' Darwin recalled in his *Autobiography*. At Cambridge Darwin took Henslow as his ideal and thereafter sought to emulate him.

Henslow himself evidently reciprocated most of Darwin's feelings. He could not miss the young man's already impressive knowledge of natural history, his enthusiasm, and his high intelligence. Nor is it likely that he would have been wholly uninfluenced by knowledge of Darwin's relationship to the great Dr Erasmus, deplore though he undoubtedly would old Dr Darwin's freethinking ways and heretical ideas on evolution.

As the two men became increasingly intimate during the academic year 1830–1, they took long walks together and Henslow frequently invited Darwin to his house for meals. There Darwin met some of Henslow's wide circle of friends, some scientists, others not. 'These men ... together with Henslow, used sometimes to take distant excursions into the country, which I was allowed to join and they were most agreeable.' In addition, there were Henslow's open evenings: 'At these parties many of the distinguished members of the University occasionally attended; and when only a few were present, I have listened to the great men of those days, conversing on all sorts of subjects, with the most varied and brilliant powers. This was no small advantage to some of the younger men, as it stimulated their mental activity and ambition.'[28]

One of the great men whom Darwin met on these occasions was William Whewell (1794–1866), mathematician and polymath, who was to become president of the Geological Society during the late 1830s and Master of Trinity College in 1841. Sometimes Darwin walked home with him after one of Henslow's evening gatherings. 'Next to Sir J. Mackintosh he was the best converser on grave subjects to whom I ever listened.'[29]

Throughout his years at Cambridge, Darwin found time for serious reading. Thus in March 1829 he was reading Gibbon's famous *History of the Decline and Fall of the Roman Empire.*[30] Other books he read with great interest were two set for his degree examination, both by William Paley (1743–1800): *Evidences of Christianity* (1794) and *Natural Theology* (1802). In the latter Paley argues that the existence of creatures showing design for living points unmistakably to there being a Great Designer, just as the existence of a watch points to there being a human designer. Darwin remarks that he studied these books 'in a thorough manner'. Their logic, he says, gave him 'as much delight as did Euclid'. He reckoned that his obtaining a good pass in his degree examination turned on his having answered well the questions on Paley's books and on Euclid.[31]

The examination was in January 1831, and the satisfactory results were known soon afterwards. To fulfil requirements for the degree, however, Darwin had to complete the academic year until June. These months enabled him to continue his serious reading. Soon after sitting his examination he was absorbed in a newly published book on the philosophy of science by John Herschel (1792–1871), *Preliminary Discourse on the Study of Natural Philosophy* (1831).The author, the son of Sir William Herschel, a German immigrant musician who by dint of self-education had become a distinguished astronomer, was himself a mathematician and astronomer of distinction. John Herschel was a friend and contemporary of Whewell, who probably recommended the work to Darwin. His book came to be recognised as an authoritative statement of the methods of science in which he advocates a hypothetico-deductive approach* strongly in keeping with current ideas.

Darwin read Herschel's book with intense interest and excitement. Writing to Fox soon after, mainly about specimens of birds which Fox was busy collecting, he adds a peremptory postscript: 'If you have not read Herschel . . . read it directly.'[33] Darwin's reading of Herschel during this last year at Cambridge, together with his conversations with Whewell, who advocated a logic of science closely similar to Herschel's, were to prove a powerful influence on all his later thinking. During the years immediately after the *Beagle*'s return, when he was deep in the construction of his theory of evolution, he reread Herschel and also a companion volume by Whewell. Thereafter he did all he could to make the exposition of his theory conform to the principles laid down by these two men.

V

Another book that Darwin read 'with care and profound interest' during his last year at Cambridge was the *Personal Narrative* (1819), of Alexander von Humboldt (1769–1859), six volumes describing his *Travels to the*

---

*In adopting a hypothetico-deductive approach a scientist advances what appears to be a plausible explanation of observations so far made and then sees to what extent new observations, and also earlier ones not previously taken into account, either support the explanation proposed or call it in question. The method needs to be used imaginatively if the resulting research is to avoid becoming sterile.

The Reverend J. S. Henslow, 1796–1861, Professor of Botany at Cambridge, whose encouragement paved the way for Darwin's career in science, aged 53 in 1849; by T. H. Maguire

The Reverend Adam Sedgwick, 1785–1873, aged 47 in 1832, Professor of Geology at Cambridge, who taught Darwin field geology but later found his species theory absurd and painful

Equinoctial Regions of the New Continent 1799–1804. This work, together with Herschel's, made a great impact: they 'stirred up in me a burning zeal to add even the most humble contribution to the noble structure of Natural Science. No one or a dozen other books influenced me nearly so much as these two.'[34] One effect of reading Humboldt was to arouse in him a determination to travel. The island of Tenerife in the Canaries had for long had a special fascination for him and he resolved to go there during the coming summer.

His first step was to stimulate an interest in the venture among a number of the younger dons he had met at Henslow's and whom he hoped might accompany him. Accordingly on one of their spring excursions he read aloud passages from Humboldt describing the glories of his favourite island. Much polite interest was expressed and one or two agreed tentatively to join the venture. Meanwhile Darwin in his enthusiastic way was thinking of nothing else: 'At present, I talk, think and dream of a scheme I have almost hatched of going to the Canary Islands,' he tells Fox in a letter of 7 April 1831. 'I have long had a wish of seeing Tropical scenery and vegetation: and according to Humboldt Tenerife is a very pretty specimen.' That Easter he paid a short duty visit to Shrewsbury after an interval of six months and then spent a week in London during which he made enquiries about ships bound for Tenerife. There were monthly sailings between June and the following February.[35]

Throughout the spring and early summer Tenerife dominated his thoughts: 'in the morning I go and gaze at Palm trees in the hot-house and come home and read Humboldt,' he tells Caroline in a letter of 28 April 1831; 'my enthusiasm is so great that I cannot hardly sit still on my chair. . . . Henslow promises to cram me in geology. – I never will be easy till I see the peak of Tenerife and the great Dragon tree; sandy, dazzling, plains, and gloomy silent forests are alternately uppermost in my mind. – I am working regularly at Spanish . . . I have written myself into a Tropical glow.' A fortnight later, writing to Fox in much the same vein, he reports that 'some good natured Cambridge man has made me a most magnificent anonymous present of a Microscope . . . one would like to know who it was, just to feel obliged to him.' The microscope had just arrived with a note declaring that the donor was in doubt 'whether Mr Darwin's talents or sincerity [were] the more worthy of admiration' and hoping that the instrument would facilitate the researches he has 'so fondly and successfully prosecuted'.[36] The donor proved to be his old friend J. M. Herbert, then embarking on a career in law, who had for long recognised Darwin's gifts and was not alone among contemporaries in predicting a brilliant future for him.[37]

By mid-June Darwin was back at Shrewsbury. Writing to Fox on 9 July from 'this stupid place' to which lack of funds was confining him, he claims that 'The Canary scheme goes on very prosperously. I am working like a tiger for it, at present Spanish and Geology, the former I find as intensely stupid, as the latter most interesting. I am trying to make a map of Shrops[shire] but don't find it so easy as I expected.'[38] Thanks to Henslow, Darwin had overcome the aversion to geology he had contracted in Edinburgh and was spending his time in Shrewsbury practising field techniques in the locality, where the geology happens to be notoriously complex. He was now regretting not having attended the lectures by the Professor of Geology at Cambridge, the Reverend Adam Sedgwick (1785–1873), especially as Henslow had arranged for him to accompany Sedgwick on the annual field trip Sedgwick was making to Wales in August.

By the end of July Darwin, unable to enlist any companions, had accepted that his dream trip to Tenerife would have to be postponed until the following year. His plan for the coming months would then be three weeks' geologising with Sedgwick in North Wales during August, shooting at Maer and Woodhouse during September, and a visit to Cambridge in October to pay his bills. These amounted to £200, he had told Fox on 11 May 1831 before leaving Cambridge, and were the reason for his being in financial straits that summer: 'the Governor has given me a 200 £ note to pay my debts, and I must be economical.' Darwin felt rather badly about these debts and, when mentioning his extravagances in after years, seems to have scaled them down by a half.[39]

By 1831 Sedgwick was far forward in the classic study he was making of the ancient rocks of Wales. In early August he reached Shrewsbury, slept the night at The Mount and set off the following day with his young apprentice. No three weeks in Darwin's life were of greater value to him than these days with Sedgwick. They traversed many complex areas of North Wales, Sedgwick often sending his student on exercises in which, following a line parallel to that of the professor, he had to bring back rocks and mark the stratification on a map. In their discussions, moreover, Darwin learned some fundamental principles of science: 'Nothing before had ever made me thoroughly realise, though I had read various scientific books, that science consists in grouping facts so that general laws or conclusions may be drawn from them.'[40]

On leaving Sedgwick in North Wales, Darwin, steering by compass, went in a beeline to Barmouth to see friends, an exciting route which led him across 'some strange wild places'. Thence he proceeded to Shrewsbury with the intention of being at Maer on 1 September for the first day of partridge shooting. There he found two letters offering him the opportunity to travel and collect on a scale far surpassing his wildest dreams.

Captain Robert FitzRoy, RN, 1805–65, in his late twenties

SEVEN

A great and uncommon opportunity 1831

I

Darwin reached Shrewsbury on the evening of Monday 29 August, and was at once given the two letters by his sisters. One was from Henslow, who explained that he had been asked by the Reverend George Peacock of Trinity, acting on behalf of the Hydrographer of the Navy, to recommend a naturalist to go as companion to Captain Robert FitzRoy*, in command of a naval vessel leaving shortly on a long cruise to survey the southern coasts of South America. 'I have stated', continues Henslow, 'that I consider you to be the best qualified person I know of who is likely to undertake such a situation – I state this not on the supposition of your being a *finished* Naturalist, but as amply qualified for collecting, observing, and noting anything worthy to be noted in Natural History. . . . Captain F. wants a man . . . more as a companion than a mere collector and would not take any one however good a Naturalist who was not recommended to him likewise as a *gentleman*. . . . The voyage is to last 2 years. . . . Don't put on any modest doubts or fears about your qualifications for I assure you I think you are the very man they are in search of.'[1]

The companion letter was from Peacock, who gave a little further information. 'Captain Fitzroy . . . sails at the end of September in a ship to survey in the first instance the South Coast of Terra del Fuego, afterwards to visit the South Sea Islands and to return by the Indian Archipelago to England. The expedition is entirely for scientific purposes . . . Captain Fitzroy is a public spirited and zealous officer, of delightful manners and greatly beloved by all his fellow officers.' Captain Beaufort (the Hydrographer of the Navy and responsible for organising the expedition) would welcome an early acceptance.[2]

Charles's immediate inclination was to accept; but his father was strongly against the idea on the grounds that it would unfit him for settling down as a clergyman, that time before sailing was too short, and that in any

*The correct spelling of FitzRoy is with a capital R. It is hardly ever used in the correspondence, however, and never by Darwin.

case he might not suit the captain. Although his father did not definitely refuse to let him go, Charles explained in a letter to Henslow written the following day, 'Even if I was to go my Father disliking would take away all energy.' That being so, he felt he must refuse the offer.[3]

On Wednesday 31 August Charles rode over to Maer, ready to be out early next morning. There he found the Wedgwoods as enthusiastic about his accepting the offer as his own family had been chilly. Fortunately there was a loophole to his father's opposition. 'If you can find any man of common sense, who advises you to go, I will give my consent,' he had told Charles. Now, Josiah II, whom his father greatly respected, favoured the idea. Plucking up his courage, Charles writes a long, apologetic letter to his father, describing how the Wedgwoods viewed the proposal and reopening the issue; he has made an exhaustive list of all his father's objections and encloses a letter from his uncle giving comments on each. Nevertheless, Charles assures his father, 'pray do not consider that I am so bent on going, that I would for one *single moment* hesitate, if you thought . . . you should continue uncomfortable.'[4]

> Dr Robert's objections, as listed by Charles, read as follows:
> 1. Disreputable to my character as a Clergyman hereafter
> 2. A wild scheme
> 3. That they must have offered to many others before me, the place of Naturalist
> 4. And from its not being accepted there must be some serious objection to the vessel or expedition
> 5. That I should never settle down to a steady life hereafter
> 6. That my accommodation would be most uncomfortable
> 7. That you consider it as again changing my profession
> 8. That it would be a useless undertaking

The comments on each by Josiah II, contained in a companion letter, are reasoned and sober and, in effect, show them to be without substance. His answers to numbers 2 and 7 are especially weighty. In response to number 2, he points out that, if he went, Charles 'would have definite objects on which to employ himself, and might acquire & strengthen habits of application, and I should think would be as likely to do so as in any way in which he is likely to pass the next two years at home.' As regards number 7, he argues that Charles is not at present absorbed in professional studies and shows no sign of becoming so. By contrast, 'his present pursuit of knowledge is in the same track as he would have to follow in the expedition.'[5]

This pair of letters, dispatched on 31 August, reached Shrewsbury overnight. Dr Robert replied immediately, withdrawing all objections and assuring his brother-in-law that, if Charles after further enquiry still wished to go, 'I will give him all the assistance in my power.' Before this note had time to reach Maer, however, Josiah II and Charles, who had interrupted his day's shooting, had set out for Shrewsbury, not realising that all opposition had already vanished. On their arrival Dr Robert was in amiable mood. Charles, however, always apprehensive about being extravagant, sought to console him by remarking how he would be 'deuced clever to spend more than [his] allowance whilst on board the *Beagle*', to which his father answered with a smile, 'But they all tell me you are very clever.'[6] Thereafter Dr Robert raised no difficulties, and Charles was left free to explore further this undreamed-of opportunity.

II

Time before sailing was short (or thought to be so) and there was much to do. Darwin's first move was to Cambridge for a long talk with Henslow. There he learned that the first man to have been approached was Leonard Jenyns, who had nearly accepted. Next Henslow had been tempted to go himself and his wife had agreed to it; but she had looked so miserable that he had changed his mind. What he gleaned about FitzRoy was favourable, but new information about the voyage in a letter from FitzRoy which dwelt at length on the many difficulties, hardships and dangers to be expected, was extremely discouraging. Although much shaken, as was Henslow, Darwin decided to go to London to meet the captain. Briefed by Henslow, Captain Beaufort (1744–1857) had written to FitzRoy commending the young man: 'I believe my friend Mr Peacock . . . has succeeded in getting a "Savant" for you. A Mr. Darwin grandson of the well-known philosopher and poet – full of zeal and enterprise and having con-templated a voyage on his own account to South America.'[7]

At their first meeting, on 5 September, Darwin was dazzled by FitzRoy, a dark, slight, handsome man hardly older than himself: 'it is no use attempting to praise him as much as I feel inclined to do,' he tells Susan in a long letter, 'for you would not believe me. – One thing I am certain of nothing could be more open and kind than he was to me.' The discouraging letter Darwin had seen at Cambridge, FitzRoy had explained, was sent because he had thought it his duty to state every thing in the worst possible point of view. . . . [He] advises me not to make my mind quite yet: but that seriously, he thinks it will have much more pleasure than pain for me.' The ship is a small one, he tells Susan, with a crew of sixty and five or six officers. Lack of space will be the biggest problem, but FitzRoy has offered to share everything in his cabin. He has a good stock of books, instruments, shotguns and rifles, so there will be much less to buy than Charles had expected. The ship is due to sail on 10 October and 'will probably be out nearly 3 years'. To Henslow he writes in the same vein; 'My dear Sir, Gloria in excelsis is the most moderate beginning I can think of. – Things are more prosperous than I should have thought possible', ending, 'There is indeed a tide in the affairs of men.'[8]

FitzRoy reciprocated Darwin's feelings. In an official letter written that same evening (5 September) to Captain Beaufort, to whom he was responsible, he states: 'I have seen a good deal of Mr. Darwin, today having had nearly two hours conversation in the morning and having since dined with him. I like what I see and hear of him, much, and I now request that you will apply for him to accompany me as a Naturalist. I can and will make him comfortable on board . . . and I will contrive to stow his goods and chattels of all kinds and give him a place for a workshop.'[9]

The decision had nearly gone the other way. A few days later FitzRoy confessed that the excessively discouraging letter he had earlier written about the expedition was a deliberate attempt to throw cold water on the scheme. Although initially keen to have a companion in the form of a naturalist, he had then taken a sudden horror at the prospect of having someone he did not like on board. Moreover, he was a high Tory, and had heard from a relative, a contemporary of Darwin's at Cambridge, that Darwin, though a good man, was a Whig. Yet another objection that had come near to making him reject Darwin, which only emerged much later, was the unpromising shape of Darwin's nose. As an ardent follower of phrenology, FitzRoy had doubted whether anyone with such a nose could possess the energy and determination demanded by the voyage.[10] It is much to Darwin's credit that he survived all these weighty objections.

The next weeks were ones of hectic preparation. In long letters to Susan, in which he asks her to send him this and arrange that, to Fox, describing his exciting prospects, and to Henslow, seeking his advice on what to take, he describes some of his activities.[11] 'I have just returned from spending a long day with Capt Fitz, driving about in his gig and shopping,' he tells Susan. FitzRoy, he says 'is all for Economy excepting on one point, viz. fire arms he recommends me strongly to get a case of pistols like his which cost £60!! and never to go on shore anywhere without loaded ones.' 'For about the first time in my life I find London very pleasant: hurry, bustle and noise are all in union with my feelings,' he tells her a few days later, but that had not prevented him from spending the previous day and a guinea to see the coronation procession of William IV. He had enjoyed the spectacle, 'but there was very little enthusiasm'.

He had learned a lot more about FitzRoy, all very favourable. The *Beagle* had already been surveying in South American waters for no less than four years, between 1826–1830, for the last two under FitzRoy's command. 'I will give you one proof of Fitzroy being a good officer,' he tells Susan, 'all officers are the same as before and ⅔ of his crew, and the eight marines, who went before all offered to come again.' Moreover, Captain King, who in a second surveying ship had been FitzRoy's senior officer on the earlier expedition and with whom Charles had been talking, 'thinks that the expedition will suit me. – Unasked he said Fitzroy's temper was perfect. He sends his own son with him as midshipman.'

From now on Charles habitually refers to FitzRoy as his 'beau ideal of a Captain', ignorant still of his Achilles' heel.

Captain King and a Mr Yarrell, zoologist and bookseller in London, have been especially helpful in advising what equipment to take for keeping and packing his specimens, which were to be given to the British Museum or a similar national collection. 'You have no idea how busy I am all day long,' he tells Henslow, 'and owing to my confidence in Capt Fitzroy I am as happy as a king.' 'The most serious objections,' he tells Fox, 'are the time (3 years) and the smallness of the vessel.'

A few days later Darwin is accompanying FitzRoy on a visit to Devonport to inspect progress. Writing from the port on 14 September, he tells Susan: 'I arrived here yesterday evening after a very prosperous sail of three days from London. . . . The vessel is a very small one; three masted, and carrying 10 guns: but everybody says it is the best sort for our work, and of its class it is an excellent vessel: new but well-tried, and ½ again the usual strength. The want of room is very bad but we must make the best of it.' She was undergoing a major refit at the time, and as Charles later notes in his diary, 'without her masts or bulkheads looked more like a wreck than a vessel commissioned to go round the world'.[12] Continuing his letter to Susan, he reports: 'I like the officers, they are evidently [a] very intelligent, active determined set of young fellows.' As far as the captain is concerned, 'Everybody praises him.' He adds that 'The time of sailing keeps on receding,' and now he hardly expects the ship to sail until 20 October. 'I am extremely glad of this as the number of things I have got to do is quite frightful. . . . I keep on balancing accounts; there are several contras, which I did not expect, but on the other hand the pro's far outweigh them.'[13]

Three days later he is back in London after a 'wonderful quick' journey by coach, and sends a further long bulletin to Susan: 'I came from Plymouth 250 miles in 24 hours and arrived this morning.' He has been in some alarm about his cabin but knows now it is 'a capital one, certainly next best to the Captain's, and remarkably light'. He will share it, he believes, with 'the officer whom I shall like best'. This was a young man of nineteen, John Lort Stokes (1812–85), who was to be mate and assistant surveyor. Their cabin was the one in which the charts would be drawn: 'in the middle is a large table, over which we 2 sleep in hammocks, but for the first two months there will be no drawing to be done. . . . Captain Fitzroy says he will take care that one corner is so fitted that I shall be comfortable in it and shall consider my home – but that also I shall always have the run of his. . . . I don't care whom you now tell for all is fixed and certain . . . this has often been a difficult task and my reason has been the only power that was capable of it: for it is most painful whenever I think of leaving for so long a time so many people whom I love.'[14]

By this time Darwin and FitzRoy, with Admiralty approval, had come to a formal agreement. The arrangement was that Darwin would be

FitzRoy's guest, and therefore unpaid, but, in FitzRoy's words, would be 'at liberty to leave the *Beagle* and retire from the Expedition when he thought proper, and that he should pay a fair share of the expenses of my table'.[15]

From London Darwin went to Cambridge for a couple of days to say goodbye to Henslow, and then on to Shrewsbury for a final visit before returning to Devonport to be ready for departure. On 28 September he writes to Henslow about some fungi found in Wales and tells him, with some satisfaction, 'My father is getting much more reconciled to the idea, as I knew he would as soon as he became accustomed to it.' The date of sailing continues to recede, however, and he is becoming restive. He has just heard the *Beagle* will not be sailing until the end of October and he has another week before he need leave Shrewsbury: 'I begin to be very anxious to start.'[16]

The delay had the advantage, however, of his being able to visit Maer and Woodhouse to say his farewells – visits for which he had thought he would not have time. Already his Maer cousin, Charlotte, now in her mid-thirties and not expecting to see him before his departure, had written to express her warm good wishes. The Wedgwood family, she says, is feeling a heavy load of responsibility for Charles's decision to go on the expedition: 'I cannot help remembering that but for the 1st September your family would have had you safe at home.' Her father and one of her younger brothers, Hensleigh, she reminds him, were the ones who had expressed a strong opinion. Having originally heard it would be a two-year voyage, they are troubled to hear it is to be three: 'that third year makes me tremble much more than I did before for the country parish and parsonage house where I should be very sorry not to see you established.'[17]

Having time on his hands, Charles then rides over to see her and other Wedgwoods at Maer, where he gives a vivid account of what he believes to be in store for him. After it, Hensleigh writes to his fiancée, a daughter of Sir James Mackintosh: 'I wonder Charles is not damped in his ardour. . . . He says that Patagonia where they are going first . . . is the most detestable climate in the world, raining incessantly, and it is one vast peat bog without a tree to be seen. The natives will infallibly eat you if they can get an opportunity. . . . It is very enterprising to go in spite of such discouraging accounts.'[18]

The unexpected addition of a third year also distresses the Mostyn Owens at Woodhouse. Fanny is especially disappointed and vexed that she has missed seeing him, owing to her being away in Devonshire. She sends him a little purse as a keepsake. Sarah too sends him a pin and a lock of hair, and reminds him of his promise to write to her in London after her imminent marriage.[19] One of their brothers, sixteen-year-old Francis, wants to join the *Beagle* as a midshipman, however, and Charles approaches FitzRoy on his behalf; but all places are filled.

During these weeks Darwin has also been corresponding with several of his friends of Edinburgh and Cambridge days. An Edinburgh friend, John Coldstream (now in practice in Leith), to whom Darwin had written enquiring about the construction of a dredge for collecting marine organisms, replied enthusiastically, giving particulars of the dredge and remarking, 'You will be a most useful man in the . . . expedition, if your Zeal in the pursuit of Science and your bodily strength remain the same as they were when I had the pleasure of seeing you here.' Another contemporary at both school and university, Frederick Watkins, now a country parson, writes saying he thinks Darwin is right to go and is sure that some day he will be ranked with famous scientists like de Candolle, Henslow and Linnaeus. An encouraging note comes also from his geology tutor, Adam Sedgwick, who plans to nominate him for membership of the Geological Society.[20]

To at least two of his friends Darwin confides his anxieties. To Fox on 19 September, after assuring him that on the whole he regards the expedition as 'a grand and fortunate opportunity', he writes: 'On the other hand there is very considerable risk to one's life and health, and the leaving for so very long time so many people whom I dearly love, is often times a feeling so painful, that it requires all my resolution to overcome it.' The diminutive size of the *Beagle* hardly inspired confidence: 'As to its safety I hope the Admiralty are the best judges; to a landsman's eye she looks very small'; but, he adds, when he thinks of all the wonderful sights he will see, 'I have moments of glorious enthusiasm.'

A few days later, to Charles Whitley, who had been his close companion in Cambridge after Fox had left, he writes: 'all is finally settled and I have signed away about half a chance of life. – If one lived merely to see how long one could spin out life – I should repent of my choice – As it is I do not.'[21]

III

By the end of September Darwin had acquired a lot of background information about the captain, the crew and the ship.

Robert FitzRoy, (1805–65), he would have learned, came of two well-known titled families. The first FitzRoy was an illegitimate son of Charles II and Barbara Villiers, Duchess of Cleveland; he had been created Duke of Grafton and died in action commanding his own ship against the French. Robert FitzRoy himself, one of the fourth generation after the first duke, was the second son of Lord Charles FitzRoy, who became a general and was subsequently Tory MP for Bury St Edmunds. An uncle, Lord William, was an admiral. Robert's mother, Lady Frances Stewart, was a daughter of the first Marquess of Londonderry and a younger half-sister of Lord Castlereagh, the famous Foreign Minister (from 1810 to his death in 1822).

Born on 5 July 1805, Robert lost his mother when he was five. Educated briefly at Harrow, he maintained the family's naval tradition by entering the Royal Naval College at Portsmouth in February 1818 at the age of twelve and a half. Forenoons were given to mathematics, the afternoons to French and drawing. Much else was crammed into the course – classics, geography and English, with especial emphasis on mechanics, hydrostatics, astronomy and the motions of the tides. FitzRoy excelled and completed the course within two years. Early 1820 he went to sea as a college volunteer (the prefix distinguished them from other volunteers who were seeking commissions by starting as officers' servants). After promotion to midshipman and serving at sea altogether four years, in the Mediterranean and South American waters, FitzRoy took his examination for promotion to lieutenant. In that he distinguished himself not only by winning the gold medal but by gaining 100 per cent of possible marks.

In the autumn of 1824 at the age of nineteen he was appointed a junior lieutenant in HMS *Thetis* and there became a shipmate of another college volunteer, Bartholomew James Sulivan, aged fifteen. The two became fast friends and were to remain shipmates for the next twelve years. Sulivan records that FitzRoy was very kind to him, offering him the use of his cabin and his books. 'He advised me what to read, and encouraged me to turn to advantage what I had learned at College by taking every kind of observation that was useful in navigation.' Sulivan sums up by describing FitzRoy as 'One of the best practical seamen in the service, [with] a fondness with every kind of observation useful in navigating a ship.'[22] For the next four years the *Thetis* was employed in a variety of duties and eventually joined the South American station, based at Montevideo. In August 1828 FitzRoy was transferred to the flagship as flag lieutenant to the admiral. His great opportunity came a couple of months later, when he was still only twenty-three.

For the previous two years two ships, *Adventure* and *Beagle*, had been surveying the coast of South America, from the Río de la Plata south to the Horn, and north again on the west coast another 1500 miles to the island of Chiloé. *Adventure* was under the command of Captain Philip Parker King and the *Beagle* of a Captain Stokes. After a gruelling time in appalling weather, with his crew sick and ship's boats lost, Stokes became so depressed he committed suicide. In October 1828 King returned with his two ships to report the casualty to the admiral at Rio de Janeiro, and the admiral ordered that FitzRoy should be put in command of the *Beagle*. FitzRoy's only requests were that Sulivan and also the master of the flagship* should be transferred to serve under him in the *Beagle*.

In January 1829, in the middle of the Antarctic summer, the two

*A ship's master was a senior warrant officer of considerable seagoing experience. Some were commissioned and reached high rank. James Cook and Bligh of the *Bounty*, both captains RN, are well-known examples.

vessels, together with an auxiliary schooner, left Montevideo to resume the survey of the maze of islands south and west of Tierra del Fuego, of which there were then only old and very inadequate Spanish charts. In this, his first command, FitzRoy excelled himself. By his courage, determination and skill he succeeded in surveying a large and complex district at the western end of the Magellan Straits, and, by both his leadership and his willingness to share the hazards and hardships of his men, earned their confidence and loyalty. Much of the surveying was done from whaleboats – large open boats propelled by sail or oars – two of which the *Beagle* carried, secured on each quarter. After the *Beagle* had been anchored in some sheltered cove, one or both these boats, under the command of FitzRoy or the master, would set out with tents and ample provisions for several weeks' surveying. Come the next Antarctic winter, the *Beagle* and the *Adventure*, which had been surveying independently in different areas, rendezvoused at a port in the island of Chiloé. There they drew their charts, rested the crews and prepared for a second cruise to the far south.

This second cruise, starting in mid-November 1829, began well enough. Once again the *Beagle* was anchored in a convenient channel and the two whaleboats set out on independent expeditions due to last one month. The local Indians, known as Fuegians, lived a life of extreme poverty and hardship, with virtually no clothes and few possessions apart from canoes and spears, and were scattered in sparse groups throughout the archipelago. Relations between them and the British sailors varied from fairly friendly to hostile. A constant problem for the sailors was the Fuegians' inveterate habit of stealing anything they could lay hands on – at which they were unbelievably adept. Now, in early February 1830, the Fuegians managed to steal one of the whaleboats. FitzRoy in the other set out immediately to recover it, but after some weeks of searching, during which he found pieces of clothing and rigging, he had to admit defeat. During the hunt they had taken two women and three children hostage, but the women slipped away overnight and FitzRoy found himself in possession of the three Fuegian children. Two were glad to be restored to their families, but one, a girl of about nine, seemed more than happy to remain. A cheerful, friendly child, she was popular with the crew and became the ship's pet. She was named Fuegia Basket (after a basket-like canoe constructed by the sailors when their whaleboat was stolen).

Fuegia's presence encouraged FitzRoy in a scheme he had been mulling over. It would be a great advantage, he thought, if some of the Fuegians could be taught English and the ways of civilisation and then returned to their native islands, where they could provide friendly contact with such other ships as might in future sail in those parts. The plan decided upon, FitzRoy managed to persuade three older Fuegians to accompany him, and, the surveying season over, the four sailed with him in the *Beagle* to his rendezvous with Captain King and the *Adventure* in Rio de Janeiro the following June.

Leaving for home in August 1830, FitzRoy, with Captain King's support, sought Admiralty authority to land the Fuegians in England and arrange for their education at his own expense, with a view to returning them to their native haunts a couple of years later.* Approval was granted in a letter stating that the Lords Commissioners of the Admiralty 'will not interfere with Commander FitzRoy's personal superintendence of, or benevolent intentions towards these four people, but will afford him any facilities towards maintaining and educating them in England, and will give them a passage home again.[23]

Landed at Plymouth, the four Fuegians, were vaccinated but one of them soon caught smallpox and died. The remaining three, comprising Fuegia herself, a boy of about fourteen named Jemmy Button and a man in his mid-twenties known as York Minster, were conveyed to London in the interior of a coach, met there by FitzRoy and taken to stay with a clergyman in Wandsworth, where they attended school. The aim was to teach them English, the plainer truths of Christianity and various practical skills. The two youngsters made good progress but York Minster was surly and uncooperative. During the summer of 1831 FitzRoy was summoned to show them to the King and Queen, who were duly appreciative.

Meanwhile, FitzRoy was concerned about arrangements for the Fuegians' return and was dismayed to learn that the Admiralty had decided not to continue the South American survey. Accordingly FitzRoy, ever generous with his own money, chartered a private vessel to take them and planned to accompany them himself. Before he set out, however, his influential relatives at Westminster prevailed on the Admiralty to honour its undertaking to give the Fuegians a passage home again. The upshot was that at the end of June 1831 the *Beagle* was recommissioned to undertake a second voyage to South American waters and, Captain King having rendered a glowing report on FitzRoy's earlier performance, FitzRoy was appointed to the command. Thus began one of the most famous voyages in British history.

IV

In addition to the further survey of the southern coasts of South America, made desirable by the rapidly increasing use of those waters by British whalers and sealers and by merchant ships returning eastabout from Australia, FitzRoy was charged with another task: to determine more accurately than before the longitude of a large number of oceanic islands as well as of the continents. This entailed carrying out a series of observations of longitude right round the world. That was the reason for the decision that, after completing her survey of the west coast of South

---

*FitzRoy's substantive rank at this time was commander. He was promoted post-captain in May 1835, during the fourth year of the *Beagle*'s second voyage.

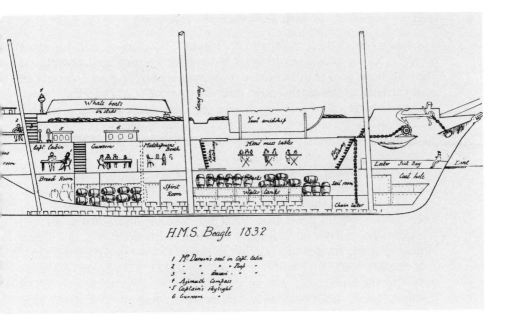

H.M.S. Beagle 1832

1 Mr Darwin's seat in Capt. cabin
2 "   "   "   " Poop "
3 "   "   " drawers "   "
4 Azimuth Compass
5 Captain's skylight
6 Gunroom "

Section of HMS *Beagle* in 1832

America, the *Beagle* should return by the much longer route, westabout across the Pacific and Indian oceans, round the Cape of Good Hope and so home.

The *Beagle* herself, launched at Woolwich in 1820, was unquestionably very small, no more than 90 feet long and about 235 tons. She had the advantage of being easily manoeuvrable in confined waters and not too difficult for oarsmen in whaleboats, to tow in and out of harbour when necessary. A square-rigged ship, she was not very stable and, according to Sulivan, required 'careful handling and management of sail'. During her first voyage south under FitzRoy she had met a severe gale and nearly capsized. That was a valuable lesson for the captain, who thereafter made an intensive study of the weather so as to forecast dangerous conditions. From those beginnings he was to become one of the founders of the science of meteorology.

Before her second voyage the *Beagle* underwent a drastic refit, described by FitzRoy as follows: 'I resolved to spare neither expense nor trouble in making our little Expedition as complete . . . as my means and exertion would allow, when supported by the considerate and satisfactory arrangements of the Admiralty. . . . I obtained permission to have the upper deck raised considerably, which afterwards proved to be of the greatest advantage to her as a sea boat besides adding so materially to the comfort of all on board. While in dock, a sheathing of two-inch fir plank was nailed on the vessel's bottom, over which was a coating of felt, and then new copper.' That added about 15 tons to her displacement. She was equipped with a number of new inventions, including lightning conductors on all three masts and the bowsprit. 'Our ropes, sails and spars were the best that could be procured; and to complete our excellent outfit, six superior boats (two of them private property) were built expressly for us and so contrived and stowed that they could all be carried in any weather.' Stores included a large quantity of lemon juice and other antiscorbutics, preserved meat, vegetables and soup, and medical supplies. There were also a great many instruments and books on board. It is evident that FitzRoy himself bore a significant proportion of the expense.

When eventually the *Beagle* sailed there were seventy-four men and youths aboard, of whom most were younger even than FitzRoy. Wickham, an older man of thirty-three, was first lieutenant; Sulivan still only twenty-one, second lieutenant; Chaffers, possibly about thirty, master; McCormick, thirty-one, surgeon; Rowlett, thirty-four and the oldest officer, purser; Stokes (no relation of the ill-fated captain of the same name), nineteen, assistant surveyor; Bynoe, twenty-eight, assistant surgeon; and a mate and assistant mate. The two midshipmen included Captain King's son, Philip, aged fourteen and Mellersh, probably a little older. One volunteer, Musters, was not yet thirteen. There were also a master's assistant, a clerk, a carpenter, a sailmaker, a ropemaker and an armourer. Some thirty seamen and a handful of cooks and stewards made up the complement, together with a sergeant and seven marines whose duties were disciplinary.

Added to this regular crew were a number of supernumeraries. They included an artist, Augustus Earle, an instrument maker (paid for by FitzRoy), servants for FitzRoy and Darwin (also paid for privately), the three Fuegians and a missionary to be settled ashore to help civilise the local inhabitants. Named Richard Matthews, he was only twenty. Last but not least among the supernumeraries was Charles Darwin, naturalist and captain's companion, now aged twenty-two.

The practice of carrying a naturalist on board a naval surveying ship was well established. On Cook's first voyage of 1768–1771 to observe the transit of Venus in Tahiti, he had aboard Joseph Banks and Daniel Carol Solander, a pupil of Linnaeus. Thereafter officers aboard survey ships were usually instructed to collect specimens of rocks, plants and animals from distant parts as one of their duties. FitzRoy himself on his first voyage to the south had regretted not having had a geologist aboard, since he suspected there might be valuable minerals in the local rocks.

As it happens, no explicit instructions to collect were given to the officers of the *Beagle* on her second voyage, but several of them did so. As a rule the ship's surgeon was expected to take the lead, and Darwin's presence as official naturalist, and in the captain's confidence, caused McCormick to take umbrage and leave the ship at Rio de Janeiro. No one was sorry to see him go. Even before sailing Darwin had dubbed him a pompous ass. Thereafter Bynoe filled the role of surgeon to everyone's satisfaction and did a lot of collecting as well.

V

In a letter to Darwin of 23 September FitzRoy had made the rather unexpected statement that 'there will be plenty of room for books'; and in his *Narrative*, written later, he writes: 'Considering the limited disposal space in so very small a ship, we contrived to carry more instruments and books than one would really suppose could be stowed away in dry secure places.'[24] The tally was indeed impressive.

In addition to the usual surveying instruments and sextants, he carried 'in a part of my own cabin' no less than twenty-two chronometers. The purpose of these was to be as certain as was humanly possible that he always had an absolutely accurate reading of Greenwich Mean Time available, a requirement indispensable for measuring longitude, which was one of his main tasks.

The size of the library aboard was no less surprising. A conservative estimate puts the number at 245 volumes, ranging in size from pamphlets to multi-volume works such as the *Encyclopaedia Britannica*. The lot would take up not less than 46 linear feet of shelf space. FitzRoy encouraged Darwin to bring any books he felt he would need, even if it meant duplicating what was there already. The combined library was kept in the cabin occupied by Darwin and Stokes and was in the charge of the captain's clerk. All books could be borrowed by the officers 'without reserve' but under strict regulations.[25]

The library included all standard works of travel and natural history, many of which were in French and some in Spanish, as well as books of more general interest. Among the latter we find the first volume of James Mackintosh's *History of England*, which had just been published. FitzRoy was a scholar and, in Darwin's words when writing to Whitley, 'very scientific and seems inclined to assist me to the utmost extent in my line'.[26]

There were two works in Darwin's own collection that were especially valued by him. One comprised the first two volumes in English translation of Humboldt's *Travels*, given him by Henslow to wish him well. The other, given him by FitzRoy, was the first volume of Lyell's *Principles of Geology*, published the previous year. Since both the work and its author were to play a decisive part in Darwin's future life, it is useful to introduce them at this point, even though Darwin did not meet Lyell until after the *Beagle*'s return.

In 1831 Charles Lyell (1797–1875) was a young anglified Scot who had been educated at Oxford and the Inns of Court in London, and had practised briefly as a barrister in the West Country. From childhood onwards, however, his first love had been natural history, especially geology; he had published his first paper on the subject in 1825, the same year he had been called to the Bar. For a couple of years he had mixed geology and law, but by the end of 1827 he had cut his legal cables and had decided to risk a career in science, aided admittedly by a modest private income. Already, while on circuit, he had 'devoured Lamarck. . . . But tho' I admire his flights, and feel none of the *odium theologicum* which some modern writers have visited him with, I confess I read him rather as I hear an advocate on the wrong side, to know what can be made of the case in good hands. I am glad he has been courageous enough and logical enough to admit that his argument . . . if worth anything, would prove that men may have come from Ourang-Outan.'[27] Many years later that unwelcome conclusion was still to prove a sticking-point and a bone of contention between him and Charles Darwin, by then a close friend and protégé.

No sooner had Lyell forsaken law than he was planning to write an ambitious book. By December 1829, having completed a nine-month geologising tour of France and Italy, he had made sufficient progress to sign a contract with the publisher, John Murray, to produce a two-volume work. He had early espoused the uniformitarian view of geological history advanced the previous century by his fellow Scot, James Hutton (1726–97), which holds that the changes in the earth's crust that have unquestionably occurred during its history are to be understood as the consequences of the same aqueous and igneous processes as are currently to be observed. That was the main thesis of his work, together with a clear statement that the age of the earth is immeasurably greater than the 4000 years calculated from an examination of the Book of Genesis by the theologians. 'I enjoy the work much as the excitement is great,' he tells his sister in February 1830; while a geologist friend predicts that the book 'will excite a sensation'.

By August that year the first volume was out and, as anticipated, it proved a bombshell. Well written and well argued, it marshalled the evidence in favour of Hutton's thesis and enthused all his supporters. By November, however, the opposition had exploded in wrath. Clinging tenaciously to the brief biblical timetable, their explanations of the geological record required them to postulate one or more gigantic happenings. Some of them, the Diluvialists, attributed all change either solely to Noah's Great Flood or else to a succession of such cataclysms. Others, the Vulcanists, invoked massive earthquakes and volcanic eruptions. Throughout the 1830s, when Lyell's second and third volumes were being published and copies reached Darwin aboard the *Beagle*, the heated debate continued. Lyell was confident of success, even though his thesis was being assaulted by most of the leading geologists of France and Germany as well as of Britain. Despite that, as early as February 1832 he was able to record that 'every day the [Royal Navy] hydrographers are coming to me for instructions. I have just drawn up some for Captain FitzRoy, who has my book, and is surveying in South America.'[28]

In view of the horror with which FitzRoy would later greet the ideas that Lyell's thesis was to engender in Darwin's mind, it is ironic that the copy of Lyell's first volume that Darwin took with him in the *Beagle* should have been given him by none other than FitzRoy himself. The fair-minded Henslow, although a confirmed catastrophist, also recommended Darwin to obtain and study the work, but warned him 'on no account to accept the views therein advocated'.[29]

VI

Having said all his farewells to family and friends in Shropshire, Darwin arrived back in London in early October, expecting to leave for Devonport a fortnight later and to be on the high seas by the end of the month. Little did he then think that a full two months after that he would still be kicking his heels in Devonport. There was to be delay after delay, initially because the *Beagle* was not ready, later because of weeks of adverse weather. The uncertainty was to prove extremely taxing.

While in London he arranged with his father's bank that they would always honour his drafts, and with Henslow that all the specimens he sent back could be stored safely in Cambridge under his watchful eye. The luggage he wants to take, he confides to FitzRoy, is 'frightfully bulky' and he is afraid much of it may have to be left behind. Sailing was postponed another week, and eventually he left for Devonport by coach on 24 October, having sent his heavy goods by steamer.

On arrival in Devonport, he found all was bustle and confusion. Going on board, he was impressed by the splendour of the fittings: 'our cabins are fitted most luxuriously with nothing except mahogany,' he tells Henslow; but he is troubled afresh by how small his own 'private corner' looks. Now he hears that the *Beagle* is not expected to sail until 20 November. 'I only wish they were a little faster,' he comments.[30]

From the time he arrived in Devonport Darwin kept a diary of his daily doings until the day of the ship's return. Usually he wrote it up each evening; but sometimes when he was unusually busy entries were retrospective. From time to time he would send instalments back to Shrewsbury, both as a way of informing the family of his activities and also for safekeeping.[31]

Darwin contrived to fill these weeks by regular long walks, usually with one or two of the ship's officers, by helping Stokes to check instruments and, when at last the ship was ready, installing his possessions in the confined space available.

Soon after arrival he was invited to dine with the gunroom officers, who regaled him with lurid stories of the initiation ceremonies meted out to novices on first crossing the Equator. Subsequently he describes the officers to Henslow as 'a fine set of fellows, but rather rough'.[32] Friendships developed steadily. The three he mentions most frequently as his walking companions are his cabin-mate, Stokes, the assistant surgeon, Bynoe, and the young midshipman, King. Wickham and Sulivan, first and second lieutenants, were responsible for getting stores aboard and making the ship ready for sailing, and consequently were extremely busy, though Sulivan sometimes accompanied him. In due course Darwin came to have great admiration for both these men. He saw a certain amount of FitzRoy, who, he found, was 'as perfect as nature can make him', dined with the admiral and was fascinated by the novelty of naval conversation; and on 12 November, with everything shipshape at last, he went aboard, where 'For the first time [he] felt a fine naval fervour'.[33]

Only in a casual entry in his diary for 13 November is there any reference to the Fuegians: they had arrived that day by steam packet in the charge of their schoolmaster and accompanied by the missionary. Not until he saw them in their natural habitat is there any sign of Darwin's fascination with peoples living in very primitive conditions.

On the following day, Admiralty instructions arrived; these, Darwin notes, were 'most perfectly satisfactory, indeed exactly what Cap. Fitz. himself wished. – The orders merely contain a rough outline. – There could not be a greater compliment paid to Cap. Fitzroy.[34] The primary object was to survey the coast of South America south of the estuary of the River Plate, to further the survey of the complex area around Tierra del Fuego and Cape Horn, and to work up the west coast of the continent as far north as possible. It was not an inviting coast, but 'the more hopeless and forbidding any long line of coast may be, the more precious becomes the discovery of a port which affords safe anchorage and wholesome refreshment'.[35] Other objects were to visit the Galapagos Islands before returning across the Pacific to complete the global observations of longitude.

A few days later Darwin reports the situation to Henslow. After giving an outline of the plans, he adds, 'I grieve to say time is unlimited, but yet I hope we shall not exceed the 4 years.' At first the voyage was to last two years, next three, and now it was to be at least four and perhaps longer. No wonder in his letter to Fox, after extolling the expedition as 'one of the grandest voyages that has almost ever been sent out', he continues, 'Time . . . is the only serious inconvenience. – Why, I shall be an old man by the time of our return.' Departure has been delayed yet again: 'Now we do not sail until the 5th of next month.'[36]

During the ensuing interval a letter arrived from Fanny Mostyn Owen describing her sister Sarah's wedding festivities, regretting his absence and fervently wishing him a safe return. Another that reached him was a long one from Henslow acting the part of Polonius. After references to the 'noble expedition' from which he hopes his young protégé will 'reap an abundant harvest of future satisfaction', he proceeds: 'If I may say so, one of your foibles is to take offence at rudeness of manners and anything bordering on ungentlemanlike behaviour, and I have observed such conduct often wound your feelings far more deeply than you ought to allow it . . . and I therefore exhort you most sincerely and affectionately never to feel offended at any of the coarse and vulgar behaviour you will infallibly be subjected to among your comrades.' Such behaviour springs, he believes, from 'mal-education and early contamination' and often hides 'real and stirling worth'. 'Take St. James's advice,' Henslow continues, 'and bridle your tongue when it burns with some merited rebuke.' Although it is no surprise that Henslow should find Darwin unduly sensitive, the advice he offers is unexpected, since it implies that at this time Darwin was given to hasty retorts. Darwin's reply is characteristically chastened: 'I am very much obliged for your last kind and affectionate letter. – I always like advice from you. . . . Recollect . . . that I am a sort of protégé of yours, and that it is your bounden duty to lecture me.'[37]

By 19 November, he notes with some relief, 'I have now a regular employment every morning taking and comparing the difference in the Barometers.'[38] He had had some good natural history walks ashore, had done a little geologising in the granite of Dartmoor, and had gossiped with a Captain Vidal, who had spent eight years surveying the African coast, during which time he had 'buried 30 young officers'. Later Captain King had impressed upon him the enormous importance of meteorology. Two days later, the paint at last dry, he carried all his books and instruments aboard but 'returned in a panic on the old subject want of room'. FitzRoy, however, solved all problems: he 'is such an effectual and good natured contriver that the very drawers enlarge on his appearance.'

On 23 November, the *Beagle* leaves the dockside, every cubic inch filled with stores and equipment including all of Darwin's, and anchors a mile out in the harbour ready for departure. Suddenly the ship comes alive as the crew sets and then furls the sails: Darwin is excited.

On Friday 2 December, his brother Erasmus arrives to say farewell. Charles enjoys his company, but is incessantly busy on last-minute chores: 'how I long for Monday even sea-sickness [which he dreads] must be better than this wearisome anxiety,' he notes in his diary. Monday the 5th at last arrives, but a heavy gale from the south forbids sailing. Darwin returns to his lodgings 'very disconsolate'. Four days pass with the gale persisting; but on the 10th the weather looks promising and by 10.00 am they are away. Erasmus stayed on board 'till we doubled the breakwater; where he left us and my misery began'. For the next twenty-four hours the ship pitched and tossed in rough seas: 'I suffered most dreadfully; such a night I never passed, on every side nothing but misery.' By noon next day they were back in harbour, foiled by the gale; and Darwin got ashore to have a good walk with the twelve-year-old volunteer, Musters – 'which considerably revived us'. For the following days 'boisterous weather' continued: 'I look forward to sea-sickness with utter dismay,' he notes.

'The ship is full of grumblers and growlers', himself not the least, he admits. 'The sailors declare there is somebody on shore keeping a black cat under a tub', which, it appears, is guaranteed to keep a ship in harbour.[39]

During the first abortive attempt to get away, an episode occurred which was to live for long in family memory. Darwin, appallingly sick, was having difficulty with his hammock and FitzRoy very kindly came and adjusted it for him. This Darwin recounted in a letter to one of his sisters (now lost), to which Caroline replied on 20 December: 'Your account of the Captain was quite sublime . . . and Papa's eyes were full of tears when he thought first of your miserable night and then of your good natured Captain in all the confusion paying you a visit and arranging your hammock.'[40] This letter, to which Catherine and Susan added paragraphs, was posted later and directed to Rio de Janeiro, where Charles received it three months later. It was the first of the monthly bulletins his sisters had undertaken to send him during the voyage and which they were to maintain to the end.

A further ten days were spent storm-bound in harbour. Darwin was contemplating his future. 'I am often afraid I shall be quite overwhelmed with the numbers of subjects which I ought to take into hand,' he enters in his diary.[41] 'It is difficult to mark out any plan and without method on ship-board I am sure little will be done. – The principal objects are 1st, collecting observing and reading in all branches of Natural history that I possibly can manage. Observations in Meteorology. – French and Spanish, Mathematics, and a little Classics, perhaps not more than Greek Testament on Sundays. I hope generally to have some one English book in hand for my amusement. . . . If I have not energy enough to make myself steadily industrious during the voyage, how great and uncommon an opportunity of improving myself shall I throw away. – May this never for one moment escape my mind, and then perhaps I may have the same opportunity of drilling my mind that I threw away whilst at Cambridge.' How loud the echoes, here, of his sisters' oft-repeated improving words.

At length, on 21 December dawn broke with a steady breeze from the north-east. Accordingly the *Beagle* set sail again; but this time everything went wrong. On leaving harbour at low spring tide the ship struck a rock, and this delayed her for a time. Next morning the wind was again round to the south-west and blowing a gale, Darwin was exceedingly sick, and when the ship returned once more to harbour the anchor became fouled. It was little comfort that many other vessels that had left with them also had to return. Never has high adventure begun with such repeated anticlimax.

Christmas was a shambles. 'The whole [day]', Darwin notes in his diary, 'has been given up to revelry, at present there is not a sober man in the ship: King is obliged to perform duty of sentry. . . . Wherever they may be, [the men] claim Christmas day for themselves, and this they exclusively give up to drunkenness.' Next day, the weather was excellent for sailing, but the ship, 'in a state of anarchy', was confined to harbour. 'It is an unfortunate beginning,' Darwin notes, 'being obliged so early to punish some of our best men.' Some were flogged, others had to sit 'for eight or nine hours in heavy chains'.[42]

A couple of days later, Darwin's thoughts were still 'most unpleasantly occupied with the flogging.' By then, however, the *Beagle* was at last making good progress to the south. The 27th was a beautiful day with 'the long wished for E. wind'. Anchor was weighed and by early afternoon 'with every sail filled by a light breeze we scudded away at the rate of 7 or 8 knots an hour'.[43] At long last the voyage had begun.

VII

Let us return briefly to consider Darwin's state of mind and health during these months of eager anticipation and repeated frustrating delay. When on 23 September Caroline Wedgwood, not expecting to see her cousin before he sailed, wrote to him from Maer, she expressed the hope that, now he had resolved to go, there would be no delay so that 'there may not be time for all the objections to rise up which they always do with much more than their real weight when there is nothing more for them to do but to torment one.' Her predictions proved, however, all too accurate. The two months Darwin spent in Devonport were, we now know from his *Autobiography*, 'the most miserable [he] ever spent . . . out of spirits at the thought of leaving all my family and friends for so long . . . [and] troubled with palpitations and pain above the heart and . . . convinced that [he] had heart disease'.[44] Neither in the diary nor in any surviving letter is there any hint of this haunting fear of a diseased heart. Evidently it was too frightening to confide even to Fox. His diary, it must be remembered, would be read by others.

The only reference to bodily symptoms during these months is a letter to his sister Susan, written only days after receiving the invitation to join the expedition, reporting that his 'hands are not quite well', which probably refers to eczema, and enquiring of his father whether 'there would be any objection to [his] taking Arsenic for a little time'.[45] No reply is on record and no further reference.

References to wearisome anxiety are frequent, however, and also many signs of misgivings about the decision to go, coupled with assertions that he was right to do so. He assures Henslow that 'Jenyns did very wisely in not coming; that is judging from my own feelings, for I am sure if I had left College some few years, or been those years older, I *never* could have endured it.'[46] After his first night at sea, during which he had 'suffered most dreadfully', he assures himself, 'I am decided I did right to accept the offer; but yet I think it doubtful how far it will add to the happiness of one's life.' Three days after sailing, when he was 'wretchedly out of spirits

HMS *Beagle* in Sydney Harbour, 1841

and very sick', his doubts about the wisdom of his decision were at their height: 'I often said before starting, that I had no doubt I should frequently repent of the whole undertaking, little did I think with what fervour I should do so. – I can scarcely conceive any more miserable state, than when such dark and gloomy thoughts are haunting the mind as have to-day pursued me.'[47]

A week later the *Beagle* was in sunnier climes. 'The day has been beautiful,' he notes in his diary, 'and I am so much better that I am able to enjoy it.'[48] Very soon he was to be absorbed by the excitement of new scenes and kept busy with a huge range of scientific observations. Thenceforward the voyage was to yield him the richest of rewards and the decision, stuck to in the face of such suffering and anxiety, was to be proved abundantly right.

EIGHT

Opportunity seized
1832–1834

I

In the event, the voyage lasted for four years and nine months and was a triumphant success.[1] The surveys planned were completed and the Fuegians restored to their native haunts, observations of longitude were made and checked at strategic points around the world, specimens of natural history – geological, botanical and zoological – collected, labelled and dispatched, and the young collector himself, reading intensively and reflecting on his observations and findings, was given time and opportunity to mature into the seasoned scientist he became. Both the captain and the naturalist were welcomed home with the greatest enthusiasm by those who had been kept informed of their manifold doings. In their respective careers each had taken a gigantic step forward.

The *Beagle* was in South American waters for all but the first two and the last thirteen months of the voyage. Outward bound, their first port of call was to be Tenerife, Darwin's dream island, but quarantine delays (due to cholera in England) led FitzRoy to depart without landing, to Darwin's manifest disappointment. Thence they sailed to Santiago in the Cape Verde Islands, where they remained for three weeks. FitzRoy was busy making observations on longitude and magnetism, while Darwin spent most days ashore taking long walks, riding to distant points – and revelling in the novelties of nature everywhere about him. After his first day a long entry in his diary ends: 'I returned to the shore treading on Volcanic rocks, hearing the notes of unknown birds, and seeing new insects fluttering about still newer flowers. – It has been for me a glorious day, like giving to a blind man eyes, – he is overwhelmed with what he sees and cannot justly comprehend it. – Such are my feelings, and such may they remain.'[2] Remain they did.

From the Cape Verdes they crossed the Atlantic to the port of Bahia, later renamed Salvador, on the north-east coast of Brazil, reached at the end of February 1832. For the next six months the *Beagle* was surveying the coasts of Brazil and Uruguay, from Bahia south to the estuarine expanses of the Río de la Plata, a distance of some 2000 miles.

After three weeks refitting in Montevideo during August, when FitzRoy and the crew were caught up in a local revolution, the *Beagle* left on a ten-week surveying cruise 400 miles south as far as Bahía Blanca, and then back to Montevideo. It was on this cruise that Darwin found the fossils of a gigantic unknown animal, which, when examined back in England, would create a stir.

Thereafter the *Beagle*'s movements were dictated by the seasons. Weather around Cape Horn was so atrocious, even in the better months, that it was prudent to confine surveying to the three months of the southern summer, December, January and February. The rest of the year was spent recovering from the rigours of these long and difficult surveys in remote areas, drawing charts of the areas surveyed, surveying those parts of the 1500 miles of coast between the estuary of the Río de la Plata and Cape Horn that lie in less taxing latitudes, and then refitting and replenishing the vessel in preparation for the next season in the south.

During the many months when the *Beagle* was either in port or planning soon to return, Darwin was ashore. At times he stayed in a place convenient for his collecting; at others he made ambitious excursions on horseback into the interior lasting several weeks, in the company of a guide. No opportunity for exploring the geology of the country or adding to his collections was lost. No one could have seized more firmly than he 'this great and uncommon opportunity'.

The summers of 1832–3 and 1833–4 were both spent around Tierra del Fuego and Cape Horn, followed in March each year by four weeks in the Falkland Islands recovering from their expeditions and doing local surveys. From April to November 1833 the *Beagle* was either in a Uruguayan port (Montevideo or Maldonado) or else surveying the coast further south. During the same months of 1834 she at first surveyed the southernmost stretches of the Patagonian coast and rivers and then threaded her way through the Straits of Magellan to the west coast. Thence, sailing north, she reached Valparaiso at the end of July and spent the next three months there.

The third southern summer, 1834–5, was again spent in southern latitudes, this time for ten weeks surveying the unknown and treacherous channels among the maze of islands off the southern stretches of the coast of Chile. During February and early March they moved further north, to Valdivia and Concepción, where they experienced and later witnessed the consequences of a severe earthquake. By early March 1835 they were back in Valparaiso to rest, draw charts and refit. The *Beagle*'s long stays in port gave Darwin opportunity for his ambitious rides and extensive exploration in the Andes.

During May and June the *Beagle* was surveying north of Valparaiso and in July sailed 1600 miles further north to Callao, the port of Lima in Peru; there she spent six weeks refitting and then was delayed, to Darwin's annoyance, by FitzRoy's interest in some old charts and papers he found in Lima. Eventually, on 7 September 1835, after three and a half years in South American waters, the *Beagle*, with her homesick crew, left the continent heading north-west to survey the Galapagos Islands before starting on the year-long journey home. During the five weeks in the islands Darwin, as usual, spent as much time as possible ashore. After brief visits to three of the islands, he stayed nine days on another, camping with a party from the ship.

From the Galapagos a twenty-five-day sail across the Pacific brought them to Tahiti, where FitzRoy had been given the unenviable task of exacting a large fine from the ruler, a fine which had been inflicted on the islanders for the murder of the master and mate of a British ship. From Tahiti they sailed west to New Zealand and thence to Sydney, which they reached in the New Year of 1836: in each place they spent ten days replenishing ship and taking observations of longitude and magnetism. Thereafter the same routine was followed at a succession of stopping places on their voyage west: Tasmania, Western Australia, Keeling Island, Mauritius, Cape Town (at the end of May), St Helena, Ascension Island and then, in early August, back to Bahia, their first port of call in South America, to complete their circle of observations. There were two more calls, the first at Santiago in the Cape Verde Islands where, over four years earlier, Darwin had enthused about the wonders of a tropical island and had first exercised his skills as a field geologist, and next at the Azores, before the *Beagle*, with her proud and weary crew, finally reached Falmouth on 2 October, 1836.

II

The *Beagle* under the command of FitzRoy was a remarkably efficient and happy ship. A strict disciplinarian, FitzRoy showed no favouritism, delegated responsibility to the excellent officers he had selected and studied the welfare of his men; and he was a splendid seaman and navigator. Unfortunately, he was also intensely sensitive to criticism, and, contrary to what Darwin had heard before sailing, on occasion could become violently angry or else deeply depressed. As a rule he recovered fast, with his recovery greatly helped by the remarkably understanding way in which his officers behaved during his bad spells. Serious though some of these episodes were, they were infrequent and never marred the morale of the crew or the success of the voyage.

Survey ships were not notable for being smart; but the *Beagle* was an exception. On entering the majestic harbour at Rio de Janeiro in early April 1832, FitzRoy took the opportunity to display the ship's capabilities in front of the many warships anchored there. Darwin was thrilled and, in the midst of a very long letter home, described the event: 'We came in first rate style, alongside the Admiral's ship, and we, to their astonishment, took in every inch of canvas and then immediately set it again: A sounding ship doing such a perfect manoeuvre with such certainty and rapidity, is an event hitherto unknown . . . – It is a great satisfaction to know that we are in such beautiful order and discipline.' Darwin himself took part in the manoeuvre, as we learn from an account (written much later) by his young friend, Philip King: 'Though Mr Darwin knew little or nothing of nautical matters he one day volunteered his services to the First Lieutenant. [On first entering Rio] it was decided to make a display of smartness in shortening sail before the numerous Men-of-War at the anchorage. . . . Mr Darwin was told off to hold to a main-royal sheet in each hand and a top-mast studding-tack in his teeth. At the order "Shorten sail" he was to let go and clap on to any rope he saw was short-handed – this he did and enjoyed the fun of it, often afterwards remarking "the feat could not have been performed without him".'[3]

When a few months later the ship was assailed by the sudden and vicious gales of southern latitudes, the certainty and rapidity of the sail drill was to prove of the greatest practical value. Its exhibition in Rio harbour was no doubt only one of the ways in which FitzRoy sought to build his crew's morale.

Already there had been other occasions for fun aboard the *Beagle*. In mid-February she had crossed the Equator and the time-hallowed ceremonies had been observed. 'In the evening . . . the officer on watch reported a boat ahead . . . and we heaved to in order to converse with Mr Neptune [who] in the morning would pay us a visit.' Next day, Darwin notes, 'We have crossed the Equator, and I have undergone the disagreeable operation of being shaved. About 9 o'clock this morning we poor "griffins", two and thirty in number, were put altogether on the lower deck [which was] dark and very hot. – presently four of Neptune's constables came to us, and one by one led us up on deck. – I was the first and escaped easily: I nevertheless found this watery ordeal sufficiently disagreeable. – Before coming up the constable blindfolded me and thus led along, buckets of water were thundered all around; I was then placed on a plank, which could easily be tilted up into a large bath of water. – They then lathered my face and mouth with pitch and paint, and scraped some of it off with a piece of roughened iron hoop. – a signal being given I was tilted head over heels into the water, where two men received and ducked me. – at last, glad enough, I escaped. – most of the others were treated much worse.' Later FitzRoy reflected, 'though many condemn it as an absurd and dangerous piece of folly, it has also many advocates. Perhaps it is one of those amusements, of which the omission might be regretted. Its effects on the minds of those engaged in preparing for its memories, who enjoy it at the time, and talk of it long afterwards, cannot easily be judged of without being an eye-witness.'[4]

Six weeks later, on passage from Bahia to Rio, the first of April had also been celebrated in customary style: 'at midnight nearly all the watch was called up in their shirts; Carpenters for a leak: quarter masters that a mast was sprung, – midshipmen to reef top-sails. . . . The hook was much too easily baited for me. . . . Sulivan cried out, "Darwin, did you ever see a Grampus. . . ." I accordingly rushed out in a transport of Enthusiasm, and was received by a roar of laughter from the whole watch.'[5]

Since so much of the voyage was spent on the tedious and repetitive operations of sounding channels and taking cross-bearings of every island and other coastal feature, opportunities for relaxation and amusement were doubly welcome. On occasions when the *Beagle* was in port with other ships, FitzRoy organised regattas. When in the vicinity of ocean rocks or tidal estuaries the crew sometimes made a great haul of fish or gathered a quantity of sea birds or their eggs. In addition to the sport, these provided a valuable change of diet. Similarly, when in harbour Darwin and his friends often went on shooting expeditions, returning on occasion with spectacular success.

The other side of the coin was danger and death. While camping in the vicinity of Rio three of the crew contracted malignant malaria and died. One was an excellent seaman renowned for his great strength and courage, a second was one of the most promising of the boys, and the third was 'poor little Musters', the volunteer hardly yet into his teens. A fourth loss occurred a year later in the Falklands when the captain's clerk was drowned trying to retrieve a bird he had shot from a densely seaweeded sea;[6] and a fifth occurred about the same time when a marine fell overboard from a small vessel he was temporarily crewing.

III

On first arriving at Bahia on 28 February 1832, Darwin had immediately gone ashore to visit the tropical forest close by. Returning to the ship he recorded his rapture. 'The delight one experiences in such times bewilders the mind. – If the eye attempts to follow the flight of a gaudy butterfly, it is arrested by some strange tree or fruit; if watching an insect one forgets it in the stranger flower it is crawling over. – If turning to admire the splendour of the scenery, the individual character of the foreground fixes the attention. The mind is a chaos of delight, out of which a world of future and more quiet pleasure will arise.'[7]

Several days were spent in this tropical paradise, and raptures added to former raptures. One long day was spent with King. 'During the walk I was chiefly employed in collecting numberless small beetles and in geologising. – King shot some pretty birds and I a most beautiful large lizard. – It is a new and pleasant thing for me to be conscious that naturalising is doing my duty, and that if I neglected that duty I should at same time neglect what has for some years given me so much pleasure.'[8] On one of these walks he pricked his knee and it went septic. Swollen and 'exceedingly painful', it confined him to his hammock for a week, to his intense frustration.

After eighteen days in Bahia and another eighteen sailing south, during which he was busy arranging his collections and studying, the *Beagle* arrived in Rio de Janeiro. There, for the first time since leaving England, he experienced 'the ecstacies of opening letters'.[9] Next, he arranged a long ride into the interior in the company of an Irishman, Patrick Lennon, who was visiting a tract of forest country he had purchased some years earlier and had placed in the hands of an agent. The journey took seven hard days of riding and another six back, sometimes ten hours in the scorching sun, sometimes by moonlight. Beautiful birds and butterflies and the extraordinary variety of the tropical forest impressed themselves indelibly on Darwin's mind. Arrived on the estate, they were witness to 'a most violent and disagreeable quarrel between Mr. Lennon and his agent', during which Lennon 'threatened to sell at auction an illegitimate mulatto child to whom [the agent] was much attached', and also to remove all the women slaves from their husbands and to sell them and their children separately in the market. 'Can two more horrible and flagrant instances be imagined?' asks Darwin in his diary.[10] Steeped as he was in the anti-slavery traditions of his family, he required no further instances of its evil to fortify his views.

Returned to base at the end of April, Darwin took up residence ashore with the ship's artist, Augustus Earle, in a delightful house they had found on the shore a few miles from Rio at Botafogo Bay. There they stayed during the months of May and June while the *Beagle* returned up the coast to Bahia in order to unravel some discrepant measurements. It was unfortunate that, while landing his gear on the beach, Darwin 'suffered on a small scale . . . the horrors of shipwreck. Two or three heavy seas swamped the boat, and before my affrighted eyes were floating books, instruments and gun cases and everything which was most useful to me. – Nothing was lost and nothing completely spoiled, but most of them injured.'[11] There followed eleven weeks of enjoyable geologising and collecting; he usually went out some distance on horseback before dismounting to engage more closely with nature. On 12 June he notes: 'Worked in the morning at yesterday's produce, a forest is a gold mine to a Naturalist and yesterdays a very rich one.' He had the help of a little Brazilian boy who had an amazing 'power of perception. – Many of the rarest animals in the most obscure trails were caught by him.' 27 June was Darwin's last day ashore and he counted his achievements. 'The number of species of Spiders which I have taken is something enormous. – The time during these eleven weeks has passed so delightfully, that my feelings on leaving Botafogo are full of regret and gratitude.'[12]

The three weeks of August 1832 spent in Montevideo, with a brief visit to Buenos Aires, were disappointing owing to political unrest which limited travel ashore; though on one day he managed to shoot a specimen

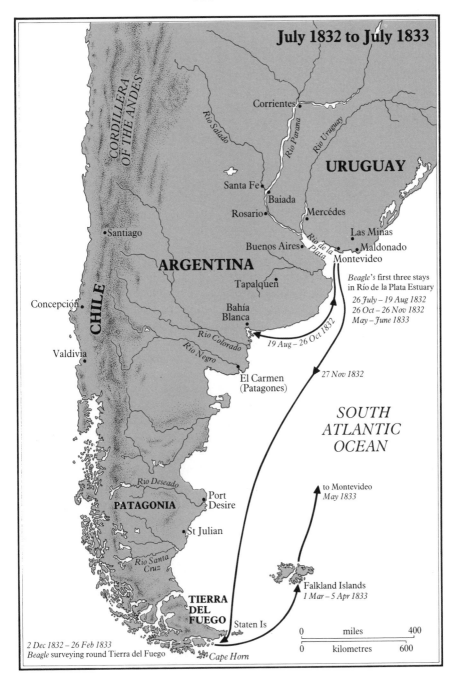

July 1832 to July 1833

CORDILLERA OF THE ANDES

Corrientes

Rio Salado

Rio Parana

Rio Uruguay

URUGUAY

Santa Fe

Baiada

Rosario

Mercédes

Las Minas

Santiago

ARGENTINA

Buenos Aires

Rio de la Plata

Maldonado

Montevideo

Tapalquen

Beagle's first three stays
in Río de la Plata Estuary

26 July – 19 Aug 1832
26 Oct – 26 Nov 1832
May – June 1833

Concepción

CHILE

Bahía
Blanca

19 Aug – 26 Oct 1832

Rio Colorado

Valdivia

Rio Negro

El Carmen
(Patagones)

27 Nov 1832

SOUTH
ATLANTIC
OCEAN

Rio Deseado

to Montevideo
May 1833

PATAGONIA

Port
Desire

St Julian

*Rio Santa
Cruz*

Falkland Islands
1 Mar – 5 Apr 1833

TIERRA
DEL
FUEGO

Staten Is

Cape Horn

2 Dec 1832 – 26 Feb 1833
Beagle surveying round Tierra del Fuego

0	miles	400
0	kilometres	600

of a large animal related to a guinea-pig that weighed 98 pounds and also to collect some beautiful snakes, lizards and beetles.[13]

The next cruise, from 19 August to 26 October, took them some 400 miles south down the Argentinian coast to Bahía Blanca and then back to Montevideo. Exploring the coast in the region of Bahía Blanca with FitzRoy and Sulivan in one of the whaleboats, Darwin came across some gigantic fossil bones. Next day, 23 September, he returned to the spot, Punta Alta, where 'to my great joy I found the head of some large animal, embedded in a soft rock'. It took him and his assistant nearly three hours to extract it and it was well after dark before he could get it on board.[14] A fortnight later he found more fossils at the same site, including a jawbone which contained a tooth. On return to Montevideo he wrote to his sister: 'I have been wonderfully lucky with fossil bones – some of the animals must have been of great dimensions: I am almost sure many of them are quite new; this is always pleasant, but with the antidiluvian animals it is doubly so. – I found parts of the curious osseous coat, which is attributed to the Megatherium. . . . this alone is enough to repay some wearisome minutes.'[15] The first specimens of the megatherium, a giant extinct creature related to the present-day armadillos, had been discovered thirty years earlier near Buenos Aires and so named by Cuvier. The only specimens in Europe were in Madrid.

Wedgwood cameo used in
anti-slavery campaign

A few weeks back in the estuary of the Río de la Plata included a week in Buenos Aires. That enabled him to enquire about local geology and to plan 'some long excursions in this unpicturesque but curious country' for when the *Beagle* returned to base after the long summer cruise to the south now imminent.

From Buenos Aires also he wrote a long letter to Henslow describing his luck with the fossil bones and announcing that he had 'fragments of at least 6 distinct animals', which included a number of teeth useful for identification purposes. There was also bad luck to report: 'by ill-luck the French government has sent one of its Collectors to the Rio Negro, – where he has been working for the last six months, and is now gone round the Horn. – So that I am very selfishly afraid he will get the cream of all the good things, before me.'[16] The Frenchman in question was a palaeontologist, A. C. V. d'Orbigny (1802–57), who was collecting in South America for the Paris Museum of natural history during the years 1826–34. The danger of losing priority to the French collectors already in the area was to emerge again later.

IV

The *Beagle* left Montevideo at the end of November 1832 for her first long cruise to the far south. Three weeks later she reached the east coast of Tierra del Fuego and anchored in the Bay of Good Success, where sixty years earlier Captain Cook had anchored during his first voyage to the South Seas. Here Darwin took the opportunity to climb one of the highest mountains in the vicinity. That entailed thrusting his way through the densest of thickets of dwarf trees, 'not above 8 or 10 feet high, but with thick and very crooked stems; I was obliged often to crawl on my knees. Altogether I reached what I imagined to be green turf; but was again disappointed by finding a compact mass of little beech trees about 4 or 5 feet high. . . . I hailed with joy the rocks covered with lichens and soon was at the very summit.'[17] He had a splendid view in every direction, but the weather looked dirty in the south-west and he prudently made his descent, not unmindful that Joseph Banks and Carl Solander, who had accompanied Cook on his first voyage, had been caught on these very hills in a snowstorm that had nearly cost them their lives.

As it turned out, the *Beagle*'s first season surveying near Cape Horn, from December 1832 to February 1833, was distinguished by the worst weather in the memory of the sealers and whalers frequenting those parts. After working down the east coast of Tierra del Fuego and making contact with the local natives, the *Beagle* managed to round Cape Horn in the teeth of a south-west gale, only to become engaged in the New Year in a fruitless effort to work a hundred miles west in order to return one of the Fuegians, York Minster, to his native island. For twenty-four days in all the ship battled with the gale coupled with a constantly adverse current.

On 9 January, after nineteen days, Darwin notes in his diary that they still had a hundred miles to go and that, 'with the miseries of constant wet and cold' and hardly an hour free of sea-sickness, his 'spirits, temper and stomach . . . will not hold out much longer';[18] but there was worse to come.

After making good progress for twenty-four hours, they came within a mile of their destination, only to be forced back by a violent squall. Wind rose to storm force, visibility was shocking, they were on a lee shore: 'The worst part . . . is our not exactly knowing where we are,' Darwin comments. By noon on the 13th the storm was at its height. 'I was anxiously watching the successive waves', FitzRoy writes in his official account, 'when three huge rollers approached, whose size and steepness at once told me that our sea-boat, good as she was, would be sorely tried . . . the vessel met and rose over the first, but . . . her way was checked; the second . . . [threw] her off the wind; and the third great sea, taking her right a-beam turned her so far over that all the lee bulwark . . . was two or three feet under water. For a moment our position was critical; but, like a cask, she rolled back again, though with some feet of water over the whole deck. Had another sea then struck her, the little ship might have been numbered among the many of her class which have disappeared.'[19] The whaleboat stowed on the lee-quarter was badly damaged and had to be cut away. That evening the wind moderated and they managed to anchor in comparative shelter behind one of the islands; they had achieved a total distance of twenty miles in twenty-four days. Inspecting his possessions the following day, Darwin notes the 'irreparable damage' caused to his drying paper and plants, which had been wetted by salt water.

Thereafter the weather turned better and the *Beagle* moved a few miles west into the Beagle Channel (so named during FitzRoy's earlier exploration of those waters). That was where Jemmy Button came from, and the next tasks were to return him to his people and to settle the missionary, Richard Matthews, in the vicinity. It then transpired that York Minster, who had decided to marry Fuegia Basket, was content to stay there too, so that the vain and dangerous attempt to return him further west had all along been unnecessary.

With the ship moored in a most excellent anchorage, secured from wind and sea, preparations were made for a long boat journey. Two boats carried the Fuegians, the missionary and a great quantity of stores. The plan was to land them at Jemmy Button's cove, build houses for them, plant a garden, and so start a settlement. Another two boats, intended to go much further, carried FitzRoy, Darwin and some fifteen men together with ample supplies. Arrived at the cove, the Fuegians were landed, together with the missionary and the extraordinary collection of stores that his society had provided for him, which included wineglasses, fine white linen and beaver hats.

On their way to the cove, groups of Fuegians were seen along the shore and their 'savage and wild' appearance made an indelible impression on Darwin. One night when the boat parties were camped ashore the Fuegians became threatening, constantly demanding they be given presents. Though their only weapons were slings and stones, they used them with such accuracy that caution was vital. During the first day or two while the settlement was being built, all was quiet and Darwin, with others, 'took long walks in the surrounding hills and woods'; but then a quarrel developed between an old man and one of the sentries and things looked ugly. 'All the goods were therefore moved to the houses and Matthews and his companions prepared to pass rather an aweful night.' By morning, however, there was peace again and the captain decided to send the two boats back to the ship. Then, with the other two, he proceeded westward to survey the whole length of the Beagle Channel to the Pacific, a distance of 120 miles, and back by a somewhat different route. The survey provided details of an alternative channel through the islands more southerly than the Straits of Magellan.

Ten days after departure the boat party was back at the settlement to find the situation desperate. 'From the moment of our leaving,' notes Darwin, 'a regular system of plunder commenced' in which Matthews had lost nearly all his possessions. 'Night and day large parties of the natives surrounded his house', and on one occasion 'a whole party advanced with stones and sticks. . . . I think we returned just in time to save his life.' Evacuation being necessary, Matthews returned to the ship with FitzRoy and his party in the two boats. 'It was quite melancholy leaving our Fuegians – amongst their barbarous countrymen,' Darwin thought. When the captain, a week later, paid them a visit the situation had improved, however. Neither FitzRoy nor Darwin liked to believe that the expense and effort of installing a nucleus of civilisation in these savage lands had failed. 'If the garden succeeds,' notes Darwin hoping against hope, 'this little settlement may yet be the means of producing great good and altering the habits of the truly savage inhabitants.'[20] A year later when they visited the district again hope would be almost extinguished.

During the long boat journey westward to the Pacific an incident occurred which had put the party in jeopardy. The scene is set by Darwin:

In many places magnificent glaciers extended from the mountains to the waters edge. – I cannot imagine anything more beautiful than the beryl blue of these glaciers, especially when contrasted by the snow. . . . One of these glaciers placed us for a minute in most imminent peril; whilst dining in a little bay about ½ mile from one and admiring the beautiful colour of its vertical and overhanging face, a large mass fell roaring into the water; our boats were on the beach; we saw a great wave rushing onwards and instantly it was evident how great was the chance of their being dashed into pieces. – One of the seamen just got hold of the boat as the curling breaker reached it: he was knocked over and over but not hurt and most fortunately our boat received no damage.[21]

FitzRoy's account gives a significant detail. After describing the scene, he proceeds:

our whole attention was immediately called to great rolling waves which came so rapidly that there was scarcely time for the most active of our party to run and seize the boats before they were tossed along the beach like empty calabashes. By the exertions of those who grappled them and seized their ropes, they were hauled up again out of reach of a second and third roller; and indeed we had good reason to rejoice that they were just saved in time; for had not Mr. Darwin, and two or three of the men, run to them instantly, they would have been swept away from us irrecoverably.[22]

This was neither the first nor last time Darwin showed himself to be one of the fittest men aboard. 'The following day' (30 January 1833), FitzRoy continues, 'we passed into a large expanse of water, which I named Darwin Sound – after my messmate, who so willingly encountered the discomforts and risk of a long cruise in a small loaded boat.' When they returned to the *Beagle*, the party had travelled 300 miles during their three-week expedition.

After two further weeks of surveying around Cape Horn in mixed weather, which included another severe gale, the *Beagle* set out for the Falkland Islands, where they arrived on 1 March. To their astonishment they saw the Union Jack flying and learned that a few weeks earlier Britain had taken possession of the islands. 'The present inhabitants consist of one Englishman, who has resided here for some years, and has now the charge of the British Flag, 20 Spaniards and three women, two of whom are negresses. – The island is abundantly stocked with animals. – there are about 5000 wild oxens, many horses, and pigs.'[23]

The *Beagle* stayed in the Falklands five weeks, refitting and doing local surveys mainly from whaleboats, with Darwin spending most days ashore studying the natural history. Thence they sailed north and at the end of April reached base at Montevideo, where they found an accumulation of mail, some of it posted as much as seven months earlier.

Meanwhile Darwin had written a long account of their doings in the wastelands of Tierra del Fuego to his sister Caroline. Referring to the incident when the glacier calved, he very characteristically made no mention of the part he had played in securing the boats, a detail he omitted also from his diary. The gale he describes as 'a sight for a landsman to remember', adding: 'The Captain considers it the most severe one he ever was in.' Future plans were still uncertain: 'I believe we must have one more trip to the South, before finally going round the Horn, or rather passing through the Straits of Magellan, for the Captain had enough of that great sea at the Cape to last him all his life. – I am quite astonished to find I can endure this life: if it was not for the strong and increasing pleasure from Nat: History I never could.'[24]

V

Back in September 1832, during the ten-week cruise south from Montevideo, FitzRoy had conceived a plan to hire two small schooners employed in sealing that he found in Bahía Blanca, to survey the coastal waters and inlets of the area. Wickham would command one and Stokes the other. 'These small craft,' FitzRoy explained, 'of fifteen and nine tons respectively, guided by their owners, who had for years frequented this complication of banks, harbours and tides, seemed to me capable of fulfilling the desired object – under command of such steady and able heads as the officers mentioned – with this great advantage; that while the *Beagle* might be procuring supplies at Montevideo, going with the Fuegians on her first trip to the southward, and visiting the Falkland Islands, the survey of all those intricacies . . . might be carried on steadily during the finest time of year.'[25] In addition to its regular crew and the naval officer in command, each vessel would have aboard a midshipman, a marine and a seaman from the *Beagle*. Admittedly, authority had not been obtained from the Admiralty for the expenses incurred, but FitzRoy was impatient to proceed and knew that to seek authority would entail a very long delay, perhaps a year. The upshot was that he hired them in his own name and sought approval retrospectively. In addressing the Board of Admiralty through Captain Beaufort, he ended: 'I believe that their Lordships will approve of what I have done; but if I am wrong no inconvenience will result to the public service, since I am alone responsible for the agreement with the owner.' In submitting FitzRoy's request to the Board, Beaufort drew attention to the fact that 'the *Beagle* is the only surveying ship to which a smaller vessel or Tender has not been attached'.[26] FitzRoy's decision, Darwin tells us, was 'hailed with joy by everyone', since it would shorten considerably the time to be spent on the east coast of the continent.[27]

The decision reached, the scheme was quickly implemented. Survey of the Argentine coast by the two little schooners went steadily ahead throughout the stormy months of the southern summer of 1832–3 while the *Beagle* was engaged around Cape Horn. In the following March, when the *Beagle* was in the Falklands, FitzRoy saw a splendid chance to purchase outright a larger vessel excellently suited to act as tender to the *Beagle* – which would allow the little schooners to be dispensed with. 'A fitter vessel I could hardly have met with,' he wrote later, 'one hundred and seventy tons burthen, oak-built and copper fastened throughout, very roomy, a good sailer, extremely handy and a first rate sea-boat.'[28] Her owner had hoped to make a fortune sealing, but the weather had been so desperately bad that he had been ruined by the venture. A forced sale enabled FitzRoy to acquire her for one-quarter her original cost; while excellent stores for her were obtained at half their value from two ships wrecked in the harbour by the gales. FitzRoy renamed her *Adventure*, a name famous in the naval surveying service since the days of James Cook. Having sent her back to Maldonado for refitting, FitzRoy wrote to Captain Beaufort at the Admiralty explaining his case and again requesting retrospective authority for his actions: 'I feel as if we could now get on fast again, and much more securely, by having so fine a craft to carry our luggage, provisions, boats etc. etc.'[29] Safety was in fact a major consideration. Shipwreck was always a possibility; and, even if the crew got safe to land, survival for long on a wild coast and a subsequent rescue would be extremely doubtful.

During the winter months of May, June and July 1833 the *Beagle* was either at Montevideo to pick up mails and stores or else at Maldonado, a small place fifty miles east, where the *Adventure* was being recoppered and where FitzRoy and his assistants could find peace and quiet to complete their charts.

This provided another opportunity for Darwin to spend a further long period ashore, for the whole of May and June in fact. Having obtained spacious, though ill-furnished, quarters in the little town of Maldonado, he set about exploring the geology of the area and collecting all the animals he could. In this he had the full-time help of a servant whom he had decided, after long thought, to engage.

In a letter of 22 May 1833 to his sister Catherine he includes a paragraph addressed to his father. After setting out the advantages of having a servant to himself, he explains that there is a man aboard who is willing to act in this capacity for a small wage. He has 'taught him to shoot and skin birds, so that in my main object he is very useful'.[30] Since Darwin finds that his annual expenses on the voyage are not high and 'it being hopeless from time to write for permission I have come to the conclusion you would allow me this expense.' Hitherto the captain had detailed a seaman always to be with him ashore; now it would be his own servant.

The man in question was Syms Covington, about seventeen years old, whose duties had been those of 'Fiddler and Boy to the poop cabin'. Darwin therefore knew him well and had already trained him for the role. The arrangement was to prove extremely successful. Covington was evidently intelligent and quick to learn. He assisted not only in collecting and skinning but in packing and labelling specimens, and also performed various secretarial duties. A few months after his appointment Darwin was giving him considerable responsibility and describing his help as 'invaluable'.

Early in this long stay ashore, Darwin undertook a twelve-day ride into the interior, in company with a local man and servant, to examine geology. At the end of his stay, with Covington's assistance, he had made an almost complete collection of birds and quadrupeds. 'The regular routine is one day shooting and picking up my mouse traps, the next preserving the animals which I take. . . . A few Reales has enlisted all the boys in the town in my service; and few days pass in which they do not bring me some curious creature.'[31] Another activity had been improving his Spanish.

At the end of May 1833 contact was made with one of the little schooners and Wickham, with King, returned to Maldonado to take command of the *Adventure*. 'They are heartily tired of their little vessels,' notes Darwin. 'It appears to have been miserable work and more than sufficiently dangerous: from the smallness of the vessels it was scarcely possible to keep anything dry.' Stokes, however, was still surveying in the other little schooner, which had lost its marine overboard in the bad weather. For Darwin one great advantage was that, with Stokes out of the *Beagle*, he had the poop cabin to himself. 'I absolutely revel in room,' he tells his sisters.[32]

Not until early July did FitzRoy receive news from the Admiralty: authority to hire the schooners had not been approved. This was a severe blow to him, since he had incurred considerable expenditure which he could ill afford. Furthermore, he had already bought the *Adventure* out of his own pocket and was also concerned that his requests had embarrassed Beaufort. 'Had either of your letters . . . reached me prior to my purchase of the *Adventure* I should hardly have risked involving you in another fracas,' he writes in a long private letter to Beaufort. 'I am now upon thorns to know the result, and what additional plague I may have caused to you by that transaction . . . a certain troubled Spirit, ycleped Conscience, is always goading me to do all I can, for the sake of doing what is *right*, without seeking for credit. . . . These are some of the reasons for occasioning my outgoings.'[33] A year later a second rejection by the Admiralty was to prove an even more severe blow to the intensely sensitive FitzRoy.

VI

At the end of July 1833 the *Beagle* again sailed on a short cruise a few hundred miles south down the Argentine coast, this time as far as the Río Negro. The two little schooners were paid off, Stokes and other crew members taken aboard, and further surveying continued by the *Beagle*, which was due to return to base within a few weeks. This gave Darwin an opportunity to embark on his longest ride of exploration, from the Río Negro north to Buenos Aires and yet further north again up the Río de la Plata as far as Santa Fe. After further travel ashore, he was back in Montevideo at the end of November in time for the *Beagle*'s departure for a second season in the far south. On 7 December, the second day out, Darwin notes in his diary: 'With a fair wind stood out of the river and by the evening were in clear water; never I trust again to enter the muddy water of the Plata. – The *Adventure* kept ahead of us, which rejoiced us all. . . . It is a great amusement having a companion to gaze at.'[34] The

ABOVE LEFT Scene aboard HMS *Beagle*, crossing the Line, 17th February 1832

ABOVE HMS *Beagle* in the Straits of Magellan, 1832

ABOVE RIGHT Bivouac ashore, Christmas 1833

RIGHT The *Beagle* beached for careening at the mouth of the Santa Cruz river, April 1834

Adventure perhaps provided also a welcome sense of security.

Progress was slow owing to light and foul winds. By 23 December, however, they had reached Port Desire (Puerto Deseado), a thousand miles south on the coast of Patagonia, where they spent a week. On Christmas Eve Darwin took a long walk, made valuable observations on the geology of the country and 'by great good luck' shot a guanaco (like a llama but rather smaller); 'it weighed without its entrails etc. 170 pounds: so that we shall have fresh meat for all hands on Christmas day.' His next diary entry runs: 'After dining in the Gun-room, the officers and almost every man in the ship went on shore. – The Captain distributed prizes to the best runners, leapers, wrestlers. – These Olympic games were very amusing; it was quite delightful to see with what school-boy eagerness the seamen enjoyed them: old men with long beards and young men without any were playing like so many children. – certainly a much better way of passing Christmas day than the usual one, of every seaman getting as drunk as he possibly can.'[35] The young men without beards were probably in their teens; and the old men with them were not very old. Over a year earlier most aboard had grown beards; Darwin's was large and black.

Early in the New Year of 1834, with the second year of the voyage complete, the *Beagle* was surveying a rocky, dangerous coast a hundred miles further south. Going ashore at San Julián, Darwin found some very interesting fossil bones, later identified as those of a giant extinct species of the llama family. It was here too that he again showed himself to be one of the fittest men aboard.

FitzRoy took a boat up the local river in search of fresh water at a place so marked on an old Spanish map. He, Darwin and four of the crew landed, all armed, and proceeded on foot. 'It turned out to [be] a very long walk,' writes Darwin; 'in the evening two of the party could not walk any further and we were all excessively tired. – It was caused by a most painful degree of thirst' in near desert conditions. Although Darwin does not say so, one of the two who collapsed was FitzRoy, who gives a more detailed account of this taxing day: 'after a very fatiguing walk not a drop of water could be found. I lay down on the top of a hill, too tired and thirsty to move farther; seeing two lakes of water, as we thought, about two miles off, but unable to reach them, Mr. Darwin, more accustomed than the men, or myself, to long excursions on shore, thought he could get to the lakes, and went to try.' One of the men volunteered to accompany him. On reaching it, they found to their great mortification that it was 'a field of snow-white salt'. The whole party then withdrew towards the boat, but FitzRoy, unable to move further, found an easily identified place and decided to lie down and sleep, with 'one man, the most tired next to me, staying with me'. Darwin and the other three struggled on and reached the boat. A relief party was then organised to take water to FitzRoy and his companion and, thus revived, both were enabled to complete the return

August 1833 to July 1834

CORDILLERA OF THE ANDES

Corrientes

Rio Salado

Rio Parana

Rio Uruguay

URUGUAY

Santa Fe
Baiada

Rosario

Mercédes

ARGENTINA

Las Minas
Maldonado

Buenos Aires

Rio de la Plata

Montevideo
4 Nov – 6 Dec 1833

Tapalquen

Valparaiso
23 July 1834

•Santiago

6 Dec 1833

•Concepción

Bahía Blanca

Rio Colorado

CHILE

Valdivia

Rio Negro

El Carmen
(Patagones) *Aug 1833*

28 June – 13 July 1834

Darwin's Rides *Aug – Dec 1833*

1 from El Carmen to Bahía Blanca
  11 – 17 Aug

2 from Bahía Blanca to Buenos Aires
  8 – 20 Sept

3 from Buenos Aires to Santa Fe
  27 Sept – 4 Oct

4 from Montevideo to Mercédes
  and return
  4 Nov – 6 Dec

Rio Deseado

PATAGONIA

Port Desire
Xmas 1833

St Julian

to Tierra de Fuego
Dec 1833 – Mar 1834

18 Apr – 8 May 1834

Rio Santa Cruz

TIERRA DEL FUEGO

Staten Is

Falkland Islands
10 Mar – 7 Apr 1834

0	miles	400
0	kilometres	600

Dec 1833 – 5 Mar 1834
Beagle surveying round Tierra del Fuego   *Cape Horn*

journey. 'No one suffered afterwards from the over-fatigue', writes FitzRoy, 'except Mr Darwin who had had no rest during the whole of that thirsty day.' After two days lying 'very feverish in bed', Darwin nevertheless was out and about geologising on the following day.[36]

At the end of January 1834 the *Beagle* entered the Straits of Magellan, where she enjoyed unexpectedly calm weather. While surveying proceeded, mainly from whaleboats, Darwin was ashore. The Patagonian Indians on the north shore of the straits were on friendly terms with the sealers and whalers, spoke a little English or Spanish, and were glad to trade fish and guanaco skins in exchange for tobacco. During late February the survey of the east coast of Tierra del Fuego was completed and they sailed round the southern tip and once again into the Beagle Channel, where they experienced a short but severe gale. FitzRoy was keen to see how Jemmy Button and his friends were faring. After they had anchored in the vicinity, a canoe came alongside, but until it was quite close, Darwin comments, they 'could not recognize poor Jemmy. It was quite painful to behold him; thin, pale, and without a remnant of clothes, except a bit of blanket round his waist; his hair hanging over his shoulder, and so ashamed of himself, he turned his back to the ship. . . . When he left us he was very fat, and so particular about his clothes, that he was always afraid of even dirtying his shoes. . . . I never saw so complete and grievous a change.'[37] Soon the old friendly relationships were established, however. He had brought 'two beautiful otter skins for two of his old friends [in the crew] and some spear heads and arrows of his own making for the Captain.' In conversation it quickly became apparent that he was now well-established, had married 'a young and very nice looking squaw', had built himself a canoe, had plenty to eat and, to the surprise of his visitors, had no desire to return to England. 'The strangest thing is Jemmy's difficulty in regaining his own language. – He seems to have taught all his friends some English.' York Minster had returned to his own country, having stolen most of Jemmy's possessions and taken Fuegia Basket with him.

For three days the *Beagle* stayed at anchor, the weather was fine and clear, the mountains north of them in Tierra del Fuego in full view and looking magnificent. This was an opportunity to determine their heights. In doing so, they discovered what FitzRoy believed to be the highest mountain in the island. This he did Darwin the singular honour of calling by his name (an honour in no way diminished by the later finding that a mountain named three centuries earlier after a Spaniard was a few hundred feet higher).

By 10 March 1834, after a fast passage, the *Beagle* was back in the Falkland Islands, which they found wracked by strife, with more in prison than out of it. There they stayed a month, enabling Darwin to go exploring again. He also had the chance to write home giving a long description of the second cruise to Tierra del Fuego and saying how fortunate he had been in finding 'some very perfect bones' at San Julián: 'There is nothing like Geology,' he assures Catherine; 'the pleasure of the first day's partridge shooting or first day's hunting cannot be compared to finding a fine group of fossil bones which tell their story of former times with almost a living tongue.'[38] Could there be higher praise than this for his new-found passion?

From the Falklands the plan was once again to spend a couple of months on the southernmost shores of Patagonia, this time in order to explore a very big river, the Santa Cruz, which rumour had it might prove navigable as far west as the Andes. Then, at long last, they would leave the east coast, pass through the Straits of Magellan and make north to the *Beagle*'s future base at Valparaiso.

Leaving the Falklands on 7 April, another fast passage brought the ship to the mouth of the Santa Cruz river. First, however, a large sandy beach and a good range of tide provided opportunity to beach the *Beagle* at high tide, inspect her for underwater damage and carry out repairs before the tide returned. Several feet of her false keel, it was found, had been carried away when the ship had struck a rock six months earlier; this was quickly made good by the ship's carpenter with timber carried aboard for the purpose.

With the *Beagle* safely anchored in the estuary, FitzRoy led a party of twenty-five men, all well armed, with three whaleboats and ample provisions for a three-week journey of exploration up the river. 'It is generally from three to four hundred yards broad,' notes Darwin, 'and in the centre about seventeen feet deep; and perhaps its most remarkable feature is the constant rapidity of the current which in its whole course runs at the rate of from four to six knots. . . . The water is of a fine blue colour with a slightly milky tinge.'

In so strong a current the only way of progressing was for the boats to be towed by a party on shore: 'the three boats were fastened astern of each other, two hands left in each, and the rest all on shore to track . . . the party which included *everyone*, was divided into two spells . . . and each of these pulled alternately for an hour and a half. – The officers of each boat lived with, eat the same food, and slept in the same tent with their crew; . . . after sunset, the first level place where there were any bushes was chosen for the nights lodgings.' Camping drill was extremely efficient so that within half an hour 'everything was ready for the night. A watch of two men and an officer was always kept, whose duty it was to look after the boats, keeping up the fires and look out for Indians; each in the party had his one hour every night.' Progress by day is described by FitzRoy: 'The order of our march was usually one or two riflemen in advance, as scouts – Mr. Darwin, and occasionally Mr. Stokes, or Mr. Bynoe, upon the heights – a party walking along the banks near the boats, ready to relieve or assist in tracking, and the eight or ten men who were dragging the three boats along at the rate of about two miles an hour over the ground, though full eight knots through the water.'[39]

The valley, which was between five and ten miles wide and bounded by flat plains a few hundred feet higher, ran nearly due east and west; within it the river followed a winding course. On a good day they made about ten miles in a straight line and perhaps fifteen or twenty as the river ran. The pebble plains contained an abundance of sea shells of recent origin. Further up they were overlaid by a blanket of basaltic lava, 300 feet thick, through which the river had carved a minor gorge.

Although they never met Indians many signs showed they were not far away. The country was arid, with low rainfall, despite being within 200 miles of the torrential rains of Tierra del Fuego. Animal life was sparse and mainly confined to the valley and 'the rugged low precipices' of the basalt. An occasional ostrich* was seen but they were very wild. The principal fauna were large flocks of guanaco, and numbers of condors which fed on the casualties. When a guanaco was shot, it was a race between the humans and the condors to decide who could get there to enjoy it. Sometimes the crew won, sometimes the condors. When they were two weeks out, 'the captain's servant shot two guanaco. Before the men could arrive to carry them to the boats the condors and some small carrion vultures had picked even the bones of one clean and white, and this in about four hours.' Next day, having travelled perhaps 130 miles from the sea, they had 'the satisfaction of seeing in full view the long North and South range of the Cordilleras. . . . We looked at them with regret, for it was evident we had not time to reach them.'[40] A couple of days later, on 5 May, with rations running low, FitzRoy ordered the return, which, in the boats, was as easy and speedy as the outward journey had been hard and slow. As we now know, they had come within a few miles of the source of all the river's water, Lago Argentino, some hundred miles long, which drains the snow from a long section of the eastern slopes of the Andes.

On reaching the estuary again, Darwin sums up the outcome: 'Almost every one is discontented with this expedition, much hard work, and much time lost and scarcely anything seen or gained. – We have, however, to thank our good fortune, in enjoying constant fine dry weather and blue skys. To me, the cruize has been most satisfactory, from affording so excellent a section of the great [geologically] modern formation of Patagonia.'[41] It seems likely there would have been less discontent had they reached the source of the river – as, without knowing it, they so nearly had done.

On 12 May 1834, with everyone embarked, the *Beagle* sailed for the Straits of Magellan, where they met with the 'bad, cold and boisterous weather' they knew all too well. There they were joined by the *Adventure* with a final instalment of letters routed via the Falklands; Darwin's were

*Officially the two species of the ostrich family found in South America are named Rheas. Darwin and FitzRoy always refer to them as ostriches, however, and that seems to have been their popular name.

dated October and November of the previous year.

During late May and early June the two ships were threading their way through the straits in wintry weather, with temperatures below freezing all day and much snow. 'This is rather miserable work in a ship,' writes Darwin, 'where you have no roaring fire; and where the upper deck, covered with thawing snow is, as it were, the hall in your house.'[42] By 10 June the ships were into the open ocean leaving behind a coast that 'is enough to make a landsman dream for a week about death, peril and shipwreck'. Their northward passage of 1700 miles to Valparaiso was frustratingly slow owing to 'furious gales from the North', which led them to put into a small port in the large island of Chiloé. A few days before arrival there the purser, Mr. Rowlett, died of natural causes, having been ill for some time. He had been on the previous cruise and had many friends in the ship; 'the funeral service was read on the quarter deck, and his body lowered into the sea; it is an aweful and solemn sound that splash of the waters over the body of an old ship-mate.'[43]

The ships stayed at Chiloé a fortnight, enabling Darwin to explore as best he could an island sparsely inhabited by Spanish-Indian peasants and blanketed by dense rain-soaked forest. Thence they departed on the final 700 miles to Valparaiso, which they reached in late July after nine days and in the much welcomed climate of blue skies, dry air and bright sun. The *Beagle* was due to spend three months there, refitting and drawing charts, before yet one more Antarctic summer surveying in southern latitudes.

As it happened, a schoolboy acquaintance from Shrewsbury, Richard Corfield (1804–97), was living as a merchant in Valparaiso and offered Darwin the hospitality of his house. Using that as a base, Darwin undertook a six-week geological excursion on horseback into the foothills of the Andes; since it was midwinter, snow made the higher slopes impassable. In late September a few days before his return he became ill and, although he struggled on geologising for another day or two, he eventually had to hire a carriage to convey him to Corfield's house. There he remained ill in bed till the end of October.[44] We do not know what the illness was, but, since Darwin put it down to drinking some 'sour new made wine' which had 'half-poisoned' him, the chances are that it was an acute gastric infection caught from something he had eaten or drunk. This view is strengthened by his telling Caroline that he is 'being sick at stomach' and that Bynoe is treating him with 'a good deal of Casteroil'.[45] In due course he made a complete recovery and was ready to join the *Beagle* again when she sailed for the south on 10 November 1834.

Darwin was not the only one to be ill at Valparaiso. FitzRoy too was incapacitated, but in a very different way.

NINE

A troubled spirit
1832–1834

About a month after the *Beagle*'s arrival in Valparaiso FitzRoy heard from Captain Beaufort at the Admiralty that the Board had again turned down his request for restrospective approval of his actions. That meant that *Adventure* had to be sold. It was a triple blow to FitzRoy, – to his *amour propre*, to his surveying plans and to his pocket. He became deeply depressed and for two months or more was in a despairing mood and incapable of decision.

We have three accounts of the breakdown, one in private letters written by FitzRoy to Beaufort, a second in a long letter Darwin wrote home shortly before the *Beagle* sailed south, and the third written retrospectively by FitzRoy in his official *Narrative*.[1]

The two private letters FitzRoy wrote to Beaufort, dated 26 and 28 September 1834, come early in the breakdown and soon after he had sold the *Adventure*. 'My schooner is sold,' he writes in the first. 'The Charts etc. are progressing slowly – They are not ready to be sent away yet. I am in the dumps. It is heavy work – all work and no play – like your Office . . . though not half so bad probably.' In the second letter he addresses Beaufort as his 'kind friend' and continues: 'Troubles and difficulties harass and oppress me so much that I find it impossible to say or do what I wish.' In listing the things that 'have made me ill and very unhappy', he starts with his having had 'to sell my Schooner', and then expresses dissatisfaction with two of his officers. He is annoyed at having to spend so long in Valparaiso and sees no hope of completing the charts before the end of October. 'I have affronted and half quarrelled with most people by shutting myself up and refusing to visit or be visited. As Captain of a Ship in a bustling sea port it is a difficult matter to keep sufficiently quiet to make such progress as one would wish. Yet to this port a vessel must come for supplies. Besides, after a long cruize, upon salt meat, it is absolutely necessary that the Crew should have fresh meat and vegetables for sufficient time to do away with all scorbutic inclinations.'[2]

Both in these letters and retrospectively in his *Narrative* FitzRoy attributes his breakdown quite explicitly to his second rejection by the Admiralty; and there is good reason to accept his account. In the *Narrative* he writes:

At this time I was made to feel and endure a bitter disappointment; the mortification it caused preyed deeply, and the regret is still vivid. I found that it would be impossible for me to maintain the *Adventure* much longer: my own means had been taxed, even to involving myself in difficulties, and as the Lords Commissioners of the Admiralty did not think it proper to give me any assistance, I saw that all my cherished hopes of examining many groups of islands in the Pacific, besides making a complete survey of the Chilian and Peruvian shores, must utterly fail. I had asked to be allowed to bear twenty additional seamen on the *Beagle*'s books, whose pay and provisions would then be provided by Government, being willing to defray every other expense myself; but even this was refused. As soon as my mind was made up, after a most painful struggle, I discharged the *Adventure*'s crew, took the officers back to the *Beagle*, and sold the vessel. Though her sale was very ill-managed, partly owing to my being dispirited and careless, she brought 7,500 dollars, nearly £1,400, and is now (1838) trading on that coast, in sound condition.[3]

Darwin's account, although contemporary, must have been derived mainly from others, since during almost all the time FitzRoy was unwell he himself was either in the Andean foothills or else ill in bed at Corfield's house. In his letter to his sister Catherine, dated 8 November 1834, he writes:

We have had some strange proceedings on board the *Beagle*, but which have ended most capitally for all hands. – Capt. FitzRoy has for the last two months, been working extremely hard and at the same time contantly annoyed by interruptions from officers of other ships: the selling the Schooner & its consequences were very vexatious: the cold manner the Admiralty (solely I believe because he is a Tory) have treated him, & a thousand other etc. etc. has made him very thin & unwell. This was accompanied by a morbid depression of spirits, & a loss of all decision & resolution. The Captain was afraid that his mind was becoming deranged (being aware of his heredetary predisposition). all that Bynoe could say, that it was merely the effect of bodily health and exhaustion after such application, would not do; he invalided & Wickham was appointed to the command. By the instructions Wickham could only finish the survey of the Southern part & would then have been obliged to return direct to England. – The grief on board the Beagle about the Captains decision was universal & deeply felt. – One great source of his annoyment, was the feeling it impossible to fulfil the whole instructions; from his state of mind, it never occurred to him, that the very instructions order him to do as much of West coast as he has time for & then proceed across the Pacific. Wickham (very disinterestedly, giving up his own promotion) urged this most strongly, stating that when he took the command, nothing should induce him to go to T. del Fuego again; & then asked the Captain, what would be gained by his resignation. Why not do the more useful part and return as commanded to the Pacific. The Captain, at last, to every ones joy consented & the resignation was withdrawn.[4]

It seems clear from Darwin's account that FitzRoy was furious with the Admiralty and effectively resigned his command in retaliation, as though saying: 'If you won't pay for my schooner I won't complete your survey.'

Two other comments on Darwin's account are called for. Whether political bias entered into the Admiralty decision is, of course, unknown but it is not impossible. The Whigs were in office and FitzRoy was well known as a Tory.

The second concerns the question of heredity. The reference to FitzRoy's 'heredetary predisposition' is to his uncle, the 2nd Marquis of Londonderry, much better known as Lord Castlereagh, who was British Foreign Secretary from 1810 until his death, by suicide, in 1822.* In those days, as in our own, the notion that all insanity is inherited was prevalent, and it clearly affected FitzRoy himself. Present knowledge, however, strongly suggests that a hereditary predisposition played little part in the condition from which FitzRoy suffered and that it can be attributed, instead, to environmental stressors.

It will be recalled that at the age of five FitzRoy lost his mother, and that such an event is apt to make a person vulnerable to subsequent depressions, especially when they meet with a further loss or major disappointment. We also know that he grew up to be burdened by 'a certain troubled Spirit, ycleped Conscience', which was 'always goading' him to do more and more. This is a state of mind found frequently in those prone to depression because an overactive conscience makes them extremely sensitive to any major failure. Further research into FitzRoy's childhood to learn more of the family events and situations before and after his mother's death would be of interest.

In addition to his many admirable qualities as a captain, FitzRoy had also some serious shortcomings. Darwin very wisely says nothing about them in his diary and, even in his letters home, is circumspect. Early in the voyage, however, having previously always referred to FitzRoy as his beau ideal, Darwin admits to his hero's failings. In a long newsy letter to Caroline at the end of April 1832 from Rio, he describes the captain. First he details FitzRoy's effect on the crew and then his behaviour towards himself: 'His candor & sincerity are to[wards] me unparalleled; and using his own words his "vanity & petulance" are nearly so. – I have felt the

---

*Castlereagh committed suicide at the age of fifty-three when obviously depressed. After his doctor had removed his razors, he piecred his jugular vein with a penknife. Rumour had it that he was being blackmailed at the time.[5]

At various times in his life, FitzRoy suffered from depressive episodes and it is well known that at the age of sixty, after another severe professional setback, he committed suicide. There is no evidence, however, of any elated moods, so that he can confidently be diagnosed as a case of unipolar depression. It is now believed that this condition, like Darwin's, is a consequence of a combination of environmental pressures, acting both early and late, and that the disposition to develop it has only light genetic loading. In these respects it contrasts sharply with the bipolar condition, which always includes manic phases, as well usually as depressive ones, and consequently is properly named as manic-depressive; and the disposition to develop it is shown now to be strongly influenced by genetic factors.

effects of the latter: but the bringing into play the former ones so forcibly makes one hardly regret them. – His greatest fault as a companion is his austere silence: produced from excessive thinking: his many good qualities are great and numerous; altogether he is the strongest marked character I ever fell in with.'[6]

Darwin's reference to having felt the effects of FitzRoy's 'vanity and petulance' is elaborated many years later in his *Autobiography* written after FitzRoy's death:

early in the voyage [in March 1832] at Bahia in Brazil he defended and praised slavery, which I abominated, and told me that he had just visited a great slave-owner, who had called up many of his slaves and asked them whether they were happy, and whether they wished to be free, and all answered 'No.' I then asked him, perhaps with a sneer, whether he thought that the answers of slaves in the presence of their master was worth anything. This made him excessively angry, and he said that as I doubted his word, we would not live any longer together. I thought that I should have been compelled to leave the ship; but as soon as the news spread, which it did quickly, as the captain sent for the first lieutenant to assuage his anger by abusing me, I was deeply gratified by receiving an invitation from all the gun-room officers to mess with them. But after a few hours Fitz-Roy showed his usual magnanimity by sending an officer to me with an apology and a request that I would continue to live with him.[7]

The other episode Darwin describes occurred four years later, in March 1835, when the *Beagle* was spending ten days in Concepción on her way back to Valparaiso after her final voyage to the south.

At Conception in Chile, poor Fitz-Roy was sadly overworked and in very low spirits; he complained bitterly to me that he must give a great party to all the inhabitants of the place. I remonstrated and said that I could see no such necessity on his part under the circumstances. He then burst out into a fury, declaring that I was the sort of man who would receive any favours and make no return. I got up and left the cabin without saying a word, and returned to Conception where I was then lodging. After a few days I came back to the ship and was received by the Captain as cordially as ever, for the storm had by that time quite blown over.[8]

In his *Autobiography* Darwin sums up his companion's deficiencies thus:

Fitz-Roy's temper was a most unfortunate one. This was shown not only by passion but by fits of long-continued moroseness against those who had offended him . . . He was also somewhat suspicious and occasionally in very low spirits, on one occasion bordering on insanity. He seemed to me often to fail in sound judgement or common sense. He was extremely kind to me, but was a man very difficult to live with on the intimate terms which necessarily followed from our messing by ourselves in the same cabin. We had several quarrels; for when out of temper he was utterly unreasonable.[9]

It seems fair to say that not many young men could have borne the FitzRoy squalls and morose calms at such close quarters and for so long.

Robert FitzRoy, aged 33 in 1838, drawn by Midshipman Philip King

Darwin was better qualified than most through his previous experience. FitzRoy and Dr Robert had a good deal in common. Both were usually generous and kind and had many other qualities to be admired. Both could also be moody, domineering, disparaging and unreasonable. In so far as Darwin had learned ways of living with his father – by avoiding confrontation, humouring him, pandering to him – those ways evidently assisted him in coping with FitzRoy. Darwin's capacity for avoiding rows was remarked on by the father of his erstwhile flirting companions, William Mostyn Owen. When much later (March 1836) he heard Charles's sisters saying how very glad they were that Charles and the captain had continued such good friends to the end of the long voyage, he commented, 'Yes, but who could quarrel with Charles?'[10] No doubt, too, it was a great help that for long spells during the voyage Darwin was living or travelling ashore.

Another advantage was that FitzRoy soon developed a liking and respect and later, I believe, much admiration for his young naturalist. As early as the ship's arrival in Bahia in March 1832, FitzRoy was reporting officially to Captain Beaufort at the Admiralty:

Mr. Darwin has found abundant occupation already, both at sea and on shore; he has obtained numbers of curious though small inhabitants of the ocean, by means of a Net made of Bunting, which might be called a floating or surface Trawl, as well as by searching the shores and the Land. In Geology he has met with far more interesting employment in Porto Praya [Cape Verde Islands] than he had at all anticipated. From the manner in which he pursues his occupation, his good sense, inquiring disposition, and regular habits, I am certain that you will have good reason to feel much satisfaction in the reflection that such a person is on board the *Beagle*, and the certainty that he is taking the greatest pains to make the most of time and opportunity.[11]

In a personal letter to Beaufort written at the same time, FitzRoy adds to the picture:

Darwin is a very sensible, hard-working man and a very pleasant mess-mate. I never saw a 'shore-going fellow' come into the ways of a ship so soon and so thoroughly as Darwin. I cannot give a stronger proof of his good sense and disposition than by saying 'Everyone respects and likes him'. He was terribly sick until we passed Teneriffe, and I sometimes doubted his fortitude holding out against such a beginning of the campaign. However, he was no sooner on his legs than anxious to set to work, and a child with a new toy could not have been more delighted than he was with St. Jago. It was odd to hear him say, after we left Porto Praya, 'Well, I am *glad* we are *quietly* at *sea* again, for I shall be able to arrange my collections and set to work more methodically.' He was sadly disappointed by not landing at Teneriffe . . . but there was no alternative.[12]

FitzRoy's account of Darwin's relations with the officers and crew is confirmed in remarks made many years later by Arthur Mellersh, who is sometimes referred to as midshipman and sometimes as mate (at the time of writing he was a vice-admiral): 'I think he was the only man I ever knew against whom I never heard a word said; and as people when shut up in a ship for five years are apt to get cross with each other, that is saying a good deal'.[13] Darwin's nickname on board was Philosopher, often shortened to Philos.

Darwin had several friends. In his April 1832 letter to Caroline he describes King as 'the most perfect, pleasant boy I ever met with and . . . my chief companion.' The first lieutenant, Wickham, 'is a fine fellow – and we are very good friends'.[14] Another whom he mentions in his letters home was Hamond, a midshipman the same age as Darwin, who joined at Montevideo and was with the ship for nearly a year (from July 1832 to May 1833), and who thus took part in the first season round Cape Horn. 'I have seen more of him than any other one and like him accordingly' is how Darwin describes him in his letter to Caroline of March–April 1833, after the cruise which, of course, Wickham and King had both missed through being engaged in the little schooners.

The *Beagle*'s officers managed to live with FitzRoy's difficulties. Most had served under him before and knew him well. They respected and admired him and had learned to avoid or tolerate his tantrums, which rarely lasted long. 'His temper was usually worse in the early morning,' recalls Darwin in his *Autobiography*,[15] and with his eagle eye he could generally detect something amiss about the ship. The junior officers when they relieved each other in the forenoon used to ask, 'whether much hot coffee had been served out this morning' – which meant 'how was the captain's temper?' 'We all jog on very well together,' writes Darwin home from Valparaiso in July 1834; 'there is no quarrelling on board, which is something to say: – the Captain keeps all smooth by rowing every one in turn.'[16]

After the episode in Concepción, when Darwin had walked out and left the ship for a few days, he recalls that poor Wickham had had to bear the brunt of FitzRoy's fury. On Darwin's return, Wickham had expostulated: 'Confound you, philosopher, I wish you would not quarrel with the skipper; the day you left the ship I was dead tired (the ship was refitting) and he kept me walking the deck till midnight abusing you all the time.'[17] Wickham, it is evident, had the measure of FitzRoy and handled him with great skill.

TEN

A voyage grievously too long
1834–1836

I

The first week of November 1834 saw the *Beagle* in Valparaiso making final preparations for her third voyage to the south. Two seasons round Tierra del Fuego, one of them exceptionally bad, together with a winter's passage through the Straits of Magellan had been more than enough for officers and crew. In October the exact whereabouts of the final season's survey was shrouded in uncertainty. 'I suspect we shall pay Tierra del Fuego another visit,' Darwin tells his sisters in a letter of 13 October, 'but of this good Lord deliver us: it is kept very secret lest the men should desert; everyone so hates the confounded country.' As it turned out they were not going so far: the main purpose was to survey round the large island of Chiloé and down the coast 250 miles to the south of it as far as the prominent Cape Tres Montes, which, to everyone's relief, was still 750 miles north of the dreaded country. 'Hurra, hurra,' Darwin writes just before sailing, 'it is fixed the *Beagle* shall not go one mile South of C. Tres Montes.'[1] Even so it was a wild rocky coast lined with a multitude of islands, the Chonos Archipelago, and noted for torrential rains.

The voyage had already lasted nearly three years, and it was well known that there were still two more to go. From now on there are occasional references to homesickness. 'I find being sick at stomach inclines one also to homesickness,' Darwin tells Caroline, writing from his sick bed on 30 October 1834. A month later he is feeling more cheerful: 'For the first time since leaving England I now see a clear and not so distant prospect of returning to you all: crossing the Pacific and from Sydney home will not take much time,' he asserts rather optimistically.[2]

With the *Adventure* sold, all stores and equipment had to be stowed in the *Beagle*, while the officers, all of whom had been taking responsibilities above their official positions, had to revert to less exalted duties. 'We are now in the same state as when we left England with Wickham for 1st Lieutenant, which part of the business anyhow is a good job. – We shall be very badly off for room; and I shall have trouble enough with stowing my collections. It is in every point of view a grievous affair in our little world; a sad tumbling down for some of the officers.'[3]

Sailing from Valparaiso on 10 November 1834, the *Beagle* arrived in San Carlos on the north coast of Chiloé eleven days later, to be greeted with the familiar gales and torrents of rain. The plan was for the *Beagle* to survey the exposed west coast of the island while a boat expedition surveyed the east. They would rendezvous in a fortnight's time at a point on the south coast about 120 miles distant. This time Sulivan was given the command of the two boats, with a crew of four officers, six men and a local surveyor, Charles Douglas, to act as pilot. Darwin went with the boats, though he spent the first three days riding through the rain-soaked forest on a track to a small port on the coast where he would embark.

Despite rain every day and usually all day, the boat party enjoyed themselves. Sulivan, whose first independent command it may have been, was in the highest spirits. Writing home, he boasted that he had 'the best singers and most diverting characters' from among the crew, and that they were 'up to anything'.[4] 'We had a remarkably pleasant boat journey along the Eastern Coast,' Darwin tells his sisters. 'You cannot imagine what merry work such a wandering journey is: in the morning we never know where we shall sleep at night. Carrying, like snail, our houses with us we are always independent; when the day is over we sit round our fire and pity all you who are confined within houses.'[5] During occasional patches of clearer weather, views of the Andean volcanoes were spectacular.

When they met the *Beagle* at the south end of the island, which they found to be thirty miles shorter in length than supposed, Darwin re-embarked on the ship, which was going much further south than the boats. As a result he missed the feast Sulivan arranged for his party on Christmas day, held on an island in a padre's house: the meal comprised a whole sheep, one side roasted the other boiled, and an immense plum pudding cooked with flour and raisins brought for the purpose and eggs obtained locally. It was a well-earned interlude in a boat-trip which would last until 18 January 1835. 'Every other day for eight weeks', writes Sulivan at the end of it, 'we were hard at work . . . I never have enjoyed such perfect good health for two months since leaving England.'[6]

Meanwhile the *Beagle* was making her way south through the Chonos Archipelago, including sheltering for three days from a gale. Darwin went ashore whenever he could, but found attempts to reach the summit of local hills almost impossible. 'As for the woods . . . I shall never forget or forgive them; my face, hands, skin – bones all bear witness what mal-treatment I have received in simply trying to penetrate into their forbidden recesses.' On one occasion, however, he managed, with a 'feeling of triumph', to reach a summit of 1600 feet, where he was rewarded by a great and extensive view. The ascent was 'so steep as to make it necessary to use the trees like ladders'.[7] A week later he climbed a

November 1834 to July 1835

5 July 1835 Copiapó

Guasco

Coquimbo

Illapel

Quillota
Valparaiso · · Mendoza

Santiago

10 Nov
1834

Curico

11 March
1835

Concepción 4–6 March
1835

Arere

Valdivia
Feb 1835

San Carlos

Chiloé Is

Chonos
Archipelago

C. Tres
Montes

Dec 1834 –
Jan 1835
Chiloé to
C. Tres Montes
and return

CHILE

ARGENTINA

URUGUAY

Buenos Aires

Maldonado

Darwin's Rides *March – July 1835*

1 transit of Andes to Mendoza and return
   18 March – 10 April 1835

2 from Valparaiso to Copiapó
   27 April – 5 July 1835

SOUTH ATLANTIC
OCEAN

PATAGONIA

Falkland Islands

TIERRA
DEL FUEGO

| 0 | miles | 400 |
| 0 | kilometres | 600 |

Cape Horn

granite peak a thousand feet higher but much easier because the granite was bare of vegetation.

On 20 December they reached their destination at Cape Tres Montes and 'put the Ship's head to the North', no doubt to everyone's relief; but, with successive gales, 'Christmas day was not such a merry one as we had last year at Port Desire'. A few days later, on the third anniversary of their leaving England, they had the surprising experience of seeing 'a man waving a shirt'. A boat was sent in and they found that he was one of a party of five men and an officer who had deserted from a North American whaler because of bad treatment. Leaving their ship by boat in the middle of the night, they had reached shore only to have their boat smashed on the rocks. There they had been marooned for fifteen months, living on shellfish and seal-flesh. They were very lucky to be rescued. On another occasion they found an island well stocked with wild goats. Eight were killed and provided fresh meat for the crew on New Year's Day 1835, celebrated in 'a heavy N W gale and with steady rain'.[8] On 18 January they were back at San Carlos, where they were met by Sulivan and his boat party.

Two days later, the volcano of Osorno, about one hundred miles to the north-east, erupted. 'It was a very magnificent sight,' Darwin notes; 'by the aid of a glass, in the midst of the great red glare of light, dark objects in a constant succession might be seen to be thrown up and fall down. . . . By the morning the Volcano seemed to have regained its composure.'[9]

The *Beagle* stayed at San Carlos for another fortnight in order to check bearings and recover from the cruise. This gave Darwin an opportunity for another ride, this time to the west coast of Chiloé, taking King with him. Then on 4 February they sailed north 150 miles to Valdivia, an early settlement a few miles up river. Here the *Beagle* stayed a fortnight, surveying up and down the coast, and Darwin had a further opportunity to explore the country and to be bitten all over by the local fleas. Here too they experienced a major earthquake, which did great damage to the town and reduced the bigger city of Concepción, 200 miles further north, to a heap of rubble.

Darwin describes his own experience. 'I was on shore and lying down in the wood to rest myself. It came on suddenly and lasted two minutes (but appeared much longer) . . . There was no difficulty in standing upright; but the motion made me giddy. – I can compare it to skating on very thin ice.'[10] In the forest no damage was done, and even in the town, where all the houses were of wood, only a few people were injured. Back in the harbour, the tide had been low: the water simply rose to the high-tide level and then receded.

During their stay at Valdivia there had been a party on board when 'the Intendente paid us a visit . . . and brought a whole boat-full of ladies', whom bad weather compelled to stay on board all night, 'a sore plague both to us and them . . . They in return gave a ball, which was attended by

Earthquake damage in Concepción, Chile, February 1835

nearly all on board' and was much enjoyed. Darwin, who had never learned to dance,[11] did not go.

Leaving Valdivia two days after the earthquake, the *Beagle* spent ten days surveying up the dangerous coast to Talcahuano, the port of Concepción. Darwin went ashore at once to inspect the coast, which 'was strewed over with timber and furniture as if a thousand great ships had been wrecked', the effect of a great wave that had inundated the area. The following day he and FitzRoy rode through Talcahuano and on to Concepción. 'The two towns presented the most awful yet interesting spectacle I ever beheld . . . In Concepción each house or row of houses stood by itself a heap or line of ruins: in Talcahuano, owing to the great wave little more was left than *one* layer of bricks, tiles and timber with here and there part of a wall yet standing up.' Only about a hundred people were known to have been killed; though, had the quake occurred at night, numbers would have been far higher. Everyone was in the habit of running out of the house immediately they felt any shock. Darwin gives a great deal of space in his diary to eyewitness accounts and speculations about the causes and consequences of the event, which made a very deep impression on him. 'To my mind since leaving England we have scarcely beheld any one other sight so deeply interesting. The Earthquake and Volcano are parts of one of the greatest phenomena to which the world is subject.'[12]

On 7 March, three days after reaching Concepción, the *Beagle* left for a flying visit to Valparaiso to obtain stores, before returning to Concepción to continue the survey up the coast. During the southern survey she had lost four of her five anchors in gales. Moreover, Concepción itself needed assistance and the *Beagle*'s errand was most timely. It was also timely for Darwin, who was thereby enabled to undertake a ride of exploration across the Andes from west to east and back, an expedition he had set his heart on.

II

On the voyage to Valparaiso Darwin wrote a long letter to his sister Caroline in which he describes events of the previous five months and plans for the future. 'The first and best news I have to tell, is that our voyage has at last a definite and certain end fixed to it. I was beginning to grow quite miserable and had determined to make a start, if the Captain had not come to his conclusion . . . I do so long to see you all again. I am beginning to plan the very coaches by which I shall be able to reach Shrewsbury in the shortest time. The voyage has been grievously too long; we shall hardly know each other again; independent of these consequences, I continue to suffer so much from sea-sickness, that nothing, not even geology itself can make up for the misery and vexation of spirit.' He gives a sketch of future plans and explains where letters should be sent: 'till the middle of November to Sydney; then till the middle of June to the Cape of Good Hope. – We expect to reach England in September 1836' (eighteen months hence).

The effects of the earthquake at Concepción he describes as 'the most awful spectacle I ever beheld . . . The force of the shock must have been immense, the ground is traversed by rents, the solid rock is shivered . . . it is one of the three most interesting spectacles I ever beheld since leaving England – A Fuegian savage. – Tropical Vegetation – and the ruins of Concepción.'

He turns then to the immediate future. After arriving at Valparaiso he planned to leave the ship for ten or twelve weeks and not join her again until the beginning of June, when she would be surveying the northern coast of Chile before proceeding on to Lima. Since now, in mid-March, it was autumn, he hoped it would 'not be too late to cross the Cordilleras; . . . I am most anxious to see a geological section of this grand range.' He planned to 'cross the Andes by the bad pass, see Mendoza [in the foothills on the Argentine side] and return by the common one. I am much afraid of this cloudy weather, if snow falls early I may be detained a prisoner on the other side!'[13]

Landed in Valparaiso, Darwin was greeted by two letters from his sisters posted in September and October the previous year. The second contained exciting news. Fox had written to them saying that he had heard 'some very flattering things said of [Charles's] exertions in Natural History by Professor Henslow'. In a postscript to his letter to Caroline, Charles adds: 'You allude to some of the fossil bones being of value, and this of course is the very best news to me which I can hear.'[14] It would be another fifteen months before a second letter, written a year later and containing even more exciting news, would eventually catch up with him, at Ascension Island.

Four days after reaching Valparaiso Darwin had organised his trans-Andean expedition, starting from Santiago on 18 March. 'I took with me my former companion, Mariano Gonzalez, and an Arriero with ten mules and the Madrina. The Madrina is a mare with a little bell round her neck; she is a sort of step-mother to the whole troop.' They took 'a good deal of food in case of being snowed up . . . and a strong passport from the President of Chili' to impress the frontier guards.[15] The expedition, described further in the next chapter, was a success and they completed the double transit, over 130 miles each way, in twenty-three days.

On his return to Santiago Darwin stayed there briefly, then geologised his way back to Valparaiso, a distance of a hundred miles, and on 17 April took up residence again with his friend Corfield. A few days later the *Beagle* arrived again from Concepción for a short visit on her way surveying up the coast. There was good news for FitzRoy: he had been promoted post-captain. Darwin went aboard, and plans for the coming months were agreed. He would ride north through the Andean foothills, some 450 miles as the crow flies, and be picked up at a small port near Copiapó.

He set out on 27 April. 'I took with me the same man [Mariano Gonzales]. . . , four horses and two mules. – We travelled in the same independent manner, cooking our own meals and sleeping in the open air.'[16] The journey took eight weeks and necessitated long hot days in desert conditions, often with only the most meagre of water rations. He found it very long and tedious and looked forward keenly to rejoining the *Beagle* and sailing for home. At the port of Coquimbo, about two-thirds of the way north, he had a brief respite in company with FitzRoy and the *Beagle*, which was refitting before the long journey across the Pacific.

The ship still had to go south to Valparaiso once more. When she got there, FitzRoy learned of the wreck of a naval vessel, HMS *Challenger*, homeward bound after serving in South American waters; she was on a wild stretch of coast south of Concepción where rescue would be difficult. The captain, Robert Seymour, a friend of FitzRoy's, had managed to get his crew ashore, but food was short and the local Indians dangerous. It was the duty of the senior officer on the station, Commodore Mason, to undertake the rescue in his ship, HMS *Blonde*: but in FitzRoy's judgement he was being timid and dilatory. FitzRoy was impatient, laid a plan and took charge, threatening the commodore with a court martial if he did not comply. The upshot was that Mason took the *Blonde* south and FitzRoy accomplished the rescue. Subsequently FitzRoy gave evidence for the defence at Seymour's court martial, pointing out that, as a result of the earthquake and the irregular elevation of the coast, which he had been measuring as part of the survey, currents had changed. Seymour was acquitted.

Darwin heard the story of the 'wonderful quarrel between the Captain and the Commodore' only after he reached Copiapó on 5 July and found Wickham temporarily in command. There he said his *adiós* with a hearty goodwill to his Spanish companion and embarked, 'very glad to be again on board'.[17]

The next major port of call was Callao, the port for Lima, where they stayed seven weeks from 19 July to 6 September, far too long for Darwin's liking. There were several reasons for this. Sulivan was still surveying the northern coast of Chile in yet another small schooner that FitzRoy had hired; the *Beagle* had to be prepared and equipped for her very long voyage across the Pacific; and FitzRoy, who only rejoined at the end of August, wanted to consult some old Spanish maps in Lima. After his promotion and the successful rescue operation his spirits were fully restored.

Darwin's frustration arose not only from his itching to start for home but also from political unrest that made it dangerous to explore ashore: 'four chiefs in arms' were battling for supremacy. The most he was able to do was to spend five very pleasant days in Lima. 'There is so much hospitality in these countries and the conversation of intelligent people in a new and foreign place cannot fail to be interesting.' Another attraction was the very elegant ladies, dressed in black elastic gowns and black silk veils which were so worn as to allow 'only one eye to remain uncovered. – But then that one eye is so black and brilliant and has such powers of motion and expression that its effect is very powerful.'[18]

Nevertheless Darwin's main concern was to be off as soon as possible for the Galapagos Islands, partly because they were 'somewhat nearer to England', as he tells Henslow in a letter of 12 August 1835, and partly 'for the sake of having a good look at an active Volcano'.[19] Although the Galapagos Islands were the last remaining survey for the *Beagle* to do, FitzRoy had so set his heart on completing the survey of the west coast of the continent that, before leaving Callao, he had bought the little schooner Sulivan had been using, put two midshipmen in charge, and left them to continue the work and return to England by merchant ship. Undaunted by previous refusals, FitzRoy once again sought retrospective authority for the expenditure and once again he was refused by the Admiralty, even though his friend Captain Beaufort recognised that the schooner would materially assist the survey.[20]

III

The Galapagos, which lie on the Equator some 500 miles from the coast of South America, consist of half a dozen big islands, ten or more miles across, and another half-dozen small ones. All are volcanic in origin. At the time of the *Beagle*'s visit, only one, Charles Island, was occupied. The population, 'nearly all people of color and banished [there] for Political crimes',[21] was about 200, governed by an Englishman, Nicholas Lawson, in the name of the state of Ecuador. Whalers visited regularly to obtain water and to collect some of the giant tortoises for food.

On arrival in the islands on 17 September 1835, FitzRoy sent off two boats under the command of Sulivan and Chaffers respectively, to start the survey. The *Beagle* herself visited the bigger islands, including Charles, where FitzRoy and Darwin called on the governor. Altogether Darwin was able to visit four of the larger islands, spending a few days on each. As usual every minute of his time was occupied in inspecting the geology of the islands and collecting all the animals and plants he could lay his hands on.

In view of the crucial part that the fauna of the Galapagos would play in Darwin's subsequent thinking about species and their origin, it is necessary to emphasise that, while he was there, by far his dominant interest was in the geology. That is mentioned in all three of the letters he wrote from Lima beforehand, to Henslow, to Fox and to his sister Caroline; but only in the last is there any mention of zoology: 'I think both the Geology and Zoology cannot fail to be interesting.'[22]

In the event he saw numberless volcanoes, small and big, ancient and modern, but not many active ones. The high ground in the island centres rises to a few thousand feet and was usually cloud-capped; consequently on their windward sides it was damp, providing such meagre supplies of water as were available. Whenever he could, Darwin walked up to the tops where the few animals and plants that inhabit these isolated islands were mostly to be found. The lower slopes, consisting of endless flows of black lava, are arid and barren and support only a few desert plants and fewer animals.

Darwin's first impressions were that the country resembled 'what we might imagine the cultivated parts of the Infernal regions' might be like: 'the stunted trees show little signs of life'. Giant tortoises and three kinds of turtle were, however, abundant and much sought after by sailors for

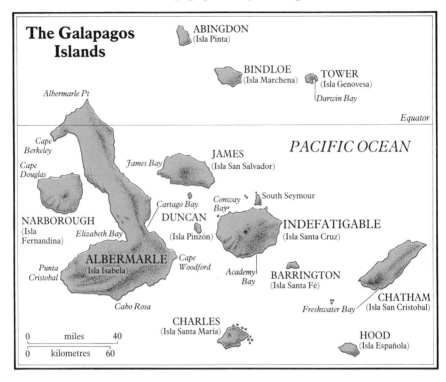

The Galapagos Islands

ABINGDON (Isla Pinta)

BINDLOE (Isla Marchena) TOWER (Isla Genovesa)

Albermarle Pt   Darwin Bay

Equator

Cape Berkeley   JAMES   PACIFIC OCEAN
Cape Douglas   James Bay   (Isla San Salvador)

Cartago Bay   Conway Bay   South Seymour

NARBOROUGH   DUNCAN
(Isla Fernandina)   Elizabeth Bay   (Isla Pinzón)   INDEFATIGABLE (Isla Santa Cruz)

ALBERMARLE   Cape Woodford
Punta Cristobal   (Isla Isabela)   Academy Bay   BARRINGTON (Isla Santa Fé)

Cabo Rosa   CHATHAM
Freshwater Bay   (Isla San Cristobal)

0   miles   40   CHARLES (Isla Santa María)   HOOD (Isla Española)
0   kilometres   60

food. The tortoises 'appeared most old-fashioned antediluvian animals'. Staying ashore on Chatham Island overnight, he records on 22 September 'having collected many new plants, birds, shells and insects'. The birds were absurdly tame and easily taken: any pool of water swarmed with them, particularly doves and finches. Another notable feature was the giant lizards, from two to four feet long. One sort, black and found by the sea, Darwin describes as 'most disgusting'.[23] Another sort, found inland on Albemarle Island and coloured an orange-yellow, he thought hideous. They were considered good to eat, however, and forty were collected for the ship.

On James Island, where Darwin camped with Bynoe and three seamen for nine days while the *Beagle* returned to Charles Island to replenish water, Darwin walked to the summit, about 3000 feet and a distance of eight miles, and slept one night up there. 'I thus enjoyed two days collecting in the fertile region.' Processions of tortoises were plodding along beaten trackways to and from the upland springs. Down near the shore, water was scarce and brackish. With the sun overhead temperatures were high. 'We should have been distressed if an American Whaler had not very kindly given us three casks of water . . . Several times during the voyage Americans have showed themselves at least as obliging, if not more so, than any of our Countrymen would have been.'[24] On 17 October the *Beagle* returned and took the party aboard. Then, after surveying round a couple of small outlying islands, FitzRoy set course for Tahiti and so began the long passage of 3200 miles across the Pacific.

The main interest Darwin had in the distinctive flora and fauna of the islands was to discover 'to what district or "centre of creation"' they belonged. Each continent, he knew, had a range of plants and animals, including fossil ones, different from those of other continents. Some of the Galapagos birds he quickly recognised as being of South American type. But what of the plants? To answer that required an expert botanist.

Those were issues concerning the plants and animals of the archipelago taken as a whole. Another issue, of no less scientific interest, was that of the distribution of species between different islands within the archipelago. After the *Beagle* returned and the specimens had been examined by the appropriate specialists, it would be found that several of the islands were tenanted by their own distinctive species. That was not a finding that could have been foreseen, however, and it is no criticism of Darwin that he failed to realise it. Admittedly the governor, Nicholas Lawson, had remarked that it was always possible to identify the island from which any particular tortoise had come, but it was only later that Darwin saw the importance of that. In his day-to-day diary it is not recorded.

The furthest he got during their five-week stay was to realise at the very end of it that some species of plant, though plentiful in one or two islands, were completely absent from others, although the climate and terrain were identical: 'It never occured to me', he writes three years later in the published version of his diary, 'that the productions of the islands only a few miles apart, and placed under the same physical conditions, would be dissimilar. I therefore did not attempt to make a series of specimens from the separate islands. It is the fate of every voyager when he has just discovered what object in any place is more particularly worthy of his attention to be hurried from it.'[25] The romantic idea that during his stay in the Galapagos Islands Darwin saw a great evolutionary light fails when examined. Before the message of the islands could be deciphered, time and assistance were necessary.

Nevertheless, towards the end of the long voyage home, during which he was busy cataloguing some of the bird specimens collected in the Galapagos Islands, he was mulling over the problem of how species are to be distinguished from mere varieties. A similar problem arose with his specimens from the Falklands, where foxes were found to differ between islands in small but significant ways. These thoughts, recorded in a notebook he was keeping, led him to conclude: 'If there is the slightest foundation for these remarks the zoology of the Archipeligoes will be well worth examining; for such facts would undermine the stability of Species.'[26] Darwin found no answers on the voyage; but he was raising some radical questions.

IV

The long journey home, more than halfway round the world, was relatively uneventful. A dozen ports were visited and up to a fortnight spent at each, with FitzRoy making observations and the ship replenishing supplies. At each one Darwin stayed as long ashore as he could and at several places undertook excursions of several days' duration. Though these were often interesting and enjoyable, the purpose of the voyage had been achieved and everyone's thoughts turned towards home. 'There never was a Ship so full of home-sick heroes as the *Beagle*,' Darwin tells a sister in a letter of February 1836 from Hobart;[27] and they were still not halfway back.

The first stop was Tahiti, which was in all ways delightful. 'Tahiti is a most charming spot,' Darwin tells Henslow. 'Every thing which former Navigators have written is true . . . Delicious scenery, climate, manners of the people, are all in harmony.'[28] The *Beagle*'s stay lasted ten days; on one, Darwin reached the summit of a hill near the anchorage, 2000–3000 feet high. From there he had a good view of a neighbouring island and was much interested in the encircling coral reef.

The following day he started on a more ambitious expedition, towards the 7000-foot centre of the island. With two Tahitian companions to act as guides, Darwin and his servant spent three days and two nights in the lush uplands. At first they moved up a valley but then had the task of scaling its precipitous sides. 'In passing from one ledge to another there was a vertical wall of rock – one of the Tahitians, a fine active man, placed the trunk of a tree against this, swarmed up it and then by the aid of crevices reached the summit – He then fixed ropes to a projecting point and lowered them for us.' 'Beneath the ledge', Darwin continues, 'the precipice must have been five or six hundred feet deep; if the abyss had not been partially concealed by the overhanging ferns and lilies, my head would have turned giddy and nothing should have induced me to consider it.'[29] In the evening his companions quickly cooked an agreeable meal and made a rustic rainproof shelter. They were following a well-known track to where a surfeit of wild bananas were growing.

Before the *Beagle* left Tahiti, the Queen and her Parliament reached agreement about the payment of the fine that FitzRoy had been given the task of collecting; the English present were greatly impressed by 'the extreme good sense, reasoning powers, moderation, candor and prompt resolution which were displayed on all sides'.[30] A farewell reception for the Queen and her chiefs was held aboard, yards manned and fireworks displayed; concern for the chronometers forbade a ten-gun salute.

Next stop was New Zealand, which, in Darwin's opinion, compared very poorly to Tahiti: the Maoris not only engaged in chronic warfare but were hideously tattooed and extremely dirty; Europeans were mostly riff-raff, living a dissolute life and setting the worst possible example. The only bright spot was the missionaries. Darwin and FitzRoy spent Christmas 1835 in their company and admired the perfect replica of an English farmstead that they had created on land bought from the Maoris. Here they left Richard Matthews, missionary designate to the Fuegians, whose elder brother was already in New Zealand. Evidently he had been aboard since being evacuated from his aborted mission, though his presence is never mentioned.

At that time there was much controversy in Europe about the effects the missionaries were having in the South Seas. In particular, a Russian traveller Otto von Kotzebue (1787–1846), had described the dampening effects of Calvinist religion on native gaiety, and had claimed that it was also the cause of wars. Both FitzRoy, who had yet to undergo his conversion to a fundamentalist faith, and Darwin judged the missionaries' activities very differently. Not only did Darwin tell both his sisters and Henslow how admirable they thought the work of the missionaries was but, when they got to Cape Town and heard the criticism, they wrote a public defence of the missionaries' work.[31]

On 12 January 1836, at the beginning of their fifth year out, the *Beagle* arrived in Sydney. To everyone's dismay there was not a single letter for the ship. 'None of you at home can imagine what a grief this is,' Darwin tells his sisters.[32]

Four days later Darwin set off on a twelve-day riding tour into the interior, going as far as Bathurst, 130 miles inland. By good fortune he fell in with a party of Aboriginal blacks, some of whom could speak a little English: 'their countenances were good-humoured and pleasant and they appeared far from such utterly degraded beings as usually represented. In their own arts they are admirable; a cap being fixed at thirty yards distance, they transfixed it with the spear delivered by the throwing stick, with the rapidity of an arrow from the bow of a practised Archer; in tracking animals and men they show most wonderful sagacity.' Later on he was taken on a kangaroo hunt by a farmer 'but had very bad sport'. They saw some fine flocks of white cockatoos, however, and 'several of the famous Platypus'. The farmer shot one, which Darwin was glad to have.[33]

On his way back to Sydney he spent a night with Captain King, who had retired from the navy and settled in New South Wales, where his father, an admiral, had been the first Governor. Darwin's friend, the midshipman Philip King, left the *Beagle* at Sydney to join his father.

About what he saw of the colony during this brief visit Darwin had mixed feelings. On the one hand he was amazed at the extraordinary economic progress it had made after so unpromising a start, on the other much 'disappointed in the state of Society. – The whole community is

rancorously divided in to parties on almost every subject', and everyone
'poor and rich . . . bent on acquiring wealth'. Ex-convicts who had made
money regarded the free settlers as interlopers. Literature was at a low
ebb and bookshops were empty.[34]

A six-day passage, the latter half cold and stormy, brought them to
Hobart, Tasmania, where they spent twelve days. Darwin was getting very
bored with the long periods spent at sea: 'a large part of our time is spent
in making passages,' he tells his cousin, Fox. 'This is to me so much
existence obliterated from the page of life. – I hate every wave of the ocean
with a fervour which you . . . can never understand.'[35]

Hobart he liked. Although it was small and relatively poor, he preferred
it to Sydney. He was introduced to the surveyor-general, who took him for
'two very pleasant rides and I passed in his house the most agreeable
evening since leaving England'. He also struggled through dense forest to
the top of Mount Wellington, 3100 feet, finding 'the labor of ascent . . .
almost as great as in Tierra del Fuego or Chiloe'.[36] He was rewarded,
however, with a most extensive view.

From 6 to 14 March the *Beagle* was in King George's Sound on the
south-west coast of Australia, which Darwin found the dullest and most
uninteresting place yet visited. Thence a seventeen-day sail north-
north-west on a long leg to the Cocos or Keeling Islands, made up of low,
circular coral reefs. Writing home from their next stop, Mauritius,
Darwin describes the islands: 'I am very glad we called there, as it has
been our only opportunity of seeing one of those wonderful productions
of the coral polypi. – The subject of Coral formation has for the last half
year, been a point of particular interest to me.'[37] He was, in fact,
developing a novel theory about how coral reefs and islands are formed.

Arrived in Mauritius at the end of April for a ten-day visit, he lost no
time exploring the town of St Louis, admiring the scenery and enjoying
the French culture. The island had been ceded to Britain at the Congress
of Vienna twenty-five years earlier and had since made much economic
progress. It remained essentially French, however, and the British
government was far from popular. The surveyor-general of the island,
John Augustus Lloyd, invited Darwin and Stokes to his country house,
and subsequently took them to see some rocks of elevated coral. 'Since
leaving England I have not spent so idle and dissipated a time,' Darwin
entered in his diary before leaving. 'I dined out almost every day in the
week: all would have been very delightful if it had been possible to have
banished the remembrance of England.'[38]

With a ship leaving shortly for England, Darwin took the opportunity to
send a long letter home giving his news since leaving Hobart. 'Whilst we
are at sea, and the weather is fine, my time passes smoothly, because I am
very busy. My occupation consists in rearranging old geological notes: the
rearrangement generally consists in totally rewriting them.' FitzRoy was
also busy all day writing up his account of the voyage. 'The Captain is daily

becoming a happier man, he now looks forward with cheerfulness to the work which is before him.' In fact, during the past fifteen months, Darwin's relations with FitzRoy had been 'very cordial', as he had written earlier from Sydney. 'He is an extraordinary but noble character, unfortunately however affected with strong peculiarities of temper. Of this, no man is more aware than himself, as he shows by his attempts to conquer them. I often doubt what will be his end, under many circumstances I am sure, it would be a brilliant one, under others I fear a very unhappy one.'[39] No words could have been more prescient.

By now everyone in the *Beagle* was desperate to get news from home and had their hopes set on the Cape of Good Hope. Since their arrival on the west coast of South America reception of letters had been extremely erratic, with some letters taking a year to reach them and others permanently missing. The last letter Darwin had received was in the Galapagos seven months earlier and, since that had been posted in Shrewsbury on 30 March 1835, he had been without news of what was happening at home for the past thirteen months. As it turned out, when the ship reached the Cape on 1 June 1836, there was only a single letter awaiting him, one from Catherine posted four months earlier. Nine months of letters, sent between April and December 1835, were 'wandering over the wide ocean'.[40] That was very unfortunate, since one of them contained exceptionally good news.

With the ship anchored in Simon's Bay together with a number of ships returning from India, Darwin at once drove up to Cape Town. Three days later he hired horses and a Hottentot groom, in 'long coat, beaver hat, and white gloves', and undertook a four-day excursion into the open and mountainous country to the north-east, noting all the geological features, the plants and the birds.[41] During the following week he took some 'long geological walks [and] dined out several days'. The high point was dinner with Sir John and Lady Herschel at their house outside Cape Town. Sir John, author of the important book on the philosophy of science which had excited Darwin so much during his last year at Cambridge, was in the middle of a four-year stay at the Cape where he was making astronomical observations of the southern sky. 'This was the most memorable event which, for a long period I have had the good fortune to enjoy,' he enters in his diary.[42] He and FitzRoy saw Herschel a few more times, as he tells Henslow in a letter: 'He was exceedingly good natured, but his manners, at first, appeared to me rather awful.' Later, in his *Autobiography*, Darwin describes Herschel as 'very shy . . . He never talked much, but every word which he said was worth listening to.'[43]

After eighteen days at the Cape they left for St Helena, arriving on 8 July for a five-day stay. Darwin immediately took up residence 'within stone's throw of Napoleon's tomb', where he noted the huge preponderance of introduced species of plant in comparison to the small number of indigenous species. 'From my central position', he writes home, 'I wandered on foot nearly over the whole Island; I enjoyed these rambles more than I have done any thing for a long time past.'[44] There was bad news about their expected arrival in England, however: the date was constantly receding. 'The next three months appear infinitely tedious and long.'

At the next stop, Ascension Island, another thousand miles nearer home, there was both good and bad news. Two of the nine missing letters of the previous year (which had arrived at Sydney after the *Beagle* left) were there, those written in October and November. In the second one, from Susan, she had written: 'Eras also says he hears that some of your letters were read at the Geological Society in London and were thought very interesting and now I will copy out another bonne bouche for you. Dr. Butler sent Papa an extract from a Letter of Professor Sedgwick's to him which was as follows about you. "He is doing admirably in S. America, and has already sent home a Collection above all praise. – It was the best thing in the world for him that he went out on the Voyage of Discovery – There was some risk of his turning out an idle man: but his character will now be fixed, and if God spare his life, he will have a great name among the Naturalists of Europe."'[45]

In his reply of 4 August, Charles tells his sisters: 'Both your letters were full of good news: especially the expressions, which you tell me Prof. Sedgwick used, about my collections. – I confess they are deeply gratifying. – I trust one part at least will turn out true, and that I shall act as I now think. – that a man who dares waste one hour of time, has not discovered the value of life.'[46] In his diary no mention is made of his receiving this momentous news, but in his *Autobiography* he describes his elation: 'After reading this letter I clambered over the mountains of Ascension with a bounding step and made the volcanic rocks resound under my geological hammer! All this shows how ambitious I was.'[47]

The bad news at Ascension concerned further delay. Because of 'some singular disagreements in the Longitudes', FitzRoy had decided to return to Bahia in Brazil, where they had been over four years earlier, in order 'to complete the circle in the Southern Hemisphere and then retrace our steps . . . to England.'[48] This entailed a journey of 2000 miles across the South Atlantic on a course west-south-west from Ascension, a direction that proved 'a sore discomfiture and surprise to those on board who were most anxious to reach England'. The *Beagle* stayed in Bahia four days, during which Darwin took several long walks: 'I was glad to find my enjoyment of tropical scenery, [despite] the loss of novelty, had not decreased even in the slightest degree.'[49]

By 20 September they were in the Azores, not previously visited. The consul kindly lent Darwin a horse and he explored the island of Terceira on two separate days. On one he went to see what was described as an active crater, but found it disappointing: nothing more than jets of steam issuing from cracks. He was compensated, however, by the sight of 'some

¶In conclusion, — it appears to me that nothing can be be more improving to a young naturalist, than a journey in distant countries. It both sharpens and partly also allays that want and craving, which as Sir. J. Herschel* remarks, a man experiences, altho' every corporeal sense is fully satisfied. The excitement from the novelty of objects, and the chance of success stimulates him on to activity. Moreover as a number of isolated facts soon become uninteresting, the habit of comparison leads to generalization. On on the other hand, as the traveller stays but a short space of time in each place, his description must generally consist of mere sketches, instead of detailed observation. Hence arises, (as I have found to my cost) a constant tendency to fill up the wide gaps of knowledge, by inaccurate & superficial hypotheses. But I have too deeply enjoyed the voyage, not to recommend to any naturalist to take all chances, and to start on travels by land if possible, if otherwise on a long voyage. He may feel assured, he will meet with no difficulties or dangers (excepting in rare cases). nearly so bad, as he before hand imagined. — In a moral point of view, the effect ought to be, to teach him, good humoured patience. unselfishness, the habit of acting for himself, and of making the best of every thing, or content

Penultimate page of Darwin's *Beagle* diary, September 1836

old English friends amongst the insects and . . . birds'. Moreover, the human population, though very poor, made an excellent impression: 'it was pleasant to meet such a number of fine peasantry; I do not recollect ever having beheld a set of handsomer young men, with more good humoured pleasant expressions.' On 25 September the *Beagle* visited the larger island of São Miguel. 'A boat was sent ashore . . . but returned without any letters, and then getting a good offing from the land, we steered, thanks to God, a direct course for England.' A week later, on 2 October, his diary reads: 'After a tolerably short passage, but with some very heavy weather, we came to an anchor at Falmouth . . . The same night (and a dreadfully stormy one it was) I started by the Mail for Shrewsbury.'[50]

During the following weeks Darwin, in a turmoil of joy, was renewing old links with family and friends and forging new ones in the scientific community. Meanwhile the *Beagle* proceeded up-Channel, first to Plymouth and later to Greenwich. There the chronometers were checked and a loss recorded of only thirty-three seconds in five years of often stormy voyage. For a while the *Beagle* was famous and many visitors came aboard, including the Astronomer Royal.[51]

FitzRoy earned high praise in many quarters. His observations were deemed of great value, and his charts, nearly a hundred of them (some still in use), of the highest quality. Recognition came in the form of a vote of thanks in Parliament and the gold medal of the Royal Geographical Society. On the *Beagle*'s next voyage, to the coast of Australia, Wickham was in command and Stokes his first lieutenant. Sulivan was appointed to command another ship to survey the Falkland Islands. So ended what is now one of the most famous voyages in British history.

ELEVEN

Geology carries the day
1832–1836

I

In recounting the story of the voyage I have omitted several salient aspects of Darwin's life during those critical years. For example, his long ambitious rides in South America have been mentioned only in passing, while his continuous correspondence with family and friends in England has only been touched upon. Moreover, nothing has yet been said about how he was reflecting on the multitudinous observations he was making nor how he was contemplating his future. We start with his activities in science.

So used are we to thinking of Darwin as the supreme biologist that it is not easy to picture him during the *Beagle* years as first and foremost a geologist. Yet that is what he was, as the many excerpts from his diary and letters presented above so plainly show. There were several reasons for this. One was the practical interests of the Admiralty – for example, FitzRoy's interest in having a geologist aboard to study the rocks of the coasts he was surveying, and Beaufort's concern to know more about the potential of coral islands and atolls to make safe harbours. A very different type of reason was the state of geology in Britain at the time and Darwin's extraordinarily fortunate contacts with it. During the weeks immediately before the offer of the voyage reached him, Darwin had been in Wales with Adam Sedgwick being trained in methods of geological fieldwork by one of the most distinguished field geologists of the day. Before sailing he had in his possession a copy of the first volume of Lyell's *Principles of Geology*, which provided a theoretical key to understanding how the various types of rock and strata might have come to occupy the particular positions they do. Looked at historically Darwin's geology is seen to stem from a remarkable combination: advanced methods of fieldwork, sophisticated theory, and a singularly gifted student capable of utilising both in an extended programme of research. In his *Autobiography* Darwin describes himself during the voyage as 'recording the stratification and nature of the rocks and fossils at many points, always reasoning and predicting what will be found elsewhere . . . I had brought with me the first volume of Lyell's *Principles of Geology*, which I studied attentively; and this book was of the highest service to me in many ways. The very first place which I examined, namely St Jago in the Cape Verde islands, showed me clearly the wonderful superiority of Lyell's manner of treating geology, compared with that of any other author whose works I had with me or ever afterwards read.'[1]

That first stop at St Jago (Santiago), only three weeks after the *Beagle* left Plymouth, did indeed decide the direction of Darwin's activities during the whole voyage; this he describes vividly in his *Autobiography*.[2] He had examined a certain cliff and had been struck by the light that was thrown on his observations when he applied Lyell's ideas. 'It thus first dawned on me that I might perhaps write a book on the geology of the various countries visited, and this made me thrill with delight. This was a memorable hour to me, and how distinctly I can call to mind the low cliff of lava beneath which I rested, with the sun glaring hot, a few strange desert plants growing near, and with living corals in the pools at my feet.' From that day forward, Darwin was addicted to geology as a field in which he could combine his enjoyment in observing and collecting with his gifts for reasoning and for proposing theories of causation. Lines written to Fox from Rio in May 1832 capture his mood during these early months: 'My mind has since leaving England [been] in a perfect *hurricane* of delight and astonishment . . . Spiders and the adjoining tribes have perhaps given me from their novelty the most pleasure . . . But Geology carries the day.'[3]

Henceforward, the collection of plants and animals, though pursued with extraordinary zeal, came second. As a science, biology was a field still without a conceptual framework that could explain the relations between the indescribable number of different species found in the world, the similarly great number found as fossils in the rocks, or how and why they have come to be distributed in place and time in the way they are. With no guiding principles, reasoning about the meaning of the items collected was difficult, and it was only towards the end of the voyage and in the months after his return home that he was able, dimly and tentatively, to discern a few promising leads. Thus towards the end of the voyage Darwin was becoming aware of the theoretical vacuum at the heart of biology; and it was, we now know, to fill that vacuum that he would be devoting so many of his later years.

II

From childhood through his university days Darwin had been accustomed to riding horses to get to places. Thus it was natural whenever horses were available in South America or elsewhere for him to use them to explore the countryside. No doubt, too, he was encouraged in the practice by the example of Humboldt, whose narrative of travels was still among his favourite reading.

In South America Darwin undertook eight of these long inland expeditions, in the company of local guides but otherwise on his own. Every one of them had as its aim greater knowledge of the geology of the country. On five of them, nights were spent in makeshift camps. Altogether these rides totalled nearly 3000 miles.

The first was in May 1833 while he was living ashore in Maldonado, fifty miles east of Montevideo. He had made friends with a Don Francisco Gonzales, who, with his servant, was willing to accompany him. These two 'were both well armed, and having plenty of friends and relations in the country, were just the people for my purpose. We drove before us a troop of fresh horses; a very luxurious way of travelling as there is then no danger of having a tired or lame one . . . I was inclined to think my guides took too much precaution with their pistols and sabres; but the first bit of news we heard on the road was, that the day before a traveller to M. Video had been found, with his throat cut, lying dead on the road.'[4]

The ride, lasting eleven days, was not very interesting, much of it through rolling green hill country. One morning they 'pursued rather a rambling course: as I was examining several beds of marble. – We crossed some fine plains abounding with cattle, here also were very many Ostriches. – I saw several flocks of between 20 and 30.' All but one night they spent in private houses, it being the custom of the country that strangers are given hospitality. That had great advantages but some snags. 'One of the greatest inconveniences . . . is the quantity you are obliged to eat. – time after time they pile heaps of meat on your plate; having [eaten] a great deal too much . . . , a charming Signorita will perhaps present you with a choice piece from her own plate with her own fork; this you must eat, let the consequence be what it may, for it is high compliment. – Oh the difficulty of smiling sweet thanks, with the horrid and vast mouthful in view!' Arrived back safely in Maldonado after covering 200 miles or more, Darwin sums up the trip: 'I am well satisfied with this little excursion, which besides an outline of the geology, has given me a very good opportunity of seeing both the country and its wild Gaucho inhabitants.'[5]

Less than three months later, in early August 1833, Darwin embarked on a much more ambitious and more dangerous excursion, or series of excursions, which would occupy him for nearly three months. With the *Beagle* sailing south again down the Argentinian coast, Darwin left the ship at the Río Negro, rode nearly 600 miles north-east to Buenos Aires, and then another 300 up the Río Paraná to Santa Fe, before eventually rejoining the *Beagle* at Montevideo for her long cruise to Tierra del Fuego and beyond.

In a brief letter home, written from Buenos Aires, he describes this 'grand expedition'. 'It is a long journey, between 500 and 600 miles, thro' a district till very lately never penetrated except by the Indians and never by an Englishman. – There is now a bloody war of extermination against the Indians.' 'The Christian army', he reports, under a very able and ruthless general, Rosas, was encamped a little north of the Río Negro and was busy clearing the whole area of Indians. To protect his lines of communication, he had established a series of posts at thirty- or forty-mile intervals where he had stationed five soldiers and a troop of horses. 'The General gave me an order for these horses. – so fine an opportunity for Geology was not to be neglected, so that I determined to start at all hazards. – The horses etc. were all gratis. My only expense (about £20) was hiring a trusty companion. – I am become quite a Gaucho, drink my Mattee and smoke my cigar, and then lie down and sleep as comfortably with the Heavens for a Canopy as in a feather bed. – It is such a fine healthy life, on horse back all day, eating nothing but meat, and sleeping in a bracing air, one awakes as fresh as a lark.'[6] Thanks to the activities of the 'Christian army', which included a great many renegade Indians, the remaining Indians had mostly moved west, where they were massing in the Cordilleras. Even so, there were marauding bands everywhere and constant vigilance was necessary. A precaution they took several times was to ride along the edge of a salt swamp with a view to riding straight out into it should they be attacked. On one such occasion Darwin's horse stumbled, resulting in his immersion in black mire. During their long ride, one of the posts with its five soldiers on the route to Buenos Aires was wiped out and the horses driven off.

This ride north-east, through unoccupied and semi-desert country, Darwin took in two stages. The first, starting on 11 August, was the 160 miles to Bahía Blanca, where he had arranged to meet the *Beagle* and where he could decide whether to continue on the much longer second stage. As it turned out, he was at Bahía Blanca for two weeks, the first before the *Beagle* arrived. He hired horses to go the thirty miles out to Punta Alta, the site of the great fossil find of the previous year. There he found the *Beagle* and spent a couple of nights aboard, telling his traveller's tales and preparing for the next stage. He was also able to check and revise particulars of the exact stratum in which the fossils were embedded and to organise yet another excavation of fossil bones, to be undertaken in his absence by his servant and an assistant.

Eventually on 8 September he started on the twelve-day second stage to Buenos Aires. This included crossing a range of hills between 3000 and 4000 feet high. He spent a couple of days exploring the area, which was steep and rugged, and, when climbing to one of the peaks, he developed cramp in both thighs. 'I presume the cause of the cramp was the great change in kind of muscular action from that of hard riding to still harder climbing. – It is a lesson worth remembering, as in some cases it might cause much difficulty.' His survey was most disappointing: 'we had heard of caves, of forests, of beds of coal, of silver and gold etc, etc., instead of all this, we have a desert mountain of pure quartz rock.'[7]

At length on 20 September they reached Buenos Aires, where Darwin stayed with an English merchant, enjoying 'all the comforts of an English house'.[8] While there he was able to catch up with his affairs, to obtain a passport and letters of introduction to Santa Fe, and to write a letter home.

Considering Darwin's political leanings and his horror of slavery, his comments about the Indian war seem rather cool. Almost the first entry in his diary runs: 'This war of extirmination, although carried on with the most shocking barbarity, will certainly produce great benefits, it will at once throw open four or five hundred miles in length of fine country for the produce of cattle.' All the Europeans supported it as a just war 'because it is against Barbarians . . . women who appear over twenty years of age are massacred in cold blood', because, he was told, 'they breed so'; the children are sold as slaves. 'Who would believe in this age in a Christian civilized country that such atrocities were committed?' he asks rhetorically; and his final comment is: 'The warfare is too bloody to last; The Christians killing every Indian, and the Indians doing the same by the Christians.'[9] Throughout his travels Darwin never doubted the advantages of economic development; nor did it occur to him that such development might be incompatible with the preservation of that rich and varied world of nature he had come so far to admire.

Within a week of arriving in Buenos Aires Darwin was off again on the third leg of this great journey. 'I shall soon be on horse back again,' he tells Caroline in his letter home; 'there is a river to the North . . . the banks of which are so thickly strewed with great bones, that they build part of the Corral with them.'[10]

On 27 September, having hired a trusted guide – 'Your entire safety in this country depends upon your companion' – Darwin started for Santa Fe and covered the 300 miles in six galloping days, including nearly eighty miles on one of them. Nights were spent at either a post-house or a ranch. At one he had his pistol stolen, but, with 'a letter of introduction to a most hospitable Spaniard', he was lent another – 'a most indispensible article'. Arrived in the district of the great bones, he hired a canoe to investigate 'two groups of bones sticking out of a cliff which came perpendicular into the water [of the Paraná]. The bones were very large, I believe belonging to the Mastodon. – they were so completely decayed and soft that I was unable to extract even a small bone.'[11]

Next day Darwin was 'unwell and feverish' and, after another day's ride on a route at risk of Indian raids, arrived in Santa Fe 'much exhausted'; the following two days he spent in bed. His plan had been then to cross the Paraná and travel east 200 miles across the province of Entre Ríos to explore interesting geological formations, including limestone with fossil shells, on the river Uruguay. Still 'not being quite well', however, he abandoned that and decided to return to Buenos Aires on one of the very large sailing ferries down the Paraná. This took no less than fifteen days, thanks to bad weather and 'the indolence of the master.'[12]

On arrival in Buenos Aires he found the city 'closely blockaded by a furious cut-throat set of rebels' and his situation dangerous. Fortunately a vessel was due shortly to leave for Montevideo and Liverpool. He therefore wrote a brief letter home describing his excursion to Santa Fe and the situation he had returned to: 'I may thank kind providence I am here with an entire throat . . . I wish the confounded revolution gentlemen would, like Kilkenny cats, fight till nothing but the tails are left.'[13] He then spent ten very disagreeable days in the city in constant danger of its being ransacked, leaving at length, without his luggage, aboard the packet for Montevideo among a crowd of refugees. Thanks to the honesty of his guide and the good offices of friends, all his luggage was forwarded to him.

Although it was already 4 November, the *Beagle* was not yet ready for the southern cruise: 'the cause of this great delay being the necessity of finishing all charts, the materials for which had been collected by the schooners'.[14] That gave Darwin another month in which to geologise. The Uruguay river, which he had hoped to approach from the west when he was at Santa Fe, could also be reached from the east. Accordingly, he undertook yet another excursion, covering about 400 miles in fourteen days, from 14 to 28 November, accomplishing his objective on a day's geologising near the town of Mercedes. Nights were again spent in either post-houses or ranches. At one he found part of the fossil head of what he supposed was a megatherium in perfect condition, which he purchased for a few shillings.

The following year, after the *Beagle* had made her second cruise to Tierra del Fuego, she reached the Falklands for her second visit there on 10 March 1834, and Darwin promptly organised a four-day ride to inspect the geology. Setting out with six horses and two gauchos, they met with cold, wet and boisterous weather, which made the ground appallingly boggy. 'I suppose my horse fell at least a dozen times and sometimes the whole six were floundering in the mud together . . . even the Gauchos were not sorry to reach the houses.'[15]

III

After her stay in the Falklands and the expedition up the Río Santa Cruz, the *Beagle* sailed right round to the west coast of the continent, arriving at Valparaiso in July 1834. There Darwin undertook three more long rides, all three to examine the geology of the Andes. The first, lasting six weeks in August and September 1834, was in the foothills around Santiago de Chile and ended in his long illness; the second was the double transit of the mountains from Santiago to Mendoza and back in March and April

there is nothing like geology; the pleasure of
the first days partridge shooting or first days
hunting cannot be compared to finding a fine
group of fossil bones, which tell their story of
former times with almost a living tongue.
After entering the St of Magellan; we had a
very interesting interview with the Patagonians,
the giants of the Older navigators; they are
a very fine set of men, & from their large
Guanaco mantles & long flowing hair, have a
very imposing appearance. — Very few, however, were
over 6 feet high, but broad across the shoulders
in proportion to this. — They have so much
intercourse with Sealers & Whalers, that they are
semi-civilized: One of them who dined with us
eat with his knife & fork as well as any
gentleman. — Many of them could talk a little
Spanish. — For observations we ran to P. Famine;
justly so called from the terrible sufferings of Sarmientos
colony. — Of this there is at now the least
vestige; every thing is covered up by the deep
entangled forest & Beech. We then returned
to the outside coast & completed the Chart
of the Eastern side. When this was finished

Page from Charles's letter to his sister Catherine, 6th April 1834 the next year; and the third the 400-mile journey north through desert country during the May and June following.

Because the first of these rides took place in late winter and early spring, it was not possible for Darwin to go high. Even so, on two occasions he reached over 6000 feet, though on the first he was nearly caught in a heavy snowfall. A major concern was to investigate the many mines in the area and much of his time was spent staying with different managers for a few days, learning about the mine and exploring the locality. A particular interest was in the widespread evidence that much of the lower land had risen from the sea in recent geological time: there were plenty of recent marine shells at an elevation of 1300 feet. Higher up there was evidence of great seismic convulsions: 'all the rocks have been frizzled melted and bedevilled in every possible fashion,' he tells FitzRoy. To his annoyance, Darwin found he was again not the first to be making geological observations in the area. 'Here also', he continues, '"the confounded Frenchmen" have been at work.' One of them, a Monsieur Claude Gay (1800–73), had given him a copy of a capable paper he had had published in Paris the previous year.[16]

The second of Darwin's Andes rides, the double transit to Mendoza and back, undertaken in March–April 1835 immediately after returning from Cape Tres Montes and the earthquake zone, was easily the most valuable scientifically and was the subject of a long and detailed letter to Henslow and another to Susan as soon as he got back to Valparaiso. The mountains here are in two ranges running north and south with a broad valley between them. The passes over each range are at about 12,000 feet, the intermediate area about 10,000 feet, and the peaks of the western range over 20,000. Since it was late in the season to be crossing, there was some danger of being snowed up in the intermediate area. As a result, Darwin notes, we 'hurried our steps more than was convenient for geology'.[17] During the tedious ascent to the higher pass, Darwin experienced some difficulty breathing, but found to his delight that on sighting fossil shells on the highest ridge he entirely forgot about it. The night spent in the intermediate valley was 'piercingly cold' and the height led to headache. Once they were over the second pass, the Portillo, descent was steep and it soon struck him that both the vegetation and the quadrupeds, and to a lesser degree the birds and insects, on the eastern side of the mountains were different from those on the western side. Evidently the mountains acted as a barrier as effective as a stretch of salt water. The way in which species are distributed geographically was becoming of major interest to him, and it was destined to remain so for the rest of his life.

Once down from the mountains, they had two day-long journeys, each of about forty miles, across a level, dry and sterile plain under an exceedingly powerful sun. It was during the night spent there that Darwin was bitten by 'the great black bug of the Pampas', which can sometimes transmit the trypanosome responsible for Chagas's disease. 'It is most disgusting to feel soft wingless insects, about an inch long crawling over ones body; before sucking they are quite thin, but afterwards round and bloated with blood.'[18] Although it has been argued that Darwin's later ill-health might have been due to his having been infected on this or some similar occasion, reasons are given in the appendix for regarding this as highly unlikely.

After a day in the irrigated oasis of Mendoza, they started back by an easier route. Another long ride across a scorching desert brought them to a point where the track rises to the first homeward pass. Darwin spent a day geologising in the district and made one of his most significant discoveries, a grove of fossilised trees. After collecting samples and making detailed notes about the geological formations of the area, he continued the return journey in unexpectedly favourable weather, admiring the wild scenery and interested in Inca ruins. The day before they reached Santiago, he began to feel unwell. The ailment, which was probably due to another gastric infection,[19] persisted for over a week, including the five days spent in Santiago; another two took him to Valparaiso, where he stayed again with Corfield. During these days of illness, Darwin records he 'saw nothing and admired nothing'.[20]

Nevertheless, he felt amply rewarded for his efforts and next day wrote his long and enthusiastic letter to Henslow of 18 April 1835 in which he describes his geological observations in considerable detail and his developing theories about the origin of the Andes ranges and their long and turbulent geological history. He was particularly proud of the 'small wood of petrified trees' he had found standing upright in relation to the sandstone strata. Before launching into detail, he warned: 'Some of the facts, of the truth of which I in my own mind feel fully convinced, will appear to you quite absurd and incredible.' In the equally technical and enthusiastic letter he wrote to Susan a few days later, he adds: 'I am getting ready my last Cargo of Specimens to send to England: this last trip has added half a mule's load; for without plenty of proof I do not expect a word of what I have written to be believed.'[21] In addition to his work in geology, he had made a collection of seeds which he was also sending to Henslow. 'All the flowers in the Cordilleras appear to be Autumnal flowerers . . . many of them very pretty. – I gathered them as I rode along on the hill sides,' he tells him. This letter took about six months to reach Henslow, just in time for parts of it to be included in material he was collecting for presentation to the Cambridge Philosophical Society.

Ten days after returning to Valparaiso, Darwin started on the last of his great rides, the 420 miles to Coquimbo and on to Copiapó. The main interest was the numerous mines at various heights in the Andean foothills. 'It was a most dreary journey,' he tells a friend in Rio, 'there is no sort of interest excepting from Geology.'[22] That had proved rewarding, however, as he explains in the letter he wrote to Henslow from Lima in

August 1835: 'This last journey has explained to me much of the ancient history of the Cordilleras', and some of his views, he says, have been revised since his letter of 18 April. Much detail follows.

Before ending his letter, Darwin makes further reference to the 'confounded Frenchmen' who were upstaging him. He had got hold of a report, published in a French journal the previous year, of the results of d'Orbigny's labours in South America. 'I experienced rather a debasing degree of vexation to find he has described the geology of the Pampas, and that I had some hard riding for nothing; it was however gratifying that my conclusions are the same, as far as I can recollect, with his results.' In later years Darwin was in touch with d'Orbigny, who identified some of the shells he had collected. Moreover, on further examination, he found he was in less agreement with the French naturalist about the age and origin of the Pampean formation than he had first supposed.[23] Darwin's anxiety concerning priorities, about which he would always feel extremely guilty, was of course natural enough in an ambitious young man eager to make his mark but, on this occasion, was thus to turn out to have been unnecessary.

IV

Throughout this prolonged voyage Darwin's links with his family were maintained by means of the regular monthly letters from his sisters and the long, informative letters he wrote back to them whenever opportunity offered, together with occasional lengthy instalments of his day-to-day diary. News of his doings was then widely disseminated, and parts of his letters and diary circulated to Wedgwood cousins and other close friends. A second channel of communication, focusing especially on his scientific activities and the cargoes of specimens he was sending back to England, was with Henslow in Cambridge. During the first two years most of the correspondence was sent by the monthly mail packet that plied between Falmouth and ports on the east coast of South America, Rio, Montevideo and Buenos Aires. During the later years delivery of letters to the *Beagle* became extremely uncertain, though Darwin's letters and cargoes seem to have reached England without difficulty, using any ships available that happened to be sailing for England at the time. When the passes were open, letters to and from Chile crossed the Andes by mule and were shipped by the Falmouth packet via Buenos Aires.

Much the biggest problem for these communications lay in the long time it took for any party to get a reply to a question. As ill-luck would have it, no less than two years elapsed between Darwin's sending his first cargo back to Henslow with a number of queries about it and his reception of Henslow's reply, which had in fact been dispatched promptly.

Henslow felt deeply responsible for having launched Darwin on this adventure and in an early letter, received in April 1832 at Rio, expressed his concern lest it prove a mistake. To this Darwin replied enthusiastically that since the *Beagle* reached the Cape Verde Islands 'it has been nearly one scene of continual enjoyment '. He had already decided that 'Geology and the invertebrate animals will be my chief object of pursuit through the whole voyage.' He was finding geology 'pre-eminently interesting', but 'One great source of perplexity . . . is an utter ignorance whether I note the right facts and whether they are of sufficient importance to interest others.' Now that he had heard the voyage might take five years, he was wondering whether he would be able to hold out to the end.[24]

He was concentrating on the invertebrate animals, both marine and terrestrial, because the vertebrates of South America were comparatively well known, whereas little or nothing was known of the huge number of invertebrates. When the ship was at sea he was using the Edinburgh-designed trawl to collect plankton. 'The invertebrate marine animals are . . . my delight,' he tells Fox in one of his letters. 'Amongst the crustacea I have taken many new and curious genera: The pleasure of working with the Microscope ranks second to geology.'[25]

From Montevideo in August 1832 he sent off his first cargo of specimens to Henslow with a long covering letter about the collection, regarding which he is apologetic and defensive. 'I am afraid you will say it is very small. – but I have not been idle and you must recollect that in lower tribes, what a very small show hundreds of species make. – The box contains a good many geological specimens. – I am well aware that the greater number are too small. – But I maintain that no person has a right to accuse me, till he has tried carrying rocks under a Tropical Sun.' He emphasises that all specimens are numbered and he has written notes about each. 'I hope you will send me your criticisms. . . ; and it will be my endeavour that nothing you say shall be lost on me.'[26]

The cargo reached Cambridge four months later, and as soon as he had had time to examine the contents Henslow wrote to reassure him: 'everything has travelled well,' he starts. 'So far from being disappointed with the Box – I think you have done wonders . . . Most of the plants are very desirable to *me* . . . Every individual specimen arrived here becomes an object of great interest . . . no one can possibly say you have not been active.' The packing had been excellent, but there were a few improvements to suggest. Henslow adds his warmest good wishes.[27]

Although dispatched by the packet to Montevideo leaving in January 1833, this letter failed to reach the *Beagle* when she was there, off and on, during the six months from May to November that year and reached Darwin only when the ship arrived in Valparaiso in July 1834. The absence of any letter from Henslow during the whole of 1833 was the most bitter of disappointments to Darwin, as he makes plain in a number of letters.

Before he eventually heard from Henslow, Darwin had dispatched three more cargoes of specimens to Cambridge. One, dispatched in

November 1832, contained the great fossil bones he had found on his first dig at Punta Alta. The covering letter ends with another apology: 'With the exception of the bones, the rest of my collections look very scanty.' A further consignment was dispatched in July the following year, with a covering letter in which he says he is 'sadly disappointed' not to have received any communication from Henslow: 'You only know anything about my collections, and I feel as if all future satisfactions after this voyage will depend solely on your approval. I am afraid you have thought them very scanty.' Yet another consignment, his fourth, was dispatched in November 1833, again from Montevideo, and consisted of several items. One contained 'nearly 200 skins of birds and animals. – amongst others a fine collection of mice of S. America'. Another was 'a bundle of seeds which I send as a most humble apology for my idleness in Botany'. A third was 'an immense box of Bones and Geological specimens'; although he was 'not feeling quite sure of the value of such bones as I before sent you'. He asks for books and advice about geology and says, once again, how anxious he is for a letter.[28]

To Fox, with whom he was also corresponding, Darwin expressed his exasperation at having received no news from Cambridge. In a letter of 25 October 1833, written while he was in rebel-controlled Buenos Aires, he describes his adventures and continues: 'I hope you will write to me . . . Excepting my own family I have very few correspondents; and hear little about my friends. – Henslow even has never written to me. I have sent several cargoes of Specimens and I know not whether one has arrived safely: it is indeed a mortification to me . . . It is disheartening work to labour with zeal and not even know whether I am going the right road.'[29]

At long last, in March 1834, when the *Beagle* reached the Falklands after the second survey around Tierra del Fuego, Darwin heard from Henslow. This letter, posted at the end of August 1833, had leapfrogged the missing one of January 1833. Henslow had received the second cargo, which included the first consignment of bones, in which, he stresses, there was the greatest interest. 'The fossil portions of the Megatherium turned out to be extremely interesting as serving to illustrate certain parts of the animal which the specimens formerly received in this country had failed to do.' William Buckland, Professor of Geology at Oxford, and William Clift, curator of the museum at the Royal College of Surgeons, had exhibited them at the recent meeting in Cambridge of the British Association for the Advancement of Science. Clift was especially eager to examine them further and describe them. 'Send home every scrap of Megatherium skull you can set your eyes upon. – and *all* fossils,' instructs Henslow, adding: 'The plants delight me exceedingly.'[30] In addition, Henslow was sending Darwin some books, including the third volume of Lyell's *Principles of Geology*, the second volume having reached Darwin in Montevideo six months earlier.

To this long-awaited letter Darwin replies immediately: 'I am quite astonished that such miserable fragments of the Megatherium should have been worth all the trouble Mr. Clift has bestowed on them . . . It is a most flattering encouragement to find Men, like Mr. Clift, who will take such interest in what I send home . . . I am very glad the plants give you any pleasure; I do assure you I was so ashamed of them, I had a great mind to throw them away.' Then, addressing Henslow as 'my President and Master', he reports on his activities in geology and zoology. He is longing for the blue skies and warm sunshine of the Pacific islands and is preparing himself 'by examining the Polypi of the smaller Corallines in these latitudes'. Dwelling on these more favourable prospects ahead, he assures Henslow: 'I will stick to the voyage.' Finally, he thanks him for the books, and asks him to thank Whewell for sending a copy of his paper on tides.[31]

Four months later, on arrival in Valparaiso, Darwin received Henslow's much-delayed letter written eighteen months earlier and also one written at the end of 1833,[32] no doubt reporting receipt of Darwin's third cargo dispatched in July that year. On reading them Darwin is jubilant and begins an immediate reply. 'You do not know how happy they have made me . . . Not having heard from you until March of this year I really began to think my collections were so poor that you were puzzled what to say: the case is now quite on the opposite tack; for you are GUILTY of exciting all my vain feelings to a most comfortable pitch; if hard work will atone for these thoughts I vow it shall not be spared . . . I have just got scent of some fossil bones of a MAMMOTH! . . . if gold or galloping will get them, they shall be mine.'[33]

Dispatch of this long letter (filling four printed pages in the published edition), covering his ride round the Andean foothills and ending with reference to his being ill in bed for six weeks, was delayed until early November, by which date he had been able to send off two more cargoes, the fifth and sixth.

On 7 August 1834, ten days after he received Henslow's two letters, one from Caroline arrived. It had been written at the end of March that year and gives news of the safe arrival of the 'immense box of bones and geological specimens' sent as part of the third cargo in November 1833. These comprised the second consignment of giant bones, some collected by Covington during the second dig at Punta Alta, others obtained up the Río Paraná, and also the very perfect part of the head of a Megatherium purchased in Uruguay. Erasmus had reported its arrival to Clift, at the College of Surgeons, and had told Caroline that Clift was beside himself with delight. 'I give you joy my dear Charles on having found these bones that delight the learned so much,' adds Caroline. Similar news reached him from his old Cambridge friend, J. M. Herbert. He had been in Cambridge in June the previous year when the British Association was meeting and had heard that 'some Geological specimens that you sent over were considered extremely valuable . . . and that you came in for a fair share of KUDOS.'[34] Fox had also heard of 'some very flattering things said of your exertions in Nat. History, by Professor Henslow', and of how 'you seem to have added much to our Gigantic Fossil Remains'.[35]

Thus, after living for two and a half years in the dark and increasingly haunted by the spectre of failure, Darwin at last learned that his zeal had not been in vain, that senior scientists found his offerings extremely valuable, and that Henslow, his 'President and Master', was after all not being critical of his efforts but was full of praise. This meant that, for a time at least, the latent or overt fears of his seniors' criticisms, engendered by his father's frequent charges of idleness and his sisters' over-zealous efforts to improve him, were allayed. True, other young men in his position, kept in the dark so long, would have been wondering how the products of their labours were being assessed, but they might have thought of explanations less self-critical than those Darwin leaned towards. Had they perhaps been self-critical during an earlier period of silence, moreover, they might have been less prone than Darwin to revert to their previous fears during a second long period of silence – as occurred during the later stages of the voyage. They might, furthermore, have revelled in unalloyed joy at all the favourable news from Cambridge instead of feeling guilty, as Darwin did, about being vain and feeling they must atone for it by working even harder. Excessive expectations of criticism and guilt over desiring or enjoying fame were forever latent in Darwin's character and ever ready to be aroused.

When Darwin received all the good news from England there were still two more years before the *Beagle* would eventually reach home. During those years he would again have no news from Henslow. This was probably because such letters as Henslow wrote failed to reach him. Meanwhile he wrote regularly to Henslow, thrice during 1835 and twice during 1836. Two of his letters were from Valparaiso. The first described the cruise to Cape Tres Montes and the earthquake; the second his double transit of the Andes, with many details of his geological observations. In the second he also gave some particulars of the final cargo he was dispatching to Cambridge, which included two bags of seeds collected in the Andes. The letter of August 1835 from Lima described his long ride north and more details and inferences about Andean geology.

Starting with the earliest observations he had made in the Cape Verde Islands, Darwin had become an enthusiast for Lyell's ideas. This he does not say clearly to Henslow, no doubt bearing in mind Henslow's early warning against accepting them. To Fox, however, he could be outspoken. 'I am become a zealous disciple of Mr. Lyell's views,' he writes from Lima. 'Geologizing in S. America I am tempted to carry parts to a greater extent, even than he does.' Although he had a considerable body of geological notes, he was far from certain, he says, whether they would be of scientific value.[36]

FOR PRIVATE DISTRIBUTION.

THE following pages contain Extracts from LETTERS addressed to Professor HENSLOW by C. DARWIN, Esq. They are printed for distribution among the Members of the Cambridge Philosophical Society, in consequence of the interest which has been excited by some of the Geological notices which they contain, and which were read at a Meeting of the Society on the 16th of November 1835.

The opinions here expressed must be viewed in no other light than as the first thoughts which occur to a traveller respecting what he sees, before he has had time to collate his Notes, and examine his Collections, with the attention necessary for scientific accuracy.

CAMBRIDGE,
Dec. 1, 1835.

Professor Henslows introduction to extracts from Darwin's *Beagle* letters, December 1835

The first of Darwin's two 1836 letters to Henslow was from Sydney in January, describing his activities in the Galapagos (all too briefly) as well as his visits to Tahiti, New Zealand and Australia, with praise for the work of the missionaries. In the second, from St Helena in July, he describes his visit to Herschel at the Cape and expresses a wish to be elected to the Geological Society in London. He also tells Henslow of 'the degree to which [he longs] to be once again living quietly, with not one novel object near me. No one can imagine it till he has been whirled round the world, during five long years in a ten Gun Brig'.[37]

In these letters Darwin, for once eschewing apologies, even shows some elation about the many observations he had been making and explanations he was proposing in geology. In South America, however, he had not done much in zoology (or so he claims). Even so, he had made 'a large collection of minute Diptera and Hymenoptera from Chiloe', and had also collected 'a genus in the family of Balanidae [barnacles], which ... lives in minute cavities in the shells of Concholepas [a species of mollusc].[38] This very peculiar barnacle was destined to play a large part in his life some years later, just as his observations of coral polyps, made earlier in the voyage, were precursors of a novel theory of coral formations he was starting to formulate, a theory deeply influenced by his knowledge of the alternating rises and sinkings of land on the coasts of South America.

In each of these five letters Darwin is either pleading with Henslow to write, adding apologetically, 'I am very unreasonable in begging for so many letters', assuring Henslow of his great delight in receiving his letters and saying how they 'always give me a fresh stimulus to exertion', or else expressing bitter disappointment that at neither Sydney nor the Cape had he received one. He suspects there may be some that have gone missing. Once again, however, he is expecting Henslow to be critical of his doings: 'it is long since I have seen your hand in writing, but I shall soon see yourself, which is far better. As I am your pupil, you are bound to undertake the task of criticising and scolding me for all the things ill-done or not done at all, which I fear I shall need much.'[39] This same fear, that Henslow will be critical, Darwin had expressed three months earlier in a letter to Caroline from Mauritius (29 April 1836): 'I look forward with no little anxiety to the time when Henslow, putting on a grave face, shall decide on the merits of my notes. If he shakes his head in a disapproving manner: I shall then know that I had better give up science, for science will have given up me. – For I have worked with every grain of energy I possess.' Strangely but characteristically, these gloomy forebodings follow a paragraph in the same letter starting: 'I am in high spirits about my geology, – and even aspire to hope that my observations will be considered of some utility by real geologists.'[40] Unfortunately, realistic hopes of today often live alongside obsolete fears deriving from times past that still live on: that was to be Darwin's fate for the rest of his life.

Had he but known it, Darwin's hopes that his geology might prove of interest to real geologists were already amply justified. Starting with Darwin's very first letter, addressed to him from Rio in June 1832, Henslow had been marking passages in Darwin's descriptions of his geological observations and zoological collections, and in November 1835 had presented a selection of them at a meeting of the Cambridge Philosophical Society. He had drawn extracts from every single letter he had received up to that time and, with minor editing, had published them as a pamphlet for limited circulation to members of the society.[41] Two days after the Cambridge meeting Adam Sedgwick had used the same material to present to the Geological Society in London. Susan's account of the stir it had caused, which finally reached Darwin in July at Ascension Island, has already been given in chapter 10. A further account appears in Caroline's letter of 29 December 1835, although this failed to reach the *Beagle* before she docked. In her letter Caroline, having thanked Charles for his letter from Lima written five months earlier, continues:

you must now hear how your fame is spreading – a note came to my Father on Xmas day from Professor Henslow speaking most kindly of you and rejoicing you would soon return 'to reap the reward of your perseverance and take your position among the first Naturalists of the day' and with the note he sent my Father some copies of extracts from your letters to him printed for Private distribution . . . in consequence of the interest which had been excited by some of the Geological notices which they contain . . . My Father did not move from his seat till he had read every word of *your* book and he was very much gratified – he liked so much the simple clear way you gave your information . . . My Father has given away a few copies of the extracts to . . . friends [including the Wedgwoods at Maer, William Mostyn Owen at Woodhouse, Fox and three others]. . . . My Father has been twice telling me not to forget his affectionate love to you and that he gives you joy with all his heart of all your laurels.[42]

Dr Robert was, indeed, extremely proud of his younger son's success. Writing to Henslow to thank him for copies of the pamphlet and for all the help he had given Charles, Dr Robert adds candidly: 'I thought the voyage hazardous for his happiness but it seems to prove otherwise and it is highly gratifying to me to think he gains credit by his observation and exertion.'[43] From now on there would be no more carping or disparaging remarks about Charles and no further concern about his becoming an idle sporting man. Henceforward Dr Robert would be a keen supporter.

TWELVE

*From prospective parson
to aspiring scientist
1832–1836*

I

During the five years of the voyage, life at Shrewsbury continued much as
before and on the whole happily. Family happenings of every kind are
recorded in the long succession of monthly letters Charles's three sisters
dispatched to him with unfailing regularity. The trickle of other letters
which kept him in touch with events in England came from Wedgwood
cousins, the Mostyn Owens of Woodhouse and from Cambridge friends
additional to Henslow. Neither Dr Robert nor Ras wrote more than a very
occasional letter, Ras claiming that Charles and he had agreed not to write
to each other and that 'Brothers never could do so.'[1] Both, however, sent
messages via the three sisters; and hardly a letter left without news of, and
kind messages from, Dr Robert.

In 1832 Dr Robert himself, now sixty-six, retired from practice, apart
from seeing a few patients near at hand. That suited him. Although much
overweight he was usually in good health and throughout Charles's
absence in good spirits. Now free of practice, he decided to see something
of England and had a new carriage built in which to make tours. Unlike his
old sulky, it seated two so that he could be accompanied by a daughter,
with coachman and manservant outside. The first trip, in November
1832, was to London for sightseeing. News reaching Shrewsbury told
that 'he does not seem so much tired by sight seeing as Caroline expected
and enjoys it all excessively'. The following May, again with Caroline, he
went to York, inspecting the new railway at Liverpool on the way. 'He is
become so spirited in touring,' reports Catherine, 'they were absent about
ten days and the tour answered most perfectly to Papa, who enjoyed it
most exceedingly and came back in so much better health than he
started.'[2] The next tour, in September 1833, was to Winchester and
Salisbury with Susan. That, however, was spoilt by a bad attack of gout
which laid him up for seventeen days. Nevertheless he had enjoyed it and
the following May went on a brief tour into Wales.

In her letters to Charles, Caroline gives a cheerful picture of their father during these years: 'he is looking very well and though since you went his powers of moving about, walking etc. are very much gone he is in every other respect quite like himself . . . he amuses himself very well . . . we go on in the old way having our game of whist and Cassino every evening.' And in March 1834 she writes: 'the methodical life he now leads suits him in every way so much better than the bustling about as he was doing when you left home. I often look back to the dread I had of his leaving off business thinking he would be so flat and dull.'[3]

The three unmarried sisters were spending most of their time at The Mount with their father, but one or other of them sometimes stayed at Maer or Woodhouse, or even on occasion visited London. Their activities at The Mount are described by Caroline in a letter of 1 September 1833: 'Susan's present hobby is [needle] work as it was when you left – she is now doing a magnificent bunch of flowers in an enormous frame. *My* hobby is a new Infant School now finished and the children and Governess all properly established in it and Catherine has a drawing rage.' Two months later she writes that she is 'so busy regulating my new Infant School' that she can think of little else.[4] Little news came from the eldest sister, Marianne, living nearby with her husband and four small boys.

Throughout these years Ras was living an idle life in London. In May 1833 Susan and Catherine were staying with Wedgwood cousins in London, and seeing a great deal of him. He was constantly in the company of another of the Wedgwood cousins, Hensleigh, and his wife, whom Ras seemed to be much in love with, though Catherine thought the real danger might be with Emma, the youngest of the Wedgwood cousins (whom Charles was later to marry). In the New Year of 1834 Caroline describes him as 'such a dissipated character . . . he seems always in good spirits and enjoys visiting about'. During the following autumn, and almost simultaneously with Charles's six weeks' illness in Valparaiso, Ras was acutely ill, probably pneumonia, but recovered under the tender care of cousins and sisters; Dr Robert had gout and was unable to travel. Charles was much relieved to hear of Ras's recovery: 'Give my most affectionate love to poor dear old Erasmus,' he requests. 'During my whole stay at Plymouth I have but one single recollection which is pleasant and that was his visit to me.' Affection was mutual. 'If he is so naughty and lazy as not to write to you,' claims 'Granny' Susan, 'I am sure he has lost no affection for you . . . he reads your letters often over and always talks with the greatest interest about you and stands up warmly for the wisdom of your expedition as it has added so much to your happiness.'[5]

To everyone's surprise, Ras took an office job with Hensleigh Wedgwood's brother-in-law at the end of 1835. He found it required legal knowledge, however, and gave it up after three weeks, preferring 'literary leisure'.[6]

In the months before the *Beagle*'s return Ras, who hitherto had been living in lodgings, acquired 'a roomy house' in Great Marlborough Street, off Regent Street. His sisters were delighted and wrote expectantly to Charles: 'it is very nice for his friends as now we can visit him comfortably whenever we like, and you too will probably find it very useful to have good quarters always ready in town.'[7] Before the year was out Charles did, indeed, find it very useful.

At Maer much was changing. Three sons and a daughter were married before the end of 1832 and, very tragically, Fanny, aged twenty-six and the second youngest, died in the cholera epidemic that swept through England that year, the first of many such epidemics. Another blow to the Maer household which occurred the following year was the serious illness of Aunt Bessy, who lost her memory and became a permanent invalid, to be cared for by her two unmarried daughters, Elizabeth, the eldest, and Emma, the youngest of the family. Thus the hospitable and gay social life of Maer came to an unhappy end.

Woodhouse too was changing, with two daughters, Sarah and Fanny, getting married and sons leaving home, two going to India. Frequent meetings with the Darwin family continued, however, and the Mostyn Owens were always eager to hear news of Charles. 'They always talk and enquire much about you at Woodhouse,' writes Susan. 'When I told Mr Owen how happy you were tears came into his eyes with pleasure – I am sure he considers you one of his children.' Occasionally Mr Owen wrote to Charles, and so did Sarah and Fanny. Current family news and fond memories of happy days spent with him at Woodhouse fill their pages. Charles reciprocates. 'Thank Fanny for her nice good natured note,' he tells Catherine from Valparaiso. 'The sight of her hand writing is enough alone to make me long for this voyage to come to some end.'[8]

II

It was not until early May, nearly five months after he had left England, that Charles's first letter home reached Shrewsbury: 'all the house rejoiced over it most heartily,' writes Susan. 'The happy account you give of yourself and all your enjoyments in the tropical world far exceeded what we most hoped for you. – Your letter has been read very often over to Papa . . . and I think he never can again . . . make his old speech of the *gaol* and the *ship*: now he has heard what a comfortable home you find it.'[9] From that time forward Charles's dispatches and the occasional instalments of his diary were greeted by the family with the utmost interest and read over repeatedly.

No one was happier to hear news of Charles than his old nurse, Nancy, who talked unceasingly about her former baby. 'Nancy begs me to tell you how very happy she is made every time we hear from you,' writes Catherine. From time to time Charles adds a postscript asking a sister to give Nancy his love, which always brings tears to her eyes. On one occasion, from the Falklands, he sends a message: 'My love to Nancy, tell her if she was now to see me with my great beard, she would think I was some swarthy Solomon come to sell the trinkets.' On receiving this, Caroline writes, 'she burst out crying. I really think poor Nancy looks forward with as much delight to seeing you again as ever my Father or any of us do.'[10]

Both of Charles's first two letters home, dispatched from Bahia in February or early March, are addressed to his father, though at the end of one he adds a postscript: 'I find after the first page I have been writing to my sisters.' Both letters are full of enthusiasm for all he was seeing and doing and express the highest of spirits. Nevertheless, he felt it necessary to add a passage to placate his father. 'Hitherto the voyage has answered *admirably* to me,' he tells him, 'and yet I am now more fully aware of your wisdom in throwing cold water on the whole scheme: the chances are so numerous of it turning out quite the reverse. – to such an extent do I feel this that if my advice was asked by any person on a similar occasion I should be very cautious in encouraging him.'[11] As it turned out, the placatory passage was quite unnecessary. The interests and enthusiasm of Charles's early letters quickly won over his father, who became deeply interested in his son's activities and full of admiration for his enterprise.

In his retirement Dr Robert was resuming his long-established interest in plants. Early in 1832 he was having a hothouse built at The Mount and was already finding it a great pleasure. 'Father . . . is in very good spirits . . . and has quite revived his old interest in flowers,' writes Caroline. 'He is going to get a Banana tree principally from your advice.' A month later, in October 1832, we learn from Catherine that 'the Banana tree is sent for . . . Papa means to call it the *Don Carlos* tree, in compliment to you.' A few months later, in March 1833 Dr Robert himself wrote Charles one of only three letters he sent him during the whole voyage, in which he expresses 'the pleasure we all feel at your still continuing to enjoy health and your voyage we are all very happy when we get a letter from you. In consequence of the recommendation in your first letter I got a Banana tree. I sit under it and think of you in similar shade. You know I never write anything besides answering questions about medicine and therefore . . . I must conclude. Your money accounts are all correct.' On receiving this Charles was delighted: 'give my best love to my Father,' he tells Caroline; 'I almost cried for pleasure at receiving it. – it was very kind thinking of writing to me.'[12]

Charles was constantly anxious lest he be spending too much money and so incurring his father's wrath. In May 1833 he reports his decision to engage a servant after thinking about it for a long time; and when eventually, a year later, he heard of his father's reactions he was greatly relieved. 'Tell my Father', he writes to Catherine, 'how much obliged I am for the affectionate way he speaks about my having a servant.' His father had, in fact, sent a message in a letter from Susan that he was '*exceedingly* glad' Charles had engaged a servant and only regretted he had not done so sooner.[13]

Meanwhile, in October 1833, while detained in rebel-held Buenos Aires at the end of his long rides, Charles was spending a good deal more than he expected and hoping his father would not be angry. 'I drew a bill a month ago for £80,' he tells Caroline. 'I am very sorry to say I shall be obliged from these great unexpected misfortunes to draw another one. – After my Father's first great growl is over, he must recollect we shall now be 8 months to the South, where as last time I can neither spend nor draw money.'[14] Here again his anxiety was unnecessary. The message he would receive in August the following year in a letter from Caroline proved most reassuring: 'My Father desires his kindest love to you and bids me to say he did not growl or grumble at the last £50 you said you drew – and he says you must not fret about money – but be as good and prudent as you can.' Caroline then reports how enthusiastic Mr Clift had been about the second consignment of fossil bones that had just arrived, and the usual news about the births, deaths and marriages that had been occurring, and ends: 'My Father is in the room and desires his kindest love, he asks me if I have told you of your fame and about the skull which I have done.'[15]

Despite these reassurances Charles continued to fret over how his father would react when hearing of his expenditure. In May 1835, when planning his double transit of the Andes, he writes to Caroline saying he anticipated spending 'a good deal of money; but I can most con-scientiously say, I never spend a dollar without thinking whether it is worth it. I am sure my Father will not grudge me a little more money than usual . . . Oh the precious money wasted in Cambridge; I am ashamed to think of it.' Back in Valparaiso a month later, preparing for his long ride north, he informs Susan that he has drawn another £100 to allow both for emergencies and for unexpected opportunities. He hopes his father will believe that 'I *will* not draw money in crossing the Pacific, because I *can not*', but, even so, he fears that 'My Father's patience must be exhausted . . . My most affectionate love to all,' he ends, 'and I pray forgiveness from my Father.'[16]

For the rest of his life, we find Charles would fret about money and, so long as his father was alive, would anticipate growls and grumbles about his extravagances.

III

Among other themes in the correspondence that illustrate Charles's relationships with members of the family are his elder sisters' persistently improving efforts and his docile acceptance of their corrections.

The second instalment of Charles's diary (referred to in the corres-pondence as his journal), dispatched from Maldonado in July 1833, reached Shrewsbury in October. Longer and more exciting than the first, it created the greatest interest: 'Your writing at the time gives such reality to your descriptions and brings every little incident before one with a force that no after account could do,' writes Caroline. A month later it was Catherine's turn: 'We are very much enjoying your [diary] now, reading it aloud to Papa in the evenings, and it meets with great success and is pronounced exceedingly entertaining . . . Papa desires me to give you his best love, and he is very glad that you are so happy and prosperous . . . [and] how very much he is pleased with your [diary].'[17] Subsequently it met with similar approval from the many others who read it.

Both Caroline and Susan, however, have some criticisms to offer. 'I am very doubtful whether it is not *pert* in me to criticize . . . I mean as to your style,' writes Caroline. Maybe Charles had been unduly influenced by Humboldt: '[You] occasionally made use of the kind of flowery french expressions he uses, instead of your own simple straightforward and far more agreeable style.' There was no such hestitation from Susan. Writing to him on 12 February 1834, Charles's twenty-fifth birthday, enclosing a small present and wishing him 'many happy *returns*', she turns to the diary, which everyone was enjoying: 'what a nice amusing book of travels it would make if printed . . . but there is one part of [it] as your Granny I shall take in hand, namely several little errors in orthography of which I shall send you a list that you may profit by my lectures though the world is between us. – So here goes.' She then lists seven words wrongly spelt with their correct forms, adding, 'I dare say these errors are the effect of haste, but as your Granny it is my duty to point them out.'[18]

Six months later, on receipt of these two sisterly letters in Valparaiso, Charles replies via Catherine: 'Thank Granny for her purse and tell her I plead guilty to some of her [two words obliterated], but the others are certainly only accidental errors – Moreover I am much obliged for Caroline's criticisms (see how good I am becoming!) they are perfectly just, I even felt aware of the faults she points out, when writing my journal.'[19]

In November 1835, towards the end of the voyage, another instalment of the diary arrived, dispatched from Valparaiso some months earlier. It was received in London and read first by Ras and Hensleigh Wedgwood, who, Susan reports, 'thinks it will make a most interesting book of travels . . . We are now reading it aloud, and Papa enjoys it extremely except when the dangers you run make him shudder. Indeed I think the escapes you have had of different dangers are quite providential . . . When I have corrected the spelling', she continues, 'it will be perfect, for instance *Ton* not *Tun*, *lose* instead of *loose* – You see I am still your Granny.' She then proceeds, without a break, to report to him what a great stir his work was making in London scientific circles and how he was expected to become 'a great name among the Naturalists of Europe'.[20]

Throughout the correspondence between Susan and Charles she

frequently signs her letters 'your most affectionate Granny', often adding, 'Susan Darwin'. Similarly, he as frequently addresses her as 'dear old Granny' or some variant of it. Caroline is more motherly: 'Do take care of yourself my dear Charles,' she warns in September 1833 when, unknown to her, he was living gaucho-style on his long ride north from Río Negro, 'you were so apt at home to over exert yourself that we are all afraid when ever we read of your enjoying yourself.' A few months earlier she had ended a long letter: 'Sitting and writing in this old school room makes me feel so Motherly to you dear Tactus' (her nickname for him). He, for his part, sees himself as the uncouth boy in need of his sisters' improving influence. Writing home at the very end of the voyage in July 1836, he expresses the fear that on his return he will have so much to say that 'I shall annihilate some of my friends. – I shall put myself under your hands,' he tells Caroline; 'and you must undertake the task of scolding as in years long gone past, and civilizing me.'[21] Thus from the start of the voyage to its very end, when Charles had turned twenty-seven, the old relationships between him and his elder sisters, whose duty it was still to scold and improve him, continued unchanged.

IV

There was, however, one issue on which Charles asserted his independence – namely where his future lay. Throughout the first year of the voyage all three sisters never ceased to remind him that his future lay in a nice quiet parsonage. As it happens, the first reminder came from his cousin, Charlotte Wedgwood, who in a long letter to Charles reports that she had just become engaged to a clergyman, Charles Langton, and is looking forward to establishing herself in a nice country parsonage and also to visiting Charles in his. Such thoughts make her 'feel more anxious that you should finish all your wanderings by settling down as a clergyman'. Next Catherine, after reading Charles's letters from his residence outside Rio, enthuses about how nice it is to think of him living quietly in a Brazilian cottage, and adds, 'but do not let the Cottage put the Parsonage out of your head ... and which we were reioiced to hear continued to be a vista to your prospects.' In the second of his letters from Botafogo Bay, dated 26 April 1832, Charles has indeed expressed these sentiments: 'Although I like this knocking about – I find I steadily have a distant prospect of a very quiet parsonage, and I can see it even through a grove of Palms.'[22]

During the second half of 1832 one sister after another endorsed his vision. 'I am very much pleased to find the quiet Parsonage has still such charms in your eyes,' writes Susan. A month later Caroline: 'I often make a day-dream of seeing you so happy in your Parsonage.' In October it was again Catherine's turn: 'My dear Charles, how I long for you to be settled in your nice Parsonage. I hope you retain that vision before your eyes.' In a letter of January 1833 Caroline pictures him in Patagonian waters: 'I do hope my very dear Charles the cold and rains whilst coasting Patagonia have not made you ill . . . if you find all these changes of Climate do not agree with your health come home and think of your snug parsonage.'[23] As it happens, her letter, dated 13 January 1833, was written on the very day that the *Beagle*, battling with the great storm off Cape Horn, came near to being swamped.

There was, however, one discordant voice in the family. In August 1832 Ras had occasion to write to his brother. Charles had asked him to buy a number of scientific books and items of equipment. After reporting on his successes and failures, Ras describes his life in London: 'I am living or rather vegetating in the quietest manner possible . . . thinking it quite an exertion if I can get round St. James's Park in the course of a day . . . I have established a very comfortable little lab. in my lodgings . . . and that and smoking fills up my day delightfully.' He deplores their Wedgwood cousin's marriage to the clergyman and longs 'to have a good groan with you over the incomparable throwing herself away'. 'I am sorry to see in your last letter', he continues, 'that you still look forward to the horrid little parsonage in the desert. I was beginning to hope I should have you set up in London . . . somewhere near the British Museum.'[24]

Although during 1832 and 1833 Charles was becoming steadily more addicted to natural history and committed to continuing the voyage, he was still from time to time clinging to ideas of becoming a country parson. To Fox, already ordained and with the same intention, he expresses these ideas in November 1832 and again in May 1833, and in similar terms. 'I hope my wanderings will not unfit me for a quiet life and that in some future day, I may be fortunate enough to be qualified to become like you a country Clergyman.' 'I often conjecture what will become of me; my wishes would certainly make me a country clergyman.'[25]

Yet his addiction to natural history and science was already well entrenched. In November 1832, writing from Montevideo just before the first cruise to Cape Horn, he thanks Caroline for letters just received – 'I assure you no half-famished wretch ever swallowed food more eagerly than I do letters' – and continues: 'I am become quite devoted to Nat. History – you cannot imagine what a fine miserlike pleasure I enjoy when examining an animal differing widely from any known genus'. The following June, when staying ashore in Maldonado, he received Caroline's suggestion that he return to the snug parsonage she pictures. He responds: 'I think it would be a pity having gone so far, not to go on and do all in my power in this my favourite pursuit'; 'I trust and believe', he continues, 'that the time spent in this voyage . . . will produce its full worth in Nat. History: And it appears to me, the doing what *little* one can do to encrease the general stock of knowledge is as respectable an object of life, as one can in any likelihood pursue.' He then paints the rosiest of pictures of the splendid prospects ahead: 'what fine opportunities for geology and for studying the infinite host of living beings: is not this a prospect to keep up the *most* flagging spirit? If I was to throw it away, I don't think I should ever rest quiet in my grave; I should certainly be a ghost and haunt the British Musuem.'[26]

After receiving Charles's vivid account of the first cruise round Cape Horn but before she had read that very clear declaration of his intentions, Catherine was expressing qualms about his future. 'I have great fears how you will stand the quiet clerical life you used to say you would return to,' she writes in September 1833. A month later, however, Susan is still hopeful: 'I quite long for you to be settled in just the same kind of manner my dear Charley' (as Charlotte Wedgwood's husband): 'I am sure I shall pitch my tent very near you in that case.'[27]

By the end of the *Beagle*'s second year out and despite Susan's lingering hopes, the barometer of Charles's future was pointing decisively away from a clerical future to a still dimly perceived scientific one. Soon after Susan's letter of October 1833, news reached Shrewsbury of the interest Charles's giant fossil bones had created at Cambridge, and when in March 1834 Charles at last learned the news his fate was probably sealed. Thereafter there was no further word from Shrewsbury about the snug parsonage, and all Charles's own letters show his increasing belief that he might be able to make a contribution to geology. That belief reinforced his decision to continue the voyage, come what may.

October 1834 was the time when Charles fell ill and was confined to bed in Valparaiso for six weeks. His letter of the 13th conveying the news reached Shrewsbury towards the end of January 1835. Catherine tells him how 'doubly anxious' everyone was to hear from him again. 'Papa charges me to give you a message from him: he wishes to urge you to think of leaving the *Beagle*, and returning home, and to take warning by this one serious illness; Papa says if once your health begins to fail, you will doubly feel the effect of any unhealthy climate, and he is very uneasy about you ... Papa is *very much in earnest* ... the time of [the] voyage goes on lengthening and lengthening every time we hear of it; we are quite in despair about it. – Do think of what Papa says, my dear Charles; his advice is *always* so sensible in the long run.' To this Caroline appends her own note, once more urging him to return home. A month later Susan expresses the family's continuing anxiety: 'Hearing of your being unwell at so great a distance is very uncomfortable and I wish with all my heart you would be sufficiently *home sick* as to proceed no further on this endless expedition.'[28]

By 30 March 1835 Charles's cheerful leter of 8 November, in which he describes his complete recovery and the *Beagle*'s imminent departure for Cape Tres Montes, had reached Shrewsbury. Caroline replies: ' – poor dear Charles it is melancholy to think of you ill and suffering for a long month and I am sadly afraid it will be very long indeed before you are as strong and able to bear climate and dangers as you have done -- We

Syms Covington, 1816–61,
Darwin's servant and
assistant aboard the
Beagle and in London.
Photographed after his
emigration to Australia in
1839

cannot help feeling very sorry for your determination of remaining in the
Beagle till the expedition is over . . . it will end by your spending the best
years of your life on shipboard . . . Papa . . . was so much affected by
thinking of you ill and forlorn that we hardly could mention your name to
him all that day – he sends you his kindest most affectionate love. I wish
you could have heard all Papa said one day when we were talking about
you.'[29]

Inevitably these appeals for him to return home were ancient history by
the time they reached him, the first probably in Lima in August 1835 and
Caroline's of March not until mid-October, when the *Beagle* was about to
leave the Galapagos on her long voyage home.

Despite Charles's oft-expressed hope he could make a contribution to
geology, he remained perplexed about his future. In Lima that August he
had received two letters from Fox, telling of his marriage and the comforts
of a clergyman's life. In reply Charles welcomes hearing from his old
friend and continues: 'This voyage is terribly long. – I earnestly desire to

return, yet I dare hardly look forward to the future, for I do not know what will become of me. Your situation is above envy . . . To a person fit to take the office the life of a Clergyman is a type of all that is respectable and happy . . . I do not know what to say.'[30]

Meanwhile Charles's sisters were becoming resigned to his future lying in science and not in the church, especially after hearing that Henslow in Cambridge and Sedgwick in London had been presenting extracts from his letters to prestigious societies. In February 1836 Susan's last letter to the *Beagle* refers admiringly to all Charles's 'fame and glory' and reflects their changed opinions: 'Papa and we often cogitate over the fire what you will do when you return and I fear there are but small hopes of you still going into the Church. I think you must turn Professor at Cambridge.'[31] The transmutation was complete.

THIRTEEN

Three fertile years
1837–1839

I

On the evening of Sunday, 2 October 1836, the *Beagle* put into Falmouth
before proceeding up-Channel to Greenwich. Darwin left the ship at
once and travelled by coach the 250 miles from Falmouth to Shrewsbury,
which he reached late at night on the 4th. There was much rejoicing. In a
note to FitzRoy he reports that he had 'found all my dear good sisters and
father quite well. My father appears more cheerful and very little older
than when I left. My sisters assure me I do not look the least different';[1]
and to Fox: 'You cannot imagine how gloriously delightful my first visit
was at home; it was worth the banishment.'[2]

Soon, however, he had to visit London to get his goods and chattels out
of the *Beagle*; and he decided to travel via Cambridge in order to visit
Henslow, to whom he writes: 'I want your advice on many points; indeed I
am in the clouds, and neither know what to do or where to go . . . My dear
Henslow, I do long to see you; you have been the kindest friend to me that
ever man possessed. I can write no more, for I am giddy with joy and
confusion.'[3]

On arrival in London, armed with advice from Henslow on whom to
see, he called on a succession of leading scientists who might help him
identify his specimens and suggest museums willing to house them.
Initially he met with much frustration, as he reports to Henslow on 30
October.[4] Everyone was intensely busy and unwilling to spare time.
Almost the only exception was Charles Lyell, at the time president of the
Geological Society, who proved extremely kind and helpful and who had
already invited him to dinner to meet the palaeontologist Richard Owen,
newly appointed as conservator and Hunterian Professor at the Royal
College of Surgeons. This, of course, was the same Richard Owen who,
during Darwin's long absence, had succeeded in destroying Darwin's
Edinburgh tutor, Robert Grant.

In his hunt for scientific assistance Darwin was particularly disgusted
by the zoologists. Not only did they appear to care little for his specimens

but when he went to one of their meetings he found them 'snarling at each other' and possessed of a 'mean quarrelsome spirit' from which he wished to distance himself. The botanists he found much more congenial. Determined though he was to do justice to his collections, the magnitude of the tasks he was setting himself was daunting and at times he felt overwhelmed. Acknowledging a note of welcome from his old Cambridge friend, Charles Whitley, he laments: 'I am at present at an utter loss to know how to begin the arrangement of specimens and observations collected during the five long years. All I know is that I must work far harder than poor shoulders have ever been accustomed to do.' A little later, however, in a letter to Fox of 6 November, he is more cheerful: 'All my affairs, indeed, are most prosperous; I find there are plenty who will undertake the description of whole tribes of animals, of which I know nothing. So that about this day month I hope to set to work tooth and nail at the geology, which I shall publish by itself.'[5]

Among the many experts whose help Darwin eventually succeeded in enlisting were several friends and colleagues from Cambridge days, including Henslow for the plants (a responsibility passed later to Joseph Hooker), his old rival beetle collector Leonard Jenyns for the fish, F. W. Hope for most of the beetles and M. I. Berkeley (1803–89) for the fungi. Others, with several of whom he would be having dealings in later years, included Richard Owen for the large fossil bones; George Waterhouse (1810–88), curator of the Zoological Society, for the mammalian and some entomological specimens; John Gould (1804–81), taxidermist to the Zoological Society, for the birds; Thomas Bell (1792–1880), Professor of Zoology at King's College, London, for the reptiles; William Lonsdale (1794–1871), librarian to the Geological Society, for the corals; and a German naturalist, C. G. Ehrenberg (1795–1876), for the infusoria.

Meanwhile Dr Robert had decided to make his younger son financially independent. This he did early in 1837 by transferring sufficient capital to bring in £400 a year. At that time this was ample for a bachelor to live on and enabled Darwin to retain the services of Covington, who continued as his assistant for nearly three years after the *Beagle*'s return. Subsequently more large sums would be transferred by father to son.[6]

II

From the day of his arrival at Shrewsbury he had been impatient to visit Maer to see his Wedgewood cousins and to express in person his gratitude to his uncle, without whose intervention he would have missed his great opportunity. At last in November he found time for the visit, to the great delight of the Wedgwood family. 'We enjoyed Charles's visit uncommonly,' writes Emma. 'We had been very handsome in inviting all the outlyers of the family to meet him . . . Caroline [Darwin] looked so happy and proud of him.'[7]

By mid-December he was able to settle down in lodgings in Cambridge to sort his geological collections. During the evenings, when not enjoying some agreeable party or other, he began work on the official version of his diary, titled *Journal of Researches* and due for publication by the Admiralty. In early January 1837 he was briefly in London to present a short paper to the geologists on the recent elevation of the coast of Chile by the earthquake, and again in mid-February to hear some very favourable comments about his work by Lyell in his presidential address to the Geological Society. News of that soon reached Shrewsbury and led to much excitement. 'My Father', writes Caroline, 'is extremely pleased by Mr. Lyell's friendship for you' and 'begs for a letter *soon*' giving as much detail as possible.[8]

Lyell was, in fact, extremely enthusiastic about Darwin's observations, since they provided some of the strongest evidence so far for his view that the great geological changes of the past can be explained as the consequences over time of the same gradual processes known to be taking place in the present. Neither gigantic floods nor vast volcanic explosions need be postulated, as his critics, the Catastrophists, maintained. The new evidence came from the earthquake at Concepción in February 1835, the effects of which had been not only observed by Darwin but also officially reported by FitzRoy. The extensive elevation of the coast that both had recorded provided firsthand and irrefutable evidence that the scale of seismic action currently occurring in various parts of the world could, over aeons of time, gradually achieve all the great changes evident in the geological record.

News of the earthquake had reached England some months after its occurrence. In October 1835 Lyell, having seen at once what the implications of the coastal elevation were for his theoretical position, had written exultantly to Sedgwick, who had been leading the Catastrophists' assault on his thesis: 'Give me but a *few* thousand centuries, and I will get contorted and fractured beds above water in Chili, horizontal ones in Sweden, etc.' A couple of months later, in another letter to Sedgwick, he returned to the topic, adding: 'How I long for the return of Darwin! I hope you do not mean to monopolise him at Cambridge.'[9] In the event Lyell lost no time in inviting Darwin to visit him at his house in Bloomsbury and their first meeting took place within a month of the *Beagle*'s return. A week later Darwin could report to Fox that he had seen Lyell several times and that he had been extremely friendly and kind. 'You cannot imagine how good-naturedly he entered into all my plans.'[10] Thus began the close friendship between the two men that was to be of major significance for Darwin, not only for his scientific career but for his emotional wellbeing too. Throughout this invaluable friendship Darwin never forgot the great difference in status that obtained between them when they had first met in 1836. In Darwin's eyes Lyell would always remain the ultimate arbiter.

In early March 1837, shortly after reading his two papers to the

Geological Society, Darwin moved permanently to London and occupied lodgings in Great Marlborough Street, off Regent Street, to be near his brother Ras. Here he was intensely busy writing his *Journal* and also found time to present two more short papers to the Geological Society, on coral reefs and the pampas, and another, to the zoologists, on the Galapagos birds.

Meanwhile the experts were at work examining parts of the vast array of animal specimens collected on the voyage, notably the fossil bones from South America which Richard Owen was finding of great interest and the birds from the Galapagos Islands found equally so by John Gould, and about which each was reaching some remarkable conclusions. It was these conclusions that, when Darwin learned about them during February and March 1837, led to his momentous decision that species are not fixed entities, as was so widely believed (not least by Lyell), but that gradually and over long periods they can become transformed into new species. In the following July he opened his first notebook, entitled *The Transmutation of Species*.

Darwin's doubts about the fixity of species had developed during the voyage, in spite of reading the second volume of Lyell's *Principles of Geology* in which the doctrine of fixity is strongly supported. His doubts had arisen when he noticed that distinctive groups of animals are found in different geographical areas. Thus many species of sloths and armadillo (including fossil species) are found in South America but apparently nowhere else, and the birds in the Galapagos resembled those on the nearest mainland but were slightly different from them. Thus, when the authoritative findings of Owen and Gould reached him, they met with a mind already well prepared for their implications.

A letter written to Fox that July describes how he was feeling about his work and how greatly encouraged he had been by the reception of his ideas at the Geological Society:

I gave myself a holiday, and a visit to Shrewsbury [in June], as I had finished my *Journal*. I shall now be very busy in filling in gaps and getting it quite ready for the press by the first of August. I shall always feel respect for every one who has written a book, let it be what it may, for I had no idea of the trouble which trying to write common English could cost one. And, alas, there yet remains the worst part of all, correcting the press. As soon as ever that is done I must put my shoulder to the wheel and commence at the Geology. I have read some short papers to the Geological Society, and they were favourably received by the great guns, and this gives me much confidence, and I hope not a very great deal of vanity, though I confess I feel too often like a peacock admiring his tail. I never expected that my Geology would ever have been worth the consideration of such men, as Lyell, who has been to me, since my return, a most active friend.

My life is a very busy one at present, and I hope may ever remain so; though Heaven knows there are many serious drawbacks to such a life, and chief amongst them is the little time it allows one for seeing one's natural friends. For

Charles Lyell, 1797–1875, geologist, aged 52 in 1849, by T. H. Maguire. Regarded by Darwin as his Lord High Chancellor in Natural Science

BELOW LEFT John Gould, 1804–81, identifier of Darwin's Galapagos birds, aged 45 in 1849, by T. H. Maguire

BELOW RIGHT Richard Owen, 1804–92, comparative anatomist, identifier of Darwin's South American fossil bones, aged 46 in 1850, by T. H. Maguire. Later a hostile critic of Darwin's theory

the last three years, I have been longing and longing to be living at Shrewsbury, and after all now in the course of several months, I see my good dear people at Shrewsbury for a week.[11]

His geological contributions, we know, had made a considerable impression long before the *Beagle*'s return to England. As early as 1833 the fossil bones of the megatherium he had sent back from Argentina had been shown at the meeting of the British Association in Cambridge and had caused great excitement. That and his scientific dispatches, which Henslow had circulated, accounted for the exceptionally warm welcome he received from Lyell and Owen, and also for his immediate election as a fellow of the Geological Society. It no doubt influenced the speed with which he was able to enlist the help of so many scientists in examining his collections and reporting their findings. It may have assisted too in his negotiations with the government for a grant to pay for the drawings and plates required for the series of monographs on his zoological specimens, each by a specialist, that he was planning – though Henslow's contacts with the MP for Cambridge, who happened also to be Chancellor of the Exchequer, clearly proved decisive. Negotiations for the grant took up some of Darwin's time during the summer months of 1837; and later on the grant itself, of £1000, caused him anxiety lest he fail to honour the obligation he had incurred as editor responsible for the series. In this matter as in so much else Darwin showed himself intensely conscientious.

The following year, 1838, saw Darwin as busy as ever on his geological studies. Early in March he presented another important paper to the Geological Society, on 'Volcanic Phenomena and the Elevation of Mountain Chains', arguing strongly in support of Lyell's self-styled 'heretical doctrines'. There was a lively debate in which all the leading members took part. Soon afterwards Lyell described the changing atmosphere to his father-in-law, Leonard Horner: 'I was much struck with the different tone in which my gradual causes was treated by all . . . from that which they experienced four years ago' when they had been treated 'with as much ridicule as was consistent with politeness in my presence.'[12] Darwin was proving a doughty recruit to whom Lyell would be for ever grateful.

From this time onward Lyell gradually replaced Henslow as Darwin's principal mentor. Not only did Darwin see Lyell far more often than Henslow but their partnership in advocating the same geological principles gave them a common cause that was lacking in Darwin's relationship with Henslow. Writing about this phase of his life in his *Autobiography*, Darwin describes how much Lyell's 'encouragement . . . advice and example' had influenced him.[13]

One regular call on his time during 1838 was editing the early numbers of the *Beagle* zoological findings, published in serial form at two-monthly intervals; this required him to write introductions to each and to describe where specimens had been found, with their geographical distribution. Another, much more exciting, was intensive work on a private project that would only be unveiled to the public twenty years later.

III

Extensive studies have now been undertaken of the content and course of Darwin's thinking and speculating about science, religion and evolution during the three years 1837–9, which were unquestionably the most fertile of his life.[14] In a series of notebooks and other manuscripts he jotted down his ideas or wrote a brief essay for his own benefit. Now in his late twenties and set on a career in science, he was eager to discover where he stood in relation to a broad array of philosophical problems. What were the proper modes of thought for a scientist to follow? How was theory related to data, and at what stage was it permissible to generalise and speculate about causes? Where did he stand in regard to ethical values, and to religious belief? Did his philosophy of science necessitate his espousing determinism or materialism? These were all problems of the greatest significance to him, not only for his own peace of mind but also for his relationship to the intellectual, political and religious world of the day.

In these notebooks can be traced the progress of his thinking. In them also the steps by which he came to construct his theory of evolution are clearly outlined, as is his recognition of the enormous problem of making his ideas intelligible and tolerably acceptable to his contemporaries. Although it is possible to pinpoint a few crucial moments when a critical step in his thinking occurred – as for instance March 1837, when John Gould gave him the results of his study of the Galapagos birds, and September 1838, when he read Malthus's *Essay on Population* – it is more accurate to describe his ideas as having formed a complex and changing cat's cradle from which emerged a new conceptual framework. Some of the excitement of these months is captured at the end of a long letter on geology that he wrote to Lyell on 14 September 1838: 'I have lately been sadly tempted to be idle – that is, as far as pure geology is concerned – by the delightful number of new views which have been coming in thickly and steadily, – on the classification and affinities and instincts of animals – bearing on the question of species. Notebook after notebook has been filled with facts which begin to group themselves *clearly* under sub-laws.'[15]

Chapter 14 gives an account of the philosophical and scientific ideas with which Darwin started and the revolutionary changes he made to them during these years which led ultimately to the *Origin*. What is striking is the courage with which he questioned the accepted doctrines and his determination to think things out for himself. The general notion of evolution was, of course, no stranger to him, since he had long been familiar with it both from his grandfather and from Lamarck. Most of their other ideas, however, he had early rejected as fanciful, and thereafter he deliberately ignored them as being misleading and confusing. Later he was to be criticised for his cavalier references to his predecessors; yet, even if at times unjust, he was unquestionably wise to clear his mind and to examine the problems afresh. No doubt it was partly for the same reason that he never discussed his scientific problems and their possible solution with others until some years later.

During this period Darwin's mind was in ferment. On the one hand were all the empirical data he had collected during the voyage and that he and his scientific colleagues were now examining; on the other were the many ideas he was culling from the wide range of books he was reading. Most of these have now been identified, and they make an extremely impressive list.[16] Among the books of travel, natural history and biography read during the second half of 1838 we find, in addition to Malthus, two books on the philosophy of science by authors with whom he was acquainted and which were to have a profound influence on him. One was Herschel's *Preliminary Discourse on the Study of Natural Philosophy*, which he had found so exciting when he first read it during his last year at Cambridge, the other a newly published work by Whewell, *Philosophy of the Natural Sciences*. The same logic for scientific thinking and reasoning was advocated by both and was adopted with the greatest care by Darwin.[17] Summing it up many years later in a letter to Lyell, Darwin describes how, in response to some bad-tempered criticism of the *Origin* from Richard Owen, he had defended his 'general line of argument of inventing a theory, and seeing how many classes of facts the theory would explain'.[18] Elsewhere he also makes clear the necessity to consider what the contrary evidence might be and what weight to give it. Thus, although he was working on the species problem in private, his many professional contacts were enabling him to keep in close touch with all the current thinking.

By the end of 1838 Darwin had found a solution to most of the problems he was wrestling with, and it needed only one more year for him to complete the basic set of ideas that he was to elaborate, illustrate and write about during the rest of his life. Nevertheless many years more would pass before he had worked out the full implications of these novel thoughts; and meanwhile they had to share a mind still steeped in assumptions that he had inevitably absorbed from the scientific and religious culture of the times – such as that of the perfect adaptation of each species within an overall beneficent design. New conceptual frameworks are not built in a day.

Even so, 1837, 1838 and 1839 were unquestionably the years of breakthrough and, consequently, of the greatest intellectual excitement; but they were years also of pervasive anxiety. The notebooks reveal how keenly Darwin was aware that the religious and political implications of his theories could prove dangerous – especially if his philosophical position turned out to be materialist, as he strongly suspected it would. Not only was materialism in those days identified with the horrors of the French Revolution, but it was being preached in England in the cause of radical political action. Furthermore, to deter intellectuals and others from propagating such ideas, laws carrying heavy punishments were in force. Darwin had been aware of all this since his Edinburgh days and also knew that scientists of the past had been persecuted and forced to recant. The conclusions he had reached on the origin of man raised especially sensitive issues. 'Man in his arrogance thinks himself a great work worthy the interposition of the deity. More humble and I believe truer to consider him created from animals,' he entered in one of his notebooks during the spring of 1838; and a little later: 'I will never allow that because there is a chasm between man . . . and animals that man has different origin.'[19] Bold though his thoughts were, he recognised that in any public statement caution was necessary. Thus in another notebook we find the entry: 'To avoid stating how far I believe in Materialism, say only that emotions, instincts degrees of talent, which are hereditary are so because brain of child resembles parent stock.'[20] By attributing an animal inheritance only to children, he hoped its implications for grown men and women might be avoided.

Despite these many difficulties, the years 1837 – 9 were, for Darwin, years of great advance when he became established publicly as a rising young scientist and, in the privacy of his notebooks, was sketching the outlines of his future famous work. Nevertheless these successes were only one side of the coin: the other was a constant nagging worry about health.

IV

The circumstances in which Darwin's worries about health began during the weeks before the *Beagle* sailed have already been described. On the one hand, as an adventurous young man who had been excited by the scientific travels of Humboldt, he was determined to make the most of his great and unexpected opportunity. On the other, as he wrote to Fox at the time (19 September 1831), 'the leaving for so long a time so many people who I so dearly love, is oftentimes a feeling so painful that it requires all my resolution to overcome it.'[21] Years later, as we have seen, he still recalled the two months he spent at Plymouth waiting for the *Beagle* to sail as the most miserable he had ever spent, 'out of spirits at the thought of leaving all my family and friends for so long a time'. Many young men would have experienced conflict; not many perhaps would have been quite so miserable and have also developed psychosomatic symptoms.

Six years later, during the summer of 1837 while working on his collections, writing up his *Journal of Researches* and lit up by his exciting new ideas on the species question, he was again worried about palpitations. By September he had consulted two leading London doctors (Henry Holland, a distant cousin, and James Clark, both later knighted) and had been urged *strongly* 'to knock off all work and go and live in the country for a few weeks'. This letter, of 20 September 1837, and subsequent ones of 23 September and 14 October, all to Henslow, show Darwin to be anxious and agitated by pressures of work.[22] He is struggling with the proofs of his *Journal* and complaining bitterly that 'the printers are so savage' and have 'bullied me so'. The strongest pressure, however, is coming from the new president of the Geological Society, William Whewell, who ever since March had been pressing Darwin to accept nomination as secretary of the society. In a long letter to Henslow of 14 October Darwin describes how 'the subject has haunted me all summer'. He proceeds to explain at great length the many reasons why he is unwilling to take the office – his 'entire ignorance of English Geology . . . [and] . . . ignorance of all languages' and especially the loss of time to work on his collections: 'I have had hopes of giving up society and not wasting an hour.' He doubts how far his health will stand the strain even without the additional work: 'I merely repeat . . . that when I consulted Dr. Clark in town, he at first urged me to give up entirely all writing, and even correcting press for some weeks. Of late, anything which flurries me completely knocks me up afterwards and brings on a violent palpitation of the heart.' At the same time he does not wish to appear selfish: 'I can neither bear to think myself very selfish and sulky, nor can I see the possibility of my taking the secretaryship'. In a state of acute indecision he ends, 'My dear Henslow, I appeal to you in loco parentis, – pray tell me what you think', and, in a final plea, protests that he must not be judged as though he had the activity of mind that Henslow himself and a few others possessed, 'though I hope never to be idle'.

In the event and very characteristically, he bowed to Whewell's pressure and accepted the secretaryship. From February 1838 he held the post (jointly with another) for three years, though throughout the third he was absent sick.

During the first six months of 1838 Darwin continued to be subject to palpitations, and also suffered from gastric upsets and headaches. He had no doubt that his symptoms were caused by pressures of work and that he was much better when he took some exercise. 'I have been riding regularly for the last fortnight,' he tells Susan in early April, 'and it has done me a wonderful deal of good'; and a few weeks later in a long letter to Caroline he again refers to his riding a good deal and his astonishment at finding pretty country within three miles of London, struck especially by the beauties of Hampstead and Highgate.[23]

In the same letter to Caroline Charles gives a vivid picture of his life and state of mind at this time. After explaining that any visit to Shrewsbury and Maer that summer would be 'cruelly hurried' owing to his various commitments, he continues: 'You being my Governess, I am bound to tell you how my books go on. I find, rather to my grief, that they grow steadily in size, and I can see no prospect of their being finished, let me work ever so hard, before three or four years'. He expects his *Journal* to be published during the autumn and a major work on geology soon afterwards (neither of which was to materialise). He continues: 'I have every encouragement to work hard in finding my opinions are thought at least worthy of attention. . . . Whewell and Lyell flatter me enough to content me about it, if I were the Greatest Gourmand in flattery. I hope I may be able to work on right hard during the next three years, otherwise I shall never have finished, – but I find the noddle and the stomach are antagonist powers . . . What thought has to do with digesting roast beef, I cannot say, but they are brother faculties.' At about this time he scrawls on a scrap of paper, 'It is very bad for one's health to work too much.'[24]

By June, having, as he records, 'lost very much time by being unwell', he decides he is in need of a break; and that a geologising trip to Scotland and a visit to Shrewsbury on his way back would do him good. 'I have not been very well of late,' he tells Fox in a letter of 15 June 1838, 'which has suddenly determined me to leave London earlier than I had anticipated. I go by the steam packet to Edinburgh – take a solitary walk on Salisbury crags and call up old thoughts of former times, then go on to Glasgow and the great valley of Inverness – near which I intend stopping a week to geologise the parallel roads of Glen Roy – thence to Shrewsbury, Maer for one day, and London for smoke, ill health and hard work.' He ends in sanguine mood: 'I really think some day I shall be able to do something on that most intricate subject species and varieties.'[25]

The so-called 'parallel roads' of Glen Roy are two raised beaches at different levels to be seen high up all round the banks of the glen and for long a source of 'wonderment and legendary story among the Highlanders' and of puzzlement to geologists. In August, after his return to London, Darwin describes the trip in a long letter to Lyell: 'My Scotch expedition answered brilliantly,' he begins. At Glen Roy 'I enjoyed five days of the most beautiful weather with gorgeous sunsets, and all nature looking as happy as I felt. I wandered over the mountains in all directions, and examined that most extraordinary district . . . It is far the most remarkable area I have ever examined.'[26] Among much else, he reports on observations he had made at a height of 2200 feet. This rapid recovery of health and spirits by means of exercise and a respite from desk work is in keeping with a diagnosis of hyperventilation and rules out any organic condition.

Returning from the north, Darwin took ship from Glasgow to Liverpool, priding himself as he had on the way north on not being seasick, and thence to Shrewsbury, where he stayed from 13 to 19 July. Here he seems to have committed to his notebooks a torrent of ideas on transmutation of species and on metaphysical subjects. It seems likely also that he had some long discussions with his father, since in the notebook on metaphysics, which he began then, there is a long series of entries beginning 'My father says . . .'[27] Towards the end of these notes he records that he had 'awakened in the night being slightly unwell and felt so much afraid though my reason was laughing and told me there was nothing'. Another notebook entry probably made at this time describes the physiological effects of fear: 'the sensation of fear is accompanied by troubled beating of heart, sweat, trembling of muscles, are not these effects of violent running away, and must not this running away have been usual effects of fear'. Perhaps significantly, it is at the end of the same entry that he emphasises the necessity of concealing his belief in materialism.[28]

In his book *To Be an Invalid* Ralph Colp has drawn attention to the fact that it was during the very same period (mid-1837 to mid-1838) when Darwin began thinking seriously about evolution and the difficulties he was confronting that he began again complaining of palpitations and also complained for the first time of gastric upsets and headaches; and on the basis of that conjunction Colp has advanced his hypothesis that Darwin's long years of ill-health are to be attributed mainly to anxiety engendered by his ideas of evolution. While the evidence suggests this may have played some part, I believe it should be seen within the context of a much more general problem, namely his deep desire to earn the approval of his father and other father-figures and, at all costs, to avoid arousing their criticism, which he was always expecting. Having accepted the role of naturalist on board the *Beagle*, Darwin felt a strong sense of responsibility both to the Admiralty and to science to ensure the results were not wasted, a responsibility that was much increased by the high value his mentors, especially Lyell and Whewell, set on his early reports and by their oft-expressed impatience to see his full results. These, it is clear from the correspondence, were the pressures that were leading him to overwork. Reading and speculating about species, he makes clear in his letter to Lyell of 14 September 1838,[29] he regarded at this time as no more than a private hobby which, because of its far-reaching and exciting prospects, tempted him to neglect his proper duties.

When fifteen years later he committed himself to presenting his revolutionary theory to his fellow scientists, however, the situation would have changed. Then, on the one hand, he would be hoping against hope that he was making a breakthrough of the greatest scientific importance which would certainly bring him fame, but, on the other, he would realise that he might be mistaken, in which case he had no doubt he would be derided as an arrogant fool. When he came to write the *Origin*, therefore, he felt he was engaging in a tremendous gamble, with everything at stake; and the uncertainty of outcome was destined to arouse in him a long period of more or less intense anxiety.

V

A main reason for Darwin's having pushed on so conscientiously with his *Journal of Researches* during 1837 was that it was to form the third part of an official government report, of which the second part was to be FitzRoy's account of the voyage and the first part Captain King's account of the earlier voyage. In the event, although Darwin's contribution was complete and set in type by November that year, delay with the other parts meant that he had to wait eighteen long months before having the satisfaction of seeing it published. Meanwhile both Lyell and Whewell were giving geological lectures in which they gratefully referred to his findings and expressed increasing impatience at the long delay in their publication.

Since Darwin's draft had to be agreed by FitzRoy, it was necessary for the two to be in touch from time to time. This was a trial for Darwin since he never knew what might arouse FitzRoy's wrath. There was only one explosion, however, – in November 1837 over Darwin's draft preface, which FitzRoy anathematised as being inadequately appreciative of the help he had received from his fellow officers.[30] Otherwise Darwin managed to keep on civil terms with the Captain. When at length the tripartite publication appeared, in May 1839, Darwin was astonished to read long chapters that FitzRoy had added to his *Narrative of the Voyage* which accounted for the very long delay.[31]

Soon after the *Beagle*'s return FitzRoy had married a very religious lady and had become converted to a belief in the literal truth of everything in the Bible. He had therefore felt it his duty to guide his readers' understanding with some reflections on the native peoples they had met with and the geological formations explored. In the first of these chapters he traces what he believed to be the Hebrew ancestry of the South American Indians as well as all the other peoples of the earth, and in the second, entitled 'A Very Few Remarks with Reference to the Deluge', he explains how the geology of South America can be understood in terms of a vast volcanic catastrophe that had accompanied the biblical Flood. 'Lyell . . . says it beats all the other nonsense he has ever read on the subject,' Darwin tells a Wedgwood cousin in a letter of October 1839; and he goes on to say how delighted he was that the FitzRoys were moving out of London. 'Although I owe much to Fitzroy, I, for many reasons, am anxious to avoid seeing much of him.'[32] Thenceforward they would meet no more than three or four times.

FOURTEEN

Darwin's revolutionary ideas

I

During the 1830s there were a number of different views current about the origins of the natural world.[1] The simplest was the biblical view that every species had been created during a single week, which Archbishop Usher had calculated occurred in 4004 BC. The findings of the geologists, however, had already shown that the age of the earth must be far greater than that. Study of fossils, greatly facilitated by the cuttings necessary for the construction of canals, was revealing some other remarkable phenomena. First, it appeared that the fossil remains in the earliest geological strata were of the simplest organisms and that subsequent strata contained fossils of increasingly complex ones, with mammals appearing only in the most recent. Secondly, a very large number of fossilised species were now extinct. Clearly these findings could not be reconciled with a single act of creation, and a multitude of different theories were advanced to account for them.

One, promulgated by Lamarck, was that an organism never really became extinct but at some point underwent a drastic transformation. Another, advocated mainly by geologists, was that on occasion a whole fauna was extinguished and replaced by a newly created and more progressive one. Both these theories thus invoked sudden catastrophic change. This did not appeal to Charles Lyell, who in his immensely influential *Principles of Geology* (1830–3) advocated the view that all geological change is extremely slow and gradual. To explain the fossil record he proposed that species had become extinct one by one as the geological conditions changed and that each was then replaced by a new and better-adapted one.

Irrespective of these different theories, there were two propositions which everyone of influence took for granted. One was that each species is distinct from all others and unchanging. Admittedly, Lamarck had proposed that occasionally a species might undergo some drastic transformation, but few accepted that. The established opinion, deriving ultimately from Plato, was that nature consists of constant types and that any deviation is subject to a powerful constraining influence and thus can only be temporary. The second basic assumption, widely held though already under attack, was that all organisms are part of a single linear scale of ever-growing perfection – the *scala naturae*. In so far as changes have occurred during geological time, they have always been for the better and have culminated in the special creation of man, the best species of all.

Thus the notion that major changes in the world's fauna and flora had taken place during geological time was prevalent, and even popular in non-academic circles, and it was often referred to as evolution. Yet, so long as the academics held that by its very nature each species was a fixed entity, the notion of the slow change of one species into another, or into several, which is the essence of evolution as it is understood today, was missing. Indeed, it was impossible.

II

When Darwin began grappling with the species problem during the voyage of the *Beagle* all the ideas in his mind were those of Lyell – not only his ideas on species but also those on science. All in all they provided Darwin with a splendid start.

Admittedly Lyell held that each species is a fixed entity and that, while some become extinct, others better adapted arise and take their place. How that happens he left open, though he favoured some form of creationism. Since, however, there was no evidence, he held further speculation to be idle. Thus it was that Lyell had posed the problem that, even before the *Beagle* docked, Darwin was busy trying to solve.

As regards the way in which the solution should be sought, Darwin very wisely took Lyell as his model. In his geological work Lyell had adopted the then radical view that the only causes it was legitimate for a scientist to postulate were those for which there is clear evidence that they are operating in the present day. This view had been formulated during the previous century by the Scottish philosopher, Thomas Reid, as a result of his reflections on Newton's thinking. It had also been advocated more recently by John Herschel, the physicist whose *Discourse* of 1830 Darwin had studied at Cambridge and again in 1838, and whom he had met in person at Cape Town. Since most scientists of the day did not adopt this rule, however, they were free to invoke almost any force or power that seemed useful. One such power, it was widely held, prevented every species from changing.*

*Unfortunately, through a major misunderstanding, Newton's work was also quoted in support of this freedom. In his explanation of astronomical observations Newton had postulated the action of gravity, looked on then as a most mysterious force. Thus, if the great Newton was allowed to advance such ideas for explanatory purposes, it was open to others to do the same. What this conclusion overlooks is that Newton had already made systematic observations of how physical bodies act on each other (e.g. a body falling to earth from a height), and it was in order to explain these that the theory of gravity had originally been advanced. As a result of the oversight, Newton's work 'let loose a tidal wave of forces and subtle fluids in science', which in almost all cases led to dead ends.[2] Freud's postulate of psychic energy to explain motivation is one example.

What, then, were the steps by which Darwin proceeded to solve the problem Lyell had bequeathed him? The first obstacle to a solution was the doctrine of species as fixed entities. Within six months of the *Beagle's* return this had been removed, thanks to Richard Owen's work on the fossils of South America and to John Gould's study of the Galapagos birds.[3]

In December 1836 Darwin had deposited a large collection of fossil bones with Owen, who had soon identified several species new to science. These had proved of intense interest to Lyell, who, on the basis of a study of living and fossil marsupials in Australia, had already been struck by the fact that the peculiar type of marsupial organisation had prevailed on that continent from remote times. Now Darwin's fossil finds demonstrated that the same principle, termed by Lyell 'the law of succession', applied also to the fauna of South America. Not only were the fossil species found there unknown elsewhere but they were of the same general form as the living species peculiar to the continent. Thus each continent had its own design of animal.

In mid-February 1837 Lyell, with Owen's permission, used these discoveries in his presidential address to the Geological Society and made sure Darwin was present to hear the exciting news. Only a few weeks later, moreover, Darwin was to hear of Gould's equally exciting verdict on the Galapagos birds.

We have already seen in chapter 10 that, shortly before the *Beagle* docked at Falmouth, Darwin, mulling over the species problem while cataloguing some of the specimens collected on the Galapagos Islands, had entered in a notebook: 'When I see these islands in sight of each other, and possessed of but a scanty stock of animals, tenanted by these birds but slightly differing in structure and filling the same place in Nature, I must suspect they are only varieties. . . . If there is the slightest foundation for these remarks the zoology of the Archipeligoes will be well worth examining; for such facts would undermine the stability of Species.'[4] The vacillation evident in this note reflects his uncertainty. On the one hand, he supposed that, although the birds of each type differed appreciably from one island to another, they could only be varieties of a single species. Yet perhaps, taken in conjunction with the fact that the tortoises on the different islands were said to differ and also that the foxes on the East and West Falklands were believed to do so too, they might be distinct but closely related species. His doubts were soon settled. In March 1837 Gould, given the task of examining the specimens at the Zoological Society, had pointed out that in the case of the mocking birds there were three distinct species each confined to its own island; not only that but, as Darwin already knew, all three were closely related to the species prevalent on the nearest mainland, South America.[5]

Gould's verdict had given Darwin's thoughts, already balanced on a knife-edge, freedom to move a long way forward. First, it must be

ABOVE An example of large-beaked finches (*Geospiza strenua*). BELOW Comparative sizes of the beaks of four species of Galapagos finches.

presumed that all three species on the Galapagos Islands were descendants of birds that had arrived from the mainland; so species were not
immutable. Secondly, the very fact that the differences between the
species were relatively slight showed that transmutation is likely to be
gradual, thus truly *evolutionary*, and *not* sudden and dramatic. Thirdly, it
showed that evolutionary change is favoured when populations are
isolated from one another. Fourthly, since several rather similar species
can evolve from a single one, it explains a number of well-known facts, for
example, that the number of species tends to multiply over time, and also
that species can be grouped together according to the degree to which
they resemble one another.

All this meant that yet another obstacle had been removed. No longer
could it be supposed that all organisms are part of a single linear scale of
ever-increasing perfection. Instead, it was evident that there is a
multiplicity of distinct lines of descent, each having at some former time
branched off some common stock. Darwin represented this shift in his
thinking by drawing tree diagrams in which larger branches give off
smaller branches and so on to the presently growing twigs. Not a few of
these lines of descent, some quite small but others big, he indicated in the
diagrams, had become extinct.

Naturally these implications of the Galapagos findings did not become
clear to Darwin all at once; but within the next two or three years he had
grasped them. Many difficulties remained, of course. One argument that
was to prove extremely difficult to rebut was the objection that the
geological record revealed no evidence of transitional forms; each species
seemed to have appeared from the first in its distinctive form. To this
Darwin always retorted that the fossil record was manifestly incomplete
and that the transitional forms had either been destroyed or else escaped
discovery. These arguments were never very convincing, however, and
the objection continued to dog him. Only when a fossil archaeopteryx,
half reptile and half bird, was found and its features described during the
early 1860s would the objection become less worrying.

III

By far the biggest difficulty of all, however, which Darwin was wrestling
with throughout 1838, was how to understand the processes that effect
these evolutionary changes. Lamarck, a strong believer in the *scala
naturae*, supposed he had solved the problem by postulating that
organisms have an 'innate tendency to perfection', a tendency expressed
in the individual as 'an inner feeling of need', which results in the
organism's effecting an adaptive change in its structure that is heritable.
To Darwin this was idle and implausible speculation lacking any
empirical foundation. For him the crucial source of clues lay in the
breeding of domestic animals, a field with which he had long been

familiar. Breeders, he knew, had been able over the course of many generations to produce distinctive breeds of each species – different breeds of cow, of dog, of pigeon and of many others too. Not only did each such breed, for example spaniel, greyhound, terrier, breed true but the differences between them were so large that, were their history to be unknown, the taxonomist would unhesitatingly suppose them to be different species. Yet these breeds had all been derived from a common ancestor by a well-known procedure, namely through constant attention to small, even minute, naturally occurring variations, and breeding only from individuals that showed variation in the direction desired; then repeating the process again and again in subsequent generations. This demonstrates that significant changes can be achieved, gradually over time, by means of selective breeding. Not only do individuals of a species vary in almost every character, even if only slightly, but some of these variations are clearly inherited.

Yet it had to be recognised that some of the breeds so produced, notably in the case of fancy pigeons, are far from being adapted to ordinary life. Thus not all variation is in a beneficial direction, as so many supposed. How, then, can it happen, if variation is random, that wild species are so exquisitely adapted to their living conditions?

Only after a number of steps, some forward, some backward and some sideways, and by taking into account observations of many kinds did Darwin find the answer. One crucial step occurred on 28 September 1838, when he read Malthus's *Essay on the Principle of Population* (1798), which impressed on him the relevance to his problem of something he already knew but had not applied: namely that, although every species produces very large numbers of young, its numbers do not increase correspondingly. That means that large numbers of each generation must die from starvation, predation or other causes, and extremely few live to breed successfully. Clearly what distinguishes the successful few from the rest is that in certain ways they are on average better adapted to survive in the environment in which they live than are the others. This process of differential breeding success Darwin termed 'natural selection', on the analogy of artificial selection used in domestic breeding. The term was not altogether well chosen however, and has led to a number of misunderstandings (see chapter 22).

The solution Darwin reached has two major components: first, the existence of plentiful individual variation that is heritable; second, superfecundity (excess production of young) and the more successful breeding of the better-adapted variants. Once grasped, the second component becomes obvious: 'how very stupid not to have thought of that', as Huxley was to remark after studying the *Origin*. What was far from obvious, however, was what caused variations in the first place, and especially why some variations are clearly responses to environmental conditions and others are not. How does it come about that some variations are manifestly inherited, others appear not to be but none the less reappear in some later generation, while others again seem not to be inherited at all? In 1838 the first steps to a solution of these problems were still three decades in the future. Meanwhile Darwin had grown up with the belief, then widely held, that the characteristics of the two parents become blended in their offspring. This mistaken assumption was one that Darwin seems never to have questioned. It led him to advance the ill-fated theory of pangenesis, and also laid him open to the well-conceived but mistaken criticisms of Fleeming Jenkin (described in chapter 25). Not until the 1930s were all these confusions cleared up.

Even so, despite this troublesome unsolved problem, by the middle of 1839 Darwin had made formidable progress; and, as we have seen, was both excited that he had developed an original and extremely promising theory and also dismayed by the appallingly difficult task he foresaw of convincing others. Twenty years were to pass and a vast amount of new evidence to be collected before he was ready to risk revealing it.

FIFTEEN

The day of days
1838–1839

I

From two sets of pencil notes, the second entitled 'This is the Question',[1] we know that during the summer of 1838 Darwin was trying to decide what sort of life he was going to lead and weighing up the pros and cons of different ways of living. Not only had he committed himself deeply to work on evolutionary problems, but as we have seen he was keenly aware that he would meet with hostile criticism: 'I fear great evil from vast opposition in opinion on all subjects of classification.' This meant, he recognised, that he would have to work out his hypothesis with great thoroughness and support it with ample evidence if the opposition was to be overcome.[2] That posed the problem of how he was to find sufficient uninterrupted time to achieve his goal. Would it be better, perhaps, to remain a bachelor? That prospect, however, appeared too bleak: 'My God,' he wrote when trying to reach a decision, 'it is intolerable to think of spending one's whole life, like a neuter bee, working, working and nothing after all, – No no won't do.' The alternative, to get married, had great attractions but daunting drawbacks, not least 'the expense and anxiety of children – perhaps quarrelling' and, emphatically, '*Loss of time*' for work. If he had many children he would have to spend time earning a living and would consequently be beset by 'anxiety and responsibility'. Moreover, were his wife to dislike living in London, he might find himself 'banished' to the country and in danger of becoming an 'indolent idle fool'. Yet marriage would provide 'Home, and someone to take care of house', distractions in the way of 'music and female chit-chat', which he thought would be 'good for one's health', and, not least, company in old age. So here again was a troublesome conflict, this time between his intensely demanding scientific ambitions and the desirability of female companionship and social recreation.

There is reason to think that these issues were among much else that Charles discussed with his father during his visit to Shrewsbury in July 1838. Ever since the *Beagle*'s return he had been financed entirely by his father. Since he could neither continue his scientific career nor contemplate marriage without an assured income, to know his father's intentions was vital. By now Dr Robert probably needed no persuasion. He knew well that his son was highly regarded by the leading scientists of the day and was undisguisedly proud of him. The outcome was that Dr Robert agreed to continue his support and also to increase it as necessary if Charles got married. The plan for Charles to make a living for himself by entering the church had been overtaken by events.

With the assurance of his father's support, Charles lost no time reaching a decision about marriage. From Shrewsbury he went to Maer for a couple of days and began courting Emma, the youngest daughter of Josiah and Bessy Wedgwood and a few months older than himself. She was his first cousin, a member of a family with whom he had spent some of his happiest days, and he had known her well since childhood. He was, however, far from hopeful (so his daughter Henrietta tells us), 'partly because of his looks, for he had the strange idea that his delightful face, so full of power and sweetness, was repellently plain'.[3] Nevertheless, with Emma long an admirer and probably eager to get married, his suit could hardly fail; and when he proposed in early November of that year she at once accepted him – 'the day of days', as he records.

The match was warmly welcomed by both families, which were already united through Charles's sister Caroline having at long last married Emma's elder brother Josiah III two years earlier. Finance was no problem, since Emma's father could make a settlement on his daughter giving her an annual income equal to Charles's. The wedding was set for the end of January 1839 at Maer.

II

When in August 1838 Charles returned to London from Maer he had much to think about. A priority was to draft a paper setting out his ideas about the geology of Glen Roy, a paper that many years later he had cause to regret. Then he had to attend to the next instalment of the *Beagle* zoology, which, he tells Lyell, he was now finding a millstone round his neck.[4] A very different activity was writing the early and fragmentary version of his *Autobiography*, covering only the first decade of his life. During September and early October he records he was reading 'a great deal on many subjects' and thinking much upon religion.[5] Although this was the time when he read Malthus and took a crucial step in his theorising about evolution, he describes these days as having been 'frittered . . . away in working on Transmutation theories'. His proper work was to complete the geology of the voyage. Speculating about species was a seductive but undesirable diversion.

It is very probable that Charles's thinking about religion at this time was prompted by his realisation that, although he and Emma had a very great

Emma Darwin, 1808–1896, aged 32 in 1840, after her marriage to Charles;
portrait by George Richmond

deal in common, they did not see eye to eye about it. She held traditional Christian views. He had never been particularly religious, though until the last year or so he had had no reason to depart from the commonly held beliefs. Now he had grave doubts. The Old Testament gave a manifestly false history of the world, and he was shocked by the image of God as a revengeful tyrant. Moreover, the evidence for Christian miracles was plainly inadequate. Yet he was unwilling to move too far from tradition. Towards the end of his life he told his close friend Joseph Hooker, 'My theology is a simple muddle.'[6]

At the time of his engagement the position he was inclined to adopt was a form of theism.[7] In a note of 16 August 1838 he writes of the 'magnificent view of the world' that results from the 'laws of harmony' implicit in his theory of evolution. 'How far grander than idea of cramped imagination that God created' an infinite number of particular species in particular places, such as the rhinoceros in Java and Sumatra and, since Silurian times, 'a long succession of vile molluscous animals'; or, phrased more succinctly a few years later, 'The existence of such laws should exalt our notion of the power of the omniscient Creator.'

III

During the last weeks of 1838 Charles and Emma were busy house-hunting and engaging servants. Emma visited London for a fortnight in December and it was then that they decided to take the furnished lease of a substantial town house with garden in Bloomsbury.* Agreeably laid out with generous square gardens, the Bloomsbury estate had been built during the previous half-century and attracted well-to-do people in the professions and the City. Among the Darwins' neighbours were Emma's brother Hensleigh Wedgwood and his wife, and also the Lyells. The bigger houses had about eight good-sized rooms (on four floors), together with a basement and attic bedrooms for some four or five servants. Thus, when Charles and Emma took up residence, there were several spare rooms in which to put visiting relatives and other guests, and to provide nursery accommodation whenever it became necessary – as it soon would. They were to live there three and a half years.

A few days after he had signed the lease Charles moved in, assisted by Covington, and found that the three days' respite from his Glen Roy paper while he moved his goods rested him 'almost as much as a visit in the country'. This was fortunate, since during her visit Emma had thought he was not looking at all well. 'Do set off to Shrewsbury and get some doctoring and then come here and be idle,' she writes after returning to Maer.[8]

*The site of the house in Gower Street is now occupied by the Darwin Lecture Theatre of University College. In the Darwins' time the address was Upper Gower Street, now the name of a northern extension of the street.

Meanwhile prospects of the approaching ceremony were alarming Charles, as he tells Emma in a letter of 7 January 1839: 'I wish the awful day was over. I am not very tranquil when I think of the procession: it is very awesome.'[9] More seriously, he was concerned whether Emma would be happy with him. A week before the wedding, and after a brief visit to Maer, he writes to her at length:

how I do hope you may be as happy as I know I shall be: but it frightens me, as often as I think of what a family you have been one of. I was thinking this morning how on earth it came about that I, who am fond of talking and am scarcely ever out of spirits, should so entirely rest my notions of happiness on quietness and a good deal of solitude; but I believe the explanation is very simple, and I mention it because it will give you hopes that I shall gradually grow less of a *brute*, it is that during the five years of my voyage (and indeed I may add these two last), which from the active manner in which they have been passed may be said to be the commencement of my real life, the whole of my pleasure was derived from what passed in my mind whilst admiring views by myself, travelling across the wild deserts or glorious forests, or pacing the deck of the poor little *Beagle* at night. Excuse this much egotism, I give it you because I think you will humanize me, and soon teach me there is greater happiness than building theories and accumulating facts in silence and solitude.[10]

To this Emma replies reassuringly: 'You need not fear my own dear Charles that I shall not be quite as happy as you are and I shall always look upon the event of the 29th as a most happy one on my part though perhaps not so great or so good as you do.' Then, aware of Charles's lack of religious faith and troubled by it, she continues: 'There is only one subject in the world that ever gives me a moment's uneasiness . . . and I do hope that though our opinions may not agree upon all points of religion we may sympathize a good deal in our *feelings* on the subject. I believe my chief danger will be that I shall lead so happy comfortable and amusing a life that I shall be careless . . . and think of nothing serious in this world or the next.'[11]

Charles's anxieties about the impending event seem to have persisted, despite the ceremony being in the village church at Maer and conducted by a cousin: a few days before the wedding he reports to Emma that he had been suffering from 'a bad headache, which continued two days and two nights, so that I doubted whether it ever meant to go and allow me to be married'.[12]

IV

Thanks to the memoir of Emma compiled by one of her daughters, Henrietta (born in 1843), we are well informed about Emma's childhood and early adult life as well as her later years. In preparing the memoir, entitled *Emma Darwin: A Century of Family Letters*,[13] Henrietta drew on many sources of information. These include what her mother told her, what she heard from her mother's elder sisters, and what is contained in the large collection of family letters and extracts from contemporary diaries which she included in her two volumes.

Emma was the youngest and much-loved member of a large and united family. She and her sister Fanny, nearly two years older, had been close companions until Fanny's untimely death at the age of twenty-six in 1832, and had always been known as 'the Doveleys.' In character the two differed greatly, as Henrietta explains:

Emma was pretty, with abundant rich brown hair, grey eyes and a fresh complexion, a firm chin, a high forehead and straight nose. She was of medium height, with well-formed shoulders and pretty hands and arms. She had a graceful and dignified carriage. . . . Fanny was short and not pretty, though with bright colouring. She was gentle, orderly and industrious. Emma had initiative, high spirits, and more ability than her sister. Her mother's nickname for Fanny 'Mrs. Pedigree' no doubt alludes to her curious tastes [which included a passion for making lists of every kind – temperatures, words in different languages, items of housekeeping]. Emma's nickname at the same time was 'Little Miss Slip-Slop', and that also is revealing as to her character. She was never tidy or orderly as to little things. But, on the other hand, she had a large-minded, unfussy way of taking life which is more common amongst men than amongst women. My father said that after he married he made up his mind to give up all his natural taste for tidiness, and that he would not allow himself to feel annoyed by her calm disregard for such details. He would say the only sure place to find a pin or a pair of scissors was his study.[14]

Emma's casual ways were well known. When she was newly grown up, a maternal aunt, who had tried hard but without success to smarten her up, had predicted that Emma would 'lark it through life'; and this, Henrietta remarks, remained true to some extent. At times she could even be a little rash, as she herself admitted after she had let the nursery-maid take a party of small children for a picnic in a nearby wood, which led to the whole party getting lost.[15]

Much in Emma's character was the natural product of her stable and loving upbringing and the easy-going education that she and Fanny received at home from their two much older sisters, Elizabeth and Charlotte. A charming picture of the way of life at Maer, and of the Doveleys when aged eleven and thirteen, is recorded in the diary of a young woman guest who spent three days there in July 1819. 'The two little girls are happy, gay, aimiable, sensible, and though not particularly energetic in learning, yet will acquire all that is necessary by their steady perseverance. They have freedom in their actions in this house as well as in their principles. Doors and windows stand open, you are nowhere in confinement.' In recording her impressions of Maer, this visitor confirms all that we know from other sources:

I never saw anything pleasanter than the ways of going on of this family, and one reason is the freedom of speech upon every subject; there is no difference in politics or principles of any kind that makes it treason to speak one's mind openly, and they all do it. There is a simplicity of good sense about them, that no one ever dreams of not differing upon any subject where they feel inclined. As no things are said from party or prejudice, there is no bitterness in discussing opinions . . . you may do as you like; you are surrounded by books that all look most tempting to read; you will always find some pleasant topic of conversation, or may start one as all things are talked of in the general family. All this sounds and is delightful.[16]

Later that year (1819) another contemporary picture of Emma and Fanny comes from the hand of Emma Allen, one of their mother's eight younger sisters who was caring for them briefly while Maer was being redecorated. In a letter to the family describing how her little party was faring she writes:

I marvel at the strength of the girls' spirits as much as I do at the perfection of their tempers. I feel now very sure . . . that an irritable feeling never arises. Fanny, to be sure, is calmness itself, but Emma's feelings would make me expect that Fanny's reproofs, which she often gives with an elder sister air, would ruffle her a little; but I have never seen that expressive face take the shadow of an angry look, and I do think her love for Fanny is the prettiest thing I ever saw. I ascribe much of Emma's joyous nature to have been secured, if not caused, by Fanny's yielding disposition; had the other met with a cross or an opposing sister there was every chance that with her ardent feelings, her temper had become irritable. Now she is made the happiest being that ever was looked on, and so much affection in her nature as will secure her from selfishness.[17]

In January 1822, when Emma was fourteen and Fanny nearly sixteen, the Doveleys went to a small boarding-school on Paddington Green, then a semi-rural village on the western outskirts of London, where they stayed one year. After that their education was continued at home, under the supervision once again of their elder sisters, Elizabeth and Charlotte. 'My mother told me they had a long morning's work, nine till one I think, and then nothing else at all to do for the rest of the day, no preparations or work of any kind.' 'I should imagine,' continues Henrietta, 'that this freedom for hours every day – to read, to think, and to amuse herself – must have greatly added to the remarkable independence of Emma's character and way of thinking. It is certainly the fact that all the sisters were well-educated women, judged by any modern standard. In languages Emma knew French, Italian and German. . . . She was capable in all she undertook, a beautiful needlewoman, a good archer and she rode, danced and skated. She drew a little, though she said herself her drawing was quite worthless. Her gift was music. She played delightfully on the piano till the very end of her life.'[18]

Only once is Emma recorded as having been abroad. This was in the winter and spring of 1826–7 when she and Fanny, aged eighteen and twenty, spent eight months in Geneva with another of their mother's many sisters, Jessie, who had married a Swiss historian, Jean Charles de Sismondi (1773–1842). It proved an enjoyable visit with much social life, a series of balls and short trips to other parts of Switzerland. In one of her letters home Emma reports that she was taking piano lessons with a German music-master and had also 'made great progress in hairdressing'.[19] Jessie de Sismondi had no children of her own and much enjoyed her nieces' eight-month visit, during which a strong bond of affecton sprang up between them.

During the autumn of 1827, when Maer was in its heyday with a constant flow of relatives and friends staying for short or long periods, 'Emma, now 19, was leading a happy girlish life, taking what parties, balls and archery meetings came in her way.' Among her other activities was teaching the village children. For some years the Wedgwood family had provided what education there was for the sixty or so local children. School could only be held on Sundays (hence the misleading name 'Sunday school'), since the children were employed during weekdays; it took place in the Maer laundry.[20]

V

At the time she accepted his proposal Emma was aware that Charles was in ill-health and that two eminent doctors regarded the illness as serious. No doubt she hoped that in due course and with her help he would recover; meanwhile she was prepared to give him whatever care he needed. In her letter of 30 December begging him to go to Shrewsbury to 'get some doctoring' she describes her concern about his health and also shows how keenly aware she was of his anxiety lest marriage intrude on his precious working time:

I am sure it must be very disagreeable and painful to you to feel so often cut off from the power of doing your work and I want you to cast out of your mind all anxiety about me on that point and to feel sure that nothing *could* make me so happy as to feel that I could be of any use or comfort to my own dear Charles when he is not well. If you knew how I long to be with you when you are not well! You must not think that I expect a holiday husband to be always making himself agreeable to me and if that is all the 'worse' that I shall have it will not be much for me to bear whatever it may be for you. So don't be ill any more my dear Charley till I can be with you to nurse you and save you from bothers.[21]

For the past six years Emma had been living a life much like those of the unmarried daughters of well-off families depicted in the novels of the contemporary authors, Trollope and Thackeray. A principal occupation had been caring for her sick mother, who was infirm and whose mind was failing – a responsibility she had been sharing with Elizabeth, her eldest, unmarried, sister.[22] There is no evidence, however, as some would have it, that Emma was a compulsive caregiver, eager to find invalids and lame ducks to minister to. All that we know of her tells against such a view.

The picture of Emma that emerges from the extensive records is of a buoyant and confident person who enjoyed life to the full and enabled others to enjoy it too. In her dealings with Charles she showed much sensitivity, as is revealed, for example, in the letter she wrote to him soon after their marriage about their different attitudes towards religion. According to Henrietta, it was Emma's profound respect for the individualities of her children and grandchildren, and also nephews and nieces, that lay at the root of her happy relations with them all. Unlike Charles's sisters, who were always intent to improve, she took people as she found them. While devoted to the welfare of her husband and chidren, she was a realist. When in later years an acquaintance remarked how interesting it must be to watch her husband's experiments, she replied simply that she did not find it so.[23] She valued Charles's scientific work, not because of its intrinsic interest nor for the fame it brought him, but because it was of such enormous importance to him, both intellectually and emotionally. Towards the end of his life she remarked that she would not wish him to go on living were he to become incapable of work.[24]

The marriage of Charles and Emma was the start of what would prove to be a happy and harmonious partnership which lasted over forty years. Apart from Charles's anxieties and health, the only problem was their difference over religion. Two letters written by Emma, carefully preserved and with a few lines at the end written by Charles, were found among his papers after his death. One had been written during the weeks after their marriage; the other when he was in poor health twenty years later. The following are extracts from her first letter.[25]

The state of mind that I wish to preserve with respect to you, is to feel that while you are acting conscientiously and sincerely wishing and trying to learn the truth, you cannot be wrong, but there are some reasons that force themselves upon me, and prevent myself from being always able to give myself this comfort. I daresay you have often thought of them before, but I will write down what has been in my head, knowing that my own dearest will indulge me.. . . It seems to me that the line of your pursuits may have led you to view chiefly the difficulties on one side, and that you have not had time to consider and study the chain of difficulties on the other, but I believe you do not consider your opinion as formed. May not the habit in scientific pursuits of believing nothing till it is proved, influence your mind too much in other things which cannot be proved in the same way, and which if true are likely to be above our comprehension.. . . Don't think that it is not my affair and that it does not much signify to me. Everything that concerns you concerns me and I should be most unhappy if I thought we did not belong to each other for ever. I am rather afraid my own dear Nigger will think I have forgotten my promise not to bother him, but I am sure he loves me, and I cannot tell him how happy he makes me and how dearly I love him and thank him for all his affection which makes the happiness of my life more and more every day.

> When I am dead, know that many times,
> I have kissed and cryed over this.
>   C.D.

SIXTEEN

A bitter mortification
1839–1842

I

At the time of their marriage, Charles was a few weeks short of thirty, Emma ten months older. They immediately took up residence in their Bloomsbury house, where Charles had already fitted out one of the attics as a museum for his collections. Almost without a break he continued with his scientific work.

A few days before their marriage Darwin had been elected a fellow of the Royal Society and a week after it he read his Glen Roy paper there. But his main preoccupation was to push on with the volume he was preparing on *The Structure and Distribution of Coral Reefs*, which, he complained, entailed his reading every account ever written of the islands of the Pacific and consulting many charts.[1] This work, begun during the previous autumn, was to take him far longer than he expected.

Meanwhile Emma was adapting to her new way of life. As a countrywoman she preferred to live in the smallish back room overlooking the garden rather than in the much larger drawing-room. In it she installed the piano given her by her father as a wedding present and on which she enjoyed playing to Charles of an evening, something she would do for the rest of their lives together. 'She had a crisp and fine touch,' reports Henrietta, 'and played always with intelligence and simplicity. But she could endure nothing sentimental, and "slow movements" were occasionally under her treatment somewhat too "allegro".'

During the first months of marriage they lived a social life, going to parties and entertaining at home. In early April they had Henslow and his wife to stay for a few days and gave a dinner party for them. This Emma describes in a letter to her eldest sister, Elizabeth, to whom she had always been especially close and now wrote frequently. Guests included the Lyells and the leading botanist of the day, Robert Brown (1773–1858). Before dinner there had been rather a long wait for one of the guests, a wait that Emma found 'rather awful'. 'Mr. Lyell is enough to flatten a party,' she continues, 'as he never speaks above his breath, so that everybody keeps lowering their tone to his. Mr. Brown, whom Humboldt calls "the glory of Great Britain", looks so shy as if he longed to shrink into himself and disappear entirely; however, notwithstanding those two dead weights, viz., the greatest botanist and the greatest geologist in Europe, we did very well and had no pauses.' Mrs Henslow kept the conversation going, and Henslow himself enjoyed meeting Brown. 'Charles was dreadfully exhausted when it was over.'[2]

At Maer Elizabeth, now forty-six, was soldiering on caring for her ageing parents and much missing the companionship of Emma. A picture of the scene at Maer and in Gower Street is given by Bessy Wedgwood's youngest sister, Fanny Allen (1781 – 1875), who was visiting her relatives at this time. 'Elizabeth has suffered from the loss of Emma more than she expected,' Fanny Allen tells a friend; 'her joy at Emma's happy prospects . . . kept her from falling back on herself and thinking of her loss, but that time must have come. Emma is as happy as possible, as she has always been – there never was a person born under a happier star than she, her feelings are the most healthful possible; joy and sorrow are felt by her in their due proportions, nothing robs her of the enjoyment that happy circumstances would naturally give. Her account of her life with Charles Darwin and in her new ménage is very pleasant.'[3]

Alexander von Humboldt, 1769–1859, German naturalist and traveller, aged 78 in 1847

A sorrow that had struck both the Darwin and the Wedgwood families at this time was the death of the baby daughter of Joe (Josiah III) and Caroline Wedgwood. Born on 13 December 1838 the baby failed to thrive and died, aged seven weeks, two days after Charles and Emma's wedding. Her loss was a terrible blow to Caroline from which she seems never fully to have recovered. Now thirty-eight, she had been preparing for the birth of her firstborn 'in an intense way' that Elizabeth Wedgwood reports she 'never saw in anyone else'.[4] Three years later another daughter was born and given the same name, Sophy, as the one who died.

During the following May, when Charles and Emma were visiting Maer, Charles's *Journal of Researches* at last made its belated appearance – 'my first-born child', as he called it. Lyell had long since seen the proofs and not only was enthusiastic but had already referred to some of the findings in one of his own papers, to Darwin's intense delight. Now that the *Journal* was published, copies could be sent to friends and colleagues. A chorus of praise followed. In a warm letter of gratitude for his copy, one geologist speaks enthusiastically of the scientific content and adds: 'What I like best, however, is the tone of kind and generous feeling that is visible in every part, so that one sees that it is the work of a plain English gentleman . . . viewing all things *kindly*.' A few months later a long and approving commentary arrived from the great Humboldt himself. In it he refers to Darwin's illustrious name and predicts an excellent future for the grandson of the poetic author of *Zoönomia*. A multitude of scientific reflections and questions follow.[5]

Heartening though the reception of the *Journal* was, there were clouds on the horizon in the shape of renewed ill-health.

II

During April and May 1839 Charles and Emma spent four weeks out of London, partly at Maer and partly at Shrewsbury – a type of combined visit to both their families which they were to make regularly for the next few years. Charles was not well: 'some reading connected with species', he records, 'but did very little on account of being unwell'. At this time Emma's eldest sister Elizabeth in a letter to an aunt describes Charles as having been 'unwell almost the whole time' and to have received some 'good doctoring' from his father.[6]

Despite ill-health, Darwin's reading on the species question had been serious. In March at The Mount, he had reread his grandfather's *Zoönomia*, and during their stay at Maer he had worked his way through Lamarck's *Philosophie zoölogique* (1809), the most ambitious and complete of Lamarck's writings on evolution, and had annotated it with great care. No doubt he had wanted to remind himself of the contents of these books and to confirm that his new ideas were indeed radically different from the old. Among other books also read at Maer was the volume of *Ethical Philosophy* by his distinguished acquaintance James Mackintosh.[7]

Mid-May to mid-August Charles and Emma spent in London, with Charles working mainly on *Coral Reefs*, when he again records having 'lost some time unwell'. In August they returned to Maer and Shrewsbury for another month, during which Charles attended the meeting of the British Association in Birmingham; but his health showed no improvement. 'During my visit to Maer,' he records, 'read a little, was much unwell, and scandalously idle. I have derived this much good that *nothing* is so intolerable as idleness.' Back in London a month later (24 October), in a long letter to Fox, he apologises for not visiting when he was with his relatives: 'during my whole visit in the country I was so languid and uncomfortable that I had but one wish and that was to remain perfectly quiet and see no one.' He then refers to Emma's pregnancy, by now seven months advanced. 'Emma is only moderately well and I fear what you said is true "she won't be better till she is worse". We are living a life of extreme quietness.' Finally, he refers to his sister Caroline's grief over the loss of her baby nine months earlier. 'I do not believe the deaths of but few babies have caused more bitter grief than hers, and I fear it will be a great drawback to her happiness through life. Goodbye my dear Fox, excuse this letter – I am very old and stupid.'[8]

A few days later Charles gives Caroline a detailed picture of their very quiet way of life. One day, he asserts, is as like another as two peas:

Get up punctually at seven leaving Emma dreadful sleepy and comfortable, set to work after the first torpid feeling is over, and write about Coral formations till ten; go up stairs and find that Emma has been down stairs about half an hour, eat our breakfast, sit in our arm-chairs – and I watch the clock as the hand travels sadly too fast to half past eleven – Then to my study and work till 2 o'clock luncheon time: Emma generally comes and does a little work in my room and sits as quiet as a mouse. – After Luncheon I generally have some job in some part of the town and Emma walks with me part of the way – dinner at six – and very good dinners we have – sit in an apoplectic state, with slight snatches of reading till half past seven – tea, lesson of German, occasionally a little music and a little reading and then bed-time makes a charming close to the day. – I fear poor Emma must find her life rather monotonous – my only comfort is how much worse it would have been if I had been in any business and nevertheless had not a better stomach. The poor thing has been but poorly every other or third day since we came back, which has been a great disappointment to me: But she is, I hope essentially going on well and undeniably growing.[9]

Emma's eldest sister Elizabeth came up to be with her during the final days of pregnancy and for the birth of her first baby, which took place on 27 December 1839. Soon afterwards her father came to see the new arrival, but Bessy, failing fast, was in no state to do so. Meanwhile, three days before the birth, Charles's health had collapsed; thereafter he remained unfit for serious work for a full eighteen months.

The fact that Darwin was unwell through most of this first year of marriage and had a major breakdown at the end of it has led some to suppose it was due in some way to Emma's excessive cosseting. A far more likely explanation is that from April onwards he was aware of the pregnancy and that as the year progressed he became increasingly anxious about Emma's safety. There is much circumstantial evidence supporting this suggestion. First, his symptoms became noticeably worse as soon as she became pregnant. Secondly, his breakdown occurred immediately before she gave birth, when there were probably signs that it was imminent. Thirdly, writing to Fox six months later, after giving much detail of his troubles he exclaims: 'What an awful affair a confinement is; it knocked me up almost as much as it did Emma herself.'[10] Finally, it may be no coincidence that it was at this time that he first suffered from 'periodical vomiting', one of the symptoms that was to trouble him most during the following years. One possibility, which inevitably remains speculative, is that unconsciously he was linking Emma's abdominal changes with the months of abdominal illness that preceded his mother's death.

As things turned out, Emma's confinement appears to have been straightforward. Charles was a proud father: 'It is a little Prince,' he tells a friend. The baby, christened William, fascinated Charles, who kept a detailed record of his development. In June he tells Fox: 'He is a charming little fellow, and I had not the smallest conception there was so much in a five month baby.'[11]

III

Charles's first serious breakdown in health, which continued throughout 1840 into the summer of 1841, is chronicled in some detail. On 7 February 1840 Emma wrote to her favourite aunt, Jessie, that Charles 'has certainly been worse for the past six weeks, and has been pretty constantly in a state of languor that is very distressing, and his being obliged to be idle is very painful to him.' Three days later she adds: '[he] is not like the rest of the Darwins, who will not say how they really are; but he always tells me how he is and never wants to be alone but continues just as warmly affectionate as ever, so that I feel I am a comfort to him. . . . It is a great advantage to have the power of expressing affection, and I am sure he will make his children very fond of him. I have been pretty well coaxed and spoilt all my life but I am more than ever now, so I hope it does one no harm, but I don't think it does.'[12] On the contrary, like others who have been truly loved in childhood, Emma was a constant source of affection and security to those around her.

The same month that Emma wrote to her aunt, Charles, in a letter to Lyell mainly about coral reefs, reports that he had seen Dr Holland, who 'now hopes he shall be able to set me going again. Is it not mortifying it is now nine weeks since I have done a whole days work, and not more than four half-days.' At about the same time he tells FitzRoy, 'my stomach as usual has been my enemy. . . . I have been obliged to give up all Geological work.'[13] Darwin records in his journal the two months after his collapse: 'In this interval read a little for Transmutation theory, but otherwise lost these whole months.'[14] In late March he writes to the Geological Society saying that, owing to the state of his health, he feels compelled to resign the office of joint-secretary.[15]

In early April, feeling rather better, he paid a brief visit to Shrewsbury on his own to consult his father. Writing to Emma, he remarks, 'I enjoy my visit and have been surprisingly well and have not been sick once.'[16] He had even resumed his *Coral* volume.

In June Charles, Emma and the baby went to Maer and from there he wrote his long informative letter to Fox in which he refers to Emma's confinement as an 'awful affair'. He had become optimistic about his health and so had his father. 'And now for myself, about whom I can now give a very good report. I have during the last six weeks been gradually, though very slowly, gaining strength and health, but prior to that time I was for nearly six months in very indifferent health, so that I felt the smallest exertion most irksome. This is the reason I have been so long without writing. I had no spirits to do anything. I have scarcely put pen to paper for the last half year and everything in the publishing line is going backwards. I have been much mortified at this, but there is no help but patience.' 'My Father', he continues, '. . . (having put a stop to periodical vomiting to which I was subject) feels pretty sure that before long I shall be quite well. . . . I am determined to obey implicitly my Father and remain absolutely quiet.'[17]

Alas! Charles's improvement was short-lived. On 4 August 1840 he records briefly, 'Taken ill', and for the next five months all correspondence ceases. A letter of 19 August written by a relative on his behalf, acknowledging the receipt of a letter, reads: 'it found him unfortunately very ill in bed'. The family stayed on at Maer until 14 November, when they returned to London. 'During this summer when well enough,' Charles records after their return, 'did a good deal of species work.'[18] As before, he evidently found species work much less taxing than grinding away dutifully at geology.

It can hardly be chance that Charles's serious relapse in August 1840 occurred just when Emma had again become pregnant. The baby, their much-loved daughter Annie, was born the following year on 2 March. Once again there is evidence of Charles's anxiety. 'Emma expects to be confined in March', he informs Fox in late January, ' – a period I most dearly wish over'. Once again, however, it appears that Emma's confinement gave no problems. 'Emma is going on pretty well,' Charles tells Lyell ten days later.[19]

Despite her burdens, Emma seems to have been her usual buoyant self during the winter of 1840–1. After paying her a visit, a long-time friend of the Wedgwood family, the novelist Maria Edgeworth (1767–1849), eldest daughter of the old Lunar Society member Richard Edgeworth, describes Emma as 'affectionate and unaffected. . . . She has her mother's radiantly cheerful countenance, even now, debarred from all London gaieties and all gaiety but that of her own mind by close attendance to her sick husband.'[20]

Although debarred from gaieties, Emma was in no way isolated. Her sisters and aunts and also Charles's sisters were frequent visitors, and they had her brother Hensleigh and his wife Fanny, with their three children, living close by. 'We find it a constant pleasure having them so near,' writes Emma. 'They often walk in to drink tea with us, and vice versa.'[21] Hensleigh was a barrister but his great interest was word origins. He was already embarked on the study that would lead eventually to the publication of his definitive *Dictionary of English Etymology* (1872), a forerunner of the great *Oxford English Dictionary* which late in life he would help to plan. Fanny, always known as Fanny Hensleigh to distinguish her from the many other Fannys in the family, was the daughter of Sir James Mackintosh by his second wife, another of Bessy Wedgwood's younger sisters. Charles, Emma, Hensleigh and Fanny had many interests and friends in common; they also enjoyed the company of Ras and his circle, which included the radical Scots essayist Thomas Carlyle (1795–1881) and his wife Jane (1801–66) and the writer Harriet Martineau (1802–76). 'I have been reading Carlyle, like all the rest of the world,' Emma tells her Aunt Jessie. 'He fascinates one and puts one out of patience. He has been writing a sort of pamphlet on the state of England called "Chartism". It is full of compassion and good feeling but utterly unreasonable. Charles keeps on reading and abusing him. He is very pleasant to talk to anyhow, he is so very natural, and I don't think his writings at all so.'[22] Hensleigh and Fanny continued to be close friends of Charles and Emma and were to prove invaluable in their support when tragedy struck in later years.

IV

Since he and Emma returned from the country in November 1840 Charles, although not yet recovered, had become more hopeful about his health. 'My strength is gradually, with a good many oscillations, increasing; so that I have been able to work for an hour or two several days in the week,' he tells Fox during January 1841. 'I am forced to live, however, very quietly and am able to see scarcely anybody and cannot even talk long with my nearest relations. I was at one time in despair and expected to pass my whole life as a miserable useless, valetudinarian but I have now better hopes of myself.' Since December he had been doing editorial work on the final number of *Birds* for the *Beagle* zoological series, and by February was drafting a paper on a problem in South American geology. This he submitted to the Geological Society in early April with the comment, 'It has been the work of such hours as I have been well enough during *two* last *months!*', and asking for it to be read on his behalf, since he would not be able to attend. During March he was able to renew his correspondence with Lyell. In one of four long letters discussing a variety of geological problems, he tells Lyell that 'it is the *greatest* pleasure to me to write or talk Geolog. with you'. During April, however, he was again 'idle and unwell' and so, predictably, spent his time sorting 'papers on Species theory'.[23]

At the end of May 1841 the family began their annual visit to Maer and Shrewsbury, and stayed altogether for two months. Describing his condition to a friend at the end of June he writes: 'I am . . . a good deal stronger than when in London, but I do not feel I shall have any mental energy for a long time and the Doctors tell me it will be some years before my constitution will recover itself.'[24] Among other activities he was amusing himself observing how humble-bees bore holes in flowers as a short cut to extracting the honey. This was to be the subject of a long letter to the *Gardener's Chronicle* in August.

For about a week in early July Charles, with William (now aged eighteen months and nicknamed Doddy) and a nursemaid, was over at Shrewsbury while Emma and the baby remained at Maer. Writing at length to Emma soon after arrival, Charles reports on his health. 'I was pretty brisk at first, but about four became bad and shivery – which ended in sharp headache and disordered stomach (but was not sick) and was very uncomfortable in bed till ten. – I was very very desolate without my own Titty's sympathy and missed you cruelly. – But today I am pretty brisk and enjoy myself.' Doddy, he says, 'is full of admiration at this new house and is friends with everyone and sits on grandpapa's knees. . . . When I had had him for about five minutes, I asked him where was Mama, and he repeated your name twice in so loud and plaintive a tone, . . . it almost made me burst out crying.'[25] A couple of days later Charles was feeling much better; but in this second long letter he again describes Doddy's puzzlement and distress at his mother's absence. Susan and Catherine were much enjoying Doddy, who 'they say is the most charming of all the children', and Charles was evidently doing so too. He proceeds to relate with obvious amusement an episode when a frog jumped near Doddy, who 'danced and screamed with horror at the dangerous monster and I had . . . to comfort him – He threw my stick over Terrace wall, looked at it as it went and cried Tatta with the greatest sang-froid and walked away.'

Charles also gives news of his father, who, now seventy-five, seemed to be ageing. The atmosphere was cheerful. 'My Father seems to like having me here; and he and the girls are very merry all day long.' Charles had used the opportunity to talk to his father about buying a house. But eruptions could still occur. 'A thunder storm is preparing to break on your head', he warns Emma, 'and which has already deluged me.' The trouble was that the nursery maid was not wearing a cap – which, Dr Robert thought, would mean that 'the men will take liberties with her'.[26]

Inevitably there were discussions regarding Charles's health, about which his father was now extremely pessimistic. 'My Father scarcely seems to expect that I shall become strong for some years,' Charles tells Lyell; 'it has been a bitter mortification for me to digest the conclusion that "the race is for the strong", and that I shall probably do little more but must be content to admire the strides others make in Science – so it must be.' Dr Robert was also gloomy about his grandson William, who, he thought, 'looks a very delicate child'.[27] These opinions, neither of which I suspect was justified, strongly suggest that much of the hypochondria in the Darwin family can be traced to Dr Robert's influence.

Despite his father's gloomy predictions, Darwin's health was much improved during the late summer and autumn of 1841. Returning to London at the end of July, he at last resumed his volume on *Coral Reefs*, after an interval of thirteen months as he records, and completed it by year-end. Furthermore, he and Emma, having made the important decision to leave London for good, began that September to look for a house, preferably about twenty miles outside the city and on a railway.

The picture Darwin gives Fox at this time, in a letter of 23 August, is almost rosy: 'We are all well here and our two babies are, I think, strong healthy ones, and it is an unspeakable comfort this – For myself I have steadily been gaining ground and really believe now I shall some day be quite strong – I write daily for a couple of hours on my Coral volume and take a little walk or ride every day – I grow very tired in the evenings and am not able to go out at that time or hardly receive my nearest relations – but my life ceases to be burthensome now I can do something.' Even so, in a further letter to Fox a month later he cannot refrain from describing himself as 'a dull old spiritless dog to what I used to be – One gets stupider as one grows older I think'.[28]

V

The occasional references to William that appear in Darwin's letters during these years, such as William's puzzlement at Shrewsbury over his mother's absence, give no indication that ever since his son's birth he had been making systematic observations of the baby's behaviour and especially how he responded to certain social situations. These results he was recording in a special diary which has only recently been published.[29]

The value for his species work of studying the development of babies had occurred to him as early as October 1838, soon after his reading of Malthus and just before he and Emma became engaged. In the notebook in which he was recording various random thoughts about man as an unusual species he has a heading 'Natural History of Babies' under which

Erasmus (Ras) Darwin, 1805–81, elder brother of Charles, aged 37 in 1841; portrait by George Richmond

Charles Darwin, aged 33, with his firstborn, William, aged 2 years 8 months in August 1842

he records questions to investigate, such as whether babies blink before experience can have taught them to avoid danger. His interest lay especially in patterns of behaviour that appear without having been learnt and in why those particular patterns should be parts of man's inherited behavioural repertoire. If his theory of natural selection were correct, he argued, they would have survival value, either currently or perhaps later on. In this connection he was especially interested in the role of emotional expressions and postures, and also of vocalisations, as means of communicating internal feelings. Studying William, he noted that although initially smiles appear to be random and without function they soon begin to communicate wellbeing and to discriminate between individuals. Similarly, the forms of crying become more differentiated. How soon, he asks himself, are infants able to understand the expressions of others? Maybe, he speculates, the development of a child's moral sense turns on the development of his capacity to anticipate how his parent will react to his actions – which, he noted, William was able to do early in his second year.

Not only was Darwin observing the ways in which certain specifically human characteristics develop during infancy but he was also noting resemblances between early human responses and those of other species. An infant crying for food, he remarks, is 'analogous to [the] cry for food of nestling-birds, which certainly is instinctive.'

His compiling this diary of William's development shows that, even if he was feeling unwell during much of 1840 and early 1841, he was far from being as idle as he so often makes out. Observing, reading, thinking, making notes, writing letters and similar activities he never counts as work. For him the word 'work' applies only to pushing on doggedly with whichever publication he is currently giving priority to. All the other activities of a studious scholar are discounted. This should be remembered when reading the repeated references in his later letters to being idle or capable of only two or three hours of work a day.

The observations Darwin made on his son, with particular reference to the early signs of his emotional life, would be drawn upon many years later for his article 'A Biographical Sketch of an Infant' (1877), after having been utilised earlier in his book *On the Expression of the Emotions in Man and Animals* (1872). Time and again, we find, the basic work on the topics of later publications was being done in these much earlier years.

VI

During the winter of 1841–2 Darwin was at last back in circulation. He began attending the Geological Society again, engaged in professional and scientific correspondence and from February onwards, for six months, was an active member of a British Association Committee on Zoological Nomenclature, although he did not attend all the meetings.[30]

He also met 'the illustrious Humboldt', who on a visit to London had expressed a wish to meet the promising young scientist.[31]

During February he was busy correcting the proofs of *Coral Reefs* but was again feeling unwell. Emma advised him to spend a few days in Shrewsbury, presumably to consult his father, and this he did during March. On arrival he felt tired and had a headache, went to bed and 'had a fit of vomiting and shivering'. 'Susan came and nursed me,' he tells Emma; 'and I am this morning *very* well and brisk and the day is bright and beautiful.' His good spirits persisted, and five days later he reports that he had been able to walk some distance, 'an immense walk for me. – The day was boisterous, with great black clouds and gleams of light, and I felt a sensation of delight, which I hardly expected ever to experience again. – There certainly is great pleasure in the country even in winter.'[32] Evidently his depression had lifted.

That spring Emma was again pregnant. Throughout this pregnancy Charles's health was tolerably good, despite a few bad patches. At the end of March he writes to Fox: 'My health has been as usual oscillating up and down, but I certainly gain strength. . . . Emma, however is uncomfortable enough all day long and seldom leaves the house, this being her usual state before her babies come into the world.' A few weeks earlier, in a letter to Susan about his relief at the safe arrival of Caroline's new baby, he had again been referring to confinements as 'horrid affairs at the best'.[33]

It was during this spring that Fox's wife died, leaving him with a number of young children, and that Darwin wrote him the letter of condolence in which he makes the astonishing statement, already referred to: 'never in my life having lost one near relation, I dare say I cannot imagine how severe grief such as yours must be.' Twelve months later, in an exchange of letters on the anniversary of Fox's bereavement, which was evidently much on Fox's mind, Darwin repeats his assertion that he had never had such an experience himself.[34]

At the beginning of May 1842 Emma preceded Charles to Maer, to start what was to be a two-month combined visit to Maer and Shrewsbury. Charles remained in London for a couple of weeks before joining her, finishing work on the proofs of *Coral Reefs* and negotiating with the printers about the final numbers of the series on the *Beagle* zoology. The government grant had already run out and he feared he would have to find the money himself. 'I came back gloomy and tired,' he tells Emma. 'I am stomachy and be blue deviled.'[35] Once he had rejoined her at Maer, however, he seems to have been much better. For example, he took the opportunity of his four week stay to summarise the ideas on evolution on which he had by now been working, on and off, for five years. This short sketch was purely for private use and was probably never shown to anyone.[36] Nevertheless it is the forerunner of the much more ambitious essay that he drafted two years later and thus is the embryo which over the years would grow to become the famous *Origin*.

The sketch completed, Darwin went on by himself to Shrewsbury for three days; then, on 18 June 1842, feeling stronger than for some time, he embarked on a ten-day trip geologising in North Wales, climbing mountains and walking long distances.[37] Once again the evidence is unmistakable: the symptoms he suffered from were not the result of physical exertion.

VII

In mid-July Charles and Emma returned to London to prepare for their coming move to the country. This move, which they had decided on two years earlier, was dictated mainly on grounds of Charles's health and in accordance with strong medical advice. There were other reasons as well. Charles loved observing animals and plants and was eager to start experiments in connection with his species work, which could only be done in the country. Moreover, both he and Emma disliked living in the Great Wen and welcomed the prospect of fresh air. After house-hunting for some time in Surrey, they had eventually decided on Down House, on the outskirts of the village of Downe* near Orpington in Kent. Although agreeably isolated, it was only fifteen miles from St Paul's and therefore reasonably accessible. The drive to the nearest railway station, over eight miles, was undesirably long; but with ten miles more and frequent trains the total journey time, Charles estimated, would be about two hours.

In a long letter of 24 July 1842 to his sister Catherine, intended also for his father's eyes, Charles gives a detailed description of the location and surrounding countryside, referring to the house itself only towards the end.

Village about 40 houses with old walnut trees in middle where stands an old flint Church & the lanes meet. – Inhabitants very respectable. – infant school – grown up people great musicians – all touch their hats as in Wales, and sit at their open doors in evening, no high-road leads through village. – The little pot-house, where we slept is a grocers-shop & the land-lord is the carpenter – so you may guess the style of the village – There are butcher & baker & post-office. A carrier goes weekly to London and calls anywhere for anything in London, & takes anything anywhere. – On the road to the village, on fine day scenery absolutely beautiful: from close to our house, view, very distant and rather beautiful – but house being situated on rather high table-land, has somewhat of desolate air – There is most beautiful old farm-house with great thatched barns and old stumps, of oak-trees like that of Shelton, one field off. – The charm of the place to me is that almost every field is intersected (as alas is our's) by one or more footpaths – I never saw so many walks in any other country – The country is extraordinarily rural & quiet with narrow lanes & high hedges & hardly any ruts – It is really surprising to think London is only 16 miles off. – The house stands very badly close to a tiny lane & near another man's field – Our field is 15 acres &

*The name of the village is spelt with an 'e', the house without.

flat, looking into flat-bottomed valleys on both sides, but no view from drawing-room, wh: faces due South except our own flat field & bits of rather ugly distant horizon. – Close in front, there are some old (very productive) cherry-trees, walnut-trees, – yew, – spanish-chestnut, – pear – old larch, scotch-fir & silver fir and old mulberry-trees make rather a pretty group – They give the ground an old look, but from not flourishing much also give it rather a desolate look. There are quinces & medlars & plums with plenty of fruit, & Morells-cherries, but few apples. – The purple magnolia flowers against house: There is a really fine beech in view in our hedge. – The kitchen garden is a detestable slip and the soil looks wretched from quantity of chalk flints, but I really believe it is productive. The hedges grow well all round our field, & it is a noted piece of Hay-land.. . .

House ugly, looks neither old nor new – Capital study 18 x 18. Dining room 21 x 18. Drawing room can easily be added to is 21 x 15. Three stories, plenty of bedrooms . . . two bath rooms – pretty good office & good stable yard & a cottage. – House in good repair.. . . I have no doubt I shall get it for one year on lease first to try – so that I shall do nothing to house at first.[38]

'Emma was at first a good deal disappointed,' he continues, but after a second visit 'is rapidly coming round'. He believes the price to be about £2200 and so about £1000 less than an alternative house they had been looking at. When later he came to purchase, his father lent him the money.

The move to Down House took place on 14 September 1842, and nine days later their third child, Mary, was born; but she survived only three weeks. In reply to a note of condolence from a sister-in-law, Emma writes: 'Our sorrow is nothing to what it would have been if she had lived longer and suffered more. Charles is well today and the funeral over, which he dreaded very much.'[39] Thereafter a shutter comes down and there are no further references to this sad event.

Simultaneously with Mary's birth and death Emma suffered another blow. Her father, Josiah II, who had developed Parkinsonism a year or so earlier, now took a major turn for the worse and became bedridden like his wife. He died on 12 July 1843 at the age of seventy-four. Bessy, now seventy-nine would live another three years. In caring for her sick parents, the devoted Elizabeth was being helped by her sister Charlotte, who with her husband Charles Langton had returned to live at Maer after he had lost his faith and resigned his parish in 1841.

Many years later in his *Autobiography* Darwin gives his own account of the years 1839 – 42: 'During the three years and eight months whilst we resided in London, I did less scientific work, though I worked as hard as I possibly could, than during any other equal length of time in my life. This was due to frequently recurring unwellness and to one long and serious illness. The greater part of my time, when I could do anything, was devoted to my work on *Coral Reefs* [published October 1842] . . . It was thought highly of by scientific men, and the theory therein given is, I think, now well established.'[40] It has remained so ever since.

SEVENTEEN

Early years at Down
1842–1846

I

Although Darwin was dedicating his life to science and not to religion, the move to Down House was in line with his earlier visions of settling down to be a country parson. From the first, he and Emma played a part in the parish, and in later years Charles was to take responsibility for the parish social clubs that normally were part of the parson's duties. Emma was a regular attender at church, the children were christened there, and within weeks of arrival their new baby, Mary, was buried in the churchyard. The roles they came to fill were part of the social structure of rural England, where the village parson and his wife were often almost the only people of education with some free time to give to social, educational and charitable activities. Emma was familiar with her role through living in the country in Staffordshire. Charles was familiar with his through his Cambridge friends, several of whom were already country parsons. One such was Fox; another, even more influential, was Henslow, who since 1839 had been living in Hitcham in Suffolk where he had been appointed vicar, and whose beneficent activities in that parish Darwin often sought to emulate. There was also the image of Gilbert White, whose *Natural History of Selborne* Darwin knew well. Despite the radical ideas Darwin had developed in science, his social values continued to be close to those of his parson-naturalist friends and had nothing in common with either revolutionary politics or militant atheism.[1] Because of this, Darwin could become close friends with the Reverend John Innes, who was vicar of Downe for sixteen years from 1846, despite the latter's Tory politics and creationist beliefs. In a letter Darwin refers to Innes as 'one of those rare mortals from which [*sic*] one can differ and yet feel no shade of animosity'.[2] When at length Innes departed (on being left family property in Scotland – which led him to insert 'Brodie' into his name), to be followed in Downe by some very unsatisfactory parsons, Darwin was to take major responsibility for parish affairs. It was in keeping with his local role that in 1857 he was appointed a county magistrate.[3]

As it happens, the parish of Downe had no vicarage and Down House had been the personal property of the previous parson, from whom Darwin bought it, together with eighteen acres including a large garden. Unfortunately the house stood very close to the lane and was wide open to public gaze – which, Charles tells Susan, he found 'intolerable'.[4] Moreover, contrary to first impressions, the house proved to be ill-built, as became evident when they began alterations. The upshot was that extensive building and outside work were undertaken during their first years there. Bow windows were added to all three storeys at the garden front, and no less than 170 yards of the lane was lowered by up to two feet, to effect privacy.

The work entailed considerable further expenditure. Fortunately Charles's father had already offered to lend the necessary money, which was gratefully accepted. By this time his father was, in fact, extremely well off, as a result of a flourishing practice and skilful investments, and was clearly willing to continue support for his gifted son. Nevertheless Charles constantly worried about money and, although he kept careful accounts, lived well within his income and invested wisely, often saw financial ruin round the corner.[5] In all likelihood he did not know how well off his father was. Moreover, it should be remembered that so far Charles had never earned a penny. Nor would he earn anything of consequence until after the *Origin* was published, nearly twenty years later. Thus it was thanks only to family money that he was able to devote himself unsparingly to a life of unbroken study.

Deeply rooted though Darwin soon became at Down, he was far from being the isolated recluse that has sometimes been suggested. On the contrary, he not only maintained all the scientific contacts and friendships he had made in London but added steadily to them. Still on the council of the Geological Society, and during 1844 a vice-president, he attended the monthly council meetings held in the afternoons while avoiding the evening scientific meetings for reasons of health. Often he stayed overnight with Ras, and occasionally spent as long as four days in London, seeing friends and visiting the zoo or the British Museum. Furthermore, there was a steady stream of invitations to friends to stay at Down for a weekend or longer. During the years 1843–6 visits were made by the Lyells and the Horners, his new friend Joseph Hooker and a number of others. Darwin was nothing if not sociable. Many years later his son Francis would describe his father as a charming host who would draw his guests out about their own interests. 'When he was excited by pleasant talk his whole manner was wonderfully bright and animated,' Francis writes, but adds: 'I think he always felt uneasy at not doing more for the entertainment of his guests.'[6]

Unfortunately the excitement of animated conversation was always a potent trigger for his symptoms, and this led him to put severe restrictions on social contacts and, when he had visitors, to ration the time he spent

with each to a brief half-hour. It also led him to restrict contacts with
neighbours. As he recounts in his *Autobiography*: 'During the first part of
our residence [at Down] we went a little into society, and received a few
friends here; but my health almost always suffered from the excitement,
violent shivering and vomiting attacks being brought on. I have therefore
been compelled for many years to give up all dinner-parties.'[7]

II

The marked improvement in Darwin's health which had begun during
the year preceding the move continued, and for the next few years his
work went steadily forward. 'Our removal has answered very well,' he tells
Fox, and, after the family had been at Down ten weeks, 'our two little souls
are better and happier – which likewise applies to me and my good old
wife'. In the spring of 1843 his account runs: 'I am *very* much stronger
corporeally but am but little better in being able to stand mental fatigue or
rather excitement, so that I cannot dine out or receive visitors.'[8] From
now on references to ill-health in letters become fewer. These early years
at Down were, indeed, years of considerable success. The family
flourished and, with much less ill-health to hinder him, Darwin was able
to complete a number of publications and, furthermore, to make great
strides with his species work.

Soon after their arrival at Down and within a few months of Mary's
birth and death, Emma was pregnant yet again. The baby Henrietta (Etty)
was born on 25 September 1843. Describing the condition of mother and
baby to Fox two months later, Charles is cheerful: Emma 'has never had
so good a recovery and there never was such a good little soul . . . she is
beginning to smile and be very charming.' As regards the house, he states
that he had nearly got the place in order and had planted an orchard. They
were living a quiet life and had only got to know one neighbour well.[9] This
was a well-off banker, Sir John Lubbock (1803–65), who was also an
astronomer and fellow of the Royal Society. Although his land marched
with Darwin's, the two had little in common and were never close. Lady
Lubbock became a friend of Emma's, however, and their schoolboy son,
another John (1834–1913), was a frequent visitor. In later years this
second Sir John, a banker and scientist like his father and also a Member
of Parliament who spoke for the scientific community in the House of
Commons, was to be among Darwin's younger friends.

During October 1843 Charles paid a brief visit to Shrewsbury. He
writes cheerfully to Emma: he is feeling 'very brisk' and is glad to know
that she is too; he has paid a call on his old nurse, Nancy, now retired and
living in her own rooms. 'She showed [me] two very old letters of my
mother, such kind and considerate ones they were and the hand very like
that of the Wedgwood family.' He then moves on to other topics: his
weight, which was 11 stone 2½ lb, Caroline's new baby daughter, about

Down House in 1872, after Darwin's many additions

Darwin's old study at Down

whom she worries incessantly, and his 'own dear three chickens', about whom he has been enthusing. He had also been having talks with his father: 'I told him of my dreadful numbness in my finger ends, and all the sympathy I could get was "Yes, yes, exactly – tut-tut, neuralgic, exactly yes yes".' Nor when he mentioned his financial worries did he get any more sympathy: '"stuff and nonsense" is all he says to my fears of ruin and extravagance.'[10]

Darwin's work during these early years at Down was conscientiously to continue the task of completing the publications arising from the *Beagle* voyage. These were principally the second and third of his three major contributions to geology, the second on *Volcanic Islands* and the third on the *Geology of South America*. Systematic work on *Volcanic Islands* was begun soon after their arrival at Down, but was interrupted in the spring of 1843 by the distractions of building activities. Characteristically he used this as a chance, perhaps an excuse, to spend time on his ever-tempting species work.[11] Another interruption came in July, when he and Emma went to Maer for the funeral of her father, Josiah II, whose death after a long illness had been expected. After going on to Shrewsbury for a day or two they returned to Down. Within two months *Volcanic Islands* was completed, and it was published in March the following year. In response to favourable comment on it from Leonard Horner, Lyell's father-in-law, Darwin insists: 'I cannot say how forcibly impressed I am with the infinite superiority of the Lyellian school of Geology over the Continental [which was still catastrophist]. I always feel as if my books came half out of Lyell's brains and that I never acknowledge this sufficiently.'[12] Meanwhile, in October 1843, the final number of the long series on the *Beagle* zoology had appeared. That left the *Geology of South America*, which would not be finished for another two years, largely because there was so much else he wanted to do.

III

Throughout these years Darwin was continuing to work on the 'species question' and, as we know from the notebooks he was still keeping, continuing to show his characteristically creative blend of observation, reading and speculation.[13] A principal part of this work was an extensive technical correspondence with a wide circle of scientists and anyone else whom he thought might have made relevant observations. Much of the correspondence concerns the outcome of breeding procedures with plants and animals. Another interest was the viability of seeds which had lain dormant over long periods or been exposed to salt water. Throughout 1843, for example, he corresponded with an amateur geologist in the Scottish borders, William Kemp, who thought he had discovered some prehistoric seeds which had none the less germinated. Darwin was excited: they might perhaps be living fossils of unknown species. It was therefore sad for both parties when in the end the plants proved to be nothing but common contemporary weeds. Nevertheless Darwin believed the seeds to have been buried for many years and thought their subsequent germination merited a note in a magazine of natural history. The note, he suggested, should take the form of a letter signed by Kemp. Darwin's offer to draft it was accepted by Kemp with the deepest gratitude, and the ghosted letter duly appeared. The correspondence provides an excellent illustration of the respect with which Darwin treated the observations of relatively uneducated men and the time and attention he was prepared to give them. In addition, he knew well that, in the absence of better data, anecdotal observations carefully checked and corroborated can be valuable.

Darwin's correspondence of 1843 is especially notable for the first exchange of letters with Joseph Hooker, newly returned from a four-year voyage to Antarctica and due soon to become Darwin's closest friend and confidant. In mid-November Darwin wrote to him and, after congratulating him on his safe return, broached a topic near to his own heart, that of the Galapagos plants which, collected during the *Beagle* voyage, had remained unexamined ever since. The original plan was that Henslow should examine them, but despite repeated prodding from Darwin he had been too busy, largely because of his migration to Hitcham. Now, with Darwin's agreement, Henslow proposed to transfer all the plants to Hooker. Fortunately Hooker was enthusiastic, since he expected Darwin's specimens would go far to supplement his own collections. Still only twenty-six and Darwin's junior by eight years, Hooker welcomed the link with the rising young scientist whose *Journal of Researches* had been a constant inspiration to him during his four years of voyaging. In his reply to Darwin, Hooker plunges straight into a detailed account of the plants he had managed to collect in the southern hemisphere, and also what he had missed and was hoping for from Darwin's collection.

Joseph Hooker had been born into the 'botanical purple'.[14] From his earliest years his father, William Hooker (1785–1865), had been Professor of Botany in Glasgow and now, from 1841 and until the end of his life, was director of the Royal Botanic Gardens at Kew. In addition, Joseph's maternal grandfather, a Suffolk banker, was also a keen naturalist. Growing up in this tradition, Joseph had from early days become an enthusiastic naturalist. Throughout his school and university years in Glasgow he had spent all spare moments working at botany and entomology, so that at the time he qualified in medicine in 1839 at the age of twenty-two he was probably the best-equipped botanist of his generation. Like Darwin, the young Hooker had been determined to travel the world as a naturalist and, thanks to his own gifts and proficiency together with his father's professional connections, had succeeded in being appointed assistant surgeon and botanist to one of the ships in Sir James Ross's Antarctic expedition the very day after he qualified in medicine. Now back in London, he was, again like Darwin, facing the task of sorting and describing the huge collections he had made on the voyage.* Thus, when they began corresponding during the autumn of 1843, the two men already had a great deal in common – family backgrounds, gifts, interests and experience. Moreover as they soon discovered, they shared all the same social and scientific values. Given such a favourable soil, scientific intimacy ripened fast, and within a few months Darwin felt sure enough of his new friend to confide in him his closest secret.

IV

Although by the autumn of 1843 it was already five years since Darwin had reached firm conclusions about the mutability of species and the roles of variation and natural selection in leading to change, he had been extremely circumspect about mentioning his ideas to anyone. In the excitement of September 1838 he could not resist referring briefly in a letter to Lyell to 'the delightful number of new views' about species that he was developing. A year later there was a similar brief reference in a letter to Henslow: 'I keep on steadily collecting every sort of fact which may throw light on the origin and variation of species'; and more recently, in a letter to George Waterhouse, the zoologist who was examining and describing the *Beagle* mammals, he had gone a little further by sketching his notion about allied species being descended from a common ancestor, though he warned that that was only 'the merest trash and hypothesis'. Now in January 1844, writing to Hooker, he goes a big step further: 'At last gleams of light have come, and I am almost convinced (quite contrary to the opinion I started with) that species are not (it is like confessing a murder) immutable'; and then, 'I think I have found out (here's presumption!) the simple way by which species become exquisitely adapted to various ends.'[15]

That summer, after their brief spring visit to Maer and Shrewsbury, Darwin wrote out the final draft of a greatly expanded version of his 1842 sketch, running in fact to 50,000 words. The new version foreshadows closely in both argument and illustrations the statement of his views published in the *Origin* fifteen years later. So important did he regard this draft that on 5 July 1844, after completing it, he wrote a memorandum to Emma in which he expressed the view that 'my sketch of my species theory' was likely to be 'a considerable step in science' and requesting her,

*The purpose of the expedition was to conduct a magnetic survey of the southern oceans and, if possible, to reach the south magnetic pole. Hooker's collecting was done on Atlantic islands on the outward and homeward voyages, on Kerguelen Island and Tasmania on the outward and at the Cape of Good Hope on the homeward. During the first Antarctic winter he collected in Tasmania (again), Australia and New Zealand with its associated islands, and during the second in the Falkland Islands and Tierra del Fuego. Much of what he collected comprised grasses, ferns, mosses, lichens, algae and seaweeds, most of which had been neglected by earlier botanical visitors.

should he meet with sudden death, to arrange its publication. In listing suitable editors, he mentions Lyell, Henslow and Owen, who 'would be very good' though unlikely to undertake it, as well as two other possibles; he also asks that a sizeable fee together with his collection of books and papers should be offered an editor as reimbursement for his labours. In later years changing relationships led to Owen's name being deleted and Hooker's added. The final change came in 1854, with 'Hooker by far best man to edit my Species volume'.[16]

During the 1840s, however, there could be no question of publication. Excited and confident though he felt about his conclusions, he was terrified of the way in which he expected his colleagues to react. They would dub him not only intolerably 'presumptuous' but 'a complete fool', he tells his old Cambridge rival and later colleague, Leonard Jenyns, in October 1844 after outlining his heterodox ideas: 'I shall not publish on this subject for several years.' Even so, he was not averse to one or two close friends seeing his sketch and giving their opinions on it: 'if I thought at some future time that you would think it worth reading,' he tells Jenyns a month later, 'I should, of course, be most thankful to have the criticism of so competent a critic.'[17] It appears there was no response from Jenyns.

It was at this time, the autumn of 1844, that Hooker, still an extreme sceptic, was starting to become interested in the species question. At the end of a very long letter to Darwin about the geographical distribution of plants in southern latitudes, he enquires: 'Pray what writings on the subject of original creation will give me the best notions of the (mad) theories of some men from Lamarck's twaddle upwards. Species (or what we call species) may be muteable but I should not think they set about it themselves so systematically as he says.' In his reply Darwin remarks that even in his most sanguine moments 'all I expect is that I shall be able to show, even to sound naturalists, that there are two sides to the question of the immutability of species; – that facts can be viewed and grouped under the notion of allied species having descended from common stocks. With respect to books on this subject, I do not know of any systematical ones, except Lamarck's which is veritable rubbish. . . . I believe all these absurd views arise from no one having as far as I know, approached the subject on the side of variation under domestication.'[18] It was, indeed, this new approach to the problem of how species might change over countless generations that proved the key to Darwin's success.

This same autumn saw the publication of an anonymous work entitled *Vestiges of the Natural History of Creation*, which caused the popular interest in the issue of creation versus evolution to reach a new peak. Written (it later proved) by a journalist and amateur geologist, Robert Chambers, it favoured evolution and was full of interesting matter, much of it accurate but some grievously mistaken. Highly readable, it became the talk of the town. Opponents of evolution were outraged and Adam Sedgwick, Darwin's old tutor in geology, savaged it in the *Edinburgh Review*. Others ridiculed it. Nevertheless Hooker was rather impressed. 'I have been delighted with *Vestiges*,' he tells Darwin, 'from the multiplicity of facts he brings together [even though] he has lots of errors'; and he jibs at some of the theory. 'After all,' he continues, 'what is the great difference between *Vestiges* and Lamarck. . . . In one place he implies that [new] species are made by the *will of the mother.*' Darwin was even more cautious: 'I have also read the *Vestiges*,' he tells Hooker, 'but have been somewhat less amused by it than you appear to have been: the writing and arrangement are certainly admirable, but his geology strikes me as bad and his zoology far worse.'[19]

During 1845 and later years speculation about who might be the author of this controversial book was rife. Writing to Fox, Darwin enquires whether Fox had read it: 'it has made more talk than any work of late and has been by some attributed to me – at which I ought to be much flattered and unflattered.' He was in fact thoroughly ambivalent, on the one hand welcoming the attention the book drew to the issue of creation versus evolution and to natural history in general, on the other anxious lest its erroneous facts and half-baked theory discredit the whole subject. During the autumn of 1845 he wrote a long letter full of professional gossip to Lyell, then on his second visit to America. Inevitably he refers to *Vestiges* and, after describing Sedgwick's hostile review, comments: 'I think some few passages [of the review] savour of the dogmatism of the pulpit, rather than of the Philosophy of the Professor['s] chair. . . . Nevertheless it is a grand piece of argument against mutability of species; and I read it with fear and trembling, but was well pleased to find that I had not overlooked any of the arguments.'[20]

Vestiges continued to sell and went through many editions despite, or perhaps because of, the savage reviews it continued to receive from scientists. Years later, after the *Origin*'s appearance, Darwin had the indignity of being told by a popular newspaper that all his ideas had been cribbed from *Vestiges*.

V

The years 1844–6 saw Darwin and Hooker becoming ever more intimate, though their opportunities for seeing each other were few. In the spring of 1844 Darwin was hoping that Hooker would pay him a visit 'in the wilds of Down'. That summer Darwin and his wife, during a few days in London, visited Kew to see Hooker, who was then seeking paid employment and meanwhile living with his parents; they much enjoyed their visit. During the autumn Darwin was trying to arrange for Hooker to meet Lyell on a weekend at Down. 'I am very glad you talk of a visit to us,' he tells Lyell; 'Young Hooker talks of coming; I wish he might meet you – he appears to me a most engaging young man.'[21] The meeting probably took place during a weekend in early December 1844 on Hooker's first visit to Down.

Joseph Hooker, 1817–1911, botanist, and intimate friend, aged 34 in 1851 by T. H. Maguire. Very slowly became an early convert to Darwin's theory

It was late that year that Hooker was at long last able to find the time to examine Darwin's Galapagos plants; and in the New Year he could tell his friend of some remarkable findings. About half the species collected, he reported, were unknown elsewhere. Furthermore, the great majority of those were confined to a single island. These results were immensely important for Darwin's thinking about evolution, since they gave him some of the most solid evidence so far that he was on the right track. 'I cannot tell you how delighted and astonished I am at the results of your examination,' he tells Hooker in a letter of 11 July 1845; 'how wonderfully they support my assertion on the differences in the animals of the different islands, about which I have always been fearful.'[22]

Hooker's report was nothing if not timely, since yet another of Darwin's activities at this time was rescuing his *Journal of Researches* from the series of official publications in which it was buried, and preparing a revised edition for commercial publication. This gave him the opportunity greatly to expand his chapter on the Galapagos by linking Hooker's findings on the plants to Gould's findings on the birds and to proceed thence to hint at a possible evolutionary explanation. The revised edition, completed and published by John Murray in August 1845, was dedicated to Lyell 'as an acknowledgement that the chief part of whatever scientific merit this journal . . . may possess has been derived from studying the well-known and admirable *Principles of Geology*'. It proved a great success, selling nearly 4000 copies before the end of 1846 – which meant that Darwin's name became known to a wide circle of intelligent laymen as well as within the scientific community. In view of the *Journal*'s long continuing sale, it was a bad mistake for Darwin to have accepted a lump sum from the publishers for the copyright, the kind of error he rarely made in matters of finance.

Meanwhile, in February 1845, Hooker's hunt for paid employment had led to the prospect of a glittering opening in Edinburgh – the chair of botany in the university. Darwin, while delighted for his friend's sake, was also dismayed. 'You will hardly believe how deeply I regret for *myself* your present prospects – I had looked forward to [our] seeing much of each other during our lives. It is a heavy disappointment; and in a more selfish point of view, as aiding me in my work, your loss is indeed irreparable.'[23] Hooker was not only a most congenial companion but also becoming an invaluable scientific colleague. Though he would remain for long far from convinced about Darwin's ideas on species, he was prepared to discuss the pros and cons in an open-minded way, and he brought a wealth of botanical knowledge to their arguments. As a guide to the world of botany Hooker's role was proving the equivalent of that long filled for the world of geology by Lyell. The numerous letters from which the extracts quoted have been culled consist mainly of extended and learned discussions of botanical or geological problems. Darwin's range of knowledge and memory for detail were prodigious.

Throughout these years Darwin's worries over health recurred sporadically. For example, in October 1844, on a visit to Shrewsbury when he received advice from his father about diet, he writes to Emma describing himself as 'your poor old sickly complaining husband'.[24] Nevertheless a few months later (February 1845) he is assuring Fox, 'I think I am decidedly better than one or two years ago, as I am able with some exceptions to do my three hours morning work', an opinion he repeats in a letter written the same month to another friend: 'We are all well, wife and children three, and as flourishing as this horrid . . . weather permits.' Yet even in his more hopeful letter to Fox he prefaces his better news by stating, 'My stomach continues daily badly'; while the following month, on 31 March, he replies to Hooker's sympathetic enquiries in rather gloomy mood: 'You are very kind in your enquiries about my health; I have nothing to say about it, being always much the same, some days better and some worse. I believe I have not had one whole day, or rather night, without my stomach having been greatly disordered, during the last three years, and most days great prostration of health: thank you for your kindness; many of my friends, I believe, think me a hypochondriac.'[25]

Hooker's concern for Darwin's health during the early months of 1845 almost certainly reflects in some degree a similar concern for his own. It was the time when he was due to start as locum lecturer in botany at Edinburgh with good prospects of succeeding to the chair when the infirm incumbent retired. But the idea of public lecturing terrified him, as he explains to his maternal grandfather in a letter of 16 January 1845:

You do not know, nor do I like to tell my Parents, how wholly unfitted I am to be a Lecturer, constitutionally in particular. I am really nervous to a degree, and though I joined debating societies on purpose and studied speeches and stood up to deliver them, I never could get two sentences on – I have earnestly endeavoured to conquer this, but without avail. I have consulted medical men, who tell me I have irritability in the action of the heart, which some have pronounced a slight disease of that organ; and this I know well, that I could never even stand up before my fellow scholars to say my lesson at school or college without violent palpitations. You know me too well to think me a coward, or, still less, to accuse me of affectation, but this I do certainly think, that I am naturally unfitted for any situation calling for a public exhibition of myself. . . . This, and this alone, has led me always to hope that I should pick up some situation where hard work and good manners were all that should be required of me. . . .

Of course I should forego all this dislike, or, as I believe, physical incapacity for lecturing, were anything so tempting as Edinbro' offered. . . . Do not think that I am frightening myself with any such bugbear as a *Heartdisease*, for I assure you I give no thought to the matter, though I cannot help feeling, from the frequency and pain of my palpitations, that I have a nervous affection there. I have no idea of its calling me away early, though I shall probably not live to your age in the ordinary course of things.

In the event Hooker accepted the lectureship, hoping he would get over his nervousness.[26]

Judging by his record of health during the Antarctic voyage and by his feats of endurance in the Himalayas a few years later, it is clear that all Hooker was suffering from was the palpitations of stage fright and that his heart was no less sound than Darwin's.[27] Although both would have benefited greatly from unequivocal reassurance from their doctors that nothing whatever was wrong, neither was to receive it, owing to the pitifully limited knowledge of the day. As things turned out, their similar if unfounded worries about health meant that they had in common yet one more area of life.

VI

During the 1840s Down House was large even for a well-to-do professional family, but, as the children multiplied, further accommodation was added. Charles had a fairly large study facing the lane. As the years rolled by and his library of books and journals expanded they were to be found in almost every room, though carefully catalogued so that their whereabouts were always known.

It was a considerable household. Charles had his own manservant and butler, Parslow, and Emma had a full domestic staff, including a nanny, Brodie, and one or more nursery-maids. There were also a coachman, with carriages and horses, and a gardener and undergardener.

Charles and Emma were considerate employers, and several of their servants stayed for long periods. First and foremost was Joseph Parslow (1809/10–98), who joined the household in Gower Street and remained until he retired on pension in 1875, having become 'an integral part of the family, and felt to be such by all visitors to the house'.[28] He married one of Emma's personal maids and, during his later years of service and after retirement, lived out in a local cottage.[29]

The Scottish nurse, Jessie Brodie (whose date of birth is unknown and who died in 1873), came from a few years' service as nanny to Thackeray's daughters* and probably, like Parslow, joined the Darwin household in Gower Street. She is described by Henrietta as 'an invaluable treasure to my mother and a perfect nurse to the children. . . . She had carrotty hair, china-blue eyes and a most delightful smile. . . . I can still see her . . . sitting in the little summer house at the end of the Sand-walk, and hear the constant click-click of her knitting-needles. . . . There she sat hour after hour patiently and benevolently looking on,

*Brodie's role with the Thackerays was a very responsible one, since she had not only to look after their three small girls, one of whom died, but also to care for their mother, who, after the third birth, developed an acute psychosis. In 1840 Thackeray put his two surviving daughters into the care of his mother, then living in Paris. It seems likely that Brodie transferred to the Darwins early in 1841 at the time of Annie's birth in March.

CHARLES AND EMMA DARWIN OF DOWN HOUSE, BROMLEY, KENT

Charles Darwin 1839 **Emma Wedgwood**
(12 Feb. 1809 –   (2 May 1808 –
19 Apr. 1882)   2 Oct 1896)

— William
(27 Dec 1839-1914)

— Anne (Annie)
(2 Mar 1841 –
23 Apr 1851)
died age 10

— Mary Eleanor
(23 Sept 1842)
died age 3 weeks

— Henrietta (Etty)
(25 Sept 1843-1930)

— George
(9 July 1845-1912)

— Elizabeth (Bessy)
(8 July 1847-1926)

— Francis
(16 Aug 1848-1925)

— Leonard
(15 Jan 1850-1943)

— Horace
(13 May 1851-1928)

└ Charles Waring
(6 Dec 1856-1858)
died age 18 months

whilst we rushed about and messed our clothes as much as we liked.'[30] To the family's distress, she insisted on leaving after Annie's tragic death in 1851 which caused her to be racked with grief.

Charles much enjoyed the children and was excellent with them (as was Emma), although as we see later he was constantly and intensely anxious about their health. A charming picture of life at Down at this time is given in a letter from Charles to Emma on one of her last visits to Maer, during February 1845:

It is really wonderful how good and quiet the children have been, sitting quite still during two or three visits, conversing about everything and much about you and your return. When I said I shall jump for joy when I hear the dinner-bell, Willy [aged five] said, 'I know when you will jump much more, when Mama comes home.' 'And so shall I,' responded many times Annie [aged four]. . . . Annie told me Willy had never been quite round the world, but that he had been a long way, beyond Leave's Green. The Babs [Etty, aged eighteen months] has neglected me much today, and would not play; she could not eat jam, because she had eaten so much at tea. She was rather fidgety, going in and out of the room, and Brodie declares she was looking for you. I did not believe it, but when she was sitting on my knee afterwards and looking eagerly at pictures, I said, 'Where is poor Mamma' she *instantaneously* pushed herself off, trotted straight to the door, and then to the green door, saying 'Kitch'; and Brodie let her through, when she trotted in, looked all round her and began to cry; but some coffee-grains quite comforted her.* Was not this very pretty? Willy told me to tell you that he had been very good and had given Annie only one tiny knock, and I was to tell you that he had pricked his finger.[31]

At the time of this visit to her old home Emma was pregnant yet again, the fifth time within six years, and the baby, George, was born on 9 July 1845. In Darwin's long letter to Hooker two days later, in which he expresses his delight at Hooker's remarkable findings in regard to the Galapagos plants, there is the briefest of mentions of the event. Apologising for not having written earlier, he explains: 'on Wednesday an upsetting event happened in the fact of a Boy-Baby being born to us – may he turn out a Naturalist. My wife is going on most comfortably.' The rest of the letter is exclusively about the Galapagos plants.[33]

Darwin's health during this pregnancy and after Emma's confinement appears to have been neither better nor worse than in the previous year, though his letter to Fox of 15 February 1845, in mid-pregnancy, records that his stomach continued 'daily badly'. Thus, if we are right in attributing his first breakdown of late 1839 continuing through 1840, and the relapse of August 1841, to his anxieties about her safety, we must conclude that after the first two babies had been born with no untoward

---

*Darwin's interest in and concern about children's responses to separation from their mother is underlined in a letter to Lyell of this period, where he takes Lyell to task for not being shocked by the atrocious practice in the American South of separating slave children from their parents.[32]

results Darwin became less apprehensive about subsequent confinements – a not unreasonable conjecture. Even so, it will be noticed that he refers to George's birth as 'an upsetting event'; and two months later, in a letter of 3 September, he tells Susan that Emma has really had 'a most suffering time' and that it has been most provoking that 'no one could come to comfort her'.[34]

This long letter to Susan is full of family news and 'all about our household and family affairs', which he knows she likes to hear. Ras has been staying at Down and seems quite prepared to stay on and help in the garden: he is not finding it as dull as he usually does. Charles then reports on his health: 'I have not been up to my average. . . . I have taken my Bismuth regularly, I think it has not done me quite so much good as before; but I am recovering from too much exertion with my Journal: I am extremely pleased my Father likes the new edition.' Later in the letter he describes the great changes going forward in the garden, which include making a new walk in the kitchen garden and 'some great earthworks' consisting of moving a mound from one area to another. 'It will make the place much snugger, though a great blemish until the evergreens grow on it. Erasmus has been of the utmost service, in scheming and in actually working; making creases in the turf, striking circles, driving stakes, and such jobs. He has tired me out several times.' More building work is planned – making a schoolroom, adding two small bedrooms, and various improvements to the servants' quarters: 'It seemed so selfish making the house so luxurious for ourselves and not comfortable for our servants, that I was determined if possible to effect their wishes.' With the sum received from Murray for the copyright of his journal he believes he can meet the expenditure from income. 'So I hope the Shrewsbury conclave will not condemn me for extreme extravagance; though now that we are reading aloud Walter Scott's life, I sometimes think we are following his road to ruin.'

Another major improvement was in hand. This was the leasing of a strip of land, a quarter of a mile from the house, from their Lubbock neighbours. This Darwin planted with a mixture of hardwoods and had a path made round its perimeter. This path, known as the Sandwalk, became Darwin's favourite exercise ground; when feeling brisk he made several circuits every day. Since it is almost a mile to walk out and back with only a single circuit, Darwin's physical fitness until nearly the end of his life can hardly be questioned.[35]

Whatever the ups and downs of Charles's health during 1845, it was certainly not too bad. In June he had been haymaking[36] and in mid-September he went to Shrewsbury at the start of a six-week absence from Down, during which he made a ten-day excursion into Lincolnshire and Yorkshire. After spending another fortnight at Shrewsbury, he returned to Down at the end of October. A principal object of his excursion was to visit a 325-acre farm at Beesby (about thirty miles east-north-east of

Lincoln and near the coast), which he had recently bought as an investment with money borrowed from his father. It was being farmed, he was advised, by an industrious good tenant, and was held to be an excellent and safe investment.[37] From Beesby he went to York to see William Herbert, an expert on hybridisation, and thence south beyond Wakefield to call on Charles Waterton (1782–1865), the eccentric squire of Walton Hall and author of the celebrated *Wanderings in South America*, who had turned his park into the first nature reserve in Britain. Darwin was familiar with Waterton's *Essays on Natural History*, which he valued for 'observations on what the world would call trifling points on Natural History [which] always appear to me very interesting'. Writing to Lyell after his return, Darwin describes Waterton as 'an amusing strange fellow. At our early dinner our party consisted of two Catholic priests and two Mulattresses! . . . It is a fine old House and the Lake swarms with water-fowl.' Darwin evidently did not know that the two dark-skinned ladies were Waterton's sisters-in-law. His wife, the daughter of a Scotsman and a South American Indian, had died in childbirth and her sisters had moved in to care for the baby.[38]

On his return journey to Shrewsbury Darwin visited Chatsworth and tells Lyell that he was 'in transports with the great Hothouse [built by Joseph Paxton]; it is a perfect fragment of a Tropical forest and the sight made me thrill with delight at old recollections.' Later, in a letter to Henslow, he says how concerned he is about the potato blight, then causing hardship and starvation in many parts of the country, and how he has followed Henslow's example in arranging for every labourer on his farm to have an allotment. His little tour, he tells Lyell, 'made me feel wonderfully strong at the time; but the good effects did not last . . . the children are the hopes of the family, for they are all happy life and spirits.'[39]

One source of anxiety for Charles during these years was the ill-health of his father. In December 1844 Dr Robert, then aged seventy-eight and at 22 stone greatly overweight, had had what was evidently an attack of angina. Reporting the event to Fox, Charles proceeds: 'He has been prevailed upon to sleep downstairs. . . . He was upon the whole very cheerful when I was there. – Illness with his figure and constitution is very dreadful.' By April the next year, however, Dr Robert was better.[40]

Emma's mother was still lingering on and had now deteriorated to a point where she recognised no one. On 31 March 1846 she died at the age of eighty-two. Maer was sold and Elizabeth bought a house in Surrey not far from where both her brother, Josiah Wedgwood III (married to Charles's elder sister Caroline), and her sister Emma were living with their families.

Maer held many happy memories for both Emma and Charles. Not only had Charles married a daughter of the house but his uncle had played a key role in his life by persuading his father to agree to his accepting the offer to sail in the *Beagle*. Since their marriage Charles and Emma had spent summer holidays there. For both of them, and for many relatives as well, the deaths of Josiah II and Bessy, and the sale of Maer, marked the end of an epoch.

Although Henrietta never knew Maer in its heyday, memories of those wonderful years lived on in the Darwin family. In her memoir of her mother she writes: 'Maer Hall . . . was so deeply beloved by the whole group that their children even have inherited a kind of sacred feeling about it. . . . My father used to say that our mother only cared for flowers which had grown at Maer.' He enjoyed recalling his visits there. 'I can remember his description of these enchanted evenings,' she writes, 'and his happy look and sigh of reminiscence, as he recalled the past, and told how nothing else was ever like it – what good talk there was . . . and how delightfully Charlotte sang, the elder cousin for whom he had a boy's admiration.' 'The picture of Maer in the old letters', she continues, 'makes me feel that few homes could have been happier, or better suited to develop a fine character. There was no idleness, but no bustle or hurry, and an atmosphere of peace and hospitality. The family were all readers, and they all loved the place and its beauty.'[41]

VII

In early October 1845, while visiting his father and sister at Shrewsbury, Darwin got news that Hooker had failed to be appointed to the chair of botany at Edinburgh. Although Hooker was much the better-qualified candidate, the Scots had preferred one of their own. In a letter Darwin expresses himself astonished and grieved at the news, and hopes Hooker will soon pay a visit to Down. Writing again a month later to commiserate, he outlines his own work programme. 'I hope this next summer to finish my S. American geology; and then to get out a little zoology and hurrah for my species work, in which according to every law and probability, I shall stick and be confounded in the mud.'[42] In the event the *Geology of South America*, which he had just resumed, took him until the end of September the following year and the 'little zoology', the study of an aberrant barnacle, would take him a great deal longer.

Throughout the following twelve months Darwin was pushing on conscientiously with *Geology of South America*, with many of his customary groans as he wrestled to revise and rewrite his draft. His regular monthly visits to London to attend council meetings of the Geological Society continued and he was constantly encouraging his friends to visit him at Down. During November 1845 he was busy organising a small gathering of young fellow scientists. In a note to Hooker about trains, he comments, 'I hope we shall have some good Nat. Hist. talk and I flatter myself I shall have the four *most* rising naturalists in England round my table and much I shall enjoy it'; and he adds: 'I returned yesterday from town, after having had four very active successful days in London.'[43] The gathering took place during the first weekend of December and included (in addition to Hooker) Edward Forbes, a naturalist who had spent eighteen months aboard HMS *Beacon* during her surveying voyage in the Mediterranean in 1841–2 and was now aged thirty; George Waterhouse, on the staff of the British Museum, who had been responsible for studying and writing the report on the *Beagle* mammals and was now thirty-five; and Hugh Falconer, a palaeontologist and botanist who had made a valuable study of Indian fossils and was now spending four years in England working on his specimens. Aged thirty-seven, Falconer was one year older than his host. Hooker, at twenty-eight, and due shortly to take up an appointment with the Geological Survey, was the baby of the party. The following week Darwin writes to tell Hooker how much he had enjoyed the weekend 'and all our raging discussions. . . . I learn more in those discussions than in ten times over the number of hours readings.'[44]

In addition to these four contemporaries, who became regular visitors – as were the Lyells when they were not geologising on the continent or in North America – guests at Down included Thomas Bell, Professor of Zoology at King's College London, who had been responsible for the *Beagle* reptiles, and Thomas Wollaston (1822–78), a specialist in the invertebrates of Madeira and other Atlantic islands. They all knew each other. A major controversy between them at this time was how to explain the presence on the Atlantic islands of animal and plant species that were related to African ones. Forbes and Wollaston held that the islands must once have been part of a large continent they named Atlantis, which had joined the islands to Africa and had subsequently sunk. Hooker was inclined to agree. Darwin, by contrast, thought this theory an inadmissable speculation in the absence of any geological evidence and sought to explain the findings by postulating the occasional transport of seeds and organisms by sea or air. Although opinions were strongly held, this and other controversies were never allowed to impair friendships.

Another scientist with whom Darwin was in communication was Richard Owen, who, he tells Hooker, 'has been doing some grand work in [the] morphology of the vertebrata'. In April 1846 he writes Owen a note saying he is anxious to have a talk with him 'chiefly about the mammifers of the Plata', and in June he reports that his old *Beagle* shipmate Sulivan has just returned from another surveying voyage to Argentina and has brought back a further haul of fossils from the Río Gallegos: 'He is anxious to have them inspected by you,' he tells Owen, 'and I should be extremely glad to be present.'[45] Later that year Sulivan with his wife and two children visited Down for a few days. Owen himself would be a visitor the following year.

After Darwin's death Hooker, contributing to Francis Darwin's *Life and Letters* of his father, gives a vivid picture of life at Down as he experienced it during visits he paid in these years:

I had many such invitations, and delightful they were. A more hospitable and more attractive home under every point of view could not be imagined – of Society there were most often Dr. Falconer, Edward Forbes, Professor Bell, and Mr. Waterhouse – there were long walks, romps with the children on hands and knees, music that haunts me still. Darwin's own hearty manner, hollow laugh, and thorough enjoyment of home life with friends: strolls with him all together, and interviews with us one by one in his study, to discuss questions in any branch of biological or physical knowledge that we had followed; and which I at any rate always left with the feeling that I had imparted nothing and carried away more than I could stagger under.[46]

Although, judging by his activities, Darwin's health during this period seems to have been reasonably good, he remained pessimistic. Writing to a German naturalist in April 1846 about some geological matters, he adds: 'My health keeps indifferent and I do not suppose I shall ever be a strong man again: everything fatigues me, and I can work but little at my writing: this summer, however, I shall get out my geology of S. America.'[47] These words sound suspiciously like those his father had used about him five years earlier (see chapter 16, page 242) and was perhaps still repeating. Since Charles had recently spent ten days at Shrewsbury, it seems likely that that was their origin.

While at Cambridge Charles had acquired the habit of taking snuff, which Emma, believing it to be bad for his health, was urging him to give up. 'I am personally in a state of utmost confusion,' he tells Hooker; 'for my cruel wife has persuaded me to leave off snuff for a month and I am most lethargic, stupid and melancholy in consequence.' Hooker sides with Emma and pleads with him to 'knock it off altogether. . . . It must hurt you and is growing a 2nd nature.' Thenceforward he did his best to ration his consumption but, according to Francis Darwin, continued the habit for the rest of his life. He also smoked, though never heavily. 'Smoking rested him,' Francis recalls, 'while snuff stirred him up and kept him going.'[48]

During June 1846 Emma took William and Annie for a three-week visit to her favourite aunt in Tenby, Maer being no longer available. Charles was left behind at Down battling with the printers over the *Geology of South America* and feeling abandoned: 'I do long to have my own wife back again,' he tells Emma. 'Yesterday was gloomy and stormy; I was sick in middle of day, but two pills of opium righted me surprisingly. . . . I have been getting on very badly with my work as it has been extremely difficult.' Next day he groans: 'the Compositor is in want of M.S. which he cannot have and I am tired and overdone I am ungracious old dog to howl. . . . Your very long letter of Monday has delighted me, with all the particulars about the children.' A little later he is telling Hooker how overworked he is feeling and how 'inexpressibly wearied' he is of South American geology.[49]

That year the British Association was meeting at Southampton during the second week of September. Darwin was looking forward to being there and meeting his friends. In a note to Jenyns thanking him for a booklet and hoping to see him in Southampton, he sums up his present condition: 'My health continues pretty well; never right and seldom very wrong, as long as I live quite quietly.'[50] In fact, the activities in Southampton were greatly to his benefit.

The visit proved an unqualified success, as he reports later to Hooker and Henslow: 'we enjoyed (wife and I) our week beyond measure,' he tells Hooker; 'the papers were all dull, but I met so many friends, and made so many new acquaintances (especially some of the Irish Naturalists) and took so many pleasant excursions – I wish you had been there.' One of the excursions had been to Winchester: 'I never enjoyed a day more in my life.' Writing in the same vein to Henslow, he adds, 'I think I shall attend the Oxford meeting' due to be held the following June (which he did), and to Jenyns, 'I enjoyed my week extremely and it did me good'.[51]

In his letter to Henslow, written in early October, he is also able to report that the *Geology of South America* is finished and due soon to be published: 'You cannot think how delighted I feel at having finished all my *Beagle* materials except some invertebrata: it is now ten years since my return, and your words, which I thought preposterous, are come true, that it would take twice the number of years to describe, that it took to collect and observe.'[52]

VIII

Throughout these years the species question is never far from Darwin's mind. In November 1845, at a meeting with Lyell's brother-in-law, Charles Bunbury, a keen amateur botanist whom he had met once before in 1842 in North Wales, he is unable to resist talking about species, as Bunbury notes in his diary. 'He avowed himself to some extent a believer in the transmutation of species, though not, he said, exactly according to the doctrine of Lamarck or of the "Vestiges". But he admitted that all the leading botanists and zoologists, of this country at least, are on the other side.' Lyell, in pressing Darwin to make this visit to meet Bunbury, whom he would find well informed and welcoming, insists: 'Your besetting sin is modesty, a rare one in this world.'[53]

Having earlier failed to get Jenyns to read his 1844 essay, Darwin very diffidently approaches Hooker. At the end of a long letter, written the same month he was talking to Bunbury, he broaches the issue. 'I wish I could get you sometime hence to look over a rough sketch (well copied) on this subject', adding deprecatingly, 'but it is too impudent a request.' Hooker, however, is too busy. 'At present,' he replies, 'I endeavour to hold aloof from all speculations on the origin of species, and wish to till . . . this part of my flora [*Flora Antarctica*] is finished.'[54] As it turned out it was to be another two years before Hooker could find time to look at it.

Robert Chambers, 1802–1871, publisher, author of *Vestiges of Creation* (1844), aged 42 in 1844

Thomas Bell, 1792–1880, zoologist, identifier of the *Beagle* reptiles, aged 59 in 1851

Edward Forbes, 1815–54, zoologist and botanist, aged 29 in 1844

Hugh Falconer, 1808–65, palaeontologist and botanist, aged 36 in 1844

In October 1846, the *Geology of South America* at last disposed of, Darwin turned his attention to the aberrant species of barnacle that he had collected on the coast of Chile some twelve years earlier. The more carefully he examined it and the more papers he read about barnacles, 'the more singular does our little fellow appear', he tells Hooker when thanking him for having very kindly made a drawing of the tiny specimen. Thus began Darwin's exhaustive study of the whole tribe of barnacles that was to occupy him for the next eight years and to delay his work on species for all that time.

This prolonged delay just when he was agog to give his mind to the great theme he had been working on for so long, formulating his hypotheses and collecting evidence for and against, has often presented a puzzle to students of Darwin's life. One explanation has been that it was the result of his acute anxiety about the rough reception he confidently expected his work would get: that it provided a good excuse for stalling. This perhaps might have played some part; but there was also a substantial reason of quite another sort.

A year earlier, in September 1845, just before Darwin's trip to the north, there had been a lively exchange of letters with Hooker. Darwin had expressed some interest in a new book on species by Frédéric Gérard, a French writer on botanical and horticultural subjects. Hooker is lukewarm. 'I am not inclined to take much for granted from anyone [who] treats the subject in his way and who does not know what it is to be a specific Naturalist himself.' He goes on to contrast Gérard's naïve opinions with those of a number of botanists distinguished for having made extensive firsthand studies in taxonomy themselves.[55]

Reading this, Darwin is cut to the quick, since he well knows that Hooker's criticism of Gérard applies equally to himself. 'How painfully (to me) true is your remark that no one has hardly a right to examine the question of species who has not minutely described many. . . . My only comfort is, (as I mean to attempt the subject) that I have dabbled in several branches of Nat. Hist: and seen good specific men work out my species and know something of geology; (an indispensable union) and though I shall get more kicks than half-pennies, I will, life serving, attempt my work.' Hooker is distressed that Darwin should have taken his criticisms of Gérard so personally and hastens to reassure him. 'Do not think I meant to insinuate that you could not be a judge from not having worked out species, for your having collected with judgement is working out species; what I meant I still maintain, that to be able to handle the subject at all one must have handled hundreds of species . . . and that over a great part . . . of the globe. These elements your toils have fulfilled and well' – in sharp contrast, he makes clear, to Monsieur Gérard, who 'is neither a specific naturalist, nor a collector, nor a traveller . . . nothing but a distorter of facts.' In reply Darwin is grateful for the 'nice note' but insists that Hooker's kind remarks make no difference to his own opinion: 'All which you so kindly say about my species work does not alter one iota my long self-acknowledged presumption in accumulating facts and speculating on the subject of variation, without my having worked out my due share of species. But now for nine years it has been anyhow the greatest amusement to me.'[56]

Thus Darwin was keenly aware that his never having made a study of any group of organisms constituted an exposed flank that he could ill afford to leave unprotected in the battles ahead. To compare his tiny aberrant barnacle from *Beagle* days with others of the family would make this deficiency good; and so, the geology of the *Beagle* at last behind him, he set to work on what was to become an enormous and definitive study.

EIGHTEEN

Too dispirited to write
1847–1849

I

In retrospect we can see that the years 1843–6 were exceptionally good ones for Darwin. The house was turning out just what he wanted, his wife was well despite repeated pregnancies, the children were flourishing, his work was proceeding steadily, and he was sufficiently fit to lead a comparatively active social life. The coming years were to be far less cheerful.

The shadow over Darwin's life was his father's failing health, ending in his death in November 1848 at the age of eighty-two. Dr Robert was suffering from an increasing degree of heart failure. He was cared for devotedly by Susan and Catherine and his condition varied, but the end was never in doubt. Charles made two visits to Shrewsbury to see his father during 1847 and another two during 1848, each visit lasting a fortnight. Throughout these months Charles's health deteriorated in parallel with his father's, leading to a crippling exacerbation of symptoms, notably sickness and depression, from July 1848 onwards. This breakdown persisted for a whole twelve months, four of them prior to his father's death and eight afterwards. Throughout this period both his work and his social life were severely disrupted.

Prior to this breakdown, however, Darwin's way of life continued relatively unaffected. His top priority was his study of barnacles, initially envisaged as no more than a year's work or possibly two. At the end of 1847, however, he was encouraged to expand the study, after which it became a gigantic undertaking. Meanwhile he was in regular contact with Hooker about botany and the species question, with Lyell about geology, and with his other scientific friends. In June 1847 he attended the meeting of the British Association in Oxford, and he was still a regular attender at council meetings of the Geological Society in London. All these activities continued until midsummer 1848.

During these years Emma produced two more babies: Bessy in July 1847 and Francis in August the next year. This brought the total to six, three of each sex. Despite these responsibilities, Emma acted as hostess to 'shoals of relations' during the summer of 1847 and also entertained some of Charles's friends.[1] The Lyells were at Down for weekends in January and September 1847 and again in February 1848. Hooker paid a long visit in January 1847 when he again met the Lyells; and in February 1848 Richard Owen, Edward Forbes and Andrew Ramsay (1814–91), a geologist who would much later become director of the Geological Survey, were among the guests.

II

Ever since he returned from the Antarctic in the autumn of 1843 Joseph Hooker had been busy preparing publications on his collections. Much of his time was spent with his parents at Kew, where he could consult his father on all matters botanical and where he also had ready access to libraries and to his father's unrivalled herbarium. Having continued for over two years on half-pay from the navy, he obtained permanent employment early in 1846 – an appointment with the Geological Survey to study British flora, extant and fossil, in relation to geology. This suited him well. Headquarters were in London and much of the work could be done at Kew. Contacts with his friends, including Darwin, presented no problems. In November 1846 Darwin had spent a day with him at Kew and had written, 'What a good thing is community of tastes, I feel as if I had known you for fifty years.'[2] Their friendship cemented, henceforward letters would be signed 'Your affectionate friend' or 'Yours affectionately'.

Darwin was particularly eager for Hooker to visit Down, not only because he wanted him to see more of Lyell but because he was impatient to get Hooker's opinion of the 1844 species sketch. He was hoping that both men would bring work to do and stay several days. In the event, the Lyells spent only a weekend in January 1847, but Hooker duly brought work and stayed ten days; when he left he was persuaded to take with him the 1844 sketch. For the next couple of months Darwin could not wait to hear Hooker's opinion. Hooker, however, was extremely busy and in mid-February had still not finished reading it. 'What an astonishing amount of work you have in hand,' writes Darwin, at once anxious to hear Hooker's verdict and guilty about pressing him too hard. 'I do most earnestly beg you not to hurt yourself: do not think of my sketch; I should never forgive myself if you look at it one minute before you have leisure and idle time: only, when you recommence it, oblige me in relooking over the marginal headings, so as to have the *whole* in view at one time.' By early March Hooker had finished reading the sketch and had made a number of notes about it, many of them favourable to the theory but by no means all. A discussion was necessary, but Darwin's projected visit to Kew at the end of the month had to be called off at the last minute on grounds of ill-health: 'I am so stomachy today,' he writes, 'that I have not heart or courage for the exertion of London & Kew.' A fortnight later he explains further: 'I should have written before now, had I not been continually unwell, and at present I am suffering from four boils and swellings, one of which hardly allows me the use of my right arm and has stopped all my work and damped all my spirits. – I was much disappointed at missing my trip to Kew.'[3]

At this time Hooker, still hardly thirty, was eager for another field trip abroad, preferably to the tropics, where the vegetation would be infinitely more varied than in the colder climes already visited. Of several plans being considered during the early months of 1847, it was an expedition to India to study the flora and geology of the eastern Himalayas that eventually materialised.

When in April that year Darwin hears that the plans look promising, he writes to Hooker: 'I congratulate you over your improved prospects about India but at the same time must sincerely groan over it: I shall feel quite lost without you to discuss many points with, and to point out . . . difficulties and objections to my species hypotheses. . . . If you have spare time, *but not without*, I should enjoy having some news of your progress. . . . By the way, I will get some work out of you, about the domestic races of animals in India.' During the six months before Hooker sailed (in November 1847) Darwin strove urgently to find opportunities to discuss the species question with him. Prior to the British Association meeting in Oxford he writes: 'I will bring the remainder of my species sketch to Oxford to go over your remarks. – I have lately been getting a good many rich facts.' For Darwin the Oxford meeting was a huge success, especially excursions with Hooker and other friends to Blenheim Park and Dropmore; though he had to refuse invitations to stay with colleagues in Oxford on grounds of health and instead stayed in lodgings, 'for then I shall have a secure solitary retreat to rest in'. The further meetings with Hooker to discuss the species sketch, which Darwin was still urgently wanting, proved difficult to arrange until late August when, his stomach 'extra well', he managed a very enjoyable two-day visit to Kew. Plans for Hooker to pay a return visit to Down before his departure miscarried, however, to Darwin's deep regret, and Darwin himself was too unwell to visit London for a last meeting. 'I shall miss you selfishly and all ways to a dreadful extent,' he assures his friend.[4]

At the time he left for India Hooker had become thoroughly familiar with Darwin's thinking but was far from being converted to it. He was impressed by the evidence that species are far more variable than other biologists supposed and also by evidence of their relationships to allied species and to their fossil predecessors in the same area. However, the notion that new species are transmutations of other ones was too big a jump. For many years to come Hooker would play two main roles in Darwin's scientific life: that of informed and sympathetic but always stringent critic and that of expert supplier of information on all things botanical, more especially geographical distribution in which both men were passionately interested.

Many years later, in 1899, Hooker gave an account of his visits to Down and the discussions he had with his host.

It was Mr. Darwin's practice to ask me, shortly after breakfast, to retire with him to his study for twenty-minutes or so, when he brought out a long list of questions to put to me on the botanical subjects then engaging his attention. These questions were sometimes answered offhand, others required consideration, and others a protracted research in the Herbarium or in the gardens at Kew. The answers were written on slips of paper, which were deposited in bags or pockets that hung against the wall within reach of his arm, each of them a receptacle devoted to a special object of inquiry. To me this operation of 'pumping' as he called it, was most instructive. I could not but feel that any information that I could give him was comparatively trivial, while what I carried away was often as much as I could stagger under. . . . These morning interviews were followed by his taking a complete rest, for they always exhausted him, often producing a buzzing noise in the head, and sometimes what he called stars in the eyes, the latter too often the prelude of an attack of violent eczema in the head, during which he was hardly recognisable. These attacks were followed by a period of what with him was the nearest approach to health, and always to activity.[5]

A characteristic described by Hooker was the enthusiasm and animation that Darwin brought to these discussions. After he had recounted an amusing story to him, Darwin would 'roar . . . with laughter and slap . . . his side with his hand, a rather common trick of his when excited'.

During the summer of 1847 Hooker had become engaged to Henslow's elder daughter, Frances; but they would not be married until after his return in March 1851. During this long engagement Hooker completed three years of adventurous and often hazardous journeying in unmapped areas of the Himalayas, sent back a great variety of seeds and young plants to be nurtured at Kew, and collected thousands of dried specimens, a significant proportion of which were new to science. Throughout he sent long technical accounts of his adventures to his father, with requests to disseminate the material to his friends, including Darwin. There was also an occasional exchange of letters between the friends, their infrequency compensated by their enormous length. In Hooker's first dispatch of February and March 1848 (before he reached the Himalayas), which runs to five long printed pages, he ends by confiding his continuing anxieties about palpitations, with a strict injunction to Darwin to keep this to himself.[6]

Darwin's reply of May 1848 comments on Hooker's news and gives some of his own: 'my confounded stomach is much the same,' he reports; 'indeed of late has been rather worse, but for the last year, I think, I have done nothing besides the Barnacles, except indeed a little theoretical paper on Erratic Boulders, and Scientific Geological Instructions for the

Admiralty volume, which cost me some trouble.' The latter, edited by Sir John Herschel, was a multi-authored manual for naval captains, which Darwin welcomed as showing that the Admiralty cared for science and would encourage captains to have naturalists aboard.[7] Although his study of barnacles was his unquestioned priority, geology continued to make heavy demands on his time; and during 1847 it had also been causing him a great deal of anxiety.

III

Early in 1847 a troublesome controversy arose about a geological opinion Darwin had expressed some nine years earlier.[8] In his paper on the 'parallel roads' of Glen Roy, written in 1838 and published by the Royal Society the following year, he had expressed the view that these raised beaches could only be accounted for by postulating that at two distinct times in the past the sea level had been much higher than it was today. This conclusion, which he described as 'inevitable', was contrary to the view, advanced by Scots geologists twenty years earlier, that the beaches had been deposited on the banks of a freshwater lake caused by a dam of rock and alluvium, which had been higher at one period than at another. Now, in March 1847, another Scots geologist, David Milne, had given a paper at the Royal Society of Edinburgh in which he presented evidence telling against Darwin's theory and supporting the earlier hypothesis.

When some months later Darwin received a copy of Milne's paper he reacted strongly. In a long letter to Lyell of 8 September 1847 he explains that there are now three hypotheses: his own, that the 'roads' are of marine origin; a second, advanced a little later than his by the Swiss-American geologist Louis Agassiz (1807–73), that they were beaches of a freshwater lake that resulted from the glen's having been blocked by ice; and now that of Milne, who supported Agassiz's view about the freshwater lake but backed the earlier view that the dam had been caused by rock, not ice. He proceeds to argue stoutly that both Agassiz and Milne are mistaken. 'Mr. Milne will think me as obstinate as a Pig,' he writes to Robert Chambers (anonymous author of *Vestiges*), who had accompanied Milne to the site; 'I abide by all I have written'. Nevertheless Darwin was upset by the controversy. 'I have been bad enough for these few last days,' he tells Hooker on 12 September, 'having had to think and write too much about Glen Roy (an audacious son of a dog . . . having attacked my theory) which made me horribly sick.'[9]

A week later, writing to Milne himself, Darwin thanks him for 'the courteous manner in which you combat me', explains that he remains unconvinced by Milne's arguments and that, having consulted Lyell, he is putting his own case in a letter to the *Scotsman*, the principal Edinburgh newspaper.[10] The letter in question, of no less than 2500 words, was rejected for publication as being far too long.

Louis Agassiz, 1807–1873, Swiss geologist, emigrated to USA in 1846.
Professor of Natural History at Harvard University, who became a leading critic
of Darwin's theory in America

Lith. de Nicolet à Neuchatel.

A. Sonrel lith.

The controversy rumbled on for another year. For some reason Darwin felt especially protective of his Glen Roy theory, and when the following summer Chambers, after a further survey, came out in support of the marine theory Darwin was much relieved. 'Glen Roy . . . is a subject . . . about which I feel much a personal interest,' he writes to Chambers, 'for I should have been more sorry to have been proved wrong on it than upon almost any other subject.' Reassuring though these findings were, Darwin was nevertheless piqued by Chambers's having used some of his own arguments while at the same time sneering at the work of his pre-decessors, and having also, in so many words, claimed the marine theory as his own. 'I do not think he has quite claims to consider that he alone has solved the problem of Glen Roy,' he complains to Lyell.[11]

That was not the end of the story, however. More than a decade later yet another Scottish geologist, Thomas Francis Jamieson (1829–1913), visited Glen Roy and found incontrovertible evidence that Agassiz had been right all along and that the 'roads' were in fact the former shore-lines of a glacial lake. 'Your arguments seem to me conclusive,' Darwin writes to Jamieson in September 1861. 'I give up the ghost. My paper is one long gigantic blunder. . . . I have been for years anxious to know what was the truth and now I shall rest contented, though ashamed of myself. How rash it is in science to argue because any case is not one thing, it must be some second thing which happens to be known to the writer.'[12] And he confesses to Lyell: 'I am smashed to atoms about Glen Roy.'[13]

The story of Darwin's part in the Glen Roy controversy is instructive on a number of counts. It shows how easily upset he was by serious criticism and how it provoked psychosomatic symptoms. It shows also what good friends he had and how grateful he was for their support. And it shows, of course, how capable he was of profiting from such criticism, painful though he found it.

IV

Darwin's study of barnacles had begun in the last months of 1846.[14] Throughout 1847 he thought of it as an exercise, limited in both scope and time, focusing on the tiny aberrant barnacle he had brought back from the south-west coast of Chile and how it resembled and differed from other barnacles of closely related species. In the course of this work he was in touch with various barnacle experts, including John Edward Gray (1800–75), who since 1840 had been Keeper of Zoology at the British Museum. Gray had had plans to make a definitive study of the group himself and had collected materials, but was too busy to do so. Learning of Darwin's interests towards the end of 1847, he suggested to Darwin that he extend the scope of his project and undertake a monograph on the whole group. By that time Darwin had realised that the traditional classifications were in a complete muddle and, when Gray made his suggestion, he was ready to fall in with it.

It will be recalled that Darwin's interest in marine invertebrates had started on the shores of the Firth of Forth more than twenty years earliei, and that during the great voyage they had been a favourite study second only to geology. Since the classifications proposed by such eminent taxonomists as Linnaeus and Cuvier were so hopelessly astray and a fresh start was therefore imperative, his decision to undertake the whole group becomes intelligible. It was a time, too, when to classify some large group was a way for a zoologist to establish his credentials: examples were Edward Forbes and Richard Owen among his friends, as well as a number of other zoologists with whom he was in correspondence.

Once launched on this enterprise Darwin began writing letters to a great range of people who might either let him borrow specimens they had already collected or else be able to make fresh collections in faraway places. For example, one of his first letters, written on the last day of 1847, was to Sir James Ross, who had commanded the Antarctic expedition on which Hooker had served and who was now setting out for the Arctic in search of the lost Franklin expedition. 'I am going to beg a favour of you', he writes to Sir James, 'which your taste for Natural History will, I hope, lead you to grant; it is to collect for me, during your ensuing expedition and preserve in *spirits* the northern species of Cirripedia or Barnacles, noting the latitude under which found, and whether the coast-rocks are abundantly covered. . . . I am now at work, and shall be for the next two years, on a Monograph on the Cirripedia; and the above specimens would be particularly valuable to me.'[15] A stream of letters along the same lines followed, but with a sharp reduction during the period of his breakdown, then resuming in full flow again from August 1849.

In March 1848 Darwin writes to Richard Owen telling him of the new microscope he has had made to his own specifications which he is finding immeasurably better for his barnacle work than anything else he knows of and urging Owen to consider acquiring one, though 'I fully appreciate the utter *absurdity* of my giving you advice about the means of dissecting. . . . When next I come to town . . . I must call on you, and report *for my own satisfaction*, a really, (I think) curious point I have made out in my beloved Barnacles.' Then, referring to the weekend Owen spent at Down six weeks earlier, he adds, 'You cannot tell how much I enjoyed my talk with you here.'[16]

This was a time when Darwin was seeing a good deal of Owen. When in London he used to call on him very early, often before breakfast, to pick his brains about osteology and problems of nomenclature arising from the barnacles. When his position was not threatened Owen could be extremely helpful, even charming; but once a rival appeared he quickly turned nasty. During May 1848 an ugly scene occurred at a meeting of the Royal Society, as Darwin recounts to Hooker. An experienced geologist and palaeontologist, G. A. Mantell, half a generation older than Owen, gave a paper in which he presented evidence that, in a study for which Owen had received the Royal Medal of the Society two years previously, Owen had misunderstood the structure of belemnites, a common fossil organism. There was 'a not very creditable discussion at meeting of Royal Society,' writes Darwin, 'where Owen fell foul of Mantell with fury and contempt about belemnites. What wretched doings come from the ardor for fame; the love of truth alone would never make one man attack another bitterly.'[17]

Among other letters written by Darwin during spring 1848 there is one to Henslow regretting that he is unable to meet him in London on one of Henslow's rare visits. Henslow had written disparagingly about the value of pure research: unless the fruits of research are of 'immediate and practical value,' he claimed, 'it is of no more use than building castles in the air'. To this Darwin objects, citing chloroform as a case in which discovery in pure science had soon been found to have a valuable application. He continues: 'I have been working very hard for the last 18 months on the anatomy etc. of the Cirripedia . . . and some of my friends laugh at me, and I fear the study of the Cirripedia will ever remain "wholly unapplied" and yet I feel that such a study is better than castle-building.' Darwin was quite wrong about its applicability: those concerned with marine fouling have found it to be of 'enormous practical benefit'.[18] However unlikely it may seem, pure research always finds application, if not sooner then later.

Darwin was to be engaged in his barnacle study until September 1854, eight years in all, but of those years he calculated two were lost through ill-health.[19]

V

During the summer of 1848 Darwin's health began seriously to deteriorate. For that year the entry in his diary reads: 'From July to end of year, unusually unwell, with swimming of head, depression, trembling – many bad attacks of sickness.'[20] Although neither in the diary nor in the correspondence is there any suggestion that the breakdown might be related to his father's terminal illness and death, it seems more than likely that that was the determining factor.

Dr Robert had had his first attack of angina in December 1844 but had then recovered. A couple of years later his condition was causing anxiety. In February 1847 Charles was planning a visit to Shrewsbury but it had to be postponed. 'I have been very unwell for all last week,' he tells Hooker, 'my Father has been ill and my visit to Shrewsbury delayed and all things gone on badly. . . . All my plans are uncertain on account of Shrewsbury.' His two-week visit began on 19 February. Soon after his return, writing to

Lyell about Glen Roy, he adds: 'My visit to Shrewsbury was rather a melancholy one, for though I found my Father better, he is much changed bodily during the last six months.' Throughout the spring of 1847, when he was trying to arrange meetings with Hooker, Charles's health was indifferent. On 14 April he enters in his diary: 'Lost several weeks by Boils and unwellness.'[21] At this time Emma was six months pregnant; and on 8 July Bessie was born.

From 22 October to 4 November 1847 Charles is again at Shrewsbury and is still suffering from boils and also from general malaise. While there he writes letters to Emma and Hooker. By this time he has adopted the practice of addressing Emma as 'Mammy' which, according to his son Francis (born the following year), he maintained for the rest of his life (except when irritated, when he called her 'Emma'). 'My very dear Mammy,' he begins, 'I had two wretched days on Friday and Saturday but the second and largest boil has just broken so I shall be, and am now, much better. I lay all day up stairs on the sofa, groaning and grumbling and reading *Last Days of Pompeii* [a well-known novel by Bulwer-Lytton published twelve years earlier]. . . . I have had plenty of time to think of you my own dearest, tenderest, best of wives. . . . Kiss the dear chldren for me. . . . Many thanks for all your very nice letters.' Writing to Hooker, he refers to the boils as his 'old evil' and continues, 'I have had two miserable days with my stomach also. . . . I cannot tell you how overdone I have been feeling lately with all fatigue.' In neither letter is there reference to his father's health. On returning home he is still 'very unwell and incapable of doing any thing'.[22]

In May of the following year, writing a long letter to Hooker in India mainly on scientific topics, Darwin moves straight from the theme of dying to his own stomach complaints in a passage that points clearly to a fear that his stomach complaint might prove fatal. There was at that time much debate in geological circles about the origin of coal, and Darwin expresses himself glad that Hooker is giving attention to the coal deposits in India. 'I shall never rest easy in Down church-yard', he continues, 'without the problem be solved by someone before I die. Talking of dying makes me tell you that my confounded stomach is much the same.'[23]

By midsummer 1848, when Charles is making another visit to Shrewsbury (from 17 May to 1 June), Dr Robert is talking openly of his own impending death. Five letters written by Charles to Emma, who is again pregnant and expecting in August, are available and give a vivid picture of his father's condition as well as his own.[24] In the first he describes his father as cheerful: he 'talked the whole evening . . . his want of breath does not trouble him at all like the dyeing sensation, which he now very rarely has . . . he thought with care he might live a good time longer.' In later ones Charles describes his father's bad nights and says he cannot help thinking that his father's health is 'rapidly breaking up'. Catherine is having 'wretched nights' but her spirits remain good.

References to his own health are mixed. Having no work with him in Shrewsbury leads him to reflect: 'being employed alone makes me forget myself: really yesterday I was not able to forget my stomach for 5 minutes all day long.' In the letter following he asks Emma to thank Willie (aged eight) and Annie (aged seven) 'for their very nice notes, which told me a great many things I wished to hear. . . . Give them and my dear Etty [five] and Georgy [four] my best love.' A day or two later he is expressing anxiety about his father's condition: 'My father had a fair night. He was very cheerful at cards, but the day here is almost continual anxiety. . . . Your letters delight me and tell me all the things I most like to hear.'

In the last letter of the series Charles has manifestly cracked up and, in his yearning for Emma's comforting presence, reveals in the clearest light the relationship that had developed between them. 'My dearest dear old Mammy,' he starts, 'I was so very glad to get your letter this morning with as good an account of the Baby [Bessy, aged ten months] as could be expected. I am so thankful you had Elizabeth [Emma's eldest sister] with you; for she of all human beings would be of the greatest comfort to you. . . . I am weak enough today, but I think I am improving. My attack was very sudden: it came on with fiery spokes and dark clouds before my eyes; then sharpish shivery and rather bad . . . sickness. . . . Today am languid and stomach bad. . . . Susan was very kind to me but I did yearn for you. Without you when I feel sick I feel very desolate. I almost doubt whether I shall be able to travel on Monday; but I can write no more now.' And he ends: 'Oh Mammy, I do long to be with you and under your protection for then I feel safe. God bless you.'

Back at Down that summer, 1848, Charles's health continues to be 'very indifferent'.[25] Because of that and Emma's impending confinement he has abandoned the idea of a weekend party of naturalists which he has hoped for. Instead, at the end of July, he and Ras take eight-year-old Willie for a week to the Dorset coast at Swanage, returning in time for the birth of a third son, Francis, on 16 August. As on previous occasions Emma's confinement seems to have been straightforward.

During the next two months Darwin is fighting depression and busy on barnacles. An event which was causing much rejoicing in scientific circles was the knighthood bestowed on Lyell by Queen Victoria: Lyell was invited to Balmoral for the ceremony and a few days' stay, and rode there the fifty miles north over the hills from the family estate at Kinnordy. 'I am delighted for your sake and for the sake of Geology,' Darwin tells him; 'for some years back [I have] most heartily abused the Government for not having long ago . . . marked your public estimation.'[26]

From 10 to 26 October Charles was again at Shrewsbury but none of his letters to Emma has survived. Dr Robert's end was clearly in sight, though he was to last another three weeks after Charles's departure. Susan and Catherine kept their brother informed. The scene just before their father died is told in a letter from Catherine: 'My father is perfectly collected and placid in his mind in every way, and one of the most beautiful and pathetic sights that can be imagined – so sweet, so uncomplaining – so full of everybody else. . . . Susan was up all last night and the greatest part of the night before; she is wonderfully able to go through her most trying part, all his directions being given to her. – He attempted to speak about you this morning, but was so excessively overcome he was utterly unable. . . . You will suffer sadly, my dear Charles. . . . I am sorry to hear of your being so unwell.' The day following Catherine wrote again giving a detailed account of their father's final hours. The previous afternoon he had become 'rather more suffering' and had failed rapidly that evening. During the early hours he had had 'a period of great suffering' and it was a mercy that he had then passed into a state of unconsciousness from which he did not recover. 'The funeral will be on Saturday, which will give you time to come. . . . God comfort you, my dearest Charles, you were so beloved by him.' Charles's daughter Etty, then six, recalled many years later that when the news reached Down she had felt awestruck and had cried bitterly out of sympathy for her father. She reports also that his journey down to Shrewsbury had been a great effort for him.[27]

Because of his condition, Charles did not start on the journey until Friday afternoon and then stayed the night in London with Ras. Next morning they travelled to Shrewsbury together. Both of them were reacting to the news of their father's death with somatic symptoms; and the four sisters were taking it for granted that Charles at least would not attend the funeral. As it turned out, Charles remained at The Mount with his eldest sister Marianne, who had also become so distraught and physically ill that she could not go. Ras had feared he would not be equal to the occasion either, but at the last moment managed to join in. In a letter to a family friend Ras described how after the service everyone in the family was sick – but, as Marianne's husband, Henry Parker, observed, entirely from their nervous feelings.[28]

VI

It is clear that Darwin was deeply distressed by his father's illness and death. On 6 February 1849 he writes to Fox apologising for not doing so earlier, 'but all the autumn and winter I have been much dispirited and inclined to do nothing but what I was forced to. I saw two very nice notes of yours on the occasion of my poor dear Father's death. The memory of such a father is a treasure to one; and when last I saw him he was very comfortable and his expression which I have now in my mind's eye serene and cheerful. Thank you much for your information about water-cure; I dislike the thoughts of it much.'[29]

During January and February 1849 he struggled to continue his usual life. He managed to attend a council meeting of the Geological Society at the end of January, having been absent for the previous six months; and he became engaged in a good-natured controversy with an expert colleague about the principles of biological nomenclature, which were causing him enormous trouble in his study of barnacles and which, he maintained, in their present application rewarded hasty and shoddy work. This was a controversy he eventually abandoned after a letter from Hooker advising him to 'drop the battle . . . you have far better work in hand'.[30]

By the end of February his symptoms were so bad and persistent tht he decided he must try the water-cure recommended by Fox that was available at an establishment at Malvern run by a Dr Gully. On 24 February, writing to Owen about some barnacles that Owen was lending him, he explains that his absence from London is due to his being 'as usual unwell. I have lost for the last 4 or 5 months at least 4/5ths of my time, and I have resolved to go . . . and spend two months at Malvern and see whether there is any truth in Gully and the water-cure: regular doctors cannot check my incessant vomiting at all.' Ten days later Emma writes to Fox on behalf of Charles: 'We really are going to set out "bag and baggage" to Malvern as soon as he is well enough. It is a great trouble taking all the household, but we think we cannot give Dr Gully's treatment a fair trial under 6 weeks or 2 months and that would be too long to leave the children even with their aunts. . . . This has been a disheartening winter with respect to his health.' Gully thought that Darwin's symptoms were due to 'nervous indigestion', which he held could not be cured in less than six months.[31] The family with governess and servants migrated to Malvern on 6 March and established themselves in a furnished house where they would stay until the end of June, over three months in all.

Dr Gully inspired great confidence in his patients: 'It was the innate feeling of his profoundness and might that gave Dr Gully such power of fascination over patients,' as a contemporary account puts it.[32] Darwin fell for this fascination almost at once. A fortnight after arriving in Malvern, he writes to his sister Susan: 'I like Dr Gully much – he is certainly an able man: I have been struck with how many remarks he has made similar to those of my father. He is very kind and attentive; but seems puzzled by my case.' In this letter Charles gives a detailed account of the regime, which starts at 6.45 am with a scrubbing in cold water for two or three minutes and then a walk for twenty, a cold water compress to be worn all day and renewed every two hours, his feet in cold water for ten minutes at noon, then another twenty-minute walk, dinner, with rest for an hour afterwards. His diet permits meat and eggs but excludes 'sugar, butter, spices, tea, bacon or anything good . . . certainly I have felt much better this week and the sickness has depressed me much less. . . . I am become perfectly indolent which I feel the oddest change of all to myself.' To this Emma appends a postscript noting that Annie, now eight, has been telling her governess all about the water-cure, and adding, 'And it makes Papa so angry' – which Charles, who is present, admits is true. A week later he writes to Fox along the same lines saying he had been 'in a much shattered condition before coming here'.[33]

During the previous December Darwin had received a long letter from Hooker, written from Darjeeling in the Himalayan foothills, but it had remained unanswered. 'What an ungrateful return for a letter which interested me so much,' he starts a reply at the end of March. 'But I have had a bad winter. On the 13th of November my poor dear Father died. . . . I was at the time so unwell that I was unable to travel, which added to my misery. Indeed, all this winter I have been bad enough . . . and my nervous system began to be affected, so that my hands trembled, and head was often swimming. I was not able to do anything one day out of three, and was altogether too dispirited to write to you, or to do anything but what I was compelled. I thought I was rapidly going the way of all flesh.' He then recounts the events that had led him to be writing from Malvern and taking the water-cure. 'I am already a little stronger,' he continues. 'Dr. G. feels pretty sure he can do me good, which most certainly the regular doctors could not. . . . I feel certain that the water-cure is no quackery. How I shall enjoy getting back to Down with renovated health . . . and resuming the beloved Barnacles.' There follows a long discourse on botanical and geological topics, with some scientific gossip thrown in.[34]

Darwin was evidently feeling a good deal better already and wrote a number of letters to friends during the following weeks. One of the first was to his old *Beagle* servant, Syms Covington. Having continued to act as Darwin's servant and assistant for nearly three years after the *Beagle*'s return, Covington, who was going deaf, had emigrated to New South Wales. Darwin had been keeping in touch with him and six years earlier, in October 1843, had reported his new address at Down and informed him he was sending him a new ear trumpet: 'You must accept it as a present from me.'[35] Now, from Malvern, Darwin writes again to Covington enquiring after his health and reporting some of his own news. His father has died and his own health has been 'very bad, and I thought all this winter I should not recover'. Now he is benefiting from the cure he is taking and he is more hopeful. He refers to the publications arising out of the *Beagle* voyage and the continuing success of his *Beagle* journal 'which you copied'. He is now employed on a large volume dealing with 'barnacles from all over the world' and hopes that Covington may be able to collect some Australian specimens for him. Instructions for packing and dispatching follow. Although he has 'not seen any of our old officers for a long time', he has news of Captain FitzRoy, who 'has command of a fine steamer frigate', and also of Sulivan, now promoted captain, who 'has gone out to settle for a few years and trade at the Falkland Islands, and taken his family with him'. Next he enquires after the Kings, father and son, also settled in New South Wales, and ends with warm good wishes.[36]

This occasional correspondence with Covington would continue until Covington's death at the age of forty-five twenty years later.

In May Darwin renewed correspondence with Henslow, repeating phrases he had already used in other letters. 'All last Autumn and winter my health grew worse and worse; incessant sickness, tremulous hands and swimming head. I thought I was going the way of all flesh.' After describing the circumstances which had brought him to Malvern and the regime he was being subjected to, he adds: 'One most singular effect of the treatment is, that it induces in most people, and eminently in my case, the most complete stagnation of mind; I have ceased to think even of barnacles!' Among much else in this letter, he expresses his intention to go to the next British Association meeting, to be held in Birmingham in September, where he is to 'be honoured beyond all measure in being one of the V.Ps [vice-presidents]'.[37]

'Indolence and stagnation of mind' are the special effects of the water-cure that Darwin had singled out a little earlier in a letter to Fox: 'Till experiencing it, I could not have believed it possible – I now increase in weight, have escaped sickness for 30 days . . . and yesterday in my walks I managed seven miles! I am turned into a mere walking and eating machine.'[38]

The whole Darwin family stayed at Malvern for over three months and finally returned to Down at the end of June. There Charles, still under Dr Gully's supervision, installed equipment which enabled him to continue with the water-cure. The previous January he had begun keeping daily notes about his health on loose sheets of foolscap. The object was first to observe the effects of hydropathy so as to regulate the regime and later to observe how different factors – travel, visitors, medicines (orthodox and otherwise), 'electric chains' and other remedies – influenced the course of illness. The record is meticulous and contains notes made daily, even hourly, of small changes in his clinical conditon.[39] In the event, this *Diary of Health* would be kept for a total of six years, ending in January 1855.

Back at Down in July Darwin continued to make good progress. Deeply grateful to Fox for having recommended the water-cure, he recounts his plans to continue the treatment for another year. 'I consider the sickness as absolutely cured. . . . The Water Cure is assuredly a grand discovery and how sorry I am . . . that I was not somehow compelled to try it some five or six years ago.'[40] On 15 July he resumed work on his beloved barnacles, limiting the daily stint to two and a half hours on Dr Gully's orders, and was soon sending more letters about the work to all parts of the world.

Darwin's account of the breakdown he suffered during his father's terminal illness and the months after his death, in which he describes himself as 'depressed', 'out of spirits' and 'melancholy', leaves no doubt that he was fairly severely depressed at that time. Many years later, in June 1862 in a letter to Hooker, he recalled that during this period he was 'utterly weary of life'.[41]

Although we can be confident that his condition was a direct reaction to his loss, it is striking that in none of the letters Darwin wrote at this time is there any hint that his symptoms, either emotional or somatic, might be linked to his father's death. Nor is there evidence of active mourning; for example, there are no references to being sad, to missing his father or to reminiscing about him. Mourning appears to have been inhibited, perhaps in order to avoid recalling resentful memories of earlier days when he had smarted under his father's contemptuous tongue. Emma, moreover, could have been of little help, try no doubt as she would have done, since her feelings for her father-in-law, which had never been warm, would have had little in common with Charles's. It thus seems possible that instead of mourning his father he became deeply pre-occupied with his own symptoms, a diversion of attention known to occur in some cases.

VII

During the autumn of 1851 Darwin's recovery from depression proceeded steadily. For ten days in mid-September he duly went, with Emma, to the British Association meeting in Birmingham, where he was one of the eight vice-presidents, and read a brief paper on barnacles. He was very disappointed that neither Henslow nor Fox was there and the meeting proved much less enjoyable than the meeting at Oxford two years earlier. On one of the excursions he had broken down and had had to return; and on the Sunday he and Emma took the opportunity to pay a brief visit to Dr Gully at Malvern. Recounting much of this to Henslow after returning to Down, he adds: 'I go on with the Water Cure very steadily and keep on deriving considerable benefit from it, as long as I live the regular life of a hermit, but I think I stand any change, even worse than formerly and my stomach has not got over the excitement of Birmingham as yet.'[42]

At the end of September he received another long letter from Hooker in which Hooker sends condolences on Dr Robert's death, thanks Darwin warmly for all the professional gossip, gives an account of his Himalayan adventures and describes some of his geological observations. Darwin answered promptly, on 12 October 1849. After discussing the geological points, he tells Hooker about the British Association meeting – 'very flat compared to Oxford' and the place dismal. He then reports on his health: 'I am going on very well, and am certainly a little better every month, my nights mend much slower than my days. . . . I steadily gain in weight and eat immensely, and am never oppressed with my food.' Apart from his work at the barnacles, he is forbidden to read anything except the newspapers, and is 'consequently terribly behind in all Scientific books'. He also confesses to being wearied by spending so much time 'at mere species describing', and adds an account of the health regime he has adopted at Down:

I have built a douche and am to go on through all the winter, frost or no frost. My treatment now is lamp five times per week, and shallow bath for five minutes afterwards; douche daily for five minutes, and dripping sheet daily. The treatment is wonderfully tonic, and I have had more better consecutive days this month than on any previous ones. . . . I am allowed to work now, two and a half hours daily, and I find it as much as I can do; for the cold-water cure, together with three short walks, is curiously exhausting; and I am actually *forced* to go to bed at eight o'clock completely tired. . . . Dr. Gully thinks he shall quite cure me in six or nine months more.[43]

There is also much else in this long letter to Hooker. At one point, after describing some of the difficulties he is encountering in his barnacle work, he protests about a recent remark of Hooker's: 'By the way, you say in your letter that you care more for my species work than for the Barnacles; now this is too bad of you, for I declare your decided approval of my plain Barnacle work over theoretic species work, had very great influence in deciding me to go on with former and defer my species-paper.' When, six months later, in April 1850, Hooker was back in Calcutta for a brief visit, he replies to Darwin's protest. 'Probably I spoke too strongly about your specific work and Barnacles,' he begins, excusing himself by describing the perilous circumstances in which his original letter had been written, and continues: 'I remember once dreaming that you were too prone to theoretical considerations about species and unaware of certain difficulties in your way, which I thought a more intimate acquaintance with species *practically* might clear up. Hence I rejoiced at your taking up a difficult genus. . . . Since then your own theories, have possessed me, without however converting me and interested as I am in the Barnacles and felt desirous of knowing in what direction they had carried your other views.'[44]

Soon after receiving Hooker's explanation Darwin replies (on 15 June 1850): 'You ask what effect studying species has had on my variation theories; I do not think much,' he begins; 'on the other hand I have been struck . . . by the variability of every part in some slight degree of every species when the same organ is *rigorously* compared in many individuals. . . . Systematic work would be easy were it not for this confounded variation which, however, is pleasant to me as a speculist [i.e. theorist] though odious to me as a systematist.'[45] In fact, as we see in chapter 20, Darwin's time-consuming study of barnacles was to prove an excellent investment, since it was destined to pay valuable dividends to his species work, still some years away in the future.

In the meantime, before this exchange of letters during the early summer of 1850, Darwin had received another of Hooker's long bulletins from the high Himalayas, this one written at the end of September 1849 from the frontier between Sikkim and Tibet. Although Hooker's expertise was botany, he was no mean geologist and this letter is almost entirely geological. 'I have been reading your Geology of S.A. with immense profit and pleasure, and have to own myself duly and truly ashamed of not having done so before,' he begins. After referring to it as 'a most capital book and extremely well written', he describes the scene of his reading: 'How you would have laughed could you have seen me perusing it with avidity at 16,000 feet where I camped for 20 days . . . lying in bed huddled up in blankets with the smallest possible tip of one finger exposed to turn the pages' because of the severity of the cold.[46]

Throughout the autumn and winter of 1849–50 Darwin's barnacle work and health regime continued unabated. In mid-October he was well enough for the Lyells to spend a weekend at Down, and in November Fox paid a visit, one of the few occasions when he stayed at Down. In December, after nearly a year's absence, Darwin resumed attendance at the council of the Geological Society in London and stayed on to hear Lyell give a paper on volcanic craters.[47] That autumn Darwin had also been well enough to sit for the Irish painter and lithographer, T. H. Maguire, who had been commissioned to produce a series of portraits of leading scientists for the Ipswich Museum. 'My wife says she never saw me with the smile, as engraved,' he tells Henslow, who had also sat for Maguire, 'but otherwise it is very like.'[48]

The year ended on a cheerful note. Darwin had received a copy of the geological report of the US Exploring Expedition to the Pacific 1838–42, written by a geologist-zoologist correspondent of his in the USA, James Dwight Dana (1813–95), and had been overjoyed to find that his views about coral reefs were strongly supported. 'I write solely from exuberance of vanity,' he tells Lyell in an enthusiastic note. 'To begin with a modest speech, I am astonished at my own accuracy!! . . . Considering how infinitely more of Coral Reefs he saw than I did, this is wonderfully satisfactory to me.' 'Farewell,' he ends. 'My boasting has done me a deal of good.'[49]

One unexpected outcome of his father's death was that Charles, his brother and four sisters were all left extremely well off. Robert Darwin's financial skills in a society with little or no taxation resulted in each of the children receiving investments that brought in no less than £8000 a year.[50] As we shall see, however, even this did not put an end to Charles's worries over money.

VIII

Except for Frank Wedgwood, who stayed on in the Potteries with his family and continued to run the factory, all the other Wedgwoods who had been living in Staffordshire moved south following the sale of Maer, and were residing not far away in Surrey or Sussex. Supported by investment income from the Wedgwood company and other sources, they pursued a life of leisure, like many other sons and grandsons of men who had built up a successful business a generation or two earlier.

Joe and Caroline were at Leith Hill Place, near Dorking. After losing their first baby, they had three more daughters, who in 1850 were eight, seven and four respectively. Henceforward Charles and Emma became fairly regular visitors there. Another of Emma's brothers, Harry, with his wife and six children, had bought a house at Woking, where Charles and Emma stayed only occasionally. Emma's sister, Charlotte Langton, with her husband and nine-year-old son, had bought a house at Hartfield, on the edge of Ashdown Forest in east Sussex; and Emma's favourite sister, Elizabeth, had had a house built nearby. Living only twenty miles from Down, both sisters welcomed visits from Emma and Charles and also from their many nephews and nieces. 'All the cousins have the happiest remembrance of visits to these two houses,' Henrietta tells us; 'there was the same atmosphere of freedom as there had been at Maer, and the surroundings were particularly delightful for children. There were streams where we fished for minnows, sand to dig in, and wild heathy commons to wander freely about.'[51] Charles and Emma enjoyed their visits to Hartfield as much as their children did, and the countryside was just what Charles liked.

NINETEEN

Grief never wholly obliterated
1850–1853

I

The year 1850 began with the birth, on 15 January, of Leonard, their eighth child and fourth son. Two days later, reporting the event to Fox, Darwin describes how labour had come on so rapidly and the pains had been so severe 'that I could not withstand her entreaties for chloroform and administered it myself. . . . The doctor got here only 10 minutes before the Birth . . . it seems she remembers nothing from the first pain till she heard that the child was born. – Is this not grand?'[1]

Throughout 1850 Darwin's health continued much improved. Writing to Hooker in early February, he apologises for having no news: 'I have never been so much cut off from all scientific friends, for I have found that interrupting the water cure does not answer.' He has been elected to the council of the Royal Society and is 'ashamed to say' he has not attended once – though he managed to do so a few days later. With no other attendances during 1850, however, he was not re-elected. Although in May he feels able to tell Fox that he has 'lately been *very* well', that is not the picture he paints to Hooker the following month: 'my life altogether is bliss compared to what it was formerly, [yet] I find I do not improve in strength to withstand excitement. . . . Everyone tells me that I look quite blooming and beautiful; and most think I am shamming, but you have never been one of those.' He now weighed 11 stone 13½ pounds, about average for his height and 20 pounds more than in March 1849 before he went to Malvern.[2] The clinical picture is fully in keeping with the diagnosis of hyperventilation.

Darwin was still taking the water-cure and following the detailed instructions sent him regularly by Dr Gully. In June Dr Gully wished to check on his patient's progress and, rather reluctantly, Darwin agreed to go to Malvern for a week. In September, although he tells Fox that 'the wondrous Water Cure . . . keeps in high favour', a few doubts are beginning to creep in. He concedes that Fox's 'aphorism that "any remedy will cure any malady" contains . . . profound truth' and is troubled by Dr Gully's credulity: 'It is a sad flaw in my beloved Dr Gully, that he believes in everything,' he confesses, instancing clairvoyance, mesmerism and homeopathy.[3]

Throughout 1850 the study of barnacles remained Darwin's top priority, and he engaged in a steady flow of correspondence about the loan of collections, acknowledging their reception, bewailing consignments that went astray (though they seem always to have been found eventually) and discussing much else of greater scientific interest. No visits to London are recorded between April, when he attended the council of the Geological Society, and December, when he next did so. However, in mid-August he and Emma stayed for six days with Caroline and Joe Wedgwood at Leith Hill Place; and in mid-October they had a further three days' break with Emma's sister, Elizabeth Wedgwood, at Hartfield. From there they went on to join their children at the seaside at Ramsgate.

Thus, after the breakdown of 1848–9, Darwin's life had resumed its former even tenor, albeit more restricted socially than earlier. Sadly, however, contrasting with this more favourable picture, there was already a dark cloud on the horizon that was to lead to tragedy the following year.

II

In the summer of 1850 their eldest daughter Annie, now aged nine and a great favourite of her parents, became unwell. Accompanied by her governess, Miss Thorley, she spent some weeks during the autumn at Ramsgate to recuperate. Her condition did not improve, however, and early in March 1851 it worsened and led to periods of vomiting. Darwin, assuming that Annie had inherited his own wretched digestion, decided to take her to Malvern to see if Dr Gully could help. Accordingly on 24 March he accompanied Annie, just turned ten, and her younger sister Etty, aged seven and a half, to Malvern together with Miss Thorley and Brodie, the nanny. After a couple of days Charles returned to London for a brief stay with Ras. Emma was seven months pregnant and remained at Down. Despite Annie's ill-health and Emma's pregnancy, Emma's next elder brother, Hensleigh Wedgwood, remarked to Ras at this time that Charles seemed healthier and happier than he had been for some years.[4]

Three weeks later the blow fell. News from Malvern was that Annie had a fever and had become dangerously ill. 'A smart bilious gastric fever' was Dr Gully's diagnosis.[5] Her father was summoned and arrived on Thursday, 17 April, to find the situation already desperate: 'she looks very ill,' he writes immediately to Emma. 'Thank God she does not suffer at all – half dozes all day. . . . You would not in the least recognize her with her poor, hard, sharp pinched features.' Although Dr Gully thought there was still hope, he was also doubtful whether she would last the night. Charles was distraught, as many years later Etty was to recall: 'I well remember his arrival and his flinging himself on the sofa in an agony of grief.'[6]

Annie was to survive another five days. Partly to relieve his own feelings and partly because he believed Emma would welcome it, each day he wrote her a long and detailed bulletin of the situation as it developed from hour to hour. On the Friday, he tells Emma, it is 'a struggle between life and death . . . she has vomited a large quantity of bright green fluid. Her case seems to me an exaggerated one of my Maer illness' (probably a reference to the first occasion when he had gastric symptoms in May 1839).

Meanwhile Emma, unable to be with Charles herself and concerned as ever about his health, persuaded her sister-in-law, Hensleigh Wedgwood's wife Fanny, to go to Malvern to be with Charles during the crisis. This we learn from a letter written by Emma's maternal aunt, Fanny Allen, who was staying at Down: 'She [Emma] is so afraid that this anxiety may injure Charles's health, which is always affected by his mind, that she has desired Fanny Hensleigh to go down to Malvern.' This was wise. Fanny, a woman of fifty and the mother of six mostly teenaged children, was a close friend and well qualified for the task of supporting Charles through this tragic time. In later years Charles was to say that he believed he could not have borne these days of anxiety and grief without Fanny there to comfort him and look after practical details.

Fanny Hensleigh arrived at Malvern on Saturday to find that Annie had rallied, and it was thought she might have turned the corner. Charles, she found, was at his wits' end. In a note to Emma, Fanny describes him as 'sadly overcome and shaken [though] he has been two little walks to-day . . . it was some relief [for him] to be doing something, though occasionally it may be too much.' Charles's anxiety made him intensely restless. 'I cannot sit still but am constantly up and down,' he tells Emma on Sunday. Annie seemed a little better, 'but I must not hope too much. The alternations of no hopes and hopes sickens one's soul. . . . It is such a relief to tell you for whilst writing to you I can cry tranquilly.' Fanny, he found, was 'an infinite comfort'. On Monday there were still hopes: 'I trust in God we are nearly safe,' he tells Emma. Fanny had sat with Annie most of the night: 'We are under deep obligation to Fanny never to be forgotten.' On Tuesday morning he was still hopeful, but by evening Annie was sinking. Deputising for Charles, Fanny informs Emma of the situation, adding that Charles 'cannot write you this himself – he is gone to lie down. . . . God support and save you for Charles's sake.'

Annie died peacefully at about noon on Wednesday, 23 April 1851. In telling Emma of the end, Charles emphasised how 'she went to her final sleep most tranquilly and most sweetly'. Then, after much further detail, he adds: 'We must be more and more to each other my dear wife.' He was thankful they had a portrait of her, a daguerreotype taken two years earlier. That evening Fanny Hensleigh in a letter to her husband describes events of the previous day: 'poor Charles was buoyed up too much and yesterday morning had written quite a hopeful letter to Emma

LEFT Charles and Emma's eldest daughter, Annie, aged 8 in 1851

RIGHT Charles and Emma's eldest son, William, aged 9 in 1853

BELOW LEFT George Darwin, aged 6 in 1851

BELOW RIGHT Henrietta Darwin, aged 5 in 1848

which he tore up but Dr Gully did not give her up till the middle of the day
– Charles was very ill all yesterday with one of his stomach attacks which
luckily made him not able to come into the room – it's most affecting to me
how he suffers constantly crying – but he says its a relief – the Funeral is
on Friday [25 April] which is a comfort so soon and he is not yet quite
decided whether he can go, but I advise him to go home tomorrow.'[8]

Charles took Fanny's advice and returned to Down to be with Emma,
for which she was thankful. Writing to Fanny before Charles' arrival,
Emma confided: 'Now I cannot help all sorts of fears for Charles which I
know are not reasonable. Now all cause for exertion is over I know he
must be ill. . . . My first feeling of consolation will be to have him safe
home again. . . . What a comfort it is to feel you are there with him.' On
the following day, while Fanny was attending the funeral at Malvern
Abbey, Emma wrote to her again: 'I cannot tell you the surprise and joy it
was to see poor Charles arrive about 6.30 yesterday. . . . He is much
better bodily than I had any hopes of and not worse in spirits and began to
notice the little ones this morning. We have done little else but cry
together and talk about our darling. He cannot express enough what a
comfort you were.' That day Charles also wrote to Fanny to thank her for
having advised him to return home and for having herself attended the
funeral: 'I know of no other human being whom I could have asked to have
undertaken so painful a task.'

Three weeks after Annie's death, on 13 May 1851, Emma gave birth to
their ninth child and fifth son, Horace.

Despite the shock of Annie's death, Charles seems not to have been in
particularly bad health during the following summer. Indeed, in July he
and Emma decided to spend ten days in London, staying as usual with
Ras, who had moved into a new house. They saw friends and also visited
the Great Exhibition at the Crystal Palace in Hyde Park.[9]

At the end of August, four months after the tragedy, Charles decided to
describe what Annie had been to him during her short but happy life in
order to recall her more vividly in the future: 'the main feature in her
disposition is her buoyant joyousness tempered by . . . her sensitiveness
. . . and her strong affection.' She was closely attached to both her parents
and much enjoyed physical contact. He refers to her 'most clinging
fondling nature' and tells how 'she would at almost any time spend
half-an-hour in arranging my hair, "making it", as she called it,
"beautiful" . . . in short in fondling me. She liked being kissed . . . and all
her habits were influenced by her loving disposition.' Always cheerful and
good tempered, 'She was very popular in the whole household'; she was
also very good with the younger children. The daguerreotype taken two
years previously 'fails entirely in expression' (no doubt largely because of
the long exposure-time required). Since then, he continues, 'her face has
become lengthened and better looking'. She had also become tall for her
age and enjoyed accompanying him around the Sandwalk. Thus, as his

eldest daughter, she was already becoming a close companion whom he was confidently expecting to continue so for many years yet. 'I always thought', he writes, 'that come what might, we should have had in our old age at least one loving soul, which nothing could have changed.'[10] To one who in childhood experienced rebuke rather than fondling, Annie's winning ways must have been exceptionally appealing. No wonder her loss proved irreparable.

Annie's death was indeed an extremely severe blow to both Charles and Emma. Many times during the final days they record the bitterness of their grief. Shortly afterwards Charles tells Ras how bitter Emma was feeling, and a few days later writes to Fox that Annie's loss was 'bitter and cruel'. This is the nearest he comes to expressing the anger that was evidently just beneath the surface. On this occasion, fortunately, all his feelings could be freely shared, first with Fanny Hensleigh, who encouraged his tears, and later with Emma herself. That, no doubt, was what enabled him to avoid the breakdown into depression and psychosomatic illness that had followed his father's death two and a half years earlier. On that occasion, it would appear, he had expressed little real feeling, and his mourning had been inhibited. Not only were his own feelings for his father bound tight in an unthinking idealisation of him, but Emma, who had never been on easy terms with her father-in-law, could not share whatever feelings Charles may have had. Now, in contrast, they felt as one.

The wounds that Annie's death inflicted on both Charles and Emma never healed. Twenty years later, in his *Autobiography* Charles notes that remembering her would still bring tears to his eyes. In the last year of his life, replying to a letter from Hooker on the death of his brother Ras, Charles contrasts the effects of the deaths of someone old and of someone young: 'Death in the latter case when there is a bright future ahead, causes grief never to be wholly obliterated.' Henrietta describes how her father 'could not bear to reopen his ˈsorrow, and he never, to my knowledge, spoke of her'. On Emma also Annie's death left an indelible mark, as Henrietta recalled when writing the memoir of her mother: 'It may almost be said that my mother never really recovered from this grief. She very rarely spoke of Annie but when she did the sense of loss was always there unhealed.'[11]

Although Charles may never have spoken of Annie, he refers to her more than once in letters of condolence to close friends who have lost a child, each time recalling the feelings of bitterness engendered by his own loss. 'There is nothing in the world like the bitterness of such a loss,' he tells Hooker, who had lost his six-year-old daughter, in September 1863. In a second letter Charles sought to hearten him by referring to the healing effects of time. 'How well I remember your feeling when we lost Annie. . . . Your grief has made me shed a few tears over our poor darling, but believe me that these tears have lost that unutterable bitterness of former days.' He was thankful that Hooker's daughter had hardly suffered, and continues: 'This was to us with poor Annie the one great comfort.'[12] The suffering of others Darwin always found unbearable.

Darwin's tendency to turn away from situations likely to cause painful emotion is never so evident as in his deliberately avoiding visits in subsequent years to Annie's grave or even to Malvern itself. Thus in October five years later, when Fox was unwell and taking the water-cure at Malvern, and wrote to Darwin telling him that he had visited Annie's grave, Darwin replies (3 October 1856): 'Thankyou for telling me about our poor dear child's grave. The thought of that time is yet most painful to me. . . . About a month ago I felt overdone in my work, and had almost made up my mind to go for a fortnight to Malvern; but I got to feel that old thoughts would revive so vividly that it would not have answered; but I have often wished to see the grave, and I thank you for telling me about it.'[13]

The same reluctance to visit Malvern is expressed in the winter of 1860–1, nearly ten years after Annie's death, when Darwin's health was precarious. In letters to Hooker, where among much else he describes the exacerbation of his symptoms, he says he has had thoughts of going to Malvern, which Emma was urging him to do. However, he never went. He gave various reasons, including unwillingness to interrupt his work; but another was his reluctance to revive memories of Annie's death.[14]

III

Not only was Annie's death a severe blow in itself but it led her parents, especially Charles, to become acutely anxious about the health of their other children. Less than a year later, on 7 March 1852, when after a brief lapse he resumes correspondence with Fox, who also had a large number of children, Darwin expresses his fear in dramatic terms: 'My fear is hereditary ill-health. Even death is better for them.' On 24 October 1852, once again in a long letter to Fox bringing him up to date with family news and bewailing the anxieties of a paterfamilias, he repeats his fear: 'but another and the worst of my bugbears is hereditary weakness'. The same words are used yet again in July of the following year.[15]

Mistaken though he certainly was, Darwin had little doubt that Annie's ill-health had been inherited from him: 'she inherits, I fear with grief, my wretched digestion,' he had told Fox before taking her to Malvern.[16] 'Her case seems to me an exaggerated one of my Maer illness,' he had written to Emma three weeks later. Now he was terrified his other children might have inherited the same trouble. Darwin's strong belief that his own gastric troubles were heritable points unmistakably to his supposing that he had himself inherited them, and that could only mean that he had done so from his mother. Whether he was aware of these ideas remains obscure, but it seems almost certain that they were present in some part of his mind. His mother's death from gastric illness and now Annie's would strengthen his belief that his own condition would also prove fatal; and this would readily account for his oft-expressed fear during his break-down of 1848–9 that he was unlikely to recover.

To what extent Darwin made these connections consciously we shall never know. All we know for certain is that, whatever the cause of Annie's death, the fear of their other children succumbing in the same way came to haunt Charles; and it explains many of the constant precautions against ill-health that came to characterise the Down household and, in later years, to be the subject of caricature.

Not only did Darwin worry about the children's health but he worried constantly also about their futures, especially the ability of his five sons to earn themselves a living. Francis in his reminiscences recalls his father's anxiety about money, which 'came in great measure from his fears that his children would not have health enough to earn their own living, a foreboding which fairly haunted him for many years.' These fears Darwin expresses repeatedly in his letters to Fox. On 7 March 1852 he writes: 'We have now seven children, all well, thank God, as well as their mother; of these seven, five are boys. . . . It makes me sick whenever I think of professions; all seem hopelessly bad, and as yet I cannot see a ray of light.' A year later, in July 1853, he writes to Fox on the birth of his (Fox's) eleventh child and commiserates with him, half jokingly and half seriously: 'Eleven children, ave Maria! it is a serious look-out for you. Indeed, I look at my five boys as something awful, and hate the very thought of professions, etc.' He then adds: 'But my bugbear is hereditary weakness.'[17]

The immediate problem that was worrying Darwin in the autumn of 1850 when Annie's illness had begun was what kind of education to give his sons – whether to expose them to the classical grind from which he had suffered or to try a school adopting a more modern curriculum. In September 1850 he enquires of Fox whether he can advise. 'I cannot endure to think of sending my boys to waste 7 or 8 years in making miserable Latin verses, and we have heard some good of Bruce Castle School near Tottenham', which he and Emma plan to inspect. Never-theless he is anxious: 'I feel that it is an awful experiment to depart from the usual course, however bad that course may be.' Has Fox any information? Such information as Fox has is favourable. Thanking him, Darwin writes to say that what he had seen for himself also seemed promising. His eldest son, William, was nearly eleven and a little 'backward for his age; though sensible and observant. I rather think we shall send him to Bruce Castle School.' Nevertheless he was 'still in an awful state of indecision' whether to plunge for the experiment or to send William to Rugby.[18] In the event Darwin shrank from the 'awful experiment' and William started at Rugby in February 1852.

In the same letter to Fox (of 10 October 1850) he tells him that he is toying with the idea of emigrating. 'I often speculate how wise it would be to start off to Australia, or what I fancy most, the middle States of N. America.' This idea appears again a month later in a long letter to Covington thanking him for the consignment of Australian barnacles just arrived and also for his news. 'You have an immense incalculable advantage in living in a country in which your children are sure to get on if industrious . . . when I think of the future I very often ardently wish I was settled in one of the Colonies, for I have now four sons (seven children in all, and more coming) and what on earth to bring them up to I do not know. . . . Many people think that Californian gold will half ruin those who live on the interest of accumulated gold or capital, and if that does happen I shall certainly emigrate.' He proceeds to enquire about the interest to be earned from a safe investment in Australia and anything else of interest about the economic situation there.[19]

In 1850 the Californian gold-rush and another in Australia were leading to anxiety about the possibility of a resulting inflation in Britain. Darwin, an avid reader of *The Times*, would have been among the first to catch this anxiety, and he remained apprehensive for another eighteen months. For example, in February 1852 he was studying an *Emigrant's Manual* and the following month was still worrying about possible effects on his investments, as he tells Fox.[20] In Britain, however, inflation did not materialise, and thenceforward Darwin makes only an occasional and not very serious reference to emigration.

In the letter to Fox of 7 March 1852 Darwin gives a picture of his current routine: 'I dread going anywhere on account of my stomach so easily failing under any excitement. I rarely even now go to London, not that I am at all worse, perhaps rather better and lead a very comfortable life with my 3 hours of daily work, but it is the life of a hermit. My nights are *always* bad, and that stops my becoming vigorous.'[21] Nevertheless, despite his describing himself as a hermit, he and Emma undertook a three-week trip to the Midlands during the early spring and a further week in Surrey during September. On 24 March they visited William, newly started at Rugby School, then went on to Shrewsbury for six days to see Charles's sister Susan, who was flourishing; Catherine was enjoying a visit to Rome. From there Charles returned to Down 'to look after the babies', while Emma visited Etruria in the Potteries to stay with her brother Frank, who was still running the Wedgwood factory. The September visit to Surrey was to Emma's brother Josiah III and Charles's sister Caroline. A month after returning to Down, on 24 October 1852, Darwin explains to Fox that, although he has been 'unusually well of late', he cannot stand change any better than formerly. 'The other day I went to London and back, and the fatigue, though so trifling, brought on a very bad form of vomiting.'[22]

1853 began with the death at the age of seventy-six of Jessie de Sismondi, Emma's favourite aunt. Since being widowed ten years earlier she had been living with three of her sisters, two unmarried and one widowed, at Tenby; distance prevented Emma attending the funeral. Throughout the year Darwin pushed on relentlessly with his barnacles, his work interrupted only by two brief family holidays. From 14 July to 4 August the whole family was at Eastbourne and then spent three days in August at Woking; from there Charles, Emma, George and Henrietta visited a military camp preparing troops for the Crimea. To their great pleasure they were shown around by none other than Captain James Sulivan, RN, formerly of the *Beagle*. Whereas in later years Charles would often complain bitterly of intense boredom on holidays, he not only enjoyed the visit to the camp but wrote to Fox from Eastbourne: 'Here we are in a state of profound idleness, which to me is a luxury.'[23]

IV

Worry dreadfully though Darwin did about his children's health, education and future, he also enjoyed their company. For two and a half years after William's birth, it will be recalled, he had made systematic observations on his son's development, with special reference to the emergence of emotional expressions; and, after Annie's birth in March 1841, he recorded a few comparisons between her development and that of William. For example, in May 1842, when Annie was only fourteen months old, he noted how much more neatly she took hold of pens and pencils than did Willy, despite his being fourteen months older and having had more practice. On the other hand, Annie showed none of the skill in throwing things that Willy had.[24] A few months later, when Willy was two years and eight months, he recorded his behaviour as manifesting 'a kind of conscience'. 'I met him coming out of dining room, with his pianofore folded up carefully and he eyeing it – I asked him what he had got there: he said "nothing . . . go away" – from his odd manner I determined to see what was concealed' (which proved to have been some yellow pickle). 'Here was natural acting and deceit,' Darwin comments.

During the following twelve months there are a few further obser-vations on Willy and Annie, recorded by Emma, and then a seven-year interval before Emma resumes. One of the first in the new series, in August 1852, concerns their third son, Francis, just turned four. Holding some nuts, Francis addresses his father: 'I'll give you lots of nuts – I'll give you one – I'll give you half the inside – It was so little I eat it all up.' The next concerns their fourth son, Leonard, aged two and a half that August. He asks his father to kiss his face – which, Emma reports, Papa did 'pretty handsomely', whereupon Lenny exclaims, 'Oh By Jo 5 – 6 – ten kisses!' A year later, when the family was holidaying at Eastbourne and Leonard was three and a half, Emma records the following: 'Papa – Well Lenny how do

Grief never wholly obliterated

Emma Darwin aged 45
with Leonard, aged 2½
in 1853

you like Eastbourne? L. (nodding towards the sea) I like that pond best –
where will they put it to when we dig in the sand? When rhodomontading.
Its only my nonsense.'

Leonard, Henrietta tells us in her memoirs, became a great favourite
and almost all the remaining entries record his various sayings, which
evidently delighted and amused his parents. In the early summer of 1854
Emma records: 'Lenny 4½ coming in all over mud up to the eyes. Papa
"Oh Lenny what have you been doing?" L. "I'd rather not tell you." P.
"Do tell me what you've been doing?" L. "Must I? Then I shan't".'
Thereafter Charles takes over the recording, which continues for another
two years. Among some three dozen entries the following are typical:

6 June 1854. Lenny after quarrelling with Horace [aged three], 'I feel that I shall
never play with Baby again, – never, in all my life' – (In half-a-minute in full
romps.)

1 February 1855. Lenny asked me 'Will you play at beggar-my-neighbour with
me, because if you won't you must.'

April 1855. Lenny was tumbling over the sofa and breaking all rules and when I
said he must not do that, He answered 'well then I *advise* you to go out of the
room'.

19 June 1855. Lenny found for me before Dinner a new Grass, so he said, 'I are
an extraordinary grass-finder, and I must keep it particularly by my side all
dinner-time'.

Charles Darwin aged 44, chalk drawing by Samuel Lawrence, 1853

24 July 1855. 'Papa I will tell you the nature of these sort of persons (meaning himself and Horace who were making a horrid mess) they like going into the mud'.

21 May 1856. Lenny [now six and a half] lying on my lap, coolly said 'Well you old ass' and being very slightly shocked, remarked 'Really, I did not mean to spurt that out'.

Since Charles himself had been brought up so very differently, it seems more than likely his amused and tolerant attitude owed a great deal to the influence of Emma.

V

From the 1850s onwards Henrietta was of an age to see her parents with some degree of objectivity, and her recollections of this time are recorded in her later descriptions of them.

My father took an unusual delight in his babies, and we have all a vivid memory of him as the most inspiriting of playfellows. Emma, as mother, was all that was tender and comfortable. Her sympathy, and the serenity of her temper, made her children feel absolutely at their ease with her, and sure of comfort in every trouble great or small, whilst her unselfishness made them know that she would never find anything a burden, and that they could go to her with all the many little needs of a child for help or explanation. Our elder cousin, Julia Wedgwood, said that in our house the only place where you might be sure of not meeting a child, was the nursery. Many a time, even during my father's working hours, was a sick child tucked up on his sofa, to be quiet, and safe, and soothed by his presence.[25]

In the evenings Charles read aloud to the children, and this, Henrietta reports, was 'a happy part of family life. Whatever my father did with us had a glamour of delight over it unlike anything else.' Emma played the piano for them and sang nursery songs. Henrietta recalls 'a troop of little children galloping round the room, whilst she played what was called the "galloping tune", composed by herself'. Untidiness never bothered her. In a letter to her Aunt Jessie, Emma contrasts herself with Charles's sister Susan: 'I saw Susan when she was at Down was rather uneasy till she had tidied away the chidren's untidiness as soon as they arose. I might be all day doing that, so I let them accumulate till the room becomes unbearable, and then call Bessy [the nursemaid] in to do it.'[26]

The old letters Henrietta had collected describing her mother's earlier years, she remarks, 'speak of her as gay and merry, and I have been told by old friends of hers that she had the charm of abounding life and high spirits.' She continues:

When I remember her as she was in my childhood, it is as serene but somewhat grave. The jokes and the merriment would all come from my father. . . . Her judgment was good, and there was about her a bright aliveness, and a many-sided interest in the world, in books, and in politics. Her utter sincerity gave a continual freshness to her opinions, and there were delightful surprises in her way of taking things. . . . Any little unexpected change in her daily habits remained a pleasure to her, instead of becoming a pain as it does to most old people. This youthfulness of nature showed itself in all her enjoyments – in her delight at the first taste of spring, and in her warm welcome of anyone she cared for. She would hurry to the front door at Down, eager for the first moment of greeting, or in summer weather she would be on the little mound which overlooks the entrance road, waiting to wave a welcome as the carriage drove up. The contrast of this outspringing warmth with her usual calm demeanour, made every arrival a kind of special festival and fresh delight which I shall never forget.

But her dignity of character was as remarkable as her light-heartedness. It would be impossible to imagine anyone taking a liberty with her, or that she should let herself be put in a false position . . . people were sometimes afraid of her at first – to my great surprise – for no one really was more approachable or less uncharitable in judgment. It is true that she was easily wearied with tediousness in people, and would flash out against their tedium, though never to them-selves. . . . She was also impatient of tedium in books and in seeing sights. I remember her saying in fun that she could see a cathedral in five minutes.

Another side of this impatience was the fact that she was a little inclined to jump to conclusions, and did not always thoroughly weigh all sides of a question. Also it was an analogous quality that made her courage, of which she had plenty, sometimes degenerate into rashness.

Nothing was ever a trouble or a burden to her, and she never made much of difficulties. It was remarkable how she infused this spirit into the household and made the servants ready to co-operate with her, often even at great inconvenience to themselves. She had a delightfully ready and thoughtful generosity.

It was therefore natural for Emma to have written regularly to the broken-hearted Brodie after she insisted on leaving the family when Annie died and returning to her home town in the Scottish Highlands, whence she made an occasional visit south to her old charges at Down.

My mother's calm strength made her the most restful person to be with I ever knew. To the very last it was always my impulse to pour out every trouble to her, sure that I should have sympathy, comfort, and helpful counsel. She was a perfect nurse in illness. Her self-command never gave way and she was like a rock to lean on, always devoted and unwearied in devising expedients to give relief, and neat-handed and clever in carrying them out.

She did not laugh much, but when she did her laugh had a frank enjoyment delightful to hear. Her voice too was sympathetic and pleasant and she read aloud clearly and well. The keenness of her sympathy never deadened. She lived with her children and grandchildren in every detail of their lives. . . . Of one thing I am sure, – that she was naturally good. I mean that I have known those who impress one as having conquered their evil tendencies, but with her there seemed no evil to conquer. Therefore, though she was the most unselfish person I have ever known, there was no trace in her of the self-suppression which is often found in those who have had to struggle for unselfishness. Her tastes, her dislikes, her whims even, were all vivid and vividly expressed, and her unselfishness did not proceed from any want of a strong personality. Everything about her was wholesome and natural; and it was impossible to imagine her having an unkind or vain thought, nor can I ever remember her making a harsh judgment.[27]

TWENTY

Everlasting barnacles, a rising star and a dark horse
1853–1854

I

By the end of 1852 Darwin's study of the 'everlasting Barnacles' was within sight of the finish. An old-established scientific society, the Ray Society, had already published the first of two volumes on *Living Cirripedia*, and arrangements were in hand for the two volumes on *Fossil Cirripedia* to be published by a more recently founded one. The amount of work still to be done, including arrangements for copious illustration, remained immense, however, and was to keep him busy for most of the next two years. The final haul on a major enterprise of this sort is always the most tedious, and before the end of 1852 Darwin was heartily sick of the barnacles. 'I hate a Barnacle as no man ever did before, not even a sailor in a slow moving ship,' he tells Fox in October. Nevertheless his first published volume was receiving high praise in scientific circles – which was reassuring. 'I am *extremely* glad to hear that you approved of my Cirripedial Volume,' he tells Fox in July 1853. 'I have spent an almost ridiculous amount of labour on the subject, and certainly would never have undertaken it had I foreseen what a job it was.'[1] Despite his hope of finishing by the end of the year, he still had another fifteen months' work in front of him.

1853 ended on a happy note. On 5 November he opened a letter from the president of the Royal Society informing him that he had been awarded the society's Royal Medal, and mentioning both his study of *Coral Reefs* and also the first volume of *Living Cirripedia*. Shortly afterwards a letter from Hooker arrived emphasising the enthusiastic support given to the proposal by the fellows of the Royal Society, especially for his barnacle study. When Thomas Bell, seconding the proposal, had picked out the barnacles for praise, Hooker writes, there 'followed such a shout of paeans for the Barnacles that you would have smiled to hear.' Darwin's reaction to the news is conveyed vividly in his reply to Hooker's congratulations: 'the [news] certainly surprised me very much, but, though the letter [from the President] was a *very kind one*, somehow, I cared very little indeed for the announcement it contained. I then opened yours and such is the effect of warmth, friendship, and kindness from one that is loved, that the very same fact, told as you told it, made me glow with pleasure till my very heart throbbed. . . . Such hearty, affectionate sympathy is worth more than all the medals that ever were or will be coined. Again, my dear Hooker, I thank you.' Characteristically, he ends by emphasising that it was ridiculous that the runner-up, a botanist ten years older, had not been awarded the medal before him.[2]

The following year Hooker himself was awarded the same medal. In a note congratulating him Darwin reflects: 'Without you have a very much greater soul than I have (and I believe that you have), you will find the medal a pleasant little stimulus; when work goes badly, and one ruminates that all is vanity, it is pleasant to have some tangible proof, that others have thought something of one's labours.'[3]

By the autumn of 1853 Hooker had been back from India for eighteen months and had lost no time marrying his fiancée, Henslow's eldest daughter. During that winter the pair had spent a fortnight at Down and, as Darwin tells Lyell (who was busy geologising in Madeira and the Canary Islands), they had brought Henslow with them 'to our extreme delight. . . . It does one good to see so composed, benevolent and intellectual a countenance.' Hooker's *Himalayan Journal*, in two volumes, had been published, and Darwin continues: 'He has honoured me beyond measure in dedicating it to me!'[4]

During the summer of 1854, with the last three barnacle volumes published, Darwin received a laudatory letter about them from none other than Richard Owen. He replies enthusiastically: 'I cannot tell you how much gratified I am at what you say about the Cirripedia. I really feel rewarded for more labour than you would readily believe it possible could have been bestowed on the work.' 'I have been very seldom in London,' he continues. 'When I was last there I called at the College to see you, but you were just gone out. Pray believe me,' he ends, 'in great state of triumph, pride, vanity, conceit, etc. etc.'[5]

At long last, in the following September, Darwin was able to inform Hooker that he was 'sending ten thousand Barnacles out of the house all over the world', and that 'I shall in a day or two begin to look over my old notes on species. What a deal I shall have to discuss with you.'[6]

The eight years Darwin spent on barnacles (less two lost through illness) were far from wasted. First, his study proved a major contribution to zoological classification. By giving close attention to their larval stages and adopting a developmental approach, he was able to demonstrate that barnacles form a major branch of the crustacea and are not molluscs as previously supposed. Secondly, during this time Darwin transformed himself from a gifted amateur in zoology into a professional held in high regard by zoological colleagues. A few years later a young comparative anatomist destined to play a major role in Darwin's life, Thomas Huxley

(1825–95), would describe Darwin's study as 'one of the most beautiful and complete anatomical and zoological monographs which has appeared in our time, and is the more remarkable as proceeding from a philosopher highly distinguished in quite different branches of science, and not an anatomist *ex professo*'.[7]

Much later, recalling events for the benefit of Francis Darwin, who was compiling the three volumes of his father's *Life and Letters*, Hooker writes:

Your father had Barnacles on the brain, from Chili onwards! He talked to me incessantly of beginning to work at his 'beloved Barnacles' (his favourite expression) long before he did so methodically. It is impossible to say at what stage of progress he realised the necessity of such a training as monographing the Order offered him; but that he did recognize it and act upon it as a training in systematic biological study, morphological, anatomical, geographical, taxonomic and descriptive, is very certain; he often alluded to it . . . as a valued discipline. . . . In conversation with me [he recognised] three stages in his career as biologist, the mere collector, in Cambridge etc; the collector and observer, in the *Beagle* and for some years after; and the trained naturalist after, and only after the Cirripede work. That he was a thinker all along is true enough. . . . Eight years so spent by any other man would establish his reputation for all time, and whether as a discipline to your father, or for its results, I cannot conceive his spending it better, at that period of his career especially.[8]

Historians of evolution theory concur. During the course of his study Darwin had been confronted among much else with the problems posed by extensive variation within a given species and the difficulty of distinguishing between species, sub-species and mere varieties. This provided him with first-hand and solid experience of the species question for when he came later to write the *Origin*.

II

Darwin's health continued to improve during 1854 and he began again making frequent visits to London. From 1854 he was for a second time a member of council of the Royal Society and is recorded as having attended sixteen meetings. Moreover, reforms were afoot at the society and a number of the most active fellows had started a club, the Philosophical Club, which dined before the society's meetings and aimed to increase attendance and stimulate papers and discussion. In March 1854 Hooker suggested Darwin should join. He replied enthusiastically on 26 March 1854: 'With respect to the Club, I am deeply interested: only two or three days ago, I was regretting to my wife, how I was letting drop and being dropped by nearly all my acquaintances and that I would endeavour to go more often to London; I was not then thinking of the Club, which, as far as any one thing goes, would answer my exact object in keeping up old and making some new acquaintances, I will therefore come up to London for every (with rare exceptions) Club Day. . . . But it

Charles Darwin, aged 45,
circa 1854

is grievous how often any change knocks me up.' Darwin was duly elected
and evidently began attending meetings immediately. On 29 May he is
writing to Hooker: 'Very far from disagreeing with me my London visits
have just lately taken to suit my stomach admirably; I began to think that
dissipation, high-living, with lots of claret, is what I want, and what I had
during the last visit. We are going to act on the same principle and . . .
have just taken a pair of season-tickets to see the Queen open the Crystal
Palace [at Sydenham on 10 June].'[9]

It was no doubt during this renewed series of visits to London that
Darwin first met Thomas Huxley, who was also a member of the Royal
Society council. Though not yet thirty, Huxley had already made a name
for himself as a comparative anatomist and had become a close friend of
Hooker's. Soon he would be invited to Down and be 'pumped' by Darwin
for specialist information. Thenceforward, the three would form a close
circle, bound together not least by the fact that Huxley, like the other two,
had also undertaken a long voyage on one of the navy's surveying ships.[10]

Thomas Henry Huxley, plain Tom in his family, was the seventh and
youngest surviving of the eight children of George Huxley, an assistant
master at a very successful school in Ealing, then a village in the country to
the west of London, and his wife, Rachel Withers, whom Thomas
strongly resembled, both physically and mentally. Ten years after his birth
the school changed hands and George Huxley moved his family back to
his home town, Coventry, where he took a modest post as manager of a

small savings bank, while his two daughters opened a little school. Thomas had attended the Ealing school but had been very unhappy there and after the move to Coventry seems to have been largely self-educated. He became an avid reader and by the age of twelve was tackling serious books, such as James Hutton's *Theory of the Earth* and William Hamilton's work on logic, and was also teaching himself German.

The year 1839, when Thomas was fourteen, saw his sisters both married to doctors. Under the influence of a brother-in-law, he decided to study medicine and in 1842 he and a brother entered Charing Cross Hospital, both of them with scholarships. There Thomas's career was shaped by a first-rate lecturer in physiology, Wharton Jones, to whom he would always feel deeply indebted. He worked extremely hard, read widely and, with his teacher's encouragement, began research. By 1845 he was able to announce his first discovery, a hitherto unknown layer of cells in the root-sheath of hair which he had observed under the microscope; this led to his first publication. Later that year he carried off the gold medal in his final medical examinations.

Once qualified, he applied for an appointment as assistant surgeon in the Royal Navy as a prompt means of earning a living. Stationed at a hospital in Portsmouth, he was quickly spotted as a young man of promise and before the end of 1846 was appointed to HMS *Rattlesnake*, leaving shortly to survey the north and east coasts of Australia. After arriving in Australian waters in July the following year, she was based at Sydney, where she stayed two or three months each of the years 1847–9 between long surveying cruises to the little-known north. Eventually she sailed for home in May 1850 and paid off at Chatham in November that year.

Unlike Darwin, who had had no duties aboard the *Beagle* and could spend lengthy periods ashore, Huxley had to remain on board during the tedious months of surveying up and down the Australian coast, the Great Barrier Reef and both sides of the Torres Straits. Huxley was neither collector nor field naturalist, and in any case those roles were filled by the official naturalist aboard, John Macgillivray. Huxley's concerns lay elsewhere. Long interested in structures (as a schoolboy he had had thoughts of becoming a mechanical engineer), he now turned his attention to the different ways in which animals are constructed and accordingly used his time to study the anatomy of freshly caught marine invertebrates, such as starfish, squid and jellyfish, which were too delicate to be preserved by methods then available. As a skilled dissector, microscopist and draughtsman, he made systematic studies of a wide range of these animals, hitherto neglected, and, finding himself in disagreement with the current ways of classifying them, proposed a radical new system – a bold step for an unknown young man. By the end of the first year's cruise he had dispatched two papers for publication to the Linnean Society and, at the end of the next, another to the Royal Society. Since out in Australia he had heard not a word of how these papers had been received, he was delighted to find on his return that they had not only been published but created a considerable stir. As a result, when the *Rattlesnake* reached England in November 1850 he was welcomed home by the scientific community with much the same enthusiasm that had greeted Darwin fourteen years earlier. Within weeks he had met Richard Owen and Edward Forbes (1815–54). Forbes was palaeontologist to the Geological Survey as well as Professor of Botany at King's College, London, and a close friend of Darwin's, and it was he who had arranged the publication of the papers Huxley had sent back from Australia. He had also been dined at the Geological Society, where he met Lyell, Horner and another Scottish geologist, Roderick Murchison (1792–1871). By June of the following year he had been elected a fellow of the Royal Society; a month later he was reading a paper at a meeting of the British Association.

Later that year Huxley wrote a long letter to a biologist friend in Australia giving him all the news and a Who's Who of the biologists of the day.[11] The two leaders, he says, are unquestionably Richard Owen and Edward Forbes, the one as deeply disliked as the other was loved and respected. 'It is astonishing with what an intense feeling of hatred Owen is regarded by the majority of his contemporaries. . . . The truth is, he is the superior of most, and does not conceal that he knows it, and it must be confessed that he does some very ill-natured tricks now and then. . . . Quite another being is the other leader of Zoological Science in this country – I mean Edward Forbes . . . he has sympathies for all, and an earnest, truth-seeking, thoroughly genial disposition which win for him your affection as well as your respect.' 'The rest of the naturalists,' he continues, 'stand far below these two in learning, originality, and grasp of mind.' There follows a string of names with critical comment on each, including that of Darwin, who 'might be anything if he had good health'.

Despite his meteoric rise in the scientific firmament, which included a Royal Medal from the Royal Society (1852), the years 1851–3 were for Huxley years of growing frustration and anxiety. Fame in science, he learned, was no guarantee of bread and butter. As a stop-gap he had obtained an extension of his appointment as an assistant surgeon with the Admiralty to enable him to write up his research findings, much as Hooker had done a few years earlier, but a permanent appointment eluded him. Chairs of natural history in Toronto, Aberdeen, Cork and London, for which he made applications, went to others. At times he thought seriously of turning his back on science and earning a living in medical practice. A principal reason for his growing exasperation was that in 1848, while the *Rattlesnake* was refitting in Sydney harbour, he had become engaged to the daughter of an English couple residing there. Having last seen each other in May 1849, they were in regular correspondence, but the many months of delay between writing a letter and receiving a reply were becoming intolerable.

Meanwhile he was extremely busy publishing further scientific papers, giving prestigious lectures at the Royal Institution, and earning a little by his pen. 1853 saw him commissioned to write a *Manual of Comparative Anatomy* and to provide a regular column of scientific news for the *Westminster Review*. He was also preparing a translation from the German of an important work on embryology by Karl von Baer (1792–1876). This was also the period when he wrote a peculiarly savage review of the tenth edition of *Vestiges of the Natural History of Creation*, the popular work first published anonymously in 1844 and still selling well.

Eventually, in the summer of 1854, Huxley's luck turned. His friend Edward Forbes was appointed to the chair of natural history at Edinburgh and left vacant the posts he held at the School of Mines and Museum of Practical Geology in central London, as well as that of palaeontologist to the Geological Survey, to all of which Huxley succeeded. Together they gave him a modest income and a convenient location from which to operate. They also enabled him to marry, which he did the following year at the age of thirty.

Huxley was to remain at the School of Mines until his retirement thirty years later and was the principal instrument of its amalgamation with two other bodies and transformation into a major academic centre for scientific and technical education, known since 1907 as Imperial College of Science and Technology. During Huxley's time there many gifted students and assistants passed through his hands, later planted by him in strategic posts in the universities of Britain, the colonies and the United States.

Huxley was a man of great energy and lively temperament. In his research he was both original and audacious; moreover, his proposals, often radical, for classifying and reclassifying members of the animal kingdom have stood the test of time. With his razor-sharp mind and great erudition he became a formidable debater and enjoyed nothing more than demolishing insincerity, cant and unsupported dogma. While protesting himself a man of peace who only took up cudgels when there was no alternative, he none the less found battling a tonic, especially when his spirits flagged as sometimes they did. Yet he was exceptionally kind and generous to friends and trusted by all.

Like Darwin, he now overworked and suffered the penalty of headaches and dyspepsia; and at times he imagined he would become an invalid. He discovered, however, that all his symptoms disappeared when he got into the country. Work for the Geological Survey proved especially useful, since it took him to Wales and Scotland and entailed plenty of long walks. For some years he also took walking and climbing holidays with friends in Switzerland, doing a little geologising on the way. He never suffered serious physical illness.

What first brought Darwin into contact with this rising star were their common interests in invertebrate anatomy and embryology. Already in

July 1851 Huxley had sent Darwin a report about some interesting research on echinoderms by a German anatomist, and a few months later Darwin had reciprocated by sending Huxley a copy of his first monograph on barnacles. Further exchanges followed and, in September 1854, when Darwin sent a copy of his second barnacle monograph, he took the opportunity of enquiring about German naturalists who might welcome receiving a copy. Meanwhile Darwin had been reading Huxley's review of *Vestiges* and had found it 'incomparably the best review' of the book he had read. He adds: 'but I cannot think but that you are rather hard on the poor author. I must think that such a book, if it does no other good, spreads the taste for Natural Science.' Then, referring briefly to his own heterodox views, he proceeds: 'But I am perhaps no fair judge, for I am almost as unorthodox about species as the *Vestiges*, though I hope not quite so unphilosophical.' In writing this review Huxley had not overlooked the opportunity to criticise Owen, though not by name. Darwin is delighted and expresses admiration for the 'exquisite and inimitable' way in which Huxley has handled the 'great Professor': 'By Heavens, how the blood must have gushed into the capillaries when a certain great man (whom with all his faults I cannot help liking) reads it!'[12] The phrase in parentheses is Darwin being charitable, a sentiment towards Owen destined soon to wear thin.

A year after this exchange, in July 1855, Darwin is congratulating Huxley on his marriage and wishing him every happiness, adding: 'I hope your marriage will not make you idle; happiness, I fear, is not good for work.'[13] By the spring of 1856 Huxley had become an occasional visitor to Down, in this role replacing to some extent Forbes, who, to everyone's deep regret, had suddenly died of a kidney complaint, shortly after settling in Edinburgh. Huxley's quick wit and entertaining conversation always charmed Darwin. In later years Darwin's son Francis recalled that after a visit his father would exclaim, 'What splendid fun Huxley is!' But, he adds, it was with Lyell and Hooker that his father had the more serious scientific arguments;[14] and, ever grateful though Darwin was to Huxley for springing to his protection and fighting all his battles, he was never reconciled to the vehemence with which Huxley assailed their foes.

III

During these same years when Huxley was establishing himself in scientific circles in London, another young man, of very different temperament, was beginning to make his mark as a naturalist. In 1852 Alfred Russel Wallace (1823–1913) returned to England from nearly five years as a professional collector of natural history specimens in the Amazon valley; and the following year he presented his findings at meetings of the Entomological, Zoological and Royal Geographical Societies.[15] In addition, he found time to publish the *Narrative* of his

Alfred Russel Wallace,
1823–1913, aged 31, in
Singapore 1854.
Independent solver of the
species problem but
insisted all credit
belonged to Darwin

Thomas Henry Huxley,
1825–95, comparative
anatomist, aged 32 in
1857. Cast himself in the
role of Darwin's Bulldog

travels before leaving England again early in 1854 for another long spell of collecting, this time in the East Indies. During his brief interlude in London Wallace did not meet Darwin; but Darwin read Wallace's papers and his *Narrative*, and so began a correspondence that a few years later was to lead to a fruitful crisis in Darwin's scientific life.

Wallace was the eighth of nine children of a feckless and impecunious solicitor. Obliged to leave school at the age of thirteen, he worked for a year in a joiner's shop in London before becoming apprenticed to his eldest brother William, who had qualified as a land surveyor. For five years from the age of fifteen he assisted his brother on surveys of parish boundaries, enclosures, railways and canals. He also became an enthusiastic naturalist and was excited to discover there were books on natural history.

In 1843 the economic depression which hit the country at that time – the hungry forties – led to a scarcity of surveying contracts and Wallace had to seek other employment. For the next year he held a residential post as a junior master at a school in Leicester, teaching English and surveying. During this time he continued his self-education and also met a like-minded contemporary with similar interests, Henry Walter Bates (1825–92). Bates was a collector of insects, especially beetles, and soon imbued Wallace with the same passion. Together they read and discussed such classics as Humboldt's *Travels in South America* and Malthus's *Essay on the Principles of Population*, both of which had as big an influence on them as they had had some years earlier on Darwin. Another book they found extremely stimulating was the newly published and anonymous *Vestiges of Creation*. Half-baked though the professionals found it, Darwin judged aright when he thought that, for all its faults, it would have the merit of arousing interest in natural history. With these two remarkably intelligent young men it did more: it called their attention to the species question and introduced them to the idea of evolution. Among other books with which they also became familiar were Lyell's *Principles of Geology* and the 1845 edition of Darwin's *Beagle Journal*.

In the autumn of 1847 Wallace, after losing his eldest brother from pneumonia and suffering a further setback after he had resumed surveying work, decided to try his fortunes overseas. Would Bates, he enquired, consider joining him in a collecting expedition to the Amazon valley? Bates proved keen, and during the coming months they prepared themselves thoroughly for the venture. The main object of the expedition was to collect specimens for sale, more especially beetles and butterflies which were in brisk demand for collectors' cabinets and were known to be both prolific and beautiful in the tropical rainforests; they also had the advantage that very large numbers could be mounted and stored in a small space. The skins of birds and mammals, and specimens of plants, would also be gathered. Since good prices could only be got for rare and unknown species, it was necessary to become familiar with those already present in collections or described in books. Some weeks were therefore spent at the British Museum, where they found the staff extremely helpful, and they also contacted Sir William Hooker at Kew. Moreover, they had to find an agent who would arrange to sell their specimens and meanwhile give them an advance. Pressing though the economic aspects of the expedition were, both Wallace and Bates nursed scientific aspirations: no less than the hope that their collections and observations would be of use towards solving the problem of species. It was thus after careful preparations and with high hopes that in 1848 these two young men, aged twenty-five and twenty-three respectively, took passage from Liverpool in a small sailing ship that landed them at Pará (now Belém) at the mouth of the Amazon.

At Pará they spent a few months collecting locally, learning about native guides and modes of travel, and acquiring knowledge of Portuguese. These preliminaries over, they moved a thousand miles up the great river in a sailing ship to start serious collecting. Since others had already collected in the more accessible parts of the interior, they aimed to go into the most remote and difficult places to find the rare and unknown specimens they sought. Having parted company, each went his own way with his own band of guides and hunters. During the following years both showed dauntless courage, surmounted appalling obstacles, survived countless dangers and made enormous collections. In addition, both were struck by how localised most species and varieties were, and how well adapted each species was to the habitat in which it was found. For both these young men geographical distribution was to become an abiding passion, and to the understanding of it Wallace was to make famous contributions.

At length in July 1852, after more than four years of hardship and exertion, interspersed with periods of rain-drenched immobility and fever, Wallace returned to Pará and took ship for home. As ill-luck would have it, the ship was carrying a cargo of a special kind of balsam used in lacquers, which overheated and set the ship ablaze. The crew and passengers took to the boats and, after ten gruelling days, were picked up; but almost the whole of Wallace's collections perished. Bates was staying on and did not return for another three years, in his case with his even larger collections intact.

Despite the hazards of collecting in unknown tropical country and the disaster that had befallen his collections, Wallace stayed only fifteen months in England before setting out on another and even longer expedition. It was during those months of 1853 that he read papers to the scientific societies and published his *Narrative of Travels in the Amazon and Rio Negro*.

Wallace had just turned thirty; but he was still shy and diffident, acutely conscious that he lacked a scientific education and much in awe of the experts. His papers created some interest, however. In one, on the butterflies of the Amazon valley, he emphasised the extreme variability of many related species and the difficulty of distinguishing species from varieties, findings that excited Darwin when he read about them in print the following year. Another paper, on his exploration of the Rio Negro (a large tributary of the Amazon) given to the Royal Geographical Society, impressed the geologist president, Roderick Murchison, sufficiently for him to help Wallace prepare for his next expedition and to obtain a free passage on a naval vessel.

Wallace was not only a successful collector but a persistent thinker, forever mulling over the possible significance of his observations for understanding the basic problems of biology. Yet at that time he was little known and would have been regarded as no more than a very dark horse among his better-educated and more confident contemporaries. Early in 1854 he set out for Singapore, intent on making another, comparable, collection of specimens in a different part of the tropics. He would be away for eight productive years.

As we have already seen, during the years when Huxley was establishing himself in the scientific circles of London and Wallace was paying his fleeting visit to England between spells of collecting in contrasting continents, Darwin was struggling forward with his everlasting barnacles and at last, in September 1854, had the satisfaction of reaching the end. There had been no family holiday that summer and, perhaps for that reason, in the following January Charles and Emma took a house in London (just off Baker Street) and were there with the family for a month. They went to concerts, which, unexpectedly, Charles enjoyed more than Emma; but the visit, Darwin tells Fox, 'turned out a great failure, for that dreadful frost just set in when we went, and all our children got unwell and Emma and I had coughs, and colds, and rheumatism nearly all the time.'[16]

Before going to London that January, Charles had discontinued his daily diary of health; the following September, with Emma, he attended the British Association meeting in Glasgow, 'but the fatigue was to me more than it was worth'.[17] He never went to another. Meanwhile, with the barnacles at last out of the way, he was free to give himself full-time to the species question for which he had been preparing so long.

TWENTY-ONE

Sometimes in triumph, sometimes in despair 1855–1858

I

The period we are now entering is one made famous by the writing and publication of *The Origin of Species*. It was a time of great activity in Darwin's life and of great emotional upheaval. It was also a time of acute and prolonged anxiety about the children's health, and one which led into several years during which, with ups and downs, his own health gave great trouble, though apparently never as badly as during the two earlier periods.

We have noted already that during the early fifties Darwin's health was much improved. This was fortunate, since from the late autumn of 1854 he was busy on his species work, collating his evidence, experimenting with plant seeds to see whether they would germinate after immersion for weeks or months in salt water, visiting gin palaces in South London to learn the secrets of breeding fancy pigeons, and writing to a great array of scientists and amateur naturalists, among whom Hooker and Fox were foremost, to gather information relevant to his great work.

At the end of a long letter to Fox of 27 March 1855 Darwin described what he was tackling:

I forget whether I ever told you what the object of my present work is – it is to view all facts that I can master (eheu, eheu, how ignorant I find I am) in Natural History (as on geographical distribution, palaeontology, classification, hybridism, domestic animals and plants etc. etc. etc.) to see how far they favour or are opposed to the notion that wild species are mutable or immutable: I mean with my utmost power to give all arguments and facts on both sides. I have a *number* of people helping me in every way, and giving me most valuable assistance; but I often doubt whether the subject will not quite overpower me.[1]

What this description omits is a statement of the double-barrelled thesis he is advancing: Species have not been created once and for all but have been evolving from primitive beginnings over vast periods of time. Furthermore, their evolution can be understood as the result of random variation within a given species and of different variants being more or less successful in surviving and reproducing themselves. The first proposition, that life as we know it today is the product of historical evolution, was far from new. On the contrary, it had been mooted repeatedly down the centuries by distinguished thinkers, including Charles's grandfather, Erasmus Darwin; but evidence in support of the proposition had never been properly marshalled and it had failed completely to oust the prevailing doctrine of creationism. The second proposition, that variation is undirected and that what we see is the product of fierce competition between variants to survive and reproduce their like, had also been proposed but was even less acceptable than the notion of evolution itself. Any such proposal had tended to have been advanced in such a low key that it went unnoticed, or else to have been aborted through pressure of the author's colleagues. In the light of history, therefore, Darwin's decision to produce a blockbuster, with all the evidence displayed and a systematic examination of all difficulties showing them to be less weighty than first appeared, was a sound one.

In this enterprise Hooker's friendship was to be of inestimable value. Since his return from India, Hooker and his newly wed wife had lived near Kew Gardens, while he devoted long hours to sorting specimens and preparing publications. His productivity was enormous. Within four years he completed two volumes on the *Flora of New Zealand* (a carry-over from the Ross expedition to the Antarctic), a first volume (with a colleague) of a 'Flora of India' which, conceived on too ambitious a scale, would never be completed in that form, and in 1854 the two volumes of his *Himalayan Journals*. During these years finances were precarious and the work could never have gone forward without the expenditure of private family money. In 1855, however, his father, now seventy, managed to persuade the authorities responsible for Kew to appoint Joseph as his assistant – a plan he had long cherished.

Sir William Hooker was to remain director of the Royal Botanical Gardens for another ten years, until his death in 1865. Since during these years his powers were failing, Joseph's post was in effect that of deputy director and entailed considerable responsibility. When eventually the directorship fell vacant, it was natural that he should be appointed; he would then hold the post for twenty years, with the greatest distinction. It was indeed during the regime of the two Hookers that Kew was transformed into the Mecca of the botanical world it has ever since been.

Hooker's residence at Kew made for easy communication with, and visits to, Darwin at Down. While, as we have seen, the two men had an enormous amount in common, in their scientific work they were in many ways complementary. Darwin took everything in natural history for his province; Hooker, master of one whole branch, with technical training in it from childhood up, and equally seized by the puzzle of how different forms of life had reached their present habitats, eagerly placed his vast knowledge and sound criticism, and his special observations during later travels, at the disposal of his inspiring friend.[2] Each vied with the other in claiming that the benefits he had received during a discussion far outweighed whatever return he might have been able to make.

During the years leading to the publication of the *Origin* Hooker, long familiar with Darwin's ideas, was nevertheless determined to think things through for himself by comparing the explanatory powers of traditional and novel theories in the light of the evidence, not least the botanical evidence he had himself done so much to expand. Perhaps at times in his criticisms of Darwin's speculations Hooker was acting as devil's advocate. Whether so or not, Darwin was always deeply grateful. For example, in letters to Hooker after talks together during the autumn of 1856, Darwin writes, on 19 October, 'fighting a battle with you clears my mind wonderfully'; and a month later, 'You never make an objection without doing much good'; and later still (undated), 'Again I thank you for your valuable assistance. . . . Adios, you terrible worrier of poor theorists'.

Not only Hooker but Lyell too had known for many years of Darwin's doubts about the fixity of species; but, unlike Hooker, Lyell had heard nothing hitherto about natural selection. During mid-April 1856, however, Lyell and his wife made one of their occasional visits to Down, where during three days the two men discussed matters of scientific interest. On the final morning Darwin for the first time expounded his natural selection theory to Lyell.[3] The momentous outcome of these discussions is described by Darwin some weeks later in a letter to Fox of 8 June: 'Sir C. Lyell was staying here lately, and I told him somewhat of my views on species, and he was sufficiently struck to suggest (and has since written so strongly to urge me) to me to publish a sort of Preliminary Essay.' In fact, Lyell's letter, written on 1 May, was couched in distinctly peremptory tones: 'I wish you would publish some small fragment of your data, *pigeons* if you please and so out with the theory and let it take date and be cited and understood.' Lyell's brother-in-law, Charles Bunbury, a botanist, had already written in the same vein.[4]

Lyell's idea was that Darwin should present a simple sketch of his views; but Darwin had promptly disagreed. 'To give a fair sketch would be absolutely impossible,' he replied, 'for every proposition requires such an array of facts . . . But I do not know what to think; I rather hate the idea of writing for priority, yet I certainly would be vexed if any one were to publish my doctrines before me.'[5] He then consulted Hooker (by letter), describing the dilemma. Shortly afterwards, and very characteristically putting ideas of priority behind him, he decided to concentrate on what he knew was bound to be a very big book.

Asa Gray, 1810–88, American botanist, Professor of Natural History at Harvard University who became the principal advocate of Darwin's theory in America

II

During the spring of 1856 Darwin entertained other scientific friends at Down. One such party comprised Hooker, Huxley and an entomologist, Thomas Wollaston (1822–78). Among the topics discussed, almost inevitably, was the species problem. Darwin and Hooker broached an evolutionary solution, but this met with strong resistance from Wollaston, who would remain a critic. Huxley had given no thought to the issue and was out of his depth. In later years he would have no recollection of the occasion.

That summer Darwin, intensively occupied on his big book, wrote a number of letters to his friends in which he first describes his labours and then attempts to disarm the savage criticism he feared by forestalling it. The language is colourful, with much hyperbole, and should not be taken literally. Even so, it illustrates the emotional strain he was under, not least because he was feeling under pressure to get the work completed and acutely apprehensive about its reception. At the end of a letter to Fox, of 8 June 1856, he confides: 'My work will be horribly imperfect and with many mistakes so that I groan and tremble when I think of it.' Evidently Fox's comments were not reassuring. 'What you say about my Essay', replies Darwin, 'is very true; and it gave me another fit of the wibber-gibbers: I hope I shall succeed in making it modest. . . . But I tremble about it.'[6] To Lyell on 8 July he refers to his work as conducted 'sometimes in triumph, sometimes in despair'; and to Hooker on 13 July he expresses revulsion at the cruelty inherent in his picture of evolution in action: 'What a book a Devil's Chaplain might write on the clumsy, wasteful, blundering low and horribly cruel works of nature!'[7]

It was July 1856 that Darwin wrote to a new scientific colleague with whom he had corresponded the previous year about the distribution and other features of the North America flora. This was Asa Gray (1810–88), a leading American botanist whom he had met through Hooker and whose thinking, Hooker had assured him, was close enough to his own. In this letter Darwin refers to his long-standing interest in how species originate and confesses to his 'heterodox conclusions', and then adds characteristically, 'I know that this will make you despise me.' In his reply Gray evidently shows a lively interest in Darwin's ideas and asks for further information. In addition, he vigorously protests any notion of despising their author. Darwin tries to explain himself: 'But I did not feel in the least sure that when you knew whither I was tending you might not think me so wild and foolish in my views . . . that you would think me worth no more notice or assistance.' Then, after referring to the severe criticism he had received from a naturalist friend, he remarks: 'I always expect my views to be received with contempt.'[8] These preliminaries over, Darwin proceeds to give Gray a brief but systematic sketch of his theoretical position. Within the year this sketch of September 1857 would be put to an unexpectedly good use.

All these self-disparaging remarks and many others like them, it must be remembered, have been abstracted from long letters in which Darwin was discussing the various scientific problems he was encountering and asking his correspondents a multitude of questions on which he wanted their help. One of these correspondents was Wallace, now far away in the East Indies. In this case, however, each was seeking information from the other and each giving as much as he was able.

Darwin's correspondence with Wallace had begun during Wallace's brief stay in England in 1853. Darwin had read Wallace's papers and his *Narrative of Travels* and had written appreciatively to him about them. Thus encouraged, Wallace had replied, and during 1854 and 1855 there was an occasional exchange of letters between them, mainly about the problems of distinguishing between species, sub-species and varieties.

After his arrival in Singapore in April 1854 Wallace collected briefly in the highlands near Malacca while learning to speak Malay, and then moved on to Borneo, where he was the guest of Sir James Brooke. In a burst of private enterprise at the turn of the century Sir James had taken possession of Sarawak, a territory on the north-west coast of the island, where he had set himself up as the first of what would prove to be a long line of white rajahs. Wallace was delighted to stay at the rajah's court while engaging guides and preparing for his expeditions into the interior. Moreover, the elderly Sir James much enjoyed the company of this intelligent, well-informed young man, whose tongue was loosed in this less than expert company. 'He pleased, instructed and delighted us by his clever and inexhaustible flow of talk – really good talk,' the rajah's secretary recalled. 'The Rajah was pleased to have so clever a man with him and it excited his mind and brought out his brillant ideas.'[9] A favourite topic, apparently, was evolution.

During one or two excursions up country to collect specimens, Wallace occasionally stayed in a Dyak long-house enjoying the lively and helpful way in which such a large number of families succeeded in living amicably together. When he was temporarily immobilised by the rainy season and lent a little house by the rajah, Wallace began to ponder over the problem which, he later reported, 'was rarely absent' from his thoughts. No one, it seemed, had thought of combining facts about geographical distribution, his own speciality, with facts about the succession of species in time, so well presented by Lyell, in the hope of casting light on the way in which species had come into existence. He therefore drafted an essay entitled 'On the Law which has regulated the Introduction of New Species', and early in 1855 sent it off by the mailboat via Singapore to London, addressed to the editor of *The Annals and Magazine of Natural History*. There it duly appeared in September that year. In lucid, cogent prose, Wallace had reviewed all the geographical and geological evidence pointing to the historical occurrence of evolution. He had ventured nothing, however, on how evolution might have proceeded.[10]

Although Darwin was an avid reader of journals, he seems not to have seen this number and it was left to Lyell to draw his attention to it. Hardly anyone else in England was the least interested, however, and such news as reached Wallace from his agent suggested it had fallen completely flat.

Fortunately, before abandoning his efforts at theory as a waste of time, Wallace received an encouraging letter from Darwin. Writing in May 1857, Darwin remarked that he could see by Wallace's paper in the *Annals* 'that we have thought much alike and to a certain extent have come to similar conclusions', that he had been keeping notes for nearly twenty years and was preparing his work for publication.[11] Darwin's news was a stimulant to Wallace, who probably received this letter in August or early September 1857 on his return to his base at the small Dutch trading port of Ternate in the Molucca Islands, over 1000 miles east of Borneo. Late in September that year Wallace writes expressing great interest in Darwin's future publication and enquiring what it will cover; and he gives an account of his explorations in the East Indies and his special study of the geographical distribution of species in the islands. He also expresses surprise that so little notice has been taken of his Sarawak essay. Darwin replies promptly and at length, on 22 December 1857:

I am extremely glad to hear that you are attending to distribution in accordance with theoretical ideas. I am a firm believer that without speculation there is no good and original observation. . . . You say that you have been somewhat surprised at no notice having been taken of your papers in the *Annals*. I cannot say that I am, for so very few naturalists care for anything beyond the mere description of species. But you must not suppose that your paper has not been attended to: two very good men, Sir C. Lyell, and Mr. E. Blyth of Calcutta, specially called my attention to it. Though agreeing with you on your conclusions in that paper, I believe I go much further than you; but it is too long a subject to enter on my speculative notions. . . . You ask whether I shall discuss 'man'. I think I shall avoid the whole subject, as so surrounded with prejudices; though I fully admit that it is the highest and most interesting problem for the naturalist. . . . I get on very slowly, partly from ill-health, partly from being a very slow worker. . . . I do not suppose I shall publish under a couple of years.[12]

At this time Wallace was continuing his correspondence with Bates, who was now back in England. In the new year of 1858 Wallace writes saying how gratified he had been by Darwin's letter, namely the earlier one, 'in which he says that he agrees with "almost every word" of my [1855] paper. He is now preparing his great work on "Species and Varieties", for which he has been collecting materials twenty years. He may save me the trouble of writing more on my hypothesis, by proving that there is no difference in nature between the origin of species than of varieties; or he may give me trouble by arriving at another conclusion; but, at all events, his facts will be given for me to work upon. Your collections and my own will furnish most valuable material to illustrate and prove the universal applicability of the hypothesis. The connection between the succession of affinities and the geographical distribution of a group, worked out species by species, has never yet been shown as we shall be able to show it.'[13] From this it is plain that, in his search for the origin of species, Wallace was getting extremely warm.

Meanwhile, throughout 1856 and 1857 and on until the summer of 1858 Darwin worked on his great book. His conflict over questions of priority and fame, perhaps fanned by Wallace, still dogged him: 'I am most deeply interested in my subject,' he tells Fox on 22 February 1857; 'though I wish I could set less value on the bauble fame, either present or posthumous, than I do, but not I think to any extreme degree: yet if I know myself, I would work just as hard, though with less gusto, if I knew that my book would be published for ever anonymously.'[14]

III

During the first two of these four strenuous years Darwin seems to have been flourishing. In mid-March 1856 he reported to Fox: 'My stomach has been much better for some months ... and I am able decidedly to work harder'; and in the autumn he asked Fox, who had recently been to Malvern, to tell Dr Gully 'that never (or almost never) the vomiting returns, but that I am a good way from being a strong man'. In mid-September, during a visit to Surrey to see Caroline and Josiah, Charles is described (in a letter from one of Emma's many aunts) as being 'agreeable, fresh and sparkling as the purest water'.[15]

Emma, who was usually in good health, had begun at this time to suffer from headaches, and these continued on and off for some years. Charles was often worried about them, and refers to them on occasion in subsequent letters to Fox. In later years Emma would tell Henrietta that Charles was always inclined to think them worse than they were. Even so, they were not negligible, since there were times when Emma needed to stay for some hours in a darkened room by herself. By early 1856 Charles had turned forty-seven and Emma forty-eight. Their seven surviving children, five boys and two girls, ranged in age from William, sixteen who was at Rugby, to Horace, just turned five. This was responsibility enough; but now Emma was pregnant yet again. Not unexpectedly she found this burdensome.[16] On 6 December her tenth child and sixth son was born. He was christened Charles Waring.

1857 was a year of hard work for Darwin on his big book and of increasing anxiety about his children. In his letters to Fox there are repeated references to overwork and its ill-effects on his health; on 22 February he writes: 'My wife agrees very heartily with your preachment against overwork, and wishes to go to Malvern; but I doubt; yet I suppose I shall have to take a little holiday sometime; perhaps to Tenby: though how

I can leave all my experiments I know not.' In the event he went for a fortnight in late April by himself to a new health establishment, Moor Park, on the borders of Surrey and Hampshire, where he was under a Dr Edward Lane. On 1 May he explains to Fox: 'I had got very much below par at home, and it is really quite astonishing and utterly unaccountable the good this one week has done me. . . . I believe that I worked too hard at home on my species-Book, which progresses, but very slowly.' As a place he much preferred Moor Park to Malvern. He especially enjoyed walking in the woods which, he tells his eldest son, 'are very wild and lonely, so just suits me'. He also liked young Dr Lane, whom he describes as well read and compares favourably with Dr Gully: 'he does not believe in all the rubbish Dr. Gully does: nor does he pretend to explain much which neither he nor any doctor can explain.'[17]

Later in 1857 Darwin visited Moor Park on two further occasions, 16–29 June and 5–12 November. From there in June he visited Selborne for the day to pay his respects to the memory of Gilbert White. On 30 October, he brings Fox up to date with his news and the conclusions he had reached about his health: 'I cannot say much for myself: I have had a poor summer, and am at last rather come to your theory that my Brains were not made for thinking, for twice I staid for a fornight at Moor Park, and was so extraordinarily better that I can attribute the difference. . . to nothing but to mental work.' In brackets he puts: 'I fell back into my old state *immediately* I returned.' Any benefits obtained from hydropathy, he believed, were secondary. 'I make slow progress in my work which is altogether too much for me.'[18]

Nevertheless and despite his forebodings, he was making headway. In late May 1858 he sent the draft of some part of the work to Hooker for comment and was enormously relieved that Hooker was approving. 'I am confined to the sofa with boils,' he replies, 'so you must let me write in pencil. You would laugh if you could know how much your note pleased me. I had the firmest conviction that you would say all my MS. was bosh. . . Tho' I should not have much cared about throwing away what you have seen, yet I have been forced to confess to myself that all was much alike, and if you condemned that you would condemn all my life's work, and that I confess made me a little low.' Then, grateful for various minor criticisms, he adds: 'believe me, I value to the full every word of criticism from you, and the advantage which I have derived from you cannot be told.'[19]

IV

During these years Darwin sometimes stayed a few days with Ras in London and, when well enough, welcomed visitors to Down. In this way he kept in touch with friends and also, on occasion, with old *Beagle* shipmates. Between 1853 and 1857, in his annual letters to Covington,[19]

Darwin reports that Captain Sulivan had half a dozen children and was earning a great reputation during service in the Baltic (in connection with the Crimean war, about the management of which, Darwin reports, there was 'terrible dissatisfaction'). By February 1857, the war over, Sulivan had been appointed to a very senior position ashore (in the Marine Department of the Board of Trade) and in doing so had 'beaten two Admirals and Captain Fitzroy who tried for the same place.' A letter to Covington of October 1853 reports that Mellersh had 'greatly distinguished himself by hard fighting with some Chinese Pirates'. 'Two or three years ago,' he continues, 'Fuegia was heard of by a sealer in the west part of the Straits of Magellan [and] . . . could still speak some English.' Captain Stokes was doing 'little now but shoot and hunt.'

During the years since Darwin had last met FitzRoy, he had followed his career with much interest and often with concern. In 1841 FitzRoy had been elected a Tory MP for Durham and had become a member of Peel's group of Progressive Tories. He spoke on a number of topics, including colonization, naval armaments and breakwaters, and sponsored a bill to introduce examinations for those aspiring to become masters or chief mates of merchant vessels. After two years in Parliament he was appointed the second Governor of New Zealand. Here his sense of fairness led him to try holding a balance between the rights of the Maoris and the pressures of the British colonists. This proved extremely unpopular and had the colonists' friends at Westminster lobbying for his removal. Though the cabinet minister responsible was not unsympathetic to FitzRoy's policies, he was handicapped defending him because of FitzRoy's failure to explain his actions. The upshot was FitzRoy's recall in 1845. He had lost much money during his time as Governor.

After further naval service in home waters in command of experimental vessels, FitzRoy's pioneering interests in meteorology led in 1853 to his appointment as head of a germinal meteorology department in the Board of Trade. That was his position when he and his wife came to lunch at Down in the spring of 1857. This lunch party was to be the last time Darwin and FitzRoy would meet.

The official duties of the post at the Board of Trade were merely to compile statistics; but FitzRoy had much more ambitious ideas. The true purpose of meteorology, he rightly held, was forecasting, and he made a major contribution by introducing a system of hoisting a large black cone at ports and harbours to indicate a threatening gale. This service was greatly appreciated by fishermen and would be continued until ultimately replaced by wireless.

V

While the anxiety that led Darwin to insist on working seven days a week was plainly responsible for much of his ill-health, anxiety about his children is likely to have been no less important.

In the first place, the baby, Charles Waring, was turning out to be retarded (it is not unlikely his was a case of Down's syndrome). In the second, Etty's health was not good; now nearly fourteen, she accompanied her father to Moor Park during the summer of 1857 and received hydropathy. Thirdly, in late August Leonard, aged seven and a half, had become ill, and Charles was terrified he would not recover. On 3 September he writes to Hooker: 'It is a strange thing, and I am sure you will sympathize with us, that for the last ten days our darling little fellow Lenny's health has failed, *exactly* as three of our children's have before, namely with extremely irregular and feeble pulse; but he is so much better today that I cannot help having hopes that, unlike the former case, it may be something temporary. But it makes life very bitter.' A few weeks later, in a letter to Fox of 30 October he writes that his children's illnesses are 'strange and heart-breaking. A man ought to be a bachelor, and care for no human being to be happy! or not to be wretched.'[20]

Lenny recovered; but Etty's ailment persisted and was to be a source of anxiety for some years. What her condition was due to is unclear, but there seems little doubt that both her parents were terrified lest she share the fate of Annie. Etty was therefore confined to bed and there she remained for months, if not years. In her reminiscences she writes: 'This year [1857] I broke down in health. The entries in my mother's diary show what years of anxiety she suffered first with one child then another. Sometimes it is my health which is thus chronicled day by day, sometimes one of the boys. Both parents were unwearied in their efforts to soothe and amuse whichever of us was ill; my father played backgammon with me regularly every day, and my mother would read aloud to me.' Elsewhere she describes how she was 'more or less ill between my thirteenth and eighteenth years' and how her father 'used to play a couple of games of backgammon with me every afternoon . . . His patience and sympathy were boundless during this weary illness.' But at times she found his concern for her a little overwhelming: 'I can recall now how on his return [from a brief visit to Moor Park] I could hardly bear to have him in the room, the expression of tender sympathy and emotion on his face was too agitating.'[21]

It is rather easy from the perspective of today's health statistics to look upon Charles and Emma as absurdly over-anxious and fussy. Yet if we look at them in the light of mid-nineteenth-century death-rates, and also in the light of their own experiences, their concern is seen more sympathetically. The tragedy of Annie's death was always with them.

Furthermore, when Emma was a young woman her sister Fanny, for long her bosom companion, had been carried off in a matter of days during an epidemic, probably of cholera, which struck the Potteries in 1832. Charles, it must be remembered, had lost his mother as a child. Although in those days deaths of children, young adults and women in labour were far more frequent than today, there is no reason to suppose that the grief they caused the survivors was any the less. Anyone who doubts this should read the family letters of the time.[22]

During the first half of 1858 Darwin was still working hard on his great book, and often feeling overwhelmed by the magnitude of his project. As he records: 'I have so much to do, and so precious little strength to do it' (31 January 1858); 'I am not so well as I was a year or two ago. I am working very hard at my Book, perhaps too hard' (8 February); 'My health has been lately very bad from overwork and on Tuesday I go for a fortnights Hydropathy. My work is everlasting' (16 April). From Moor Park, where he stayed from 20 April to 3 May, he wrote a large number of letters – to Emma and his son William telling them of his activities, and others to Hooker and Lyell on scientific matters. During the last few days, he tells Fox (8 May), he had felt 'splendidly well . . . and walked one day two miles out and back'. Back at Down, however, he was 'hard at work again as usual' and his health soon deteriorated.[23]

Although during the early months of 1858 the situation at Down was bad enough, there was much worse to come. In the latter half of June Etty became acutely ill with a condition initially suggesting diphtheria but later diagnosed as scarlet fever, and one of the nursery-maids contracted it too. No sooner was Etty over the worst than the baby got it; and he died on 28 June. A second nursery-maid then went down with it. Following the urging of Fox, the other children were evacuated from Down on 2 July to stay with Emma's eldest sister, Elizabeth, in nearby Hartfield. Charles and Emma remained at Down caring for Etty and the two nurse-maids. In a note to Hooker three days later Charles reports: 'We are become more happy and less panic-struck now that we have sent out of the house every child, and shall remove H [enrietta] as soon as she can move . . . . You may imagine how frightened we have been. It has been a most miserable fortnight.'[24] In this epidemic of scarlet fever no fewer than six children in the village of Downe died. By 9 July Charles, Emma and Etty were able to join the other children at Hartfield, and the whole family then went on to Sandown in the Isle of Wight to convalesce.

The epidemic had been a harrowing experience and during it Darwin describes himself to Hooker as prostrated and unable to do anything. The baby's death was a shock but in the long run could also be regarded as merciful. In later years Henrietta recalls how her parents had felt about him: 'Both my father and mother were infinitely tender towards him, but, when he died in the summer of 1858, after their first sorrow they could only feel thankful.'[25]

VI

By a cruel chance this family crisis coincided with a professional one. In mid-June 1858, just before the epidemic broke, Darwin received the manuscript of a new paper by Wallace, entitled 'On the Tendency of Varieties to Depart Indefinitely from the Original Type', and requesting it be forwarded to Lyell. The paper had been written in February in Ternate, where Wallace had been detained by a sharp spell of fever, during which 'in a flash of light', as he later described it, he had reached a radical solution to the species problem. On reading it Darwin at once realised that Wallace was advancing a theory of variation and natural selection identical to his own. In conveying and commending the script to Lyell, Darwin remarks with resignation: 'Your words have come true with a vengeance – that I should be forestalled. . . . I never saw a more striking co-incidence. . . . So all my originality, whatever it may amount to, will be smashed.' Nevertheless he adds, 'my book, if it will ever have any value, will not be deteriorated; as all the labour consists in the application of the theory.'[26]

There followed for Darwin an appalling conflict between his desire for priority and fame and his sense of honour. Wallace's paper clearly deserved publication and this he must arrange. At the same time his own 1844 essay, read by Hooker many years previously, showed that he had developed the very same ideas independently of Wallace. Yet he had had no plans to publish anything until his big book was complete. Would it therefore be honourable to rush into print now? On 25 June, with the family panic-stricken by the epidemic and the baby critically ill, Darwin lays his dilemma before Lyell and invites his judgement, apologising at the end for his 'trumpery feelings'. The following day, still agonising, he writes again, this time adding as a postscript: 'I have always thought you would make a first-rate Lord Chancellor; and I now appeal to you as a Lord Chancellor.'[27] To Hooker he writes in a similar vein.

The solution to the dilemma is well known. Lyell and Hooker, though keenly alive to Darwin's twenty year gestation, ruled it a dead-heat. Wallace's paper together with an extract from Darwin's essay (with part of the sketch he had sent Asa Gray the previous autumn) should be presented together at a meeting of the Linnean Society and then published in its journal. The meeting took place almost immediately, on 1 July, three days after the baby's death. Darwin, in a state of shock, was not there; and both the papers were read by the secretary of the society. Both Lyell and Hooker spoke briefly, impressing on the audience the need to give the papers serious attention; 'but', in Hooker's words,

there was no semblance of discussion. The interest excited was intense, but the subject too novel and too ominous for the Old School to enter the lists before armouring. It was talked over after the meeting, 'with bated breath'. Lyell's approval, and perhaps in a small way mine, as his lieutenant in the affair, rather overawed those Fellows who would otherwise have flown out against the doctrine, and this because we had the vantage ground of being familiar with the authors and their themes.'[28]

Publication took place the following August. Thereafter, when writing to Wallace, Darwin always referred to 'our theory'. Conversely Wallace, keenly aware of the twenty years during which Darwin had been working on the problem and collecting the evidence, never failed to give precedence to Darwin. They became close friends, and their correspondence reveals how many were their agreements and how unexpected their few differences. Thus ended one of the happiest stories in the history of science.

Those days of late June 1858 had, however, been very far from happy ones for Darwin. Exchanges with Hooker about the Wallace paper are laced with news and condolences about the children's illnesses and the baby's death. As regards the latter Darwin writes on the 29th, 'I cannot think now on the subject but soon will', and in a second letter the same evening, 'I am quite prostrated and can do nothing'; then, with reference to the Linnean Society plans, he ends: 'I will do anything. God bless you my dear kind friend. I can write no more.'[29]

TWENTY-TWO

My abominable volume
1858–1859

I

On 17 July the family reached the Isle of Wight for what was to be nearly four weeks of convalescence, spent partly at Sandown and partly at Shanklin. The next day Charles got news that his eldest sister, Marianne, had died after a long illness at the age of sixty. It was a 'blessed relief', he tells Fox, 'after long continued and very severe suffering'.[1] Her five children, now all grown up, made their home with Susan at The Mount.

No sooner had the family settled in at Sandown than Darwin reaches what was to be a momentous decision about his work. Now that his ideas have been made public he recognises that it is urgent for him to set out more fully both the ideas and the evidence on which they rest as soon as possible. A paper or possibly a series of papers in the *Linnean Journal* is his first idea, and on 20 July at Sandown he starts work on what he calls his 'Abstract'. At the end of the month he reports to Hooker:

This is a very charming place and we have got a very comfortable house. But I cannot say the sea has done H[enrietta] or L[eonard] much good. Nor has my stomach recovered from all our troubles. I am very glad we left home, for six children have now died of scarlet fever in Downe . . . .

I pass my time by doing daily a couple of hours of my Abstract, and I find it amusing and improving work. I am most heartily obliged to you and Lyell for having set me on this.'[2]

Back at Down Darwin resumes work on the 'Abstract'. Gradually it is borne in on him that it will be longer than he first supposed and by mid-October he is telling Hooker that he expects it to 'run into a small volume, which will have to be published separately'. By April 1859 he is negotiating with the publisher, John Murray. Darwin, who sees the volume as only a very preliminary work, proposes the title: *An Abstract of an Essay on the Origin of Species and Varieties through Natural Selection*; but Murray insists on something shorter. The title they agree to is *On the Origin of Species*, with the addition *by Means of Natural Selection* relegated to a subordinate position. By late April the whole manuscript, in a fair copy done by the village schoolmaster, is with the printers. By mid-June the galley proofs begin arriving and Darwin is horrified by what he regards as his bad English and lack of clarity. As a result he works like a Trojan revising the galleys, apologising repeatedly to Murray for doing so. At last, on 1 October 1859, he is able to enter in his diary: 'Finished proofs (thirteen months and ten days) of Abstract on *Origin of Species.*' The first edition is published on 24 November and all 1250 copies are sold to the trade on the first day.[3]

This account is no more than the bare bones of what has been an intensive effort, constantly fighting his 'accursed' stomach, and interspersed with no less than four brief visits to Moor Park in order to drive the 'horrid species' out of his head and so relax for a short spell before resuming.[4] During these months there are no reports of the children's being ill, and even Henrietta seems to be getting better.

The prospect of intense criticism of his ideas is always with him, however. So preoccupied is he with it, indeed, that in a striking lapse he imagines it coming even from Hooker, who, though long hesitant about going the whole way with him, had always been strongly supportive. On receiving Hooker's reassuring reply, Darwin apologises for his error (13 October 1858): 'the truth is, that I have accustomed myself, partly from being quizzed by my non-naturalist relations, to expect opposition and even contempt, that I forgot for a moment that you are the one living soul from whom I have constantly received sympathy.'[5]

In fact by the autumn of 1858 Hooker's outlook had changed considerably, thanks to many years of argument with Darwin and the recent convincing presentation of the new ideas by Darwin and Wallace at the Linnean Society. Accordingly, in his current work Hooker was applying Darwin's theories and finding the results illuminating. Hooker's slow conversion to his friend's theoretical outlook is well described in a letter he was to write to a botanist friend, William Harvey (1811–66), shortly after the publication of the *Origin*. Warning Harvey against too hasty an adverse judgement, Hooker writes: 'Give time, abate prejudice, and let your ideas clarify, which they assuredly will in time. Remember that I was aware of Darwin's views *fourteen years* before I adopted them, and I have done so *solely* and *entirely* from an independent study of plants themselves.'[6]

During the autumn and winter of 1858–9 Hooker was busy on the final botanical publication arising from the Ross expedition to the Antarctic fifteen years earlier, namely the *Flora of Australia and Tasmania*. In a long and scientifically significant introductory essay of over a hundred pages he demonstrated that Darwin's theories were not only better explanations of the perplexing problems of botanical affinity and geographical distribution than the creationist ideas he had espoused formerly but also raised a host of fascinating questions for research. Since in the event his work would appear in the autumn of 1859 a few weeks before the publication of the *Origin*, it would mean that, so far as plant life is concerned, Hooker's monograph would provide strong advance evidence in favour of Darwin's position. It would mean also that Darwin would already be assured of the public support of at least one distinguished botanist.

Throughout these crucial months of 1858 and 1859 there is a frequent interchange of letters between the friends, with Darwin reporting progress on his 'Abstract' and on the ups and downs of his health. There is also much scientific discussion, with Darwin constantly asking Hooker for facts about the geographical distribution of plants. When drafts of his chapters are available he sends them to Kew for comment and is profuse in his thanks for the help obtained.

From time to time during 1858 and 1859 Darwin also gives information about himself to Fox. In a letter of 13 November 1858 he is optimistic, hoping he can go to press in the spring. Moreover, a recent 'very pleasant week at Moor Park' had been a success: 'Hydropathy and idleness did me wonderful good and I walked one day 11½ miles – a quite Herculean feat for me!' Throughout this correspondence Darwin is quite explicit that it is his work that brings on the symptoms. For example, in February 1859, during a further three weeks at Moor Park, he writes: 'I have been extra bad of late, with the old severe vomiting rather often and much distressing swimming of the head . . . . My abstract is the cause, I believe of the main part of the ills to which my flesh is heir to; but I have only two more chapters and to correct all and then I shall be a comparatively free man.'[7] A month later, on 24 March 1859, he writes again to Fox:

We are all pretty well, and our elder daughter is improving. I can see daylight through my work, and am now finally correcting chapters for press. . . . I am weary of my work. It is a very odd thing that I have no sensation that I overwork my brain; but facts compel me to conclude that my Brain was never formed for much thinking. We are resolved to go for two or three months, when I have finished, to Ilkley [another hydropathic establishment] or some such place, to see if I can anyhow give my health a good start, for it certainly has been wretched of late, and has incapacitated me for everything. You do me injustice when you think that I work for fame; I value it to a certain extent; but if I know myself, I work from a sort of instinct to try to make out truth.'[8]

Having completed the manuscript during April, he decides to take yet another break at Moor Park. Reporting his plan to Hooker on 18 May, he explains that his health has quite failed and that he is not fit enough to read through some proofs on plant distribution that Hooker has sent him for comment. Ten days later he says he is feeling better and can deal with Hooker's proofs, continuing: 'I had . . . great prostration of mind and body, but entire rest, and the douche, and "Adam Bede", have together done me a world of good.' Nevertheless, by July he is again incapacitated and writing to Hooker on the 2nd: 'I have been bad, having had two days of bad vomiting owing to the accursed Proofs – I shall have to go to Moor Park before long.' There he goes for another week later that month from

19 to 26 July. Throughout August he is working on the galleys doing so much rewriting that during September he has to spend some further weeks correcting the revised versions. On 1 September he reports progress to Hooker, adding that he is 'incapable of doing anything whatever, excepting three hours daily work at proof sheets. God knows whether I shall ever be good for anything again. . . . I had a terribly long fit of sickness yesterday, which makes the world extra gloomy today.'[9]

On 23 September, within a week of finishing the proofs, he writes a long letter to Fox in which, apologising for not having written earlier, he explains that he has been in 'an absorbed, slavish and overworked state', and that his health had been 'as bad as it well could be all summer.' 'Thank Heaven,' he continues, 'I have at last as good as done my Book . . . So much for my abominable volume, which has cost me so much labour that I almost hate it.'[10]

Earlier in the year Darwin had expressed his forebodings about the future to Wallace. At the end of a long letter of 25 January in which he expresses admiration for the generous spirit in which Wallace had responded to the news of the decision by Lyell and Hooker that his paper should be coupled with Darwin's at the Linnean Society meeting, Darwin wishes Wallace good health and all success in his work. He then adds: 'I look at my own career as nearly run out. If I can publish my Abstract and perhaps my greater work on the same subject, I shall look at my course as done.'[11] At the time this was written Darwin was not quite fifty.

Reading these and other letters gives the impression that throughout 1859 Darwin was striving to fend off depression. Concluding his letter to Fox of 23 September 1859, he explains that he will try 'to keep to my resolution of being idle this winter. But I fear ennui will be as bad as a bad stomach.'[12] It was a dilemma: work and its accompanying somatic symptoms; or absence of work and its accompanying ennui, which the context strongly suggests means depression.

II

When at last Darwin had come to present his ideas he followed faithfully the method advocated by Herschel and adopted by Lyell. Set out in modern terms, it comprises the three steps: first, making observations, asking questions and seeking explanations; secondly, constructing an explanatory model; thirdly, examining the adequacy of the model by applying it to new data and, whenever possible, to data derived from experiment. In advanced sciences today this procedure is followed systematically;* in Darwin's day it was not only exceptional but mistrusted by the philosophers.

*In the early stages of a new science, before a tolerably adequate model has been constructed, the procedure cannot be followed; and, in default of something better, schools of thought, usually rivalrous, become established.

In Darwin's work the historical sequence had been: first, the array of observations he had made during the voyage, leading to questions about species and their distribution in time (the fossil record) and in space (on islands and continents). The second step, model-making, had been accomplished during the three extraordinarily fertile years of 1837–9. The third step was to be his application of the model to a vast array of observations, some old, some new, some made by himself, including the results of his imaginative experiments, but most of them derived from books and journals and from replies to questions put to his huge circle of specialist correspondents. A most important part of the third step was his systematic examination of the many difficulties that he was aware of.

It has been unfortunate that in his own descriptions of his scientific procedures Darwin uses words and phrases that have misled readers and have resulted in the misconceived criticism that his methods were largely speculative and deductive. Thus, he tells us in his *Autobiography* that he adopted 'the true Baconian method', which is usually interpreted to mean amassing facts unguided by theory and then deducing a theory from them. Moreover, where we would say he built an explanatory model, Darwin refers to himself as 'speculating'. The fact is that Darwin was one of the first scientists to adopt what has become the current method. This is made explicit in Darwin's Introduction to his great work.

In this Introduction Darwin starts by referring to the observations he had made when on board HMS *Beagle*, which he says, 'seemed to me to throw some light on the origin of species – that mystery of mysteries, as it has been called by one of our greatest philosophers'. A little later he continues:

it is quite conceivable that a naturalist reflecting on the mutual affinities of organic beings, on their embryological relations, their geographical distribution, geological succession, and other such facts, might come to the conclusion that each species had not been independently created, but had descended, like varieties, from other species. Nevertheless, such a conclusion, even if well founded, would be unsatisfactory, until it could be shown how the innumerable species inhabiting this world have been modified, so as to acquire that perfection of structure and co-adaptation which most justly excites our admiration.'

Then, after pointing to the inadequacies of some current ideas, he describes how he had found illumination from a study of the breeding of domestic animals, and he proceeds to formulate his novel theory:

As many more individuals of each species are born than can survive; and as, consequently, there is a frequently recurring struggle for existence, it follows that any being, if it vary, however slightly in any manner profitable to itself, under the complex and sometimes varying conditions of life, will have a better chance of surviving, and thus be *naturally selected*. From the strong principle of inheritance, any selected variety will tend to propagate its new and modified form.

Thereafter in his Introduction he describes the contents. In the first four chapters he is setting out the reasoning leading to this fundamental theory; in the next five he is examining the many difficulties he sees and their possible solution; and in the final four, before the recapitulation and conclusion, he is reviewing some of the many observations derived from a great variety of sources that can be understood better when viewed in the new perspective – better, that is, than in the perspective of biblical creationism. These observations include the succession of changes seen in fossil organisms from the most ancient times up to the present, their geographical distribution, and their mutual relationships as demonstrated in their anatomy, embryology and rudimentary organs.

In the first four chapters, in which he is formulating his theory, Darwin begins with the established principles by which different breeds of domestic animals have been produced, namely by the rigorous selection of individuals that have some desired characteristic in more marked degree than others and breeding only from them. That can be termed 'artificial selection'. In the next three chapters he argues that, in an analogous way, the striking differences between species and genera can be understood as the consequences of an equally rigorous selection for breeding purposes of individuals that show variations that make them and their progeny better able than other variants to survive and reproduce in their current environment. That he termed 'natural selection'. Although Darwin found the analogy compelling, others were misled. Already by 1860 he was regretting not having substituted 'natural preservation' for 'natural selection', but by then it was too late. Wallace never ceased to be worried by the misunderstanding to which Darwin's metaphor continued to give rise, and as late as July 1866 would be pleading with him to make a change; but there was no easy solution.[13]

To complement Darwin's account of his work it is necessary to describe also what the *Origin* omits. First, there are no references either to his predecessors or to the sources of his data. Since the volume does not pretend to be more than an abstract of a bigger work, however, these omissions are excusable; though they did not appear so to his critical contemporaries. What to the academics was even less excusable was that he had failed to open with a proper discussion of the philosophical issues, as was both customary and, they held, necessary. Instead, he had plunged straight into the scientific task of presenting data and considering how they are best to be explained. Though today the procedure may be taken for granted, for Darwin to do so was to break a mould.

III

On 3 October 1859, true to his resolution, he went to a hydropathic establishment at Ilkley in Yorkshire. His first impressions were not favourable, however, as he tells Fox on 5 October: 'I always hate everything new and perhaps it is only this that makes me at present detest

ON

THE ORIGIN OF SPECIES

BY MEANS OF NATURAL SELECTION,

OR THE

PRESERVATION OF FAVOURED RACES IN THE STRUGGLE
FOR LIFE.

By CHARLES DARWIN, M.A.,

FELLOW OF THE ROYAL, GEOLOGICAL, LINNÆAN, ETC., SOCIETIES;
AUTHOR OF ' JOURNAL OF RESEARCHES DURING H. M. S. BEAGLE'S VOYAGE
ROUND THE WORLD.'

LONDON:
JOHN MURRAY, ALBEMARLE STREET.
1859.

Title page of the first edition of *The Origin*

the whole place.' He then urges Fox to join him. A few days later he managed to rent a house and on 17 October Emma and the family arrived. The stay, however, was something of a disaster. Darwin sprained his ankle and also suffered from boils; and the medical proprietor did not impress him. Moreover, although the visit to Ilkley was conceived as a long break from work, he continued with all his scientific correspondence, writing some very long letters. He had arranged for the publishers to distribute pre-publication copies of the *Origin* to a number of friends and colleagues: first and foremost Hooker, Lyell and Huxley; then three from his old Cambridge days, Fox, Henslow and Sedgwick; next Richard Owen, Hugh Falconer, John Philips (a geologist) and his close neighbour and amateur botanist, John Lubbock; finally four overseas, Wallace, Asa Gray, Agassiz and Augustin de Candolle (a Swiss botanist). To all of them he wrote personal letters begging them to let him have their opinions. To several he attempted to forestall the hostile criticism he expected by adding apologies for the book's heterodox contents – to Henslow, whom he addresses as 'my dear old master in Natural History', 'I fear . . . that you will not approve of your pupil in this case'; to Richard Owen, 'I fear that it will be abominable in your eyes'; and to Hugh Falconer, who had already accused him of perverting Hooker, 'Lord how savage you will be, if you read it, and how you will long to crucify me alive!'[14]

The family did not leave Ilkley until 7 December. Towards the end of their time Darwin was busy making corrections and minor revisions for the reprinting which Murray was calling for urgently.

Throughout the stay Darwin was on tenterhooks over how his closest colleagues would greet the book. The previous year he had decided that he would be able to tolerate all the savage criticism he was anticipating provided Lyell, Hooker and Huxley approved his ideas. Since Hooker had seen many of the chapters in proof and had expressed himself favourably, about him Darwin now felt confident. Huxley, having devoured his pre-publication copy within days, wrote enthusiastically to Ilkley on 23 November. Not for many years, he said, had a work on natural history science 'made so great an impression on me, and I do most heartily thank you for the great store of new views you have given me'. Darwin replied immediately; 'I should have been more than contented with one quarter of what you have said. Exactly fifteen months ago, when I put pen to paper for this volume, I had awful misgivings; and thought perhaps I had deluded myself, like so many have done, and I then fixed in my mind three judges, on whose decision I determined mentally to abide. The judges were Lyell, Hooker and yourself. It was this which made me so excessively anxious for your verdict.'[15]

That left Lyell. Earlier in the summer, Lyell had asked if he might see the proofs when available, and Darwin had replied enthusiastically on 28 June that he would send them 'as soon as ever I can get a copy . . . ready . . . and if you approve of it, even to a moderate extent, it will be the highest satisfaction which I shall ever receive.' A couple of months later, on 2 September, Darwin had forwarded the sheets, reminding Lyell: 'Remember that your verdict will probably have more influence than my book in deciding whether [my] views . . . will be admitted or rejected.'[16] On his arrival at Ilkley a month later Darwin was still awaiting the great man's verdict. No one's opinion weighed more heavily with him and he was deeply anxious about what it would be.

Three years earlier Darwin's hopes that Lyell would be a supporter had run high, if only because, as he had long recognised and as Huxley was later to emphasise, the geological principles which Lyell had formulated were an essential basis for his own thesis. Moreover, in June 1856, soon after reading the 1844 essay, Lyell had written encouragingly; and this had led Darwin to report to Hooker on 13 July 1856; '[Lyell] is coming round at a railway pace on the mutability of species, and authorizes me to put some sentences on this head in my preface.' Subsequently he had advocated the presentation of the Darwin and Wallace papers to the Linnean Society. Nevertheless, a few months later Lyell's opinion remained in doubt, as Darwin had explained to Wallace on 25 January 1859: 'You ask about Lyell's frame of mind. I think he is somewhat staggered, but does not give in, and speaks with horror, often to me, of what a thing it would be . . . if he were "perverted". But . . . I think he will end by being "perverted".'[17]

During the following September, after sending Lyell the proofs, Darwin writes to him further: on the 20th 'as I regard your verdict as far more important . . . than [that] of any other dozen men, I am naturally very anxious about it . . . let me beg you to keep your mind open'; and ten days later, just before departing for the ill-starred visit to Ilkley: 'I look at you as my Lord High Chancellor in Natural Science. . . . I shall be deeply anxious to hear what you decide.'[18]

Soon after reaching Ilkley Darwin received the verdict. In a long letter dated 3 October 1859, from a house on the family estate in Scotland where he had been reading the proofs, Lyell expresses admiration: 'It is a splendid case of close reasoning, and long substantial argument throughout so many pages.' He then makes a large number of useful suggestions for minor revisions and additions when Darwin comes to prepare the next edition. But he also raises a considerable number of difficulties, and in one passage he expresses his old-standing reservations: 'I have long seen most clearly that if any concession is made, all that you claim in your concluding pages will follow.' Then, emphasising that the argument cannot but apply to man as well as to other species of animal and plant, he adds: 'It is this which has made me so long hesitate.'[19] Thus Lyell's verdict continued to be 'not proven'.

Within a few days of receiving Lyell's letter Darwin, troubled that Lyell should still be so noncommittal, replies at great length (on 11 October), in fact in nearly 2500 words. After thanking him for giving so much time and thought, he proceeds to consider one by one each of Lyell's difficulties. He agrees that there is no halfway house: 'I think you will be driven to reject all or admit all: I fear by your letter it will be the former alternative.' By the end, however, he is more hopeful: 'If you think enough, I expect you will be perverted and if you ever are, I shall know that the theory of Natural Selection is, in the main, safe.' Such hopes appeared to be fully confirmed when a month later he received a letter from Hooker (dated 21 November 1859), who had been reading his pre-publication copy of the complete work. After a reference to 'your glorious book', Hooker continues: 'Lyell, with whom we are staying, is perfectly enchanted and is absolutely gloating over it.'[20]

As a result of this information or, perhaps more likely as a result of a letter from Lyell which has not survived, Darwin writes an exultant letter on 23 November:

My dear Lyell – You seemed to have worked admirably on the species question; there could not have been a better plan than reading up on the opposite side. I rejoice profoundly that you intend admitting the doctrine of modification in your new edition [of the *Manual of Geology*]; nothing, I am convinced could be more important for its success. I honour you most sincerely. To have maintained in the position of master, one side of a question for thirty years, and then deliberately give it up is a fact to which I much doubt whether the records of science offer a parallel. For myself also, I rejoice profoundly; for thinking so many cases of men pursuing an illusion for years, often and often a cold shudder has run through me, and I have asked myself whether I may not have devoted my life to a phantasy. Now I look at it as morally impossible that investigators of truth, like you and Hooker, can be wholly wrong, and therefore I rest in peace.[21]

Thus, even if he was to be execrated as he so confidently expected, he now felt sure he had three stalwart friends to support him, including his all-important Lord High Chancellor.

While still at Ilkley, and only days after the *Origin* was published on 24 November, Darwin received the first salvo in the bombardment he had long anticipated. It came from his old teacher, the geologist Adam Sedgwick, and his comments were scathing. In the course of a very long letter, in which he praises Darwin's erudition, he dismisses the theory and the conclusions as ridiculous and dangerous: 'I have read your book with more pain than pleasure. Parts of it I admired greatly, parts I laughed at till my sides were almost sore; other parts I read with absolute sorrow, because I think them utterly false and grievously mischievous.'[22] Darwin, seeking support, sent a copy of the letter to Lyell with the comment: 'it is terribly muddled, and . . . the first page seems almost childish.'[23]

In her memoirs Henrietta recalls the two months that the Darwin family spent at Ilkley: 'It was a miserable time, bitterly cold, he was extremely ill, and suffering, and I also was ill, the lodgings were wretched and I look back on it as a time of frozen horror.' Earlier in their stay Darwin, at the end of a letter to Hooker (27 October or 3 November) dealing with problems of geographical distribution of Australian animals and plants, gives a grim account of his condition: 'I have been very bad lately; having had an awful "crisis" one leg swelled like elephantiasis – eyes almost closed up – covered with a rash and fiery Boils: but they tell me it will surely do me much good – it was like living in Hell.'[24] It was thus in this anxious and suffering state that the author was celebrating the publication of what was to become one of the most famous books in the history of science.

IV

On their return journey to Down the family spent a couple of days in London. This enabled Darwin to sample opinion in the capital, as he relates in a long letter to Lyell of 10 December 1859 – through which, it should be noted, there runs the implicit assumption that Lyell is now supporting his theory.[25] One visit was to Sir Henry Holland, who, as a distant cousin, had often advised the family on matters of health ever since Darwin first consulted him in 1838. Sir Henry had been reading the *Origin* and was much influenced by it, greatly to Darwin's satisfaction: he 'found him going immense way with us . . . good, as showing how wind blows'.

A second visit, by contrast, left him dumbfounded. This was to his former colleague, Richard Owen, who had examined and identified the great haul of fossil bones he had sent back from South America and who had frequently advised him about problems of anatomy and nomenclature during the barnacle years. Owen was now at the height of his career. Three years earlier, having fallen out with the authorities at the Royal College of Surgeons, he had been appointed to the newly created and influential post of superintendent of the Natural History Department of the British Museum. Since he was now recognised as a world authority in the field of comparative anatomy, Owen's opinion would carry weight. Continuing his letter to Lyell and with insistence he repeat nothing, Darwin describes the very long interview: 'Under garb of great civility, he was inclined to be most bitter and sneering against me . . . He was quite savage and crimson at my having put his name with defenders of immutability. When I said that was my impression and that of others . . . he then spoke of his own position in science and that of all the naturalists in London . . . with a degree of arrogance I never saw approached.' Darwin's repeated efforts to mollify his critic all misfired. At the end he thanked Owen for his correction of a technical point in the *Origin*, which referred to similarities between bears and whales, and explained how in consequence he had deleted the passage in the revised edition. 'Oh have you,' retorted Owen, 'well I was more struck with this than any other passage; you little know of the remarkable and essential relationship between bears and whales.' Nothing Darwin could say was right.

Nevertheless they parted with expressions of high civility which, Darwin adds, 'on reflexion I am almost sorry for. – He is the most astounding creature I ever encountered.' A few months later an anonymous and vitriolic review would appear, readily identifiable as the work of Owen.

During his stay in London one more influential opinion about the *Origin* reached Darwin, as he tells Lyell in a postscript. 'I have heard by [a] round about channel that Herschel says my Book "is the law of higgledy-pigglety" . . . If true this is great blow and discouragement.'

Controversy was mounting and opinion polarising. Bitter criticism there might be; yet for Darwin there was one great comfort – all three friends whose opinions he valued most now seemed firmly on his side.

V

Alas! Darwin's confidence that Lyell was at last ready to subscribe publicly to his theory was soon proved mistaken. In fact, Lyell would continue to suspend judgement on Darwin's thesis for several years yet, thereby causing him constant anxiety and repeated disappointment, which was to end in serious breakdown. That being so, it is only fair to look at the situation from Lyell's point of view.[26]

From the time that he first heard Darwin describe it, Lyell had a firm and detailed grasp of the theory's main features. Furthermore, he realised at once not only that it was of the first importance for the sciences but also that it had far-reaching implications both for religion and for man's ideas about his place in the world. It raised, in fact all the troublesome issues that Lamarck's theories had raised and against which he had repeatedly argued ever since he had first read the French biologist's book nearly thirty years earlier. Shortly after being inducted into the secrets of Darwin's new and far more convincing version of evolution theory in April 1856, Lyell got wind of the radical ideas on species that had been expressed during the meeting between Hooker, Huxley, Darwin and Wollaston, who was Lyell's informant. 'I cannot see how they can go so far and not embrace the whole Lamarckian doctrine,' he noted in his journal; and some months later (February 1857) he wrote: 'The ordinary naturalist is not sufficiently aware that when dogmatizing on what species are, he is grappling with the whole question of the organic world and its connection with the time past and with Man.'

In contrast to youngish men like Huxley and Hooker, who in 1857 were thirty-two and forty respectively and without any earlier commitments on the species question, Lyell was already sixty and had long since committed himself publicly to the traditional idea that species are fixed and immutable; colleagues therefore looked to him to defend it. To abandon it would be a major step – intellectually, professionally and emotionally. Above all, it would require him to swallow the unpalatable idea that, so far from being a special creation, man was descended from the brutes. To adjust to these revolutionary changes of outlook Lyell needed time, just as Hooker had. Darwin, by contrast, sought instant support. It was a tragic conflict.

It was a misfortune for Darwin that Lyell's slowly changing views were progressing in the pattern of two steps forward and one step back. Since Darwin was intensely sensitive to every sign and hint of Lyell's views, his hopes were thus repeatedly raised only to be dashed again. In fact, much had happened in Lyell's scientific thinking since 1856. First, a number of exciting fossil finds had shown that man had been present on earth for far longer than anyone had previously believed. Secondly, there had been the meeting at the Linnean Society at which the Darwin and Wallace papers had been read. Finally, almost simultaneously with the appearance of the *Origin* was the publication of Hooker's Introduction to his *Flora of Tasmania* in which, on the basis of extensive botanical evidence, he advances powerful arguments in favour of Darwin's theories. Lyell was deeply impressed and, at the end of an enthusiastic letter to Hooker of 19 December 1859, had written; 'The first two notes of page vii are very interesting, and show what grand speculations and results "the creation by variation" is capable of suggesting and one day of establishing.'[27] A few months later, in his private journal, he would sum up his views on the *Origin*: 'Mr. Darwin has written a work which will constitute an era in geology and natural history to show that [compared to creationism] the rival hypothesis of unlimited variability is the more probable of the two, and that the descendants of common parents may become in the course of ages so unlike each other as to be entitled to rank as distinct species, from each other or from some of their progenitors.' This conclusion, however, would always be qualified so far as man is concerned. Meanwhile Darwin was kept on tenterhooks.

VI

As already noted, Huxley's reaction to the *Origin* was one of instant enthusiasm. Although explained in part by his mercurial temperament, it none the less presents a puzzle, since hitherto he had been little interested in evolution and, ignorant of Darwin's theory, regularly expressed views inconsistent with it.

Huxley, it must be remembered, was no field naturalist. Describing himself in a brief autobiography, he writes: 'I am afraid there is very little of the genuine naturalist in me. I never collected anything, and species work was always a burden to me; what I cared for was the architectural and engineering part of the business.'[28] Problems of variation, heredity and natural selection lay far outside his range of interests, not only prior to reading the *Origin* but afterwards as well.

When in 1854 Huxley had been appointed naturalist to the Geographical Survey in succession to Forbes, he had found himself in strange waters. Fossils had never interested him and at first he had resisted the idea of studying them. In time, however, he had accommodated to his new duties and in due course became an expert palaeontologist. During the 1850s a great debate was raging in geological circles. Some thought there was clear evidence of progression in the fossil record – namely that, working from the most ancient rocks to the most recent, animals and plants of each class become progressively more varied in form, complex and specialised. That was Darwin's view and used by him as important evidence for evolution. It was also the view of most contemporary field naturalists. Others, including Lyell, held that there was no such evidence, that the fossil record was so fragmentary and inadequate that firm conclusions were impossible. Huxley followed Lyell. Indeed, one of the principal criticisms he had levelled at the hapless author of *Vestiges* was that the latter had based so much of his case on the mistaken tenet of progressionism. In Huxley's view discussions of this sort were nothing but idle speculation, made worse when the advocates of progressionism, notably Lamarck, invoked mysterious and scientifically illicit forces, such as an internal drive towards perfection, to account for the changes they alleged to have occurred.

In any case, what especially impressed Huxley in his new role of palaeontologist was that there are a multitude of species that have persisted unchanged through aeons of geological time. That, of course, is true; but by generalising his findings to include all species he reached some strange conclusions. Unimpressed by the fact that no one had found fossil reptiles in geological formations earlier than the Triassic or fossil mammals before even later formations, and committed to the unchanging character of every organism, he felt free to predict that it was only a matter of time before the fossil remains of reptiles, birds and mammals would be found in the most ancient of rocks; and that might be so even for man. As late as June 1859, a few months before publication of the *Origin*, he expressed those views in a long memorandum to Lyell. Thus, contrary to how he later described his position during these early years – namely as having been strictly neutral and agnostic – at this time Huxley was in reality holding views antithetic to Darwin's.[29]

Not unexpectedly, these anti-progressionist views, voiced emphatically by Huxley in his lectures at the Royal Institution, worried Darwin. In a letter of 10 June 1855 Darwin thanks Huxley for a copy of one of the lectures and expresses regret that the evidence he musters against progressionism should be so persuasive: 'I had hoped things had been in a slight degree otherwise.' A little later, in a letter to Hooker, while conceding that in the matter concerned Huxley might be right, he adds, 'Yet I think his tone very much too vehement, and I have ventured to say so in a note to [him].'[30]

It was probably in 1854 or early 1855 that Huxley had his first serious scientific discussion with Darwin. Describing it thirty years later, he recounts how he was expressing his 'belief in the sharpness of the lines of demarcation between natural groups and in the absence of transitional forms, with all the confidence of youth and imperfect knowledge. I was not aware at that time', he continues, 'that he had then been many years brooding over the species question; and the humorous smile which accompanied his gentle answer, that such was not altogether his view, long haunted and puzzled me.' Soon after that interview there was the meeting at Down in late April 1856 to which Darwin had invited Huxley together with Hooker and Wollaston, and during which radical ideas about species had been expressed. It is striking that in later years Huxley should have had so little recollection of the meeting; he hazarded that any opinions critical of traditional ideas that he might have expressed were probably in 'counterblast to Wollaston's conservatism'. The ringleader he felt sure, must have been Hooker. Plainly this first hearing of Darwin's heterodox views on this occasion had little influence on Huxley. Three years later, just before the *Origin* appeared, he concluded one of his many specialist papers with an uncompromising assertion of his anti-progressionist position.[31]

Yet, despite these sharp differences on matters scientific, the friendship between the two men flourished. Apart from occasional meetings, more often probably in London than in Down, they wrote regularly to each other exchanging information and offering criticism. For example, during 1857 we find Darwin expressing gratitude for some advice Huxley had given on a matter of embryology; and in subsequent discussions, on issues of classification, Darwin is evidently grateful for the challenging arguments his young friend advances. But it was Huxley who was the chief beneficiary of these exchanges, and during the late 1850s he was not only developing a deep respect and affection for the older man but had learned to value his ideas and criticism. A letter from Huxley to Hooker of early 1858, in reply to some criticism of Hooker's, is revealing of relationships between members of this intimate circle. 'I always look upon any criticism as a compliment, not but what the old Adam in T.H.H. *will* arise and fight vigorously against all impugnment, and irrespective of all odds in the way of authority, but that is the way of the beast. Why I value your and Tyndall's and Darwin's friendship so much is, among other things, that you will pitch into me when necessary.'[32]

Such criticisms as Darwin offered were in fact very gentle, often regretting the violence with which his young friend expressed his opinions, and counselling moderation. On one of the many occasions when Huxley had crossed swords with Owen and had sent Darwin an account of the dispute, Darwin warns him against being too combative, adding, 'your father confessor trembles for you. I fancy Owen thinks much of this doctrine of his; I never from the first believed it.' A little later, after thanking Huxley for his 'very pleasant note', he proceeds: 'It amuses me to see what a bug-bear I have made myself to you; when having written some very pungent and good sentence it must be very disagreeable to have my face rise up like an ugly ghost.'[33]

During the years when Huxley's friendship with Darwin was growing closer his quarrels with Owen were growing fiercer. The mix was explosive: on the one hand an established figure, arrogant and jealous of his position, on the other an upstart twenty years younger who cared nothing for seniority or authority. In March 1858 Huxley writes a long letter full of news to his sister Lizzie, the only member of his family with whom he was intimate and who, with her doctor husband and several children, had emigrated to Tennessee. 'You want to know what I am and where I am', he starts, and there follows a long list of his various posts and distinctions. 'Considered a rising man and not a bad fellow by his friends – *per contra* greatly over-estimated and a bitter savage critic by his enemies. Perhaps they are both right. I have a high standard of excellence and am no respecter of persons, and I am afraid, I show the latter peculiarity rather too much. An internecine feud rages between Owen and myself (more's the pity).'[34] Apart from disagreements on scientific matters and the professional rivalry resulting, relations between the two had been soured when a couple of years earlier Owen took advantage of facilities provided for him at the School of Mines to arrogate to himself Huxley's title as Professor of Palaeontology there.[35] Three months after writing to his sister, Huxley gave a prestigious lecture at the Royal Society on the anatomy of the vertebrate skull, on which Owen had written extensively, and utterly destroyed the older man's position; and who should have been in the chair but Owen himself.

On the issues that divided the two rivals Darwin's position varied. Often he agreed with Huxley but not always. For example, although later proved mistaken, on the development of the vertebrate skull he had been inclined to believe Owen's account. What is particularly ironic is that on the central issue of the fossil record it was Owen who favoured progressionism whereas Huxley was against it.

After the Darwin and Wallace papers at the Linnean Society in July 1858 Huxley was, of course, aware that Darwin was writing on the theme of transmutation of species, but he knew singularly little of what he was going to say: Darwin never sent him drafts for comment as he did to Hooker. It might well be, he thought, that Darwin believed that when one species is transmuted into another the change occurs by a jump from a parent of one species to progeny of another, as though a mare suddenly gave birth to a zebra.[36] Thus he was totally unaware of Darwin's theory of infinitely gradual change occurring over immense numbers of generations, and of Darwin's picture of one species differentiating over time into a number of diverse though related species.

It is therefore all the more to Huxley's credit that as soon as he had read Darwin's great work he recognised it at once as the epoch-making contribution it has proved to be. In his initial outburst of praise and gratitude of 23 November 1859, he realises he must read it repeatedly in order to grasp the full implications of his friend's revolutionary ideas and also that there are a number of points about which he has reservations. He foresees clearly that Darwin is likely to be the target of 'considerable abuse and misrepresentation'. 'Depend upon it,' he continues, 'you have earned the lasting gratitude of all thoughtful men. And as to the curs who will bark and yelp, you must recollect that some of your friends . . . are endowed with an amount of combativeness which (though you have often and justly rebuked it) may stand you in good stead. I am sharpening up my claws and beak in readiness.'[37]

What impressed Huxley beyond all else about the *Origin* was the high quality of the scientific argument and the wide range of biological and geological data explained by it. Whatever its limitations, Darwin's theory provided by far the most plausible working hypothesis for understanding many puzzling phenomena. It was therefore vital that it be given a fair hearing and not be destroyed by ignorant prejudice. Thus, knowing well Darwin's aversion to controversy and his own skill and appetite for it, Huxley from the first cast himself in the role of Darwin's champion. 'I am Darwin's bulldog,' he announced. Darwin was deeply grateful. In an exchange of letters at the end of the famous year of 1859, he concludes, 'Farewell, my good and admirable agent for the promulgation of damnable heresies!'[38] The stage was set for the dramas to come.

TWENTY-THREE

Awful battles and staunch friends
1860–1862

I

From the moment the *Origin* was published it generated the most intense interest and controversy. A month after publication *The Times* carried a three-column review. Although it was anonymous, as was the custom, the accuracy of the content and the hard-hitting style spoke loudly of Huxley's doing, and so it proved. Private letters and public reviews followed fast. Thus it came about that during the 1860s Darwin's scientific life was dominated by reactions to the *Origin*: preparations of revised editions and arrangements for translations; a voluminous correspondence about the theories; attempts to clarify misunderstandings; and efforts to supplement the work with material that had earlier been destined for the big book. Darwin was later to remark that being the author of the *Origin of Species* was almost a full-time job.

Although Darwin did his best to inure himself against criticism, he was in fact keenly sensitive to it. A man given to 'acute sensitiveness to praise and blame' is how Huxley later described him.[1] As a result, these were years of stress and strain and it was merciful that throughout he had the strong support of both Hooker and Huxley, and also, though only for a short time, the belief that Lyell could be counted on.

Only if we imagine ourselves back in the intellectual climate of the mid-nineteenth century is it possible to comprehend the varied reception given to the *Origin*. There were three main groups of readers. First were the orthodox theologians whose response was highly predictable. Next were the large number of fairly uncritical general readers (of whom Darwin's contemporary, the poet Tennyson, was one) whose interest in evolution had been captured by the half-baked but popular work on the subject, *Vestiges of Creation*. For many of those readers, the *Origin* was probably regarded as another essay in the same vein, only a good deal tougher to read. Neither the criticisms of the theologians nor the enthusiasms of the general readers were of much consequence to Darwin, however. Those whom he was trying to convince were the third group, the philosophers and scientists, and it was they who, with some exceptions, advanced the most weighty objections. For example, there had already been a number of serious discussions of the problems Darwin was dealing with and many ideas advanced other than naïve creationism; yet none of these had he mentioned. In particular, he seemed unaware that, since species are known to be fixed entities, it is a contradiction in terms to talk about one species becoming transformed into another. Herschel, we have seen, was so affronted by the suggestion that variation is random, not directed, that he dubbed it the law of higgledy-piggledy. In any case, the whole way in which Darwin was arguing his thesis was inadmissible.

Since Darwin was a revolutionary thinker, there is no wonder that his work met with misunderstanding and hostility. What is surprising is the speed and extent to which his ideas, if not agreed with, transformed the intellectual climate of the late nineteenth century.[2]

While Darwin deeply disliked the personal attacks directed against him, and was often troubled initially by the adverse arguments of fellow scientists, the only criticisms that led him to change his mind proved to be those of the engineer and mathematician Fleeming Jenkin and the physicist William Thomson (Lord Kelvin). They it was who would lead him in later editions of the *Origin* to put greater weight than earlier on the inheritance of acquired characters, a change we now know to have been sadly mistaken.

II

On 7 January 1860 the publishers produced a second printing of the *Origin* which, since it contained a number of revisions, many of them suggested by Lyell, was technically a second edition. More comments were arriving from friends and colleagues who had been sent pre-publication copies. At the end of January 1860 Darwin received a copy of an enthusiastic letter written to Hooker by Asa Gray, to whom it will be remembered Darwin had already confided his ideas on evolution. Gray, who for over forty years held the chair of natural history at Harvard University, had written in reply to a letter from Hooker expressing admiration for the *Origin*. Gray concurred (5 January 1860): 'It is done in a *masterly manner.* . . . It is crammed full of most interesting matter – thoroughly digested – well expressed – close, cogent, and taken as a system it makes out a better case than I had supposed possible.' Gray then refers to the hostile attitude of his close colleague in Cambridge, Massachusetts, Louis Agassiz – who some years earlier had solved the Glen Roy problem: 'Agassiz, when I saw him last had read but a part of [the *Origin*]. He says it is *poor – very poor*!! (entre nous). The fact [is] he is very much annoyed by it. Tell Darwin this. . . . As I have promised, he and you shall have fair play here.' He explains that he is starting to write a review for the March number of the influential American *Journal of*

Science and Arts.[3] Gray was to be as good as his word. In an obituary many years later Hooker describes him as 'one of the first to accept and defend the doctrine of Natural Selection . . . so that Darwin . . . regarded him as the naturalist who had most thoroughly gauged the *Origin of Species* and as a tower of strength to himself and his cause'. Gray's tireless advocacy led Huxley to write: 'Among evolutionists . . . Asa Gray . . . fought the battle splendidly in the United States.' Already in early 1860 battle lines had been drawn in the USA. Gray, as the great proponent, quickly arranged for an American edition, which appeared on the 22 May that very year.[4] Agassiz remained a hostile critic until the end of his life.[5]

In Britain also there was hostile criticism. During the early spring of 1860 a long article appeared in the prestigious and powerful *Edinburgh Review* attacking both theory and author. This Darwin recognised immediately as being by none other than Richard Owen. Fortunately it so happened that Hooker and Huxley were staying at Down when the copy of the *Edinburgh Review* arrived and, since it attacked the views of all three friends in an equally savage manner, they gave one another support. Writing to Lyell on 10 April, Darwin describes the event: 'I have just read the *Edinburgh [Review]* which is without doubt by Owen. It is extremely malignant, clever and I fear will be very damaging. He is atrociously severe on Huxley's lecture and very bitter against Hooker. So we three *enjoyed* it together. Not that I really enjoyed it for it made me uncomfortable for one night; but I have got quite over it today . . . It is painful to be hated in the intense degree with which Owen hates me.'[6] This hatred, they had no doubt, was due to envy. Writing to Henslow on 8 May, Darwin explains: 'Owen is indeed very spiteful. . . . The Londoners say he is mad with envy because my book has been talked about; what a strange man to be envious of a naturalist like myself, immeasurably his inferior.'[7]

Thereafter Owen came to occupy a special place in Darwin's emotional life. Confiding his feelings to Hooker on 15 April 1861, he writes: 'in simple truth I am become quite demoniacal about Owen – worse than Huxley. . . . But I mean to try to get more angelic in my feelings; yet I never shall forget his cordial shake of the hand, when he was writing as spitefully as he possibly could against me.' Try as he might to become more angelic, it was the demoniacal feelings that lingered on. In a letter to Asa Gray of 23 July 1862 he refers to Owen as 'one of my chief enemies (the sole one who has annoyed me)'; and six months later he writes to Huxley (10 January 1863), referring to their mutual enemy: 'I believe I hate him more than you do.' On this occasion their charge against Owen was that he had made unauthorised use of the observations of a colleague (Hugh Falconer). 'I am burning with indignation,' Darwin had written to Hooker on 3 January; 'I could not get to sleep till past three last night for indigestion.'[8] When in later years Darwin reflected on his critics, he remarked of Owen: 'His power of hatred was certainly unsurpassed.'[9]

Throughout these years both Hooker and Huxley were towers of strength. Huxley's review in *The Times*, a fruit of instant opportunism, ensured serious discussion: 'it may make some of the educated mob who derive their ideas from the *Times* reflect,' he tells Hooker. 'And whatever they do, they *shall* respect Darwin.' Yet Huxley's enthusiasm was not always matched by his grasp of Darwin's ideas. Early in 1860 he was to give a lecture 'On Species and Races' at the Royal Institution, in which he planned to discuss evolution. Darwin was delighted, offered him drawings of pigeon varieties as visual aids and took tickets to attend; but the content proved a great disappointment. 'I succeeded in persuading myself for twenty-four hours that the lecture was a success,' he tells Hooker. 'Parts were eloquent and good, and all very bold; and I heard strangers say, "What a good lecture!" I told Huxley so.' 'After conversation with others and more reflection,' he continues, 'I must confess that as an exposition of the doctrine the lecture seems to me an entire failure. I thank God I did not think so when I saw Huxley; for he spoke so kindly and magnificently of me, that I could hardly have endured to say what I now think. He gave no just idea of Natural Selection.'[10]

Those who have studied Huxley's later works are agreed that an understanding of Darwin's key ideas – random variation, the survival of varieties best adapted to do so, and the history of life on earth as best represented by the metaphor of a branching tree – continued to escape him, despite his famous assertion that when he had first made himself master of the central idea of the *Origin* he had said to himself, 'How extremely stupid not to have thought of that.'[11] In consequence he would never contribute to the development of Darwin's theory. Nevertheless, in the public mind he was completely identified with it – which ensured its respect. Moreover, in the role of Darwin's bulldog, Huxley performed the indispensable function of maintaining Darwin's morale.

It should be noted that, of Darwin's three closest friends, Lyell, Hooker and Huxley, it was only Hooker who both understood the basic principles of the theory and was also in agreement with it. Admittedly he had a few reservations – for example, whether Darwin was extending his theory of natural selection too widely[12] – but these were comparatively minor. For these reasons Hooker would continue to be the friend in whom Darwin could confide with the least reservation.

Lyell's position was the reverse of Huxley's. He had a very clear grasp of the theory but a deep dislike of its implications. Thus during the early months of 1860 Darwin's expectations about him were still fluctuating. In a letter to him of 8 April, in which he describes how he and his friends had reacted to Owen's review, Darwin has occasion (when referring to some work on pigs) to remark: 'By the way it is a great blow for me that you cannot admit the potency of natural selection. The more I think of it, the less I doubt its power for great and small changes.' Yet six weeks later, on 18 May, he feels able to write to Wallace in optimistic mood. First he lists

Lyell among the 'geological converts', and then proceeds: 'Lyell keeps as firm as a tower, and this autumn will publish on the Geological History of Man, and will then declare his conversion which now is universally known.'[13] Thus in mid-1860 Darwin was feeling sure Lyell would declare in favour of evolution as a historical occurrence even if not in favour of natural selection as the effective agent.

III

To the worry and stress arising from Darwin's work there was added chronic and at times acute anxiety about the health and future of his children. Although by 1860 the eldest, William had turned twenty and would soon start a banking career in Southampton, the others were much younger, ranging from Henrietta, sixteen, down to Horace, not yet nine. During the spring of 1860 Etty's health deteriorated again and for the next twelve months caused her father 'incessant anxiety', as he reported to Fox on 18 October.[14] Although the following year was a better one, there was further intense anxiety in the summer of 1862 when Leonard, then aged twelve, was recovering from a dangerous fever. Thus, though it is convenient to deal separately with the scientific and the family problems with which Darwin was grappling, it must be remembered that anxieties caused by the one were constantly interacting with anxieties caused by the other. Throughout the next six years, 1860–5, Darwin's health was never very good and during two periods, July 1863 to spring 1864 and six months in 1865, was very bad. As usual he consulted a number of doctors and took a great variety of remedies, particulars of which are given in much detail by Ralph Colp in his book *To Be an Invalid*.

Throughout 1860 Darwin's health was indifferent. He had put himself under a new doctor, whose treatment at first seemed promising but, as always happened, later proved disappointing. On 22 March he tells Fox: 'I shall go to my grave, I suppose, grumbling and growling with daily, almost hourly, discomfort.' A couple of months later, on 18 May he tells Fox of the critical attacks that were falling 'thick and heavy' on him and claims unconvincingly that he now has a 'case-hardened hide'.[15] Nevertheless the following month, his stomach having 'utterly failed',[16] he decides on another visit to Dr Lane's establishment, which had moved from Moor Park to Sudbrook Park at Richmond-on-Thames. There he stayed for ten days, days during which the famous debate on evolution was taking place at the British Association meeting at Oxford, where Huxley and Hooker, both in fighting mood, trounced the Bishop of Oxford, Samuel Wilberforce, an able man who knew nothing of science.

The debate took place on Saturday, 30 June, and on the Monday evening Darwin received a long exultant account of it from Hooker. After describing the scene, Hooker continues:

The meeting was so large that they had adjourned to the library, which was crammed with between 700 and 1000 people, for all the world was there to hear Sam Oxon.

Well, Sam Oxon got up and spouted for half an hour with inimitable spirit, ugliness and emptiness and unfairness. I saw he was coached up by Owen [who was present] and knew nothing, and he said not a syllable but what was in the Reviews; he ridiculed you badly and Huxley savagely. Huxley answered admirably and turned the tables, but he could not throw his voice over so large an assembly, nor command the audience; and he did not allude to Sam's weak points nor put the matter in a form or way that carried the audience. The battle waxed hot. Lady Brewster fainted, the excitement increased as others spoke; my blood boiled, I felt myself a dastard; now I saw my advantage; I swore to myself that I would smite that Amalekite, Sam, hip and thigh if my heart jumped out of my mouth, and I handed my name up to the President (Henslow) as ready to throw down the gauntlet. . . . [It] became necessary for each speaker to mount the platform, and so there I was cocked up with Sam at my right elbow, and there and then I smashed him amid rounds of applause. I hit him in the wind at the first shot in ten words taken from his own ugly mouth; and then proceeded to demonstrate in as few more:

(1) that he could never have read your book, and
(2) that he was absolutely ignorant of the rudiments of Bot. Science. I said a few more on the subject of my own experience and conversion, and wound up with a very few observations on the relative positions of the old and new hypotheses, and with some words of caution to the audience. Sam was shut up – had not one word to say in reply, and the meeting *was dissolved forthwith*, leaving you master of the field.[17]

Most accounts of this famous debate omit reference to Hooker's role and give the day to Huxley. There are good reasons for this. Huxley's polemics, in which he replied with matching contempt to the bishop's contemptuous query whether it was on his mother's side as well as on his father's that he was descended from the apes, appealed to the layman and received maximum publicity. Hooker's contribution, springing from a much better grasp of the issues, appealed to the scientists. Another reason was that, when in 1885 Francis Darwin was compiling the *Life and Letters* of his father, the modest Hooker dissuaded him from publishing his exultant letter as he feared it was 'far too much of a braggart epistle'. This, together with many printed accounts of Huxley's devastating retort (that he was not ashamed to have an ape as an ancestor but would be ashamed to be connected with a man who used great gifts to obscure the truth), has meant that Hooker's critical intervention has been forgotten. The effect it had on the audience is nevertheless endorsed by Lyell, who had heard that, after the bishop had been much applauded, opinion had been 'quite turned the other way, especially by Hooker'.[18]

Immediately on reception of Hooker's letter on 2 July, Darwin replies:

I have been very poorly, with almost continuous bad headache for forty-eight hours, and I was low enough, and thinking what a useless burthen I was to myself

Since Lamarck's time almost all competent naturalists have left speculations on the origin of species to such dreamers as the author of the *Vestiges*, by whose well-intentioned efforts the Lamarckian theory received its final condemnation in the minds of all sound thinkers. Notwithstanding this silence, however, the transmutation theory, as it has been called, has been a "skeleton in the closet", to many an honest zoologist and botanist who had a soul above the mere naming of dried plants and skins. Surely, has such an one thought, nature is a mighty and consistent whole, and the providential order established in the world of life must, if we could only see it rightly, be consistent with that dominant over the multiform shapes of brute matter. But what is the history of astronomy, of all the branches of physics, of chymistry, of medicine, but a narration of the steps by which the human mind has been compelled, often sorely against its will, to recognize the operation of secondary causes in events where ignorance beheld an immediate intervention of a higher power? And when we know that living things are formed of the same elements as the inorganic world, that they act and react upon it, bound by a thousand ties of natural piety,¹ is it probable, nay is it possible, that they, and they alone, should have no order in their seeming disorder, no unity in their seeming multiplicity, should suffer no explanation by the discovery of some central and sublime law of mutual connexion?

Paragraph from Huxley's anonymous review of
The Origin in *The Times*

Protagonists in the Oxford debate of 1860:
T. H. Huxley, 1825–1895 and OPPOSITE
Sam Oxon (Samuel Wilberforce), 1805–73

and all others, when your letter came and it has so cheered me; your kindness and affection brought tears into my eyes. Talk of fame, honour, pleasure, wealth, are all dirt compared to affection. . . . I am astonished at your success and audacity. . . . I have read lately so many hostile views, that I was beginning to think that perhaps I was wholly in the wrong and that Owen was right when he said the whole subject would be forgotten in ten years; but now that I hear that you and Huxley will fight publicly (which I am sure I never could do), I fully believe that our cause will in the long run prevail.[19]

The following day he writes in the same vein to Huxley: 'I had a letter from Oxford written by Hooker late on Sunday night giving me some account of the awful battles which have raged about species at Oxford. He tells me you fought nobly with Owen . . . and that you answered the B. of O. capitally. . . . I honour your pluck; I would have soon have died as tried to answer the Bishop in such an assembly.'[20] Owen himself had not spoken but the bishop was speaking from Owen's brief which claimed that there is a radical difference between a human brain and that of an ape. Huxley had also studied primate brains and held there was no such difference. Inevitably he had seized the opportunity to refute Owen's opinion once more. The feud lived on.

Among the various speakers who supported the bishop was none other than FitzRoy, as Darwin would have learned later from reports of the debate in the weekly journals.[21] As a pioneer meteorologist, FitzRoy had been elected FRS nine years earlier, supported by both Darwin and Beaufort. At the Oxford meeting he had earlier given a paper on the history of severe British storms; and towards the end of the debate he intervened to voice his regret at the publication of Mr Darwin's book and to deny Mr Huxley's claim that it was a logical arrangement of facts. He had, he said, often expostulated with his old comrade of the *Beagle* for entertaining views contradictory of the first chapter of Genesis. That, Darwin knew well, FitzRoy regarded as a conclusive argument.

The *Evening Star* of the following day carried an account of the meeting, giving half its space to the debate:

The soundness or unsoundness of the Darwinian theory gave rise to a long and very animated discussion. The Bishop of Oxford, in a speech of great power and eloquence, which produced a marked effect upon the audience, denounced the theory as unphilosophical, as one based upon mere fancy instead of facts, and one which, in its effect, was degrading to the dignity of human nature. He alluded, in a forcible manner, to the weight of authority which had been brought to bear against it – to such men as Sir B. Brodie and Professor Owen – both of whom, with many others eminent for their scientific attainments, had opposed it; and he denied that the supporters of the theory could adduce one single fact to prove that the alleged change from one species to another had ever taken place. Professor Huxley, in reply, alluded to his lordship as an 'unscientific authority', and then proceeded to defend the Darwinian theory in an argumentative speech, which was loudly applauded. Several other speakers, including Admiral Fitzroy, Dr Hooker, Mr. Lubbock, Dr Beale, and Mr Purdy, spoke on the question, and, so far as we could judge, the new Darwinian theory, whatever may be its real merits in a scientific point of view, has no small number of supporters amongst the members of the Association.

Though honours were even, the publicity was entirely to Darwin's advantage. That was his own view.

Later in July, writing to Huxley a second time, he gives mature judgement: 'From all that I hear from several quarters, it seems that Oxford did the subject great good. It is of enormous importance, the showing the world that a few first-rate men are not afraid of expressing their opinion.'[22]

Concurrently, another first-rate man was doing great good in the USA. During July, August and October the *Atlantic Monthly* carried three articles by Asa Gray expounding and supporting Darwin's ideas. So pleased was Darwin with them that he arranged for them to be republished in Britain, where he believed they made many converts.[23]

IV

Meanwhile, since late April Etty's health had again been giving rise to acute anxiety. In his letter to Fox of 18 May 1860 Charles reports that she had 'now been 3 weeks ill with *odd* fever, partly [illegible word], partly typhoid; . . . it has harassed us much.' More than once Charles called in Sir Henry Holland, now one of the leading London physicians. In early July, soon after Charles's return from Sudbrook Park, he and Emma took Etty on a visit to Emma's eldest sister, Elizabeth, at Hartfield, where they stayed until the end of the month. Charles continued intensely anxious about Etty and gave her almost compulsive attention. Writing on 28 August from Down to Lady Lyell, Emma comments on his constant anxiety and on the beneficent role of his work: 'Charles is too much given to anxiety, as you know, and his various experiments this summer have been a great blessing to him.' She then adds: 'I have also succeeded pretty well in teaching myself not to give way to despondency, but live from day to day. We had the bad luck at Hartfield to fall into the hands of a desponding medical man, and it was really a great injury to us. . . . We then had a visit from Sir Henry Holland who cheered us again.'[24]

Intense preoccupation with Etty's health continued and led to their spending two months during the autumn at Eastbourne (from 22 September to 16 November). 'We came here for chance of the sea doing Etty good,' Charles writes to Fox on 18 October, 'and it has certainly to a certain extent succeeded. At one time [during] this illness I gave up all hopes of her recovery, but she does gain strength at a snail's pace, and now suffers from indigestion and weakness.'[25] Although apparently Charles makes no reference at this time to Annie's illness and death nine years earlier, the resemblance of the two girl's symptoms must constantly have been in his mind. His mother had died of gastric trouble; and so had

Annie. Now it must have seemed Etty was going the same way. 'I have done little of my regular work this summer,' he tells Fox, 'chiefly owing to incessant anxiety and [illegible word] on account of Etty.'

Later in the same letter Darwin notes that his correspondence about the *Origin* was continuing to be 'gigantic' and that he was also amusing himself 'with a little natural history of other kinds'. Here he is referring to the various experiments that Emma had mentioned as having been such a great blessing to him since they took his mind off his worries. The experiments concerned sundew (*Drosera*), a small fly-eating bog-plant with which he had become fascinated while at Hartfield in July. Another botanical interest that had been stimulated during the same visit was the fertilisation of orchids by insects. In this casual way, during the year after the *Origin's* publication, began Darwin's strikingly original contributions to yet another of the natural sciences.

To start with Darwin had won distinction as a geologist; next he had turned zoologist and was winning fame as the author of the *Origin*; now in 1860 he began twenty years of botanical experiments that would initiate a number of novel lines of research in plant physiology. His persisting anxiety, destructive though it was to his health and happiness, impelled him to engage in endless diversionary study, and this, coupled to an extraordinarily fertile mind and retentive memory, played its part in the enormous contributions he had already made and was still to make to the natural sciences.

Francis Darwin tells how his father regarded his botanical experiments as a 'rest or holiday' from the trials of marshalling facts and reasoning about them, required by works like the *Origin* and its successors.[26] Already in January 1860, as soon as the second edition of the *Origin* was out, Darwin had begun work on another great compilation, *The Variation of Animals and Plants under Domestication*, which was to include the extensive data he had collected, intended originally for inclusion in the big book. This work had been interrupted by his visits to Sudbrook Park and Hartfield; and there he had become seduced by his discovery of the carnivorous activities of *Drosera*. As a result the rest of the year was spent in its study, first at Down, then during the two months at Eastbourne, and finally back at Down. Simultaneously he was conducting 'an immense correspondence with Lyell', in which he replied patiently and at length to the succession of difficulties that his old master continued to find in his theories. At the end of one of these letters (12 September), Darwin apologises for his idleness: 'I have been of late shamefully idle, i.e. observing [*Drosera*], instead of writing and how much better fun observing is than writing.'[27]

During the visit to Eastbourne Darwin wrote a series of letters to his old Cambridge tutor, Henslow, whom he was consulting about his observations on *Drosera* 'as I am so ignorant of vegetable physiology'. Along with the botanical questions, Charles charts Etty's initial improvement

OPINIONS

OF

MEN OF LIGHT & LEADING

And of the TIMES Newspaper, &c.,

ON

THE DARWIN CRAZE.

"A Gospel of Dirt."—THOMAS CARLYLE.

"I venture to think that no system of Philosophy that has ever been taught on earth lies under such a weight of antecedent improbability."
THE DUKE OF ARGYLL, in the *Contemporary Review.*

"The subtle sophistries of his (Huxley's) school are doing infinitely more mischief than the outspoken blasphemy of Bradlaugh."
J. M. WINN, M.D., M.R.C.P.

"The Science of those of his books which have made his chief title to fame, the "Origin of Species," and still more the "Descent of Man," is not Science but a mass of assertions and absolutely gratuitous hypotheses, often evidently fallacious. This kind of publication and these theories are a bad example, which a body that respects itself cannot encourage."—LES MONDES.

(Darwin having been refused membership, as a correspondent with the French Academy of Sciences, on the ground of the unscientific character of his books.)

BY

THE REV. F. O. MORRIS, B.A.,

Rector of Nunburnholme, Yorkshire,

AUTHOR OF "A HISTORY OF BRITISH BIRDS,"

Dedicated by permission to Her Most Gracious Majesty the Queen.

LONDON: W. S. PARTRIDGE & CO., PATERNOSTER ROW.

PRICE ONE PENNY.

Collection of adverse opinions of Darwin's theory (published in 1885) and subsequent relapse. On 26 October, a month after arriving, he reports: 'My poor girl improved during the first four weeks here, but has had this last week a fearful attack, and is much exhausted, and we are much dispirited about her. – When we shall be able to take her home I cannot conjecture.' A fortnight later however, he notes on 10 November that she is a little better: 'We return home this afternoon as my poor dear girl is now just strong enough to bear removal.'[28]

Darwin had always kept in touch with Henslow, and contact became easier after Hooker married Henslow's daughter. After Henslow's departure from Cambridge to become a country parson in Suffolk, their correspondence was usually about botany. Darwin was forever seeking information, which Henslow gladly supplied. In addition, Henslow got children of his parish to collect the seeds of wild flowers that Darwin asked for. Henslow was no theorist, and Darwin never referred to his evolutionary interests in his letters. Nevertheless Henslow kept his links with science and attended meetings of the Cambridge Philosophical Society. Soon after the *Origin*'s publication, the society had held a meeting at which Sedgwick and others had attacked Darwin. Describing the event to his son-in-law, Henslow writes on 10 May 1860: 'I got up . . . and stuck up for Darwin as well as I could, refusing to allow that he was guided by any but truthful motives. . . . I believe I succeeded in diminishing, if not entirely removing, the chances of Darwin's being prejudged . . . I do not disguise my own opinion that Darwin has pressed his hypothesis too far, but at the same time I assert my belief that his Book is (as Owen described it to me) the "Book of the Day".' Henslow asks that Hooker forward his letter to Darwin, who writes to thank him 'for so generously defending me as far as you could against my powerful attackers. . . . Believe me my dear Henslow I feel grateful to you on this occasion and for the multitude of kindnesses you have done me from my earliest days in Cambridge.'[29]

Shortly afterwards Henslow's strong sense of fair play proved of incalculable value when, by chance, he happened to be in the chair when the stormy debate blew up at Oxford.

V

On 22 November 1860 Darwin heard from his publisher that yet another edition of the *Origin* was called for.[30] This was an opportunity to deal with numerous misunderstandings and other difficulties that had been revealed in the reviews; the necessary expansions led to the addition of twenty pages. It was also an opportunity to make good the omission from the first edition of any mention of his many forerunners in the study of species and their possible evolution, an omission commented on acidly by Owen and justified by Darwin on the grounds that the book was no more than an abstract of a definitive work. In the third edition, therefore, he included a twelve-page 'Historical Sketch'. This has often been criticised as perfunctory.[31] Generous though Darwin always was to those whose empirical observations he found useful, he barely acknowledged those whose ideas had influenced him. By far the most unexpected feature of the 'Sketch' is the dismissive way in which he refers to the contribution of his eminent grandfather, Erasmus Darwin, who receives mention only in a footnote as having preceded Lamarck in advancing certain erroneous opinions. Work on the third edition was completed in January 1861 and it was published in April. Meanwhile, during 1860 a rather unsatisfactory German edition had appeared, with a chapter by the translator, H. G. Bronn, in which he advances a number of objections of his own to Darwin's thesis.[32] Nevertheless the fact that the *Origin* was stirring interest in Germany was a source of satisfaction. A Dutch edition had also appeared.

At the turn of the year Darwin was still acutely worried about Etty and again suffering symptoms of his own. In a letter to Hooker of 4 December 1860 thanking him for botanical information, Darwin reports of Etty that though 'the Doctors do not despair, I almost do'; and then adds a postscript: 'I believe I shall have to go soon for some water cure, I cannot sleep and my heart is almost always palpitating.' To Fox a fortnight later he writes, 'I have been of late rather below my low mark'; and to Hooker on 15 January 1861 he says: 'I continually suspect I shall soon entirely fail; my stomach keeps bad heart all day and night.'[23] It was at this time that he had ideas of going to Malvern again, but refrained from doing so for fear it would revive painful memories of Annie's death almost ten years earlier (as recounted in chapter 20).

It was also about this time that Emma wrote her second letter to Charles regretting his absence of religious faith, to which he again appended his initials, and which was found later with his papers.[34] (The first, it will be remembered, had been written shortly after their marriage; see chapter 15.) The letter ends:

I feel presumptuous in writing this to you. I feel in my inmost heart your admirable qualities and feelings and all I would hope is that you would direct them upwards, as well as to one who values them above everything in the world. I shall keep this by me till I feel cheerful and comfortable again about you but it passed through my mind often lately so I thought I would write it partly to relieve my own mind.

God Bless you. C.D. 1861

Of Emma's outlook on religion Henrietta writes:

In our childhood and youth she was not only sincerely religious . . . but definite in her beliefs. She went regularly to church and took the Sacrament. She read the Bible with us and taught us a simple Unitarian Creed, though we were baptized and confirmed in the Church of England. In her youth religion must have largely filled her life, and there is evidence in the papers she left that it distressed her, in her early married life, to know that my father did not share her faith. . . . I remember once, when I was a girl, her telling me that she had often felt she could only bear her anxiety by saying a prayer for help.'[35]

That spring, March 1861, Darwin received bad news. Henslow, his tutor and friend, was dying. Hooker was nursing him at the rectory in Suffolk and was encouraging Darwin to visit. This put Darwin into an acute conflict. On the one hand he felt he ought to go, on the other he feared how it would affect him. On 23 April he writes Hooker a long letter explaining his dilemma: 'I write now only to say that if Henslow, you thought, would really like to see me, I would of course start at once. The thought had once occurred to me to offer, and the sole reason why I did not was that the going with the agitation would cause me probably to arrive utterly prostrated, I should be certain to have severe vomiting afterwards. . . . I doubt whether I could stand the agitation at the time.' At the end of the letter he repeats what he had said earlier: 'I should *never* forgive myself if I disappointed the most fleeting wish of my master and friend to whom I owe so much.'[36]

Sad to say, Darwin never went, and Henslow died the following month, aged sixty-five. He had played a crucial role in Darwin's life and been a steadfast friend. It is difficult not to link Darwin's failure to go with earlier occasions when he had found mortal illness and death almost more than he could bear.

Despite this bad start, 1861 was to prove a better year than the three previous ones. In early February Darwin had written to Hooker that Henrietta's health was improving and that she 'can sometimes get up for an hour or two twice a day. . . . Never to look to the future or as little as possible is becoming our rule of life.' Her improvement seems to have continued, since by midsummer she had recovered. Meanwhile, he tells Hooker in early February, he 'was crawling on most slowly, with my volume of "Variation under Domestication".'[37]

During early April Darwin spent four enjoyable days in London staying with Ras (who had recently moved to a house in Queen Anne Street, off Harley Street) and meeting a number of friends, including Lyell, Robert Chambers, author of the *Vestiges*, and Thomas Bell (1792–1880), the dental surgeon and zoologist who had described the reptiles collected during the *Beagle* voyage. After returning to Down he writes a long letter to Hooker on 15 April: 'I dined with Bell at the Linnean Club . . . dining out is such a novelty to me that I enjoyed it. Bell has a real good heart.' He had called on Chambers, and had had 'a very pleasant half-hour's talk – he is really a capital fellow'; and with Lyell he had had 'a splendid long talk' about his geological work in France: 'You may guess how splendid,' he adds, 'for he was many times on his knees, with elbows on the sofa.' Lyell's eccentric behaviour when excited by a topic was a familiar sight to his friends. Then, commenting on yet another episode in the feud between Huxley and Owen, he writes: 'Huxley's letter was truculent, and

I see everyone thinks it too truculent': 'but,' he continues in a passage already quoted, 'in simple truth I am become quite demoniacal about Owen – worse than Huxley.'[38]

Constant irritant though Owen was and would continue to be, Darwin's admirers were on the increase. At the British Association meeting in Manchester that year Henry Fawcett (1833–84), a young man destined shortly to hold the chair of political economy at Cambridge, had spoken strongly in defence of the scientific method employed by Darwin in the *Origin*. Darwin was grateful, since that was still a favourite topic for attack by his opponents. In writing to thank Fawcett, Darwin makes some scathing criticisms of the atheoretical empiricism that critics seemed to advocate: 'You will have done good service in calling the attention of scientific men to means and laws of philosophising. . . . About thirty years ago there was much talk that geologists ought only to observe and not theorise; and I well remember someone saying that at this rate a man might as well go into a gravel-pit and count the pebbles and describe the colours. How odd it is that anyone should not see that all observation must be for or against some view if it is to be of any service.'[39]

Darwin had not been at Manchester. Instead, on 1 July, the family went to Torquay, where they had an unusually successful eight-week holiday, accompanied as usual by Ras. 'The boys were full of enjoyment', and Emma took Etty for a little tour round Dartmoor, 'the only one Emma ever took in all her married life'. Furthermore, Charles was also in better shape. Three weeks after arriving he writes to Lyell: 'This is quite a charming place, and I have actually walked, I believe, good two miles out and back, which is a grand feat.'[40] He had, of course, taken work with him, but it was another of his new botanical hobbies, the fertilisation of orchids, not the great two-volume compilation on *Variation in Animals and Plants* which was to be a burden on him for several years yet.

Though feeling rather guily at neglecting *Variation*, Darwin continued working on orchids for the rest of the year. It gave him the utmost pleasure to puzzle out the various ingenious devices which different species had developed to enable their fertilisation to be accomplished by some particular species of insect. Hooker sent him specimens from Kew. From Torquay on 27 July Darwin replies acknowledging receipt of a consignment: 'You cannot conceive how the Orchids have delighted me.'[41] Since during this period his health seems not to have been much trouble, work on the orchids appears to have been the occupational therapy he needed.

It proved, however, a good deal more than occupational therapy. The work demonstrated that even seemingly trivial variations of structure had a valuable adaptive function and that arguments to the contrary, repeatedly advanced by critics, were groundless. Not surprisingly, the manuscript in which Darwin was presenting his findings outran a journal article and he offered it to Murray, who wisely jumped at it. Published on 15 May 1862, it received a chorus of praise from the botanists.[42]

Meanwhile, in March 1862, a French edition of the *Origin* had appeared. As in the case of Bronn's German edition, the translator, Mademoiselle Royer, had added some uncalled-for opinions of her own, though this time naïvely enthusiastic: 'in many places where the author expresses great doubt,' Francis Darwin comments 'she explains the difficulty, or points out that no real difficulty exists.'[43]

VI

During these years Wallace was still out in the East Indies, pursuing his collecting in the remotest islands, including some months in New Guinea. In February 1860 he returned to his base in Ternate, where his 1858 paper had been conceived and written during an inspired week while suffering from fever. There he found waiting for him the copy of the *Origin* sent him by Darwin. From the moment he read it he became the warmest of admirers. To one old friend he writes with generous enthusiasm: 'I have read it through five or six times, each time with increasing admiration. It will live as long as the *Principia* of Newton.' To another, Bates, he proceeds: 'I do honestly believe that with however much patience I had worked and experimented on the subject, I could *never* have approached the completeness of this book, its vast accumulation of evidence, its overwhelming argument, and its admirable tone and spirit. I really feel thankful it has *not* been left to me to give the theory to the world.'[44]

Wallace's letter to Darwin dated 16 February 1860 has not survived but its contents can be partly guessed. On receiving it in May, Darwin replies immediately: 'your letter has pleased me very much, and I most completely agree with you on the parts [of the *Origin*] which are strongest and which are weakest. . . . Before telling you about the progress of opinion on the subject [which he later does at length], you must let me say how I admire the generous manner in which you speak of my book. Most persons would in your position have felt some envy or jealousy. How nobly free you seem to be of this common failing of mankind. But you speak far too modestly of yourself. You would, if you had my leisure have done the work just as well, perhaps better, than I have done it.'[45]

It was not until the spring of 1862 that Wallace at last returned to England and began sorting his gigantic collection of specimens. In August he visited Darwin at Down, any hint of rivalry long extinguished. Step by step they became more intimate.

In May 1864 there is a characteristic exchange of letters. Darwin writes appreciatively to Wallace about an article he had recently published in the *Anthropological Review* discussing the evolutionary status of man. At the end of his long reply Wallace describes how he sees their respective contributions to evolution: 'As to the theory of Natural Selection itself, I shall always maintain it to be yours and yours only. You had worked it out in details I had never thought of, years before I had a ray of light on the subject, and my paper would never have convinced anybody or been noticed as more than an ingenious speculation, whereas your book has revolutionised the study of Natural History and carried away captive the best men of the present age. All the merit I claim is the having been the means of inducing you to write and publish at once.'[46]

Although for some years the self-educated Wallace remained diffident about entering the heated public controversy about evolution and was overawed by the distinguished champions on each side, he gradually became a most effective participant. After writing a succession of competent descriptive papers, during the following decade he would produce a distinguished and pathbreaking work on the *Geographical Distribution of Animals* (1876).

At this point it is interesting to ask how great was the coincidence that Darwin and Wallace should both have come to advance the same revolutionary theory in the middle of the nineteenth century? Light is cast when the sequence of events is traced.

The steps by which Wallace reached his conclusions were almost identical to those followed twenty years earlier by Darwin. Both of them as young men had become familiar with the idea of evolution, Darwin from his grandfather, Wallace from the *Vestiges*. Similarly, both had, early in their careers, read and digested Lyell's *Principles of Geology*. During long years as field naturalists both had become steeped in the facts and problems of geographical distribution. Both, moreover, had been struck by the ubiquity of variation and the frequent difficulty of distinguishing varieties from species. To each of them the solution had come in a flash of light when he suddenly saw the relevance to the problem of Malthus's thesis, namely that the powerful propensity of every species to propagate requires that each has a high death-rate, especially among eggs, seeds and young, if its numbers are to remain as stable as they normally do.

As the younger man Wallace had certain advantages. For example, he had read the second edition of Darwin's *Beagle Journal* and had taken note of the remarkable facts about the animal and plant species in the Galapagos Islands that Darwin reports in that edition: this we know from Wallace's having used them in his Sarawak paper. It may well be, moreover, that the perspicacious Wallace had read a good deal between the lines of the guarded passages in which Darwin hints at his ideas on evolution in that edition, and that he had been more influenced by them than he realised. Finally, Wallace had the advantage of knowing that he was not alone in tackling the great problem of species, that no less a naturalist than Darwin believed it could be solved. Nevertheless, even with these advantages Wallace's was a great achievement. Carl Pantin (sometime Professor of Zoology at Cambridge), who had examined all Wallace's scientific contributions, believes indeed that, had Darwin not produced the *Origin*, Wallace could well have filled his place by writing his own book in his own way.[47]

VII

Though 1861 had been a better year for Darwin and the family, further anxieties were close ahead. First, he was worried about Horace, now aged eleven. 'We have of late had much anxiety about our youngest Boy, who has failed in some way, but worse than other of our children,' he tells Fox in a letter of 12 May 1862.[48] Then, later in the summer, serious illness again visited Down. This time it was Leonard, then a boy of twelve, who, Henrietta recalls, 'had scarlet fever most dangerously, and hung between life and death for weeks'.[49] Charles was distraught. Writing to Asa Gray on 23 July to acknowledge receipt of two large packets that he had not yet looked at, he explains:

we have been in fearful distress, and I could attend to nothing. . . . I despaired of his life; but this evening he has eaten one mouthful and I think has passed the crisis. He has lived on port wine every three-quarters of an hour day and night.. . . Children are one's greatest happiness, but often and often a still greater misery. A man of science ought to have none – perhaps not a wife; for then there would be nothing in this wide world worth caring for, and a man might (whether he could is another question) work away like a Trojan. I hope in a few days to get my brains in order, and then I will pick out all your orchid letters.[50]

No sooner had Leonard recovered, however, than Emma, 'at the end of her long period of nursing . . . caught the fever herself and was very ill'. The fever struck her at Southampton, where the family was staying overnight with William on their way to convalesce in Bournemouth. When the local doctor talked about all the possible complications of Emma's illness Charles became 'sick with terror' and thereafter always recalled 'with indignation' the Southampton doctor's carelessness in doing so.[51] Writing again to Asa Gray from Southampton on 21 August, Darwin bemoans: 'We are a wretched family, and ought to be exterminated. We slept here to rest our poor boy on his journey to Bournemouth, and my poor dear wife sickened with scarlet fever and had it pretty sharply, but is recovering well. There is no end of trouble in this weary world. I shall not feel safe till we are all at home together, and when that will be I know not.' September was spent in Bournemouth, whence he writes to Fox. After thanking him for his sympathy, he continues: 'I have never passed so miserable a nine [?] months. . . . All the misery has shaken me a good deal.' Then, a week later, he writes: 'All Darwins ought to be exterminated.'[52] Before their return to Down he had had ideas of going on to Cambridge for the last days of the British Association meeting there, but in the end decided not to go.

Throughout 1862 more reviews of the *Origin* arrived and also letters, many of them welcome ones from old friends and new scientific acquaintances, others, occasionally amusing, from cranks. All were answered. To H. W. Bates, the close friend of Wallace, who had made brilliantly original studies of mimicry in butterflies,* he sends warm congratulations on 20 November and ends a long letter: 'How gets on your book? Keep your spirits up. A book is no light labour. I have been better lately, and working hard, but my health is very indifferent. How is your health?'[53]

At this time Bates was busy preparing a book describing his travels in South America. Published the following spring under the title *The Naturalist on the river Amazons*, it called forth Darwin's highest praise: 'it is the best book of Natural History Travels ever published,' he writes enthusiastically to the author. 'Nothing can be better than the discussion on the struggle for existence.'[54] Others also valued Bates's works. In 1864 he was appointed assistant secretary to the Royal Geographical Society (a post he would hold until his death in 1892) and in 1881 he was elected a fellow of the Royal Society.

At the end of 1862 Hooker in a letter to a botanist friend sums up Darwin's achievements and scientific reputation:

Darwin still works away at his experiments and his theory and startles us by the surprising discoveries he now makes in Botany; his work on the fertilization of orchids is quite unique – there is nothing in the whole range of Botanical Literature to compare with it, and this, with his other works, 'Journal', 'Coral Reefs', 'Volcanic Islands', 'Geology of Beagle', 'Anatomy etc. of Cirripedes' and 'Origin' raise him without doubt to the position of the first Naturalist of Europe, indeed I question if he will not be regarded as great as any that ever lived; his powers of observation, memory and judgement seem prodigious, his industry indefatigable and his sagacity in planning experiments, fertility of resources and care in conducting them are unrivalled, and all this with health so detestable that his life is a curse to him and more than half his days and weeks are spent in inaction – in forced idleness of mind and body.[55]

---

*The process whereby a non-poisonous insect comes to show the same warning colour patterns as a poisonous one, thus enabling it to escape predation.

TWENTY-FOUR

A fearful disappointment
1863–1867

I

The year 1863 began with Darwin pushing on with *Variation of Animals and Plants under Domestication*, a comprehensive work presenting an array of evidence that extends and underpins much of the argument in the *Origin*. He also continued his scientific correspondence, much of it with overseas admirers, and was especially pleased with a set of lectures Huxley had published on the *Causes of Organic Nature* in which he lavishes praise on the *Origin* and which Darwin thought would do much to disseminate knowledge of natural history. During the first days of January, as we have seen, he was upset by Owen's having made unauthorized use of Falconer's work and was 'burning with indignation about it'. This led to an outbreak of eczema which, he tells Falconer, had 'taken the epidermis a dozen times clean off; but I have been knocked up of late with extraordinary facility'. To his great regret, he was unable to come to London to see his friends.[1] A month later, however, he and Emma spent ten days in town staying with Ras – a change that brought much benefit: 'wonderfully improved', he tells Hooker in mid-February after their return to Down.[2]

At that moment a blow fell which had a devastating effect on him.

During the past couple of years Darwin had been confident that Lyell, in his new book on the geological history of man, was going to declare himself in favour of evolution. Although its appearance had been expected much earlier, publication was not until February 1863, when it appeared under the title *The Antiquity of Man*. Darwin read it immediately and described his reactions in a letter to Hooker. When he first turned over the pages and saw that Lyell had discussed the subject of species, he had thought Lyell 'would do more to convert the public than all of us', but on reading further he had found himself utterly mistaken. After all his high hopes, this was an appallingly bitter disappointment.

In his letter to Hooker of 24 February, after expressing admiration for much in the book, he proceeds: 'but I am deeply disappointed (I do not mean personally) to find that his timidity prevents him giving any judgement. . . . I had hoped he would have guided the public as far as his own belief went.' Then, at the end of this long letter, he remarks: 'The Lyells are coming here on Sunday evening to stay till Wednesday. I dread it, but I must say how much disappointed I am that he has not spoken out on species.' Two days later he writes similarly to Huxley: 'I am fearfully disappointed at Lyell's excessive caution in expressing any judgement on Species or [on the] origin of Man.'[3]

Darwin's health deteriorated at once. In a further letter to Hooker on 5 March he reports: 'I have been having very bad 10 days with much sickness and weakness, and have been obliged to stop the Lyells. It breaks my heart, but Emma says, I believe truly, that we must all go for two months to Malvern. It is very pricking after London doing me so much good.'[4] Having stopped the visit, Darwin writes to Lyell on 6 March:

I have been of course deeply interested by your book. I have hardly any remarks worth sending, but will scribble a little on what most interested me. But I will first get out what I hate saying, viz., that I have been greatly disappointed that you have not given judgement and spoken fairly out what you think about the derivation of species. I should have been contented if you had boldly said that species have not been separately created, and had thrown as much doubt as you like on how far variation and natural selection suffices. . . . I think the *Parthenon* is right, that you will leave the public in a fog. . . . But I had always thought that your judgement would have been an epoch in the subject. All that is over with me.[5]

On receiving Darwin's letter Lyell, clearly much concerned, first writes to Hooker on 9 March: '[Darwin] seems much disappointed that I do not go farther with him, or do not speak out more. I can only say that I have spoken out to the full extent of my present convictions, and even beyond my state of *feeling* as to man's unbroken descent from the brutes.' Two days later he explains to Darwin:

I think the old 'creation' is almost as much required as ever, but of course it takes a new form if Lamarck's views improved by yours are adopted . . . .

But you ought to be satisfied, as I shall bring hundreds towards you, who if I treated the matter more dogmatically would have rebelled.

I have spoken out to the utmost extent of my tether so far as my reason goes, and farther than my imagination and sentiment can follow, which I suppose has caused occasional incongruities.

In a second long explanatory letter to Darwin a few days later, on 15 March, Lyell makes clear what the sticking point is: 'I remember that it was the conclusion he [Lamarck] came to about man that fortified me thirty years ago against the great impression which his arguments first made on my mind.' Yet, Lyell proceeds, judged by the standard of his times Lamarck had made some good points about the slow changes that had occurred in the organic and inorganic world. Then, defending himself, he adds, 'Have I not at p. 412 put the vast distinction between you and Lamarck as to "necessary progression" strong enough . . .? I am sorry you have to go to Malvern. The good of the water-cure is abstinence from work; a tour abroad would do it, I am persuaded, as effectually and more profitably. I hope my long letter will not task you too much . . . . Hooker, not having heard from you, is growing anxious, and hopes it is . . . not because of serious ill-health.'[6] Evidently Lyell is also anxious. As usual he signs himself, 'Ever affectionately yours'.

During this flurry of letter-writing Lyell's constant reference to Lamarck's work becomes a red rag to Darwin. Already in a letter of 12 March Darwin had stated his objections: 'Lastly, you refer repeatedly to my view as a modification of Lamarck's doctrine. . . . I believe this way of putting the case is very injurious to its acceptance. . . . [Lamarck's is] a wretched book, and one from which (I well remember my surprise) I gained nothing.' Next day he tells Hooker of his feelings: 'I have grumbled a bit in my answer to him at his *always* classing my work as a modification of Lamarck's.' A few days later (17 March) he is apologising to Lyell for having complained, but cannot resist repeating his opinion that, for him, Lamarck's is 'an absolutely useless book'. Then, in explanation, he adds: 'Perhaps this was owing to my always searching books for facts, perhaps from knowing my grandfather's earlier and identically the same speculation.' He ends by telling Lyell how favourably the *Origin* is being greeted in Germany, France and America.[7]

Deeply disappointing to Darwin though Lyell's attitude was, it is again necessary to look at the situation from Lyell's point of view. It was now seven years since he had first learned of Darwin's theory. During the last three his reason had been telling him that Darwin would in the end be proved right. Yet that was a deeply unpalatable conclusion, and one he still could not bring himself to accept. (Hooker, it should be recalled, had taken fourteen years to make up his mind.) As it turned out, although Lyell became increasingly impressed by the powerful explanatory value of Darwin's theory and commended it strongly to his friends, he continued to baulk at its application to man.[8] Thus he never came out unequivocally in favour of Darwin's theory, keen supporter of Darwin as scientist and personal friend though he continued to be. For many a scientist in Darwin's position such hesitation would no doubt have been disappointing; but only for someone so intensely in need of approval and support from an older man would it prove traumatic.

The poor state of Darwin's health, which had deteriorated immediately after the crushing disappointment, continued through the spring and summer.[9] One of the many symptoms that had troubled him over the years was eczema, and he held the view that so long as he had eczema he was in better general health. For example, after referring to his cancellation of the Lyells' visit in the letter of 5 March to Hooker, he had continued: 'A good severe fit of Eczema would do me good'; and three months later, on 23 June, again to Hooker, he writes that his eczema had stopped and that without it he felt 'languid and bedeviled'. During these months he consulted a skin specialist and also yet another physician, Dr William Jenner. For a couple of weeks in late April and early May he and Emma visited her sister Elizabeth at Hartfield and then on for a few days more to Joe and Caroline at Leith Hill Place; but after their return to Down Darwin tells Fox, on 23 May, 'the change did me no good and I have been mostly in bed for the last week from my old evening sickness. . . . All this everlasting illness has stopped my work much.' At the end of this gloomy letter he makes further reference to Horace: 'Our youngest boy is a regular invalid with severe indigestion, clearly inherited from me.'[10]

At Hartfield the previous year Emma's sister Charlotte Langton had died at the age of sixty-five after a longish illness during which Emma had often visited her. In October 1863, after eighteen months of widowhood, Charles Langton married Darwin's youngest sister, Catherine, now aged fifty-three.

<h2 style="text-align:center">II</h2>

There was indeed no improvement in Darwin's health during the summer months of 1863. Nevertheless, until mid-July he pushed on doggedly with *Variation of Animals and Plants*, which had occupied him since the beginning of the year. He had in fact been making remarkable progress – during the first three months of the year three chapters, during April and May another five and a further two chapters up to 20 July.[11] Thereafter his condition deteriorated sharply, including vomiting every morning, so that for the next nine months he was unable to do any serious work at all. The evidence strongly suggests that this breakdown was a reaction, only slightly delayed, to Lyell's having failed to give him the support for which he was so desperately eager and on which he had been so confidently counting – the fearful disappointment, to use his own words.

Despite having heard that Dr Gully was seriously ill, the family moved to Malvern on 2 September, almost certainly on Emma's initiative. They rented a house and Charles undertook a modified course of hydropathy. On 6 October he reports to Hooker: 'I am very weak and can write little. My nervous system has failed and I am kept going only by repeated doses of brandy.' When Dr Gully recovered, however, he decided that Darwin was not strong enough to bear the water treatment. The family therefore returned to Down on 14 October. Meanwhile Horace had been receiving treatment for his indigestion and, Emma reports, had been put on to 'a better system'.[12]

Four weeks after their arrival in Malvern Emma had given a progress report to Fox (on 29 September). In it she describes how it was only with difficulty that she had found Annie's grave, which she had been eager to do, and how shocked she had been that the stone had been removed. Subsequently it had been found and replaced. Whether Charles had had courage enough to visit the grave remains unclear.[13]

Writing many years later, Francis Darwin describes his father's condition during the autumn and winter at Down: 'He returned [from Malvern] in October, and remained ill and depressed, in spite of the hopeful opinion of one of the most cheery and skilful physicians of the day.' This was Dr William Brinton, a specialist in diseases of the stomach, who in a recent book had emphasised 'undue intellectual exertion' and 'mental anxiety' as first among the causes of dyspepsia.[14] After Brinton's visit to Down, Darwin informs Hooker of the verdict on 10 November: 'he does not believe my brain or heart are primarily affected, but I have been so steadily going downhill, I cannot help doubting whether I can ever crawl a little uphill again. Unless I can, enough to work a little, I hope my life may be very short, for to lie on a sofa all day and do nothing but give trouble to the best and kindest of wives and good dear children is dreadful.' In another note referring to his father's condition during the winter of 1863–4, Francis again refers to it as a 'period of ill-health and depression' during which his father 'despaired of ever being able' to utilise his notes on the evolution of man.[15] Thus, although Francis Darwin is the only one to use the word 'depressed', it seems evident that this is the word that most aptly describes his father's condition.

A series of weekly bulletins addressed to Hooker records the ups and downs of Darwin's health, on one day rather better and on the next worse again. In November he reports six days with no vomiting, but on 5 December: 'I have had a bad spell, vomiting every day for eleven days.' In the same letter he sympathises with Hooker about illness (or threat of it) in the family and proceeds: 'Nothing is so dreadful in this life as fear; it still sickens me when I cannot help remembering some of the many illnesses our children have endured.'[16]

During the same month Emma gives an account of Charles's condition to Fox, an account apparently at variance with a diagnosis of depression: 'He is wonderfully cheerful when not positively uncomfortable. He does not feel the least temptation to disobey orders about working for he feels quite incapable of doing anything. His good symptoms are losing no flesh and having a good appetite so that I fully hope that in time he will regain his usual standard of health which is not saying much for him.'[17]

During the early months of 1864 Darwin's condition, as revealed by his regular bulletins to Hooker, was little changed. Even so, it is clear that he was reading scientific literature and engaging in a certain amount of correspondence. For example, on 1 January 1864 he writes to Wallace to tell him of Gray's strong praise of his (Wallace's) papers. Spread through the letter are various references to his own condition: 'I am still unable to write otherwise than by dictation. . . . Now, although I cannot read at present, I much want to know . . . [and there follows a quantity of

Asa Gray, aged 57 in 1867

Alfred Russel Wallace, aged about 40,
circa 1863

questions]. It will be many months before I shall do anything.'[18] Several of his letters to Hooker, moreover, include references to a Scottish gardener, John Scott, with whom during the previous year he had been having a long correspondence about the fertilisation of orchids. Although Scott was largely self-educated, Darwin had a high opinion of his potential, had arranged for one of his papers to be published in the *Linnean Journal* and was eager to get him a suitable post. Letters on these issues were sent by Darwin at intervals throughout this ill-fated winter.[19] In one of them he very characteristically advises Scott: 'Do not work too hard to injure your health.'

Returning to Darwin's own health, we learn some details from a letter to Hooker written on 22 February 1864: 'You ask about my sickness – it rarely comes on till 2–3 hours after eating, so that I seldom throw-up food, only acid and morbid secretion; otherwise I should have been dead. . . . On my well days I am certainly stronger.'[20] During all these months he was nursed by Emma, assisted by his manservant Parslow, who had been with him many years. Emma and Henrietta read to him light romantic novels which amused him.

During March he was again in the care of Dr William Jenner, whose treatment he thought was doing him much good, so that by April he was 'gaining vigour'. Nevertheless, Emma thought it would still be unwise for Fox to visit them at Down, as he had proposed. Explaining the position, Emma writes on 6 May 1864: 'I must tell you how ill Charles has been since we were at Malvern. He has had almost daily vomiting for 6 months, and it was becoming a great anxiety that it should be stopped. . . . Dr. Jenner. . . . has succeeded in stopping [it] and he has been 3 weeks free from it, but I am afraid of the least exertion bringing it on till the stomach has more recovered its strength. . . . The day we saw you in London last spring has been almost the last time of his being tolerably well. He is still in his room and goes to bed more than once a day, but he walks out of doors and occupies himself a good deal with experiments with his flowers.'[21]

One consequence of Charles's liking for botanical experiments had been that he had built himself a greenhouse. When he was feeling a little stronger than usual he liked to go there – which entailed a walk of rather more than 100 yards. 'I am getting better, I almost dare to hope permanently;' he writes to Huxley on 11 April; 'for my sickness is decidedly less – for twenty-seven days consecutively I was sick many times daily, and lately I was five days free. I long to do a little work again.' Yet earlier in the same letter he had remarked, with some insight: 'I feel it in myself possible to get to care too much for Natural Science and too little for other things.'[22] In reply (18 April) Huxley, who was also given to overwork, seems to support these sentiments by urging Darwin to be careful: 'pray don't think of doing any work again yet'. By May, however, Darwin was working two or three hours a day, no longer on *Variation*, but instead on his much-loved botanical experiments which, he tells Hooker on 5 May, 'makes a wonderful difference in my life'. Once again it proved excellent occupational therapy, so that by month-end he was writing cheerfully to Asa Gray: 'Your kindness will make you glad to hear that I am nearly as well as I have been of late years, though a good deal weaker.' The recovery was maintained, much to the delight of his friends. In June Hooker paid a visit to Down during which they discussed Darwin's experiments, and Gray wrote to say how 'heartily rejoiced' he was to hear the good news.[23]

III

During the summer of 1864 Darwin had suddenly become lit up watching the movements of climbing plants. On 2 June he writes to Hooker: 'I have a sudden access of furor about climbers. Do you grow *Adlumia cirrhosa?* . . . Could you have a seedling dug up and potted? I want it fearfully, for it is a leaf climber and therefore sacred.'[24] In due course the results of his experiments would be published as a long article in the *Linnean Society Journal* for 1867 (with a second edition appearing in a separate monograph in 1875). Once again his occupational therapy was proving scientifically productive.

By the early autumn Darwin was feeling well enough to resume his more serious work. Writing to Gray on 13 September to thank him for his friendly note, he proceeds: 'I have less strength (though still gaining same and now at least living downstairs) than formerly and after my two hours work glad to be quite idle. I have little to say; for my soul has been absorbed with climbing plants, now finished and tomorrow I begin again after 13 months interruption on *Variation under Domestication*.' On 23

September, to Hooker, he describes his feelings on starting again: 'I have been looking over my old MS., and it is as fresh as if I had never written it; parts are astonishingly dull, but yet worth printing, I think; and other parts strike me as very good. I am a complete millionaire in odd and curious little facts, and I have been really astonished at my own industry whilst reading my chapters on Inheritance and Selection. God knows when the book will ever be completed, for I find that I am very weak and on my best days cannot do more than one or one and a half hours' work. It is a good deal harder than writing about my dear climbing plants.'[25] He would be working on *Variation* until 22 April the following year, when his health would break down yet again.

During mid-October a visit to Down by the Lyells is described by Darwin to Hooker on the 20th: 'The Lyells have been here, and were extremely pleasant, but I saw them only occasionally for ten minutes, and when they went I had an awful day; but I am now slowly getting up to my former standard. I shall soon be confined to a living grave and a fearful evil it is.' The rest of the letter deals as usual with a variety of geographical and botanical problems.[26]

In early November 1864 Darwin was informed that the Royal Society was conferring on him its highest honour, the Copley Medal. Congratulations came from his many friends; once again, he explained, the warmth of their affection meant far more to him than 'the round bit of gold'. He had been proposed for it the previous year but opposition was too strong, much to Lyell's indignation. It had again been strong this year, Lyell tells Darwin. 'Huxley alarmed me by telling me a few days ago that some of the older members of the Council were afraid of crowning anything so unorthodox as the "Origin". But if they were so, 'they had the good sense to draw in their horns.'[27] Whatever Lyell's reservations about Darwin's theories, he had none about Darwin the scientist.

Inevitably, Darwin was not present in person to receive the medal at the Royal Society's anniversary meeting on 30 November. Writing to Hugh Falconer, who had seconded the proposal, he explains: 'I find that on my good days, when I can write for a couple of hours, that anything which stirs me up like talking for half or even a quarter of an hour, generally quite prostrates me, sometimes even for a long time afterwards. I believe attending the anniversary would possibly make me seriously ill.' On the evening of the meeting Lyell gave an after-dinner speech and wrote subsequently to Darwin that he had made a 'confession of faith as to the 'Origin. . . . I said I had been forced to give up my old faith without thoroughly seeing my way to a new one. But I think you would have been satisfied with the length I went.'[28] Had Lyell made his declaration in print two years earlier, as Darwin had so confidently expected, we can hardly doubt that it would have pleased him far more than ever the medal could.

To Fox Darwin writes appreciatively on 30 November: 'I was glad to see your handwriting. The Copley being open to all sciences and all the world, is reckoned a great honour; but excepting from several kind letters, such things make little difference to me. It shows, however, that Natural Selection is making some progress in this country, and that pleases me. The subject is safe in foreign lands.' He continues: 'As for myself, I fear I have reached my sticking point. I am very weak and continually knocked up, but able most days, to do from 2 to 3 hours work, and all my Doctors tell me this is good for me; and whether or no, it is the only thing which makes life endurable to me. I am slowly crawling on in my work on *Varieties under Domestication* occasionally amusing myself with a little Botanical work.' The same month Emma writes to one of her aunts: 'I do not feel easy to leave Charles for a night, he is so subject to distressing fainting feelings and one never knows when an attack may come on.'[29]

IV

During the early months of 1865, despite indifferent health, Darwin still pushed on doggedly with *Variation*. Regular letters to Hooker describe a temporary despair at the inability of doctors to help. After enquiring of Hooker on 7 January whether he knows a good man, Darwin adds: 'but I know it is folly and nonsense to try anyone'. A month later he reports, 'I have been having 5 or 6 wretched days, miserable from morning to night and unable to do anything', then adding, 'but am much better today'. On 6 April he bewails, 'I work a little every day with groans and sighs and am as dull as a fig. – It is hopeless and useless'; and he then enquires whether there is 'any man better than Jenner for giving life to a worn out poor Devil'. A fortnight later his condition had deteriorated to the point where he had to cease work. He asked Jenner to come to see him, but reports subsequently to Hooker (4 May) that 'Jenner . . . is evidently perplexed at my case'.[30]

It was then that he recalled that a few months earlier he had received a book from a Dr John Chapman describing his newly devised ice-cure. On 16 May he wrote to Dr Chapman requesting him to come to Down, and shortly afterwards he sent him the extensive notes about his symptoms already quoted in the Prologue. The ice-cure, however, proved unsuccessful, and he continued in grievous ill-health throughout the summer months. Describing his condition to Fox on 25–26 October, he writes: 'I have had a bad time for the last six months and have been able to do no scientific work. . . . I have not gone out of my grounds for the last 12 months.'[31] Darwin's friends were alarmed by his condition. Writing to the German zoologist Ernst Haeckel that summer, Huxley informs him that Darwin had been 'very ill for more than a year past, so ill, in fact, that his recovery was at one time doubtful. But he contrives to work in spite of fate, and I hope that before long we shall have a new book from him.'[32]

Not unexpectedly, Emma sometimes found her task of caring for Charles a strain. 'I have often taken a little to gardening this summer.' she writes to her aunt Fanny Allen, 'and I often felt surprised when I was feeling sad enough how cheering a little exertion of that sort is. I also like cutting and carving among the shrubs, but as my opinion is diametrically opposite to the rest of the family, I don't have my own way entirely in that matter.' Glimpses of Emma and Charles at this time are provided by this aunt in letters to her friends. On 26 June 1865 she writes: 'What a life of suffering his is, and how manfully he bears it! Emma's, dear Emma's cheerfulness is equally admirable.' A fortnight later she writes again: 'I had one of Emma's charming letters yesterday. She had waited for a good moment [for] Charles, and his *four* days of tolerable wellness had given spirits to give me the treat of a letter.'[33]

There is a great deal in this account to suggest that throughout the six months, April to September 1865, Darwin was again suffering from fairly severe depression. In addition to all the depressive remarks in his letters – 'wretched', 'miserable', 'hopeless and useless', 'a worn out poor Devil' – it will be recalled that among the numerous symptoms described in his notes for Dr Chapman he listed 'hysterical crying'. Moreover, there is a recollection recorded many years later by Darwin's son Leonard which almost certainly refers either to this period or to the breakdown of 1863–4 and which strongly supports a diagnosis of depression: 'As a young lad I went up to my father when strolling about the lawn, and he, after, as I believe, a kindly word or two, turned away as if quite incapable of carrying on any conversation. Then there suddenly shot through my mind the conviction that he wished he was no longer alive. Must there not have been a strained and weary expression on his face to have produced in these circumstances such an effect on a boy's mind?'[34] Leonard was in his early teens during the period of his father's two breakdowns.

It is difficult to discern what event may have triggered this period of depression. There is no evidence of any particularly distressing criticism of his theories. Nor is there reason to think that he was more worried than usual about the health of Emma or the children. By now the seven survivors were at an age when they were less vulnerable to acute infections. The youngest, Horace, had turned fourteen in May 1865 and William was twenty-five. The three other boys were at school or university and doing well; while the two girls, Henrietta (aged twenty-two) and Bessy (eighteen) were at home and so far as is known in good health.

Since there appears to have been no recent event that might have triggered this episode, it is worth considering whether there is evidence of its being an anniversary reaction, namely a reaction on the anniversary of an earlier bereavement. The deaths of Darwin's mother and father do not qualify as possibilities, since they occurred in July (1817) and November (1848) respectively. Annie's death, however, might conceivably be relevant, since it occurred in April (1851) – which made April 1865 the fourteenth anniversary. No other evidence supports this idea, however, though memories of Annie's death are never far from his mind. They are expressed in a long letter Darwin wrote to Hooker at this time (27 September 1865). Hooker's father had died recently, at the age of eighty, and Darwin had evidently written a note of condolence. To this Hooker had replied comparing his feelings on losing his father with those he had after losing a young child. In this next letter Darwin writes movingly: 'I fully concur and understand what you say about the difference of feeling in the loss of a father and child. I do not think anyone could love a father much more than I did mine, and I do not believe three or four days ever pass without my still thinking of him, but his death at eighty-four caused me nothing of that insufferable grief which the loss of poor dear Annie caused. And this seems to be perfectly natural, for one knows that for years previously that one's father's death is drawing slowly nearer and nearer while the death of one's child is a sudden and dreadful wrench.'[35]

Although during the months from May to December 1865 Darwin did no work on *Variation*, he was by no means entirely idle. For example, he tells Hooker in the letter quoted above of the books he has been reading, which include E. B. Tylor's *Researches into the Early History of Mankind* and W. E. H. Lecky's *The Rise of Rationalism in Europe*, both published this year. Continuing his letter, he proceeds (most misleadingly) to say: 'I confine my reading to a quarter or half hour per day in skimming through the back volumes of the Annals and Magazine of Natural History, and find much that interests me.'[36] Time and again one has the strong impression that, when Darwin refers to the amount of time he is able to work, he is excluding from his calculations a great deal of time spent reading journals and books and also writing or dictating long technical letters to scientific friends.

A striking example of this off-the-record work was that, even during May 1865[37] when his health was crumbling, Darwin was busy drafting a thirty-page essay on pangenesis, a new theory of heredity on which he set much store, which he planned to include as the final chapter of *Variation*. Doubting how it would be received, he writes to Huxley on 27 May seeking his opinion. Huxley is not impressed. On 12 July Darwin replies thanking him warmly for his comments and proceeding: 'I do not doubt your judgement is perfectly just, and I will try to persuade myself not to publish. The whole affair is much too speculative.'[38] In the event, however, he did publish the theory, which proved wholly mistaken. Some of the factors that led him to take this wrong turning are discussed in the next chapter.

Yet another activity of 1865 was looking over the *Origin* in preparation for a second French edition. 'I am as it were, reading the *Origin* for the first time,' he tells Hooker, 'for I am correcting for a second French edition: and upon my life, my dear fellow, it is a very good book, but oh! my gracious, it is tough reading.'[39]

In early May 1865 Darwin heard sad news of FitzRoy, whom he had last seen in 1857 when he and his wife had lunched at Down. For the past

Robert FitzRoy, after his
promotion to Vice-
Admiral in 1863

twelve years FitzRoy had been head of the meteorology department at the
Board of Trade, collecting statistics and initiating a forecasting service.
Although he had his forecasting successes, he also had his failures –
which is hardly surprising considering the state of the science and his
totally inadequate staff. That spring his forecasts proved especially
unsuccessful; his mistakes were seized upon and he was pilloried in the
press. Eventually, on 28 April, a sensitive and deeply depressed FitzRoy
followed his uncle Castlereagh's example by cutting his throat. Sulivan
was at the funeral and sent Darwin an account. Reporting the event to
Hooker, Darwin comments: 'What a melancholy career he has run with
all his splendid qualities.'[40] Since Darwin was already in low spirits when
he received the news, it could not have been responsible for his becoming
depressed. Yet it would probably have added to his sense of hopelessness
and may well have fuelled his feelings that life is not worth living.

V

Darwin's recovery from the 1865 breakdown can in all likelihood be
attributed in some part to medical advice of a novel kind. In September of

that year he called in yet another prominent London physician, Dr Henry Bence Jones, (1814–73), whose prescription included dieting and more exercise. Darwin strongly approved of the dieting and grew more optimistic. Describing the regime to Hooker on 27 September, he writes: 'I am sure he has done me good by rigorous diet. I have been half-starved to death and am 15 lb lighter, but I have gained in walking power and my vomiting is immensely reduced. I have my hopes of again some day resuming scientific work, which is my sole enjoyment in life.'[41] His condition improved and, despite a setback in November resulting from a visit to Ras in London and to see Bence Jones, he was able to resume work on *Variation* at the end of December.

The other and perhaps more important part of the Bence Jones regime was more exercise. Darwin himself was advised to ride every day and Emma was to have a drive in the carriage. Charles acquired a reliable cob and his daily ride became a major new feature of his life. The following account is drawn from the memoir of his father by Francis: 'we had the luck to find for him the easiest and quietest cob in the world. . . . He enjoyed these rides extremely, and devised a number of short rounds which brought him home in time for lunch. . . . I think he used to feel surprised at himself, when he remembered how bold a rider he had been, and how utterly old age and bad health had taken away his nerve. He would say that riding prevented him thinking much more effectually than walking.' In a letter of August 1866 he tells Fox how much he was enjoying riding again and that he believed it improved his health.[42]

In addition to advising a rigorous diet and more exercise, it may be that Bence Jones played some part in influencing Emma to take Charles away on holiday whenever she thought he was overworking, as thenceforward she regularly did.

Other evidence of how much better Darwin was during 1866 is given by his having attended a Royal Society soirée on 27 April. A short time before this he had grown the beard that is so characteristic a feature in all the later portraits. In a letter to her aunt, Fanny Allen, Emma describes the occasion: 'The greatest event was that Charles went last night to the Soirée at the Royal Soc. . . . He saw every one of his old friends . . . [but] was obliged to name himself to almost all of them, as his beard alters him so much.' During the evening he was much in demand and was presented to the Prince of Wales (later to be King Edward VII). Among those present was Dr Bence Jones, who, Emma reports, 'received [Charles] with triumph, as well he might, it being his own doing.'[43]

The improvement in Darwin's health that had begun during the autumn of the previous year was maintained throughout 1866, with only a few setbacks, and those of limited duration. This was in spite of the deaths of two of his sisters.[44] On 2 February Catherine, the sister one year younger than him who had married her widower less than three years earlier, died at the age of fifty-five after having returned with her husband

Family group at Down House, circa 1866. Left to right: Leonard, Henrietta, Horace, Emma, Bessy, Francis and a school-friend

Erasmus (Ras) Darwin, 1804–81, aged about 60

to stay with Susan at the family home at Shrewsbury. A few months later, on her sixty-third birthday in October, Susan, who had earlier kept house for her father and had never married, died also. She had been ill for several years. 'Ras was particularly depressed by the death of Susan who had been his favourite sister. Charles, of course, had a recurrence of his illness; and the Mount, which Emma noted had seemed so sunny and yet was so sad, was put up for auction.' Charles did not travel to Shrewsbury and so did not attend either funeral. During that year he left Down on only three occasions – for a few days in Surrey at the end of May, and two visits, each of a week, to Ras in London.[45]

Darwin's health was so much better in 1866 that he was 'able to work some hours daily', as he tells Wallace in July.[46] His principal activity was grinding on with *Variation*, though early in the year this was interrupted for ten weeks by his having to prepare yet another edition of the *Origin*, the fourth. In it he included references to a number of recent publications, though subsequently he was much vexed to find he had forgotten important works by two of his friends, one on Arctic plants by Hooker, the other on mimicry in butterflies by Bates. The new edition (of 1250 copies, making 7500 in all) appeared in June. Later in the year Darwin was corresponding with Victor Carus (1823–1903), a leading German zoologist, who was using the recent edition of the *Origin* for a new and much-improved translation destined to become the second German edition.

At long last in December 1866 the draft of *Variation* was almost complete and the following January it was delivered to Murray. For no less than six years the work had been a burden to him; yet even now there was to be another year before it was done. Apart from a short break in February 1867 when he began looking over his notes on man, he was engaged for eight months, from mid-March to mid-November, revising and often rewriting the proofs of *Variation*. In doing so he was horrified to find that the work ran to two volumes, each longer than the *Origin*, and he began to feel that its value in no way justified the years he had spent on it. In a letter to Hooker of 17 November 1867 he refers to the revision as having been an 'awful job' and, after its publication in January 1868, writes to him: 'I have been for some time in despair about my book and if I try to read a few pages I feel fairly nauseated . . . it is not worth a fifth part of the enormous labour it has cost me.'[47] Nevertheless, after publication it was much praised and sold well.

Despite Darwin's groans over *Variation*, 1867 was a much better year than earlier ones. He was riding every day and there are no reports of his having had to knock off work because of ill-health. 'You are quite right about riding,' he tells Fox on 8 February; 'it does suit me admirably, and I am very much stronger.'[48] Although severe criticism of the *Origin* (from the physicists) was in the offing, it had not yet broken, while honours multiplied. From Prussia, for example, came their highest honour, Knight of the Order *Pour le Mérite*. Not least important was that there were now far fewer grounds for anxiety about the family. Panic over childhood fevers was in the past and, to Darwin's astonishment, the boys were beginning to distinguish themselves academically. Two of them, George (twenty-two) and Francis (nineteen) were doing well at Cambridge. For the annual celebrations of May week they invited their mother, their sister Bessy (twenty) and two other young ladies to join them – an entertainment which Emma greatly enjoyed. Later in the summer, Emma and some of the children went to London for the evening to see some farewell performances by Kate Terry. Henrietta describes the scene: 'We had at that time two fast little grey horses, and we drove the six miles to Bromley, our nearest station, in the open carriage. It was enchanting summer weather, and the drive back in the starlight summer night was almost the most delightful part of the nearly unheard of dissipation, which my mother was as eager about as any one of us.'[49]

The improvement in Darwin's health was to continue, despite a few temporary setbacks. The year 1866 could therefore be looked back upon later as having been a turning-point.

VI

In 1867 the British Association held its annual meeting in Liverpool under the presidency of Thomas Huxley. To enable Mrs Huxley to accompany him, Emma very kindly proposed that the seven Huxley children and their two nurses should spend a fortnight at Down, and this they did. Leonard Huxley (1860–1933), the third child and eldest son, was then aged seven and in later years recorded his memories of the visit. That spring

a whole tribe of us were transplanted from London to the country delights of the old house at Down. The air of peace and happy interest still seems to issue from the wise and kind personalities of our host and hostess, pervasive but never invasive. . . . At breakfast time each morning Darwin would come in to greet us – tall, white bearded, impressive, his kind blue eyes beaming on us from under the penthouse of his brows. . . . the old man would always have a cheery word for us.

Leonard Huxley also recalled Darwin's occasional visits to his father at their house in St John's Wood during the late sixties and early seventies:

When in London he was able to pay brief visits to his scientific friends, choosing the early morning. . . . I well remember his arrival. . . . at my father's house somewhere between half-past nine and ten and the special preparations made for him. . . . But half-an-hour was the limit of his stay . . . and in order to economize time he would have ready written on a slip of paper the particular questions he wished to discuss.[50]

TWENTY-FIVE

An odious spectre
1868–1871

I

The two volumes of *Variation* were published at the end of January 1868. Since almost the whole of the first printing of 1500 copies was sold immediately, a second, of 1250, was put in hand. 'This has done me a world of good,' Darwin writes to Hooker early in February, 'for I had got into a sort of dogged hatred of my book. And now there has appeared a review in the *Pall Mall* which has pleased me excessively, more perhaps than is reasonable'; and he signs himself 'Your cock-a-hoop friend'. Francis Darwin, commenting on this review, suspects his father to have been especially gratified by the following passage: 'We must call attention to the rare and noble calmness with which he expounds his own views, undisturbed by the heats of polemical agitation which those views have excited, and persistently refusing to retort on his antagonists by ridicule, by indignation, or by contempt. Considering the amount of vituperation and insinuation which has come from the other side, this forbearance is supremely dignified.'[1] In view of the emotional turmoil engendered in him by these hostile criticisms, Darwin's achievement in excluding it from his book is indeed impressive.

While almost the whole content of the volumes was empirical, there was one speculative chapter, in which Darwin advances his hypothesis of pangenesis. This was his brave attempt to account for the transmission to progeny of those variations that have proved themselves favourable to survival and reproduction. While that process was central to his theorising, he had for many years been keenly aware that he did not understand it. What causes variations in the first place? Which are heritable and which not? When parents differ in some character, what determines the form that character will take in the offspring? The trouble was that at that time there was no theory of genetics to draw upon. Furthermore, in spite of observations of his own that pointed in other directions, he remained.wedded to certain traditional ideas which we now know to be mistaken. One such was the age-old belief in the heritance of acquired characters – an idea commonly attributed to Lamarck but in fact long antedating him. Another was the belief of breeders that the first sire to mate with a female influences the progeny not only of that mating but of all subsequent ones. A third was the belief that the different character-istics of the two parents become blended in their offspring, an error Darwin adhered to despite his having told Huxley a decade earlier that he was inclined to think that 'true fertilisation will turn out to be a sort of mixture and not true fusion, of two distinct individuals'.[2]

The theory he advanced, which he termed pangenesis, postulates that the germ cells consist of 'gemmules', which are constantly produced and thrown off by each separate part of the organism and carried to the germ cells in the bloodstream. Ill-based as it was, the theory proved totally wrong. Darwin was a bold theoriser and often showed remarkable prescience, but he was not immune to following false trails.

Ironically, it was during the very years when Darwin was working on pangenesis that Mendel was performing the botanical experiments that, when their importance was recognised many years later, were to lay the foundations for the modern theory of genetics.

As usual Darwin confidently expected criticism for his theory of pangenesis. When sending copies of *Variation* to Huxley, he writes: 'I never received a note from you in my life without pleasure; but whether this will be so after you have read pangenesis, I am very doubtful. Oh Lord, what a blowing up I may receive.' Pangenesis was indeed destined to receive a very mixed reception from Darwin's scientific friends. A few were enthusiastic, including Wallace and Lyell, and that gave enormous pleasure; but the majority were critical – Huxley, Hooker, Bates and Carus. None the less Darwin retained his belief in its promise. Disappointed that Hooker was among the critics, he asserts his position: 'You will think me very self-sufficient when I declare that I feel *sure* if Pangenesis is now stillborn it will, thank God, at some future time reappear, begotton by some other father, and christened by some other name.' Earlier, when sending proofs for Asa Gray to read, he had confided: 'The chapter on Pangenesis will be called a mad dream. . . ; but at the bottom of my own mind I think it contains a great truth.'[3]

II

No sooner were the proofs of *Variation* off his desk towards the end of 1867 than Darwin resumed work on man. Back in the spring, when he had briefly looked over his notes while awaiting the proofs of *Variation*, he had supposed it might make an extra chapter for that work; now he expected it to be a 'very small volume'. In the end it became two substantial volumes, published in February 1871 under the double title *The Descent of Man, and Selection in Relation to Sex.*

Although this was one of his later works, written around the time he turned sixty, Darwin's interest in the nature of man was already engaging his attention during those exciting years 1837– 9 after his return from the *Beagle* voyage. During those years, it will be remembered, not only was he working on his *Journal of Researches* and presenting original papers in geology but he was reading widely and reflecting deeply on problems of philosophy. Among several substantial works that he had read and annotated critically were Whewell's *History of the Inductive Sciences* (three volumes, published in 1837) and Mackintosh's *General View of the Progress of Ethical Philosophy* (1832). The latter he was reading while staying with Emma at Maer in May 1839 during the first year of their marriage. Stimulated by Mackintosh's idea, he had then written a long critical essay on what would now be called social and emotional psychology, in which he outlines theories not dissimilar to those current today in sociobiology (though expressed in a very different language).[4] The essay starts as follows: 'Looking at Man, as a naturalist would at any other Mammiferous animal, it may be concluded that he has parental, conjugal and social instincts, and perhaps others. The history of every race of man shows this, if we judge him by his habits, as another animal. These instincts consist of a feeling of love (and sympathy) or benevolence to the object in question.' He then discusses the problem of moral conflict between the short-term pleasures of indulging 'a passion' and the long-term satisfactions of following 'social instincts', namely acting in accordance with altruistic feelings. In the course of his argument he notes: 'In a dog we see a struggle between its appetite or love of exercise and its love of its puppies; the latter generally soon conquers. . . . But, whereas a dog acts without reflection, the case of man is different.' After considering also the anatomical and physiological evidence he has no doubt that man must be classified as one of the primates but as 'having unusual mental powers'. In January 1839 he had noted: 'It is only our natural prejudice, and that arrogance which made our forefathers declare that they were descended from demi-gods, which leads us to demur to this conclusion.'[5]

Thus we find that most of the main themes of his current work on man were already in Darwin's mind before 1840, thirty years earlier; but, like his ideas on evolution, they were not to be divulged to the public until decades later. When writing the *Origin* he had first had the notion of including a chapter on man but had then deliberately avoided doing so, judging it prudent to establish his main thesis first by drawing his evidence only from studies of other species. As he had told Wallace in December 1857 in reply to the latter's enquiry whether he would discuss man, he had decided to avoid the whole subject as being too surrounded by prejudice.[6]

Now in the late 1860s the position was very different. The historical fact that animals and plants have evolved over time was becoming a well-established and respected opinion; and there was growing a lively interest in man's origins – his antiquity as seen in the fossil record, his relation to the apes and monkeys, differences between human races. Furthermore, not only had three of Darwin's closest friends already published on the subject – Huxley in his *Zoological Evidences as to Man's Place in Nature* (1863), Lyell in his *Antiquity of Man* (1863) and Wallace in a long article in the *Anthropological Review* in 1864 – but several other scholars had done the same. Now Darwin was preparing to publish his own work on man. Prior to publication he was, inevitably, filled with apprehension. In late 1869, however, Huxley very kindly offered to read the proofs and was evidently reassuring. Very grateful, Darwin replies: 'Your offer has just made all the difference, that I can now write ... with a feeling of satisfaction instead of vague dread.'[7]

The Descent of Man, it has often been noted, should really have been two books – the first limited to man and the second given to the role that sexual selection plays in evolution. As it turned out, sexual selection occupies over two-thirds of the whole.

In working on man, Darwin gave much thought to the differences between the various races and how these might have arisen. This led him to the idea that preferential selection for mating purposes of individuals of the opposite sex who have certain special characteristics, such as beauty in a female or strength in a male, might play a major part. This in turn led him to consider the possible role of such selection in the whole range of animal species from molluscs onwards. To check his facts he began, early in 1868, to engage in an extensive correspondence with a wide range of specialists who had studied one or another group of animals. In thanking one of them in June that year for 'all the curious facts about the unequal number of the sexes in Crustacea' we find him adding characteristically, 'but the more I investigate the subject the deeper I sink in doubt and difficulty'.[8]

The modern view is that, while sexual selection probably plays a part in accounting for the evolution of certain features in some species, Darwin seriously exaggerated its role. The hypothesis led to much valuable research, however, in this respect differing greatly from the theory of pangenesis, which was to prove completely stillborn.

The first serious blow Darwin received to his theory of pangenesis came during the summer of 1870. His second cousin, Francis Galton (1822–1911), was busy putting the theory to empirical test. If, as proposed, each cell in the body is continually discharging gemmules into the bloodstream which, when lodged in the sperm and ova, become the basis for heredity, Galton argued that transfusing the blood of a black rabbit into a grey one should affect the colour of the progeny of the grey. Early trials proved negative, however. In March 1870 Emma, writing to Henrietta, describes the situation: 'F. Galton's experiments (viz. injecting black rabbits blood into grey and *vice versa*) are failing, which is a dreadful disappointment to them both. F. Galton said he was quite sick with anxiety till the rabbits' *accouchements* were over, and now one naughty creature ate up her infants and the other has perfectly commonplace ones. He wishes this experiment to be kept quite secret as he means to go on, so don't mention.'[9] Later experiments were to be no more successful.

III

While the work on *The Descent of Man* was Darwin's main occupation during the years 1868–70, there were, of course, a number of interruptions. March 1868 saw him and Emma spending a month in London. In letters to the naturalist J. J. Weir inviting him to visit Down (as he did the following September together with the Hookers and Wallaces) Darwin explains that his state of 'health is so precarious [that] I can ask no one who will not allow me the privilege of a poor old invalid; for talking tries my head more than anything, and I am utterly incapable of talking more than half an hour except on rare occasions.' Meanwhile, in London, he is being 'overwhelmed both with calls and letters; and alas! one visit to the British Museum of an hour or hour and a half does for me the whole day. . . . We remain here till April 1st, and then hurrah for home and quiet work.'[10]

Unfortunately, within a couple of months of their return Darwin's symptoms grew so bad that he 'could do nothing'. After three weeks he and Emma with some of the children went off on holiday to Freshwater in the Isle of Wight. Here, within a couple of days, he was already feeling better, as he wrote to Hooker on 17 July. The poet William Allingham was staying nearby, and in his diary describes Darwin as 'yellow, sickly, very quiet'[11] – which suggests he might have had an attack of jaundice. Whatever it was, he seems to have picked up fairly quickly.

Henrietta gives a glowing account of their five-week stay: 'It was a beautiful summer, and we had a very entertaining time. Mrs. Cameron . . . friend of Watts and Tennyson, was sociable and most amusing, and put my father and Erasmus Darwin, who was with us, into great spirits. It was there she made her excellent photograph of my father.' Julia Cameron (1815–79) was a gifted early photographer, famous for her portraits. Darwin noted on his photograph that he liked it 'very much better than any other'. For some years Tennyson, who was born in the same year as Darwin, had been living at Freshwater. '[He] came several times to call on my parents,' Henrietta writes, 'but he did not greatly charm either my father or my mother.' From a letter to Fox of 21 October, we learn that Darwin had actually enjoyed the holiday.[12]

An event that had given Darwin especial pleasure early in their stay was receiving good news of Leonard: he had passed second in the entrance examination for the Royal Military Academy at Woolwich, where, after training, he would be commissioned in the Royal Engineers. 'I must write to someone, else I shall burst with pleasure at Leonard's success,' he tells Horace.[13]

Charles Darwin, aged 60, photographed by Julia Cameron, July 1869

At Freshwater he was, as usual, continuing to write long letters to friends and colleagues. Hooker was President of the British Association that year and in his presidential address at Norwich was planning to rebut allegations that belief in the theory of natural selection was on the wane; and he had asked Darwin to let him have information supporting the rebuttal. In his reply Darwin, after describing the extensive sales of the *Origin* in English and other languages, calls attention to a historical fact that had long been a great comfort to him,[14] namely that 'a man so extraordinarily able as Leibnitz' had rejected the Newtonian theory of gravitation, 'which seems to everyone now so certain and plain'. 'The truth', he continues, 'will not penetrate a preoccupied mind.' By late August 1868 Darwin, back at Down, was delighted to hear of the success of Hooker's address; and he writes to say how grateful he is to him for the 'eulogium . . . passed on me [which] makes me very proud'. For some years now he had taken special satisfaction from the knowledge that the historical fact of the evolution of species had become widely accepted, which he felt was far more important than the special view about it he had advanced. 'Personally, of course, I care much about Natural Selection,' he had told Asa Gray in 1863; 'but that seems to me utterly unimportant compared to the question of Creation *or* Modification.'[15]

IV

The next major interruption came at the end of 1868 when Darwin had to prepare another edition of the *Origin*, the fifth. This took him about seven weeks (until mid-February 1869) and, as he wrote to Wallace on 22 January, cost him 'much labour'. In this edition a number of changes were made which have incurred criticism from later biologists. In June 1867 a hostile article on the *Origin* had appeared in the *North British Review* by the Professor of Engineering at Glasgow, Fleeming Jenkin. In it he had not only poured contempt on Darwin's arguments but had advanced serious criticism of the possible efficacy of natural selection as an agent of change on the basis of mathematical considerations. Jenkin demonstrated that, given the current theory of blending inheritance which Darwin unthinkingly adopted, the chances of favourable single heritable variations becoming incorporated in a population were infinitesimally small. This was a criticism which, though based on false premises, Darwin could not see his way to rebut. 'Fleeming Jenkin's arguments have convinced me', he tells Wallace.[16]

Not only did Jenkin's argument carry weight but another and possibly even weightier criticism had emanated from the same city, voiced by no less a person than William Thomson (later Lord Kelvin), the premier physicist of the day. After having made some earlier statements about the rate at which the earth appeared to be cooling, Thomson in 1865 launched a direct attack on the views held by the geologists. Sophisticated calculations, he explained, showed that the age of the earth was far shorter than the geologists supposed and that the aeons required to enable evolution to occur in accordance with Darwin's theory were mere figments of imagination. Once again it proved later that the critics were wrong: Thomson had supposed the earth to be cooling far faster than it was, since as yet there was no knowledge of the counteractive effects of radioactivity within the planet.

When a scientist is met with substantial criticism of the kinds advanced by Jenkin and Thomson and which he cannot answer, he is faced with a dilemma. Does he shift his position by modifying his theory? Or does he, after scrutinising his evidence afresh and believing it sound, hold his ground and await further evidence? Either course can be defended. At first Darwin was inclined to await further evidence.[17] In the end, however, he retreated. Writing to Victor Carus in May 1869, the month of publication of the new edition, he describes some of the changes he has made: 'Many of the corrections are only a few words, but they have been made from the evidence on various points appearing to have become a little stronger or weaker. Thus I have been led to place somewhat more value on the definite and direct action of external conditions; to think the lapse of time as measured by years, as not quite so great as most geologists have thought.'[18]

As a result of this retreat, which proceeded further in the sixth and final edition published in January 1872, the last two editions are much less satisfactory than earlier ones. In particular, the inheritance of acquired characters, which had occupied only a subordinate place in the first edition, was now given a major role. This meant that the environment, instead of being seen as a pressure that selects existing spontaneous variations, came to be regarded as the *cause* of such variations. The geneticist C. D. Darlington, who is especially critical of the retreat, notes a little acidly that Darwin never referred in print to Jenkin's argument and that this change back to the traditional theory 'was produced by imperceptible modifications of successive editions'.[19]

Darwin found the criticisms of Jenkin and Thomson extremely disturbing. As he had remarked some years earlier to a friend, 'A man is as tender of his theories as of his children.'[20] Now, in a letter of 31 January 1869 to an unknown correspondent, he writes: 'I am greatly troubled at the short duration of the world according to Sir W. Thomson for I require for my theoretical views a very long period before the Cambrian formation.' In April he is telling Wallace that 'Thomson's views of the recent age of the world have been for some time one of my sorest troubles'; and a couple of years later (12 July 1871) says that Thomson haunts him 'like an odious spectre'. Wallace himself had from the start deplored Darwin's inclination to retreat: 'Variations of every kind are always occurring in every part of every species,' he insists, 'and therefore favourable variations are always ready when wanted. . . . I would put the burthen of proof on my opponents.'[21]

Since this retreat to the traditional and, as we now know, mistaken ideas has met with sharp criticism and argument, it is of interest to read how Darwin himself viewed his change of opinion; this he describes in the first edition of his *Descent of Man*:

I now admit . . . that in the earlier editions of my *Origin of Species* I probably attributed too much to the action of natural selection or the survival of the fittest . . . I may be permitted to say as some excuse, that I had two distinct objects in view, firstly, to show that species had not been separately created, and secondly, that natural selection had been the chief agent of change, though largely aided by the inherited effects of habit, and slightly by the direct action of the surrounding conditions. . . . If I have erred in giving to natural selection great power, which I am far from admitting, or in having exaggerated its power, which is in itself probable, I have at least as I hope, done good service in aiding to overthrow the dogma of separate creations.[22]

V

Ironically, over the problem of man it was Wallace who proved hesitant and Darwin bold. In a review of the most recent editions of Lyell's standard works on geology, published in the *Quarterly Review* of April 1869, Wallace claimed that, although variation and natural selection could account unaided for the evolution of all other species and also for the human body, they could not account for the development of man's huge brain. That, he insisted, had evolved in advance of its having had any selective advantage: a higher intelligence, he suspected, had been guiding the selective processes responsible. Darwin had had warning of Wallace's defection and, before reading the article, had expressed his deep anxiety: 'I hope you have not murdered too completely your own and my child.' After reading it he was no less horrified. Writing to Wallace on 14 April, he praises everything else in the article, adding only: 'As you expected, I differ grievously from you, and I am very sorry for it. I can see no necessity for calling in an additional and proximate cause in regard to man.'[23]

Wallace was not the only one of Darwin's supporters to jib at going the whole way. Although Lyell in the most recent edition of his *Principles of Geology* had confessed his conversion to an evolutionary viewpoint (a change of position to which Wallace pays handsome tribute), he shared the latter's reservations regarding man. Darwin, writing to Lyell about another matter on 4 May 1869, is full of admiration for Wallace's article; 'but', he continues, 'I was dreadfully disappointed about Man, it seems to me incredibly strange. . . . But I believe that you will not agree quite in all this.' Darwin was right. In his reply Lyell, after sharing in Darwin's admiration for Wallace's article, continues, 'as I feel that progressive development or evolution cannot be entirely explained by natural selection, I rather hail Wallace's suggestion that there may be a Supreme Will and Power which . . . may guide the forces of law and nature.'[24] Asa

Gray also was not convinced that variations are random, and suspected that they were biased in a favourable direction. A lesson that emerges is that innovators must expect that even their most enthusiastic supporters may not be prepared to go the whole way but may wish to compromise at some point between the new scheme and the old, however illogical that compromise may appear, and may well be.

It was not only Wallace, Lyell and Gray who were being hesitant, however. Huxley, for all his enthusiasm, was being slow to utilise evolutionary ideas. Indeed, it was not until the German biologists, to whom he was close, had integrated them into their own tradition that Huxley made use of them. The Germans were systematists and during the mid-sixties were applying evolutionary ideas to their task of disentangling the genealogical and phylogenetic* relationships of the living and fossil species they were studying. Since members of that school were not interested in the process, natural selection passed them by. It is striking that Huxley also makes no reference to it in any of his work.[25]

Huxley, though notably bold in his defence of Darwin against the critics, was in fact extremely cautious when it came to questions of theory. He never felt confident of Darwin's position, thinking that current ignorance regarding the origins and heritability of variations rendered the theory excessively speculative. He himself felt much happier dealing with purely empirical problems. As far as science was concerned, to the end of his life he remained the comparative anatomist.[26] But Huxley was a great deal more than just a distinguished anatomist. From the time he was appointed to the School of Mines he had been active in promoting the spread of scientific and technical education and had been giving an enormous number of popular lectures and addresses. During the 1860s, moreover, he was becoming recognised nationally as the leading spokesman for science in government circles. As a result, he was now engaged in a host of public activities, starting with the Fishery Commission (to which he was appointed in 1863), but most of them concerned with education, whether at primary, secondary or university level, and in consequence he was hardly more than a spare-time scientist. Considering all his other commitments it is remarkable he managed to achieve as much as he did. His friends, however, bewailed the diversion of a talented scientist to what they saw as less important work.

As far as Huxley's research is concerned, the trigger that led to his belated application of evolutionary ideas, which he first did in his study of dinosaurs, seems to have been an important work, published in 1866, by Ernst Haeckel (1834–1919) of Jena, a rising young German zoologist whom Darwin also had recently got to know. Since 1865 they had been corresponding regularly, and in October the following year Haeckel had visited Down, where his boisterous manner had left mixed feelings.[27] In

*'Phylogenetic' refers to the evolutionary development through geological time of one or more species from their earliest forms through intermediate forms and into their most recent ones.

Germany he had become a vigorous exponent of Darwin's ideas, so vigorous in fact that Darwin was worried lest it be counter-productive. During correspondence in May 1867, following the publication a few months earlier of Haeckel's book, Darwin writes of his concern lest Haeckel 'excite anger . . ., anger so completely blinds everyone, that your arguments would have no chance of influencing those who are already opposed to our views. Moreover, I do not at all like that you, towards whom I feel so much friendship, should unnecessarily make enemies, and there is pain and vexation enough in the world without more being caused.' In the event, Haeckel made plenty of enemies, but this had its uses. According to one German observer, Haeckel 'concentrated on himself . . . all the hatred and bitterness which Evolution excited in certain quarters, [so that] in a surprisingly short time it became the fashion in Germany that Haeckel alone should be abused, while Darwin was held up as the ideal of forethought and moderation.'[28]

Haeckel's name has lived in history as the author of the theory of recapitulation, according to which an embryo, during its development, represents in succession the adult forms of its various ancestors. Although soon discredited by more careful work, the theory has seemed plausible enough to the layman. In consequence it has had a remarkably long and influential life outside biology. It has inspired theories of education and it also forms the basis for Freud's theory of libidinal phases which for the first three-quarters of this century dominated psychoanalysis.[29]

VI

After the brief relapse in the summer of 1868, Darwin's health continued reasonably good during the winter of 1868–9. But in April 1869 he had a bad accident out riding: 'His quiet cob Tommy stumbled and fell, rolling on him and bruising him seriously. It was a great misfortune, for Tommy was soon considered to be unsafe for him to ride, and he never afterwards found a quite suitable horse.'[30] (Nevertheless, in the summer of the following year, while he and Emma were staying with their banker son outside Southampton, he was again riding every day and much enjoying it.)

The early summer of 1869 saw the family on holiday at Caerdeon, near Barmouth in Wales. During the 1860s Charles was always averse to holidays and while the Welsh holiday was being planned, partly to help him get over the riding accident, we find Emma describing to Henrietta how 'poor F.' was far from enthusiastic about it but more or less resigned to going. Leonard (nineteen) and Horace (eighteen), she adds, were 'very crazy on the scheme'. They stayed there for seven weeks from 10 June until the end of July. On their way the family stopped in Shrewsbury to visit The Mount, now occupied by strangers. They were shown over the house but could not take their time. 'I remember my father's deep disapppointment', writes Henrietta, 'as he said, "If I could have been left alone in the greenhouse for five minutes, I know I should have been able to see my father in his wheel-chair as vividly as if he had been there before me."'[31]

In the event, while Leonard and Horace enjoyed themselves thoroughly, for their father the holiday was not a success. Writing to Hooker ten days after their arrival, he describes the splendid view from the house: 'Old Cader [Idris] is a grand fellow, and shows himself off superbly with every changing light'; but, he continues: 'I have been as yet in a very poor way; it seems as soon as the stimulus of mental work stops, my whole strength gives way. As yet I have hardly crawled half a mile from the house, and then have been fearfully fatigued. It is enough to make one wish oneself quiet in a comfortable tomb.' This picture of her father is confirmed by Henrietta: 'Our summer at Caerdeon . . . which would have been otherwise very enjoyable, was spoilt by my father's continued illness.'[32]

Once he was home, it seems, Darwin's health picked up. He and Emma visited London, as usual staying with Ras. In mid-November 1869 Charles writes to Hooker in cheerful mood: 'We had a very successful week in London, and I was unusually well and saw a good many persons, which, when well, is a great pleasure to me. I had a jolly talk with Huxley among others. And now I am at the same work as before, and shall be for another two months . . . , and I am sick of [it].' The work in question was the extensive study of the role of sexual selection in evolution. A little later, however, he was cheered by the note from Huxley, mentioned earlier, offering to read the proofs, which gave him 'a feeling of satisfaction instead of vague dread'.[33]

Heartened by Huxley's kind offer, Darwin pushed on with *The Descent of Man* throughout 1870 and completed it by year's end. Fortunately his health was holding up. This was largely due, perhaps, to Emma's insisting he take proper holidays. Describing his condition to Henrietta on 19 March 1870, she writes: 'F. is wonderfully set up by London, but so absorbed about work and all sorts of things that I shall force him off somewhere before very long.'[34] Emma was successful, and during the year the pair made two visits to see their sons: in May they went to Cambridge to see George (twenty-five) and Francis (twenty-two) and in August they stayed with William (thirty) in Southampton.

Cambridge held many attractions for Darwin. Both his sons were doing well academically and were staying on after taking their degrees. In the mathematics tripos George had come second and had gone on to win a major prize. There were also old friends to see. Describing the visit in a letter to Hooker of 25 May, Darwin writes: 'Last Friday we all went to the Bull Hotel in Cambridge to see the boys, and for a little rest and enjoyment. The backs of the Colleges are simply paradisaical. On Monday I saw Sedgwick who was most cordial and kind. . . . His affection and kindness charmed us all' – his savage attack on the *Origin* of ten years previously evidently quite forgotten. 'My visit to him was in one way unfortunate,' Darwin continues, 'for after a long sit he proposed to take me to the museum, and I could not refuse, and in consequence he utterly prostrated me. . . . I have not recovered the exhaustion yet. Is it not humiliating to be thus killed by a man of eighty-six . . .? . . . But Cambridge without Henslow was not itself; I tried to get to the two old houses, but it was too far for me.'[35]

During June 1870 Darwin renewed correspondence with his old *Beagle* shipmate, James Sulivan, now Admiral Sir James, KCB. Congratulating him on his well-deserved distinctions, Darwin proceeds:

On the other hand, I am sorry to hear so poor an account of your health; but you were surely very rash to do all that you did and then pass through so exciting a scene as a ball at the Palace. It was enough to have tired a man in robust health. Complete rest will, however, I hope, quite set you up again. As for myself, I have been rather better of late, and if nothing disturbs me I can do some hours work every day. I shall this autumn publish another book partly on man, which I dare say many will decry as very wicked. I could have travelled to Oxford, but could no more have withstood the excitement of a commemoration than I could a ball at Buckingham Palace.

He had been invited to receive an honorary degree by Oxford University but had declined it on the score of ill-health. Before ending his long letter to Sulivan, Darwin thanks him for his 'kind remarks about my boys. Thank God, all give me complete satisfaction; my fourth [Leonard] stands second at Woolwich, and will be an Engineer Officer at Christmas.'[36]

Henrietta also came in for a share of praise from her proud father. During the spring of 1870 she was in the south of France and was reading proofs of the early part of *The Descent of Man* which he had sent her. 'My dear H.,' he writes,

I have worked through (and it is hard work), half of the second chapter on mind, and your corrections and suggestions are *excellent*. I have adopted the greater number, and I am sure they are very great improvements. . . . You have done me real service; but, by jove, how hard you must have worked, and how thoroughly you have mastered my M.S. . . .
Your affectionate, and admiring and obedient father,
C.D.[37]

During this time Emma also was reading the proofs of *The Descent of Man*, but she found a good deal that troubled her. Expressing her misgivings about one of the chapters to Henrietta, she writes: 'I think it will be very interesting, but that I shall dislike it very much as again putting God further off.'[38]

Charles's and Emma's second visit of the year, to William in Southampton, was as successful as the earlier one to Cambridge.

LEFT Sir Charles Lyell in later years

BELOW LEFT Reverend Adam Sedgwick in later years

RIGHT Joseph Hooker, aged about 55, circa 1872

Describing it to one of her aunts, Emma writes: 'We are very comfortable here. . . . Charles rides in the morning, and there are a great variety of pretty rides and walks. We talk and read of nothing but war [the Franco-Prussian war]. . . . Charles . . . manages to be idle and gets through the day with short walks and rides.'[39]

On their return home from these days of idleness, Charles plunged at once into revising the later proofs of the *Descent*, which were finally completed in mid-January of the following year. In late February 1871, a few days after Darwin's sixty-second birthday, the two volumes were published. The first printing of 2500 copies sold remarkably well and a further 5000 copies were called for before the end of the year. Although there were hostile reviews, including one in *The Times* written, Darwin tells his publisher, by someone who 'has no knowledge of science, and seems to me a wind-bag full of metaphysics and classics', most were respectful and many guardedly favourable.[40]

In a more recent assessment of Darwin's contribution, Sir Arthur Keith, himself a distinguished anatomist, expresses admiration for the care with which Darwin amassed his evidence: 'To know the structure of man's body is usually supposed to be enough to keep an anatomist busy for a lifetime. Darwin in the *Descent* did make a few minor blunders which were easily put right; they did not invalidate the rightness of his argument.'[41] The first two chapters display the anatomical evidence of man's primate origins. Next, Darwin considers the far more controversial question of whether it is plausible to regard man's mental powers and moral faculties as having the same beginnings. That in these respects there is a gulf between man and other species is not denied; but, Darwin argues, it is not as wide as usually supposed. Having seen human life in the raw in South America, not only the rude existence of the Indians of Tierra del Fuego but also the savagery of the colonising whites, he thinks it easy to overrate both the mental powers and, especially, the moral dispositions of the human species. In a similar way, he thinks there is a marked tendency to underestimate the intelligence and socially co-operative behaviour of other species. These are lessons, I believe, that a century later many have still to learn.

TWENTY-SIX

A perfectly uniform life
1871–1872

I

By the new year of 1871 Darwin had been writing and publishing on evolution for fifteen years with only an occasional break. Three major works were complete (the *Origin*, *Variation* and *Descent of Man*); but another two years were required before he felt free to devote himself exclusively to his favourite pastime, botanical experiments. First he was eager to work up his extensive notes on the expression of emotion, and next he had the troublesome job of preparing yet another edition of the *Origin* and answering yet more of the hostile criticism directed against his theories. For most of these two years his health was reasonably good, though during the summer of 1871 he had a recurrence of symptoms and was unable to work for two months.

True to his habits Darwin began his labours on the expression of the emotions on 17 January 1871, precisely two days after he had finished revising the final proofs of *The Descent of Man*. By the end of April he had completed the first draft, which, when returned from the printers as galleys, would as usual have to undergo extensive revision. Owing to his having to give time to the new edition of the *Origin*, revisions were not completed until late August of the following year, 1872, with publication of the work, entitled *The Expression of the Emotions in Man and Animals*, occurring at the end of November. The work is really an extension of his study of man and would have made a much more suitable second half to the *Descent* than the chapters on sexual selection.

Darwin's interest in the expression of emotion has been traced to the time when he was a very young medical student in Edinburgh.[1] In December 1826, when not yet eighteen, he is recorded as having been present at a meeting of a student scientific society at which a paper was read criticising a recent book by Sir Charles Bell, *Anatomy of Expression*. Bell had maintained that man is endowed with certain muscles solely for the purpose of expressing his emotions. From that time onwards Darwin was interested in the question and there are many entries on the subject in

his notebooks of 1837–9. Moreover, as already noted, as soon as his first child, William, was born in December 1839, he had begun making observations. Thus, when ultimately in January 1871 he began working up his notes, he was gathering the fruits of over forty years' interest in the subject.

Contrary to the thesis advanced by Sir Charles Bell, Darwin sought to show not only that the facial musculature in humans bears a close resemblance to that in other primate species but that the forms in which the various emotions are expressed in different species of primates and also in other mammals are sufficiently alike as to support his hypothesis of biological affinity. That implied, among much else, that the emotions and their expression in man are in some degree genetically pre-programmed (to use modern terminology). To support this hypothesis Darwin collected data from many fields. One field was other countries and cultures. When someone is surprised or angry, for example, does he show the same facial appearance and gestures no matter what his country, race or culture? Another field was the inmates of mental hospitals, whose expressions, he subsequently decided, were of a piece with those of the sane, though sometimes tragically intense and prolonged. A third was infants, in whom, he believed, it might be possible to observe 'the pure and simple source' from which our expressions spring. Whereas for several fields he had to rely mainly or wholly on the observations of correspondents, the observations of infants were his own.[2] So too were some of the observations of emotional expression in other species. Monkeys and apes ... he watched in the London Zoo. Dogs were ... many years he had owned them as pets. the truth of ... Darwin was able to demonstrate, first, that in ... In No... ... of emotional expression and of understanding across ... cultures, and, secondly, that there is a considerable degree of continuity also across species. Thus man's emotional expressions are as much a product of his evolution as are his anatomy and physiology.

Darwin's previous books had sold so well that Murray decided on a first printing of no less than 7000 copies. Moreover, when the book appeared in November 1872, three-quarters were sold at once, which led Murray to print another 2000. This proved a mistake, however, since sales thereafter were slack and a second edition, which would have included a mass of further notes on the subject, was not called for until after the author's death.[3]

Expression of the Emotions received several favourable reviews and a few hostile ones. In a perspicacious article in the *Quarterly Journal of Science*, Wallace remarks on Darwin's 'insatiable longing to discover the causes of the varied and complex phenomena presented by living things' and notes that in Darwin's case 'the restless curiosity of the child [seems] never to

have abated its force'. On the other side, a theologian describes the book as 'the most powerful and insidious' of all the author's works.[4]

In scientific circles the book has had a chequered career. After Darwin's death it was for long neglected – a tragedy for the study of socio-emotional development which, lacking an evolutionary perspective, almost expired in the wastes of behaviourism and the jungle of psychoanalysis. In recent years, however, with the growing interest in an ethological approach to the understanding of man's emotional life and behaviour, Darwin's work has become recognised as a classic first contribution to the subject.

II

No sooner had Darwin completed the first draft of *Expression of the Emotions* at the end of April 1871 than he turned his attention to preparing the new edition of the *Origin*. A principal reason was that his publishers wanted an edition that would sell more cheaply. Another was that Darwin himself wanted to deal with the criticisms of his theory advanced in a recently published book entitled *On the Genesis of Species* by a zoologist, St George Mivart. This he had read in January 1871 while working on *Expression of the Emotions*, and had been much shaken by the tone and power of its attack. In correspondence with Wallace, on 30 January, he complains that 'Mivart is savage or contemptuous about my "moral sense"', and on 9 July expresses his dismay at the 'great effect against Natural Selection' that Mivart's book was having.[5]

Mivart's argument was that any characteri ̇ ̇   ̇ ̇ as the long neck of a giraffe or the complex structure of an eye, w   ̇   ̇   would contribute to survival, would have no surviv ̇ Thus there could be no possibility of its infl ̇ and breeding, which were central to Darwin's ̇

This was in fact a difficulty that Darwin had h ̇   ̇n ̇   res ̇ed with and discussed. Even very small differences, h ̇ ̇ ̇d decided, could in certain circumstances confer an advantage, and he had therefore believed the problem could be solved. Nevertheless, he was deeply disturbed by the attack and far from confident he would be able to counter it effectively. Moreover, there was further hostile criticism of him in the July number of the *Quarterly Review*, in a review of the *Descent of Man* which, although anonymous, was readily identifiable as also being by Mivart. As he tells Hooker in a letter of 16 September, Darwin was especially incensed by the way in which he thought Mivart had misrepresented his ideas and by the contrast between Mivart's public attack and his private assurances: 'You'd never read such strong letters Mivart wrote to me about respect towards me, begging that I would call on him, etc. etc.' yet in the *Quarterly Review* he shows the greatest scorn and animosity towards me, and with uncommon cleverness says all that is most disagreeable. He makes me the

most arrogant, odious beast that ever lived . . . It has mortified me a good deal.'[6]

Throughout this crisis Darwin was in frequent correspondence with Wallace, who proved a tower of strength in providing both scientific advice and emotional support. On 12 July, at the end of a long postscript, Darwin describes his feelings: 'God knows whether my strength and spirit will last out to write a chapter versus Mivart and others; I do so hate controversy and I feel I should do it so badly.' To this Wallace replies encouragingly: 'Dear Darwin, – I am very sorry you are so unwell, and that you allow criticisms to worry you so. Remember the noble army of converts you have made and the host of the most talented men living who support you wholly.'[7]

That autumn Huxley entered the arena. While on summer holiday with his family in Scotland at St Andrews, where he was introduced to golf, he read Mivart's book and review and also the article of 1869 by Wallace expressing reservations about the applicability of natural selection to man. Roused to action, he began drafting a hard-hitting article defending Darwin and attacking the critics. Apprised of Huxley's plan, Darwin writes back gratefully on 21 September: 'Your letter has pleased me . . . to a wonderful degree. It quite delights me that you are going to some extent to answer and attack Mivart. . . . I never dreamed that you would have time to say a word in defence of the cause you have so often defended. It will be a long battle after we are dead and gone . . . Great is the power of misrepresentation.' Ten days later proofs of Huxley's article arrived. Darwin is enthusiastic: 'There are scores of splendid passages, and vivid flashes of wit . . . I must tell you what Hooker said to me a few years ago. "When I read Huxley, I feel quite infantile in intellect." By Jove I have felt this throughout your review.'[8]

vember, on sending Haeckel a copy of his article 'Mr Darwin's Critics', which had just appeared in the *Contemporary Review*, Huxley explains his motives: 'The dogs have been barking at his heels too much of late.' These same sentiments are expressed again some years later when, taken to task for the acerbity of his criticisms, Huxley retorts: 'I declare that for the last twenty years I have never attacked but always fought in self-defence, counting Darwin, of course, as part of myself, for dear Darwin never could nor would defend himself.' Darwin was indeed always grateful for his bulldog's interventions, even though on this occasion, as on others earlier, the scientific content of Huxley's rebuttal left a good deal to be desired.'[9]

As so often before, the misgivings Darwin had been expressing in his letters to Wallace proved misplaced. The relevant passages in his new edition of the *Origin*, while recognising the critical nature of the problem raised by Mivart, were effectively argued, moderate and dignified in tone. Subsequent work on the problem has shown Darwin to have been right and Mivart's criticisms mistaken.

Alfred Wallace, aged 46, in 1869

Darwin's work on the new edition continued during the autumn of 1871 and it was not until January that he dispatched the final proofs. Publication followed soon after. Since this was to be the final edition and was for long regarded as the standard one, it was unfortunate that it was on poor paper and in small print. Even more unfortunate were some of the revisions, especially those by which Darwin sought to meet the ill-founded criticisms of Sir William Thomson and Professor Fleeming Jenkin by resorting to the theory that acquired characters are inherited.

III

During the summer of 1871, while grappling with Mivart's criticisms and the 'odious spectre' of Sir William Thomson, Darwin, not unexpectedly, was in poor health. At the end of the year, in a letter to Haeckel of 27 December, he remarks: 'I have had bad health this last summer, and during two months was able to do nothing.'[10] It is not clear exactly which these months were, but the evidence suggests July and August.

On 9 July, writing to Wallace, Darwin concludes with the remark: 'I have been rather seedy, but a few days in London did me much good; and my dear good wife is going to take me somewhere, *nolens volens*, at the end of this month.' Accordingly before the end of July they went to stay with Hensleigh and Fanny Wedgwood at a house, Haredene, near Guildford in Surrey, that they had been lent for the summer. Thankful to have Henrietta as a travelling companion, Emma notes in a letter to her eldest sister: 'Charles was so giddy and bad at Croydon I could not leave him.'[11]

By the end of August Charles and Emma had returned to Down for the marriage of their daughter, Henrietta. Now twenty-eight, she had become engaged earlier that year to a thirty-nine-year old bachelor, Richard Litchfield, a scholar, philosopher and philanthropist who was one of the founders of the Working Men's College. Writing to her after she had embarked on a long honeymoon in Switzerland, Charles recalls the happiness she had always given him and concludes: 'I shall miss you sadly. But there is no help for that . . . I have had my day and a happy life notwithstanding my stomach; and this I owe almost entirely to our dear old mother who, as you well know is as good as twice-refined gold.' On the same occasion Emma thanks Henrietta for a very kind letter and adds: 'If I don't get my head turned amongst you all it will be a wonder; but I feel it like F. making me out to be so very ill always, only a proof of his affection, and therefore he does not succeed in making me think myself so very sick or so very good.'[12]

The year 1871 ended with the youngest of Darwin's five sons, Horace, now twenty, passing a critical classics examination at Cambridge. Writing to congratulate him on 15 December, Charles continues: 'I am so glad, and now you can follow the bent of your talents and work as hard at Mathematics and Science as your health will permit.'[13] Horace had never

CHARLES AND EMMA DARWIN'S GROWN UP CHILDREN

William 1877 Sara Sedgwick
(1839-1914)   (1839-1902)
banker, Southampton

Henrietta (Etty) 1871 Richard Litchfield
(1843-1930)   (1831-1903)
editor of *Family Letters*   lawyer & philanthropist

George 1884 Maud du Puy
(1845-1912)   (1861-1947)
Professor of Astronomy &
Experimental Philosophy,
Cambridge

               Charles
               (1887-1962)
    2 sons   Physicist, Master,
  2 daughters Christ's College,
               Cambridge
               William

Elizabeth (Bessy)
(1847-1926)
lived at home

Francis 1874 ① Amy Ruck 1883 ② Ellen Crofts
(1848-1925)   (1850-1876)   (1856-1903)
reader in Botany,
Cambridge
editor of father's *Life & Letters*

1 son   1 daughter
Bernard
(1876-1961)

Leonard 1882 ① Elizabeth Fraser 1900 ② Mildred Massingberd
(1850-1943)   (1846-1898)   (1868-1940)
Major, Royal Engineers
President, Royal Geographical Society

Horace 1880 Ida Farrer
(1851-1928)   (1854-1946)
Founder, Cambridge Scientific
Instrument Company

1 son, Erasmus, killed in action (1881-1915)

1 daughter, Ruth, served on Board for Psychiatric Hospitals
(1883-1973)

1 daughter, Nora ———— Alan Barlow
           (1885-1989) (1881-1966)
           edited Charles Darwin's *Autobiography*
           and related works

been good at exams. Now he would proceed to a career as an inventor and the founder of a very successful company.

A character in the story about whom there is a strange silence is Bessy, the second surviving daughter of Charles and Emma. In 1871, aged twenty-four and unmarried, she was, as custom demanded, still living at home. Nevertheless, despite her constant presence in the house, only very occasionally does her name appear in any of the mountain of family letters, and even then only as happening to be of the party. The questions arise, therefore, what do we know of Bessy and what was her role in life?

Evidently much less able than her brothers and her sister, Henrietta, four years her senior, Bessy was of a retiring disposition and willing to stay in the background doing odd jobs around the house and garden. The only information about her readily available comes from a few pages in the book *Period Piece*, written by her niece, Gwen Raverat. Since, however, this niece was not born until 1885, her description of Bessy belongs to the period after Charles's death, and so is given in the Epilogue. Meanwhile, Bessy's shadowy presence should not be forgotten.

Another figure about whom little is written is Joseph Parslow, who had by now served the family for thirty years and had seen his master become famous and seven of the children grow up. 'Among the faithful servants memory calls up,' writes Leonard Huxley about his visits to Down during the 1870s was 'the round figure, white-haired and apple-faced, of Parslow the butler – a veritable pillar of the house, without whom one could hardly picture the place.'[14] In 1875 Parslow would retire to live with his wife and son in the village. He was succeeded by William Jackson, who would serve until the end of Darwin's life.

The relapse during the summer of 1871, almost certainly caused by Mivart's attack, was to be the last occasion when Darwin had to give up work because of psychosomatic symptoms. There were no doubt many reasons for this improvement, not least that Emma saw to it that he had frequent, if often short, breaks from his work. Thus in February 1872 they were in London for a week or so 'for the sake of rest', as Charles puts it when explaining to the distinguished German biologist, August Weismann (1834–1914), who had sent a reprint, that it would be some little time before he would be able to read it.[15]

Most of 1872 was spent revising the proofs of *Expression of the Emotions*, and the last sheets were returned to Murray on 22 August. Francis thinks that writing the book had proved 'a somewhat severe strain' and cites a letter to Haeckel written at this time: 'I have resumed some old botanical work, and perhaps I shall never again attempt to discuss theoretical views. I am growing old and weak, and no man can tell when his intellectual powers begin to fail.'[16] A few weeks later Emma decides to intervene. Writing to her aunt, she explains: 'Yesterday 3 sons went in different directions to look for a house for us, as I have persuaded Charles to leave home for a few weeks. The microscopic work he has been doing with sundew has proved fatiguing and unwholesome, and he owns he must have rest. Horace came home the fortunate one, like the youngest brother in a fairy-tale. He had found nice lodgings on Sevenoaks Common.' Charles and Emma were there during October. 'We return home on Saturday after three weeks of the most astounding dullness, doing nothing and thinking of nothing,' Darwin tells Huxley. 'I hope my Brain likes it – as for myself it is dreadful doing nothing.' Complain though he might, these breaks in routine organised by Emma seem always to have done him good. This he admits in a revealing letter of 29 October addressed to Fox after their return. 'Three weeks of extreme dullness has done me some good; but my strength fails more and more and I find I require a rest every 6 weeks or 10.'[17]

Darwin ends this letter by claiming that 'Three of my sons are ailing more or less, and have inherited my poor constitution.' The three in question include George and also Horace, about whose alleged ill-health Charles had often complained in earlier letters to Fox.[18] In view of Emma's remark about Charles making her out to be so very ill always, we cannot help being doubtful how seriously to take these anxieties about the sons.

When in November *The Expression of the Emotions* was published, he sent a copy to his old flirting partner, Sarah Mostyn Owen of Woodhouse, now married to a judge, with a long letter recalling the very happy days he had spent with her and her family: 'no scenes in my whole life pass so frequently or so vividly before my mind as those which relate to happy old days spent at Woodhouse. I should very much like to hear a little news about yourself and other members of your family . . . I have had many years of ill-health and have not been able to visit anywhere. As long as I pass a perfectly uniform life, I am able to do some daily work in Natural History, which is still my passion, as it was in old days, when you used to laugh at me for collecting beetles with such zeal at Woodhouse.' Very characteristically he adds to this letter his familiar groan: 'Excepting from my continued ill-health, which has excluded me from Society, my life has been a very happy one; the greatest drawback being that several of my children have inherited from me feeble health.'[19]

IV

In his invaluable reminiscences Francis Darwin has given a lively portrait of his father during his later years and a detailed account of his daily routine.[20] Rising fairly early, Darwin would take a short turn round the garden at about 7.30 am and then back for a solitary breakfast at 7.45. From 8 to 9.30, a period he regarded as the best time in his day, he worked in his study. Next he spent an hour in the drawing-room, reading letters addressed to him and listening to family letters read aloud by Emma. If the post was light, there might be time for a short instalment of the novel Emma was reading to him. At 10.30 am he returned to his study for another ninety minutes of serious work. From 12.15 until one o'clock, when he had lunch, was the time for his principal walk or, for a few years, the time for his ride. Sometimes he confined himself to a few turns round the Sandwalk, sometimes he went further afield. Occasionally Emma went with him, though less often as she grew older.

After lunch he would lie on the sofa reading *The Times* right through, and taking a lively interest in all the news. From two o'clock to three he wrote letters. Short ones he wrote himself, but the longer ones to scientific friends he dictated from a rough draft. At one time Henrietta helped with these letters, later it was Francis; but it appears that as often as not it was Emma who took the dictation. At three o'clock Charles went upstairs to rest for an hour on his bed, while Emma read the current novel to him; but promptly at 4 pm he was down for another walk. Retreating to his study at 4.30, he worked for a further hour, after which he might spend a short time idle in the drawing-room. Next, another rest on his bed, with more novel reading by Emma. In his later years he took to smoking a cigarette or two during his afternoon and evening rests. Sometimes after a bad night he would fall asleep and thereby miss an episode of the novel. 'He had a great horror of drinking', and took only an occasional glass of sherry or other wine.

Dinner was at 7.30, though often he preferred to eat a light high tea while the rest of the family had something more substantial. Next came the celebrated two games of backgammon with Emma, a time often of high spirits, Charles exulting when he won and lamenting bitterly or exploding in mock-anger when he lost. There followed a period of an hour or so when he read some scientific work, groaning miserably when wrestling with some difficult German book or paper. Then, after perhaps half an hour of Emma or some guest playing the piano, he withdrew to his room and was in bed by 10.30. Often he slept badly, lying awake or sitting up in bed suffering much discomfort. Francis continues: 'He was troubled at night by the activity of his thoughts, and would become exhausted by his mind working at some problem which he would willingly have dismissed. At night, too, anything which had vexed or troubled him in the day would haunt him.'[21]

That was the routine, day in day out, weekdays and Sundays alike. Emma always played her part. 'During my father's last years,' Henrietta writes, 'her whole day was planned out to suit him, to be ready for reading aloud to him, to go his walks with him, and to be constantly at hand to alleviate his daily discomforts.'[22]

No account of Darwin's working life would be complete without an emphasis on the meticulous care with which he stored his books and journals and filed his voluminous notes. Every room in Down House became lined with books, each one carefully coded and catalogued. The same care was extended to his finances, every item of expenditure, however trivial, being entered in his account books. When during his working day he found time for all this additional labour is not recorded.

The most intimate account of Charles and Emma during the later years of their marriage is also given in Francis's reminiscences, though much of it is in passages omitted from the 1885 published version. In recalling his father's feeling for his mother, Francis writes:

All the sympathy and tenderness of his nature came out [in his relationship with her]. Rejoicing in all that gladdened her, and feeling with her in any sorrow or anxiety . . . I remember quite well the tone of distress in which he spoke when he heard she had a headache and wasn't coming down . . . They used to laugh at one another in a pleasant way. He chiefly at mother's power of mislaying things and for [the] tendency in her accounts to get mixed up – She would laugh at his impatience or at some odd precaution or fidgetty arrangements, or at some of his simple or naive sayings. . . . Her pet [name] for him was Younigger (pronounced all in one) or 'My nigger' – He generally called her Mammy or some form of that or mother – I think when he called her 'Emma' he was not feeling so much at ease. For instance when fidgetted about something going wrong in her accounts which put his wrong.

They were a model couple in the way in which the machinery of their joint life worked. My mother was always consulted about everything, but the ultimate decision of anything important really rested with my father; and my mother always seemed perfectly happy that it should be so. On the other hand he was glad to be managed in all little things – He often said in fun that the woman was the real master of the house. . . . She used to go and scold him for talking too long with guests etc. This was very useful to him, as it gave an easy way of leaving the room before he was tired out. He would tell her beforehand that she was to send him away early.

In the innumerable books which they read aloud I think their tastes agreed fairly well except that my father was more tolerant of dullness and sometimes was willing to go on with a book which my mother found unbearable. In the matter of science she was naturally not able [to] take a share. . . . My father used to tell how at one of the British Association meetings . . . he had said 'I'm afraid this is very dull for you' and how my mother had placidly answered 'No not duller than everything else'.[23]

V

In Darwin's letter to Horace congratulating him on passing his exam, he adds a paragraph about scientific discovery:

I have been speculating last night what makes a man a discoverer of undiscovered things; and a most perplexing problem it is. Many men who are very clever – much cleverer than the discoverers – never originate anything. As far as I can conjecture the art consists in habitually searching for the causes and meaning of everything which occurs. This implies sharp observation, and requires as much knowledge as possible of the subject investigated.[24]

He might have added that, since causes are never manifest, the only way of proceeding is to propose a plausible theory and then test its explanatory powers against further evidence and in comparison with the powers of rival theories. This he was constantly doing, as Francis emphasises in his 'Recollections' of his father: 'He often said that no one could be a good observer unless he was an active theoriser. . . . It was as though he was charged with theorising power ready to flow into any channel on the slightest disturbance, so that no fact, however small, could miss releasing a stream of theory . . . but fortunately his richness of imagination was equalled by his power of judging and condemning the thoughts that occurred to him.' Theories have to be tested, certainly, but they must not be condemned unheard, and that made him 'willing to test what would seem to most people not at all worth testing. These rather wild trials he called "fool's experiments", and enjoyed extremely.'[25]

Since most theories prove to be untenable, advancing them is a hazardous business and requires courage, a courage that Darwin never lacked.

TWENTY-SEVEN

Almost an Indian summer
1873–1877

I

The last decade of Darwin's life was remarkable for his improved health, greater general contentment, and a vast output of published work. Changes likely to have been responsible were widespread recognition of his scientific achievements with a corresponding reduction in hostile criticism; limiting his work to empirical studies and avoiding controversial theory; the fact that his children were prospering and no longer subject to dangerous illness; and not least Emma's constant devoted care and the regular holidays she insisted on.

Evidence regarding his improved health and happiness comes from several sources. Shortly after Charles's death in April 1882, Emma, replying to a letter from son William, writes: 'I have been reading over his old letters. I have not many, we were so seldom apart, and never I think for the last 15 or 20 years, and it is a consolation for me to think that the last 10 or 12 years were the happiest (owing to the former suffering state of his health, which appears in every letter).'[1]

The picture is endorsed by Francis, who, having qualified in medicine, never practised but instead was devoting himself to botanical research. He lived in the village and acted as his father's secretary and research assistant. Reflecting on these years, he writes:

During the last ten years of his life the state of his health was a cause of satisfaction and hope to his family. His condition showed signs of amendment in several particulars. He suffered less distress and discomfort, and was able to work more steadily. . . . In later years he became a patient of Sir Andrew Clark*. . . . It was not only for his generously rendered service that my father felt a debt of gratitude to Sir Andrew Clark. He owed to his cheering personal influence an often-repeated encouragement, which latterly added something real to his

---

*Dr Andrew Clark (1826–1893), a prominent London physician, first attended Darwin in 1873, the year that his former physician Dr Bence Jones died. He was not created a baronet until 1883, thus remaining plain Dr Clark during Darwin's lifetime.

happiness, and he found sincere pleasure in Sir Andrew's friendship and kindness towards himself and his children.[2]

Yet another witness testifying to this improvement is Darwin's new manservant William Jackson, who is reported to have replied to a neighbour enquiring about Darwin's health: 'Master's illnesses nowadays are nothing to what they used to be.'[3] (Since Jackson had not been with the family before 1875, he was presumably quoting a common opinion.)

Since in Darwin's letters of the period the familiar groans about his health appear with regularity, and during the last couple of years his physical health was clearly beginning to fail, it seems likely that the principal improvement in his condition lay in his suffering less anxiety and less depression. Whatever the reason, a main effect was that he had no further breakdown and was thus able to maintain his regular work routine without further interruption.

Darwin's extraordinary productivity during this decade stands in stark contrast to his oft-repeated assertions of earlier years that he was worn out and incapable of doing anything further. The list of his publications shows five new books, seven new editions of earlier works and the reprinting of an eighth, and thirty-three scientific notes or longer papers. In addition, he continued to participate in an extensive scientific correspondence on matters botanical, zoological and geological, to keep abreast of scientific publications and to comment on works in English, French and German sent him by colleagues and admirers. Moreover, new editions of his earlier works were continually being called for, and these often required extensive revision which caused him much pain and grief.

The five new books all report the results of observations and experiments carried out at Down, many of them in conjunction with Francis. In each case the originality of the book lies in its being a study of function. In what way, Darwin asks, do certain structures and movements of plants contribute to their survival and reproduction? What are the effects, beneficial or otherwise, of the activities of earthworms? Although such questions arose naturally in the mind of someone steeped in an evolutionary approach, they did not cross the minds of those working in the biological tradition of the day. Thus the reception of Darwin's work by the established botanists, who confined themselves to descriptive and taxonomic issues, was a mixed one. Some were excited by their novelty, others frowned on it. 'Many of the Germans are very contemptuous about my making out the use of organs,' he tells a friend; 'but . . . I for one shall think it the most interesting part of Natural History.'[4]

Another feature of these last years was the steady stream of honours Darwin received, some from Britain, many more from other countries. In Britain he had already received the highest honour his fellow scientists could confer, the Copley Medal of the Royal Society, and high honours had already been given also by Sweden (1865) and Prussia (1867). Now during the 1870s he was elected an honorary member of the most prestigious scientific societies in most of the leading countries: Germany (both Prussia and Bavaria), Austro-Hungary, Italy, Belgium, Denmark, the United States and Argentina. Moreover, another form of honour was awarded him. From Germany came an album containing the portraits of 154 men of science, including some of the most famous scientists in the world. Darwin described it to Haeckel as 'by far the greatest honour' he had ever received. From Holland he received a similar album of distinguished Dutch students of natural history.

Among French scientists Darwin's work was less acceptable – which may have been due partly to his cavalier treatment of Lamarck. Much to Lyell's indignation, when in 1872 Darwin was proposed for election to the Zoological Section of the French Institute he received only one-third of the votes. This was explained by an eminent member in a letter to the French press. What had led to Darwin's exclusion, he wrote, was 'that the science of those of his books which have made his chief title to fame – the *Origin of Species*, and still more the *Descent of Man*, is not science, but a mass of assertions and absolutely gratuitous hypotheses, often evidently fallacious. This kind of publication and these theories are a bad example, which a body that respects itself cannot encourage.'[5] Eventually, in 1878, Darwin was elected a Corresponding Member of the Botanical Section, which he regrded as 'a good joke' in view of his slender knowledge of botany.

In his own country, it will be remembered, Darwin had been unable to accept an honorary degree offered by Oxford. In 1877, however, his own university, Cambridge, invited him, and this time he accepted. Another British honour he appreciated was the Baly Medal of the Royal College of Physicians. No national honour was ever offered;* but when he died public acclaim demanded he be buried in Westminster Abbey.

II

The year 1873 opened with Darwin correcting the proofs of the second edition of his book *On the Movement and Habits of Climbing Plants*, and then resuming work on another botanical book, *The Effects of Cross and Self Fertilisation in the Vegetable Kingdom*. Other activities included notes to *Nature* on 'Inherited Instinct' and on 'Perception in the Lower Animals', and a steady flow of correspondence with scientific friends.

At this time, Francis Galton, Darwin's second cousin, was strongly advocating a policy of eugenics and had published an article in *Fraser's Magazine* entitled 'Hereditary Improvement'. What he proposed was to improve the human species by means of differential breeding: 'a sentiment of caste among those who are naturally gifted' should be built up and a policy adopted to give them various social preferences. In

*The two honours for which today he would have been held supremely well qualified, the Order of Merit and the Companion of Honour, were not instituted intil 1902 and 1917 respectively.

addition, a society should be founded to keep a register for breeding purposes. In his reply to Galton's letter, Darwin points out a number of practical difficulties, of which the greatest, he thought, 'would be in deciding who deserved to be on the register; . . . Though I see so much difficulty,' he concludes, 'the object is a grand one; . . . yet I fear [it is] utopian.'[6]

In March Charles's work programme was interrupted. On Emma's initiative, they took a house in London near to Henrietta and Richard Litchfield, and stayed there a month. 'Charles had much rather stay at home', Emma writes to her ageing aunt, 'but knows his place and submits.' During this visit Emma and Lady Lyell instigated a plan to raise funds to enable Huxley to take time off to recover his health and strength. For the past fifteen months he had been in a bad state, anxious, depressed and dyspeptic, and a three months' cruise in the Mediterranean to Cairo the previous spring had given only temporary relief. Charles joined actively in the ladies' project and a sum of over £2000 was raised. Charles next had the delicate task of persuading Huxley to accept it. 'He sent off the awful letter to Mr. Huxley yesterday, and I hope we may hear tomorrow,' writes Emma. But all was well and Huxley accepted gratefully.[7]

Huxley's breakdown had begun at the end of 1871.[8] He was having a house built in St John's Wood for his growing family, two sons and five daughters, but in November a neighbour had initiated a lawsuit claiming the work had led to flooding of his house. This had caused Huxley very great anxiety lest he be saddled with heavy costs just when his finances were being stretched to the limit by the building. By June 1872 the claim had failed but legal expenses remained. With a vast number of public commitments for which he received no payment and with no private money, Huxley's finances were always fragile, and not helped by a regular allowance to a sister whose husband had become incapable.[9] On receiving Darwin's letter of 23 April 1873 with the generous donation from his many friends, Huxley exclaimed, 'What have I done to deserve this?', but the relief from financial anxiety was such that he accepted it.

Even so, he continued to suffer from 'severe mental depression', to use Hooker's words, and was once again ordered by his medical adviser to take a trip abroad.[10] To that, however, 'he offered a stubborn resistance'. At this point Hooker stepped in: 'being myself quite in a mood for a holiday, I volunteered to wrestle with him, and succeeded, holding out as an inducement a visit to the volcanic region of the Auvergne.' On 2 July 1873 they set out 'loaded with injunctions from his physician as to what his patient was to eat, drink and avoid, how much he was to sleep and rest, how little to walk and talk, etc., that would have made the expedition a perpetual burden to me had I not believed that I knew enough of my friend's disposition and ailments to be convinced that not only health but happiness would be our companions throughout.' Hooker was right.

Within days Huxley's spirits revived. Arrived in the Auvergne, the two friends, Hooker aged fifty-six and Huxley forty-eight, enjoyed long hill walks with some gentle geologising; and within ten days the invalid was climbing 4000 feet to a peak seven miles distant. After a month of this therapeutic companionship, Hooker returned home and Huxley was joined by his wife and son. By the end of August he was himself again and ready to resume his multifarious duties which, in addition to his heavy teaching load at the School of Mines, included being secretary of the Royal Society, serving on the Royal Commission on Scientific Instruction and membership of the London School Board.

III

Back at Down in the spring of 1873 and with the proofs of *Climbing Plants* finished, Darwin returned to the study of his beloved *Drosera*, the tiny plant that feeds on insects. Then in early August, no doubt again on Emma's initiative, they made a first visit to Thomas Farrer and his second wife, the daughter of Hensleigh and Fanny Wedgwood, whom he had recently married. Farrer (later Lord Farrer) was a senior civil servant who lived in a comfortable house at Abinger in Surrey. He was a keen botanist and had had some correspondence with Darwin during the previous four years. From now on they became close friends. Henrietta describes the scene: 'This pleasant friendly house was now added to the very few places where my father felt enough at ease to pay visits. In general he considered his health debarred him from such pleasures. He much enjoyed Mr. Farrer's talk.' He also liked walking on the common. After Darwin's death Lord Farrer recalled: ' here it was a particular pleasure of his to wander, and his tall figure, with his broad-brimmed Panama hat and long stick like an alpenstock, sauntering solitary and slow over our favourite walks is one of the pleasantest . . . associations I have with the place.'[11]

After Abinger, Charles and Emma went to stay with William at Basset, just outside Southampton. This had for long been a favourite place to visit, their *séjour de la paix*, as they liked to call it.

In September soon after their return to Down, Darwin had an attack which has suggested a brief episode of cerebral anoxia – a shortage of oxygen to the brain due to the blood supply being temporarily reduced. In a letter to Hooker dated 12 September Darwin described it as 'much loss of memory and severe shock continually passing through my brain'. Dr Clark was called in and was reassuring. Later the same month Darwin wrote again to Hooker: 'Dr. Clark is convinced that the brain is affected only secondarily for which thank God, as I would far sooner die than lose my mind. Clark is doing good by an abominable diet.' In fact Darwin 'recovered remarkably quickly', to use Emma's words, and soon began work again. 'I think with invalids', she writes to her aunt, 'unusual health "goes before a fall". I hardly ever saw him so well as the Sunday and

Monday before his attack.' Any benefits there may have been from the
diet soon evaporated. In December he was telling Huxley, 'The great
benefit at first was, I believe, merely due to a change, and changes of all
kinds are at first highly beneficial to me.'[12]

Later that autumn Charles and Emma went to London to stay for the
first time in Henrietta and Richard's house in Bryanston Square,
Marylebone. To protect Charles, Emma insisted he saw none of his
friends except the Huxleys. 'We shall stay a week,' she had told Henrietta
before the visit. 'I should like to stay 10 days but I don't think I shall
compass that.' Charles was deeply absorbed observing the night-time
behaviour of an Indian plant he was studying. '[He] went to see it last
night,' continues Emma. 'It was dead asleep, all but its little ears which
were having most lively games, such as he never saw in the day-time.'[13]

Back at Down in November Darwin's botanical studies were rudely
interrupted by his having to prepare a second edition of *The Descent of
Man*. This he found a most unwelcome chore, since he was by then
immersed in the writing of his book on *Insectivorous Plants*, to the study of
which he had returned whenever possible ever since he first observed
Drosera in 1860. 'I never in my lifetime regretted an interruption so much
as this new edition of the *Descent*', he told Wallace; and a few weeks later
wrote to Huxley: 'The new edition of the *Descent* has turned out an awful
job. It took me ten days merely to glance over letters and reviews with
criticisms and new facts. It is a devil of a job.' Completion of the revisions
took him until the end of March the following year, when, as Francis puts
it, 'he was able to return to his much loved *Drosera*'.[14]

The four and a half months Darwin was working on the revision of
Descent was broken by a brief visit in the new year to Ras in London. At
that time spiritualism had become a fashionable interest and to amuse the
company his son George had hired a medium. 'We had grand fun,'
Charles writes on 10 January 1874: the medium 'made the chairs, a flute,
a bell, and candlestick, and fiery points jump about in my brother's dining
room, in a manner that astounded everyone. . . . The Lord have mercy on
us, if we have to believe in such rubbish.' Subsequently, in a letter to
Huxley, Darwin describes, very plausibly, how he thinks it was done.
Emma remained noncommittal and unimpressed.[15]

On 11 May, answering a letter from Fox, Darwin as usual gives a brief
account of his own health: 'I have been rather better of late, but I never
pass six hours without much discomfort.' Commenting on Fox's
reference to their advancing years, Darwin finds that old age is not
without its advantages: 'I think one takes everything more quietly, as not
signifying so much.'[16]

The summer of 1874 saw the first of the five Darwin sons get married.
Francis, now twenty-six, married Amy Ruck, aged twenty-four, from
Wales. They took a house in Downe village and Francis continued to act
as assistant to his father.

During August Charles and Emma spent about a fortnight with William at Basset, where they were joined by George. In a letter to Leonard, who had recently sailed with an expedition to New Zealand to observe and photograph the transit of Venus, Emma writes describing their 'most successful and peaceful stay with dear old William. F. says he has not felt so rested and improved and full of enjoyment since old Moor Park days. . . . Our expeditions . . . have chiefly consisted in driving as far as N. Stoneham Park and getting out for a short walk. I had no idea it was so charming and pretty, and F. finds he was quite mistaken in thinking he had succeeded in crushing out his taste for scenery, or that for a beautiful garden, which he saw yesterday in such a blaze of sun. . . . The Bessemer Steam-boat is to be launched in 3 weeks. I don't despair of taking F. across some day' (presumably to the Isle of Wight).[17]

Later that year, at the meeting of the British Association in Belfast, the president (Professor J. Tyndall, a physicist and long-time friend of Huxley's) gave a brilliant address on the history of evolution culminating in an eloquent analysis of the *Origin*. This led Lyell to write a congratulatory note to Darwin: 'You and your theory of Evolution may be fairly said to have had an ovation.'[18]

For the rest of 1874 Darwin was drafting his manuscript on *Insectivorous Plants*, though he had one further interruption when he was called upon to revise his book on *Coral Reefs*, by then a classic. New facts were added, the whole book revised, and the later chapters almost rewritten. The new edition appeared later the same year.[19]

IV

In 1874 Lyell was in his late seventies but still actively geologising, despite his growing blindness. Early in 1875, however, in his seventy-eighth year, he died; his wife had died two years earlier. Writing to Lyell's long-time secretary, Darwin remarks how completely Lyell had revolutionised geology and how he never forgot that almost everything he himself had done in science he owed to the study of Lyell's works. Rejoicing with Hooker that Lyell was to be buried in Westminster Abbey, he added that he had been asked by members of the family to be one of the pall-bearers but had declined, fearing he would fail in the midst of the ceremony.[20]

Another death of significance to the family occurred a few months later. Emma's maternal aunt, Fanny Allen, to whom so many of Emma's letters are addressed, died aged ninety-four; she had been in good health to the end.

Meanwhile Darwin was busy trying to complete *Insectivorous Plants*. Francis remarks that his father seemed to have been 'more than usually oppressed by the writing of this book' and quotes a letter written to Hooker during February: 'You ask about my book and all that I can say is that I am ready to commit suicide; I thought it was decently written but find so much wants rewriting, that it will not be ready for the printers for two months,'[21] In the event it was completed in March and published in early July 1875. Of the first printing of 3000 copies, 2700 were sold.

During February and March that year Darwin sat for the first of what would be three official portraits in oils, each commissioned by an academic body. Walter Ouless, RA (1848–1933), was asked by Darwin's old Cambridge college, Christ's, to paint a head and shoulders. Darwin found the sittings 'a great fatigue', but his son Francis thought well of the portrait and was later to describe it as 'the finest representation of my father that has been produced'. Darwin's own opinion was conveyed in a letter to Hooker: 'I look a very venerable, acute, melancholy old dog; whether I really look so I do not know.'[22]

From early in the 1870s vivisection had been causing controversy and a movement to have it banned had become increasingly vocal. Already in 1870 the British Association had set up a committee to consider the issues, and in March 1871 we find Darwin expressing strong views in reply to questions put to him by a biologist colleague: 'I quite agree that it is justifiable for real investigations on physiology; but not for mere damnable and detestable curiosity. It is a subject which makes me sick with horror, so I will not say another word about it, else I shall not sleep tonight.'[23] By 1875 some form of legislation was being proposed, but before acting the government decided on a Royal Commission, which began its work in July.

Meanwhile Darwin had been trying to clarify his ideas on the subject and in early January he had written a long letter to Henrietta, who had raised the subject and had evidently wanted him to sign an anti-vivisection petition. In reply he explains that he is concerned to see vivisection strictly controlled but also to ensure that serious physiological investigation be permitted. Thus, he writes, on the one hand he has 'rejoiced at the present agitation' but, on the other, he 'is certain that physiology can progress only by experiments on living animals'. The proposal 'to limit research to points of which we can now see the bearings in regard to health etc.' he regards as 'puerile'. 'I have long thought physiology one of the greatest sciences, sure sooner, or more probably later, greatly to benefit mankind; but, judging from all other sciences, the benefits will accrue only indirectly in the search for abstract truth.' In conclusion he tells Henrietta, 'I cannot at present see my way to sign any petition without hearing what physiologists thought would be its effect, and then judging for myself.'[24]

During early April, after Charles had finished *Insectivorous Plants*, he and Emma paid a short visit to Henrietta and Richard in London. About this visit he writes to Hooker on 14 April; 'I worked all the time in London on the vivisection question; and we now think it advisable to go further than a mere petition.' Richard Litchfield had drawn up a sketch of a bill.

Darwin proceeds to list a number of prominent scientists who are supporting the move and says they 'wish me to see Lord Derby, and endeavour to gain his advocacy with the Home Secretary'. He is arranging for a copy of the draft to be sent to Hooker, whose support as president of the Royal Society was essential. 'Pray let me have a line from you soon.'[25] Hooker gave his support and the draft went forward.

Darwin's role in the vivisection debate was not yet ended, however. The Royal Commission was taking evidence and requested him to attend a session, which he did on 8 November. Emma, writing to Leonard, tells how the chairman 'came to the door to meet him and he was treated like a Duke. They only wanted him to repeat what he had said in his letter (a sort of confession of faith about the claims of physiology and the duty of humanity) and he had hardly a word more to add.'[26] In due course an Act regulating vivisection was passed, though controversy continued.

For a month from early June 1875 Charles and Emma were at Abinger Hall with the Farrers – a move designed to give Charles a long break from work. After their return to Down he describes the circumstances of the visit: 'I was quite knocked up and worried with the subject so that I had to take a month's complete rest away from home.'[27] Ralph Colp states that 'the subject' was the book on *Insectivorous Plants*;[28] but there were two other matters that may well have been worrying Darwin also. One was his political responsibilities over vivisection, the other the renewed attack both on him personally and on his theories by Mivart.

In July the previous year (1874) Mivart had published some severe criticisms of the first edition of the *Descent of Man*, claiming that Darwin did 'not exhibit the faintest indication of having grasped' certain elementary distinctions and principles. Now, in his new book, *Lessons from Nature*, Mivart continued his campaign in what Wallace describes as 'a violent attack [in] unusually strong language'. Among other things Darwinians were accused of 'unscrupulous audacity' and a 'conspiracy of silence'. The following year Wallace, in his review of Mivart's book, once again springs to Darwin's defence, for which on 17 June 1876 Darwin expresses himself as deeply grateful.[29] Fortunately, this kind of personal attack on Darwin and his theories was no longer in vogue, but on the occasions when they did erupt they were certainly distressing.

Back at Down in early July 1875 Darwin began two months' work preparing a second edition of *Variation*, which included extensive rewriting of the chapter on pangenesis. That done, he resumed work on the next book, *The Effects of Cross and Self Fertilisation in the Vegetable Kingdom*, the first draft of which would occupy him until early May of the following year.

One of the few enthusiasts for Darwin's theory of pangenesis was George John Romanes (1848–1894), an able young man of Scottish descent and private means, who during the early 1870s was doing physiological research in the newly founded Physiology School at

Charles Darwin, aged 66, etching from a painting by Walter Ouless, RA, 1875

George Romanes, 1848–94, physiologist and youthful admirer of the aging savant. Aged 43 in 1891

Down House photographed by Leonard Darwin, 1877

Cambridge.[30] He was a tremendous admirer of Darwin and was therefore beside himself with joy when in 1873 a letter he wrote to *Nature* on the colour of fish led to a 'friendly little note' from the great man himself. A correspondence developed and a year later Romanes was invited to Down. 'From that time began an unbroken friendship, marked on one side by absolute worship, reverence and affection, on the other by an almost fatherly kindness and a wonderful interest in the younger man's work and in his career. Mr. Darwin met him [at Down], as he [Romanes] often used to tell, with outstretched hands, and a bright smile, and a "How glad I am that you are so young!"' Thereafter Romanes made regular visits to Down once or twice a year. Later on, during the years 1875–78 when Romanes was working at University College, London, Darwin usually visited him whenever he was in town.

Romanes had two research interests at this time. As regards the first, pangenesis, he was planning experiments hoping to obtain evidence supporting the theory, and Darwin was naturally delighted. The second, which proved more successful, was the nervous systems of marine invertebrates, for example jellyfish. As these were plentiful on the east coast of Scotland from June onwards, he could experiment on them there while staying at his mother's old home, where he had fitted out a small laboratory. Later in the summer he could vary his experimental work with a day or two's shooting. On one occasion he sent Darwin a present of game. Darwin replied thanking him and then, echoing the dire warnings of his father when he himself was a keen young shooting man, added, 'I hope you are well and strong and do not give up all your time to shooting', and then threatens playfully, to take Romanes's wife to task should he 'turn idle'.

V

During the first four months of 1876 Darwin had an uninterrupted spell completing the first draft of *Cross and Self Fertilisation*, at the end of which he and Emma spent a fortnight with Hensleigh and Fanny Wedgwood at Hopedene, between Dorking and Guildford in Surrey. From there on 29 May he writes a long letter to Romanes, mainly about pangenesis, and ending: 'We have come here for rest for me, which I have much needed; and shall remain here for about ten days more, and then home to work, which is my sole pleasure in life.' A week later he writes to Wallace congratulating him on his recently published *magnum opus*, which Darwin had evidently been reading at Hopedene: 'You have written, as I believe, a grand and memorable work, which will last for years as the foundation for all future treatises on Geographical Distribution.'[31] Darwin's prediction was to prove correct.

Back at Down he started preparing a second edition of his book on the fertilisation of orchids, and during the afternoons continued with his brief

Autobiography, which he had begun at Hopedene and finished on 3 August. Next day Emma writes to Leonard at Malta, on his way back from New Zealand, 'The time passes so quickly in our methodical life that I find I have been 10 days without writing to you. . . . F. has finished his Autobiography and I find it very interesting', adding that others less familiar with his life 'would find it more so'. 'The summer keeps on blazing away,' Emma tells Leonard., 'F. has taken to sit and lie out which is wholesome for him.' From time to time the even flow of life was broken by visitors, some distinguished, others mere sightseers eager to get a glimpse of 'the great man himself'. Among the distinguished were several Germans, whom Emma found a little trying: 'Häckel came on Tuesday. He was very nice and hearty and affectionate, but he bellowed out his bad English in such a voice that he nearly deafened us. However, that was nothing to yesterday.' She proceeds to describe a lunch party with two German professors, one deaf but with a nice wife: 'anything like the noise they made I never heard. Both visits were short and F. was glad to have seen them.'[32]

During August and September 1876 Darwin was correcting proofs of *Cross and Self Fertilisation*, which was published later that year (1500 copies). All appears to have been running smoothly that summer, and there is a letter to his son George, written on 13 July, showing Darwin in high spirits. First he rejoices that George's work in astronomy is going so well and that his papers are to be presented to the Royal Society: 'I know I shall feel quite proud.' Next he lists the exploits of his other sons in their diverse fields – scientific instrument making, botany and military engineering: 'Horace goes to lecture on his dynamo at Birmingham. Frank is getting on very well with Dipsacus and has now made experiments which convince me [of the validity of a finding] about which I was beginning to feel horrid doubts. Leonard going to build forts. O Lord, what a set of sons I have, all doing wonders.'[33]

That autumn Francis's wife, Amy, gave birth to a boy, the first of Darwin's grandchildren. He was named Bernard. This happy event was marred by tragedy, however: Amy died. In the published sources there is no record of how this affected Charles. On Emma, however, Henrietta reports the effect was far-reaching: 'The shock and the loss had a deep effect . . . and I think made her permanently more fearful and anxious.' Some years later, soon after Charles's death, Emma spoke of her feelings to Henrietta: 'I feel I can bear your father's loss. I felt I couldn't bear Amy's.'[34]

After Amy's death, Francis and Bernard came to live in Down House with Charles and Emma. 'The baby was a great delight to both my parents,' records Henrietta, 'and my mother took up the old nursery cares as if she were still a young woman. Fortunately, little Bernard was a healthy and good child so there was not much anxiety, but it greatly changed her life. She wrote: "your father is taking a great deal to the Baby.

We think he (the Baby) is a sort of Grand Lama, he is so solemn".'[35] During subsequent years there are often references to Bernard in Emma's letters. Although he had a nanny, Emma clearly took joint responsibility with Francis until he married again in 1883.

During the last months of 1876 Darwin was continuing his botanical experiments, the results of which would be reported in his next book, *The Different Forms of Flowers on Plants of the Same Species*. In December he and Emma were in London, staying with Ras. From there he writes in good spirits to a botanical friend. He had been to a meeting of the Royal Society especially to see Hooker presiding and was deeply disappointed he was not there. There were compensations, however. 'My outing gave me much satisfaction. . . . I saw lots of people, and it has not done me a penny's worth of harm, though I could not get to sleep till nearly four o'clock.'[36]

During the first months of 1877 Darwin was hard at work on *Different Forms of Flowers*, which appears to have caused him less anxiety and distress than the previous book. He and Emma then had a long June holiday during which they stayed first with the Farrers at Abinger, next with Joe and Caroline at Leith Hill Place nearby and finally with William at Basset. Charles seems to have been in good spirits throughout.

At Abinger Darwin renewed his longstanding interest in the activities of earthworms. In one of her almost daily letters to Henrietta, Emma tells her that 'F. was made very happy by finding two very old stones at the bottom of the field, and he has now got a man at work digging for the worms.'[37] Francis reports that the old stones were in fact the remains of a building of Romano-British times, and that finding them afforded his father an opportunity to see 'the effects produced by earthworms on the old concrete floors, walls etc.' Subsequently Darwin wrote to his host: 'I cannot remember a more delightful week than the last. I know very well that E. will not believe me but the worms were by no means the sole charm.' Three years later Darwin began his experimental studies of the activities of earthworms, which were reported in 1881 in his last major publication.

After moving on to stay with William at Basset, Charles and Emma, with George's help, undertook a long day trip to see Stonehenge. Emma had her misgivings: 'We are really going to Stonehenge tomorrow,' she tells Henrietta. 'I am afraid it will half kill F. – two hours rail and a twenty-four mile drive [twelve each way] – but he is bent on going, chiefly for the worms, but also he has always wished to see it.' Two days later she is writing: 'We started from here at 6.45 a.m. on a most lovely day only alarmingly hot.' The old soldier placed there to keep guard 'was quite agreeable to any amount of digging', but, adds Emma, 'they did not find much good about the worms who seem to be very idle out there. . . . I was not so tired as I expected and F. was wonderful, as he did a great deal of waiting out in the sun.'[38]

Back at Down, Darwin began systematic observations and experiments, the results of which were later to appear in the book *The Power of Movement in*

Plants. By the autumn Francis reports, 'his enthusiasm for the subject was thoroughly established'. 'I am all on fire at the work,' Darwin tells a friend.[39] By then the previous volume, *The Different Forms of Flowers* had been published (1250 copies), and also a short paper in the new journal, *Mind*, in which he reported the observations he had made nearly forty years previously on the early years of his first-born child, William.

November 1877 saw two enjoyable events. The first was the marriage of this same William, now turning thirty-eight, to an American of the same age, Sara Sedgwick. She had been known to William and his parents for nearly ten years, having visited England from time to time with her sister and brother-in-law and stayed in the vicinity of Down. Charles and Emma welcomed their new daughter-in-law with enthusiasm.[40]

The second great event was the honorary degree Darwin received at Cambridge. Emma writes a long and entertaining letter to William, who was unable to be there:

Bessy and I and the two youngest brothers [Leonard and Horace] went first to the Senate House and got in by a side door, and a most striking sight it was. The gallery crammed to overflowing with undergraduates, and the floor crammed too with undergraduates climbing on the statues and standing up in the windows. There seemed to be periodical cheering in answer to jokes which sounded deafening; but when F. came in, in his red cloak, ushered in by some authorities, it was perfectly deafening for some minutes. I thought he would be overcome, but he was quite stout and smiling and sat for a considerable time waiting for the Vice-Chancellor. The time was filled up with shouts and jokes, and groans for an unpopular Proctor, Mr. . . . , which were quite awful, and he looked up at them with a stern angry face, which was very bad policy. We had been watching some cords stretched across from one gallery to another wondering what was to happen, but were not surprised to see a monkey dangling down which caused shouts and jokes about our ancestors, etc. A proctor was foolish enough to go up to capture it and at last it disappeared I don't know how. Then came a sort of ring tied with ribbons which we conjectured to be the 'Missing Link'.[41]

At long last the vice-chancellor arrived and the ceremony began. While the public orator was struggling through 'his very tedious harangue, [he was] constantly interrupted by the most unmannerly shouts and jeers.' The ceremony over, 'everybody came up and shook hands. Of all days in the year I had a baddish headache, but managed to go and enjoyed it all. . . . I felt very grand walking about with my LLD. in his silk gown.'

The following day Darwin met a lot of friends, and there followed 'a brilliant luncheon at George's'. In a note to George after their return home, his father writes: 'I enjoyed my stay at Cambridge to a very unusual degree, owing chiefly to you good boys.' The same cheerful mood pervades the letter Darwin writes to Fox soon afterwards on 2 December: 'As for myself I am better than usual and am working away very hard on the physiology of plants. We had a grand time of it in Cambridge and I saw my old rooms at Christ's where we spent so many happy days.'[42]

TWENTY-EIGHT

Last years
1878–1882

I

During 1878 and 1879, Darwin continued in better health and, with much appreciated help from Francis, continued happy and busy with his botanical experiments. Moreover, following the pattern of recent years, Emma organised regular breaks in Charles's working routine.

During both years Darwin's main occupation was studying movement in plants – for example, flowers closing at dusk and the curling movements of climbers – and trying to formulate some general principles to account for them. Another botanical problem he attacked was the function of bloom on the leaves of certain plants. During the spring of 1879 he also spent some weeks working on the biography of his grandfather,the great Erasmus Darwin, the publication of which was to lead to a most unfortunate and unnecessary controversy the following year. Meanwhile, during 1878 and 1879 there seem to have been few events to cause him anxiety or distress.

1878 saw Charles and Emma away from Down on three occasions. The first was a fortnight during the spring with the newly married William and Sara at Basset; this Charles describes in a note to a botanist friend on 29 April as 'a fortnight's complete rest, which I required from too hard work'. The next was an ambitious round of visits during August, and finally a week in London during November with Ras 'for a little rest which I much needed', as he tells a friend.[1]

The August visits comprised five days with Joe and Caroline at Leith Hill Place, another five days with the Farrers at Abinger, and finally a week at Barlaston, in Staffordshire, for a visit to Emma's brother Frank, who was continuing as manager of the Wedgwood works. While planning this series of visits, Emma tells Henrietta: 'It is almost incredible that F. should agree, and I am afraid not coming home after ten days absence will be very serious.' In the event Emma's misgivings proved well founded. From Barlaston Charles writes a long technical letter to Romanes on 20 August, ending: 'Thank Heaven, we return home on

Thursday, and I shall be able to go on with my humdrum work, and that makes me forget my discomforts.'[2]

Back at Down during the autumn Darwin was able to celebrate the great success of his astronomer son George, who had joined the debate about the age of the earth with a brilliantly original paper, 'On the Influence of Geological Changes on the Earth's Axis of Rotation', which had greatly impressed Sir William Thomson, Darwin's old and much-feared critic. In it George had drawn attention to various influences that should be taken into account in estimating the age of the earth which Thomson had neglected. Whereas some of these influences pointed to a greater age than Thomson had estimated, others supported his position. In either case George's reputation was made and the direction of his future work determined. Henceforward he would have Thomson as his friend and supporter. Darwin marked the occasion with an enthusiastic letter:

Down, Oct. 29th [1878]

My Dear Old George,

I have been delighted with your letter and read it all with eagerness. You were very good to write it. All of us are delighted, for considering what a man Sir William Thomson is, it is most grand that you should have staggered him so quickly, and that he should speak of your 'discovery etc' and about the moon's period. I also chuckle greatly about the internal heat. How this will please the geologists and evolutionists. That does sound awkward about the heat being bottled up in the middle of the earth. What a lot of swells you have been meeting and it must have been very interesting.

Hurrah for the bowels of the earth and their viscosity and for the moon and for the Heavenly bodies and for my son George (F.R.S. very soon).

Yours affectionately

C. Darwin[3]

Another pleasant surprise of that autumn was a letter from a complete stranger, a Mr Anthony Rich, who was without children and had decided to leave his considerable fortune to Darwin and his family. 'I never before heard of a bequest to a man for what he has been able to do in science,' he tells his eldest son.[4]

1879 had much in common with the previous year. Charles and Francis continued to work hard on *The Power of Movement in Plants*. When he started to draft the book during the spring we hear some familiar groans: 'I am overwhelmed with my notes,' he tells a friend, 'and almost too old to undertake the job which I have in hand – i.e. movements of all kinds. Yet it is worse to be idle.' During the summer he is more optimistic. Writing to Victor Carus regarding a possible German translation, he proceeds, 'Together with my son Francis, I am preparing a rather large volume on the general movements of Plants and I think we have made out a good many new points and views . . . we have been working very hard for some years at the subject.' During the autumn he was still drafting and tells Asa Gray on 24 October: 'I have written a rather big book – more is the pity . . . and I am now just beginning to go over the M.S. for the second time, which is a horrid bore.'[5]

Meanwhile Emma had made sure Charles would have some breaks. First they spent a week in May at Basset, whence Emma reports to Henrietta: 'I am afraid F. does a little too much work but it quite keeps off *ennui*, which might be powerful in this dismal cold weather.'[6] On the return journey they called in for a few days to see Joe and Caroline at Leith Hill Place. In mid-June Charles, most reluctantly, gave up two whole days' work to sit to William Richmond (1842–1921), who, commissioned to paint a portrait for which members of Cambridge University were subscribing, visited him at Down. William Richmond (later Sir William, RA) has left a brief record of the sitting in some reminiscences of his life and in a letter to his father, George Richmond (1809–96), who forty years earlier had been commissioned by Emma's father, Josiah II, to paint watercolour portraits of his newly married youngest daughter and also of his new son-in-law. In this letter William Richmond describes Darwin as 'the most modest man I ever met', and refers to the difficulty he had had in getting him to talk. There was, however, one topic that Richmond raised that struck a spark, namely the long-lasting influence of childhood memories. 'I asked Mr. Darwin', Richmond records in his memoirs, 'which of the years of a child's life were the most subject to incubative impressions; his answer was: "without doubt, the first three." This appeared to be a rash statement from so cautious a thinker, but the reason he gave was that the brain at that period is entirely formed – it is a virgin brain adapted to receive impressions, and although unable to formulate or memorize these, they none the less remain and can affect the whole future life of the child recipient.' 'I know by experience that Mr. Darwin's statement is true,' comments Richmond.[7]

As it turns out, neither of the Richmond portraits is successful. George Richmond makes the coming young scientist of 1840 look like a prim dandy, while the much more ambitious oil of the distinguished savant in the scarlet gown of an honorary doctor of laws by William Richmond was the target of stern criticism from Darwin's family when, some months later, they saw the finished version. 'I thought it quite horrid,' writes Emma to Henrietta, 'so fierce and so dirty'; while Francis reports that in his view 'neither the attitude nor the expression are characteristic of my father'.[8]

In August 1879, a month after the sitting, Charles and Emma, with other members of the family, ventured on a month-long holiday to Coniston in the Lake District. Henrietta gives a glowing account:

My father enjoyed the journey there with the freshness of a boy – the picnic luncheon, and the passing country seen from the train. Even missing the connection at Foxfield, and being hours late, did not daunt his cheerfulness. One expedition was made to Grasmere. My father was in a state of enthusiastic delight, jumping up from his seat in the carriage to see better at every striking moment. During this visit they also had the interest and pleasure of making friends with Ruskin. I remember very well his first call on them and his courteous manner: his courtesy even included giving my father the title of 'Sir Charles'.[9]

That autumn the youngest of the five Darwin sons, Horace, now twenty-eight, became engaged to Thomas Farrer's only daughter, Ida, aged twenty-five; they were married in the new year. Henrietta describes how this marriage 'added a great happiness to my mother's life, as Ida became another daughter to her'.[10]

Darwin's concern for the welfare of his friends was expressed afresh during 1879 when he initiated a proposal that Wallace should be granted a government pension. The idea was taken up by other distinguished scientists and Darwin was overjoyed when the plan succeeded. Early in the new year he received a letter from the Prime Minister himself telling of the decision. 'How extraordinarily kind of Mr. Gladstone to find time to write under the present circumstances,' he tells Hooker. 'Good Heavens! how pleased I am.'[11]

II

1880 began with a touching family event – the present of a fur coat to their father by his five sons and two daughters. Bought in secret, it was placed in his study while he was resting upstairs so as to be a surprise. Francis, who watched to see the effect, describes the scene to his sister: 'I think the coat exploded very well. I left it on the study table, furry side out and letter on the top at 3, so that he would find it at 4 when he started his walk. . . . You will see from Father's delightful letter to us how much pleased he was. He was quite affected and had tears in his eyes when he came out to see me. . . . I told mother just before so that she might come and see the fun.' In a brief note thanking them all for the magnificent present, Darwin ends: 'The coat, however, will never warm my body so much as your dear affection has warmed my heart. My good dear children, Your affectionate Father, Charles Darwin. N.B. I should not be myself if I did not protest that you have all been shamefully extravagant to spend so much money over your old father, however deeply you may have pleased him.'[12]

Later the same month another explosion occurred in the Darwin world, this time of a most unpleasant sort. A misunderstanding, in part Darwin's fault, arose out of the small book about Darwin's grandfather, Dr Erasmus Darwin, on which he had been working with a lively interest for six weeks during the spring of the previous year, and which was published in November 1879. The book is a composite work made up of two brief biographies of Dr Erasmus: one is a translation by Darwin of an article by a German botanist, Ernst Krause (1839–1903), the original of which had been published in the German journal *Kosmos* in a number celebrating

Charles Darwin's seventieth birthday in February 1879; the other, which despite being much longer appears in the book as merely 'a preliminary essay by Charles Darwin', is what in chapter 1 above is referred to as a 'Memoir' of his grandfather.

Shortly after publication of this work, and to Darwin's dismay, an extremely hostile letter appeared in the influential weekly, the *Athenaeum*, written by a young acquaintance of Darwin's, Samuel Butler (1835–1902). Butler was the grandson of Darwin's old headmaster at Shrewsbury of the same name, the Reverend Samuel Butler, and the son of one of his contemporaries at Cambridge, Thomas Butler (1806–86), with whom he had collected beetles at Barmouth fifty years earlier. After a spell of sheep farming in New Zealand, Samuel Butler the younger had become a full-time author whose works included the very successful satire, *Erewhon* (1872). For a time he was an enthusiastic admirer of Darwin, with whom he corresponded. Later, however, he began to study the earlier evolutionists, Buffon, Erasmus Darwin and Lamarck, and came greatly to prefer their ideas. Although no scientist, he ventured a work, *Evolution Old and New*, in which he argued strongly for the earlier ideas and against those of the *Origin*. As it happened this book was published in May 1879, after Krause's original article in German and six months before the English translation, for which Darwin was responsible.

The trouble arose because Darwin had sent Krause a copy of Butler's book, and Krause, when preparing a version of his article for English translation, included some new passages, one of which was strongly critical of Butler. Through an oversight, a note referring to the changed version had been omitted – which made it seem as though the criticism had appeared in the original article. In early January 1880, therefore, Butler wrote to Darwin asking for an explanation, to which Darwin replied immediately, stating that, should a reprint be called for, he would add a note drawing attention to the change. Not satisfied with this, Butler decided to publicise his complaint by writing his letter to the *Athenaeum*. Printed in the issue of 31 January 1880, Butler's letter casts aspersions on Darwin's character in phrases such as 'he must have perfectly well known' that he had substituted one version of an article for another, and that this substitution had been deliberately concealed.

A full account of the controversy is given in an appendix to Nora Barlow's edition of Darwin's *Autobiography*.[13] What is evident is that Butler was spoiling for a fight. A generation younger than his target, Butler was clearly trying to draw attention to himself by criticising his distinguished senior. A public controversy with the great man himself would add fuel to the fire he was busy igniting.

Inevitably, after reading the *Athenaeum* letter Darwin was incensed. He at once drafted a reply suitable for publication, but before dispatching it he sent it to London for advice and comment from Henrietta and Richard Litchfield. Both strongly advised against sending it. 'Not one reader in a thousand will make head or tail of the grievance,' wrote Richard. 'If you answer him you bring about exactly the result he most wants, which is to fill people's heads with the notion that your book [on Erasmus Darwin] is in some way a reply or rejoinder to his: in fact you make it a "Darwin–Butler affaire" as the French would say – and this is what will delight him.' In a letter to George, who was abroad at the time, Emma describes the consternation: 'We have been greatly excited by Butler's attack. . . . F. wrote an answer to it and sent it up by John [the coachman] to show it to Richard and Henrietta. John brought back a most sensible letter from Richard giving all the reasons against taking any notice of it. . . . [Butler's] is an odious spiteful letter but so tedious and confused. . . . As F. had a satisfactory reply to make I was in favour of his sending it; but I have changed my opinion and F. is going to send his [draft] reply and Richard's letter to Huxley and abide by his opinion. . . . F. was much bothered at first but will now cast it off his mind.'

Opinion in the family was much divided. Francis was keen a reply be sent; Emma and Leonard wavered; Henrietta and Richard were much against: hence the plan to seek Huxley's opinion. Although agreeing this move, Richard was apprehensive that Huxley, being himself 'horribly pugnacious, . . . would naturally be for fighting', while Charles 'hoped to God Huxley would say NO'. Huxley obliged: 'I say without the least hesitation burn your draft and take no notice whatever of Mr. Butler. . . . Has Mivart bitten him and given him Darwinophobia? Its a horrid disease.' In accordance with Huxley's judgement, no reply was sent.

At the end of the year Butler returned to the attack in a new book, *Unconscious Memory*. Once again the Darwin family was hopelessly divided about a public reply and this time decided to appeal to the biographer and critic Leslie Stephen (1832–1904), who was a friend of the family. Replying to Darwin on 12 January 1881, Stephen has no doubts: 'When you tell me that it pains you to be called a liar in your old age, I can quite understand it. To hear you called a liar makes me wish to give somebody such a slap in the face as he would have cause to remember. But I also reflect that you and your friends are bound also to remember your position and to avoid undignified squabbles. . . . My opinion about the matter is perfectly distinct and unhesitating. I think you should take no further notice of Mr. Butler whatever.'

Although this thoroughly disagreeable experience, which plagued Darwin on and off throughout 1880, was of a kind that would formerly have affected his health, on this occasion it appears not to have done so. During the spring he was working hard on the manuscript and later the proofs of *The Power of Movement in Plants*. In early April he and Emma spent some days at Abinger. Charles was suffering from a bad cough, and the change helped him.[14] By the end of May, with the proofs of *Movement in Plants* dispatched, they took another break, staying a fortnight with William and Sara at Bassett. Just before they left Down a book had arrived from the French biologist, Alphonse de Candolle. Writing to thank him for it on 28 May, Darwin continues 'As for myself I am taking a fortnight's rest after sending a pile of M.S. to the printers, and it was a piece of good fortune that your book arrived as I was getting into my carriage, for I wanted something to read whilst I was away from home.' He then gave a brief account of the contents of his own new book: 'I think that I have succeeded in showing that all the more important great classes of movement are due to the modification of a kind of movement common to all parts of all plants from their earliest youth. . . . P.S. It always pleases me to exalt plants in the organic scale.'[15]

Back at Down during the summer, Darwin resumed his study of the activities of earthworms and started a series of experiments. In characteristic style, Emma describes the proceedings to Leonard: 'F. has no proof sheets and has taken to training earthworms but does not make much progress, as they can neither see nor hear. They are, however, amusing and spend hours in seizing hold of the edge of a cabbage leaf and trying in vain to pull it into their holes.'[16] Worms, Charles had observed, spend time dragging leaves into their burrows. His experiments were designed to discover the size of leaf they can manage and which edge or corner of the leaf they select to drag in first. He also devised a number of ways of checking his estimates of the amount of soil they moved and, in the ensuing book, added much about their habits and natural history.

During August Charles and Emma stayed for the first time with Horace and Ida in Cambridge. 'It was arranged that they should go in a through carriage from Bromley, having a special train across London to King's Cross,' reports Henrietta. Her father's comfort 'was a good deal disturbed by the quantity of trouble the shunting gave,' but Emma enjoyed the journey. 'They both did and saw a great deal, my father especially enjoying a lunch in Frank Balfour's rooms. My Mother went to Trinity Chapel to hear the organ.' After returning to Down, Darwin writes to Balfour on 4 September referring to topics in botany and embryology they had discussed and ending: 'Our recent visit to Cambridge was a brilliant success to us all, and will ever be remembered by me with much pleasure.'[17] Frank Balfour (1851–82) was a brilliant young scientist who was killed in a climbing accident in the Alps shortly after Darwin's own death.

Early in November *The Power of Movement in Plants* was published and 1500 copies were immediately disposed of to the trade. 'The book was widely reviewed, and excited much interest among the general public,' reports Francis. There was even a leading article about it in *The Times*, which began: 'Of all our living men of science none have laboured longer and to more splendid purpose than Mr. Darwin.'[18] As it happened, this was read by an old friend of his youth, Sarah Mostyn Owen of Woodhouse (now Mrs Haliburton), with whom he had corresponded briefly eight years earlier. Writing to congratulate him, she reminded him that he had said as a boy that if the local newspaper ever alluded to him as 'our deserving fellow townsman' his ambition would be amply gratified. Darwin replies enthusiastically on 22 November:

Your letter has done more than please me, for its kindness has touched my heart. I often think of the old days and of the delight of my visits to Woodhouse, and of the deep debt of gratitude I owe to your father. It was very good of you to write. I had quite forgotten my old ambition about the Shrewsbury newspaper; but I remember the pride which I felt when I saw in a book about beetles the impressive words 'captured by C. Darwin'. . . . This seemed to me glory enough for any man! I do not know in the least what made the *Times* glorify me, for it has sometimes pitched into me ferociously. I should very much like to see you again, but you would find a visit here very dull, for we feel very old and have no amusement, and lead a solitary life. But we intend in a few weeks to spend a few days in London and then . . . perhaps you could come and lunch with us.[19]

In due course a meeting took place at Ras's house.

Charles and Emma were indeed growing a little old, and 1880 saw the deaths of three of their near-contemporaries: Charles's old friend William Darwin Fox, Emma's eldest brother Joe, and her eldest and favourite sister Elizabeth.

Fox had retired from his parish in Cheshire to Sandown in the Isle of Wight, where he had been living for some years with his wife before his death at the age of seventy-five. The correspondence between him and Darwin had been maintained, with one or two letters each way most years. The last were in 1878, when Fox had given news of his daughter's serious illness and subsequent death and Charles had written letters of condolence.

In March of 1880 Emma's brother Joe died at the age of eighty-five. Caroline stayed on at Leith Hill Place and seemed in good spirits when Charles and Emma visited her the following December.[20] Already eighty, Caroline would survive another seven years, outliving both her younger brothers.

Emma's eldest sister Elizabeth, to whom she had always been close, had come to live in a small house in the village of Downe in 1868. 'There she spent the last twelve years of her life,' records Henrietta, 'happy with her garden, her little dog Tony, her devoted servants, helping her village neighbours, and sheltered by my mother's constant love and care.' She was a regular visitor to Down House and always given a warm welcome. 'Her little bent figure had been a familiar sight to us all as she came into the drawing room, leaning on her stick and followed by her dog Tony.'[21] In November 1880 at the age of eighty-five, after a year of ill-health, she died. She was much missed.

III

Until May 1881 Darwin was hard at work on earthworms, with a brief spell in London at the end of February staying with Henrietta and

Richard. Writing on 27 February to George, who was in Madeira, Charles describes how they 'had seen lots of people. . . . We came up that I might attend Burdon Sanderson's Lecture at the Royal Institution on the movement of plants and animals compared. He gave a very good lecture. I was received with great honour and placed . . . alongside the Chairman and was applauded on my entrance!' Evidently he had asked George to look out for wormcastings in Madeira. He thanks him for doing so, adding, 'It is hopeless where the soil is dry. Perhaps you may see some whenever you go into the interior.' After reporting his pleasure at 'the triumph of the Ladies at Cambridge' (a vote permitting women to take tripos examinations), he adds: 'We had F. Galton to Down on last Sunday. He was splendid fun and told us no end of odd things.'[22]

Francis's son Bernard, now aged four and a half, was still the only grandchild and was still living with his father and grandparents in Down House. In illustration of her mother's sympathetic concern for him, Henrietta quotes her account of his reactions when he was losing his nanny through her marriage in the spring of 1881: 'We had some trouble with poor Bernard yesterday. He mistook his father to say that Nanna would come after he was in bed. So yesterday morning I found I must tell him the truth or really deceive him. At first I told him that she was at Mrs. Parslow's and he should go and see her. He said, "I shall soon have her out of Mrs. Parslow's." When I told him she was going to be married, his poor face crumpled up and he said, "I don't like it that way at all." He cried very quietly but could not get over it for some time.' When he first saw his nurse after her marriage he said to her, 'You ought to have told me Nana, you ought to have told me.'[23]

Controversy over vivisection was still rumbling on. In April Darwin received an enquiry from the professor of physiology at Uppsala University asking for his views on the subject, to which Darwin replied candidly and at length; and a few days later he felt impelled to write to *The Times* defending his fellow scientists from a hostile attack which had appeared in its columns the previous day. Explaining his action to his young friend George Romanes, he writes on 22 April: 'I thought it fair to bear my share of the abuse poured in so atrocious a manner on all physiologists.'[24]

During these last years, Darwin and Romanes were in regular correspondence. Romanes's interests in the mental capacities of animals was drawing them together even further, and his book, *Mental Evolution in Animals*, published in 1883, contains a posthumous essay on instinct by Darwin himself. Subsequently Romanes published another work in which he carried the argument further, *Mental Evolution in Man* (1885). A copy of this was among the books salvaged from Freud's library after he left Vienna, and has marginal markings in Freud's hand.

The principal holiday in 1881 was a second visit to the Lake District in June. This time they took a house in Patterdale for the month. 'I think that this visit to the Lake country was nearly as full of enjoyment as the first,' writes Henrietta. 'It was an especial happiness to my mother for the rest of her life to remember her little strolls with my father by the side of the lake. I have a clear picture in my mind of the two often setting off alone together for a certain favourite walk by the edge of some fine rocks going down into the lake.' Emma describes one occasion: 'The day has turned out even more beautiful than the first Sunday. We all, but F., went in the boat, as far as the How Town landing-place, where we got out. Bernard was with us, dabbling his hand in the water and very quiet and happy. It was very charming up among the Junipers and rocks. . . . F. got up to his beloved rock this morning, but just then a fit of his dazzling came on and he came down.'[25] (In view of subsequent events, it seems not unlikely that the fits of dazzling were due to failing circulation.)

For Charles the holiday was not a great success. Replying on 15 June to a letter from Hooker, who at the time was terribly busy, Darwin writes from Patterdale: 'I am rather despondent about myself, and my troubles are of an exactly opposite nature to yours, for idleness is downright misery to me, as I find here, as I cannot forget my discomfort for an hour. I have not the heart or strength at my age [seventy-two] to begin any investigations lasting years, which is the only thing which I enjoy; and I have no little jobs which I can do. So I must look forward to Down graveyard as the sweetest place on earth. This place is magnificently beautiful and I enjoy the scenery, though weary of it; and the weather has been very cold and almost always hazy.' After their return home he describes the holiday to Wallace in the same depressed tones: 'the scenery is quite charming, but I cannot walk and everything tires me, even seeing scenery. . . . What I shall do with my few remaining years of life I can hardly tell. I have everything to make me happy and contented, but life has become very wearisome to me.'[26]

In the event Darwin had only another nine months to live; and it seems he was already beginning to fail. Nevertheless he persevered with his botanical work with Francis, determined to continue till the end. An interruption came in the first week of August, when he was required in London to sit for yet another portrait, one which had been commissioned by the Linnean Society from a young artist, John Collier (1850–1934), who had recently married one of Huxley's daughters. In contrast to his experience with William Richmond two years earlier, this time Darwin felt able to relax. 'Collier was the most considerate, kind and pleasant painter a sitter could desire,' Darwin remarked afterwards. Though many who were familiar with the sitter thought Collier's the best of the portraits, Francis Darwin did not agree: 'There is a certain expression in Mr. Collier's portrait which I am inclined to consider an exaggeration of the almost painful expression which Professor Cohn has described in my father's face.' Francis preferred the Ouless portrait of 1875: 'According to my feeling,' Francis records, 'it [Collier's picture] is not so simple or strong a representation of him as that given by Mr Ouless.'[27]

Sir Joseph Hooker, aged 64
portrait by John Collier, 18

Punch cartoon, circa 1881

Charles Darwin, aged 72 portrait by John Collier, 1881

Darwin's new study (formerly
billiard room) first occupied by
him in 1881

While in London for the sitting with Collier, Charles and Emma stayed with Ras. On 26 August 1881, only a fortnight later and in his seventy-seventh year, Ras died after a short illness and 'without any great suffering'; he was buried at Down. He had always been much loved by his many nephews and nieces. Acknowledging letters of condolence from his friends, Darwin writes to Hooker: 'The death of Erasmus is a very heavy loss to all of us, for he had a most affectionate disposition. He always appeared to me the most pleasant and clearest headed man, whom I have ever known. London will seem a strange place to me without his presence.' To Farrer he writes: 'He was not, I think, a happy man, and for many years did not value life, though never complaining.' This judgement is echoed by Henrietta: 'He was weary of life and the constant burden of ill-health, but for us all the loss was irreparable.'[28]

Since Ras had left his not inconsiderable fortune to Charles, the latter found himself even better off than before. Furthermore, Anthony Rich still insisted on adhering to his plan to leave all his money to the family, despite Darwin's having apprised him of the recent change in the family's finances. All this meant that there was more than enough to provide for Emma and each of the seven children after he died. Darwin decided, therefore, to use some of his resources to finance research in biology and geology. In botany a project of especial interest to him was the compilation of a complete index of all plants known to botanists, together with the numerous and confusing synonyms that each had accreted over the years and that had plagued him repeatedly in his work, and including also the geographical distribution of each. This would be done at Kew, where Hooker had long presided. For zoology he approached Huxley, and for geology a Professor Judd, who subsequently described their meeting: 'He was most anxious to devote what he could spare to the advancement of Geology or Biology. He dwelt in the most touching manner on the fact that he owed so much happiness and fame to the natural history sciences which had been the solace of what might have been a painful exist-ence. . . . I was much impressed by the earnestness, and, indeed, deep emotion, with which he spoke of his indebtedness to Science and his desire to promote its interests.'[29]

During the autumn of 1881 and on into 1882 two problems in plant physiology were engaging Charles and Francis: one was the function of bloom on leaves, work which was to remain uncompleted, the other the action of carbonate of ammonia on roots. To Henrietta on 23 November 1881 Emma writes: 'F. is at last getting some rewards for these months at the microscope, in finding out something quite new about the structure of roots. However, it makes him work all the harder now.'[30] This study resulted in Darwin's two last papers, both of them read for him to the Linnean Society (presumably by Francis) during the following June.

During October 1881 Darwin's last book, *The Formation of Vegetable Mould, through the Action of Worms, with Observations on their Habits*, was published and created extraordinary interest. 'Conclusions so wide and so novel and so easily understood, drawn from the study of creatures so familiar, and treated with unabated vigour and freshness, may well have attracted many readers,' explains Francis. In November Darwin is telling a friend: 'My book has been received with almost laughable enthusiasm, and 3500 copies have been sold!!!' Three months later, on 4 February 1882, he tells his benefactor, Anthony Rich: 'I have been plagued with an endless stream of letters . . . ; most of them very foolish and enthusiastic; but some containing good facts which I have used in correcting yesterday the "Sixth Thousand".'[31] Three years later the total would be 8500, a sale greater relatively than that of the *Origin*. Once again Darwin's eye for significant detail combined with his immense perseverance had produced a classic, minor though it is. Moreover, as one perspicacious reviewer pointed out, the work had a basic scientific lesson to teach, namely, the cumulative importance in geological and biological time of the infinitely little.

During the same month that the book on earthworms was published, Charles and Emma spent a week in Cambridge, staying with Horace and Ida, who was seven months pregnant. After their return, Emma tells William and Sara: 'I think F. is quite set up by our happy week in Cambridge. We saw many pleasant people. . . . Our chief dissipation was going to King's.'[32]

Two months later, on 13 December 1881, Charles and Emma left Down for yet another visit, this time to stay with Henrietta and Richard in London. It was during this visit that Charles suffered his first unmistakable heart attack. He had called at the house of George Romanes, who gives the following account:

I happened to be out, but my butler, observing that Mr. Darwin was ill, asked him to come in. He said he would prefer going home, and although the butler urged him to wait at least until a cab could be fetched, he said he would rather not give so much trouble. For the same reason he refused to allow the butler to accompany him. Accordingly he watched him walking with difficulty towards the direction in which the cabs were to be met with, and saw that, when he had got about three hundred yards from the house, he staggered and caught hold of the park-railings as if to prevent himself from falling. The butler therefore hastened to his assistance, but after a few seconds saw him turn round with the evident purpose of retracing his steps to my house. However, after he had returned part of the way he seems to have felt better, for he again changed his mind, and proceeded to find a cab.[33]

Apparently Darwin returned safely to the Litchfields' house, and in due course also to Down. On Sunday, 8 January 1882, Leslie Stephen and his group of 'Sunday Tramps'* arrived. 'Charles was delightful to them and enjoyed their visit heartily,' Emma later recalled.[34] By the end

---

*The nickname given to the Sunday Walking Club that Stephen had founded.

of February, however, he was suffering anginal attacks almost daily. Despite that, one afternoon in early March he ventured on his own as far as his favourite Sandwalk, where he had a fairly bad attack. He managed to get home, but thereafter his condition became obviously more serious and Sir Andrew Clark and other doctors were called in. 'He suffered from distressing sensations of exhaustion and faintness,' records Francis, 'and seemed to recognise with deep depression . . . that his working days were over. He gradually recovered from this condition, and became more cheerful and hopeful.' With ups and downs he struggled on, attended constantly by Emma. On good days they sat in the garden together. On 10 April George returned from a visit to the West Indies. Although Charles was not up to talking for very long, he enjoyed George's news. On 17 April Emma notes in her diary: 'Good day, a little work, out in garden twice.'[35] The 'little work' was recording the progress of an experiment on which Francis was engaged during the latter's temporary absence. On the night of the 18th he had a severe attack. Emma and Francis were there to support him, while Bessy and Henrietta, who had arrived, did the nursing. The following day at 3.30 pm he died peacefully.

Although the family would have preferred him to have been buried at Down as he himself had been expecting, many people thought otherwise. On 26 April the funeral took place in Westminster Abbey. Among the group of ten distinguished pallbearers were his old friends Hooker, Huxley, Wallace and Lubbock.

In this work, for reasons given in the Preface, it has not been possible to do justice to the magnitude and variety of Darwin's scientific contributions, nor to the multitude of productive research programmes to which his work has given rise. As the years pass and his achievements are studied and reappraised, his status as a scientist is seen to grow ever greater. To present that side of his life another biography is required, a biography written by an author much better qualified than I am to assess Darwin's place in the history of the geological and biological sciences, his place, indeed, in the unfolding history of science itself. To close this study it must therefore suffice to draw on the verdict of Ernst Mayr, doyen of scholars in evolutionary biology, when he opened a conference held at Darwin College, Cambridge, in June 1982 to commemorate the centenary of Darwin's death. After reviewing Darwin's achievements and describing him as an intellectual revolutionary, Mayr summed up what he saw as the most evident ingredients of Darwin's greatness:

A brilliant mind, great intellectual boldness, and an ability to combine the best qualities of a naturalist-observer, of a philosophical theoretician, and of an experimentalist. The world has so far seen such a combination only once and this accounts for Darwin's unique greatness.[36]

Epilogue

I

After Charles's death Emma mourned him deeply, but took great comfort in her many happy memories and in her knowledge of what she had been able to be to him. In the form of a little diary, she wrote down notes of memories she wished to keep fresh in her mind. Henrietta gives a number of extracts.[1] Some are episodes of the recent past which Charles had enjoyed; others are recollections of the warmly affectionate relations between Charles and his sons and daughters. Many are of things Charles had said to her, especially those of his last days: 'I am not the least afraid of death'; 'Remember what a good wife you have been to me'; and, during an attack, 'I shall bear it better if you are awake'.

As the months passed Emma began to rebuild her life. She felt that the winters in the great empty house at Down would be too lonely and decided to live in Cambridge, where she already had two sons. Moreover, it was a better location for Francis's botanical work. She therefore bought a house, The Grove, just outside the centre of the town with a mature garden and well-grown trees.* By November 1882 she had moved there, together with Francis and his son Bernard, (now six years old) and also Bessy, the unmarried daughter. Down house was retained. Emma spent the summer months there and was joined for holidays by many members of the family.

A second grandson had been born the previous December. The son of Horace and Ida, he had been given the long-used family name of Erasmus. Now a year old, and living nearby, he was a great source of pleasure to Emma: 'Rasmus called in his pram, driven by Ida. I was pleased at his putting out his arms to me as soon as he saw me, and trotting about the room quite tame,' she tells Henrietta on 18 January 1883.[2]

During the following summer Francis became engaged to Ellen Crofts, a lecturer at Newnham College, and they were married soon afterwards.

*The house and adjacent properties are now occupied by the women's college, New Hall.

They decided to build a house adjacent to The Grove; this was a special pleasure for Emma, since Bernard could now come and go as he pleased between his father's house and her own. Furthermore, Horace and Ida decided to do the same, making a large Darwin colony on the Huntingdon Road.

Henrietta describes how her mother always kept busy. She made a lot of new friends and read extensively. 'The number of books she read and her original way of looking at them, her interest in contemporary politics and her power of entering into other people's lives, made her company refreshing and exhilarating.' But she became a little deaf and tended to avoid large parties.[3]

Meanwhile the two bachelor sons had both got married, Leonard in 1882 to Elisabeth Fraser, the sister of a brother officer, and George in 1884 to Maud Dupuy from Philadelphia. Leonard had no children; but George and Maud produced four. Altogether Emma lived to enjoy the company of four grandsons and five granddaughters, all of them living nearby in Cambridge. Although she did not always see eye to eye with her daughters-in-laws' methods with them, she held her tongue and, as a result, relations between them were warm and happy. Henrietta avers: 'I think it may be said that there was never from beginning to end one instant's jar in their many years of close intercourse.'[4] The four months at Down each summer with large gatherings of family around her were special treats for Emma.

Within a year of his father's death Francis began work on the three volumes of *Life and Letters*, which were published in 1887. Henrietta describes her mother's feelings: 'My mother had beforehand a shrinking dread of publicity, but the truth and feeling with which it was written changed her fear into satisfaction, and it became only a happiness to her.'[5] Before it went to press, however, there were to be anxious, indeed heated, family conferences. The *Autobiography*, which Charles had written in the summer of 1876 and to which he had added numerous passages in subsequent years, was to appear in the first volume. In it Charles had given some account of his religious beliefs, and the question arose whether they were better omitted. Henrietta held strongly that they should be. According to Leonard, 'She felt that on religious questions [the *Autobiography*] was crude and but half thought-out, and that in these circumstances it was not only unfair to his memory to publish it but that he would have objected strongly.' Francis disagreed, holding firmly that the publication should be complete. Emma, the evidence suggests, sided with Henrietta and the controversial passages were duly omitted.[6]

Only in 1959 was a complete edition of the *Autobiography* published under the editorship of Horace's daughter Nora, who in her Introduction gives an account of the episode. Perhaps it is best explained, she comments, 'by divided loyalty amongst the children between the science of their father and the religion of their mother; though the differences of view that existed [had] caused no estrangement between the parents'. The heat of the controversy within what was otherwise a singularly united family, Nora Barlow suggests, is only intelligible in the light of the scientific-religious storm that had raged during the previous two decades.

Emma lived to be eighty-eight, dying peacefully at The Grove in October 1896. In her old age she continued alert and for the most part healthy. Reading, needlework, writing letters, playing patience, delighting in the birdsong of spring, and enjoying visits from friends and relations, she passed her days. Her memories she kept warm and whenever she was at Down she visited those places that Charles had especially enjoyed and in which they had spent happy hours together.

II

Emma was not the only character in this story to live to a ripe old age. All but one of their children lived to be older than their father – an eloquent answer to his chronic anxieties about hereditary ill-health. All the sons, moreover, made their mark in life; while, as readers already know, Henrietta became the family chronicler and editor of the great store of family letters.

William lived to be seventy-four, dying in 1914. Retiring from the Southampton Bank soon after being widowed in 1902, he moved to London to a house close to Leonard's in Kensington. Among the grandchildren's many uncles he was their favourite. He was also the only one said to be entirely free of hypochondria. This information, and much else of what follows in this section, comes from the memoirs of George's daughter Gwen.[7]

George was the shortest lived of the seven sons and daughters, though he lived to be sixty-seven. Appointed to the Plumian Chair of Astronomy and Experimental Philosophy a year after his father's death, as had been predicted, he had a distinguished academic career. Much of his later work was on the evolution of the solar system, a development of the paper of 1876 that had so impressed Sir William Thomson. Later he served on many scientific committees dealing with subjects such as tidal theory and meteorology. In 1905 he was conspicuously successful as president of the British Association when it met in South Africa. Soon afterwards he was knighted and, before his death in 1912, he received many further honours. One of his last activities was to preside at the International Congress of Mathematicians in the summer of 1912.

To the end he is said by a colleague to have retained a certain boyish eagerness, as though always on the lookout for adventure; and like his father he was modesty itself.[8] This picture is amplified by his daughter, who describes him as most affectionate, warm and open as a father, though his 'spirits were quickly up and quickly down'. George was one of the two sons whose health was always a worry. After taking his degree he

Emma Darwin, aged 73 in 1881

had a spell of digestive troubles and general weakness, for which he sought a cure at spas in England, Germany and France. From 1873, it was reported, he improved under the care of Sir Andrew Clark. His daughter is confident it was mostly hypochondria.

Francis, the third son, lived to be seventy-seven. The only one of the children to be interested in natural history, he continued the studies in plant physiology he had begun at Down with his father. Although appointed lecturer and later reader in the Cambridge Botany School and, like George, elected a fellow of the Royal Society (1882), he declined to apply for the chair when it fell vacant. He had little ambition, his niece tells us, and hardly cared at all for the honours which came to him. The latter included a knighthood in 1913 and several honorary degrees. For some years he served on the council of the Royal Society and he was its foreign secretary from 1903 to 1907. In 1908 he followed in George's footsteps as president of the British Association.

Francis, Gwen Raverat tells us, 'was always apt to suffer from fits of depression . . . [which] had no doubt been accentuated by the shock from which he never recovered: the death of his young wife, Amy . . . after this he continually expected the worst about everything.'[9] His pessimism can hardly have been helped by the death of his second wife, Ellen, in 1903, when he was still only fifty-five. Ten years later he was married for a third time, to a widow, Florence Maitland.

Francis will always be remembered as the author and editor of the three volumes of the *Life and Letters* of his father, published in November 1887, and (with a co-author) of the two further volumes of letters published in 1903. An important additional service was his editing and publishing in 1909 of the two preliminary essays on evolution written by his father in the years 1842 and 1844. The applause that greeted the three volumes of *Life and Letters* delighted him. 'Frank says he has lost all modesty,' his mother tells a friend in a letter of 20 December 1887, 'and I hope it is partly true. His nature is to doubt and disparage everything he does.'[10] – much like his father she might have added. Another side of his personality, also like his father, is presented by a colleague who describes how his 'delightful sense of humour endeared him to his many friends and made him the best of company'.[11] He was a good musician and devoted to the English countryside.

The fourth son, Leonard, proved to be the longest lived of the family, dying in 1943 at the age of ninety-three. According to his niece, he explained that the reason he had gone into the army was that 'he was afraid of being afraid'. During his twenty years as an officer in the Royal Engineers he was either an instructor or engaged in some special scientific mission; he did little routine military duty. In 1890 he resigned in the rank of major on the grounds that his health was not very good. Three years later he stood for Parliament as the Liberal-Unionist candidate in the Staffordshire constituency of Lichfield and won the seat

– much to his mother's delight. Three years later, however, he lost it and never again stood. None the less he continued to be active in public life, being successively president of the Geographical Section of the British Association, president of the Royal Geographical Society (1908–11) and president of the Eugenic Society (1911–28). In the latter role he became a strong advocate of the differential breeding policies for humans that had been proposed a generation earlier by Francis Galton and were regarded so sceptically by Darwin.

Like Francis, Horace lived to be seventy-seven, dying in 1928. Never good at academic work, he none the less became a most successful inventor and scientific engineer. When in 1885, with a friend, he founded a small company to make scientific instruments, no one in the family was very optimistic about the venture; they always referred to it simply as 'the shop' meaning 'workshop'. Yet it prospered and in the spring of 1895 was able to move to a new factory built for it on the outskirts of Cambridge. A few months before she died Emma was able to visit Horace in his new quarters: 'I liked seeing the Shop on Sunday. It is a perfect situation, surrounded with gardens and so quiet.'[12]

As time went on 'the shop' became well known as the Cambridge Scientific Instrument Company and contributed materially to the growth of the science schools in the university. Horace himself designed many of the instruments. His practice was to soak himself in the scientific problem to be solved, after which he was usually able quickly to evolve a solution. When in 1909 an Advisory Committee for Aeronautics was set up by government, Horace became principal adviser on instrumentation; and during the First World War he was appointed chairman of the Inventions Committee. Like two of his elder brothers, Horace was elected a fellow of the Royal Society, in 1903, and was knighted in 1918. Horace, his niece tells us, shared with his elder brother George the burden of 'weak health'. As the youngest surviving child, he had been delicate as a boy and had perhaps been over-protected by Emma. When in later life he was ill, he did not worry over details as George and Henrietta did, 'but he did enjoy the extra affection he received at those times'.[13]

Despite her long years of ill-health during adolescence, Henrietta lived to be eighty-six and was the last but one to die. She and Richard had no children and lived in London. Together they worked on the two volumes of family letters, which were first published in a privately circulated edition in 1904. A year later Richard died at the age of seventy-three. Soon afterwards Henrietta moved to a villa in Surrey with a garden and small wood. In 1915 the public edition of the letters was published, with a few, but sometimes significant, omissions.

Concern for her husband's health and her own was, according to her niece, Henrietta's main preoccupation in life. In an entertaining chapter in her memoirs, Gwen Raverat quotes one of the rhymes composed one Christmas by her cousin Bernard:

Question: Fussy people Darwin's are
Who's the fussiest by far?
Answer: Several aunts are far from calm,
But Aunty Etty takes the palm.

Although she was hospitable and kind to her nephews and nieces, they none the less found staying with her a little stifling. Clearly an able woman, who, we are told, could easily have ruled a kingdom, she was sadly short of an occupation for most of her life.

After Emma's death, Bessy moved to a small house in Cambridge where she lived to be seventy-eight. Like Henrietta, she had no occupation. Among her activities were regular visits to the workhouse to read to the old people. The only picture we have of her comes from her niece, who describes her in later years as very stout and nervous, and not good at practical things: 'she could not have managed her own life without a little help and direction now and then; but she was shrewd enough in her own way, and a very good judge of character. She showed great daring in being sometimes rather sceptical about Aunty Etty's ill-health; for Aunt Etty always maintained her position as the older and cleverer sister. . . . Relations between [them] remained the same to the end of their lives: Aunt Etty rather superior and impatient; and Aunt Bessy submissive, but a little resentful and critical.'[14] No doubt in a less gifted family Bessy would have come into her own. As it was she was overshadowed.

III

Among the nine grandchildren several have become known to the public. Bernard was for many years a journalist on the staff of *The Times*, known mainly for his golfing column and 'third' leaders. His younger half-sister, Frances, under her married name Frances Cornford, was one of the Georgian poets.

Gwen, the eldest of George and Maud's four, was a successful artist under her married name, Gwen Raverat, and the author and illustrator of the amusing memoir *Period Piece: A Cambridge Childhood*. Charles, her younger brother, became a leading physicist and the fifth generation of Darwins to be a fellow of the Royal Society. In later years he became master of his grandfather's old Cambridge college, Christ's.

Among Horace and Ida's three, Erasmus was killed in action in France in 1915 – which cut short a promising career in engineering. Ruth became a power for good in the mental hospital world during her time as a member of a strangely titled body, the Board of Control, members of which inspected and advised on the care of mental patients. Late in life she married her widowed colleague on the Board, W. Rees Thomas. Finally Nora, under her married name Nora Barlow, became the skilled editor of several of her grandfather's works, thus making available a great deal of material until then buried in the archives.

IV

Among Darwin's five longest and closest friends, the two oldest had died before him: Lyell in 1875 and Fox in 1880. That left Hooker, Huxley and Wallace, all of whom were to live many years longer. Another colleague, Darwin's 'former friend and [later] bitter enemy', Richard Owen, although five years older, also survived him, living another ten years and dying at the age of eighty-eight.

Owen had had an extremely distinguished career, receiving the highest of scientific honours before he was fifty, a decade or more before they would be bestowed on his younger rival, Darwin. From 1856, when he became responsible for the natural history collections in the British Museum, his work had focused mainly on the fossil skeletons of extinct animals and included a definitive study of the dinosaurs. He had also pressed for proper accommodation for the collections and played a leading part in persuading the government to erect a large new building for them. This would become the Natural History Museum in South Kensington, eventually opened in 1881. Owen became the first director and was rewarded with a knighthood.

An excellent conversationalist and given to much old-world courtesy, Owen had early attracted the attention of the Prince Consort, who arranged for him to give lectures to the royal children. Moreover, as early as 1852 the Queen had given him a house, Sheen Lodge in Richmond Park, to live in. He mixed freely with his many prominent contemporaries and had the ear of prime ministers; but he was neither liked nor trusted by his scientific colleagues: 'no man could say harder things of an adversary or a rival' runs the entry in the *Dictionary of National Biography*. 'Unfortunately, he grew so addicted to acrimonious controversy that many who followed kindred pursuits held somewhat aloof from him, and in later life his position among scientific men was one of comparative isolation.' From first to last jealousy gnawed his soul.

At the time of Darwin's death, Thomas Huxley was still only fifty-seven and in full harness, dean of the National School of Science in South Kensington, into which the School of Mines had been transformed, and shortly to be elected president of the Royal Society after having served for ten years as a joint secretary. Three years later, however, ill-health forced him to retire from both posts, and in 1889 he left London for Eastbourne. There he continued to write, mainly on matters philosophical, theological and sociological. At the time of his death in 1895 at the age of seventy, he was drafting a critical review of Arthur Balfour's *Foundations of Belief*.

Between 1865 and 1885 Huxley had combined in a remarkable way four distinct roles: that of scientist doing original research; that of advocate of pure science as an educational discipline; that of populariser of biological science; and that of adviser to a number of public bodies.

During the years 1862–8 he had sat on four royal commissions; and during 1870 to 1884 on another six. Among the topics covered were fisheries, scientific education, Scottish universities and vivisection. During his later years Huxley was the recipient of a great many honours, including a number of honorary degrees and membership of countless foreign scientific societies. In 1888 he received the Copley Medal of the Royal Society and, the year before he died, the newly instituted Darwin Medal. One of his last public appearances was in Oxford in 1893, when he gave the first Romanes lecture on the theme 'Evolution and Ethics', two topics that had interested him all his life. The previous year he had been appointed a privy councillor.

Huxley was survived by his widow, two sons and four daughters. His elder son, Leonard, who became a publisher, edited his father's *Life and Letters* (1900) and subsequently the *Life and Letters* of Joseph Hooker (1918). He was also the father of three Huxley grandsons who have become well known, two of them as biologists, Sir Julian and Sir Andrew, and the third as a writer, Aldous.

In 1894, a year before Huxley's death, Darwin's young friend George Romanes died prematurely at the age of forty-six. Today he is best known from the annual lecture he endowed at Oxford, to be on any topic of high current interest in the fields of art, literature or science. The first lecture was given by Thomas Huxley, the fiftieth by Julian.

At the time of Darwin's death Joseph Hooker was sixty-five and had established a reputation as the leading authority on the geographical distribution of plants. His knowledge had come from expeditions to every continent, the last having been in 1877 when he spent several months in the USA at the invitation of the US Geological Survey. With Asa Gray and others he visited the Rocky Mountains in Colorado and Utah. After each of his many expeditions he had published weighty reports of his findings. In addition to all this firsthand experience of the distribution of living plants, he had acquired substantial knowledge of fossil plants during his ten years as botanist to the Geological Survey.

During 1873–7 Hooker was president of the Royal Society at a time when Huxley was one of the joint secretaries. Together they made a major contribution to plans for the voyage of yet another government research ship, HMS *Challenger*, which circumnavigated the globe in the years 1873–6; subsequently Hooker oversaw the publication of its reports.

In 1885, three years after Darwin's death, Hooker retired from the directorship of Kew which he had held for twenty years and which had entailed heavy and at times disagreeable administrative burdens. Having built himself a house accessible to Kew, he continued his scientific work unabated. Between 1883 and 1897 he was engaged in completing the seven volumes of the *Flora of British India*, in which are described close on 17,000 species, a large proportion by Hooker himself.

As might be expected, Hooker received many honours: a knighthood in

Francis Darwin, 1848–
1925, assistant to and
biographer of his father.
Reader in Botany at
Cambridge

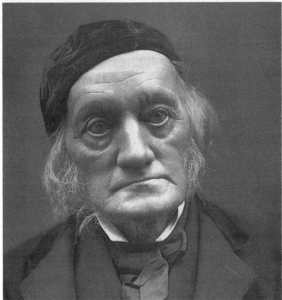

Sir Richard Owen, aged
about 85 circa 1890

Thomas Huxley, aged about 65 circa 1890

Alfred Wallace, in old age

1877, the Copley Medal of the Royal Society ten years later, honorary degrees from Oxford, Cambridge and Edinburgh (among others), and distinguished recognition from Germany, Sweden and France. On his ninetieth birthday in 1907 he was presented with the Order of Merit. Despite his many honours, however, Hooker never got over the stage-fright of his youth. After receiving the Copley Medal and giving a speech, he writes to Huxley: 'The success of my after dinner homily at the R.S. is to me far more wonderful than getting the Copley. You who are one of the few who know how morbidly nervous I am – can guess my condition of two days' nausea before the dinner, and 2 days illness after it. I am not speaking figuratively. It is mere nervous upset.'[15]

Mentally vigorous and active to the end, Hooker lived until December 1911, when he died peacefully in his sleep at the age of ninety-four. Following his own express wish he was buried at Kew and not in Westminster Abbey as was proposed.

Like Hooker, Alfred Wallace survived to enjoy a productive old age. After Darwin's death he became the embodiment of 'Darwinism', the name he insisted on giving to the twin theories of evolution and variation with natural selection. In 1885 he was invited to Boston, Massachusetts, to give the Lowell lectures. This was an invitation he welcomed as giving him an opportunity to visit yet another continent to see the fauna and flora, and also to visit his elder brother John, who had settled in San Francisco. Once in the United States he was lionised both in Boston and in Washington, and was able to earn enough from lecturing to work his way across the continent and back via Quebec. While in California with his brother he visited the Yosemite Valley and also heard from Senator Stanford and his wife of their plans to build a university in memory of their son, whom they had lost three years earlier.

Back home Wallace continued active in the cause of evolution. In 1889 he published an extended version of his lectures under the title *Darwinism* and seven years later another volume, *Method of Organic Evolution*. When in the new century, after Mendel's work had been rediscovered, some influential Mendelians began challenging the theory of variation with natural selection, Wallace stood his ground. He pointed out, correctly as it proved, that the simple extrapolation of the early laboratory findings to the complex world of nature was illegitimate and misleading.

Evolution, however, was not Wallace's only interest. Since his youth he had been a radical in politics and was never afraid to point out the deficiencies of capitalism and the contrast between the conditions of the wealthy few and those of the impoverished many. This did not always recommend him to potential employers, so that he and his wife and two daughters were often in straitened circumstances. Wallace, though, was of an endearingly sanguine disposition – as sanguine, indeed, as Darwin was gloomy.

Many honours came to Wallace, although a little belatedly. In 1889

Oxford gave him an honorary degree, and three years later, at the age of seventy, he was invited to accept election to fellowship of the Royal Society. For some reason, however, he refused, and it was not until 1905 that he accepted.

In 1908 the Linnean Society staged a splendid celebration of the fiftieth anniversary of the meeting when the two papers by Darwin and Wallace had been read to a bemused audience. A number of special medals had been struck for the occasion, and Wallace, who received one, was asked to reply on behalf of the recipients, among whom was Hooker. Although nearly eighty-six, Wallace made an excellent speech, in which he insisted, as ever, that all the credit for the ideas was Darwin's. Contrasting the twenty years of laborious collecting of evidence by Darwin with his own flash of insight and hastily written paper, he went on: 'I was then (as often since) the "young man in a hurry": *he*, the painstaking and patient student. . . . It was really a singular piece of good luck that gave to me any share . . . it was only Darwin's extreme desire to perfect his work that allowed me to come in.'[16]

That was certainly true. None the less Wallace had made his own distinctive contribution to science, notably his *Geographical Distribution of Animals* of 1876; and he had amply earned both the Copley Medal of the Royal Society and the Order of Merit, both of which he received in the anniversary year. This was a remarkable climax for this self-taught and modest man.

Five years later in 1913, at the age of ninety, Wallace died peacefully, alert and active to the end. Thus passed the last of Darwin's gifted band of friends and protectors.

Darwin's ill-health in the light of current research

I

The case for thinking that Darwin may have suffered from Chagas's disease, an idea that received enthusiastic and influential acceptance from biologists during the 1960s, rests partly on the course of the illness and the nature of the symptoms and partly on the fact that in South America he was undoubtedly at risk of becoming infected.

The course of the disease is exceedingly variable. In some cases there is an acute illness, in others none. Should chronic symptoms develop – which does not always occur – they do so after a latent period which may last as long as twenty years. Such symptoms are due to the slow and varied destruction of neurones and muscle cells, giving rise to pathology of the cardiac and gastro-intestinal systems. The symptoms come and go and may include dysphagia (difficulty in swallowing), regurgitation of food, vomiting or constipation, as well as cardiac failure.

In supporting the case for the diagnosis, the principal advocates, Saul Adler (1959) and Ralph Bernstein (1984), point to the fact that Darwin was undoubtedly bitten by the relevant bug, as he himself records in his *Beagle Journal*.[1] While in South America, moreover, he suffered an acute fever which kept him in bed for six weeks. Subsequently, the symptoms from which he suffered, after what might have been a latent period of about five years, were largely cardiac and gastro-intestinal. The improvement during the last decade of his life, Bernstein suggests, might have been 'an asymptomatic or quiescent chronic disease process [which] continued until four months before his death.' Thus the unusual sequence of Darwin's complaints is sufficiently consistent with the course of some cases of Chagas's disease for the diagnosis to appear a possibility.

There are, however, a number of difficulties. A relatively minor one is that the acute fever from which Darwin suffered in Chile in October 1834 occurred six months *before* he records having been bitten by the bug, which was in March 1835. If the illness was due to infection with the trypanosome, therefore, he must have contracted the infection on some earlier occasion. That, however, is by no means impossible, since he had been sleeping rough in infested areas on and off ever since the *Beagle* arrived in South American waters.

A far weightier objection, of course, is that at least one of Darwin's symptoms, palpitations, was present before the *Beagle* set sail, and possibly his gastric trouble as well.[2] Not only does Bernstein fail to mention this but he makes no attempt to rebut the many other arguments against the diagnosis that Woodruff (1965) advances in his substantial article. What causes infection, Woodruff points out, is not simply the bites of the bugs but contamination of the wound by their excreta; most of the local inhabitants who contract the disease, moreover, do so only after having been exposed to the bug over periods of several years. Furthermore, as remarked in the Prologue, there is abundant evidence that the situations that led to Darwin's developing symptoms were social and psychological rather than any entailing physical exertion.

II

Weighty evidence that Darwin's symptoms were caused by hyper-ventilation is outlined in the Prologue. There are many useful reviews of current opinion and research regarding the condition. Some approach it physiologically, e.g. C. Bass & W. Gardner (1985) and L. C. Lum (1987), others psychologically, e.g. M. Gelder (1986) and G. A. Hibbert (1985). All emphasise the role of both and the malignant interaction between them. For a brief and lucid introduction there is nothing better than a paper by H. R. Lazarus and J. J. Kostan (1969).

Symptoms of the condition are protean. Among those in Darwin's written list are: palpitations, flatulence and nausea, trembling or shiver-ing, blurred vision, paraesthesias (tingling sensations), faintness, becoming easily and chronically tired, and fear of dying. Other common symptoms include dizziness, headaches, emotional sweating, and chest pains on activity or from emotion.

Once the condition is suspected, diagnosis is often fairly easy. For example, in early cases, disordered breathing, in which rate and rhythm change rapidly and breathing is confined to the thorax without con-tractions of the diaphragm, may be obvious. In chronic cases, however, overbreathing is usually not evident because rate of respiration is normal and the increased volume of air inspired at each breath not apparent. For such patients diagnostic tests are available. A standard test is to ask the patient to breathe deeply at a rather fast rate (forty breaths per minute) for three minutes. Symptoms such as dizziness, unsteadiness and blurred vision commonly start within half a minute; other symptoms take a little longer. After three minutes chest pains occur in about half the patients. A great advantage of the test is that it demonstrates to the patient how his symptoms come to be produced. Differential diagnosis is fully discussed by R. Brashear (1983) and the emotional influences causing the condition by G. Magarian (1982) and C. Bass and W. Gardner (1985).

It is hardly unexpected that hyperventilation should be initiated when a person is in a distressed condition, since it is common knowledge that emotion affects breathing: a well-known example is the deep spasmodic sighing characteristic of acute grief. When these changes in breathing are studied systematically, moreover, it is found that hyperventilation is both a common and normal response to any stressful situation. Whereas in most people such overbreathing is of limited duration, there is a minority in whom it tends to persist or else to be readily reactivated by reminders of the event. These are the people who are likely to develop symptoms; and they are also the people, mentioned in the Prologue, who tend to avoid making any reference to whatever situation it may be that is distressing them.

A persistent avoidance of reference to distressing situations by psychosomatic patients, or to the distressful emotions that are normally aroused by them, is the subject of much research, most of it stimulated by a study of J. C. Nemiah and P. E. Sifneos, who in 1970 drew attention to the condition, for which they coined the term 'alexithymia'. In a review of subsequent research Ahrens and Deffner (1986) point out that the inability to express distressful feelings is evident only when a patient is reminded of the particular events and situations in which he has been personally involved and does not occur in situations contrived for experimental purposes. Recent studies of interest are those by C. Z. Malatesta, R. Jonas and C. E. Izard (1987) and by J. W. Pennebaker and J. R. Susman (1988).

The related finding, also referred to in the Prologue, is that such a person does not need to be consciously aware of having been reminded of the event for it to affect his breathing. Although in some quarters this statement might appear speculative, it is now confirmed by careful experimental research carried out by a group led by Dr Peter Nixon, a consultant cardiologist at Charing Cross Hospital in London, assisted by a research cardiologist, Dr Leisa Freeman, and a clinical psychologist, Mr Ashley Conway. In one of their studies patients suffering from hyperventilation syndrome were reminded under hypnosis of some continuing situation or event known or strongly suspected from previous interviews to have distressed them. This led to an increase in their breathing, which in turn resulted in a marked fall in the level of carbon dioxide in their blood. A control group treated in the same way showed no such changes. (Freeman, Conway and Nixon, 1986: Conway, Freeman and Nixon, 1988). Further work by the same group (Nixon and Freeman 1988) suggests that, for clinical purposes, the much simpler procedure of instructing the patient to recall and then to dwell consciously on a time or place when he had experienced typical symptoms, while physiological changes are simultaneously being measured, may well be sufficient in a majority of cases (and in conjunction with standard procedures) to clarify the nature of the patient's psychosomatic condition and to confirm its psychological origin. Findings such as these are supported by those from a number of related experiments, for example, those of A. Mathews and C. MacLeod (1986).

Treatment of the condition includes both physiotherapy and psychotherapy. Physiotherapy consists, first, of demonstrating to the patient how readily his symptoms are brought on when he overbreathes; training him in better modes of breathing; and then rehabilitating him back to ordinary life and work, which may include helping him confront situations that formerly brought on the symptoms and that consequently he has been systematically avoiding. Essential though such measures are, they are insufficient without trying to help the patient deal with the emotional problems that have made him prone to overbreathe in the first place.

Psychotherapy can usefully start by encouraging the patient to talk about his anxieties, especially the thoughts and feelings he has during an attack, as well as details of the situations in which attacks tend to occur. This can lead on naturally to helping him explore more extensively events and situations in his life that have caused him stress and anxiety. A feature of psychotherapy to which I attach especial importance is the role of the therapist as a companion in their joint exploration of these distressing events and of the painful thoughts and feelings the patient had at the time – thoughts and feelings that in the past he may have been strongly discouraged from expressing. The object of this procedure, which a patient may be very reluctant to engage in, is to help him gradually gain insight into the high degree to which the anxieties and forebodings with which he is viewing current situations is the product, without his knowing it, of the distressing events he has experienced during his childhood. With the aid of such insight the patient is encouraged to look afresh at the relevance of these past experiences to how he is thinking and feeling about the situations he is meeting during the course of therapy, and to do so in the light of his present-day knowledge of the world and of the motives of the people in it. A brief account of this variation of psychoanalytic psychotherapy can be found in a book by the present author.[3]

III

Believing as many do that Darwin's symptoms were responses to stress, psychiatrists and other medicals have advanced a great range of ideas in attempts to explain them. Proposals fall into two complementary categories:

1 Theories that implicate social situations that he was in during his adult life. Some of those proposed as having been pathogenic persisted over long periods; others were clearly defined events or situations of a stressful nature encountered by him at particular times.

2 Theories that implicate factors thought to have made him specially vulnerable to conflictual situations and stressful life-events. Some of these proposals focus on possible heritable factors; others call attention to emotional problems stemming from family relationships during his childhood and adolescence.

Some of the theories in the first category ascribe Darwin's symptoms to social situations that he was in for continuous periods after the *Beagle* voyage. Of these there are three that I believe to have little substance. One, proposed in an early paper by Douglas Hubble (1943) and presented as the major influence by George Pickering (1974), is a conflict between his scientific aspirations and social distractions. According to Pickering, 'the cause of Darwin's psychoneurosis . . . was the conflict between his passionate desire to collect convincing evidence for his hypothesis and the threat imposed on his work by social intercourse'. This is to promote what can have been no more than a secondary gain to the role of prime motive.

A second factor, invoked also by both Hubble (in a later paper, 1953) and by Pickering (1974), is what they conceive to have been Emma's excessive cosseting of her husband. According to Pickering, 'Emma loved looking after invalids'; in Hubble's words, there was 'environmental overcare . . . The perfect nurse had married the perfect patient.' These ideas are certainly encouraged by the entertaining descriptions of members of the Darwin family given by one of Charles and Emma's granddaughters, Gwen Raverat (1952); but they spring, it seems to me, from a grave misjudgement of Emma's character and a total neglect of the situation she found herself in. It may well be that with present knowledge she could with advantage have behaved differently; but it must be remembered that Charles's medical advisers, not knowing better, led both of them to believe he was physically affected.

A third factor, advanced initially by the geneticist C. D. Darlington (1959) and favoured by Hedley Atkins (1974), is conflict between what were seen in Darwin's day to be the adverse religious consequences of evolution theory and Emma's religious beliefs. Admittedly Emma was concerned that Charles was not a believer – he describes himself as having become an agnostic[4] – but there is scant evidence that she was troubled by the apparent conflict between evolutionary theory and religion that so occupied Victorian intellectuals. The fact that she helped correct the proofs of the *Origin*[5] and did everything she could in other ways to facilitate his work tells against the idea.

A further defect of each of these hypotheses, and a crucial one, is that none makes any attempt to explain why Darwin's symptoms developed when they did, nor why at three periods in his life they became so very much worse.

Yet another situation present over a long period, and the one regarded by Ralph Colp (1977) as the overriding one, concerns 'Darwin's feelings about his evolutionary theory', especially the difficulties he foresaw from the first in presenting it in a convincing light to his scientific colleagues and, after the *Origin* was published, the hostile criticism he met with from some of them. In presenting this theory Colp takes careful account of the timing of events and presents much relevant evidence. For instance, there can be little doubt that Darwin's intense concern about how his theories would be received, not only by hostile critics but, as Colp points out, especially by his friends and supporters among senior colleagues, was a major factor at the time of his persisting ill-health during 1859 and the early 1860s. A special blow was Lyell's unexpected failure publicly to endorse Darwin's theories when the latter's hopes were running high in 1863. That ranks unmistakably as a clearly defined stressful life-event of the kind referred to earlier.

Deeply significant though the reception of his work undoubtedly was for Darwin's emotional well-being during later years, before and after publication of the *Origin*, there were other events and situations occurring earlier that were no less so. For example, when, soon after the *Beagle*'s return, his symptoms became troublesome he was desk-bound in London writing up his findings and under much pressure from senior scientists which he found it impossible to resist. Other stressful situations concerned his family life. These included Emma's repeated pregnancies, the frequent and often serious illnesses of the children, and his father's final illness and death. Not only did these situations provoke intense anxiety and/or depression in Darwin but they almost certainly account in large part for the marked worsening of his symptoms at certain times in his life. Although several students of his ill-health have noted the relation between the death of his father in 1848 and the worsening of his symptoms at that time, only Colp, it seems, has picked out Emma's pregnancies and the children's illnesses as likely also to have been of consequence. Even so, despite his presenting much new and important evidence, Colp in his book assigns to these situations no more than a secondary role and adheres to his view that Darwin's anxieties about his theoretical ideas played the dominant part. Thus, although I find myself in agreement with much of Colp's evaluation of the events and situations that caused Darwin anxiety and distress, differences of emphasis remain. There are also some differences between us in how we understand the origin and nature of his vulnerability.

IV

Stressful life-events of the kinds mentioned are, of course, likely to cause more or less acute anxiety and distress in every human being. Only in a minority, however, do they lead to a breakdown in which daily life cannot be carried on or is carried on only with the greatest difficulty. Any theory (such as the one presented here) that implicates stressful life-events as contributing to psychological breakdown must therefore also explain why one person is especially vulnerable to such events and another is not.

Although nature and nurture are complementary and constantly interacting, theories to account for increased vulnerability have tended hitherto to emphasise either hereditary influences or else environmental ones. What this means is that some theories postulate so adverse a genetic loading that there is a high chance of its being expressed even in a fairly benign environment, whereas other theories postulate so adverse an environment that it is likely to cause disturbed development even given a fairly average heredity. In the literature on Darwin's ill-health, theories with each of these emphases have been advanced, since his hyper-sensitivity to stressors has been widely recognised as calling for explanation.

Among those who invoke a strongly inherited susceptibility is Arthur Keith, a surgeon and physical anthropologist who claims that 'the constitution which made him [Darwin] liable to so many disorders was inherited'; and he adds, 'this indeed was his own opinion which, of course, weighs heavily with me.'[6] This view is strongly supported by Hedley Atkins, a fellow surgeon, and also by a psychiatrist, W. C. Alvarez (1959). All draw attention to what they believe to be an undue incidence of psychiatric disorder in the Darwin family. The evidence for that, presented in detail by Colp, is far from convincing, however; while, even if it were shown that there was such a clustering, there are good reasons for believing that it would probably not have been due to an adverse genetic loading. First, current findings in genetics show that the constellation of anxiety and depressive symptoms from which Darwin often suffered is not among the psychiatric conditions now known to have a significantly high genetic loading (Owen and Murray, 1988). Secondly, current epidemio-logical studies are confirming the findings of those working in family psychiatry and family therapy that psychological disorder is frequently transmitted through a family microculture in which disturbed relation-ships and vulnerable personalities in one generation produce disturbed relationships and vulnerable personalities in the next. Moreover, there are also families in which a disaster that has affected one member adversely has affected other members adversely as well, albeit, as often happens, in different ways. Until recently these alternative explanations of the clustering of cases in certain families have been seriously neglected. The assumption that the explanation can lie only in an adverse genetic loading is now shown to have been made much too readily.

The alternative possibility – that Darwin's vulnerability to stressful situations was mainly a consequence of emotional problems stemming from difficult family relationships during his childhood and adolescence – has for long been the subject of suggestions by those of a psychoanalytic orientation. Thus Edward J. Kempf (1918), Douglas Hubble (1943,

1946), Rankine Good (1954) and Phyllis Greenacre (1963) all draw attention to his difficult relations with his father, for which there is indeed plenty of evidence. A particular theory, favoured especially by Greenacre, picks out unconscious hostile feelings for his father as having been responsible for Darwin's symptoms. The only student of the problem to point to what I believe to be the great relevance of Darwin's feelings for his mother, however, is the early psychoanalyst, Edward J. Kempf (1918), whose ideas have been almost completely neglected (even by Colp, who does no more than mention his name).

The significantly increased incidence of depressive and related disorders in those who have lost their mother during childhood, for long the subject of controversy, is now well attested as a result of the research of a London group led by George Brown and Tirril Harris. In three separate epidemiological studies, carried out with exemplary care, it was found that women aged between eighteen and sixty-five who had lost their mother before their eleventh birthday were two to three times more likely to become depressed when they met with a severely adverse life-event, notably another loss or threat of loss, than were women who had not done so. Although for practical reasons these studies have so far been confined to women, there is no reason to suppose the findings for men would be materially different. The research group has many publications to its credit, of which the most relevant are an article by George W. Brown, Tirril Harris and Antonia Bifulco (1985) and a book by Tirril Harris and her two colleagues (in preparation) on the long-term effects of early loss of parent. Clinical reports provide complementary evidence.

For fifty years descriptions of adults whose current emotional problems have been traced during therapy to a childhood bereavement have been published in psychoanalytic journals. In most such cases the patient is unable to recall much about the lost parent or having had any particular feelings about the loss. Yet, after the patient has begun to trust his therapist to be understanding, a situation may arise that reminds him of the loss, details about it are recalled, and feelings, long asleep, come flooding in. The same sequence can also occur outside therapy, as the following account, given by a middle-aged woman in a research interview, illustrates.[7]

Mrs W., a working-class woman of forty-six who had lost her mother as a child, gave the following account. She was aged six when her mother died. She had been told nothing about it and, she said, 'You wasn't allowed to ask. It was the type of family where everything was kept out of the way.' She had felt 'nothing' after the loss and could never cry. A few weeks afterwards she had been found in a dazed state, bumping into lamp-posts. She had been unable to recall where she had been going; all she could remember was a bandage having been put on her head. Some years later she had come across a slip of paper with the date of her mother's death on it. The date, she said, had stuck in her mind, and each year since then she had thought of her mother on that date.

When she was eighteen it happened by chance that she overheard a neighbour telling another how Mrs W.'s mother had committed suicide because her husband (Mrs W.'s father), was having an affair with the woman he subsequently married. On hearing this, and much to her surprise, Mrs W. had cried for the first time and had grown violently angry. Subsequently she had experienced an intense urge to find her mother's grave. Thus, although to all appearances Mrs W. had been unaffected by her mother's death, somewhere in her mind there persisted an unexpressed potential for angry protest, for sorrow and for search.

I am postulating that, had he embarked on psychotherapy, Darwin would have discovered similar feelings within himself. He might also have recalled some of the items he was preoccupied with after his mother's death, in particular ideas about what might have caused her fatal illness.

When, as in the cases of both Mrs W. and Charles Darwin, a child is given no information about illness, death or the hereafter and is not allowed to ask questions, he is left to speculate about such matters, matters that are of the greatest concern to him. If he is given no guidance, his speculations may light on one or more of a host of highly irrelevant possibilities that seem ridiculous to the adults around him. In the technical literature these are often called phantasies, but a better name for them is hypotheses which, because built on fragmentary information, are mistaken. Given patience, their origin can usually be traced to something the child has observed and misinterpreted or else heard and misunderstood.

One such hypothesis is a child's belief that he himself may in some way be responsible for his parent's death. This belief, which creates an appallingly heavy load of responsibility for a child to bear, can arise all too easily from remarks made by exasperated adults attempting to control a child. Remarks such as 'If you go on like that you'll make mother ill' or 'One of these days you children will be the death of me' are construed literally; and they are recalled guiltily should the parent then become ill or die. Whether Darwin entertained ideas of this sort is unclear, though an occasional remark in his letters is a little suggestive. There are, however, two conclusions he seems definitely to have drawn after his mother died. One is that gastric symptoms indicate an illness likely to prove fatal; the second that the tendency to develop such illness is hereditary. These ideas are only expressed clearly when he was in a depressed state after his father's death, though they were probably never far from his mind.

V

From the foregoing it will be seen that the model of psychological and psychosomatic disorder that is being invoked to account for Darwin's troubles is a multifactorial one. This implies not only that factors of many different sorts contribute to the onset of disorder but that the interaction between them may be much more powerful than the sum of their respective influences when acting alone. It is a model that has long been employed in physiological medicine and is now becoming established in psychological medicine as well.

In this type of model, causal factors are classified into four types:

1 predisposing
2 provoking
3 contributing
4 symptom-specifying.

Predisposing factors influence the structure of an organism, usually during its development, thereby determining in large part the degree to which it is vulnerable in the long term to a *provoking* factor. To produce disorder, factors of both types are necessary: neither is sufficient on its own. In physiological medicine, for example, the degree of a person's susceptibility to a specific infection is a predisposing factor and his exposure to that infection is the provoking one. *Contributing* factors are of several sorts. Some influence vulnerability in the short term; for example, cold and wet may make a person more vulnerable to infection than he would otherwise be, though only temporarily. Others may increase an individual's likelihood of meeting with a provoking factor; for instance, living in a certain area may determine exposure to a particular pathogen. Others again may exacerbate a disorder already present. *Symptom-specifying* factors account for the particular form that an illness takes in any one individual. Such factors are often obscure, and the riddle of diverse symptomatology is more often than not left unanswered.

Whereas a multifactorial model of this sort is usually taken for granted in the field of physiological medicine, it is only in recent years that it has become exploited in psychological medicine.

Notes

To save space, abbreviations are used for sources which appear more than a few times in the following notes.

A	*The Autobiography of Charles Darwin*, ed. Nora Barlow, 1958
B & HW	Barbara and Hensleigh Wedgwood, *The Wedgwood Circle 1730–1897*, 1980
CC I, II, III, IV,	*The Complete Correspondence of Charles Darwin*, ed. F. Burkhardt and S. Smith, 1985–8; vol. I, 1821–1836; vol. II, 1837–1843; vol. III, 1844–1846; vol. IV, 1847–1850
CFL I, II	*Emma Darwin: A Century of Family Letters 1792–1896*, 2 vols, ed. Henrietta Litchfield, 1915 edition
1904 *CFL* I, II	ditto, 1904 edition
Colp (1977)	Ralph Colp, Jr, *To Be an Invalid*, 1977
D	*Charles Darwin's Beagle Diary*, ed. R. D. Keynes, 1988
Dar.	Unpublished material in the Darwin archives in Cambridge University Library
D & H	*Darwin and Henslow: Letters 1831–1860*, ed. Nora Barlow, 1967
Fox	Unpublished letters from Charles Darwin to W. D. Fox in the library of Christ's College, Cambridge
Hooker *LL* I, II	*Life and Letters of Sir Joseph Dalton Hooker*, 2 vols, ed. L. Huxley, 1918
Huxley *LL* I, II, III	*Life and Letters of Thomas Henry Huxley*, 3 vols, ed. L. Huxley, 1900
Keith	Arthur Keith, *Darwin Revalued*, 1955
King-Hele	D. King-Hele, *Doctor of Revolution: The Life and Genius of Erasmus Darwin*, 1977
LL I, II, III	*The Life and Letters of Charles Darwin*, 3 vols, ed. Francis Darwin, 1885
Lyell *LL* I, II	*Life, Letters and Journals of Sir Charles Lyell, Bt*, 2 vols, ed. K. M. Lyell, 1881
Memoir	Charles Darwin, 'Preliminary Notice' to Ernst Krause, *Erasmus Darwin*, 1879
ML I, II	*More Letters of Charles Darwin*, 2 vols, ed. Francis Darwin and A. C. Seward, 1903
Raverat	Gwen Raverat, *Period Piece: A Cambridge Childhood*, 1952
Record	*The Beagle Record*, ed. R. D. Keynes, 1979
Wallace *LL* I, II	*Alfred Russel Wallace: Letters and Reminiscences*, 2 vols, ed. J. Marchant, 1916
W, W/M	Unpublished material in the Wedgwood archives in the library of the University of Keele

Prologue
1 *A*, 79
2 *A*, 115
3 Adler (1959)
4 Woodruff (1965)
5 Bernstein (1984)
6 *CC* II, 255
7 *LL* I, 109
8 Pickering (1974)
9 Hubble (1943)
10 *A*, 79–80
11 *CC* II, 47; original emphasis.
12 *LL* I, 10
13 *CC* II, 298
14 Atkins (1974)
15 In this section I am deeply indebted to the findings of Dr Peter Nixon, Dr Leisa Freeman and Mr Ashley Conway of Charing Cross Hospital, London. See also the appendix.
16 Freud (1895)
17 Lum (1987)
18 Hibbert (1985)
19 Engels (1985)
20 *LL* I, 112
21 *CFL* II, 117
22 *LL* II, 360
23 Fox, 145; letter to Hooker of 27 September 1865, quoted in Colp (1977), 86; Wallace *LL* I, 160
24 *CFL* II, 177
25 *LL* I, 130
26 L. Darwin (1929)
27 *LL* I, 127–8
28 *A*, 60–8

Chapter 1
1 Information in this chapter derives from King-Hele and B & HW
2 In this section I am indebted to King-Hele, especially the last chapter, and also to Gruber's important work, *Darwin on Man* (1974), ch. 3.
3 *A*, 122

Chapter 2
1 This description from Anna Seward's *Memoirs of the Life of Dr Darwin* (1804) is taken from King-Hele (p. 40), from which I have also drawn other information about Mary Howard.
2 This letter was first published as a note to the 1959 edition of Charles Darwin's *Autobiography*, edited by Nora Barlow, pp. 223–5.
3 This was written a century later by Robert's son Charles, in 'The Life of Erasmus Darwin', which he published in 1879 as a preliminary notice to an essay (translated from the German) by Ernst Krause. Later

quotations from this publication are referred to as Memoir.
4 Memoir.
5 B & HW, 70.
6 B & HW, 74.
7 Memoir, 36.
8 King-Hele, 22. Evidence regarding Dr Erasmus's treatment of other people is well reviewed in King-Hele, 46–7.
9 Memoir, 70 and 36.
10 Memoir, 76.
11 Memoir, 31–2.
12 From a note in Charles Darwin's M notebook begun in summer 1838, quoted in Gruber and Barrett (1974), 269.
13 Memoir, 83–4.
14 Memoir, 75.
15 Memoir, 76.
16 Information in this and subsequent paragraphs is drawn from B & HW, 61.
17 Eliza Meteyard, *A Group of Englishmen* (1871), 260–1.
18 B & HW, 117.
19 *A*, 56.
20 *A*, 29.
21 *A*, 30.
22 *A*, 31.
23 See Gruber and Barrett (1974), 340.
24 Memoir, 84.
25 *A*, 39–40.

Chapter 3
1 W 35–26456; *CFL* I, 68.
2 W 35–26442.
3 W 35–26474.
4 See B & HW, 174; and letters from Bessy Wedgwood to Fanny Allen, 3 January 1816 (W/M 68), and from John Wedgwood to Josiah II, 2 February 1816 (W 28–20117).
5 Susannah to Josiah II, 17 March 1816; (W 35–26480.)
6 W 35–26489.
7 W 27–19835.
8 W 28–20399.
9 B & HW, 181.
10 B & HW, 181.
11 *CFL* I, 138–9.
12 Barlow (1945), 9.
13 The earlier account, which ends when he was aged eleven and which I refer to as the 'Fragment', was found among his papers after his death. It was first published in 1903 in the first chapter of *ML* I and republished in *CC* II, 438–42.
14 *A*, 22.
15 W 165; W 35–26459, letter from Dr Robert to Josiah II, 20 August 1813.
16 *A*, 22.
17 *A*, 22, footnote by Charles's son Francis.
18 *A*, 23.

19 *A*, 22–3.
20 *A*, 23, footnote by Nora Barlow.
21 *A*, 24.
22 *A*, 25.
23 *A*, 25.
24 Dar. 112.
25 *A*, 27–8.
26 Colp (1985).
27 W 35–26594 and 35–26597.
28 *A*, 44.
29 *A*, 45–6.
30 *A*, 42–3.
31 *CC* I.
32 Information for this section comes from contemporary letters, some in the Wedgwood archives, others printed in *CFL*. In the latter volumes Charles's daughter Henrietta Litchfield, who knew her aunts in later life, gives her own impressions. See also Barlow (1945), Ch. 1.
33 W/M 74.
34 W/M 76.
35 *CFL* I, 141.
36 *CC* II, 29 and 85.
37 *A*, 42.
38 W/M 68.
39 The manuscript of Francis Darwin's 'Recollections' of his father (Dar. 140.4) contains a number of passages that were omitted from the version published as chapter 3 of *LL* I. (Although in the manuscript the sister being described is referred to as Caroline, the context makes it clear that the reference is to Catherine.)
40 *CFL* II, 184.
41 Vorzimmer (1977).
42 *LL* I, 10–11.
43 Memoir, 86.
44 Barlow (1945).
45 W/M 74.
46 W/M 74.
47 *CFL* II, 184.
48 *A*, 28.
49 *LL* I, 11.
50 Dar. 140/3.
51 *A*, 126

Chapter 4
1 B & HW, 195–6; *CC* I, 505.
2 Quoted by Moore (1985), 475–6.
3 Francis Darwin's 'Recollections', *LL* I, 120 and 140.
4 *LL* I, 154; L. Darwin (1929).
5 *LL* III, 219–20.
6 *LL* I, 158.
7 *LL* I, 124.
8 *LL* III, 53.
9 *LL* III, 53.
10 *LL* I, 141.

11 *A*, 27 and 26.
12 Hooker *LL* I, 495–6.
13 Quoted in article by John Durant in *The Times Higher Education Supplement* 31 May 1985.
14 See, for example, the conclusions reached by a group at Yale University, who, after reviewing nearly a hundred research studies, call attention to a significant group of patients who are apt to develop panic attacks and depressive episodes, either sequentially or simultaneously (Breier, Charney and Heninger, 1985).
15 The evidence for the conclusions regarding childhood mourning and also evidence supporting the notion of segregated systems active outside consciousness are reviewed in *Loss: Sadness and Depression* (Bowlby, 1980).
16 *CC* II, 315–16.
17 Raverat.
18 See Bowlby (1980)

Chapter 5
1 *A*, 49 and 47; *CC* I, 25.
2 Extracts from the records of Edinburgh University Library, subsequently lost, were published anonymously in 1888 and are referred to in *CC* I, 19, note 6.
3 *A*, 48 and 46.
4 *A*, 27.
5 *CC* I, 301.
6 *CC* I, 20.
7 *CC* I, 22 and 24.
8 *CC* I, 28–9.
9 *CC* I, 37.
10 *CC* I, 35–7.
11 *CC* I, 39.
12 *A*, 53–4.
13 See the unpublished parts of Francis Darwin's reminiscences, Dar. 140(3).
14 *A*, 53 and 49.
15 *CC* I, 71, note 6.
16 *CC* I, 35.
17 This information, and much else regarding Darwin's second session at Edinburgh, comes from an article by Ashworth (1934–5).
18 *A*, 52.
19 Quoted in Ashworth (1934–5).
20 Quoted in Ashworth (1934–5).
21 Egerton (1967).
22 Information in this paragraph and the quotation come from Ashworth (1934–5).
23 Information about Robert Grant comes from Desmond (1984).
24 *A*, 49.
25 This note, made by Henrietta for her brother's edition of the *Life and Letters* of their father but not included in the

published work, was found later at Down House and is reproduced in Jesperson (1948–9), from which the quotation is taken.
26 *A*, 49.
27 Desmond (1984).
28 *A*, 51.
29 *A*, 56.
30 *A*, 57.
31 *A*, 54–6.
32 For an account of the Wedgwood pottery and the part played by Josiah II, Josiah III and Frank, see B & HW, chs 19, 23 and 24.
33 *A*, 55.
34 *A*, 54.
35 *A*, 54–5.
36 Dates of birth of the five girls in the family are not given in *CC* I, but those of the five sons are. Since we know from a Wedgwood letter (see chapter 5, p. 20) that Sarah was seventeen in November 1820, she was evidently born in 1803 and so the eldest of the family. Fanny, and probably Caroline also, came between their two brothers, William (born 1806) and Arthur (1813).
37 *CC* I, 28; 40–1; 170; 213–14.

Chapter 6
1 *CC* I, 112, note 3.
2 At the age of twenty-seven, on returning from the *Beagle* voyage, he weighed 10 stone 8 lb; but he had added another stone three months later (*CC* I, 505, note). In contrast to his father, he remained thin until the end of his life (*LL* I, 111).
3 *A*, 60
4 *A*, 58.
5 *CC* I, 66, 92, 99.
6 *CC* I, 95 and 71.
7 Quoted by Allen (1976).
8 *A*, 62; *CC* I, 81.
9 *CC* I, 56–7 and 59.
10 *LL* I, 168.
11 *CC* I, 64 and 70.
12 *A*, 63; *CC* I, 90, note 1.
13 *CC* I, 88.
14 *CC* I, 74.
15 *CC* I, 74.
16 *CC* I, 81.
17 *CC* I, 75 and 106.
18 *CC* I, 85, 89, 101.
19 *CC* I, 98 and 124; *A*, 66–7.
20 Colp (1985), 371, note 59. Colp gives his reference to the US edition of *Life and Letters* I, 332 note.
21 Ruse (1975)
22 *A*, 64 and 60.
23 *CC* I, 102 and 104.
24 *CC* I, 104, note 3.
25 *A*, 64–5.

26 *CC* I, 109–10.
27 *A*, 64–6; *LL* I, 186–8.
28 *A*, 67; *LL* I, 187.
29 *A*, 66.
30 *CC* I, 79.
31 *A*, 59.
32 Ruse (1975)
33 *CC* I, 118.
34 *A*, 67–8.
35 *CC* I, 120; *A*, 68; *CC* I, 125.
36 *CC* I, 122–3.
37 *A*, 67; Herbert's letter of April 1832, *CC* I, 224.
38 *CC* I, 224.
39 *CC* I, 123; Dar. 140 (3).
40 *A*, 69–70.

Chapter 7
1 *CC* I, 128–9. Sources for this and subsequent chapters include *Charles Darwin's Beagle Diary* (1988) and *The Beagle Record* (1979), both edited by R. D. Keynes, Darwin's *Journal of Researches*, 2nd edition (1845), and the biography of *Robert FitzRoy* by H. E. L. Mellersh (1968).
2 *CC* I, 129–30.
3 *CC* I, 131.
4 *A*, 71; *CC* I, 133.
5 *CC* I, 134.
6 *CC* I, 135; *A*, 72.
7 *CC* I, 136.
8 *CC* I, 140–2.
9 *CC* I, 143, note 1.
10 *A*, 72.
11 *CC* I, 143–8.
12 *D*, 4.
13 *CC* I, 154–5.
14 *CC* I, 155–6.
15 *CC* I, 164 note.
16 *CC* I, 170–1.
17 *CC* I, 164–6.
18 B & HW, 215.
19 *CC* I, 166–73.
20 *CC* I, 151–2, 157–9.
21 *CC* I, 162–4, 167–8.
22 These passages from Sulivan's *Autobiography* are quoted by Mellersh (1968).
23 Quoted by Mellersh (1968).
24 *CC* I, 167; Mellersh (1968), 70.
25 *CC* I, appendix IV.
26 *CC* I, 151.
27 Lyell *LL* I, 168. Information about Charles Lyell here is drawn from this source.
28 Lyell *LL* II, 371.
29 *A*, 101.
30 *CC* I, 176–7.
31 A new edition of the *Beagle Diary* has recently appeared (edited by R. D. Keynes, 1988) and is drawn on extensively in what follows. After the *Beagle*'s return Darwin

used much of the diary material for his official account of the voyage, published under the title *Journal of Researches of the Voyage of the Beagle*. Even so, much else was omitted, while facts and ideas arising after his specimens had been examined by experts were added. Darwin himself referred to the contemporary record as his 'Journal', but, to distinguish the two versions, it has become the custom to refer to it as his diary.

32 *CC* I, 176.
33 *D*, 5–6.
34 *D*, 7.
35 Quoted by Mellersh (1968).
36 *CC* I, 179–80, 182.
37 *CC* I, 183–4, 186.
38 *D*, 7.
39 *D*, 10–15.
40 *CC* I, 187.
41 *D*, 13.
42 *D*, 15–16.
43 *D*, 17.
44 *CC* I, 164–5; *A*, 79–80.
45 *CC* I, 143.
46 *CC* I, 180.
47 *D*, 12 and 18.
48 *D*, 19.

Chapter 8
1 There are two good accounts of the voyage, both beautifully illustrated: *The Beagle Record* ed. R. D. Keynes (1979); and Alan Moorehead, *Darwin and the Beagle* (1971)
2 *D*, 22–3.
3 *CC* I, 220 and 221, note 2.
4 *D*, 36–7 and 37, note 1.
5 *D*, 49.
6 *D*, 71 and 145.
7 *D*, 42.
8 *D*, 44.
9 *D*, 51.
10 *D*, 58.
11 *D*, 61.
12 *D*, 74 and 77.
13 *D*, 93.
14 *D*, 106–7.
15 *CC* I, 276.
16 *CC* I, 280.
17 *D*, 126.
18 *D*, 131–2.
19 *Record*, 102.
20 *D*, 141–3.
21 *D*, 140.
22 *D*, 140, note 1.
23 *D*, 145.
24 *CC* I, 302–5.
25 *D*, 102–3, note 1.
26 Mellersh (1968), 131.
27 *D*, 102.

28 *D*, 149 note.
29 *Record*, 133.
30 *CC* I, 312.
31 *D*, 160.
32 *D*, 159–60; *CC* I, 313.
33 *Record*, 143–4.
34 *D*, 207.
35 *D*, 208–9.
36 *D*, 214–15 and 215, note 1.
37 *D*, 226–7.
38 *CC* I, 379.
39 *D*, 232–3 and 237, note 1.
40 *D*, 237.
41 *D*, 239.
42 *D*, 240.
43 *D*, 244–5.
44 *D*, 250–62.
45 *CC* I, 410–11.

Chapter 9
1 Quoted in *Record*, 222.
2 *Record*, 238–9.
3 Quoted in *D*, 264.
4 *CC* I, 418.
5 Hyde (1959)
6 *CC* I, 225–7.
7 *A*, 74.
8 *A*, 75.
9 *A*, 73.
10 *CC* I, 394.
11 Quoted in *D*, 205, note 2.
12 Quoted in *D*, 205, note 1.
13 *Record*, 42.
14 *CC* I, 226.
15 *A*, 73.
16 *CC* I, 393.
17 *A*, 75.

Chapter 10
1 *CC* I, 411 and 418.
2 *CC* I, 411 and 418.
3 *CC* I, 411.
4 Quoted in *Record*, 246.
5 *CC* I, 434.
6 Quoted in *Record*, 247.
7 *D*, 274–5.
8 *D*, 274–7.
9 *D*, 280.
10 *D*, 292.
11 Unpublished recollections of Francis Darwin, Dar. 140 (3).
12 *D*, 296 and 304.
13 *CC* I, 433–5.
14 *CC* I, 413 and 435.
15 *D*, 304–5.
16 *D*, 324.
17 *D*, 343–4.
18 *D*, 349–50.
19 *CC* I, 461–2.
20 *D*, 351, note 1.

21 *D*, 355.
22 *CC* I, 458.
23 *D*, 351–2, 354, 353.
24 *D*, 361–3.
25 *Journal of Researches* (1839), 474–5, quoted in *D*, 360, note.
26 Barlow (1963).
27 *CC* I, 489.
28 *CC* I, 485.
29 *D*, 371.
30 *D*, 379.
31 *CC* I, 479, note 3.
32 *CC* I, 482.
33 *D*, 398, 401–2.
34 *D*, 405–6.
35 *CC* I, 491.
36 *D*, 409.
37 *CC* I, 495.
38 *D*, 422.
39 *CC* I, 495–6, 483.
40 *CC*, I, 497.
41 *D*, 425.
42 *D*, 427.
43 *CC* I, 500; *A*, 107.
44 *D*, 427; *CC* I, 501–2.
45 *CC* I, 469.
46 *CC* I, 503.
47 *A*, 82.
48 *CC* I, 503.
49 *D*, 432 and 433.
50 *D*, 439, 441, 447.
51 For information in these paragraphs, see Mellersh (1959).

Chapter 11
1 *A*, 77.
2 *A*, 81.
3 *CC* I, 232–3.
4 *D*, 154.
5 *D*, 156–9.
6 *CC* I, 330–1.
7 *D*, 184.
8 *D*, 191.
9 *D*, 172, 180–1.
10 *CC* I, 331.
11 *D*, 204, 192–3.
12 *D*, 194.
13 *CC* I, 342–3.
14 *D*, 198.
15 *D*, 229–31.
16 *CC* I, 406.
17 *D*, 306.
18 *D*, 315.
19 A letter of 25 June 1835 from an acquaintance in Valparaiso, with whom Darwin was in correspondence about geology, thanks him for a letter of 29 May and continues: 'I was sorry to hear that your rebel stomach had been annoying you again; (*CC* I, 450).
20 *D*, 323.

21 *CC* I, 440–4, 446.
22 *CC* I, 463.
23 *CC* I, 462 and 463, note 1.
24 *CC* I, 199, 236–9.
25 *CC* I, 316.
26 *CC* I, 250–2.
27 *CC* I, 392–4.
28 *CC* I, 279–81, 321–2, 351–3.
29 *CC* I, 344–5.
30 *CC* I, 327–8.
31 *CC* I, 368–71.
32 No copy of this letter has survived.
33 *CC* I, 397–402.
34 *CC* I, 372–4, 374–7.
35 Report by Fox relayed by Darwin's sister Catherine: *CC* I, 412–14.
36 *CC* I, 460.
37 *CC* I, 499–500.
38 *CC* I, 437.
39 *CC* I, 437, 462, 500.
40 *CC* I, 495–6.
41 *CC* I, 239, note 1.
42 *CC* I, 473–4.
43 *CC* I, 473.

Chapter 12
1 *CC* I, 229.
2 *CC* I, 284 and 318.
3 *CC* I, 301 and 374.
4 *CC* I, 329–30, 346.
5 *CC* I, 359, 459, 429.
6 *CC* I, 474.
7 *CC* I, 488–9.
8 *CC* I, 300, 235, 394.
9 *CC* I, 234.
10 *CC* I, 275, 382, 409.
11 *CC* I, 205.
12 *CC* I, 269, 274, 301, 312.
13 *CC* I, 392 and 337.
14 *CC* I, 343.
15 *CC* I, 372–4.
16 *CC* I, 435, 447–8.
17 *CC* I, 345 and 356.
18 *CC* I, 345 and 366.
19 *CC* I, 392.
20 *CC* I, 469.
21 *CC* I, 346, 302, 501–2.
22 *CC* I, 197, 254, 227.
23 *CC* I, 256, 271, 275, 290.
24 *CC* I, 258–9.
25 *CC* I, 286, 316.
26 *CC* I, 277, 311–12.
27 *CC* I, 337.
28 *CC* I, 424, 426, 429.
29 *CC* I, 438.
30 *CC* I, 460.
31 *CC* I, 489.

Chapter 13
1 *CC* I, 506.

2 *CC* II, 11.
3 *CC* I, 507–8.
4 *CC* I, 512–14.
5 *CC* I, 511, 516.
6 Keith, 221–2.
7 *CFL* I, 273.
8 *CC* II, 7.
9 Lyell *LL* I, 457–9, 460–1.
10 *CC* I, 514 note, 517.
11 *CC* II, 29.
12 Lyell *LL* II, 39–41.
13 *A*, 83–4.
14 See the studies of Gruber and Barrett (1974), Manier (1978), Ospovat (1981) and Sulloway (1982b).
15 *CC* II, 107.
16 *CC* IV, appendix IV.
17 Ruse (1975)
18 *LL* II, 241.
19 Items 196, 197 and 223 in the C notebook: see Gruber and Barrett (1974), 452; Moore (1985), 453. The dating here and elsewhere in this chapter derives from Moore (1985).
20 Gruber and Barrett (1974), 276.
21 *CC* I, 163.
22 *CC* II, 47–52.
23 *CC* II, 80 and 84.
24 *CC* II, 85; Barlow (1958), 233.
25 *CC* II, 431, 91–2.
26 *ML* II, 171–3; *CC* II, 96.
27 Moore (1985).
28 Entries 54 and 57 in the M notebook, transcribed in Gruber and Barrett (1974) 275–6.
29 *CC* II, 107.
30 *CC* II, 57–8.
31 Mellersh (1968).
32 *CC* II, 236.

Chapter 14
1 For material in this chapter I am indebted to articles by Ernst Mayr, M. J. S. Hodge, D. L. Hull and G. E. Allen, in Bendall (1983). These present the results of the many detailed studies of the contents of the notebooks Darwin kept during the fertile years from 1837 to 1842, trace the steps by which he reached his main theories, and discuss his achievements in the light of philosophies of science, both those of Darwin's own day and those now current.
2 Hull (1983).
3 For the sequence of events, see Sulloway (1982b).
4 *CC* I, xix.
5 It has been widely stated that the group of Galapagos birds that influenced Darwin's thinking was the group known as Darwin's

finches. After examining the evidence, Sulloway (1982a) shows this to be a myth. Darwin had, in fact, failed to label his specimens adequately. Moreover, because of the complexity of the group, it required many more specimens and a knowledge of the theory of adaptive radiation before their relationships could be understood. Similarly, Darwin's collection of Galapagos tortoises was sadly deficient and it was only some years after the voyage that he came upon an earlier report, published in 1815, that recorded the real evidence regarding the distinct island forms (Sulloway, 1982b).

Chapter 15
1 Reproduced in *CC* II, appendix IV. Unless otherwise stated all quotations in this paragraph are from this source.
2 Quoted by Colp (1977), 17, from Darwin's *Notebooks on Transmutation of Species*, edited by Sir Gavin de Beer (1960–7).
3 *CFL* II, 1.
4 *CC* II, 105.
5 *CC* II, 432.
6 *ML* I, 321.
7 The quotations that follow are derived from Moore (1985).
8 *CC* II, 159, 149–50.
9 *CC* II, 159–60.
10 *CC* II, 165–6.
11 *CC* II, 169.
12 *CC* II, 170–1.
13 The first edition, for private circulation only, appeared in 1904. The second, public edition, with a few passages deleted, was published in 1915.
14 *CFL* I, 61–2.
15 *CFL* II, 80–1.
16 *CFL* I, 59–60.
17 *CFL* I, 134–5.
18 *CFL* I, 61–2.
19 *CFL* I, 187–8.
20 *CFL* I, 210, 141–2.
21 *CC* II, 150.
22 B & HW, 219.
23 *CFL* I, 48.
24 Henrietta Litchfield to Francis Darwin, 18 March 1887, Dar. 112, quoted by Colp (1977).
25 *CC* II, 171–2.

Chapter 16
1 *A*, 98.
2 *CFL* II, 40–1.
3 *CFL* II, 36–7.
4 *CFL* II, 28.
5 *CC* II, 104, 96, 199, 218–22.

6   *CC* II, 433; *CFL* II, 42.
7   Vorzimmer (1977)
8   *CC* II, 433, 234–5.
9   *CC* II, 236.
10 *CC* II, 269–70.
11 *CC* II, 250, 269.
12 *CFL* II, 51–3.
13 *CC* II, 253, 254.
14 *CC* II, 434. Starting in August 1838 Darwin kept a small notebook which he called his journal, in which he recorded the periods when he was away from home, the progress and publication of his work, and important events in the family life (*CC* II, 430). Entries are extremely brief and rarely more than one to a month.
15 *CC* II, 260.
16 *CC* II, 261–3.
17 *CC* II, 269–70.
18 *CC* II, 273, 434.
19 *CC* II, 279, 286–7.
20 *CFL* II, 56.
21 B & HW, 236.
22 *CFL* II, 52.
23 *CC* II, 279, 289, 284, 434.
24 *CC* II, 292
25 *CC* II, 293–4.
26 *CC* II, 295–6.
27 *CC* II, 298, 293.
28 *CC* II, 303–5.
29 The circumstances which led Darwin to keep this diary and the nature of its contents are the subject of an article by Keegan and Gruber (1985).
30 *CC* II, 311, 435.
31 *A* 107.
32 *CC* II, 313–14.
33 *CC* II, 316, 312.
34 *CC* II, 315–16, 352–3.
35 *CC* II, 318.
36 *LL* II, 10.
37 *A*, 99.
38 *CC* II, 323–5.
39 *CFL* II, 78.
40 *A*, 98.

Chapter 17
1   Moore (1985).
2   Quoted by Stecher (1961), 232.
3   Moore (1985).
4   *CC* II, 360.
5   Atkins (1974).
6   *LL* I, 139.
7   *A*, 115.
8   *CC* II, 345, 352–3.
9   *CC* II, 409.
10 *CC* II, 399.
11 *CC* II, 435.
12 *CC* III, 54–5.
13 Kohn and others (1982).

14 This phrase and much else in this paragraph comes from Hooker *LL*.
15 *CC* II, 238, 378; *CC* III, 1–2.
16 *CC* III, 43–5.
17 *CC* III, 67–8, 85.
18 *CC* III, 72, 79.
19 *CC* III, 101–3, 107–8.
20 *CC* III, 180–1, 258.
21 *CC* III, 28, 48, 55–7.
22 *CC* III, 216. See Sulloway (1982a, 1982b, 1984) for the development of Darwin's thinking about evolution, especially during the years 1835–45.
23 *CC* III, 139–40.
24 *CC* III, 86, 68.
25 *CC* III, 141–3, 165–6.
26 Hooker *LL* I, 194–5.
27 It is stated in Hooker's biography that while in Madeira on the outward voyage to the Antarctic he suffered 'a sharp attack of rheumatic fever' (Hooker *LL* I, 91). Whatever the ailment may have been, there seems to be no evidence that it was really rheumatic fever.
28 Recollection of Joseph Hooker in Darwin *LL* I, 318.
29 Freeman (1978).
30 *CFL* II, 86.
31 *CC* III, 134.
32 *LL* I, 341.
33 *CC* III, 216.
34 *CC* III, 247.
35 Woodruff (1965).
36 *LL* I, 338.
37 *CC* III, 157.
38 *CC* III, 332, 258; Blackburn (1989).
39 *CC* III, 258–60.
40 Fox, 70; *CC* III, 180.
41 *CFL* I, 51–2.
42 *CC* III, 264.
43 *CC* III, 272.
44 *CC* III, 274–5.
45 *CC* III, 311, 314, 323.
46 *LL* II, 26–7.
47 *CC* III, 310.
48 *CC* III, 311–12; Dar. 140(3).
49 *CC* III, 325–7.
50 *CC* III, 332.
51 *CC* III, 346, 354.
52 *CC* III, 350.
53 Bunbury *LL* I, 214; *CC* III, 236–7.
54 *CC* III, 264, 282.
55 *CC* III, 250.
56 *CC* III, 252–6.

Chapter 18
1   *CC* IV, 57.
2   *CC* III, 366.
3   *CC* IV, 15, 28, 29.
4   *CC* IV, 29–30, 45, 47, 87.

5   Hooker (1899).
6   *CC* IV, 118.
7   *CC* IV, 139.
8   A detailed account of the controversy is given in an editorial note in *ML* II, 171–3.
9   *CC* IV, 71, 74.
10 *CC* IV, 75.
11 *CC* IV, 148, 152.
12 Quoted by De Beer (1959).
13 *ML* II, 188.
14 For information regarding Darwin's study of barnacles, I am indebted to appendix II of *CC* IV.
15 *CC* IV, 101.
16 *CC* IV, 125–6.
17 *CC* IV, 140.
18 *CC* IV, 127–8; 129, note 5.
19 *A*, 117.
20 *CC* IV, 384.
21 *CC* IV, 10–11, 24, 343.
22 Dar. 140(3); *CC* IV, 91–4.
23 *CC* IV, 139.
24 *CC* IV, 142–7.
25 *CC* IV, 158.
26 *CC* IV, 167.
27 *CC* IV, 181–3; *CFL* II, 119–20.
28 B & HW, 249–50.
29 *CC* IV, 209.
30 *CC* IV, 204.
31 *CC* IV, 219, 223, 224, note 2.
32 Quoted by Colp (1977), 195.
33 *CC* IV, 224–6.
34 *CC* IV, 227–8.
35 *CC* II, 395–6.
36 *CC* IV, 229–30.
37 *CC* IV, 235–6.
38 *CC* IV, 234.
39 Colp (1977), 44, 51–3.
40 *CC* IV, 246.
41 *LL* III, 270.
42 *CC* IV, 256.
43 *CC* IV, 268–70.
44 *CC* IV, 270, 327–8.
45 *CC* IV, 344.
46 *CC* IV, 260–2.
47 *CC* IV, 385.
48 *CC* IV, 303.
49 *CC* IV, 284–5.
50 B & HW, 250.
51 *CFL* II, 106.

Chapter 19
1   *CC* IV, 302–3.
2   *CC* IV, 310–11, 335, 343–5, 336, note 3.
3   *CC* IV, 353–4.
4   *CFL* II, 132; B & HW, 250.
5   Where not otherwise stated, information in this section comes from a detailed article by Colp (1987).
6   *CFL* II, 132.

7   *CFL* II, 122; B & HW, 250.
8   This and the subsequent three letters are in the Wedgwood archives at Keele University (W/M 310).
9   B & HW, 250.
10 *LL* I, 132–4.
11 *A* 98; *LL* III, 228; *CFL* II, 137.
12 Dar. 115, quoted in Colp (1987).
13 Fox, 100.
14 Colp (1977), 70.
15 *LL* I, 382, 384, 387.
16 Fox, 78a.
17 *LL* I, 121, 381, 386–7.
18 *CC* IV, 354, 362.
19 *CC* IV, 368–9.
20 *CC* IV, 370, note 4.
21 Fox, 80.
22 *LL* I, 383–4.
23 Fox, 84.
24 These observations and others quoted below are drawn from *CC* IV, appendix III, which is devoted to Darwin's observations on his children.
25 *CFL* III, 45.
26 *CFL* II, 156, 154, 99.
27 *CFL* II, 46–8.

Chapter 20
1   *LL* I, 386–7.
2   *CC* IV, 406; *LL* I, 388–9.
3   *LL* II, 44.
4   *LL* I, 390–1.
5   Quoted in De Beer (1959).
6   *LL* I, 395.
7   *CC* IV, 402.
8   Hooker *LL* II, 299–300.
9   *LL* II, 42; *ML* I, 78.
10 Information on Huxley is derived mainly from the *Life and Letters* by his son Leonard Huxley and from Bibby's biography (1959).
11 Huxley *LL* I, 91–5.
12 *ML* I, 74–5.
13 Huxley *LL* I, 129.
14 *LL* I, 142.
15 Information on Wallace is drawn mainly from *Letters and Reminiscences*, ed. Marchant (2 vols. 1916), and the biography of Wallace by Annabel Williams-Ellis (1966).
16 *CFL* II, 156; Fox, 87.
17 Fox, 96.

Chapter 21
1   *LL* II, 49.
2   This passage follows closely one in Hooker *LL* I, 497. Other particulars, including the quotations from Darwin's letters in the next paragraph, are derived from the same source.

3 Evidence that this was the first time is presented by Wilson, who also prints the extract from Lyell's letter to Darwin of 1 May 1856: Wilson (1970), xlv–xlvii.
4 Stauffer (1975), 8.
5 *LL* II, 67–8.
6 *LL* II, 71.
7 Stauffer (1975), 9; *ML* I, 94.
8 *LL* II, 78–9, 120–1.
9 Quoted by Williams-Ellis (1966).
10 Professor Carl Pantin (1959) describes this essay as 'far the most important "pre-Darwinian" contribution to the theory of evolution'.
11 *LL* II, 95.
12 *LL* II, 108–10.
13 Quoted by Pantin (1959).
14 *LL* II, 94–5.
15 Fox, 97, 100; *CFL* II, 158–9.
16 Fox, 86; *CFL* II, 205, 162–4.
17 Fox, 101–2, 103.
18 Fox, 104.
19 *ML* I, 109.
20 Published in De Beer (1959)
21 Quoted by Colp (1977), 56.
22 *CFL* II, 163; *LL* I, 136–7.
23 B & HW, 219; Jalland (1986).
24 *LL* II, 111–12; Fox, 113.
25 *LL* II, 126.
26 *CFL* II, 162–3.
27 *LL* II, 116–17.
28 *LL* II, 117–19.
29 Hooker *LL* II, 301.
30 *LL* II, 119–20.

Chapter 22
1 Fox, 118.
2 *LL* II, 132.
3 *LL* II, 138, 205.
4 *LL* II, 151.
5 *LL* II, 138–9.
6 Hooker *LL* I, 519–20.
7 Fox, 119, 106.
8 *LL* II, 150.
9 *LL* II, 158–9, 163–4.
10 Fox, 122.
11 *LL* II, 145–7.
12 Fox, 122.
13 *LL* II, 346; *ML* I, 267–71.
14 *D & H*, 200; De Beer (1968), 77–8; *LL* II, 216.
15 *LL* II, 231–3.
16 *ML* I, 125; *LL* II, 165.
17 *ML* I, 96; *LL* II, 146.
18 *LL* II, 166, 169–70.
19 Lyell *LL* II, 325–6.
20 *LL* II, 208–15, 228.
21 See Wilson (1970); *LL* II, 229–30.
22 *LL* II, 247–50. Although the date of this letter is given in *Life and Letters* as 24

December, there is good reason to think it was written on 24 November and so reached Darwin while he was still at Ilkley.
23 *ML* I, 136.
24 *CFL* II, 187; Dar. 115.
25 This letter is in the library of the American Philosophical Society and is printed in part in *LL* II, 240–1.
26 Lyell's gradually changing opinions about Darwin's theory from the time Darwin first expounded it to him in April 1856 are well documented in the *Scientific Journals on the Species Question* kept by Lyell from 1856 to the end of 1861, which have been edited with a valuable Introduction by L. G. Wilson (1970). Further information is available in Lyell's letters, covering these and later years, in Lyell *LL* II.
27 Lyell *LL* II, 328.
28 Quoted by Bartholomew (1975), whose article 'Huxley's Defence of Darwin' I have drawn on extensively in this section. See also Ospovat (1981) and Desmond (1982).
29 Huxley *LL* I, 173–4; II, 187–8.
30 *ML* I, 81–2 89–90.
31 Huxley, *LL* II, 196; Bartholomew (1975).
32 *ML* I, 97.
33 Huxley *LL* I, 157.
34 *ML* I, 102–3.
35 Huxley *LL* I, 158.
36 Bibby (1959), 72.
37 Huxley *LL* I, 173–4.
38 *LL* II, 232.
39 *ML* I, 131.

Chapter 23
1 *LL* II, 179.
2 Mayr (1983).
3 Commonly known as *Silliman's Journal* after the founder and editor; *LL* II, 268.
4 *ML* I, 455, note.
5 *LL* II, 268, 256; *ML* II, 175 note.
6 *LL* II, 300–1. Because Owen was still alive when *Life and Letters* was published Owen's name was omitted.
7 *ML* I, 149.
8 *ML* I, 185, 203, 232; quoted by Colp (1977), 72. See *ML* I, 226–8, for an account of Owen's behaviour that Charles Darwin and his friends found so outrageous.
9 *A*, 104–5.
10 Huxley *LL* I, 177; *ML* I, 139.
11 See Bartholomew (1975), Desmond (1982); *LL* II, 197.
12 *ML* I, 135.
13 Wallace *LL* I, 141–2.
14 Fox, 130.
15 Fox, 127, 128.
16 Quoted by Colp (1977), 68.

17 Hooker *LL* I, 526–7.
18 Hooker *LL* II, 303; Huxley *LL* I, 184; Lyell *LL* II, 335.
19 *LL* II, 323.
20 *LL* II, 324.
21 Mellersh (1968).
22 *LL* II, 324.
23 *LL* II, 370–1.
24 Fox, 128; *CFL* II, 177.
25 Fox, 130.
26 *LL* I, 150.
27 *LL* II, 345, 341.
28 *D & H*, 212, 214.
29 *D & H*, 205–7.
30 *LL* II, 351.
31 e.g. Eiseley (1958), Darlington (1959).
32 *LL* II, 346 note.
33 Dar. 115(i); Fox, 130a; Dar 115(ii).
34 Barlow (1958), 237–8.
35 *CFL* II, 173–5.
36 Dar. 115.
37 *LL* II, 360–1.
38 *ML* I, 184–5.
39 *ML* I, 194–6.
40 *CFL* II, 178; *LL* II, 376.
41 *LL* III, 262, 264.
42 *LL* III, 265–72.
43 *LL* II, 387 note.
44 These letters are quoted in Williams-Ellis (1966), 163, where the date of Wallace's return to Ternate is mistakenly given as December 1961.
45 *LL* II, 309.
46 *ML* II, 36.
47 Pantin (1959).
48 Fox, 132.
49 *CFL* II, 178.
50 *ML* I, 202.
51 *CFL* II, 178; from Francis Darwin's reminiscenses, Dar. 140 (3).
52 *LL* II, 383; Fox 134–5.
53 *LL* II, 393.
54 *LL* II, 381.
55 Hooker, *LL* II, 32–3.

Chapter 24
1 *LL* III, 2–3; *ML* I, 228.
2 Quoted by Colp (1977), 73.
3 *LL* III, 8–9; *ML* I, 237–9.
4 Quoted by Colp (1977) 74.
5 *LL* III, 11–12.
6 Lyell *LL* II, 361–6.
7 *LL* III, 14–17.
8 See his letters of 1868 and 1869 to the Duke of Argyll, Haeckel and Darwin in Lyell *LL* II, 431–42.
9 Unless otherwise indicated, information and quotations in this pragraph and subsequent ones are derived from Colp (1977), 74– 81.

10 Fox, 139.
11 *LL* III, 1.
12 Fox, 141.
13 Fox, 140, 141.
14 *LL* III, 1; Colp (1977), 219.
15 *LL* III, 1–2, 89.
16 Colp (1977), 76; *ML* II, 337.
17 Fox, 142.
18 *ML* I, 245.
19 *ML* II, 302–32.
20 Quoted by Colp (1977), 77.
21 Fox, 143.
22 *ML* II, 326; *ML* I, 247.
23 Colp (1977), 79–80.
24 *ML* II, 342.
25 Quoted by Colp (1977), 80; *LL* III, 27.
26 *ML* I, 251–2.
27 Lyell *LL* II, 384.
28 *ML* I, 257; *LL* III, 29.
29 *LL* III, 27–8; Fox, 145; *CFL* II, 182.
30 Information in this paragraph and the next is derived from Colp (1977), 81–6.
31 Fox, 146.
32 Huxley *LL* I, 267.
33 *CFL* II, 182–3.
34 L. Darwin (1929).
35 *LL* III, 39–40.
36 *LL* III, 40.
37 As the authority for this date, Colp (1977) cites R. C. Olby, 'Charles Darwin's Manuscript of Pangenesis', *British Journal for the History of Science* 1, (1963), 250–63.
38 *LL* III, 43–4.
39 *LL* III, 31.
40 Quoted by Colp (1985), 390.
41 Quoted by Colp (1977), 225.
42 *CFL* II, 185; *LL* I, 117–18; Colp (1977), 86.
43 *CFL* II, 184.
44 Information and the quotation given in this paragraph come from B & HW, 288.
45 *LL* III, 42.
46 Wallace *LL* I, 175.
47 *LL* III, 75.
48 Fox, 147.
49 1904 *CFL* II, 216.
50 Huxley (1921).

Chapter 25
1 *LL* III, 76.
2 *ML* I, 103.
3 *ML* I, 287; *LL* III, 78, 73.
4 This essay, together with much other material of great interest, was found in a bundle labelled 'Old and Useless Notes'. All this material is transcribed in Gruber and Barrett (1974); see especially pp. 398–403.
5 Transcribed by De Beer (1963).
6 *LL* II, 169.

7 *ML* II, 40.
8 *LL* III, 97.
9 *CFL* II, 197.
10 *ML* II, 68–9.
11 Diary first published 1907; Penguin edition (1985), 184.
12 *LL* III, 92; *CFL* II, 190; Fox, 149.
13 *CFL* II, 190.
14 See letter to Lyell of 23 February 1860, *LL* II, 289–90.
15 *ML* I, 305; *LL* III, 101; *LL* II, 371.
16 *LL* III, 107.
17 *ML* I, 313–14.
18 *LL* III, 109.
19 Darlington (1959). In his preface to a facsimile of the first edition of the *Origin*, Mayr (1964) argues that Darwin's retreat was less great than critics have made out.
20 *CC* IV, 130.
21 Quoted in Eiseley (1958), 235, from a letter in the possession of the American Philosophical Society; *LL* III, 115, 146; letter of July 1866, Wallace *LL* I, 142–3.
22 I am indebted to Himmelfarb (1959) for calling attention to this passage in the *Descent*, volume 1, pp. 152–3.
23 *ML* II, 39; *LL* III, 115–16.
24 *LL* III, 116–17; Lyell *LL* II, 441–2.
25 Di Gregorio (1982).
26 Bartholomew (1975)
27 *CFL* II, 223.
28 *LL* III, 68–9.
29 Sulloway (1979).
30 *CFL* II, 195.
31 *CFL* II, 192, 195.
32 *LL* III, 106; 1904 *CFL* II, 226.
33 *ML* I, 316; *ML* II, 40.
34 *CFL* II, 197.
35 *LL* III, 125.
36 *LL* III, 126.
37 *CFL* II, 196–7.
38 *CFL* II, 196.
39 *CFL* II, 198 (the first sentence is in the 1904 edition only).
40 *LL* III, 139.
41 Keith, 144.

Chapter 26
1 Gruber and Barrett (1974).
2 Darwin's observations on William were published separately in 1877 in the journal *Mind*, vol. 2, pp. 285–294. They are reprinted in Gruber and Barrett (1974).
3 *LL* III, 171.
4 *LL* III, 172.
5 *LL* III, 136, 144.
6 *ML* I, 333.
7 *LL* III, 146; Wallace *LL* I, 269.
8 *LL* III, 148–50.

9 Huxley *LL* I, 363; Huxley *LL* II, 427; Bartholomew (1975).
10 *ML* I, 335.
11 Wallace *LL* I, 265; *CFL* II, 204.
12 *CFL* II, 204–5.
13 *CFL* II, 207.
14 Huxley (1921)
15 *ML* II, 95.
16 *LL* III, 171.
17 *CFL* II, 210; *ML* II, 442–3; Fox, 151.
18 Fox, 132, 139, 145.
19 *LL* III, 174.
20 *LL* I, 108–60.
21 *LL* I, 124.
22 *CFL* II, 254.
23 Dar. 140 (3).
24 *CFL* II, 207.
25 *LL* I, 149.

Chapter 27
1 *CFL* II, 255.
2 *LL* III, 355.
3 Quoted by Colp (1977), 288, from an article by L. A. Nash, 'Some Memories of Charles Darwin', *Overland Monthly*, 77 (San Francisco, 1921).
4 *LL* III, 324.
5 *LL* III, 224 note.
6 *ML* II, 43.
7 *CFL* II, 212.
8 For details of Huxley's breakdown see Huxley *LL* I, chs 26 and 27.
9 Bibby (1959).
10 Quotations are from Hooker's retrospective account given to Leonard Huxley for inclusion in his father's *Life and Letters* (Huxley *LL* I, 390–1).
11 *CFL* II, 213–14.
12 *CFL* II, 214; for most of the other information in this paragraph I am indebted to Colp (1977), 88–9.
13 *CFL* II, 216.
14 *LL* III, 175–6.
15 *LL* III, 187–8; *CFL* II, 217.
16 Fox, 153.
17 *CFL* II, 218.
18 *LL* III, 189–90.
19 *LL* III, 181.
20 *LL* III, 197.
21 *LL* III, 328.
22 *LL* III, 195.
23 *LL* III, 200.
24 *LL* III, 202–3.
25 *LL* III, 204.
26 *CFL* II, 221.
27 This letter, addressed to Dr Maxwell Masters, a British horticulturalist, is in the USA.
28 Colp (1977), 89.
29 *LL* III, 184–5.

30 Geison (1978). Quotations are from the Life and Letters of George John Romanes by his widow, Ethel Romanes (1896).
31 ML I, 364; ML II, 12–13.
32 CFL II, 223.
33 CFL II, 224.
34 CFL II, 225, 255.
35 CFL II, 225.
36 ML II, 408.
37 CFL II, 225.
38 CFL II, 226.
39 LL III, 329–30.
40 CFL II, 229–30.
41 CFL II, 230–1.
42 CFL II, 230–1; Fox, 155.

Chapter 28
1 ML II, 421; LL III, 331.
2 CFL II, 231–2; ML II, 48.
3 CL II, 233; since George Darwin's paper was published in 1877, the date Henrietta assigns to the letter may be a year too late.
4 CFL II, 234.
5 LL III, 332.
6 1904 CFL II, 297.
7 Stirling (1926), 264, 101.
8 CFL II, 248; LL III, 222.
9 CFL II, 238.
10 CFL II, 238.
11 LL III, 228–9.
12 CFL II, 239.
13 All quotations referring to the Butler affair are taken from this work, pp. 167–219.
14 LL III, 240.
15 LL III, 332–3.
16 CFL II 241.
17 CFL II, 240; ML II, 424–5.
18 LL III, 334 and 335 note.
19 LL III, 334–5.
20 CFL II, 243.
21 CFL II, 189, 242.
22 CFL II, 244–5.
23 CFL II, 246.
24 LL III, 206.
25 CFL II, 246.
26 ML II, 433; LL III, 356.
27 LL III, 223. Professor Cohn, a German, visited Down in 1876, and shortly after Darwin's death published what Francis describes as 'a pleasantly written account' of his visit in the Breslauer Zeitung.
28 LL III, 228 and note; CFL II, 247.
29 LL III, 352–3.
30 CFL II, 249.
31 LL III, 218, 217.
32 CFL II, 248–9.
33 LL III, 357.
34 CFL II, 253.
35 LL III, 357; CFL II, 251–3.
36 Mayr, 1983; see also volumes edited by Bendall (1983) and Kohn (1985).

Epilogue
1 CFL II, 253.
2 CFL II, 261.
3 CFL II, 269.
4 CFL II, 276–7.
5 CFL II, 261.
6 The account of Henrietta's views was given by Leonard Darwin to his niece, Nora Barlow, many years later: Barlow (1958), 12.
7 Raverat.
8 Dictionary of National Biography 1912–1921.
9 Raverat, 191.
10 CFL II, 280.
11 Dictionary of National Biography 1922–1930.
12 CFL II, 309.
13 Raverat, 204.
14 Raverat, 146–7.
15 Hooker LL II, 309.
16 Wallace LL I, 113–14.

Appendix
1 Journal of Researches 1845, p. 330.
2 See CC II, 255.
3 Bowlby (1988), 137–57.
4 A, 94.
5 LL I, 153.
6 Keith, 220.
7 Theresa Jacobsen, personal communication.

Bibliography

Very extensive information on Darwin's life, work and health exists. Although a large amount has already been published and more is appearing almost every day, much is still available only in the archives at Down House, Cambridge University Library and the Library of the American Philosophical Society in Philadelphia, or else scattered in small lots or as single items in other collections around the world.

There are a great many published volumes containing parts of the enormous correspondence in which Darwin himself engaged with relatives, friends and other scientists, as well as volumes of letters in which reference is made to him, written by his relatives or by his scientific colleagues. Most of these volumes date from the period 1885–1915 and are listed on pp. 467. While they contain an enormous amount of value, they also have limitations, as Janet Browne has pointed out in a study published in 1978. For example, when the printed versions are compared with such manuscripts as still exist, omissions, errors of transcription and dating are found. Moreover, the editorial matter, usually compiled by a relative belonging to a younger generation, relies heavily on recollections of friends and other relatives, which are apt to be inaccurate or biased and are sometimes apocryphal.

It is therefore fortunate that in more recent years new editions of some of these letters have appeared, together with many letters previously unpublished and much valuable editorial matter. The supreme example is the series of volumes containing the *Complete Correspondence of Charles Darwin*, under the general editorship of Frederick Burkhardt and Sydney Smith, which, starting in 1985, is in course of publication by Cambridge University Press. In the present work I have been able to draw on only the first four of these volumes, which cover the years up to 1850. Additional volumes, each containing correspondence covering three or four further years, are being produced at the rate of about one a year.

Other works that have appeared under modern editorship are Darwin's *Autobiography*, edited by his granddaughter Nora Barlow (1958), and the *Diary* Darwin kept during the *Beagle* voyage, edited by Richard Keynes (1988). Whereas the *Autobiography* is tantalisingly brief, the *Beagle Diary*, taken in conjunction with the letters he wrote to relatives and friends in England, provides a detailed and vivid picture of his activities, thoughts and feelings during the five most eventful and critical years of his life. For an understanding of Darwin's emotional and intellectual development, the letters and *Beagle Diary* are far more illuminating than the retrospective account of the voyage that he gives in the well-known volume he published after his return, commonly referred to by the abbreviated title *Journal of Researches.*

During the *Beagle* voyage and for several years afterwards Darwin kept a sequence of notebooks in which he entered brief notes on a great variety of topics containing ideas that occurred to him during reading or after a conversation. Many refer to the species problem, particularly to the special case of the human species. In his numerous notes on human emotion, many derived from introspection, there are ideas about anxiety, anger and depression that would repay much more intensive study than I have been able to give them. Until recently only parts of this heterogeneous mass of material had been transcribed and published, mostly by De Beer (1960) and by Gruber and Barrett (1974), and these have been my sources. Now, however, a comprehensive edition has appeared, *Darwin's Scientific Diaries 1836–1842*, compiled by a group of editors under the leadership of Frederick Burkhardt (1987).

Two books that I have found especially useful for the light they throw on the economic circumstances, cultural traditions and personal relationships of the Darwin and Wedgwood families are Desmond King-Hele's biography of Erasmus Darwin (1977) and Barbara and Hensleigh Wedgwoods' *The Wedgwood Circle* (1980). The latter gives a panoramic picture, derived from the Wedgwood archives, of family life in three large and much intermarried families, the Wedgwoods, the Darwins and the Allens. Within these families letter writing was a skilled and highly practised art, especially among sisters, cousins and aunts. Whereas the Darwin archives are significantly silent about Darwin's mother, the Wedgwood archives yield valuable information.

For a description of Darwin's ill-health, both of the course of his symptoms and of the many theories that have been advanced to account for them, Ralph Colp's *To Be an Invalid* (1977) is indispensable.

Among publications arising from the centenary of Darwin's death, the symposium *Evolution from Molecules to Men*, edited by D. S. Bendall on behalf of Darwin College, Cambridge (1983), provides a comprehensive, though technical, survey of the current state of the scientific and intellectual revolution that Darwin set in train. *The Blind Watchmaker* by Richard Dawkins (1986) presents the best general account of evolution currently available to the non-specialist reader.

Finally, mention must be made of R. B. Freeman's compilation, *Charles Darwin: A Companion* (1978), a veritable encyclopaedia of everything a reader might wish to know about Darwin or his relatives, friends and colleagues. To this source I am indebted for many of the facts and figures given in this biography.

Publications relating to Darwin

ADLER, S. (1959) 'Darwin's illness', *Nature*, 10 October, pp. 1102–3

ALLEN, D. E. (1976) *The Naturalist in Britain*, London: Allen Lane (Pengiun Books)

ALVAREZ, W. C. (1959) 'The nature of Charles Darwin's lifelong ill-health', *New England Journal of Medicine*, 261, 1108–12

ASHWORTH, J. H. (1934–5) 'Charles Darwin as a student in Edinburgh 1825–27', *Proceedings of the Royal Society of Edinburgh*, 55, 98–101

ATKINS, H. (1974) *Down: The Home of the Darwins*, London: The Royal College of Surgeons of England

BARLOW, N. (ed.) (1945) *Charles Darwin and the Voyage of the 'Beagle'*, London: Pilot Press

BARLOW, N. (ed.) (1958) *The Autobiography of Charles Darwin*, London: Collins

BARLOW, N. (ed.) (1967) *Darwin and Henslow: Letters 1831–1860*, London: John Murray

BARTHOLOMEW, M. (1975) 'Huxley's defence of Darwin', *Annals of Science*, 32, 525–

BENDALL, D. S. (ed.) (1983) *Evolution from Molecules to Men*, Cambridge: Cambridge University Press

BERNSTEIN, RALPH E. (1984) 'Darwin's illness: Chagas' disease resurgens', *Journal of the Royal Society of Medicine*, 77, 608–9

BIBBY, C. (1959) *T. H. Huxley: Scientist, Humanist and Educator*, London: Watts

BLACKBURN, J. (1989) *Charles Waterton: Conservationist and Traveller*, London: The Bodley Head

BOWLBY, J. (1965) 'Darwin's health', letter to *British Medical Journal*, 10 April, p. 999

BROWNE, J. (1978) 'The Charles Darwin–Joseph Hooker correspondence: an analysis of manuscript resources and their use in biography', *Journal of the Society for the Bibliography of Natural History*, 8, 351–66

BURKHARDT, F., AND SMITH, S. (eds) (1985–8) *The Complete Correspondence of Charles Darwin*, vols I-IV, Cambridge: Cambridge University Press

BURKHARDT, F., AND OTHERS (eds) 1987) *Darwin's Scientific Diaries 1836–1842*, Cambridge: Cambridge University Press

COLP, R., JR (1977) *To Be an Invalid: The Illness of Charles Darwin*, Chicago: Chicago University Press

COLP, R., JR (1985) 'Notes on Charles Darwin's autobiography', *Journal of the History of Biology*, 18, 357–401

COLP, R., JR (1987) 'Charles Darwin's "insufferable grief" ', *Free Associations*, 9, 7–44

DARLINGTON, C. D. (1959) *Darwin's Place in History*, Oxford: Blackwell

DARWIN, C. (1845) *Journal of Researches into the Natural History and Geology of the Countries visited during the Voyage of H. M. S. Beagle round the World*, 2nd edn, London: John Murray

DARWIN, C. (1859; facsimile reprint, 1964) *On the Origin of Species*, with an introduction by Ernst Mayr, Cambridge, Mass.: Harvard University Press

DARWIN, C. (1871) *The Descent of Man, and Selection in Relation to Sex*, 2 vols, London: John Murray

DARWIN, C. (1879) 'Preliminary notice to E.Krause, *Erasmus Darwin*, London: John Murray

DARWIN, F. (ed.) (1887) *Life and Letters of Charles Darwin*, 3 vols, London: John Murray

DARWIN, F. (1912) 'Fitzroy and Darwin 1831–36', *Nature*, 88, 547–8

DARWIN, F., AND SEWARD, A. C. (eds) (1903) *More letters of Charles Darwin*, 2 vols, London: John Murray

DARWIN, L. (1929) 'Memories of Down House', *The Nineteenth Century and After*, 106 (July – December), 118–23

DAWKINS, R. (1986) *The Blind Watchmaker*, London: Longman (reprinted Penguin, 1988)

DE BEER, G. (1959) 'Some unpublished letters of Charles Darwin', *Royal Society Records*, vol. 14, pp. 12–66

DE BEER, G. (1960) 'Darwin's notebooks on transmutation of species', *Bulletin of the British Museum (Natural History) Historical Series 2*, 23–83

DE BEER, G. (1963) *Charles Darwin: Evolution by Natural Selection*, Edinburgh: Nelson

DESMOND, A. (1982) *Archetypes and Ancestors: Palaeontology in Victorian London 1850–1875*, London: Blond & Briggs

DESMOND, A. (1984) 'Robert E. Grant: the social predicament of a pre-Darwinian evolutionist', *Journal of the History of Biology*, 17, 189–223

DI GREGORIO, M. A. (1982) 'The dinosaur connection: a reinterpretation of T. H.Huxley's evolutionary view', *Journal of the History of Biology*, 15, 397–418

EGERTON, F. N., III (1967) 'Darwin's early reading of Lamarck', *Isis*, 67, 452–6

EISELEY, L. (1958) *Darwin's Century*, New York: Doubleday

FREEMAN, R. B. (1978) *Charles Darwin: A Companion*, Folkestone: Dawson, Anchor Books

GEISON, G. L. (1978) *Michael Foster (1836–1907) and the Cambridge School of Physiology: The Scientific Enterprise in Late Victorian Society*, Princeton, NJ: Princeton University Press

GILLISPIE, C. C. (1960) *The Edge of Objectivity: An Essay in the History of Scientific Ideas*, Princeton, NJ: Princeton University Press

GOOD, R. (1954) 'The origin of the *Origin*: a psychological approach', *Biology and Human Affairs*, October, pp. 10–16

GREENACRE, P. (1963) *The Quest for the Father*, New York: International Universities Press

GRUBER, H. E., AND BARRETT, P. H. (1974) *Darwin on Man*, New York: E. P. Dutton

HIMMELFARB, G. (1959) *Darwin and the Darwinian Revolution*, London: Chatto & Windus

HOOKER, J. (1899) 'Reminiscenses of Darwin', *Nature*, 22 June, pp. 187–8

HUBBLE, D. (1943) 'Charles Darwin and psychotherapy', *Lancet*, 30 January, pp. 129–33

HUBBLE, D. (1946) 'The evolution of Charles Darwin', *Horizon*, 14, 74–85

HUBBLE, D. (1953) 'The life of the shawl', *Lancet*, 26 December, 1351–4

HULL, D. L. (1983) 'Darwin and the nature of science', in D. S. Bendall (ed.) *Evolution from Molecules to Men*, Cambridge: Cambridge University Press

HUXLEY, L. (ed.) (1900) *Life and Letters of Thomas Henry Huxley*, 3 vols, London: Macmillan

HUXLEY, L. (1918) *Life and Letters of Sir Joseph Dalton Hooker*, 2 vols, London: John Murray

HUXLEY, L. (1921) *Charles Darwin*, London: Watts & Co

HUXLEY, T. H. (1888) 'Obituary of Charles Darwin', *Proceedings of the Royal Society*, 44, i–xxv; reprinted in T. H. Huxley, *Darwinian Essays*, New York: D. Appleton & Co, 1897

HYDE, H. M. (1959) *The Strange Death of Lord Castlereagh*, London: Heinemann

JALLAND, P. (1986) *Women, Marriage and Politics 1860-1914*, Oxford: Oxford University Press

JESPERSON, P. H. (1948–9) 'Charles Darwin and Dr Grant', *Lychnos*, pp. 159–67

KEEGAN, R. T., AND GRUBER, H. E. (1985) 'Charles Darwin's unpublished "Diary of an infant": an early phase in his psychological work', in *Contributions to a History of Developmental Psychology: International Wm T. Preyer Symposium*, ed. G. Eckhardt et al., Berlin: Mouton, pp. 127-45

KEITH, A. (1955) *Darwin Revalued*, London: Watts

KEMPF, E. J. (1918) 'Charles Darwin – the affective sources of his inspiration and anxiety neurosis', *Psychoanalytic Review*, 5, 151–92

KEYNES, R. D. (ed.) (1979) *The Beagle Record*, Cambridge: Cambridge University Press

KEYNES, R. D. (ed.) (1988) *Charles Darwin's Beagle Diary*, Cambridge: Cambridge University Press

KING-HELE, D. (1977) *Doctor of Revolution: The Life and Genius of Erasmus Darwin*, London: Faber & Faber

KOHN, D. (ed.) (1985) *The Darwinian Heritage*, Princeton, N.J: Princeton University Press.

KOHN, D., SMITH, S., AND STAUFFER, R. C. (1982) 'New light on the foundation of the *Origin of Species*: a reconstruction of the archival record', *Journal of the History of Biology*, 15, 419–42

KRAUSE, E. (1879; facsimile reprint, 1971) *Erasmus Darwin*, with a 'preliminary notice' by Charles Darwin, London: John Murray

LITCHFIELD, H. E. (1904) *Emma Darwin: A Century of Family Letters*, 2 vols, Cambridge: University Press (privately printed)

LITCHFIELD, H.E. (1915) *Emma Darwin: A Century of Family Letters 1792–1896*, 2 vols, London: John Murray

LYELL, K. M. (ed.) (1881) *Life, Letters and Journals of Sir Charles Lyell, Bart*, 2 vols, London: John Murray

LYELL, MRS HENRY (ed.) (1906) *The Life of Sir Charles J. F. Bunbury, Bart*, 2 vols, London: John Murray

MANIER, E. (1978) *The Young Darwin and His Cultural Circle*, Dordrecht: Reidel

MARCHANT, J. (1916) *Alfred Russel Wallace: Letters and Reminiscences*, 2 vols, London: Cassell

MAYR, E. (1964) Introduction to facsimile of the first edition of *On the Origin of Species*, Cambridge, Mass.: Harvard University Press

MAYR, E. (1983) 'Darwin, intellectual revolutionary', in D. S. Bendall (ed) *Evolution from Molecules to Men*, Cambridge: Cambridge University Press

MELLERSH, H. E. L. (1968) *Fitzroy of the Beagle*, London: Hart-Davis

METEYARD, E. (1871) *A group of Englishmen (1795–1815): Being Records of the Younger Wedgwoods and their Friends*, London: Longmans Green

MOORE, J. R. (1985) 'Darwin of Down: the evolutionist as squarson-naturalist', in D. Kohn (ed.), *The Darwinian Heritage*, Princeton, NJ: Princeton University Press

MOOREHEAD, A. (1971) *Darwin and the Beagle*, Harmondsworth: Penguin

OSPOVAT, D. (1981) *The Development of Darwin's Theory: Natural History, Natural Theology, Natural Selection 1838-1859*, Cambridge: Cambridge University Press

PANTIN, C. F. A. (1959) 'Alfred Russel Wallace, FRS, his essays of 1858 and 1855', *Notes and Records of the Royal Society of London*, 14, 67–84

PICKERING, G. (1974) *Creative Malady*, London: George Allen & Unwin

RAVERAT, G. (1952) *Period Piece: A Cambridge Childhood*, London: Faber

ROMANES, ETHEL (1896) *The Life and Letters of George John Romanes*, London: Longmans Green

RUSE, M. (1975) 'Darwin's debt to philosophy', *Studies in the History and Philosophy of Science*, 6, 154–81

STAUFFER, R. C. (ed.) (1975) *Charles Darwin's Natural Selection: Being the Second Part of his Big Species Book written from 1856 to 1858*, Cambridge: Cambridge University Press

STECHER, R. M. (1961) 'The Darwin-Innes Letters', *Annals of Science*, 17, 201–58

STIRLING, A. M. W. (1926) *The Richmond Papers*, London: William Heinemann

SULLOWAY, F. J. (1979) *Freud, Biologist of the Mind*, New York: Basic Books

SULLOWAY, F. J. (1982a) 'Darwin and his finches: the evolution of a legend', *Journal of the History of Biology*, 15, 1–53

SULLOWAY, F. J. (1982b) 'Darwin's conversion: the *Beagle* voyage and its aftermath', *Journal of the History of Biology*, 15, 325–96

SULLOWAY, F. J. (1984) 'Darwin and the Galapagos', *Biological Journal of the Linnean Society*, 21, 29–59

VORZIMMER, P. J. (1977) 'The Darwin reading notebooks (1838–1860)', *Journal of the History of Biology*, 10, 107–53

WEDGWOOD, B. AND H. (1980) *The Wedgwood Circle 1730-1897: Four Generations and their Friends*, London: Studio Vista/Cassell

WILLIAMS-ELLIS, A. (1966) *Darwin's Moon: A Biography of Alfred Russel Wallace*, London and Glasgow: Blackie

WILSON, L. G. (1970) *Sir Charles Lyell's Scientific Journals on the Species Question*, New Haven; Conn.: Yale University Press

WOODRUFF, A. W. (1965) 'Darwin's health in relation to his voyage to South America', *British Medical Journal*, 1, 747–8

Studies of Psychological and Psychosomatic Illness

AHRENS, S., AND DEFFNER, G. (1986) 'Empirical study of alexithymia: methodology and results', *American Journal of Psychotherapy*, 40, 430–47

BASS, C., AND GARDNER, W. (1985) 'Emotional influences on breathing and breathlessness', *Journal of Psychosomatic Research*, 29, 599–609

BOWLBY, J. (1969, 1973, 1980) *Attachment and Loss*, 3 vols, London: Hogarth Press; New York: Basic Books

BOWLBY, J. (1988) *A Secure Base*, London: Routledge; New York: Basic Books

BRASHEAR, R. (1983) 'Hyperventilation syndrome', *Lung*, 161, 257–73

BREIER, A., CARNEY, D. S., AND HENINGER, G. R. (1985) 'The diagnostic validity of anxiety disorders and their relationship to depressive illness', *American Journal of Psychiatry*, 142, 787–97

BROWN, G. W., HARRIS, T., AND BIFULCO, A. (1985) 'Longterm effects of early loss of parent', in M. Rutter, C. Izard and P. Read (eds), *Depression in Childhood: Developmental Perspectives*, New York: Guilford Press

CONWAY, A. V., FREEMAN, L. J., AND NIXON, P. G. F. (1988) 'Hypnotic examination of trigger factors in the hyperventilation syndrome', *American Journal of Clinical Hypnosis*, 30. 296–304

ENGELS, W. D. (1985) 'Skin disorders', in H. Kaplan, A. Freedman and B. J. Saddock (eds), *Psychiatry*, 4th edn, Baltimore, Md: Williams & Wilkins, pp. 1178–84

FREEMAN, L. J., CONWAY, A., AND NIXON, P. G. F. (1986) 'Physiological responses to psychological challenge under hypnosis in patients considered to have the hyperventilation syndrome', *Journal of the Royal Society of Medicine*, 79, 76–83

FREUD, S. (1895) 'On the grounds for detaching a particular syndrome from neurasthenia under the description "anxiety neurosis"', *Standard Edition of Freud's Works*, vol. 3, pp. 92–115, London: Hogarth Press, 1962

GELDER, M. G. (1986) 'Panic attacks: new approaches to an old problem', *British Journal of Psychiatry*, 149, 346–52

HARRIS, T. O., BIFULCO, A. B. AND BROWN, G. W. (in preparation) *Childhood Loss of Parent and Later Depression*, London: Routledge

HIBBERT, G. A. (1985) 'Ideational components of anxiety, their origin and content', *British Journal of Psychiatry*, 144, 618–24

LAZARUS, H. R., AND KOSTAN, J. J. (1969) 'Psychogenic Hyperventilation and death anxiety', *Psychosomatics*, 10, 14–22

LUM, L. C. (1987) 'Hyperventilation syndromes in medicine and psychiatry', *Journal of the Royal Society of Medicine*, 80, 229–31

MAGARIAN, G. (1982) 'Hyperventilation syndromes: infrequently recognized common expressions of anxiety and stress', *Medicine*, 61, 219–36

MALATESTA, C. A., JONAS, R., AND IZARD, C. E. (1987) 'The relation between low facial expressivity during emotional arousal and somatic symptoms', *British Journal of Medical Psychology*, 60, 169–80

MATHEWS, A., AND MACLEOD, C. (1986) 'Discrimination of threat cues without awareness in anxiety states', *Journal of Abnormal Psychology*, 95. 131–8

NEMIAH, J. C., AND SIFNEOS, P. E. (1970) 'Affect and fantasy in patients with psychosomatic disorders', in O. W. Hill (ed.), *Modern Trends in Psychosomatic Medicine*, London: Butterworth

NIXON, P. G. F., AND FREEMAN, L. J. (1988) 'The "think-test": a further technique to elicit hyperventilation', *Journal of the Royal Society of Medicine*, 81. 277–9

OWEN, M. J., AND MURRAY, R. M. (1988) 'Blue genes; three genes linked to bipolar affective disorder', *British Medical Journal*, 297, 871–2

PENNEBAKER, J. W., AND SUSMAN, J. R. (1988) 'Disclosure of traumas and psychomatic processes', *Social Science and Medicine*, 26, 327–32

Who's Who

AGASSIZ, Jean Louis Rodolphe (1807–73) Swiss geologist and zoologist. Professor of Natural History, Neuchâtel, 1832–46. Emigrated to the United States in 1846. Professor of zoology and geology, Harvard University, 1847–73. Criticised Darwin's theories as 'unscientific' and 'mischievous'.

ALLEN, Catherine (1765–1830). Emma's aunt, second daughter of John Bartlett Allen. Married Sir James Mackintosh as his second wife in 1798.

ALLEN, Frances (Fanny) (1781–1875). Emma's aunt, youngest daughter of John Bartlett Allen, unmarried.

ALLEN, Jessie (1777–1853). Emma's aunt, sixth daughter of John Bartlett Allen, married Jean Charles Leonard Simonde de Sismondi in 1819.

BAER, Karl Ernst von (1792–1876). Anatomist and embryologist. Professor at Königsburg University, 1817–1834. Active member of the Academy of Sciences in St Petersburg, 1834–67. Accepted Darwin's views on evolution with some reservations.

BASKET, Fuegia (1821–93?) A Fuegian girl brought to England in 1830 by Robert FitzRoy. In 1833 was returned to Tierra del Fuego in the *Beagle*. Married York Minster.

BATES, Henry Walter (1825–92). Naturalist and traveller. Author of *The Naturalist on the river Amazons*, 1863, highly regarded by Darwin. Assistant Secretary, Royal Geographical Society, 1864–92. FRS, 1881.

BEAUFORT, Francis (1774–1857). Naval officer; retired as Rear-Admiral in 1846. Hydrographer to the Navy, 1832–55, and organised *Beagle* voyage. Recommended Darwin to FitzRoy. FRS, 1814.

BELL, Thomas (1792–1880). Dental surgeon at Guy's Hospital, 1817–61. Professor of Zoology at King's College, London, 1836; President, Linnean Society, 1853–61; described the reptiles from the *Beagle* voyage. FRS, 1828.

BENCE JONES, Henry (1814–73). London physician, attended Darwin in September 1865–.

BENTLEY, Thomas (1730–80). Liverpool businessman who became friend and partner of Josiah Wedgwood I from 1768.

BOAT MEMORY (d. 1830). A Fuegian man brought to England in 1830 by Robert FitzRoy, Died of smallpox in Plymouth.

BOULTON, Matthew (1728–1809). Metal manufacturer in Birmingham; joined by James Watt and founded firm of Boulton & Watt in 1773. Member of Lunar Society.

BRIGGS, Mark. Darwin family coachman at The Mount, Shrewsbury.

BRINDLEY, James (1716–72). Civil-engineer; surveyed and built the Grand Trunk canal linking the Mersey and Trent rivers. Member of Lunar Society.

BRODIE, Jessie (d. 1873). The Darwin children's nurse at 12 Upper Gower Street and Down House, 1842–51. Left after Annie Darwin's death.

BROWN, Robert (1773–1858). Botanist. Librarian to Joseph Banks, 1810–20. Keeper of the botanical collections, British Museum, 1827–58. Described plants brought back from the first voyage of the *Beagle*. FRS, 1810.

BUNBURY, Charles James Fox, 8th Baronet (1809–86). Amateur botanist. Collected plants in South America, 1833–4; South Africa 1838–9. Married Frances Horner, Charles Lyell's sister-in-law, in 1844. FRS, 1851.

BUTLER, Reverend Samuel, I (1774–1839). Headmaster of Shrewsbury School, 1798–1836, while Darwin was there. Bishop of Lichfield and Coventry, 1836–9.

BUTLER, Samuel, II (1835–1902). Son of Revd Thomas Butler (1806–86), who was Darwin's contemporary at Cambridge, and grandson of Revd Samuel Butler I. Author and controversialist: *Evolution Old and New*, 1879; *Unconscious Memory*, 1880.

BUTTON, Jemmy. One of the Fuegians Robert FitzRoy brought to England in 1830 and returned to Tierra del Fuego in 1833.

BYERLEY, Thomas (1747–1810). Nephew, assistant and, from 1790, partner of Josiah Wedgwood I.

BYNOE, Benjamin (1804–65). Naval surgeon, 1825–63. Assistant surgeon in the *Beagle*, 1832–7; treated Darwin during his illness at Valparaiso.

CANDOLLE, Alphonse de (1806–93). Professor of Natural History and director of the botanic gardens, Geneva, 1835–50. Author of *Géographie botanique raisonnée*, 1855. Foreign member, Royal Society, 1869.

CARLYE, Thomas (1795–1881). Essayist and historian; close friend of Darwin's brother Ras and of Emma's brother, Hensleigh Wedgwood.

CARUS, Julius Victor (1823–1903). German zoologist. Professor of Comparative Anatomy, Leipzig, 1853. Translated Darwin's works into German.

CHAFFERS, Edward Main. Master of the *Beagle* during Darwin's voyage.

CHAMBERS, Robert (1802–71). Publisher, writer and amateur geologist. Anonymous author of *Vestiges of the Natural History of Creation*, 1844.

CHAPMAN, John (1822–94). Physician; MD, St Andrews, 1857. Advocated the application of an ice-bag to the spine as a remedy and treated Darwin in 1865.

CLARK, Andrew (1826–93). Fashionable London physician. Attended Darwin in 1873 and again in 1881 and 1882. Baronet, 1883; FRS, 1885.

CLIFT, William (1775–1849). Naturalist, curator of the Hunterian Museum at the Royal College of Surgeons, 1793–1844; identified South American fossils found by Darwin. FRS, 1823.

COLDSTREAM, John (1806–63). MD, Edinburgh, 1827. Practitioner in Leith, 1829–47. Friend of Darwin at Edinburgh University.

COOK, James (1728–79). Naval officer and distinguished navigator. Circumnavigated the world, 1768–71 and 1772–5. FRS, 1776.

CORFIELD, Richard Henry (1804–97). Darwin's contemporary at Shrewsbury School, 1818–19. Darwin stayed at his house in Valparaiso in 1834 and 1835.

COVINGTON, Syms (1816?–61). Darwin's servant in the *Beagle* from 1833; remained with him as assistant, secretary and servant until 1839, when he emigrated to Australia.

CUVIER, Georges (1769–1832). French systematist, comparative anatomist, palaeontologist and administrator. Foreign member, Royal Society, 1806.

DANA, James Dwight (1813–95). American geologist and zoologist.

Naturalist with the United States Exploring Expedition to the Pacific, 1838–42. Professor of Geology, Yale University, 1856–90. Foreign Member, Royal Society, 1884.

DARWIN, Anne Elizabeth (Annie) (1841–51). Darwin's eldest daughter, whose death was a tragic blow to her parents.

DARWIN, Bernard Richard Meirion (1876–1961). Son of Francis Darwin and grandson of Charles and Emma; essayist; golf correspondent of *The Times*, 1908–53.

DARWIN, Caroline Sarah (1800–88). The second of Charles's elder sisters. Married Josiah Wedgewood III (Joe) in 1837.

DARWIN, Charles I (1758–78). Eldest son of Erasmus I and uncle of Charles of the *Origin*. Medical student at Edinburgh. Died of acute infection.

DARWIN, Elizabeth (Bessy) (1847–1926). Darwin's fourth and youngest daughter, unmarried and lived at home.

DARWIN, (Emily) Catherine (1810–66). Darwin's younger sister. Married Reverend Charles Langton as his second wife in 1863.

DARWIN, Emma (1808–96). Youngest daughter of Bessy and Josiah Wedgewood II of Maer Hall. Married Charles Darwin, her first cousin, in 1839.

DARWIN, Erasmus I (1731–1802). Charles Darwin's grandfather. Physician, naturalist and poet; proposed an evolutionary theory similar to that later expounded by Lamarck. Member of Lunar Society. FRS, 1761.

DARWIN, Erasmus II (1759–99). Second son of Erasmus I and uncle of Charles of the *Origin*; lawyer, committed suicide.

DARWIN, Erasmus Alvey (Ras) (1804–81). Charles Darwin's elder brother. Attended Shrewsbury School, 1815–22, Christ's College, Cambridge, 1822–5, and Edinburgh University, 1825–26. Qualified MB Cambridge but never practised. Lived a leisured life in London from 1829. A close friend of Hensleigh Wedgwood, Thomas Carlyle and Harriet Martineau. Unmarried.

DARWIN, Francis (1848–1925). Charles Darwin's third son. Trinity College, Cambridge. Collaborated with his father on several botanical projects, 1875–82. Lecturer in botany, Cambridge University, 1884; Reader, 1888–1904. Compiled the three volumes of his father's *Life and Letters* (1887) and two further volumes of *More Letters* 1903. FRS, 1882.

DARWIN, George Howard (1845–1912). Charles Darwin's second son. Trinity College, Cambridge, mathematician; Plumian Professor of

Astronomy and Experimental Philosophy, Cambridge University, 1883–1912. FRS, 1879.

DARWIN, Henrietta Emma (1843–1927). Charles Darwin's third daughter. Married Richard Buckley Litchfield, 1871. Edited *Emma Darwin: A Century of Family Letters*, 1904 and 1915.

DARWIN, Horace (1851–1928). Charles Darwin's fifth and youngest son. Trinity College, Cambridge. Designed scientific instruments; founded the Cambridge Scientific Instrument Company in 1885. Mayor of Cambridge, 1896–7. FRS, 1903.

DARWIN, Leonard (1850–1943). Charles Darwin's fourth son. Attended the Royal Military Academy, Woolwich; commissioned in Royal Engineers, 1871; retired as major, 1890. Served on scientific expeditions, including those for the observation of the transit of Venus, 1874 and 1882. Instructor, School of Military Engineering, Chatham, 1877–82; Intelligence Department, War Office, 1885–90; Liberal Unionist MP, Lichfield division of Staffordshire, 1892–5. President, Royal Geographical Society, 1908–11.

DARWIN, Marianne (1798–1858). Charles's eldest sister. Married Dr Henry Parker in 1824.

DARWIN, Mary (1740–70). Daughter of George Howard and the first wife of Erasmus Darwin I; grandmother of Charles Darwin of the *Origin*.

DARWIN, Robert Waring (1766–1848). Charles Darwin's father. Third son of Erasmus Darwin I by his first wife, Mary Howard. Physician: MD, Leiden, 1785; FRS, 1788. Married Susannah, eldest daughter of Josiah Wedgwood I, in 1796.

DARWIN, Susan Elizabeth (1803–66). The third of Charles's elder sisters; unmarried; cared for her father, and lived at The Mount, Shrewsbury, until her death.

DARWIN, Susannah (Sukey) (1765–1817). Charles Darwin's mother. Eldest daughter of Josiah Wedgwood I. Married Robert Waring Darwin in 1796. Died after chronic illness when Charles was eight years old.

DARWIN, William Erasmus (1839–1914). Charles Darwin's eldest child. Christ's College, Cambridge. Banker in Southampton.

EARLE, Augustus (1793–1838). Artist in the *Beagle*, 1831–2; left at Montevideo because of illness.

EDGEWORTH, Maria (1767–1849). Novelist of Irish life, eldest daughter of Richard Edgeworth and friend of Josiah II and Bessy Wedgwood.

EDGEWORTH, Richard Lowell (1744–1817). Civil engineer and inventor. Member of the Lunar Society.

EDWARD. Servant of the Darwin family at The Mount, Shrewsbury.

EHRENBERG, Christian Gottfried (1795–1876). German naturalist, microscopist and traveller. Studied the infusoria, including specimens from the *Beagle* voyage. Foreign member, Royal Society, 1837.

EYTON,, Thomas Campbell (1809–90). Shropshire naturalist and collector of bird skins and skeletons. Darwin's friend and Cambridge contemporary. Examined birds from the *Beagle* voyage.

FALCONER, Hugh (1808–65). Palaeontologist and botanist. Superintendent of the botanic gardens at Saharanpur, 1832, and Calcutta, 1848; Professor of Botany, Calcutta Medical College, 1848–55. In later years close friend of Darwin's. FRS, 1845.

FARRER, Thomas Henry (1833–84). Barrister and civil servant, 1873 married Euphemia (Effy), daughter of Hensleigh Wedgewood, as his second wife; lived at Abinger Hall, Dorking, Surrey, a favourite house for Darwin to visit in later years.

FITZROY, Robert (1805–65). Naval officer, hydrographer and meteorologist. Captain of the *Beagle* during Darwin's voyage. Author of *Narrative of the Surveying Voyages of the Adventure and Beagle*, 1839. MP for Durham, 1841–3. Governor of New Zealand, 1843–5. Chief of the meteorological department of the Board of Trade, 1854–65. Vice-admiral, 1863. FRS, 1851.

FORBES, Edward (1815–54). Zoologist, botanist and palaeontologist. Professor of Botany, King's College, London, 1842. Palaeontologist with the Geological Survey, 1844–54. Professor of Natural History, Edinburgh University, 1854. FRS, 1845.

FOX, William Darwin (1805–80). Clergyman and naturalist; Darwin's second cousin and intimate friend; near contemporary at Christ's College, Cambridge; introduced him to entomology; lifelong correspondent. Rector of Delamere, Cheshire, 1838–73. Retired to Sandown, Isle of Wight.

FRANKLIN, Benjamin (1706–90). American scientist, diplomat and statesman. Inventor of lightning conductor and member of Lunar Society.

GALTON, Francis (1822–1911). Charles Darwin's cousin. statistician and eugenist. Author of *Hereditary Genius* 1869.

GAY, Claude (1800–73). French naturalist and traveller who surveyed the flora and fauna of Chile before Darwin's visit.

GOULD, John (1804–81). Self-taught ornithologist and artist. Taxidermist to the Zoological Society of London, 1826–81. Described the birds collected on the *Beagle* expedition. FRS, 1843.

GRANT, Robert Edmond (1793–1874). Scottish zoologist. Befriended Darwin in Edinburgh, 1825–7. Professor of Comparative Anatomy and Zoology, University College, London, 1827–74. FRS, 1836.

GRAY, Asa (1810–88). American botanist. Fisher Professor of Natural History, Harvard University, 1842–72. Devoted time to the Harvard Botanic Garden and herbarium. First met Darwin on visit to Kew in 1850s and became friend and supporter. Foreign member, Royal Society, 1873.

GRAY, John Edward (1800–73). Zoologist; keeper of zoology at the British Museum, 1840–74; made over his collection of barnacles for Darwin to study. FRS, 1832.

GULLY, James Manby (1808–83). Physician. Studied medicine in Paris and Edinburgh. Practised in London, 1830–42. In 1842 he set up a hydropathic establishment in Malvern where he treated many famous people. Darwin was his patient for some years from March 1849.

HAECKEL, Ernst Heinrich (1834–1919). German zoologist and physician. Professor of Zoology at University of Jena from 1865. Strongly supported Darwin's theories and promulgated them in Germany.

HARRIS, James. British trader at the Rio Negro, Patagonia, from whom Robert FitzRoy hired two small schooners during 1832–3 for surveying parts of the coast too shallow for the *Beagle*.

HENSLOW, Reverend John Stevens (1796–1861). Clergyman, botanist and mineralogist. Professor of Mineralogy, Cambridge University, 1822–7; Professor of Botany, 1827–61. Extended and remodelled the Cambridge Botanic Garden. Rector of Hitcham, Suffolk, 1837–61. Darwin's teacher and friend at Cambridge and later.

HERBERT, John Maurice (1808–82). St John's College, Cambridge. Fellow, 1832–40. Barrister, 1835. County Court Judge, South Wales, 1847–82. Close friend of Darwin's at Cambridge.

HERSCHEL, Sir John Frederick William (1792–1871). Astronomer, mathematician and philosopher of science. Author of *Preliminary Discourse on the Study of Natural Philosophy*, 1831. Carried out astronomical observations at the Cape of Good Hope 1834–8, where Darwin visited him in June 1836. Dubbed Darwin's theory 'the law of higgledy-piggelty'. FRS, 1813. Baronet, 1838

HOLLAND, Henry (1788–1873). Prominent London physician; distant cousin of the Darwins and Wedgwoods. Physician to Queen Victoria,

1852, and created baronet 1853. Attended Darwin family at Down House. FRS, 1816.

HOOKER, Joseph Dalton (1817–1911). Botanist. Assistant surgeon to the Antarctic expedition of James Clark Ross, 1838–43, and published the botanical results of the voyage. Botanist to the Geological Survey, 1845. Collected plants in the Himalayas, 1848–50. Assistant director, Royal Botanic Gardens, Kew, 1855–65, and succeeded his father as director, 1865–85. Specialist in taxonomy and plant geography. Close friend and confidant of Charles Darwin. FRS, 1847; PRS, 1873–8; knighted, 1878; OM, 1907.

HOOKER, Sir William Jackson (1785–1865). Botanist. Regius Professor of Botany, University of Glasgow, 1820–41. First director of the Royal Botanic Gardens at Kew, 1841–65. Father of Joseph Dalton Hooker. FRS, 1812. Knight, 1836.

HOPE, Frederick William (1797–1862). Entomologist and clergyman. Prominent beetle collector whom Darwin met in 1829; gave Oxford University his collection of insects, some of which had been sent him by Darwin from Australia, and founded a professorship of zoology at Oxford, 1849. FRS, 1834.

HORNER, Leonard (1785–1864). Linen draper, amateur geologist and educationalist. Factory Commissioner, 1833–60. President of the Geological Society, 1845–7, 1860–2. Father-in-law of Charles Lyell. FRS, 1813.

HUMBOLDT, (Friedrich Wilhelm Heinrich) Alexander von (1769–1859). Eminent German naturalist, traveller and author. Explored equatorial South America, 1799–1804; travelled in Siberia, 1829. Foreign Member, Royal Society, 1815.

HUTTON, James (1726–97). Scottish natural philosopher and geologist. Propounded a uniformitarian view of geological history in his *Theory of the Earth*, 1795, taken up and developed by Charles Lyell.

HUXLEY, Thomas Henry (1825–95). Zoologist, comparative anatomist, essayist and educator. Assistant surgeon, HMS *Rattlesnake*, surveying east coast of Australia, 1847–9. Lecturer, Royal School of Mines, 1854–84. Fullerian Professor at the Royal Institution, 1863–7. Close friend of Darwin's from 1855 and polemical supporter of his theory. FRS, 1851; PRS, 1883–5.

INNES, Reverend John (1817–94). Clergyman, Trinity College, Oxford. Perpetual curate of Downe, 1846; vicar, 1860–9. Left Downe in 1862 after inheriting property in Scotland. Changed his surname to Brodie Innes *c.* 1860.

JENKIN, Henry Charles Fleeming (1835–85). Engineer. Professor of

Engineering at University College, London, 1865, and at Edinburgh, 1868. Advanced strong technical arguments against Darwin's theory of natural selection. FRS, 1865.

JENYNS, Reverend Leonard (1800–93). Naturalist and clergyman. Vicar of Swaffham Bulbeck, Cambridgeshire, 1828–49. Fellow beetle collector and friend of Darwin's at Cambridge. Described the *Beagle* fish specimens.

KING, Philip Gidley (1817–1904). Eldest son of Captain Philip Parker King, RN. Midshipman in the *Beagle*, 1831–6. Left ship to join father in Australia, 1836.

KING, Philip Parker (1793–1856). Naval officer and hydrographer. Commander of the *Adventure* and *Beagle* on the first surveying expedition to South America, 1826–30. Settled in Australia. FRS, 1824.

KRAUSE, Ernst (1839–1903). German botanist; author of biography of Erasmus Darwin which Darwin translated into English with long preliminary essay, 1879.

LAMARCK, Jean Baptiste Pierre Antoine de Monet de (1744–1829). French naturalist; botanist at the Jardin du Roi, 1788–93; Professor of Zoology, Muséum d'Histoire Naturelle, 1793–1829; author of *Philosophie zoölogique*, 1809. Believed in spontaneous generation and the progressive development of animal types; proposed a theory of transmutation.

LANE, Edward Wickstead (?–1889). Medical practitioner and proprietor of hydropathic establishment at Moor Park, near Farnham, Surrey, later at Sudbrooke Park, near Richmond-on-Thames. Darwin spent many brief periods at Dr Lane's, starting in 1857.

LANGTON, Reverend Charles (1801–86). Clergyman. Trinity College, Oxford. Rector of Onibury, Shropshire, 1832–40; lost his faith and resigned living. Married Charlotte Wedgwood, 2nd daughter of Josiah II, 1832. After her death, married Darwin's younger sister Catherine, 1863.

LANGTON, Charlotte (1797–1862). Daughter of Bessy and Josiah Wedgwood II of Maer Hall; and second of Emma Darwin's elder sisters. Married Reverend Charles Langton, 1832. Resided at Maer, 1840–6, and at Hartfield Grove, Sussex, 1847–61.

LINNAEUS (Carl von Linné) (1707–78). Swedish botanist and zoologist. Enunciated principles for defining species and genera and established a system for the classification and nomenclature of living organisms.

LUBBOCK, John William, 3rd Baronet (1803–65). Astronomer,

mathematician and banker. First Vice-Chancellor of London University, 1837–42. Owner of large estate and neighbour of Darwin's at Downe. FRS, 1829.

LUBBOCK, John, 4th Baronet (1834–1913). Banker, politician and naturalist. Son of Sir John William Lubbock and a neighbour of Darwin's at Downe. Studied entomology and anthropology. An active supporter of Darwin's theory of natural selection. Liberal MP and spokesman for science in Parliament. FRS, 1858. Created first Baron Avebury, 1900.

LYELL, Charles (1797–1875). Barrister and geologist. Professor of Geology, Kings' College, London, 1831–3. President of the Geological Society, 1834–6 and 1849–50. Author of *Principles of Geology*, 3 volumes, 1831–3. Scientific mentor and friend of Darwin's. Inherited estate at Kinnordy, Forfarshire. FRS, 1826. Knight, 1848. Baronet, 1864.

LYELL, Mary Elizabeth (1808–73). Eldest child of Leonard Horner. Married Charles Lyell in 1832. No children.

McCORMICK, Robert (1800–90). Naval surgeon in the *Beagle*, 1831–2, who resented Darwin's role as naturalist. Left ship on grounds of ill-health.

MACGILLIVRAY, William (1796–1852). Scottish naturalist and ornithologist. Conservator of the Royal College of Surgeons' Museum in Edinburgh, 1822–41, where Darwin got to know him. Professor of Natural History, Aberdeen, 1841–52.

MACKINTOSH, Sir James (1765–1832). Philosopher and historian. Professor of Law and General Politics at the East India Company College, Haileybury, 1818–24. By his first wife was father of Frances (Fanny), wife of Emma's brother Hensleigh Wedgwood. Married secondly Emma's aunt, Catherine Allen, 1798.

MAGUIRE, Thomas Herbert (1821–95). Irish lithographer and portraitist. Lithographer to the Queen, 1854. Produced a series of portraits of men of science known as the Ipswich Museum portraits, which included portrait of Darwin made in 1849, and published by George Ransome 1851.

MALTHUS, Reverend Thomas Robert (1766–1834). Clergyman and political economist. First Professor of History and Political Economy at the East India Company College, Haileybury, 1805–34. Quantified the relationship between growth in population and food supplies in his *Essay on Population*, 1798. FRS, 1819.

MANTELL, Gideon Algernon (1790–1852). Physician, geologist and palaeontologist and noted collector of fossils. Secretary, Geological Society, 1841–2. Vice-president, 1848–9. FRS, 1825.

MARTENS, Conrad (1801–79). Landscape painter; joined *Beagle* as artist as replacement for Augustus Earle, 1833–4. Settled in Australia.

MARTINEAU, Harriet (1802–76). Author, reformer and traveller; close friend of Darwin's brother Ras.

MILNE, David (afterwards Milne-Home) (1805–90). Scottish advocate and geologist; criticised Darwin's explanation of the parallel roads of Glen Roy.

MIVART, St George Jackson (1827–1900). Barrister and biologist. Lecturer in biology, St Mary's Roman Catholic College, Kensington. Author of *The Genesis of Species*, 1871, in which he strongly criticised *The Origin of Species* and *The Descent of Man*.

MURCHISON, Roderick Impey (1792–1871). Geologist noted for his work on the Silurian system. Director of Geological Survey, 1855. Influential figure in the Geological Society, British Association for the Advancement of Science, and Royal Geographical Society. FRS, 1826. Knight, 1846. Baronet, 1866.

MURRAY, John (1808–92). Publisher and author of guidebooks. Darwin's publisher from 1845.

MUSTERS, Charles (d. 1832). Volunteer 1st class in the *Beagle*: died of fever at Rio de Janeiro.

NANCY. Darwin's childhood nurse who continued for many years with the Darwin family at The Mount, Shrewsbury.

ORBIGNY, Alcide Charles Victor Dessalines d' (1802–57). French palaeontologist who explored in South America, 1826–34. Professor of Palaeontology, Muséum d'Histoire Naturelle, Paris, 1853.

OWEN, Arthur Mostyn (1813–96). Second son of William Mostyn Owen, Sr, of Woodhouse. Attended Shrewsbury School, 1827–8, and the East India Company College, Haileybury, 1829–31. Indian Civil Service, 1832–8. Shooting companion of Darwin's before the *Beagle* voyage.

OWEN, Fanny (Frances) Mostyn (? 1810–). Second daughter of William Mostyn Owen, Sr, of Woodhouse. Married Robert Myddleton Biddulph of Chirk Castle, Denbighshire, in 1832. A close friend of Darwin's before the *Beagle* voyage.

OWEN, Sarah Harriet Mostyn (1804–). Eldest daughter of William Mostyn Owen, Sr. of Woodhouse. Married first Edward Hosier Williams of Eaton Mascott, near Shrewsbury in 1831 and second

Thomas Chandler Haliburton in 1856. A close friend of Darwin's before the *Beagle* voyage.

OWEN, William Mostyn, Sr., Squire of Woodhouse, Shropshire. Taught Darwin to shoot and enjoyed his company.

OWEN, William Mostyn (1806–68). Eldest son of William Mostyn Owen, Sr, of Woodhouse. Major, Royal Dragoons. Shooting companion of Darwin's before the *Beagle* voyage.

OWEN, Richard (1804–92). Comparative anatomist. Assistant conservator of Hunterian Museum, Royal College of Surgeons, 1827, and Hunterian Professor, 1836–56; Superintendent of the Natural History departments, British Museum, 1856–84. Described the *Beagle* fossil mammal specimens; later bitter critic of Darwin's theories. FRS, 1834. Knight, 1884.

PALEY, Reverend William (1743–1805). Anglican clergyman and theologian. Author of *Natural Theology*, 1802.

PARKER, Henry (1788–1856). MD, Edinburgh, 1814. Physician to the Shropshire Infirmary. Married Darwin's eldest sister Marianne in 1824.

PARSLOW, Joseph (1809/10–98). Darwin's manservant at Gower Street, c. 1840, and butler at Down House until 1875.

PEACOCK, George (1791–1858). Tutor in mathematics at Trinity College, Cambridge, 1823–39. Lowndean Professor of Geometry and Astronomy at Cambridge University, 1837. Asked by Captain Beaufort to recommend a naturalist to join the *Beagle* voyage. FRS, 1818.

PRIESTLEY, Joseph (1733–1804). Unitarian minister and distinguished chemist. Member of Lunar Society. Emigrated and died in USA.

ROMANES, George John (1848–94). Biologist, worked at University College, London, and later Oxford. Author of *Animal Intelligence*, 1882, *Mental Evolution in Animals*, 1883. Close friend of Darwin's from 1874 onwards. FRS, 1879.

ROSAS, Juan Manuel de (1793–1877). Argentine cattle rancher. Governor of Buenos Aires, 1829–32, and ruled as dictator of Argentina, 1835–52.

ROSS, James Clark (1800–62). Naval officer and polar explorer. Discovered the north magnetic pole in 1831. Commanded expedition to the Antarctic in which Joseph Hooker served, 1839–43, and search expedition for John Franklin, 1848–9. Rear-Admiral, 1856. FRS, 1828.

SABINE, Edward (1788–1883). Army officer, retired as general; astronomer and physicist; carried out studies of geomagnetism. Secretary of the British Association for the Advancement of Science, 1838–59. FRS, 1818. PRS, 1861–71. Knighted, 1869.

SARMIENTO, Pedro (1532–1608?). Spanish navigator who surveyed the Straits of Magellan and set up the unsuccesful colony later known as Port Famine. Highest mountain in area named after him.

SEDGWICK, Reverend Adam (1785–1873). Geologist and clergyman. Woodwardian Professor of Geology at Cambridge University, 1818–73. Taught Darwin elements of field geology and remained a friend despite strong criticism of the *Origin*. FRS, 1821.

SISMONDI, Jean Charles Leonard Simonde de (1773–1842). Swiss historian. Married Emma's aunt Jessie Allen in 1819.

SMALL, William (1734–75). Scots physician and mathematician. Settled in Birmingham and acted as convenor of the Lunar Society.

STOKES, John Lort (1812–85). Naval Officer. Served in the *Beagle* as midshipman, 1826–31, and as mate and assistant surveyor, 1831–7. Continued in naval service; admiral, 1877.

STRICKLAND, Hugh Edwin (1811–53). Geologist and zoologist. An advocate of reform in zoological nomenclature. Consulted by Darwin during his study of barnacles. FRS, 1852.

SULIVAN, (Bartholomew) James (1810–90). Naval officer and hydrographer. Second lieutenant in the *Beagle*, 1831–6; surveyed the Falkland Islands and coast of South America, 1838–46; served in Baltic, 1854–5. Naval officer in Maritime department of Board of Trade, 1856–65; Admiral, 1877.

THOMSON, William (1824–1907). Astronomical physicist. Professor of Natural Philosophy, Glasgow, 1849–99. Advanced strong technical arguments against Darwin's theories. FRS, 1851; PRS, 1890. Knighted, 1866. 1st Baron Kelvin, 1882.

THORLEY, Miss. Governess at Down House, 1850–6. Present at Anne Darwin's death in Malvern, 1851.

USBORNE, Alexander Burns. Master's assistant in the *Beagle*, surveyed the coast of Peru after the *Beagle* had left for the Galapagos Islands, 1835–6.

WALLACE, Alfred Russel (1823–1913). Naturalist, traveller and collector. Advanced theory of variation and natural selection in 1858 independently of Darwin, but always described it as Darwin's theory. Main publications: *Geographical Distribution of Animals*, 1876; *Darwinism*, 1889. FRS (1892), 1905; OM, 1908.

WATERHOUSE, George Robert (1810–88). Naturalist. A founder of the Entomological Society, 1833. Curator, Zoological Society, 1836–43. On the staff of the natural history department of the British Museum, 1843–80. Described the mammalia and entomological specimens from the *Beagle* voyage.

WATERTON, Charles (1782–1865). Naturalist, traveller in Guiana and a pioneer conservationist. In 1845 visited by Darwin, who admired his *Essays on Natural History*, 1838.

WATT, James (1736–1819). Scots engineer. Developed a much improved steam-engine and joined Matthew Boulton in Birmingham to found firm of Boulton & Watt in 1773. Member of Lunar Society.

WEDGWOOD, Charlotte (1797–1862). Second surviving daughter of Bessy and Josiah Wedgwood II and elder sister of Emma's. Married Reverend Charles Langton in 1832.

WEDGWOOD, Elizabeth (Bessy) (1764–1846). Eldest daughter of John Bartlett Allen of Cresselly, Pembrokeshire. Married Josiah Wedgwood II in 1792; mother of Emma.

WEDGWOOD, Emma (1808–96). Youngest daughter of Bessy and Josiah Wedgwood II of Maer Hall. Married Charles Darwin, her cousin, in January 1839.

WEDGWOOD, Frances (Fanny) (1806–32). Fourth daughter of Bessy and Josiah Wedgwood II and next before Emma: as an inseparable pair they were known as the Dovelies. Died early unmarried.

WEDGWOOD, Frances Mackintosh (Fanny) (1800–89). Daughter of Sir James Mackintosh by his first wife. Married Hensleigh Wedgwood in 1832 and known as Fanny Hensleigh.

WEDGWOOD, Francis (Frank) (1800–88). Master-potter and managing partner in the works at Etruria until 1876. Third son of Bessy and Josiah Wedgwood II and one of Emma's elder brothers. Married Frances Mosley in 1832.

WEDGWOOD, Hensleigh (1803–91). Barrister and philologist. BA, Christ's College, Cambridge, 1824; Fellow, 1829–30. Metropolitan police magistrate, Lambeth, 1832–7. Registrar of metropolitan carriages, 1838–49. Fourth son of Bessy and Josiah Wedgwood II and next brother before Emma. Married Frances Mackintosh in 1832.

WEDGWOOD, John (1766–1844). Banker and horticulturist. A founder of the Horticultural Society of London, 1804. Eldest son of Sarah and Josiah Wedgwood I. Married (Louisa) Jane Allen in 1794, second daughter of John Bartlett Allen.

WEDGWOOD, Josiah I (1730–95). Master-potter who founded the

Wedgwood pottery works at Barlaston and Etruria, Staffordshire. Close friend of Dr Erasmus Darwin and member of Lunar Society. Married cousin Sarah (Sally) Wedgwood and was father of Susannah (Sukey), Charles Darwin's mother. FRS, 1783.

WEDGWOOD, Josiah II (Jos) (1769–1843). Of Maer Hall, Staffordshire. Master-potter of Etruria; partner in firm. MP for Stoke-on-Trent, 1832–4. Married Elizabeth (Bessy) Allen in 1792, and father of Emma.

WEDGWOOD, Josiah III (Joe) (1795–1880). Of Leith Hill Place, Surrey; eldest son of Bessy and Josiah Wedgwood II, and brother of Emma. Married Caroline Darwin in 1837, second of Charles's elder sisters.

WEDGWOOD, Sarah (Sally) (1734–1815). Married Josiah Wedgwood I in 1764 and gave birth to Susannah (Sukey), Charles Darwin's mother.

WEDGWOOD, Sarah (Elizabeth) (1778–1856). Youngest daughter of Sarah (Sally) and Josiah Wedgwood I, and Charles and Emma's aunt, unmarried.

WEDGWOOD, (Sarah) Elizabeth (1793–1880). Eldest daughter of Bessy and Josiah Wedgwood II, who cared for Emma when a child; unmarried. Resided at Maer till 1847, at The Ridge, Hartfield, Sussex, 1847–62, and at Downe from 1868.

WEDGWOOD, Thomas (1771–1805). Fourth son of Josiah Wedgwood I. Published researches on heat and light, 1791–2, and developed concept of photography. Friend and patron of Samuel Taylor Coleridge. Died early unmarried.

WHEWELL, William (1794–1866). Mathematician and philosopher of science. Tutor at Trinity College, Cambridge, 1823–38; Master, 1841–66. Professor of Mineralogy at Cambridge University, 1828–32; Professor of Moral Philosophy, 1838–55. President of Geological Society, 1837–40, and persuaded Darwin to become secretary, 1838–40. Author of *History of the Inductive Sciences*, 3 volumes, 1837. FRS, 1820.

WHITE, Gilbert (1720–93). Naturalist and clergyman. Author of *The Natural History and Antiquities of Selborne*, 1789, much admired by Darwin.

WICKHAM, John Clements (1798–1864). Naval officer. First lieutenant in the *Beagle*, 1831–6. Commander of the *Beagle*, 1837–41, surveying the Australian coast. Emigrated to Australia, 1842; Government Resident in Queensland, 1853–60.

WHITLEY, Reverend Charles Thomas (1808–95). Clergyman. Attended Shrewsbury School, 1821–6, and St John's College, Cambridge;

friend of Darwin's. Reader in Natural Philosophy and Mathematics at Durham University, 1833–55. Vicar of Bedlington, Northumberland, 1854–95.

WILBERFORCE, Reverend Samuel (1805–73). Bishop of Oxford, 1845–60. Leading critic of Darwin's theories in the Oxford debate of 1860. FRS, 1845.

WITHERING, William (1741–99). Physician and botanist. Chief physician to the Birmingham General Hospital. Active member of the Lunar Society. FRS, 1785.

YARRELL, William (1784–1856). Zoologist and bookseller in London. Author of standard works on British birds and fishes. Advised Darwin on equipment for *Beagle* voyage.

YORK MINSTER. A Fuegian man brought to England in 1830 by Robert FitzRoy; returned to Tierra del Fuego in the *Beagle* and married Fuegia Basket.

Index

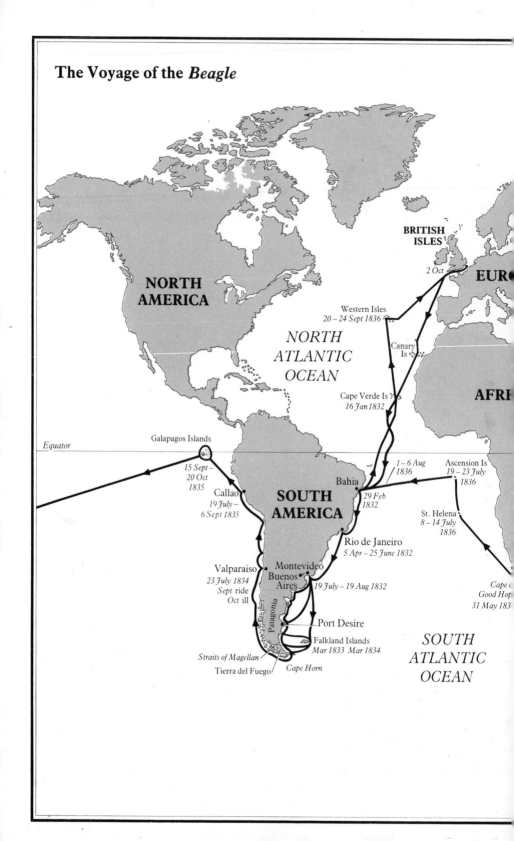

The Voyage of the *Beagle*

NORTH AMERICA

SOUTH AMERICA

NORTH ATLANTIC OCEAN

SOUTH ATLANTIC OCEAN

BRITISH ISLES

EUR

AFRI

2 Oct

Western Isles
20 – 24 Sept 1836

Canary Is

Cape Verde Is
16 Jan 1832

Equator

Galapagos Islands
15 Sept –
20 Oct
1835

Callao
19 July –
6 Sept 1835

Bahia
29 Feb
1832

1 – 6 Aug
1836

Ascension Is
19 – 23 July
1836

St. Helena
8 – 14 July
1836

Rio de Janeiro
5 Apr – 25 June 1832

Valparaiso
23 July 1834
Sept ride
Oct ill

Montevideo
Buenos
Aires   19 July – 19 Aug 1832

Cape
Good Hop
31 May 183

Port Desire

Patagonia

Straits of Magellan
Tierra del Fuego

Falkland Islands
Mar 1833 Mar 1834

Cape Horn